GREEK CULTURE IN THE ROMAN WORLD

EDITORS

SUSAN E. ALCOCK
Brown University

JAŚ ELSNER
Corpus Christi College, Oxford

SIMON GOLDHILL
University of Cambridge

MICHAEL SQUIRE
King's College London

The Greek culture of the Roman Empire offers a rich field of study. Extraordinary insights can be gained into processes of multicultural contact and exchange, political and ideological conflict, and the creativity of a changing, polyglot empire. During this period, many fundamental elements of Western society were being set in place: from the rise of Christianity, to an influential system of education, to long-lived artistic canons. This series is the first to focus on the response of Greek culture to its Roman imperial setting as a significant phenomenon in its own right. To this end, it will publish original and innovative research in the art, archaeology, epigraphy, history, philosophy, religion, and literature of the empire, with an emphasis on Greek material.

Recent titles in the series

The Maeander Valley: A Historical Geography from Antiquity to Byzantium
PETER THONEMANN

Greece and the Augustan Cultural Revolution
A. J. S. SPAWFORTH

Rethinking the Gods: Philosophical Readings of Religion in the Post-Hellenistic Period
PETER VAN NUFFELEN

Saints and Symposiasts: The Literature of Food and the Symposium in Greco-Roman and Early Christian Culture
JASON KÖNIG

The Social World of Intellectuals in the Roman Empire: Sophists, Philosophers, and Christians
KENDRA ESHLEMAN

ROMAN FESTIVALS IN THE GREEK EAST

This study explores the development of ancient festival culture in the Greek East of the Roman Empire, paying particular attention to the fundamental religious changes that occurred. After analysing how Greek city festivals developed in the first two Imperial centuries, it concentrates on the major Roman festivals that were adopted in the Eastern cities and traces their history up to the time of Justinian and beyond. It addresses several key questions for the religious history of later antiquity: Who were the actors behind these adoptions? How did the closed religious communities, Jews and pre-Constantinian Christians, articulate their resistance? How did these festivals change when the empire converted to Christianity? Why did emperors not yield to the long-standing pressure of the Church to abolish them? And finally, how did these very popular festivals – despite their pagan tradition – influence the form of the newly developed Christian liturgy?

FRITZ GRAF is Distinguished University Professor and Director of Epigraphy at the Ohio State University. He has published widely on Greek mythology, local cults in ancient Asia Minor, eschatological texts from Greek graves, and ancient magic.

Religion and Identity in Porphyry of Tyre: The Limits of Hellenism in Late Antiquity
AARON JOHNSON

Syrian Identity in the Greco-Roman World
NATHANIEL J. ANDRADE

The Sense of Sight in Rabbinic Culture: Jewish Ways of Seeing in Late Antiquity
RACHEL NEIS

Roman Phrygia: Culture and Society
PETER THONEMANN

Homer in Stone: The Tabulae Iliacae in their Roman Context
DAVID PETRAIN

Man and Animal in Severan Rome: The Literary Imagination of Claudius Aelianus
STEVEN D. SMITH

Reading Fiction with Lucian: Fakes, Freaks and Hyperreality
KAREN NÍ MHEALLAIGH

Greek Narratives of the Roman Empire under the Severans: Cassius Dio, Philostratus and Herodian
ADAM M. KEMEZIS

The End of Greek Athletics in Late Antiquity
SOFIE REMIJSEN

ROMAN FESTIVALS
IN THE GREEK EAST

From the Early Empire to the Middle Byzantine Era

FRITZ GRAF

CAMBRIDGE
UNIVERSITY PRESS

University Printing House, Cambridge CB2 8BS, United Kingdom

Cambridge University Press is part of the University of Cambridge.

It furthers the University's mission by disseminating knowledge in the pursuit of
education, learning and research at the highest international levels of excellence.

www.cambridge.org
Information on this title: www.cambridge.org/9781107092112

© Fritz Graf 2015

This publication is in copyright. Subject to statutory exception
and to the provisions of relevant collective licensing agreements,
no reproduction of any part may take place without the written
permission of Cambridge University Press.

First published 2015

Printed in the United States of America by Sheridan Books, Inc.

A catalogue record for this publication is available from the British Library

Library of Congress Cataloguing in Publication data
Graf, Fritz.
Roman festivals in the Greek East : from the early empire to the Middle
Byzantine Era / Fritz Graf.
pages cm
Includes bibliographical references.
ISBN 978-1-107-09211-2
1. Festivals – Rome.   2. Festivals – Greece.   3. Rites and ceremonies – Rome.
4. Rites and ceremonies – Greece.   5. Rome – Social life and customs.
6. Rome – History – Empire, 30 BC – AD 476
7. Greece – History – 146 B.C.–323 A.D.   I. Title.
DG125.G73   2015
292.3'8 – dc23
2015015126

ISBN 978-1-107-09211-2 Hardback

Cambridge University Press has no responsibility for the persistence or accuracy of
URLs for external or third-party internet websites referred to in this publication,
and does not guarantee that any content on such websites is, or will remain,
accurate or appropriate.

For Sarah

Contents

Preface	*page* xiii
List of abbreviations	xv
Introduction	1
PART I FESTIVALS IN THE GREEK EAST BEFORE CONSTANTINE	9
1 Greek city festivals in the Imperial age	11
Introduction	11
Imagining festivals	13
Tradition and innovation in Greek festivals	18
Eastern splendors	32
Criticizing festivals	51
Conclusions	58
2 Roman festivals in eastern cities	61
Introduction	61
Roman festivals in Syria Palaestina	66
Further Roman festivals	86
Conclusions	98
PART II ROMAN FESTIVALS IN THE GREEK EAST AFTER CONSTANTINE	103
Introduction	103
3 Theodosius' reform of the legal calendar	105
The imperial rescript	105
Theodosius as law-giver in summer 389	107
Theodosius' reform of the legal calendar of the City of Rome	114
The reception of Theodosius' text	123
4 Contested festivals in the fourth century	128
The Christian contestation of the Kalendae Ianuariae	128
Councils and emperors	146

5	The Lupercalia from Augustus to Constantine Porphyrogennetos	163
	Augustus and the Lupercalia in the Imperial age	163
	Pope Gelasius and the Lupercalia in late-fifth-century Rome	168
	Constantine Porphyrogennetos and the Lupercalia in tenth-century Constantinople	175
	Transformations of a festival	181
6	John Malalas and ritual aetiology	184
	Introduction	184
	Rhomos and double kingship	185
	Romulus and the Brumalia	189
	Brutus and the Consilia	192
	Conclusions	199
7	The Brumalia	201
	The Bruma in the Latin West	201
	The Brumalia in Constantinople	208
	From Bruma to Brumalia	212
	The Christian contestation	214
	The disappearance of the Brumalia	217
8	Kalendae Ianuariae again, and again	219
	Kalandai in twelfth-century Constantinople	219
	Vota and *ludi votivi*	221
	Postscript from Muslim North Africa	224
9	Christian liturgy and the imperial festival tradition	226
	Introduction	226
	Christian liturgy in Jerusalem	227
	The Jerusalem liturgy and ancient festivals	229

PART III CHRISTIANITY AND PRIVATE RITUAL 239
    Introduction 239

10	Incubation in a Christian world	241
	Introduction: a spa in the Holy Land	241
	Past scholarship	245
	Pagan incubation	246
	Dreaming among Christians	248
	Incubation among the Christians	253
	Narratives of dream healing	263

11	Magic in a Christian Empire	268
	Augustine and magic	268
	Magic in imperial legislation	273
	Amulets and the Christians	288
	Church and state	294

Epilogue: The persistence of festivals and the end of sacrifices	305
The tenacity of festivals	306
Bottom up and top down	314
The end of sacrifice, and the continuity of festivals	318

References 323
Index 355

Preface

This book has been a long time in the making. It began its life as a project on Roman festivals that should go beyond the antiquarianism that at the time, in the 1990s, still characterized part of the studies on Roman cult. The first steps in this project were made during a sabbatical from Basel that I spent in 1996/97 at the University of Chicago and that was made possible by Christopher Faraone and Bruce Lincoln. I first publicly explored my methodology in the *Lectio Teubneriana* of 1997 on the Roman festival year, which was still fully and only concerned with the time between Caesar and Augustus, Cicero and Ovid. But this easy and fast trajectory was soon derailed when I realized that there was evidence for Roman festivals beyond the well-documented periods from Varro to Ovid, and beyond the city walls of Rome, from the Greek East during the Imperial age well into the Christian centuries of both Romes, the Eastern and the Western one. The 1999 Grey Lectures in Cambridge gave me the first opportunity to deal systematically with this evidence and to put it into a framework of Greek city festivals and the Christian opposition, manifested in the exciting sermons of Augustine that François Dolbeau had just published and that gave me a first entry into the debates of the Christianizing fourth and fifth centuries. I thank my Cambridge hosts, Mary Beard and David Sedley, for a great time, and my patient audience for their rich input in what was then still very much a learning enterprise. My years at Princeton helped me to enter the worlds of post-Second Temple Judaism and late antique Christianity, mostly thanks to the generous friendship of Peter Schäfer and Peter Brown.

More than a decade has gone by since then. Although other obligations sidetracked me sometimes, the elapsed time has offered enough time for prolonged reflection and deepened my interest in the way the Mediterranean world turned from many gods to one through the work of ever-changing prophets, some more radical than others, but few as open to compromise as the emperors and their administration. Some leisure to push forward with this and to read my way into the vast continent of Christian sermons, council acts, and law codes was granted by fellowships from the American Council of Learned Societies and the Guggenheim Foundation, to whom I am immensely grateful. The final touches were added during a stay at the Lichtenberg Kolleg in Göttingen where Heinz-Günther Nesselrath and Ilinca Tanaseanu-Döbler were my generous hosts; the debates with them and with the Lichtenberg fellows helped again consolidate things. Other impulses came from my former Academic home, the University of Basel, where during several summers my successor Henriette Harich-Schwarzbauer graciously invited me to teach Roman religion, from the Republic to Late Antiquity; I thank her and the Basel colleagues Joachim Latacz and Anton Bierl for having me temporarily back. During the years at The Ohio State University, I could rely on the treasures of the Epigraphy Center and the reliable help and advice of its staff members, Wendy Watkins and Phil Forsythe.

Among the many colleagues who gave me input and incentive, I mention again Mary Beard and add Jan Bremmer, Gideon Bohak, Peter Brown, Angelos Chaniotis, David Frankfurter, Peter Schäfer, John Scheid, and my Ohio State colleagues David Brakke, Tom Hawkins, Anthony Kaldellis, and Tina Sessa.

I owe more than I can describe to the long discussions, steady help, and sometimes intellectual provocation of Sarah Iles Johnston, colleague and companion for many years, who kept me sane and on course even during my years as department chair.

I thank Michael Sharp and the editors of this series for welcoming the manuscript and improving its content and form in many helpful ways, and the staff of Cambridge University Press, especially my editor Emma Collison and copy-editor Malcolm Todd, for carefully and patiently assisting in moving the text from the manuscript to the printed book.

Abbreviations

When I abbreviate names or works of ancient authors, I follow the conventions of the *Oxford Classical Dictionary* (third edition) and of Lampe, respectively. The same is true for periodicals and series where, however, I have often preferred to give the full name.

What follows, then, is a list of abbreviations not found in *OCD³* or Lampe.

Basilika	see Bibliography at Scheltema and Van der Waal (1955)
BE	*Bulletin épigraphique*
BMCR	*Bryn Mawr Classical Reviews*
CIG	*Corpus Inscriptionum Graecarum*
CIL	*Corpus Inscriptionum Latinarum*
CJ	*Codex Justinianius*, ed. Paul Krueger. Corpus Iuris Civilis II (Berlin: Weidmann, 1877)
Const. Sirm.	*Constitutiones Sirmondianae*, in: *CTh* ed. Th. Mommsen and P. M. Meyer
Copt. Enc.	*The Coptic Encyclopedia*
CTh	*Codex Theodosianus*, ed. Theodor Mommsen and Paul M. Meyer (Berlin: Weidmann, 1905)
DNP	*Der neue Pauly*
FGrH	*Die Fragmente der griechischen Historiker*, ed. Felix Jacoby *et al.*
FiE	*Forschungen in Ephesus*
I.Cret.	*Inscriptiones creticae, opera et consilio Friderici Halbherr collectae*, ed. Marguerita Guarducci (Rome: Libreria dello Stato, 1935–1950)
I.Didyma	*Didyma. Teil 2: Die Inschriften*, ed. Alfred Rehm and Richard Harder (Berlin: Reimer, 1958)

I.Ephes.	Die Inschriften von Ephesos, ed. Hermann Wankel. IKS 11:1–8,2 (Bonn: Habelt, 1979–1984)
IKS	Inschriften griechische Städte aus Kleinasien
ILS	Inscriptiones Latinae Selectae, ed. Hermann Dessau (Berlin: Weidmann, 1892–1916)
I.Milet	Inschriften von Milet, ed. Peter Herrmann. Milet: Ergebnisse der Ausgrabungen und Untersuchungen 6 (Berlin: De Gruyter, 1998)
I.Priene	Inschriften von Priene, ed. F. Hiller v. Gaertringen (Berlin: Reimer, 1906)
I.Stratonikeia	Die Inschriften von Stratonikeia, ed. M. Çetin Şahin. IKS 21 (Bonn: Habelt, 1981ff.)
Iscrizioni di Cos	Iscrizioni di Cos, ed. Mario Segre (Rome: "L'Erma" di Bretschneider, 1995, 2007)
IvP	Die Inschriften von Pergamon, ed. M Fränkel. Altertümer von Pergamon 8 (Berlin: Spemann, 1890/1895)
Lampe	G. W. H. Lampe, A Patristic Greek Dictionary (Oxford: Clarendon Press, 1961)
LSCG	Frantizek Sokolowski, Lois sacrées des cités grecques (Paris: Boccard, 1969)
Mansi	Sacrorum conciliorum nova et amplissima collectio, ed. Giovan Domenico Mansi (Paris: Welter, 1901–1927)
OLD	The Oxford Latin Dictionary
OMS	Louis Robert, Opera Minora Selecta. Epigraphie et antiquités grecques. 7 vols. (Amsterdam: Hakkert, 1969–1990)
RAC	Reallexikon für Antike und Christentum
SIG^3	Sylloge Inscriptionum Graecarum, ed. Wilhelm Dittenberger, 3rd edn. (Leipzig: Hirzel, 1915–1924)
StEGO	Steinepigramme aus dem griechischen Osten, ed. Reinhold Merkelbach and Josef Stauber (Bonn: Habelt, 1998–2004)
ThesCRA	Thesaurus Cultus et Rituum Antiquorum (Los Angeles: The J. Paul Getty Museum, 2004–2006)

Introduction

Festivals, secular or religious, their changing history, and their power of persistence as the most vivid expression of communal life have always attracted me. Living on another continent, I have come to realize that growing up in Switzerland had in part shaped this fascination. A remote part of the country still celebrates the *Kalendae Martiae*, or rather, in the local Ladin language, the *Chalanda Marz*; they were made famous to two generations of Swiss children through Alois Carigiet's splendid pictures that illustrate the story of *Schellenursli*, the boy who found the largest cowbell. Modern Chalanda Marz is a festival performed by boys to drive out Winter, as the explanation goes, with the ringing of cowbells, the larger and louder the bell the better: this is far from the Roman Matronalia, the funk they induced in Horace, and the fiery anger they provoked in Tertullian, but it fascinates the historian all the more; Chalanda shares with many other festivals the irrelevance of its aetiology, and the fate of having become a children's entertainment. Stodgy Zurich, my home for two decades, celebrates another expulsion of Winter in its *Sechseläuten*, James Joyce's "Sexaloitez." The rite is a solemn, even sometimes pompous self-presentation of the local bourgeoisie, with a parade of the city elite disguised in historical costumes or wearing their officer's parade uniforms: hence the joke in Joyce's word play. The final, spectacular act, when the bells of Zurich's city church strike ("*läuten*") six, is the burning of a paper snowman, loaded with explosives, atop a high pyre; young men (and nowadays women) on horseback circle the burning and exploding pyre. Its Frazerian paganism only thinly veils its nineteenth-century invention; this taught me the existence and importance of invented traditions long before I came across Hobsbawm and Ranger's celebrated book. Looking back, then, this world made me receptive for the vicissitudes of Lupercalia that were reinvented as a courtly Spring ritual in tenth-century Byzantium, or of the Kalendae Ianuariae that tenaciously survived in many guises in the medieval societies around the Mediterranean Sea, including as a children's game in

Islamic North Africa, despite the attacks by Jewish rabbis, Christian bishops, and Muslim clerics over many centuries.

This book treats festivals in the eastern half of the Roman empire in the millennium between the reigns of Augustus and Constantine Porphyrogennetos. In past scholarship, Greek and Roman festivals have fared somewhat better than other aspects of the religions of the Imperial age, but neither was at the center of scholarly attention in the way especially sacrifice was in the last half-century, or mysteries were in the age of Cumont. With the exception of the ruler cults treated in several seminal monographs, from Lucien Cerfaux and Jean Louis Tondriau (1957) through Fritz Taeger (1960) and Simon Price (1984) to Duncan Fishwick's many volumes (1987–2005), and the mystery cults whose treatment is slowly evolving from under the shadow of Franz Cumont, the religions in the Imperial period did not fare too well until very recently. By now, the splendid survey of Mary Beard, John North, and Simon Price has opened Rome's Imperial religion to a wider group of readers and scholars, successfully moving away from the concentration on Republican (or even pre-Republican) religion that has been the inheritance of Wissowa and Dumézil. On the Greek side, it was mainly epigraphical studies on Asia Minor that brought more information and insight on the religions of the Imperial Age, but with a much smaller impact: epigraphy is still perceived as, and is indeed, a specialist's domain and usually overlooked by the historians of ancient religion, despite the efforts of scholars such as Louis Robert, John Scheid, Michael Wörrle, Kevin Clinton, and Angelos Chaniotis.

Festivals, on the other hand, have mostly been treated as a problem of historical and antiquarian reconstruction, with the books of William Warde Fowler (1899), Martin P. Nilsson (1906), and Ludwig Deubner (1932) setting the pace and several later monographs revisiting the evidence and adding new material, without opening up new perspectives.[1] There are exceptions. The conference volume on *La fête, pratique et discours* that Françoise Dunand edited in 1981 is remarkable for its interest in the contemporary reflection about festivals, and Walter Burkert's 1992 attempt to find an inherent logic in the sequence of festivals during the Athenian year remains the most promising attempt to find over-arching structures in the linear sequence of the festival calendar; it inspired me when I reflected on Rome's festivals in my Teubner Lecture. Only during the past decade, however, have collective volumes on ancient festivals multiplied, all of them the result of seminars and conferences, and some have focused on the

---

[1] An idiosyncratic attempt with not much resonance outside Italy is Sabbatucci (1988).

Imperial epoch – most importantly the volumes edited by Christian Landes and Jean-Michel Carrié (2007), and by Jörg Rüpke (2008b). Other editors of such collections are more generally interested in festivals and contests of all ages – such as the volumes of André Motte and Charles Ternes (2003), Sinclair Bell and Glenys Davies (2004) and J. Rasmus Brandt and Jon W. Iddeng (2012).

A few scholars, most recently and explicitly Brandt and Iddeng, were explicitly trying to move away from what they defined as an "empirical-positivist" approach, and they are gaining some new ground, although not all the studies in Brandt and Iddeng's collection live up to the onerous claim; the definition and the classification of festivals in Greece and Rome need more discussion, and the term "empirical-positivist" with its polemical undertones does not always do justice to the subtle precision of earlier studies, or their implicit theoretical models.[2] Nilsson (1906), for one, is more shaped by the patient precision of its data than by its soft Frazerian theorizing, and it is the precision, not the concession to a now defunct theory, that has guaranteed its survival; and the same is true for more recent individual case studies. A monograph such as Michael Wörrle's 1988 presentation of an inscription of Hadrianic times that contains the files of an agonistic foundation in small-town Oinoanda remains a model to follow, even if it can be described (or descried) as "empirical-positivist"; the same is true for most contributions in the collection edited by Peter Wilson (2007), with its programmatic subtitle "Documentary Studies," especially its opening contribution by William Slater, which takes account of the epigraphical evidence.

When they reflect on the function and purpose of ancient festivals, most scholars have followed an implicit or explicit Durkheimian paradigm, expanded towards a Geertzian understanding of festivals as expressing social order and power structures, sometimes with a whiff of Turnernian *communitas* added for additional attraction. This selective methodology was mostly put to a convincing use, given the collective nature of festivals and the irrelevance of "theological" interpretations even in Christian antiquity – especially when they avoided the mysticism that beckoned as a temptation in Turner's approach. Myths and gods did not matter much, as Walter Burkert discovered when he discussed the festival at the terebinths of Mamre, and as became clear when I reflected on the Christian reception of pagan festivals – it was only late antique Christian leaders and late-nineteenth- and twentieth-century scholars whose ideological concerns insisted on the importance of theology

---

[2] The same is true for the (overused) term "empirico-positivist" in Phillips (2007).

for festivals.[3] For the present book – at least for the chapters on the Christian transformation of ancient festivals – the most important model was not Durkheim's, Geertz's, or Turner's classical books but Mona Ozouf's splendid and patient *La fête révolutionaire* of 1976, a book that is as much about the need of any articulated human group to celebrate festival as it is about conscious and ideology-driven change of the festival's calendar and character, and that should be compulsory reading for all who work on late antiquity and the transition to the Christian religions.

This book treats a small selection from among the many festivals that either the city on the Tiber or any city of the Roman East celebrated. I treat these festivals because, in the world of ancient festivals, they constitute a double paradox and surprise: they are translocal, and they survive the transformation of the polytheist world into monotheist Christianity (and, in one case, one step further into monotheist Islam). This caught my interest, and raised questions. (This, by the way, is the first and almost last time in this book that I will use the term "polytheist," which I do not use as an overly politically correct way of avoiding "pagan" but as a descriptive term. Otherwise, I will unhesitatingly use "pagan" to describe aspects of the non-Christian, or non-Jewish, traditional religious systems of the ancient world that are far from uniform as to ritual forms or doctrinal contents, not to mention both the obvious facts that monotheism was thought of long before the rise of Christianity, or that the description of Christianity as monotheist contradicts living religious reality.[4])

Handbooks teach us that festivals in the ancient world were radically local, confined to one city and even to one of its subgroups, as expressions of group identity and specificity; the many monographs with a local name in their title, including Rome, bring that point easily home.[5] Translocal festivals such as the tribal Panionia or the panhellenic Olympia conformed to the pattern but enlarged the group beyond one city; festivals in single cities that were related by concern or divinity or both still took specific local forms, such as Thesmophoria or Dionysia, or the festivals of the ruler cult from Hellenistic kings to Roman emperors. Only with the rise of Christianity did some festivals become global, driven by a global religious creed – or, to remain more modest, pan-Mediterranean in the extensive sense the term is used by historians such as Cyprian Broodbank – and even

---

[3] Burkert (2012), 42: "There seems to be no common religious dogma for the festival, no 'theology' of the event, no authoritative sacred tale."
[4] See the reflections in Cameron (2011), 14–32 and Jones (2012), followed by Cribiore (2013), 7.
[5] On Rome and the export of the festival calendar (or refusal thereof) see Feeney (2007), 209–211; for a list of local studies on Greece see the introduction to the 1995 reprint of Nilsson (1906), ix*.

then adding some local colors. The spread of a traditional city festival to another city is almost unheard of before the Imperial age, and the spread from the Roman West to the Greek East is even more surprising. But surprise is the mother of curiosity. Of these Western city festivals, I want not only to know how they arrived in the East, where they were celebrated, and how and why they changed their form, and sometimes their name, over the course of the centuries; I also want to know whether and how this changed the very conception of festival.

Some of these festivals survived into a Christian empire – not as a pagan survival that was destined to disappear with "full" Christianization, but as a festival in its own right, albeit sometimes tolerated rather than wholeheartedly embraced by radical bishops.[6] This calls for a set of other questions: What were the forces that kept such a festival alive despite the strong opposition of severe Christian theologians, and how does a festival shed its connection with the pagan gods to become acceptable and accepted in a Christian world? What are the reconceptualizations necessary to do this, and what was their effect on how festivals were understood?

The topic is not entirely new. A few individual festivals have received scholarly attention in the past, most prominently the best-attested case, the Kalendae Ianuariae; but Michel Meslin's 1970 book-long investigation was mainly interested in the Latin West before the rise of Christianity: Christianization is sketched rather cursorily, despite the long-standing and well-documented opposition of local bishops.[7] Two other late festivals were the subject of learned doctoral dissertations. John Crawford treated the Brumalia in his 1916 Harvard thesis, a thorough investigation but written in Latin, which impeded its reception; half a century later, A. W. J. Holleman focused his Amsterdam dissertation more narrowly on pope Gelasius' resistance against the Lupercalia.[8] A few other late antique festivals received some attention as well but do not feature in this book because they are confined to the Latin West, as the Volcanalia, or did not originate in Rome although they were celebrated there, as the Maiouma or the festivals of Isis, or they remained family celebrations, as the Rosalia.[9]

The book has a relatively straightforward plan. Chapter 1 is exclusively Greek and deals with festivals in some Eastern cities of the first centuries of

---

[6] On such festivals see e.g. Aug. *Epist.* 17.1 or 91.8.
[7] See Kaldellis (2011) on the Byzantine Kalendae. [8] Crawford (1914–1919); Holleman (1974).
[9] Volcanalia: Opelt (1970). Maiouma: Greatrex and Watt (1999); Belayche (2004). Isis: Alföldi (1937) Rosalia: Kokkinia (1999); on the army ritual Hoey (1937).

the Imperial Age. The chapter cannot be, nor does it want to be, the much-needed supplement to Nilsson's *Griechische Feste*, which concentrates almost entirely on the pre-Roman centuries even when he uses a large amount of later information from inscriptions as well as from Pausanias. Rather, the chapter is a loose series of case studies that aims to understand the specific forms festivals took in the Greek cities of the Imperial age, distinct and different from the polis festivals of Archaic, Classical, and Hellenistic Greece. The evidence is mostly epigraphical, and among the flood of inscriptions from the period I have selected a few cases that allow for broader generalizations and make clear how and why these imperial cities could absorb the insertion of Roman city festivals.

Chapter 2 deals with Roman festivals in the East before Constantine. The most interesting and most detailed evidence comes from the Rabbinic debates about idolatrous festivals in Iudaea Palaestina. These discussions, preserved in the Jerusalem Talmud, mark the earliest moment when such festivals in an Eastern province become visible to scholarship, and the rabbis' attempts to articulate opposition to them sheds invaluable light on the complexities of religion in the Empire. Compared to this coherent body of texts, the rest of the evidence is sketchy and as haphazard as the adoption of Roman festivals outside Rome.

With the third chapter, we move beyond Constantine, his foundation of a second Rome that closely followed its Western sibling, and his tolerance that opened the world to Christianity, with its new festivals. The chapter concentrates on one legal text with vast consequences, the reform of the legal calendar of Rome codified by the first Theodosius in Rome in early August of 389. Given the high walls that surround the study of Roman law, breached by a few pioneers such as John Matthews and Fergus Millar, the text has not yet received the attention it deserves among the historians of ancient religions, including early Christianity. But the law code put together on the order of the second Theodosius has remained a constant source of fascination to me, and I have come to understand how it stands next to *Iliad* and *Odyssey*, the *Aeneid*, the Septuagint and Vulgate as the most influential books from the ancient world.

The chapter on Theodosius' law gave me the occasion not just to look at new Christian festivals, but also to look at the Christian opposition to older pagan festivals, not least the festivals of Rome that became festivals of the Empire. Chapter 4 looks in more detail at these debates. Given the imperial protection of many traditional festivals, the opposition of powerful bishops to them was also an opposition to the imperial government. But this was never explicitly stated, with good reasons. In a world where "even for the most courageous, many topics were taboo," in Peter Brown's formulation, indirect criticism was the most that was permitted.[10]

The rest of the book turns to the centuries after Theodosius I, and does not always stay away from the West. Chapter 5 deals with the Lupercalia, the festival that was already in existence when Romulus founded the city, at least according to the Roman historians, and that not only survived impressively long, until at least the time of Constantine Porphyrogennetos, but also underwent several radical and sometimes spectacular transformations in order to accomplish this survival. I look into the resistance to the festival by pope Gelasius and into the radically changed form it took, centuries later, in Byzantium under Constantine Porphyrogennetos.

Chapter 6 looks at the mythical aetiology for late Roman festivals. Even in the Christian centuries, myth still remained important; it survived and flourished because it was still disguised as history. The chapter is devoted to the one historian whose aetiological Roman stories were most influential throughout Byzantine history, John Malalas, the contemporary of Justinian. His narration of Rome's origins between Romulus and Brutus contains the explanation of several festivals. Although these stories are sometimes derided (or plainly ignored) by the historians of ancient religion and mythology, they were important to explain and legitimize customs of Justinian's time to the contemporary world, and to those who came later.

The Brumalia, the topic of Chapter 7, is another Roman festival that survived beyond Constantine Porphyrogennetos. Unlike Kalendae and Lupercalia, it received its name only in Constantine's city; but it had a Western predecessor in the Bruma already vilified by Tertullian. The chapter follows the history of this seasonal celebration, from its modest form as a household festival in the second century CE to its development into the almost month-long festival celebrated by the Byzantine court.

Another festival of *longue durée* is the Kalendae Ianuariae. This festival, already treated in earlier chapters, especially in Chapter 2 in its Palestinian context, will be treated again in Chapter 8 in its Byzantine form. The neglect of its later Greek appearances by Meslin has been somewhat corrected recently: thus, my chapter is both a summary of recent scholarship in the framework of the present book, and an outlook to the festival's survival and transformation in later times.

In many ways, what had started as an investigation into the presence of a few Roman festivals in the cities of the Greek East turned also into a

---

[10] Brown (2012), 56.

narration of how paganism disguised itself in a Christian world, to the dismay of many bishops but to the delight of the crowds. Chapter 9 looks at another aspect of the same transformation and analyzes the Jerusalem liturgy, as known especially through the report of Egeria, on the background of the phenomenology of Roman festivals developed in the preceding chapters; the analysis stresses both continuities and radical changes.

The final two chapters follow this thread of Christianization in two topics that might surprise in a book on festivals: incubation and magic. The examination of these rituals of the individual are intended as a contrast to the collective festivals; as often, such a contrast throws the object of research into greater relief.

Incubation (Chapter 10) was an integral part of healing rituals in the pagan world, most impressively in the cult of Asklepios. But incubation in some form made its way also into Christian cult; even today scholars regard this still through the eyes of the Frazerian Ludwig Deubner, as if it were a pagan survival. Through several case studies, the chapter tries to understand what incubation in a Christian ritual context really meant, and whether scholars are really justified to import the pagan term into a new world.

The following chapter on the Christianization of pagan magic (Chapter 11) returns to the intersection of ritual and Roman law. Strictly speaking, Christian bishops rejected magic as fiercely as they rejected the Kalendae or Brumalia. Constantine, however, in his legislation on sorcery, had left a loophole that future generations were to exploit, once again provoking the ire of bishops, even against more pliable popes. Constantine had permitted rites to protect the crops from damage, and later usage extended this to the amulets that protected the individual from harm. Not unlike the festivals, these rites survived under the umbrella of legal protection.

The epilogue does not only pull the threads of a complex argument together. It also attempts a synthesis driven by two questions: Why did festivals survive, despite the onslaught of generations of bishops and their collective outcries? And how does this intersect with the problem recently made prominent in two independent investigations, namely the end of sacrifice, given that in the most pervasive view of pagan festivals sacrifices are at their very core? Earlier scholars sometimes had attempted an answer by resorting to general anthropological needs of *homo ludens*; this does not appeal to me. I will instead try to stay inside the historical specificity of the centuries with which this book is dealing and with people firmly embedded in their time and society.

PART I

*Festivals in the Greek East
before Constantine*

CHAPTER I

Greek city festivals in the Imperial age

Introduction

O Greece, you perform all this beautifully and fittingly, offering, as far as it is possible, lavish sacrifices and organizing a most glorious contest of behavior, strength and speed, and you preserve all the traditions of festivals and mysteries that came from the past. But think also about this: "Ill now is the care that is taken of you; you are wretched with age and unkempt, and your garments are unseemly to see."[1]

Thus ends Dio Chrysostom's *Olympikos*, the theological oration on the statue of Zeus in Olympia, delivered in Olympia during one of the three games between 97 and 105 CE. It is a surprising and ambivalent peroration. Dio acknowledges that the Greeks were still performing all the festivals that their tradition had handed down to them, and they were performing them beautifully and lavishly: witness the Olympic Games where he is speaking just now. However, Dio also sees a limitation. They were doing so "as far as possible" or, as Liddell-Scott-Jones somewhat pedantically translate ἐκ τῶν παρόντων, "according to the present circumstances"; and Odysseus' words about his father grow out of this cautionary and "oddly pessimistic" note that the orator has inserted into his praise. The biological metaphor he is using – noble Greece has reached a "dismal old age," as has noble Laërtes – suggests that a restoration of the former glory is as impossible to achieve for Greece as is rejuvenation for mortal humans. There is thus a tension between the

---

[1] Dio, *Or.* 12.85: τάδε μὲν οὕτως, ὦ σύμπασα Ἑλλάς, καλῶς καὶ προσηκόντως ἐπιτελεῖς, θυσίας τε θύουσα ἐκ τῶν παρόντων μεγαλοπρεπεῖς καὶ δὴ καὶ τὸν εὐκλεέστατον ἀγῶνα τιθεῖσα <ὡς> ἀπ' ἀρχῆς εὐεξίας καὶ ῥώμης καὶ τάχους, ὅσα τε ἑορτῶν καὶ μυστηρίων ἔθη λαβοῦσα διαφυλάττεις. ἀλλὰ ἐκεῖνο φροντίζων σκοπῶ, ὅτι "αὐτήν σ' οὐκ ἀγαθὴ κομιδὴ ἔχει, ἀλλ' ἅμα γῆρας λυγρὸν ἔχεις αὐχμεῖς τε κακῶς καὶ ἀεικέα ἕσσαι." (Translation after R. Lattimore, 1965); the citation Hom. *Od.* 24.249f. For the date see Russell (1992), 16.

"lavish" (μεγαλοπρεπής) performance and the "dismal" and "foul" (λυγρός and ἀεικής) general circumstances.

Dio is not the only Greek author to complain about the present circumstances and their signs of a breakdown of the former greatness. His contemporary Plutarch discussed the silence of many oracles as a similar sign of decline, and saw it happen even in Delphi, where the Pythia at least was still speaking, even if in prose, unlike in many local oracular shrines all over Boiotia that had become entirely mute. The end of his dialogue *On the Obsolescence of the Oracles* sounds even more pessimistic than Dio's *Olympikos*: "There are some [the speaker, Plutarch's brother Lamprias, says] who assert that the things above the moon also do not endure, but give out as they confront the everlasting and infinite, and undergo continual transmutations and rebirths."[2] Although there is some ambiguity here as well – Plutarch, the Platonic philosopher, did not subscribe to the Stoic view his brother is embracing –, it still shows how these men could see the plight of their society and understand it as part of a larger, almost cosmic and teleological phenomenon. In the same dialogue, Plutarch also remarks that in his own time all of Greece would be unable to muster the three thousand hoplites one single city, small Megara, had dispatched to fight the Persians at Plataia, more than half a millennium earlier.[3]

What Pausanias saw happening when traveling the country several decades later seems to agree with Plutarch's assessment. His descriptions of the still existing antiquities and his rich record of the stories connected with them contrast with the many sanctuaries he saw in ruins, and that never made it back from the dismal times during the first century BCE. For many ancient and modern readers, Pausanias thus seems to echo what Cicero's friend Sulpicius famously had noticed two centuries earlier, when sailing from Aigina towards Megara and recording Greece's former glory: Aigina, Megara, Piraeus, Corinth "were once booming cities but look now razed and destroyed."[4] Sulpicius tells this story in order to talk Cicero out of his debilitating grief for his daughter; he might well have been exaggerating as much as Plutarch was when talking about contemporary population figures. Nevertheless, the passages still seem to reflect the general feeling of an irrevocable decline.

---

[2] *De defectu oraculorum* 51, 438D: εἰσὶ δ' οἳ καὶ τὰ ἐπάνω φάσκοντες οὐχ ὑπομένειν, ἀλλ' ἀπαυδῶντα πρὸς τὸ ἀΐδιον καὶ ἄπειρον συνεχέσι χρῆσθαι μεταβολαῖς καὶ παλιγγενεσίαις (translation F. C. Babbitt, Loeb edition).
[3] *Ibid.* 8, 414A.
[4] Cicero, *Ep. ad familiares* 4.5.4 *quae oppida quodam tempore florentissima fuerunt, nunc prostrata ac diruta ante oculos iacent.*

Despite the Augustan peace and the spectacular liberation of Greece by Nero, pessimism persisted well into the second century; the loving care expended by Trajan and Hadrian did not change much. Only administrators – optimistic by profession, if not nature – contradicted this. The quietly efficient Pliny, sent to Bithynia to deal with the problems of the province, noted that the provincials sacrificed much less because of the ascent of Christianity, but he was confident that his own measures were turning the tide: "Temples, almost deserted, have begun to receive visitors again, and many festivals that have been omitted for some time are again performed."[5] And later in the century, orators agreed; Aelius Aristeides could praise the peace brought by Rome as granting a perpetual holiday to the gods throughout the cities of the civilized world.[6]

Modern scholars, as dazzled by Periklean Athens as Plutarch was or seduced by the remnants of hoary rituals in Archaic Greece, have been influenced by this pessimistic reading: Greek religion in the Empire is boring at best, only a shadow of its former glory. Most scholarly accounts of Greek religion still end with Alexander the Great, as does Burkert's or the less voluminous books that came later. Nilsson, who in his History of Greek Religion bravely persisted to the very end of Greek religion (writing a *Handbuch* has its obligations) introduced his section on "Die römische Zeit" with the very passages I just alluded to and adds a few more, and his first sentence evokes the destructions of the Roman civil wars in Greece in a powerful image: "Verblutet, verödet lag das alte Griechenland ... da" – bloodless, a victim of Roman violence, never to rise again.[7]

Imagining festivals

Talking about festivals

But one has to listen to Dio or, for that matter, to Pliny more carefully than this, or just read Pausanias with a less biased eye to realize that the festival tradition did not only survive but was thriving during the centuries before Constantine, after a difficult period between Sulla and Nero. Other authors concur. Not half a century before the battle at the Milvian Bridge, the rhetor Menander wrote a short treatise on epideictic oratory. In it, he still counted festivals among the central elements of praise of a

---

[5] Plin. *Ep.* 10.96, the citation from para. 10 *prope iam desolata templa coepisse celebrari, et sacra sollemnia diu intermissa repeti.*
[6] Ael. Aristid. *Or.* 26.97–99.   [7] Nilsson (1951), 310.

Greek city. An important expression of justice in a city, he says, is its piety (εὐσεβεία), which means both being θεοφιλής, "beloved by the gods," and φιλόθεος, "god-loving." The dichotomy feels somewhat pedantic and smacks of the classroom; but it is illustrative of how these men understood their religion. The φιλοθεότης of cities expresses itself "in many ways: whether they instituted rites (τελετάς); whether they preserved the many traditional festivals by offering the largest number of sacrifices of the finest quality; whether they have built many sanctuaries, both for numerous gods and numerous shrines for each of them; and whether their priests are performing their duties correctly."[8] It deserves to be kept in mind that correctness – whether defined by tradition or any other panhellenic norm – is the criterion by which the merit of rituals and ritual specialists is judged. And since epideictic praise of a city usually finds its place at a festival, the orator is advised "to dwell at some length on each occasion, be it a festival, a fair or a gathering for an armed, an athletic or a musical contest."[9] Even in the years after the middle of the third century – when, according to Nilsson, "die alte Religion schwand hin" ("traditional religion melted away")[10] – there were occasions where an orator could praise the festival tradition as if nothing had happened at all since the days of Homer, Solon, and Perikles.

Those experts of public speaking, of course, were using these very festivals to advertise their art and to compete with each other, and thus they needed the piety of the cities. If Menander was sounding a critical note, it was not about the piety of the contemporary cities, but that of his contemporaries as individuals: "Nowadays," he remarks, "it is difficult to find piety in an individual, although many cities rightly claim common piety and zeal for the gods."[11] This constructs a dichotomy between thriving public and dwindling private religiosity that might surprise the modern observer, who is familiar with the opposite development in the later third century with the rise not only of Christianity, but of a host of mystery cults. But this might just be the problem Menander remarked

---

[8] Menander Rhetor, *Dihaeresis* p. 362.25–30 Spengel: τὴν δ' αὖ φιλοθεότητα, ὥσπερ ἔφην, κριτέον ἰδίᾳ μέν, εἰ τῶν πολιτῶν ἕκαστος τῆς περὶ τοὺς θεοὺς θεραπείας ἐπιμελεῖται, δημοσίᾳ δὲ κατὰ πολλοὺς τρόπους, εἰ τελετὰς κατεστήσαντο, εἰ πολλὰς ἑορτὰς ἐνόμισαν, εἰ πλείστας θυσίας ἢ ἀκριβεστάτας, εἰ πλεῖστα ἱερὰ ᾠκοδόμησαν ἢ πάντων θεῶν ἢ πολλὰ ἑκάστου, εἰ τὰς ἱερωσύνας ἀκριβῶς ποιοῦνται· ἀπὸ γὰρ τούτων αἱ τῶν πόλεων φιλοθεότητες σκοποῦνται.
[9] *Ibid.*, p. 365.30 χρὴ τοίνυν τῶν πανηγυρικῶν πλείστην διατριβὴν περὶ τὸν καιρὸν ἕκαστον ποιεῖσθαι, οἷον εἰ ἑορτὴ εἴη ἢ πανήγυρις ἢ σύνοδος ἐν ἀγῶνι ἢ ἐνοπλίῳ ἢ γυμνικῷ ἢ μουσικῷ.
[10] Nilsson (1951), 331.
[11] Menander, *Dihaer.* p. 362.30 ἣν μὲν οὖν τῶν καθ' ἕνα σπάνιον ἐν τοῖς <νῦν> χρόνοις εὑρεῖν, τῆς δὲ κοινῆς εὐσεβείας καὶ περὶ τοὺς θεοὺς σπουδῆς πολλαὶ ἀντιποιοῦνται πόλεις.

upon. He defines private piety as "the care of every citizen for the worship of the gods" (εἰ τῶν πολιτῶν ἕκαστος τῆς περὶ τοὺς θεοὺς θεραπείας ἐπιμελεῖται). This understands worship as addressed to the (traditional) gods, and leaves it to individual initiative; but individual initiative to perform traditional sacrifice seemed flagging, or choosing other objects. The cities – that is, their wealthy elites – were more eagerly clinging to the religious traditions than everybody else. However, many individuals might have felt tempted to join those who hesitated to perform sacrifices and followed either the skeptical views of Lucian on sacrifice or the vegetarian and Pythagoreanizing doctrines propagated by Porphyry, or who might even have been tempted by a religion that did not count as religion at all in this resolutely traditionalist view, Christianity.[12] If so, it resonates not only with Pliny's complaint about the decline of temple cult in Christianized Bithynia a century and a half earlier, but even more so with the motives behind the attempt of the emperor Decius (ruled 249–251), a contemporary of the orator Menander, to force all free citizens of the empire to offer sacrifices to their gods. It also resonates with the clear-sighted analysis of Géza Alföldy, who long ago pointed out that after the middle of the third century traditional religion was gaining in importance among the imperial elites.[13] For Rome – which must have seen the same tensions and would still see them more than a century later – Herodian's history, written around 240 CE, demonstrates the vitality of the official religious life and both the historian's own interest and the implied interest of his Greek readers in these matters.[14] Herodian himself watched the splendor of the *ludi saeculares* of 204 CE, under Septimius Severus:

> In his reign we saw every kind of spectacle in all the theaters simultaneously, rituals and night-long revels celebrated in imitation of the Mysteries. The people of that day called them the Secular Games when they learned that they would be held only once every hundred years. Heralds were sent throughout Rome and Italy bidding all to come and see what they had never seen before and would never see again.[15]

---

[12] On Lucian see Belayche (2011); Graf (2011b).
[13] Alföldy (1989). On Decius see especially Rives (1999) and Selinger (2004; first German edition 1994).
[14] See Alföldy (1989), 71.
[15] Herodian 3.8.10: εἴδομεν δὲ ἐπ' αὐτοῦ καὶ θέας τινῶν παντοδαπῶν θεαμάτων ἐν πᾶσι θεάτροις ὁμοῦ, ἱερουργίας τε καὶ παννυχίδας ἐπιτελεσθείσας ἐς μυστηρίων ζῆλον· αἰωνίους δὲ αὐτὰς ἐκάλουν οἱ τότε, ἀκούοντες τριῶν γενεῶν διαδραμουσῶν ἐπιτελεῖσθαι. κήρυκες γοῦν κατά τε τὴν Ῥώμην καὶ τὴν Ἰταλίαν διεφοίτων καλοῦντες ἥκειν καὶ θεάσασθαι πάντας ἃ μήτε εἶδον μήτε ὄψονται. (Translation after Edward C. Echols, 1961).

This might be hyperbole, and we shall have to see how far it reflects the reality of Greece's cities under the emperors that is visible in the epigraphical record. But first we turn to another bit of literature.

Describing festivals

Hyperbole is more often found in the novelistic descriptions of urban life and religion than in the historian's narrations. But as successful texts these descriptions resonate with the feelings of their readers, who, after all, were all performers or onlookers of a variety of rituals as well; it makes sense to see what they have to say about the religious life of their cities.

In his "Ephesian Tales" (*Ephesiaka*), written not later than the second century, and presumably already in the first, Xenophon of Ephesos introduces his hero and heroine as key performers in the annual procession from the city of Ephesos out to the shrine of Artemis.[16] The description evokes all the splendor and wealth of a rich performance – "the sacred objects, the torches, the baskets, the incense burners, then horses, dogs and hunting gear," finally the youthful performers, fifty maidens led by Anthia, "daughter of Megamedes and Euhippe" (giving her all the civic legitimization she needs and, in the aristocratic sounding names, her social status), "clad in a purple dress that ended at her knees and her elbows, and in a fawn skin; she carried a bow and hunting spears, and dogs went with her." This was impressive enough, but the spectators remained even more impressed by the final group of fifty young men, led by young and beautiful Habrokomes. "A large crowd had assembled to look on, locals and foreigners"; and they all would later participate in the less orderly occasion of the sacrifice and, presumably, the banquet in the shrine.[17]

A much longer and, in its detailed splendor, much richer account is given in the "Ethiopian Tales" (*Aethiopika*) of Heliodorus when he describes the Delphic procession for the penteteric sacrifice at the grave of Neoptolemus.[18] The description, written considerably later than

---

[16] Xenophon, *Ephesiaka* 1.2.2–3.1. Dating any of the Greek novels is notoriously difficult. For Xenophon see the recent discussion in Whitmarsh (2013), 36, 41–42 (42 "the evidence for dating Xenophon . . . is . . . tenuous"; 36 "probably first century CE"); but see Ruiz-Montero (1999), 306: "his novel . . . mirrors the religious and social atmosphere of the 2nd cent. to a greater degree than others."

[17] Xenophon, *Ephesiaka* 1.2.2–3.1. The name Megamedes is only attested as the name of a πύργος, a fortified estate in Hellenistic Teos, *CIG* 3064.30, an inscription that D. W. S. Hunt (1947) discussed under the title "Feudal Survivals in Ionia."

[18] Heliodor. *Aethiop.* 2.34–3.6; the procession described in 3.1–5. On the date see the overview by Fusillo, *DNP* 5.289; the resonances with Philostratus' *Life of Apollonius of Tyana* make a date in the

Xenophon's, parades first a hecatomb of black bulls with gilded horns and garlanded with flowers that are led by picturesquely rustic Thessalians, then a large group of lesser sacrificial animals with their attendants, followed by flutists and syrinx-players, fifty virgins in two dancing groups, one with flower baskets, the other with baskets full of cakes and incense burners, balancing both baskets and burners on their heads while dancing and singing a hymn to Thetis and Achilles. Fifty mounted ephebes in white cloaks follow, their Thessalian horses adorned with rich silver trimming. At the very end, on a chariot pulled by two white cows, rides the youthful priestess of Artemis, in a purple cloak and sporting a bow and arrows. It is a dazzling performance, whose sights, sounds, and smells Heliodorus' rich and intricate ecphrasis catches beautifully.[19]

These novelistic processions are not only events full of grandiose beauty, they are also filled with erotic attraction. Beauty provokes erotic longing, and novels deal with erotic passion and suffering, ἐρωτικὰ παθήματα. Xenophon is somewhat more explicit than Heliodorus: Anthia consistently had rejected Eros, and the god was about to take the same revenge that his mother had taken on Apuleius' Psyche. At the same time, the Ephesians were fully aware of the erotic possibilities of the event: "It was" – the narrator informs us – "a custom at this festival to find husbands for the maidens and wives for the ephebes."[20] Far from being simple "escortings" of sacred objects or sacrificial animals, as some scholars think who rely too much on the etymology of the word πομπή, these processions are sensuous multimedia events; and this is true not just for those in the ancient novels, as we shall presently see.[21] Although it is correct that in Greek and Roman sacrificial rituals, processions served one main purpose, to escort the sacrificial animals from outside the sanctuary to the altar in the sanctuary where they would be sacrificed, from early on in their history Greek processions seemed especially apt to carry additional symbolic and aesthetic values and to become the main expression of festivity, beauty, order,

---

earlier third century rather attractive to me. On the procession and the resonances with Xenophon see Whitmarsh (2013), 45, who dates Heliodorus "probably fourth cent." (36).

[19] On which see Hardie (1998).
[20] Xenophon 1.2.3: ἔθος ἦν ἐκείνηι τῆι πανηγύρει καὶ νυμφίους ταῖς παρθένοις εὑρίσκεσθαι καὶ γυναῖκας τοῖς ἐφήβοις.
[21] On πομπή as "escortings" see e.g. the otherwise excellent paper by Kavoulaki (1999) that follows Robert Parker's lead on the terminology; the translation is one-sided at best and overlooks the perspective of the spectators. In many cases, the inscriptions make it clear that the πομπή serves to transport, πέμπειν, the sacrificial animals to the altar (e.g. *IG* ii² 334, a.335/4, on the Panathenaia); when we deal with an escort as in the Athenian procession to Eleusis (*IG* ii² 1078, see below), the verb used is παραπέμπειν, not πέμπειν alone. On Hellenistic processions, their aesthetics and their politics, Chaniotis (2013).

and plenty, perhaps even more so than the banquet at the other end of the tripartite structure of procession, sacrifice, and banquet that so often figures in honorary decrees to express what Louis Robert memorably termed the "gratefulness of the belly." And certainly both processions and banquets were much more visible than the sacrifices with their ritual killing that, according to modern theorists, from Mauss to Vernant and Burkert, was at the center of the ritual. If they were right, it was a center that was more often hidden than revealed, except in the polemics against animal sacrifice.[22]

Tradition and innovation in Greek festivals

A festival of Akraphia in Boiotia

In many places, actual ritual reality came close to these fictionalized descriptions, not only in the cities that had traditionally been Greek, from Magna Graecia to Ionia: in the cities further east, during the imperial centuries Rome's "tenuous and erratic control" at the time when Augustus came to power was quickly replaced by a genuinely felt expression of Greekness.[23] Literary texts, however, are somewhat reticent about this process. Almost all the information comes from the rich inscriptions of the period, especially the extended honorary decrees that cities customarily dedicated to their many benefactors, that range from the first to the third centuries, and that come from the Greek mainland as well as from many cities throughout Anatolia.[24]

Maybe the single most memorable body of texts are the three inscriptions from Boiotian Akraphia in honor of Epameinondas, son of Epameinondas, a benefactor of his own city, Akraiphia, and a prominent figure in the politics of Greece under Caligula and Nero; his cult activities raise important questions as to the festival culture of his time and are thus a good starting point for this discussion.[25] Epameinondas served as an

---

[22] Van Straten (1995), 103 already pointed out how few images reproduce the actual killing of the sacrificial animal – and the novelists' descriptions still seem to echo this quasi-silence. In recent work on sacrifice, scholars have begun to rethink the centrality of ritual killing in ancient religions: see esp. Smith (1987) and McClymond (2008).

[23] For an overview of the Roman East, see Millar (1993) (the quotation on p. 27) and Sartre (2001) and (2005); see also Sartre (1995).

[24] For two case studies of the Imperial epoch, see Chaniotis (2003) and Graf (2011a).

[25] The embassy and the honors conveyed to Epameinondas *IG* vii 2711; the honors by Akraiphia for a series of local benefactions *IG* vii 2712; Nero's proclamation *IG* vii 2713; the entire file again in Kantiréa (2007), 208–213. On *IG* vii 2712, see Graf (2011a), 107–110, with earlier bibliography in 108

ambassador from the "Federation of the Greeks" to Caligula on the occasion of his accession in 37 CE; he was later responsible for inscribing Nero's proclamation of Greek freedom on a large marble stele in his home town – the only copy of this momentous document we still have – and he engaged intensively with the cult life of his own town. As a gymnasiarch, he organized the annual festival for the gods of the gymnasium, Hermes, Herakles, and the emperors, with its sacrifice of bulls, βουθυσία, and the ensuing banquet for all citizens, and he did the same at the Sebasteia, the local festival that honored the imperial house.

But most importantly in the context of this book, he devoted himself and his vast financial resources to the Ptoia, the festival of Apollo Ptoios held in the sanctuary on mount Ptoion, fifteen stadia above Akraiphia in the densely wooded hills; a few decades later, the Boiotian native Plutarch would insist on just how deserted and lonely the region was.[26] When Epameinondas entered office, the contest – and presumably with it the sacrifices of the Ptoia and the oracular activities of the god's shrine – had been omitted for the last thirty years. Once elected *agonothetes* of the Ptoia (perhaps upon his own initiative), Epameinondas reinstated the annual sacrifices, the oracles, and the ancient contest. But he went beyond this and also restored the regional network that came with the festival: he invited sacred embassies (θεωρίαι) from other cities, and he enhanced its prestige and splendor by combining the contest with the cult of the emperors, founding τὰ μεγάλα Πτοῖα καὶ Καισηρεῖα, a contest that seems to have been celebrated every sixth year.[27] At the second celebration of the "Great Ptoia and Kaisareia," Epameinondas "performed the traditional great processions and the traditional dance of the *syrtoi*" (τὰς δὲ πατρίους πομπὰς μεγάλας καὶ τὴν τῶν συρτῶν πάτριον ὄρχησιν). One would like to know more about these processions and dances. The natives knew what they were but they did not tell us; perhaps understandably, they preferred to record in great detail the opulent meals that Epameinondas offered to the men and ephebes in the sanctuary, and those that his wife gave to the women and girls in her home.

We can guess some of the ritual details, however. The gender segregation suggests that some of the contests were athletic – Hellenistic inscriptions from the Ptoion attest to both athletic and musical contests, as do some texts of the second century CE.[28] Feeding the ephebes in the sanctuary

---

n. 14. On the frequency of the local festivals with their contests in late Hellenistic Boiotia see Knoepfler (2004), esp. 1249.

[26] *De defectu* 8, 414A; Pausanias 9.23.5–6.   [27] Kantiréa (2007), 178–180.
[28] *IG* vii 2727 and 2728 (1st cent. BCE); 4151 and 4152 (2nd cent. CE); 2726 (after 211 CE); see also 4154.

along with the men means that they played a major role in the processions, as they did in other cities, most impressively in Xenophon's novelistic Ephesos.[29] The most exciting, and most enigmatic, detail however is the restoration of a traditional dance. Ancient texts rarely talk about such restorations, nor do they give us other evidence for the Akraiphian custom.[30] Its name, *syrtoí* (or *syrtaí*), must mean "those in long trailing robes"; such robes are attested for contemporary theatrical performances of tragedies, but they were also characteristic for some elites in Archaic Greece.[31] I thus imagine these dancers to be not unlike the Whirling Dervishes of Konya, only that the costume was associated in later Greece with the pre-Classical past.[32] Given the gap of thirty years or one generation in the performance of this dance, I also wonder how many of its details were still remembered by former onlookers or performers; at the time of its restoration, these people were middle-aged or older. It might thus be that many details were much more a creative reconstruction and invention of a tradition rather than a true restoration.[33] The text, of course, stresses the traditional character of dance and procession. What counted to his contemporaries was that Epameinondas had connected his troubled present again with a glorious past, and what mattered was the unquestioned belief that he brought the age-old dance of the *syrtoi* back. Nobody cared overmuch whether the details were historically correct or not: the reconstruction served the necessities of a community's life, not of an antiquarian's interests.

In order better to understand Epameinondas' intentions, we need to look at the history of the Ptoion.[34] The sanctuary with its oracle was flourishing already in the later Archaic age, as shown by the many statues of kouroi that

---

[29] Theatrical performances, on the other hand, are characterized as "ornaments," συνκοσμοῦντας τὴν ἑορτήν; we don't know whether there were musical contests as well.

[30] A possible parallel is Petzl (1982), 2.1: 141 no. 654, a fragmentary honorary decree for two sisters who as *theologoi* were concerned with a girls' dance connected with a "festival of the *mystai*."

[31] The Ἴωνες ἑλκεχίτωνες meet annually on Delos, *Homeric Hymn to Apollo* 147; see also the story of Theseus arriving in Athens in such a robe, Pausanias 1.19.1.

[32] The contemporary dances of the Whirling Dervishes suffered a similar fate. In 1925, Atatürk abolished the Mevlevi Derwish Order; its dances were reinstated only in 1960 with the help of the illustrious Orientalist Hellmut Ritter (1892–1971) whose rather dramatic life had brought him to Istanbul in 1926, where he continued a remarkable career that in Germany had been curtailed by a prison sentence for homosexuality; see van Ess (2014) and Josef van Ess, "Ritter, Hellmut," in: *Encyclopaedia Iranica*, on line at www.iranicaonline.org/articles/hellmut-ritter (accessed January 2015).

[33] The term "invention of tradition" was coined by Hobsbawm and Ranger 1983 (for Victorian Britain).

[34] A summary in Schachter (1981), 52–73, with earlier bibliography.

were dedicated there. The fame of its oracle motivated Mardonios, the Persian general of king Xerxes, to send an envoy asking about the war's outcome; the polyglot god answered in the ambassador's native Carian.[35] The Boiotian Confederacy (*koinon*) made it into its main oracular shrine, at least after the reconstitution of the *koinon* after 338 BCE, and it entrusted Akraiphia with the oversight over the sanctuary, replacing Thebes in this prestigious but also costly role. At the latest after 312, the Confederacy began to dedicate tripods in the sanctuary.[36] Around 228 BCE, the Ptoia festival and its contest was a part of the religious self-definition of the *koinon*, according to the preserved decrees from several Boiotian cities that, in response to a high-powered embassy from Akraiphia, all agreed to send an embassy (*theoría*) with a sacrificial bull to be paraded in the procession.[37] Some fifty years later, an oracle of Trophonios ordered the Boiotians "to dedicate the city of Akraiphia to Apollo Ptoios"; since the same oracle also ordered them to dedicate the town of Lebadeia to Zeus Soter and Trophonios, the initiative for this move must have come from the Boiotian Confederacy or the Delphic Amphictyony that at the same time guaranteed the inviolability of the territory of Akraiphia and confirmed a sacred truce during the Ptoia. The two decrees that guaranteed divine protection to the city were inscribed in Akraiphia on one large stele, together with a third text in which a certain Kapillos, son of Straton, from Larymna on the Euboian Gulf, donated money for the festival. The oracular shrine and the festival celebrated for the oracular god brought the city fame and internationally guaranteed security, and the grateful citizens wanted to record this impressive role for generations to come.[38] Even the catastrophe of 146 BCE turned out not to be lethal: the Confederacy, and with it the festival of the Ptoia, were revived, albeit celebrated with less splendor. Around 100 BCE, Akraiphia expressed its gratitude to a local benefactor who, like Epameinondas, served as agonothetes of the Ptoia and "abundantly and lavishly offered sacrifices to the gods and banquets to the citizens."[39] Private benefaction seems to have taken the place of the

---

[35] Hdt. 8.135, repeated by Plutarch, *De defectu* 5, 412 A and Pausanias 9.23.5–6.
[36] Schachter (1981), 67.
[37] See *IG* vii 351 = Petrakos (1997), 213 no. 304, line 11: πέμπειν βοῦν ἀπὸ τῆς πόλεως εἰς τὰ Πτώϊα καὶ αὐτοὺς συμπομπεύειν καὶ τἆλλα πάντα πράττειν καθάπερ καὶ ἐν ταῖς λοιπαῖς θυσίαις γέγραπται, αἷς ἡ πόλις θύει ἐν τῶι κοινῶι Βοιωτῶν, "to send a bull from the city to the Ptoia and to participate in the procession, and to do everything else as it is written for the other sacrifices that the city performs in the Boiotian confederacy."
[38] *IG* vii 4135 (*amphiktyones*), 4136 (oracle of Trophonios), 4137 (donation for the Ptoia).
[39] *IG* vii 4148: ἐκτενῶς δὲ καὶ λαμπρῶς καὶ τοῖς θεοῖς τὰς θυσίας καὶ τοῖς πολίταις τὰς εὐωχίας παρέσχηται.

Confederacy as main sponsor: this foreshadowed the thirty years in which, according to the decree for Epameinondas, the cult and its oracle were altogether abandoned because private benefaction also had ceased to help.

This history helps us to grasp the magnitude of Epameinondas' undertaking. When seen against the backdrop of the earlier reforms of the festival and the efforts of Hellenistic benefactors, it becomes clear that he did not just enhance an existing tradition or contribute his own funding because money had become an issue.[40] Much more ambitiously, he aimed to give back to Akraiphia the preeminent position the city had held in the Boiotian Confederation, thanks to the oracle that advised the *koinon* and to the Ptoia in which Akraiphia helped the *koinon* to represent itself. One should read his interactions with the emperors, the embassy to Caligula and the intercession with Nero, in the same vein. Now, in the middle of the first century CE, it was not enough for an individual Boiotian city to be recognized by the members of the Boiotian Confederacy or the Delphic Amphictyony. These bodies had become shadows of their former selves, and the real power resided with the emperor in faraway Rome. When he offered to be an ambassador to the emperor on behalf of all Greeks, Epameinondas did not only gain the recognition of the other cities for his Akraiphia (represented in the person of its most powerful and, presumably, most wealthy citizen), but he connected these cities – and of course Akraiphia and himself – directly to the imperial power. To enlarge the traditional Ptoia with a cult for the emperor and his house, to turn them into "Great Ptoia and Sebasteia," was a step as logical as it was necessary on the level of religious politics.

This manipulation of the ritual tradition that combines reconstruction with innovation shows the ambivalent status of the new civic elite of the Greek cities. They were furthering the status of their cities in a Greek world where the past was the most valuable commodity, but at the same time they were also furthering the interest of the new ruling power, Rome, and, of course, their own.

Twenty years later, the same Epameinondas was involved in a much larger and more momentous reconstruction of the Greek past. When in 67

---

[40] As was the case at the time: see the decree in Robert (1935) (= *SEG* 15.330), the honors for three citizens who had helped in a difficult time (ἐν τῇ τῆς χώρας ἀπωλείᾳ), when the eponymous magistracy had to be taken over by (the temple funds of) Zeus Soter and when "the sacrifice for Apollo Ptoios and the emperor Tiberius (in the gymnasium) should have been performed, but one could not find funding to perform the honors for the gods," ἔδει δὲ τὴν προσήκουσαν τῷ θεῷ Ἀπόλλωνι Πτωίωι καὶ Τιβερίῳ Καίσαρι Σ[ε]βαστῷ Γερμανικῷ γενέσθαι θυσίαν, πόρος δὲ οὐδεὶς εὑρίσκετο ὅθεν τὰ εἰς τοὺς θεοὺς ἐπιτελεσθῇ.

CE Nero decreed that the mainland Greeks should be given back their ancient freedom, Epameinondas, now high priest of the provincial imperial cult, had the text of the decree inscribed on two stelai, one on the agora of Akraiphia next to an altar of Nero Zeus Eleutherios, the other one in the sanctuary of Apollo Ptoios.[41] The new altar in Akraiphia, whose existence the decree nearby explained, stood next to an older altar dedicated to Zeus Soter, the god who had saved the Greeks from the Persians at the battle of Plataia in 478 and who was also worshipped as Zeus Eleutherios in his Plataian sanctuary.[42] The new god Nero blended easily in with older deities. Existing older templates helped the Greeks to adapt and integrate new political facts.[43]

We can thus understand the activity of Epameinondas as a re-founder of a traditional cult in the larger framework of his overall activity for his city, for Boiotia, and for the mainland Greeks. In his wider political activities, he mediated the interests of these Greeks inside the new power structure of imperial Rome, in which the political realities must have been rather complex: Akraiphia itself had no direct access to the emperor, but was part of several larger structures, the Boiotian League that combined all cities of Boiotia, the Panhellenes, and the province of Achaea with its proconsul. To the Greek cities that had no military and virtually no economic power left, the main asset was their past that could be translated into a claim of cultural power; and the Romans perceived it as such, not the least Nero when he freed the Greeks. The restoration of past cultural events (games, dances, oracles) thus could be seen as bolstering these claims: it is the beginning of an activity that gained momentum under the philhellenic emperors Trajan and Hadrian in the second century and has been dubbed by scholars, in its literary form, the Second Sophistic. Seen in this context, which points to some political urgency, it becomes even clearer why the accuracy of the revived tradition did not matter.

We do not know how well Epameinondas succeeded in the long term. The omission of a festival is reflected only by silence in the record, and only in exceptional cases can we see how a new cult collapsed. We might wonder what happened to the phallos procession in Beroia after the Roman

---

[41] *IG* vii 2713 (= *SIG*³ 814), 56–57 (a. 67 CE).
[42] On Zeus Eleutherios of Plataia, see Strabo 9.2.31 (p. 412C) and Pausanias 9.2.5; the epiclesis is attested in other places.
[43] A precursor was Theophanes of Mytilene, the friend of Pompey, to whom the Mytilenaians dedicated a statue as [θ]έῳ Δ[ὶι Ἐλευθε]ρίῳ Φιλοπάτριδι Θεοφάνη τῷ σωτηρι καὶ εὐεργέτᾳ καὶ κτίστᾳ δευτέρῳ τᾶς πάτριδος, "to the god Zeus Eleutherios Philopatris Theophanes, the savior, benefactor and second founder of our country," *IG* xii 2163b. Other emperors followed suit: see the material collected by Taeger (1960).

governor in the earlier second century CE, L. Memmius Rufus, moved 1,000 denarii from a donation for the procession over to the funding of the local *gymnasion*, but we do not really know whether it ceased to exist altogether.[44] We can, however, understand how a local foundation without a tradition such as the Euaresteia of Oinoanda, founded after 220 CE by the wealthy orator Iulius Lucius Pilius Euarestos, rather quickly collapsed after the death of the founder.[45] Plutarch, two generations younger than Epameinondas, complains about the disappearance of all Boiotian oracles except that of Trophonios, and Pausanias, as we saw, had no interest in the sanctuary in the woods above Akraiphia, for whatever reason.[46] But victor inscriptions of the second and early third centuries CE attest to the existence of at least a musical contest called Ptoia Kaisareia, with victors from several Greek cities.[47] It might well be that after Epameinondas the cult ceased again and that, after a longer interruption, another wealthy founder revived what he knew to be a venerable tradition – perhaps no less a patron than Herodes Atticus, whose daughter Elpinike Regilla was honored by the Akraiphians.[48] Unlike obscure private foundations, an institution already mentioned in Herodotus must have attracted any imperial sponsor eager to bring back Greece's ancient splendor.

Restorations and invented traditions

Similar efforts are visible elsewhere. In about 220 CE, when inscriptions still recorded victors in the Ptoia Kaisareia of Akraiphia, the Athenians decreed how their ephebes would participate in the annual procession to Eleusis that opened the Mystery festival. Not unlike Xenophon's Ephesian ephebes (or those of Akraiphia), they would march at the head of the several thousands of initiates who came to Athens from the entire empire, "in full armor, wearing a wreath of myrrh and marching in formation"; and they would participate "in the sacrifices, libations and paeans along the route." Although the text tells us that by doing so the ephebes would become "more pious men," ἄνδρες εὐσεβέστεροι, the visual effect of all this was not lost on the Athenian law-makers either. In their decree, they emphasized the "orderliness," κόσμος, of the procession: κόσμος is both

---

[44] Nigdelis and Souris (2005); Gauthier and Hatzopoulos (1993).   [45] Chaniotis (2004), 296.
[46] Plut. *De defectu oraculorum* 5, 411F.
[47] *IG* vii 2727 and 2728 (1st cent. BCE); 4151 and 4152 (2nd cent. CE); 2726 (after 211 CE); see also 4154.
[48] The honors: *Bulletin de Correspondance Hellénique* 16 (1892), 464 no. vii; see Schachter (1981), 72 n. 5.

an aesthetic and a moral category, and the official overseeing the ephebes in Athens and elsewhere was the κοσμητής.

This is not the first time the ephebes were involved in the Eleusinian mysteries, of course: already the late Hellenistic inscriptions that praise the service that they and their *kosmetes* rendered to the cults of the city described how they marched in several city processions, and how at the Mysteries they "met the sacred objects and led them out again, and similarly Iakchos"[49]; Iakchos is the god whose image was carried at the head of the great procession of the initiates from Athens to Eleusis. The inscription of about 220 CE deals with a restoration of this role of the ephebes. Both in the repeated insistence on tradition (τὰ πάτρια) and the intention to "avoid any interruption and neglect of our piety towards the Two Goddesses" (24), one can sense problems that in the past had led to this very interruption and neglect. Once again one also wonders how many of the details of the restored ritual were correctly remembered and how many were the result of discussions and negotiations among the civic and religious leaders involved in the restoration.[50] Change even in this most venerable ritual of Athens was possible, after all. A few decades earlier, Herodes Atticus, another very generous and very powerful benefactor, introduced white cloaks for the ephebes instead of the traditional black ones that Herodes, and with him the Athenian assembly that had to vote on it, perceived as not being festive enough.[51]

Herodes Atticus was conscious that he changed a custom. In most other cases, we can only wonder whether the men who claimed to have restored τὰ πάτρια were aware of the degree of invention they brought to their restorations – given that they legitimated their elevated social position with their embeddedness in cultural traditions, I think rather not; no other elite member had the power of Herodes Atticus. Thirty years ago, Eric Hobsbawm and Terence Ranger realized that many traditions in nineteenth-century Europe were in reality inventions that were legitimized, consciously or unconsciously, by the claim of traditionality.[52] In my Swiss world, I would count the Basel *Fasnacht* and the Zurich *Sechseläuten* among them, the former a restoration of the traditional

---

[49] *IG* ii² 1006.9 ἀπήντησαν δὲ καὶ τοῖς ἱεροῖς καὶ προέπεμψ[α]ν αὐτά, ὁμοίως δὲ καὶ τὸν Ἴακχον.
[50] *IG* ii² 1078 = *LSCG* 8; see Chaniotis (2003), and in Dignas and Trampedach (2008), 25–26. The quotation, l. 24 ὅπως μηδέποτε τοῦτο ἐκλε[ιφθείη με]δὲ ὀλιγωρηθείη ποτὲ τὰ τῆς εὐσεβείας [τῆς εἰς τὼ θε]ώ.
[51] Philostrat. *V.Soph.* 2.1, 550; the aition for the black cloaks, the murder of Kopreus, shows that black was understood as a color of mourning and guilt.
[52] Hobsbawm and Ranger (1983).

Carnival by infusing it with elements taken from the world of Renaissance mercenaries, the latter a wholesale invention in the template of "pagan" fertility cults. Neither Akraiphia's traditional dance nor the Athenian restoration of the mystery procession might have gone as far as these modern examples, but their characterization as invented traditions is useful. It is a background to keep in mind when dealing with the world of festivals in the Roman Empire, as long as one is fully aware that to assume the invention of a specific tradition in the Imperial world is not meant as a judgment on the value and authenticity of the invented institution, but rather that it signals an extreme case of its flexibility and adaptability.[53]

But of course not all cases of restoration might hide invention. In an unassuming honorary decree from the village of Almoura in Lydia, villagers honored one P. Aelius Menecrates, a citizen who had received Roman citizenship under Hadrian (this dates the text before or around the mid-second century) and who possessed the concomitant wealth. As the decree says, he "dedicated and consecrated to the priestess of Demeter the basket set in silver that was missing in the mysteries of Demeter" and invited the carriers of the basket in the annual procession to a banquet in his private house, together with the village magistrates.[54] The procession obviously was important to the village and needed the sacred basket for carrying the sacred objects. We do not know why it was missing: maybe it was made of wickerwork and finally had given out, or it was made from silver and had been stolen (if silver was an innovation, as it well might have been; we are not told so). The important thing is that Aelius Menecrates felt it his civic duty to donate a new silver basket for the rite.

Given the scarcity of our data, it is not always possible to discern whether we deal with restoration or innovation, intentional or not. The most intriguing case is that of the mystery festival of the Great Gods in Messenian Andania. Pausanias connected it with the very foundation of the Messenian state, but recent scholars rather viewed it as wholesale invention by a powerful member of the local elite, one Mnasistratos; this

---

[53] On the problem of reading invention of a tradition in a (misguided) opposition to authenticity see the anthropological protest of Briggs (1996) or Clifford (2004/2013), 20/56: "the rather narrowly political invention of tradition analyzed by Hobsbawm and Ranger (1983), with its contrast of lived custom and artificial tradition." I remain convinced of its usefulness as a tool of the historian, despite its problems – that we cannot always know when extreme adaptability becomes invention (often a somewhat arbitrary decision), and that to put such a stress on tradition as such is a nineteenth-century invention; see Prickett (2009).
[54] Pleket (1970), 61 no. 4 ("2nd century A.D., (post)Hadrianic period").

then would be a clear case of an invented tradition. Either in 92/91 BCE or, more likely, in 24/25 CE, the festival received a lengthy and systematic codification of its rules of performance sanctioned by an oracle; the text is preserved in two impressive marble stelai.[55]

The mystery cult was performed at a sanctuary about ten kilometers outside the city of Andania, the Karneiasion; and as in Eleusis and other places, there was a procession from Andania to the Karneiasion that brought the cult officials with the sacred objects from the city to the sanctuary. At its head marched Mnasistratos, the wealthy benefactor who had made the new form of the cult possible by donating the sacred books. He was followed by the priest and priestess of the mystery divinities and the administrative officials of the mysteries; after them, the maidens led the carts with the boxes that contained the sacred objects, the very core of the ritual. This conceptual center of the procession was followed first by the "sacred women," then "sacred men," selected initiates (both adults and adolescents) who played a key role in the organization of the cult. They were dressed in white felt caps and, as all the initiates, in a white dress and cloak; the women were riding on chariots. There followed a group of functionaries from the local cults of Demeter. At the end, slaves led the relatively modest sacrificial animals, two sows, one of them pregnant, a boar, a ram, and a sheep. The order in which the groups – maidens, sacred women, and men – walked was determined either by lot or by a governing body; the somewhat unusual fact that the sacred women had precedence over the sacred men derives either from the key role of women in Demeter's cult, or from the fact that the chariots with the women immediately followed those with the sacred objects, or from both. The text does not mention the initiates proper, but one can safely assume that they followed after the sacrificial animals, presumably in a loose group without a given order. We only learn that the πρωτομύσται, perhaps "those initiated the first time," were wearing a special headdress, the στλεγγίς, which later was exchanged against a laurel wreath: I assume that these visual signs differentiated neophytes and more senior initiates, contributing to the visuality of the experience.[56]

---

[55] *IG* v 1.1390 (*LSCG* 65). See the editions and commentaries by Deshours (2006) and Gawlinski (2011). On the date: the inscription gives "the 55th year" as the year in which some future construction will take place (l. 90): this is most likely the following year. Past scholars assumed that time-reckoning here followed the Messenian year; mostly for palaeographical reasons, Petros Themelis has twice argued for the Actian era. See Pirenne-Delforge (2010), 224, who agrees with this late date.

[56] On the πρωτομύσται see Deshours (2006), 133.

Undisguised innovations

Besides innovations like these that hide under traditions, there are those that do not disguise their novelty. Sometimes, conscious innovation is born from economic pressure and administrative intervention by a Roman authority. We saw the case in the gymnasium of Beroia where the governor curtailed the traditional phallos procession, to allocate some of the money elsewhere.[57] An earlier instance of a similar Roman intervention comes from Ephesos; here, the ephebes not only marched in the annual procession of the Artemisia that Xenophon described, they were also singing the hymns for the goddess and the emperors in the respective celebrations. At least they did so after a reform by Paullus Fabius Persicus that is known through a lengthy although fragmentary epigraphical file.[58] In about 44 CE, this capable Roman administrator looked into the deplorable state of the city's finances and made them disband the expensive professional singers (*hymnodes*) "for whom not a small amount of the city's revenue is spent," to replace them with the ephebes, "whose age, social position and capability of learning," as he shrewdly observed, "make them more apt for this office, but who also will offer this service without pay."[59] It deserves notice how highly the Ephesian cult authorities valued hymn singing in their liturgies; the proconsul was aware of it and did not want it to cease but replaced it with an alternative that he thought better both in terms of public finances and civic education.

Nor did the proconsul – as he underscored – intend to disband all professional choirs in his province: he was aware that his letter to the Ephesians could and would be used as a legal precedent all over the province of Asia, as imperial letters were used as legal guidance all over the empire.[60] Thus, he singled out the professional *hymnodes* in the imperial cult at Pergamon as a body that should under all circumstances continue its services. He realized that it was not a good idea for a governor to appear to be interfering with the imperial cult and with the pride of a

---

[57] Nigdelis and Souris (2005); Gauthier and Hatzopoulos (1993).
[58] Reconstructed in *I.Ephes.* 17–19.
[59] *I.Ephes.* 17 lines 54–55 = *I.Ephes.* 18D lines 4–8: εἰς οὓς οὐκ ὀλίγον μέρος τῶν τῆς πόλεως ἀναλίσκεται προσόδων ... ἐφήβο[υς] δὲ,| ὧν καὶ ἡ ἡλικία καὶ ἡ ἀξία καὶ ἡ πρὸς τὸ μαθεῖν ἐπιτηδειότης τοιαύτη μᾶλλον ἁρμόζει λειτουργίᾳ, [ταύτην χ]ω[ρὶς] | ἀργυρίου παρέχεσθαι τὴν χρείαν.
[60] On the principle see Matthews (2000), 13–16. The principle is easily extended to the proconsul, who in his province "has the fullest right to lay down the law" (*cum plenissimam autem iurisdictionem proconsul habeat*, Ulpian, *Dig.* 1.16.7.2) and "he has a more ample legal power than anybody else except the emperor" (*maius imperium in ea provincia habet omnibus post principem*, Ulpian, *Dig.* 1.16.8).

provincial association whose members all belonged to the elite and often were Roman citizens.[61]

This high esteem of hymn singing continued throughout the Imperial epoch; if in Ephesos the ephebes simply replaced professional singers in their ritual function, in other places ephebic singing was introduced without impacting the professionals. In the early third century, and in a city further inland, Stratonikeia in Caria, the city's assembly decided to revive the boys' choir in the sanctuary of Hekate that had been neglected because their fathers were reluctant to dispatch their young sons for this duty; the assembly intervened at the initiative of their influential secretary Sosandros, the son of a priest and himself a former high priest of the Imperial cult and husband of a priestess. The assembly also decreed that thirty noble boys should walk every day to the *bouleuterion*, "clad in white, wreathed, and carrying in their hand boughs," to sing a hymn for the two main city divinities, Zeus Panamaros and Hekate, whose intervention more than two centuries earlier had saved the city from the marauding troops of Caesar's former lieutenant Labienus and who thus deserved all possible honors.[62] Half a century later, the Didymean Apollo still recommended the singing of hymns as the most pleasing form of cult he could imagine.[63]

This same interest in hymn singing manifests itself also in another way in the epigraphical record. Starting in the mid-fourth century BCE, inscriptions preserve numerous hymns inscribed in stone, with Delphi and Epidauros as the main centers, but other places demonstrating a similar interest, including the tiny city of Erythrai in Ionia with a paean to Asklepios and, on the same stone but in a somewhat later letter style, another one to king Seleukos Nikator, who died in 281 BCE.[64] But again, the Imperial epoch shows much more. Two significant series of late inscriptions attest to the daily singing of hymns, whose texts were recorded on a stone "hymn-book" for the use of singers or worshipers, even if some of the hymns were considerably older and as famous as the hymn of Ariphon to Hygieia.[65] From the vicinity of

---

[61] On this body see Friesen (2001), 104–116; Price (1984), 90.
[62] *LSAM* 69 = *I.Stratonikeia* 1101; for the very well-placed family see *I.Stratonikeia* 264–266. See Chaniotis (2004), 296–300; on the Labienus episode Roussel (1931) is still valuable.
[63] *I.Didyma* 217; see Harder (1956) and Peek (1971).
[64] Delphi: Furley and Bremer (2001), nos. 2.3, 2.5, and 2.6 (all inscribed between 4th cent. and 128 BCE); Epidauros: *ibid*. nos. 6.2–5, 6.7 (inscribed between mid-4th cent. BCE and 3rd cent. CE); Erythrai: *I.Erythrai* 205 (the paean for Asklepios also in Furley and Bremer 2001, no. 6.1).
[65] See Furley and Bremer (2001), no. 6.3. Compare also the paean of an anonymous poet to Asklepios whose oldest text was inscribed in about 380/360 BCE in the Asklepieion of Erythrai – much later examples come from Ptolemais in Egypt (under Nerva), Athens and Dion in Macedonia (2nd cent. CE); Furley and Bremer (2001), no. 6.1.

Athens – presumably from a shrine of Telesphoros – in 1688 Hessian troops brought a stone to Kassel in Germany that in the third century CE was inscribed with four hymns, the first being a morning hymn to Hygieia;[66] and several stones from Epidauros, inscribed between the second and fourth centuries CE, together constitute a similar late antique collection, with one stone carrying the remark "at the third hour," ὥραι τρίτηι.[67] Already Aelius Aristides attests to a morning prayer in the Asklepieion of Pergamon, and a very fragmentary Epidaurian inscription from around 200 CE preserves tantalizing morsels of information on ἡμερείσια [ἱερά], "daily rituals" – maybe a long-standing tradition originating from Epidauros rather than an invention in later times.[68]

The lavish invention of a new ritual or festival, however, is very common in these centuries, usually in some connection with the cult of the emperors. Among the many epigraphical documents that attest to such new foundations throughout the Imperial age, two stand out because of the wealth of details preserved to us through long inscriptions: the processions founded under Trajan by C. Vibius Salutaris in Ephesos, and the musical contest of the Demostheneia in Oinoanda, named after their otherwise unknown founder, C. Iulius Demosthenes, and founded in 124 CE, when the emperor Hadrian was staying in the East.

As is typical for many of these foundations of the Imperial epoch, both festivals are known through an epigraphical file that documents their foundation, from the founder's will to the permits from the Roman authorities and the honorary decree of their respective cities. The Demostheneia, one of the many Hellenistic and Imperial festivals named after their founder and sponsor, lasted from Artemision 1 to Artemision 22 and was celebrated every fourth year. It comprised processions and sacrifices for Apollo Patroos and the emperor, a market day (*panegyris*) and three days for meetings of the Council and the Assembly, and a rich program in musical contests, from trumpeters and heralds to tragedies and comedies; at the end, the founder added three days of paid entertainment by professional mimes and one day of athletic contests for citizens.[69] The festival thus inscribes itself into the phenomenology of many other imperial festivals, with the worship of the Roman ruler on its first day as the

---

[66] *IG* ii² 4533; one of the hymns, the paean of Ariphron, also in *IG* iv² 1.132.
[67] Furley and Bremer (2001), 2:268, following Maas (1933), 154–155.
[68] Ael. Aristid. *Hieroi Logoi* 1.280, p. 453 Dindorf; *IG* iv² 1.472 add. = *LSS* 25.
[69] Extensively discussed by Wörrle (1988); on the performance of tragedy and comedy see Nervagna (2007).

prelude to a much larger local event, and the program of the musical contests following a more or less standardized schedule. Whereas the founder himself prescribed the details of the musical program and determined the prize money for the victors (lines 38–46), the city in its own decree ruled on the details of the organization and the processions and sacrifices: in the daily procession, ten newly elected Sebastophoroi were to carry unidentified "imperial images" (τὰς σεβαστικὰς εἰκόνες, 62), an image of the city's ancestral Apollo, and a silver altar through the theater, together with an impressive number of animals, some of which were sent from outlying villages. In a complex blend of innovation and tradition, the new festival combined the international attraction of lavish spectacles with an emperor cult that by now had become almost routine in these cities, given the readily available imperial images, and with its own cult of an ancestral (πατρῷος) Apollo in whose sacrifices both the city and the villages on its territory were involved;[70] it deserves some attention that the founder seems to focus on the spectacles whereas the city made all the decisions that had to do with the ritual and the detailed organization.

The processions founded by another provincial Roman, C. Vibius Salutaris, in 104 CE in Ephesos is much more original, if not unique.[71] The procession is part of a much larger bequest that we again know through a large epigraphical file whose contents reached from Salutaris' bequest with a later addition, through two decisions of the Ephesian council on organizational details and the decree of the assembly to accept Salutaris' bequest, to honor him with the greatest honors, and to inscribe the text on two stelai, to a letter from the Roman governor who signed off on this decision.

The bequest for the procession orders the creation of nine large statues of the goddess Artemis and twenty-two images (busts) of silver (with some gilding) which on all the major events of the town were to be carried in procession from the Artemision through the city and back – at the sacrifice at the first New Moon of the year (that is, the start of the Ephesian political year); at the monthly assemblies; at the festivals of annual Sebasteia and Soteria and the penteteric Ephesia; and "whenever the city officials should find fit." The images were kept in the *pronaos* of the sanctuary of Artemis, "seven stadia" (a bit more than half a mile) outside the town.[72] They were to be carried by the "gold-bearing" victors in the sacred contests and the

---

[70] Wörrle (1988), 216: the images belonged "zum festen Devotionalienbestand der Stadt."
[71] The texts collected in *I.Ephes.* 27. Most important, Rogers (1991) (with the Greek text and an English translation); but see also Portefaix (1993).
[72] "Seven stadia": Xenophon, *Ephesiaka* 1.2.2.

priests and accompanied by the *neopoioi*, the stewards of the Artemision, and their beadle; they were carried on the Sacred Way towards the city. At the Magnesian gate, the southeastern of the two gates that looked towards the sanctuary (a third, monumental gate opened towards the harbor), the ephebes took over from the *neopoioi* and led the images through the *Kuretenstrasse*, one of the three monumental streets of the city, to the theater. Here they were exhibited in a predetermined order during all the assemblies. At the end, the ephebes walked them out through another monumental street, the *Marmorstrasse* or Marble Street, and finally handed them back to the personnel of the Artemision at the Koressian gate, the northern gate. Unlike Demosthenes in Oinoanda, whose foundation was centered around the penteteric spectacles, Salutaris' was centered on the processions that were regularly repeated throughout the year and for which specific new images were vital; we shall see below how the visuality created by leading its thirty-one rich and glittering images through the city was used to give expression to political concepts and tensions in the contemporary world

Eastern splendors

> Là, tout n'est qu'ordre et beauté,
> Luxe, calme et volupté.

Looking at the above and similar descriptions, the overall impression of festivals in the imperial epoch was that of order, splendor, and plenty; the refrain from Baudelaire's *Invitation au voyage* almost imposes itself. Order appears not only as a cognitive category to evoke social structures, as it did already at the procession of the Athenian Panathenaia or of Mnasistratos in Andania, it is also an aesthetic category that shapes the festivity of the event. The descriptions in the novels focus on festivity only, to the exclusion of every other aspect, and we can safely assume that this reflects the attitude of their readers as well, who carried their real-life expectations into their reading. In general, a festival is a time of heightened joy of life: "A festival is not a time when you bring a sacrifice moaning and expecting jail, but when you offer sacrifices and libations absolutely free of any fear," as Libanius puts it in a letter that advises a governor against too aggressively pagan policies.[73] Accordingly, in this world ἑορτή can become a metaphor

---

[73] Liban. *Epist.* 135.4, to Alexander, an appointee of Julian (see *Epist.* 811, to Julian); see on this ill-guided affair Bowersock (1978), 104–105. See also e.g. *Or.* 45.23 or *Epist.* 1329 on the reality and the norm of festivals.

for any joyful occasion[74]. The possibility of erotic attraction is very much part of it, as the novels show; and already the Eleusinian initiates in Aristophanes' *Frogs* were singing about a girl's breast that was delightfully visible through the rags worn in the mystery procession.[75] The joke points to the incongruity of sexual desire in Demeter's mysteries, which could lead to its conscious exclusion: the rules of the mysteries of Andania explicitly prohibit diaphanous dress for girls and women. In the same comedy, the slave Xanthias is also excited about the smell of roasted pork: eating and drinking are central to every festival, and remain so throughout antiquity and beyond.[76]

The intention of temporary enjoyment was not always so clear and outspoken as in the foundation of one Aurelius Marcus who in 237 CE gave money for "a festival of Happiness," εὐφροσύνης ἑορτή, in his small town of Orkistos in Eastern Phrygia: even if εὐφροσύνη does not refer to happiness as such but to one of the Charites (which seems less convincing to me), the joyful occasion that suspended the hard life in the mountains of Central Anatolia must have been most welcome to his fellow citizens.[77] The longer such a festival lasted, the more occasion for splendor and enjoyment there was: instead of one day only, several days became almost the norm, be it the ten days of the new Ptoia, the twenty-two of the Demostheneia, or an entire month, a ἱερομηνία, as the Ephesians decreed: in about 160 CE, true to their inclination for grandiosity, they decided to devote the entire month of Artemision to their festival of Artemis, and they justified it by pointing out not only how powerful and widely accepted the goddess was all over the world, but also how Ephesos would become "more famous and happy for all the time to come."[78] Everything that could be perceived as distracting from the feeling of high festivity was removed – to the extent that Herodes Atticus changed the famous black cloaks of the

---

[74] E.g. Liban. *Epist.* 65.1, 258.1, 1004.1.4; *Declamat.* 48.1.56. [75] *CIG* 2811, 2812.
[76] Aristophanes, *Frogs* 338.
[77] For the inscription see Buckler (1937), a foundation and its acceptance by a decree of Orkistos, both fragmentary and known through two independent readings made by W. M. Ramsay and J. R. S. Sterret; shortly afterwards, the locals destroyed the stone. The festival name is never fully preserved, and εὐφροσύνη is my suggestion for Buckler's [εὐδαιμ]οσύνη – epigraphically, both fit the space, and the latter is a noun that is almost unattested outside the writings of Archytas and the Doric Pseudopythagorica, the former very common, especially in the context of festivals to which already the Hesiodic names of the three Charites refer, Aglaia ("Splendor"), Thalia ("Good Cheer"), and Euphrosyne; see Rouché (1989) in her commentary on no. 35: "As well as the general sense of delight, εὐφροσύνη has a specific sense of banquet and the joy of a festive occasion, a meaning which continues into the late empire."
[78] *I.Ephes.* 24B (= *LSAM* 31) lines 33f. πόλις ἡμ[ῶν ἐνδοξότερα] τε καὶ εὐδ[αιμονεστερα] εἰς τὸ[ν ἅπα]ντα διαμενεῖ χ[ρόνον]; ἐνδοξότερα for Ephesos, thank to the goddess, already in l. 10.

ephebes into white ones, and that, according to his apocryphal acts, John the Evangelist was arrested by the Ephesians when he took part in the annual Artemis festival in a black dress.[79]

Heightened visuality contributes a large part of this splendor, besides the beauty of order and the richness of the *mis-en-scène*. The descriptions of the novelists, being extrapolations of what one hoped to see in one's own city, already showed this. The many processions developed into colorful pageants that, at least in Heliodorus, would need only floats to be comparable to contemporary events. Be it the splendor of ephebes in shining armor marching in formation, as in Athens, or the large number of selected sacrificial animals, all cleaned and garlanded, as in Oinoanda, or the well-ordered officials on foot and on chariots that formed the procession in Andania: all this appealed mainly to the sense of vision. The divinities were represented by large images carried in these processions, such as the seven images of Artemis in the Salutaris procession in Ephesos. Sometimes, the gods were made present by priests in disguise, and not only in the case of Charikleia and Anthia in their novels: the same could happen in actual ritual. Christian bishops attacking pagan rituals brought forward the charge of incorporating "the heathen demons" by wearing masks during processions.[80] Outside the novels, the only detailed description of such a rite comes again from Pausanias and concerns the often discussed Laphria in Roman Patrai, reshaped and refounded by Augustus. Here, at the festival of Artemis Laphria – a cult presumably transferred to Patrai from Kalydon – the citizens solemnly walked out from the city to the sanctuary of Artemis, and the priestess of Artemis imitated in person the image of the goddess: "First they perform a very magnificent procession for Artemis, and the virgin priestess rides at the end on a chariot drawn by stags." The following day, they burned birds and all sorts of wild animals alive to the goddess, in a rather gruesome spectacle that Pausanias had watched personally.[81] The sacrifice is without parallels and cannot be very old; that the disguise of the priestess recalls the novelistic heroines makes it appear as archaizing rather than archaic, far from Martin Nilsson's "echt altertümliches Opfer."

---

[79] Herodes: see above, n. 51. John: Acts of John, in: *Acta Apostolorum Apocrypha* 2.1 Bonnet (1898) = Hennecke (1965), 236. – On the opposition between black clothes and festivals see also Plut. *Arat.* 53.4, 1051E.
[80] See below, Chapter 3.
[81] Pausanias 7.18.12. See Nilsson (1906), 218–220. For more recent discussions, see Piccaluga (1981); Pirenne-Delforge (2006) and (2008), 227f.

Greek city festivals in the Imperial age

Festivals need crowds, onlookers as well as performers; some could be labelled sacred ambassadors, θεωροί, others we would call tourists: the markets catered to both, as well as to the locals.[82] Pausanias is silent about the visitors of the Laphria in Patrai, but the rite must have been attractive to them. In Sparta, the traditional rite of stealing cheese from the altar of Artemis Orthia was changed into a much bloodier contest of endurance during which the boys were beaten by their seniors until they drew blood, and in the presence of the small and awe-inspiring image of the goddess, brought, legend said, by Orestes from the savage Taurians.[83] While this change of ritual happened before Cicero's time, perhaps during the transformation of the Spartan state under Nabis, in imperial times the Spartans had built a theater around the famous altar in order to open up the spectacle for the many interested foreigners who were attracted by this rite.[84]

Despite some rather spectacular changes in Imperial times, not all is new and typical only of the Imperial age. Hellenistic benefactors were praised for their lavish banquets, such as the *stephanephoroi*, the eponymous magistrates in small Priene, who when entering into office invited "all the tribesmen" to a banquet in their own home, or at least everyone ("the citizens, the resident aliens, the foreigners, the former slaves and the houseslaves") to a dessert, γλυκυσμός:[85] the times were economically strained, and these invitations were more than just an embellishment of daily life.[86]

Orderliness, εὐταξία, is already part of the standard praise in the late Hellenistic ephebic inscriptions of Attica: their disciplined and well-ordered public performances enhanced the fame and glory of the polis.[87] Good order combined with dangerous speed was even more impressive:

---

[82] See Rutherford (2013) and Perlman (2000).
[83] The new form of the rite is often mentioned in imperial texts, and Philostratus has even Apollonius of Tyana discuss it, *VA* 6.20; Libanius *Or.* 1.23 still mentions it.
[84] On the theater temples Hanson (1959) and Nielsen (2002).
[85] *I.Priene* 108 and 109 (120/100 BCE), 114 and 133 (after 84 BCE).
[86] I hope to show elsewhere how such large sacrifices could stimulate the local economy.
[87] See *IG* ii² 1006.58 (about the *kosmetes*) μέγιστον δὲ νομ[ίσ]ας εἶναι κόσμον τῆι πατρίδι τὴ[ν] εὐταξίαν αὐτῶν καὶ ἀνδρείαν [κ]α[τε]σκεύασεν αὐτὸν ἄξιον τῆς τοῦ δήμου προαιρέσεως πρέπουσαν ἑαυτῶι ἀγωγὴν ποιησάμενο[ς] καὶ ἀξίαν τ[ο]ῦ [τ]ε δήμου καὶ αὐτῶν τῶν ἐφήβων, ("judging that their orderliness and manliness would be the greatest ornament for the city, he established it worthy of the people's decision and made the training fitting his own dignity and worthy of the people and the very ephebes"); see *ibid.* 40 (about the ephebes) [ἐπα]ινέσαι τοὺς ἐφήβο[υς τοὺς ἐπ]ὶ Δημητρίου ἄρχοντος [καὶ στεφ]ανῶσαι αὐτοὺς χρυσῶι στεφάνωι εὐσεβείας ἕνεκεν τῆς πρὸς τοὺς [θεοὺ]ς καὶ εὐταξίας [ἧς ἔχοντ]ες διατετελέκασιν ἐν ὅλωι τῶι ἐνιαυτῶι καὶ φιλοτιμίας τῆς εἰς τὴν βουλὴν καὶ τὸν δῆμον ("to praise the ephebes in the archonship of Demetrios and crown them with a golden crown because of their piety towards the gods, the orderliness that they maintained during the entire year, and their effort shown to the council and the people").

Xenophon advised that the skillful participation of cavalry in procession was "most welcome to gods and onlookers alike."[88]

Other things are attested earlier as well. We saw how Aristophanes' audience was aware of the erotic possibilities of the mystery procession; in the solemn cult of Demeter, the incongruity of an exposed female breast was perceived as titillating. The same procession was led by Iakchos, "the chief leader of the Mysteries," ἀρχηγέτης τῶν Μυστηρίων – at some point in the form of his image, carried by a special priest, the ἰακχαγωγός whose title, however, does not precede the Imperial age.[89] More impressively, when Philipp II wanted to impress the Greek world, he organized a lavish festival in Aigai that combined the marriage of his daughter Kleopatra with sacrifices and contests, including a procession that "carried the images of the twelve gods made with marvelous craftmanship and shining wealth ... and as the thirteenth his own."[90] Vibius Salutaris in Ephesos simply had more images and more precious metal, and was not a Macedonian king, but a former Roman administrator; new elites tend to adopt older forms of display.

The same concerns are visible elsewhere and as early, for example in early fourth-century BCE Eretria, as again shown by a decree of the assembly. The citizens debated "how to perform the Artemisia most beautifully, and have sacrifices from as many people as possible." The answer was a lavish musical contest with generous prize money and, less commonly, with the obligation upon the contestants to contribute to the musical introduction of the main sacrifice. As in Lycian Oinoanda half a millennium later, the villages on Eretria's territory were asked to contribute an animal to the sacrifice, in this case a choice ox; a procession with all the musicians who had participated in the contest displayed all animals, the most beautiful one walking first. There was thus a beauty contest for the animals as well, as in other places, "so that the procession and the sacrifice are as beautiful as possible."[91]

Tensions

Festivals are periods cut out from the continuity of time, as sanctuaries are cut out from the continuity of space. Both cut-outs have to be filled, and

---

[88] Xenophon, *Hipparchikos* 3.2–4.
[89] See Clinton (1974), 96–97 and (1992), 64–71; see also Geominy (1989), 263, who assumes that he was represented by a priest.
[90] Diodorus 16.92.5.
[91] *LSCG* 92.40 ὅπως ἂν ὡς καλλίστη ἡ πομπὴ καὶ ἡ θυσία γένηται. Beauty contests of sacrificial animals are known e.g. from Kos (*LSCG* 151A), or from Bargylia, Blümel (1997 and 2000), see also Hotz (2005).

the way they are filled is the result of negotiations between many claims and tensions, and thus is highly informative of contemporary society and religion, and of the groups that play important roles. One obvious strain arose from the interactions between the city and its benefactors; another one existed between the city's status as a Greek town and its role as part of the Roman Empire – a tension that the emperor cult with its emphasis on the ruler only partly resolved.

City and benefactor
The relationship between a city and its benefactors has been amply discussed in the mainly French scholarship on euergetism – in many notes on relevant inscriptions (but never in the promised book) by Louis Robert, then in the books by Paul Veyne and Philippe Gauthier.[92] This research was mainly confined to the Hellenistic era, although the phenomenon lived on into imperial times, practically unchanged except that the imperial power structure added complications.

The interest of the city and it benefactors did not always coincide, and the two sides offered different things to be negotiated: money and the qualities that the German attribute to a "Macher," someone who achieves results, on the side of the benefactor, symbolic capital in the form of manyfold honors on the city's side. The city wanted to assert itself to the outside world, against the neighboring cities, rivals in fame and importance, but also against the dominant power of the Romans, the emperor and his governor; the benefactor needed to assert himself against the many other contenders for power among the elites of the city, the province, or the Empire. Ephesos introduced its sacred month in order to outshine all neighbors, and it spent huge amounts of money without much regard to its desolate financial situation in order to organize splendid festivals, not because the city was hedonistic but because the authorities in their turn thought the gain in symbolic capital to be worthwhile; it needed the realism of a Roman administrator to start thinking otherwise.

Usually, the cities gratefully accepted the gifts of their benefactors, and gained from it. The small town of Rhodiapolis in the Rhodian hinterland, otherwise unremarkable for centuries, suddenly gained fame because her most important citizen, Heraclitus son of Heraclitus, a physician and medical writer whom the Athenians had praised as "the Homer of medical writing," built a temple of Asklepios and Hygieia and instituted local Asklepieia;[93] without being too cynical, one might conjecture that this

---

[92] See Veyne (1976) and Gauthier (1985).   [93] *TAM* II 910.

brought as much fame and additional income to him as it brought to his city. More commonly, the contests that were introduced all over the Greek East by benefactors who sometimes became eponymous founders, or chose a famous name such as Olympia, or dedicated it to an important Roman – the Demostheneia in Oinoanda,[94] Nikekrateia in Tralles,[95] Philomenieia or Aphrodisia Philemonia in Aphrodisias, or the contest of sculptors called Lysimacheia Tatianeia in the same city,[96] and the Tyrimneia in Thyateira,[97] or the contest described as ἀγὼν ὁ ἐκ τῶν Φλαβίου Λυσιμάχου διαθηκῶν "contest according to the will of Flavius Lysimachos" in Aphrodisias,[98] to name but a few – were backed by their respective cities and their councils because they promised fame and business for the city without much additional cost.[99]

Only when they really despaired – because the responsible authorities refused the money, or there was no benefactor in sight – did individual sanctuaries and cults turn to the Roman authorities to ask for money in order to continue their rituals, "the sacrifices and libations for the god and the emperor for victory and eternal permanence [of the dynasty], and for large harvests."[100] The proconsul then sometimes wrote a rather painful official letter – as when the Milesian priest of the August Kabeiroi (σεβαστοὶ θεοὶ Κάβιροι), an otherwise unknown Timon, son of Menestor, turned to Caecina Paetus, proconsul after 37 CE and later famous for his spectacular suicide, in order to obtain from the city the usual contributions for his cult; in a tight economic situation, the city authorities might have been tempted to hope that the priest would want to forego compensation, or refer the priest to the proconsul when the cult had elements of ruler cult anyway, as the August Kabeiroi did. Paetus, however, acted as if he had not understood and pointed out to the Milesians that the "sacrifices and rituals" of the Kabeiroi had been an annual tradition and better be continued and financed by the state "as it had been the custom every year" (καθὼς κατ' ἐνιαυτὸν ἔθος ἐστίν).[101]

In this case, we do not know where the money came from, whether the city or Timon paid up, or a benefactor did. The interests of the benefactors

---

[94] SEG 38.1462. [95] I.Ephes. 27A lines 48, 94; 27B lines 210f., 268–272.
[96] (Aphrodisia) Philomenieia: CIG 2811, 2812; REG 19 (1906), 250 no. 146; MAMA 8.506. Sculptors: MAMA 8.519 = Rendiconti dell'Accademia dei Lincei 26 (1971), 189–197. See BE 1972.414; Reynolds (1982), 189.
[97] I.Smyrn 668 (honors of Smyrna for a victor in the contest in Thyateira).
[98] Reynolds (1982), 57 (under Commodus, 180/190 CE).
[99] See Ziegler (1985); Wörrle (1988), with the important review by Mitchell (1990); van Nijf (2001).
[100] Inscription from Sardis, dated 188/189: Malay (1999), no. 131.
[101] I. Milet I:9 no. 360, cf. VI:1 p. 125.

themselves did not necessarily coincide with those of the cities, and negotiations were needed, in order to determine how much money went towards which honors. Usually, these negotiations remain invisible to us (and might well have been invisible to most citizens as well): all we see are the honorary decrees, both Hellenistic and Imperial. Sometimes things become a bit more visible – when a benefactor could not make up his mind, or when the two parties could not agree. Pliny asked Trajan for advice when one Iulius Largus (who was unknown to him), made him his heir and wished that he spend the inherited money either on a building or a contest in honor of the emperor; Trajan let Pliny decide, and we do not know what came out of it.[102] The ambitious building program that Dio Chrysostom planned for his home town, Prusa, ran into difficulties when some citizens opposed the demolition of some older buildings for historical reasons, as they claimed; in the background, there was envy and elite competition. Dio was incensed: his opponents defended those empty shells, he argued, "as if they were the Propylaia, the Parthenon, the Samian Heraion, the temple of Didyma or the one of Artemis at Ephesos."[103]

Dio was not alone with such problems. The emperor Antoninus Pius, who endorsed the building program of his friend P. Vedius Antoninus III in Ephesos, did so against the manifest reluctance of the Ephesians, who obviously would have preferred, as the emperor phrased it, "shows and distributions and the spectacles of games" to new buildings.[104] This case also shows how easily – though not exactly elegantly – a well-placed benefactor could bulldoze his way over the decisions of his city. No wonder that, instead of receiving the usual public honors, a statue with the honorary decree inscribed on its base, Vedius had himself to display an inscription that spelled out the emperor's recognition.

There is at least one other case where an elite member decided in favor of utility instead of pleasure. In the reign of Commodus, Dionysios son of Dionysios, the priest of the local Apollo in a small Lydian town, decided to spend the money tradition wanted him to expend on banquets (ὑπὲρ τῶν εἰς τὰ δεῖπνα ἀναλωμάτων) on ameliorating the water

---

[102] Plin. *Ep.* 10.75 and 76. [103] Dio, *Or.* 40.8.
[104] *I.Ephes.* 1491 (= *SIG*³ 850), a. 145/146 CE. See also *I.Ephes.* 1493, where the emperor again endorses and joins Pollio's program as that of someone "who enhances the beauty of his city and the splendor of the province" (tentatively restored as α[ὔξοντι τὸ κά]λλος τῆς [πόλεως] καὶ κό[σμο]ν τῆ[ς Ἀσίας]). See the dossier in Kalinowski (2002) and, on the type of imperial letter to which these documents belong, Kokkinia (2003). The emperor shares his rejection of entertainment with the moralists: see Diogenes of Oinanda, frg. 2, col. iii Smith: "theaters ... and baths and perfumes and ointments, which we have left to the masses."

supply.[105] As far as we can see, there were no major problems with the economy, so the decision had most likely the same reason that Antoninus Pius had for his recommendation. The text is inscribed on a building block and must come from whatever construction – most likely an aqueduct – Dionysios financed.

Such rerouting of funds, then, was not unique at the epoch; according to a letter of Hadrian, it was happening often, and cut both ways.[106] Not everybody was happy with the abolition of games and spectacles for more utilitarian reasons – not just the crowds that loved to be entertained, but also the entertainment industry itself. Earlier in the century, in his letter from the later months of 134 CE, Hadrian reassured the "Guild of Itinerant Stage Artists of Dionysos" (σύνοδος θυμελικὴ περιπολιστικὴ τῶν περὶ τὸν Διόνυσον τεχνιταί) that he would not tolerate "that a city would use the money set aside for games by an imperial law, a city decree or a private foundation for other expenditures or the construction of a building." Such a misappropriation, as they saw it, alarmed the professional artists and athletes who spent money on travel only to find out, when they arrived, that the contest had been cancelled.[107] The emperor was willing to grant an exemption to a city in distress, such as a famine when one needed funds to buy wheat; but he insisted that the request should be addressed to him. One wonders whether ameliorating the water supply qualified for such an imperial exemption, and whether Dionysios the son of Dionysios had written to the emperor.

City and emperor

This brings up the second tension, that between the city that viewed itself as autonomous and the sometimes painful restrictions on autonomy that the imperial power structure brought with it. Hadrian's letters to the artists of Dionysos reveal an emperor who was willing to override the decrees of the cities in the interest of maintaining the spectacles and thus preserving the good will of the Guild.[108] Being connected with the governor's or the emperor's court gave individuals and cities an edge, because it could secure the success of petitions for imperial backing or for privileges for oneself or for one's community. The imperial letters to Ephesos and Aphrodisias show how a powerful citizen with imperial patronage could efficiently undo even a decision by the assembly; and honorary decrees regularly

---

[105] Malay (1999), 115 no. 127. [106] Petzl and Schwertheim (2006), line 8.
[107] Petzl and Schwertheim (2006), a long inscription from Alexandreia Troas.
[108] Petzl and Schwertheim (2006), 36.

point out the services that good connections had brought to the city. Even in a place as far away from any metropolis as among the Arillenoi and Thamoreitai on the Lydian countryside, we find a local community handsomely honoring its priest of Zeus Driktes and his wife, the priestess, with a golden crown for having obtained the privilege of a fair from the proconsul T. Aurelius Fulvius, who was in office in 134/135 CE; the priest dutifully thanked his god with a dedication for his help in the undertaking.[109]

The most common expression of this new order of things was the addition of the imperial cult to an existing festival. After Simon Price's work, it has become common knowledge that this was more than an empty political gesture: it expressed the new order and its complexities in a religious code. By being worshiped, the emperor had become part of the civic pantheon: after all, he was ὁ ἐπιφανέστατος θεός (*deus praesentissimus*), "the most helpful divinity," as his benefactions towards any individual city demonstrated; as an all-powerful benefactor, he remained ἐπιφανέστατος even when he had become a Christian.[110] The Greeks in their entirety promoted Nero to Zeus Eleutherios and Hadrian to Zeus Panhellenios, manifestations of the most powerful Olympian.[111] At the same time, the emperor represented a political system that was not always comfortable and needed constant attention and maintenance, and his representatives were very concrete forces to be reckoned with in political negotiations. Only Tiberius once pointed out that he needed only "very modest honors, befitting a human."[112] Thus, the cities had to take care of Rome's over-arching power and, at the same time, project the very best image of themselves.

The procession of Salutaris again

Program and form

The iconographical program behind the procession funded by C. Vibius Salutaris in Ephesos beautifully expresses these complexities; it is wrong

---

[109] Malay (1994), 152 no. 523, with a good commentary.
[110] ἐπιφανέστατος is used of Gaius in Cyzicus, *SIG*³ 799.9, or of Claudius in Maroneia, *SEG* 53.659; the augusti Diocletian and Maximianus and their ἐπιφανέστατοι Καίσαρ[ες] dedicated a silver statue to the local Zeus in the hinterland of the Skamander, *I.Ilion* 3.96. See also the milestones under Geta in Halikarnassos, *BSA* 1955, 106–7 no. 33b, and under Diocletian, Maximian, Constantius I, and Galerius in Ephesos, *I.Ephes.* 3603. Christian emperors, e.g. Constantinus II in Delphi, *SIG*³ 903 C, or Constans *ibid.* 903 D; see Barceló (2003). Compare ἐπιφανής (σωτήρ) e.g. for Hadrian in Nikomedeia, *TAM* IV 1.401, or Samos (as Zeus Olympios, mostly also σωτήρ καὶ κτίστης) in a series of small altars (erected during a visit, as often?) *IG* xii:6, 503–526; see next note. For ἐπιφανής as a divine epithet in the Hellenistic and Imperial epochs, see L. Robert, *passim*.
[111] See Taeger (1960), passim; Jones(1999), 11f.
[112] The famous response to the city of Gytheion, *SEG* 9,922f. = Ehrenberg and Jones (1955), no. 102.

and short-sighted to label it simply as political propaganda, as has been done.[113] The twenty-nine images that he had made, and to which two months later he added two more, were carried through the city several times a year, in an order determined by the sponsor, and then exposed in the theater during the people's assemblies and other events. In a first group of images, there were nine different statues of Artemis: a golden image with two silver stags that reproduces the traditional cult image of the goddess, and eight silver images of the goddess with a torch, in an individual iconography that is not always accessible to us, both because of the allusiveness of the text written for natives ("another silver Artemis with torch, similar to the one in the exedra of the ephebes"), and the damage to the stone.[114] These nine large statues (ἀπεικονίσματα, "representations") thus develop an Artemisian theology, talking about the main goddess of Ephesos and her complex figure, whose power and fame determined the city's perception from within and without.

At the same time Artemis was represented as clearly distinct both from the city of Ephesos and from Rome, which each received their own set of statues; the same bipolarity between Ephesos and the Artemision is expressed in the decision to have the documents of the foundation inscribed both in the theater and in the sanctuary. Fifteen images represent Ephesos' present and past: its institutions, Demos, Boule, Gerousia, Ephebeia, and the six tribes; its geographical landmark, the Pion mountain; and its four founders, the heroes Euonymus, the pre-Ionian settler,[115] and Androklos, the Ionian founder of the city,[116] king Lysimachus, the second founder, and the emperor Augustus, who transformed Ephesos into the foremost city of Western Asia, μητρόπολις τῆς Ἀσίας. Augustus opens up the purely Greek history and traditions of Ephesos to Rome, although the inscription itself resolutely understands Augustus as part of its own Ephesian present, since he is also the religious focus of the tribe Sebaste. There is thus a reason for Augustus' inclusion in this Ephesian group and his exclusion from the five purely Roman images – Trajan, the actual ruler

---

[113] The program is outlined by Salutaris' letter, *I.Ephes.* 27; political propaganda according to Portefaix (1993).
[114] *I.Ephes.* 27B lines 168: ὁμοίως καὶ ἄλλη Ἄρτεμις ἀργυρέα λαμπαδηφόρος, ἐ[μφερής]|τῆι ἐν τῆι ἐξέδρηι τῶν ἐφήβων.
[115] The name is missing in *I.Ephes.* 27B line 191, but the supplement (Ε[ὐωνύμου]) is confirmed by the logic of the list that combines a hero and a tribe, here the tribe of the Euonymoi.
[116] The name is missing in *I.Ephes.* 27B line 183 but the supplement (suggested by R. Merkelbach), although conjectural, makes sense: Androklos, the founder, cannot be absent, and the tribe that is combined with the missing hero is the Karenaioi whose ancestors helped the Ephesians against the children of Androklos: Rogers (1991), 109.

at the time of the first procession, and his wife Plotina; the Roman Senate; the Equestrian Order, to which Vibius Salutaris belonged; and the Roman people. The way these images are grouped articulates their relationship. The images of Trajan and Plotina, the ruling emperor and his empress, are standing alone in no other combination, while the other images pair an Ephesian and a Roman institution: the Roman senate and the Ephesian *boule*, the *populus Romanus* and the Ephesian *gerousia*, the equestrian order and the *ephebeia*. This changes only when the images talk about the subdivisions of the city itself, where Augustus goes with the tribe *Sebaste*, the demos of Ephesos with the tribe of the Epheseioi, and so on. The Roman institutions are represented as parallel to and on the same hierarchical level as the Ephesian ones; only the ruling emperor and his empress transcend this parallelism of structures. Vibius Salutaris and his Ephesian partners thus cleverly used the medium of the procession to talk about the city of Ephesos and its relationship to Rome, and to assert Ephesian claims vis-à-vis Rome's power. The claim of Ephesos is lofty: the city insists on its Greek, Ionian autonomy under the umbrella of the one ruling emperor. At every major festival of Ephesos, the procession publicly and visibly negotiated the tensions behind this claim.

The two images that Salutaris added three months later pose their own questions. One is Athena Pammousos, dedicated to the *paides*, the citizen boys: the statue underlines their ongoing education, with an Athena as patroness of education that feels more Roman than Greek. The other image represents Sebaste Homonoia Chrysophoros, uniting imperial Rome with the main contests whose victors are the *chrysophoroi* who carry the images, and with Concord, in a way that make one wonder whether there was an actual need for concord in this specific group of athletes, or between the athletes, the city, and Rome.

By structuring space, the medium of the procession had always visualized complex relationships or concepts. Already in Archaic and Classical Greece, it articulated the relationship between a city and a powerful sanctuary on its borders, between Argos and the Heraion, Athens and the sanctuary of Eleusis, Miletus and the sanctuary of Didyma, and it gave visual expression to complex communities and their power structures, such as the Athenian state in the Panathenaian procession, or the Augustan ruling class in the procession attested on the frieze of the Ara Pacis. But compared to those earlier examples, the Ephesian procession innovated in order to do this in a much more reflective way, expressing normativity rather than symbolizing reality: rather than using, as those processions did, real people as signs for communication, Salutaris used allegorical images, images that are more easily given the desired shape.

In Archaic and Classical Greece, processions such as this one that connected an outlying sanctuary with its city were all centrifugal, moving outwards from Miletus to Didyma or from Argos to its Heraion: the center continuously conquered its outlying territories.[117] Vibius' procession performed a much more complex movement, in an intricate play with changing actors and shifting centers.

The procession started at the Artemision outside the city, entered the town at the Magnesian Gate and marched through one of the three monumental streets to the theater, where the images were exhibited for a while. Then it moved through a second monumental street to a different gate, the Koressian Gate, and back to the sanctuary. All the images were exhibited or stored in the *pronaos* of the shrine, both for exhibition and for safekeeping under the protection of the divinity. On the surface, this is not a linear but a circular movement. But it was articulated and broken up into several steps. In the first step, the procession treated the sanctuary as the center. The images were always carried by the victors in the large city contests, who were also called *chrysophoroi* and who appear connected both with the city and the sanctuary. On the first leg of the procession, from the Artemision to the Magnesian Gate, the images were guarded and accompanied by the stewards (νεοποιοί) of the sanctuary, its beadle (σκηπτοῦχος), and its priests. As soon as the procession reached the Magnesian Gate, the constellation changed. It became centripetal, with the city as the center, as the actors demonstrate: now, the Ephesian ephebes, the annual army of young citizens, replaced the stewards and their beadle as honor and security guards, brought the images to the theater, and exhibited them there at predetermined spots and in the triads of Artemis, hero or Roman personification, and Ephesian institution. The second step reversed this movement: once the event in the theater ended, the ephebes led the images from the theater to the Koressian Gate, in a centrifugal procession towards the sanctuary. At the gate it again turned centripetal, with the sanctuary as its center: the ephebes handed over the image to the personnel of the Artemision.

Why this complex choreography? One reason is the status of the sanctuary and the city: although nominally a city shrine and in certain respects depending on the city, it was always not just spatially separated from the city, had its own priesthood and personnel, and an international fame very much of its own. The city – with the large theater where the citizens met monthly for their business of running the community – and

---

[117] On these categories see Graf (1996).

the sanctuary of Artemis far outside the city walls were thus performing a closely orchestrated balancing act, with neither one conquering the other nor submitting to a conquering push: each respected the other's status, in a relationship that would have been unthinkable in the Age of the Polis but that was made possible under the umbrella of the Roman Empire. It was a movement between two poles, the sanctuary and the theater.

But of course this could have been expressed by a straight line, in and out along the same route. The circle, or rather curve, if perceived from the vantage point of the city, from the Magnesian Gate to the theater and from there to the Koressian Gate, still needs an explanation. The answer has to make a distinction between the human actors of the procession, and the images that were escorted. The human actors changed at the two gates, from the representatives of the temple to those of the young citizens and back to the temple staff: on this level, the temple and the city are the two poles of the action whose relationship has to be negotiated. The images, however, remain the same, and all three components of their tripartite combination remain stable throughout the entire ritual: no image is added or subtracted at a gate, and as triads they are exposed in the theater during the Ephesian assemblies. This reflects the fact that, for Ephesos, Artemis is "the goddess who presides over our city," ἡ προεστῶσα τῆς πόλεως ἡμῶν θεὸς Ἄρτεμις, as a decree from about 160 CE says: while the human actors change, the goddess remains the same, and she binds together sanctuary and city.[118] Thus, it should not surprise that three statues of Ephesian Artemis with many breasts have been found in the Prytaneion, the political center of the city with the eternal fire of Hestia, among them the "Beautiful Artemis Ephesia," as the excavators called her.[119] On the other hand, the city had some political influence on the sanctuary: when Paul angered the Ephesian silversmiths, they assembled in the theater, not the sanctuary, and it was the γραμματεύς, the official secretary of the assembly, who calmed them down, not a priest.[120]

But again: why this circular movement? It appears to be caused by the necessity that all these images, and especially those of Artemis, make contact with most of the city. Ephesos had three main gates, the Magnesian in the East, the Koressian in the North, and the triple Harbor Gate towards the Sea; and it had three monumental streets from the three gates to the city center with agora and theater, the *Kuretenstrasse*,

---

[118] *LSAM* 31 = *I.Ephes.* 24B.
[119] Fleischer (1973), 14–15, nos. E 45 ("Grosse Artemis Ephesia"), E 46 ("Schöne Artemis Ephesia"), E 47 ("Kleine Artemis Ephesia").
[120] Acts 19:23–35.

the Marble Street plus Stadium Street that, despite the excavators' nomenclature, are one street only, and the much shorter, and still not well understood, Arkadiane that connects the city center with the harbor and that appears much more as an elongated marketplace than a street proper. The procession used two of the three gates and the two long monumental streets, but did not enter Arkadiane: to enter it would have necessitated turning the entire procession in a full circle at its harbor end and returning to Marble Street, a logistically almost impossible move; thus, it was practical reasons that kept the procession away from a third leg. In other words: the way in and the way out do not cancel each other out semantically as they would if the procession used the same route both ways; by using a different way out from the way in, it opens itself up to a new meaning, that of designating the space as relating to the symbols carried. Ephesos is thus designated as Sacred City of Artemis, as Guy Rogers saw. But it is also designated as the civic space of the Ephesians, and as part of Rome.

I thus feel tempted to connect the semantics of the Ephesian procession with the circular processions that we know much better from Rome where the circular movement is in their names: they are the Amb-arvalia or *ambarvale sacrificium*, the procession round (ἀμφί) the fields, and the *amburbium sacrificium*. Both are basically sacrificial processions: Servius defines both with the phrase *quod urbem* [resp. *arva*] *ambit victima*, "because the sacrificial animal goes round the city or the fields," and the long and detailed description in Cato's *De Re Rustica* similarly talks about "leading the *suovetaurilia*, the animal triad of pig, sheep and ox" that maximizes the animal sacrifice, round the fields (*circumagi*).[121] Cato also makes it clear what all this is about: his farmer has to invoke Mars, the god of the fields, and to say, among other things, "to take care to purify my farm, my land and my ground around whichever part you think that these *suovetaurilia* have to be driven or carried."[122] The animals thus are the pointers to the land with which the god should be concerned; the circular movement guarantees that all relevant land is included. The Ephesian movement with the images through the city, from one gate to its center to the other gate, along the two main arteries of the city, does the same for Artemis, only with less spatial precision and a higher interest in political landmarks, as again Rogers pointed out: it indicates the area that is ruled by the city goddess Artemis, the political entity Ephesos.

---

[121] Serv. *Buc.* 3.77; Cato, *Rust.* 141.

[122] *Rust.* 141 *uti illace suovitaurilia fundum agrum terramque meam quota ex parte sive circumagi sive circumferenda censeas, uti cures lustrare.*

Being Roman in Ephesos
The main ingredients in this procession thus are the images, those of the goddess, the heroes, and the emperors, and the personifications or allegorical images. This use of allegorical images has no real parallel in other Greek processions, as far as I can see. To some degree, it recalls Roman *pompae* where sometimes the very common *tituli*, the inscribed signs, were supplemented or replaced by allegorical statues: according to a fragmentary frieze from the arch of Titus, his triumphal procession of 81 CE exhibited an image of the river god Jordan; and in the *pompa funebris* of the emperor Pertinax of 193 CE, "there followed all the populaces he had conquered, represented in bronze statues in their native dress."[123] It is thus likely that the combination of divine images with those of the imperial house looked at the Roman *pompa circensis* rather than at Greek models: one of the main changes in the circus procession of the Julio-Claudian epoch was the addition of images of the deceased members of the imperial house at the head of the procession. At least in one case we hear that an image – the bust of Marcellus – was not only carried in the procession but placed during the performance of the games near the entrance of the circus in the same way Salutaris had his images being placed in the theater during the entire duration of the assemblies.[124]

Such a Roman influence on the processional representations should not surprise us. The sponsor himself, C. Vibius Salutaris, was very conscious of being both a Roman and a Greek, a councilor of Ephesos and an administrator and official of the emperor, Salutaris in Latin and Σαλουτάριος in Greek.[125] The texts that set up his copious foundation are all written in Greek, and this is true not just for the decrees of the Ephesian assembly and Salutaris' letters to the Ephesians where Greek goes without saying, but also for the letters of the Roman proconsul, C. Aquilius Proculus, and the praetorian legate, P. Afranius Flavianus, who both had to approve the foundation: these officials routinely used Greek to communicate with Greek authorities.[126] Greek in these documents thus is a given. It is different in another group of texts. We still have several of the bases that were to hold the images Salutaris donated during the assemblies in the

---

[123] See *ThesCRA* 1.45 no. 57 (Cassius Dio 75.4.5 on Pertinax); 48 no. 77 (Titus); see also 49 no. 78.
[124] Reconstructed by Arena (2009). On images in processions see also Edelmann (2008), who overstresses the importance of the theater.
[125] In the same way as the Roman *primopilaris* became the Greek πριμοπιλάριος, to avoid an ending that in Greek ears sounded feminine.
[126] We need a study on the bilingualism of Roman officials in the Greek East comparable to Rizakis (2008) on the bilingualism of the Greek elites in imperial times.

Ephesian theater: their texts are all bilingual, with an identical text except for the dedication that refers to the specific image, the final dating formula, and two explanatory additions in the Greek text that are absent in the Latin. Here is one, to Artemis and the Augustan Tribe, that preserves Salutaris' full *cursus honorum*:[127]

[Dian]ae ^{vacat} Ephesiae et
[ph]yle ^{vacat} Sebaste
C(aius) [Vi]bius, C(aii) f(ilius), Vof(entina), Salutaris, promag(ister) portuum provinc(iae) Sicilia[e,] item promag(ister) frumenti mancipalis, praefec(tus) cohor(tis) Astur[u]m et Callaecorum, trib(unus) mil(itum) leg(ionis) XX[II]
  Primigeniae
P(iae) F(idelis), subprocurator provinc(iae) Mauretaniae Tingitanae, item provinc(iae) Belgicae Dianam argenteam, item imagines argentea[s] duas, unam divi Aug(usti), [a]l̤i[a]m phyles, sua pecunia fecit ita, ut omni ecclesia in theatro supra bases ponerentur; ob quarum dedicationem in {in} sortitionem sex phylaes consecravit HS(sestertiis) XXXIII CCCXXXS.
Ἀρτέμιδι Ἐφεσίᾳ καὶ φυλῇ Σεβαστῇ Γ(άϊος) Οὐείβιος, Γ(αΐου) υἱός,
Οὐωφεντείνα, Σαλουτάριος, ἀρχώνης λιμένων ἐπαρ-
[χ]είας Σικελίας καὶ ἀρχώνης σείτου δήμου Ῥωμαίων,
ἔπαρχος σπείρης Ἀστούρων καὶ Καλλαίκων, χειλί-
αρχος λεγιῶνος ΚΒ Πρειμιγενίας Πίας Φιδήλεως, ἀν-
τεπίτροπος ἐπαρχείας Μαυρετανίας Τινγιτανῆς καὶ
ἐπαρχείας Βελγικῆς, Ἄρτεμιν ἀργυρέαν καὶ εἰκόνας
ἀργυρέας δύο, μίαν θεοῦ Αὐγούστου καὶ ἄλλην τῆς φυλῆς, ἐκ
τῶν ἰδίων ἐποίησεν· ἅτινα καθιέρωσαν, ἵνα τιθῆνται κα-
τ' ἐκκλησίαν ἐν τῷ θεάτρῳ [ἐ]πὶ τῶν βάσεων, ὡς ἡ διάταξις αὐτοῦ περιέχει· καθιέρωσεν δὲ καὶ εἰς κλῆρον ταῖς ἓξ φυλαῖς
δηνάρια ΗΤΛΓ ἀσ(σάρια) Ϛ.
ἐπὶ ἀνθυπάτου Γ(αΐου) Ἀκυιλλίου Πρόκλου, γραμματεύοντος Τιβ(ερίου)
  Κλαυδίου Ἰουλιανοῦ,
φιλοσεβάστου καὶ φιλοπάτριδος, ^{vacat} τὸ Β.

> To Artemis of Ephesos and the August Tribe, C. Vibius, son of Gaius, (of the tribe) Ufentina, Salutaris, deputy head of the ports of the province of Sicily, deputy head for grain contracts [*in the Greek:* of the Roman people], prefect of the cohort of Asturians and Callaecans, military tribune of the 22nd legion Primigenia Pia Fidelis, deputy procurator of the province of Mauretania and Tingitana, the same of the province of Belgium, has had made at his own expense a silver Artemis and two other silver images, one of the divinised Augustus, the other one of the tribe, so that at every meeting in the theater they would be put on their bases [*in the Greek:* as the legal

---

[127] *I.Ephes.* 28–36 (I cite no. 29). Note also the carefully Greek declination of φυλή: genitive singular *phyles* (8), dative singular *phyle* (2), dative plural *phylaes* (10).

instruction provides]; for their dedication he consecrated 33,330 and a half sesterces [*in the Greek:* and 6 asses] for drawing by lot among the six tribes. [*In the Greek:* (Given) under the proconsul C. Aquilius Proclus [i.e. 104 CE], when Tiberius Claudius Iulianus, lover of the emperor and of his home city, was secretary for the second time.]

The intended audience of these texts, with their careful distinction between the two worlds – including the precise declination of the Greek technical term *phyle* in the Latin text and the distinction between Roman Salutaris and Greek Σαλουτάριος – must have been both the citizens of Ephesos and any Roman official and visitor who chanced to pass through the city.[128] Again, as in the allegorical images, we perceive a manifest intention of mediating between Ephesos and Rome, the Greek East and the Roman West.

It would be important to know more about Salutaris' background, but "the man behind this foundation largely remains a shadow."[129] The Ephesians called him their citizen. At the same time he must have been born a Roman citizen, as his *tria nomina* indicate; they contain no Greek element – on the contrary, he takes some care to Hellenize his Roman cognomen. One would like to know more: the Ephesians refer to "the good character" of his father, or rather "the good situation," ἀγαθὴ διάθεσις, which must include the wealth that results from and confirms good qualities. It is tempting to think that this father was a Roman businessman and knight with formal residence in Ephesos (*civis Romanus Ephesi consistens*) and as such a member of the *conventus* of resident Roman citizens.[130] It remains unclear whether it was his son only or already the father and his progeny upon whom the city conferred citizenship. At any rate, being Roman must have been a large part of the self-definition of these men, and a Roman audience must have been always included in their public proclamations; after all, Ephesos, the site of the imperial cult and the governor's residence, had its share of Romans, residents or visitors. And Salutaris is not the only prominent Epheso-Roman whose background

---

[128] The only other bilingual text preserved from Vibius is the dedication of an image of his "friend" M. Arruntius Claudianus, a fellow administrator and official, *I.Ephes.* 620, made perhaps during his second tenure as praetorian legate of Asia.

[129] Rogers (1991), 16, who collects all the available evidence (16–19).

[130] The key passage is *I.Ephes.* 27A lines 14–19: Γάϊός] τε Οὐίβι[ος Σαλο]υτάριος, ἀ|νὴρ ἱππικῆς τά[ξε]ος, γένει καὶ ἀξίᾳ διάσημος, στρατείαις τε καὶ | ἐπιτροπαῖς ἀ[πὸ] τοῦ κυρίου ἡμῶν αὐτοκράτορος κεκοσμημένος,| πολείτης ἡ[μέτε]ρος καὶ τοῦ βουλευτικοῦ συνεδρίου, πρὸς πα[τρός | τε ἀγ]αθῇ χρώμ[ενος δι]αθέσι: "C. Vibius Salutaris, a man of the equestrian order, conspicuous by birth and personal worth, and adorned with military commands and procuratorships by our lord emperor, a citizen of our city and a member of the council, regulating his life well as his father did" (translation after Guy M. Rogers). On the *conventus* of the *cives consistentes* see Van Andringa (2003).

remains hazy to us. In a similar way, we do not know whether Publius Vedius Antoninus (whom we meet first under Hadrian) went back to a native family that received its citizenship more than a century earlier, through Augustus' powerful friend Vedius Pollio who for a while did business in Ephesos, or whether Publius just belonged to another Italian family who resided in the city. And although his adoptive son with the sonorous name Marcus Claudius Publius Vedius Antoninus Phaedrus Sabinianus, perhaps the first senator to come from Ephesos, started out in life as M. Claudius Phaedrus, the Greek cognomen does not make him a freedman (even if we did not know that he was elevated to senatorial rank), given that his father was the solidly Roman knight M. Claudius Sabinus. We can suspect that at some point there was a Greek Phaidros who received Roman citizenship from a Claudius and left his now cognomen wandering through his family. Greek and Roman identities were deeply intertwined in these fascinating but hazy elite members of provincial cities.[131]

Being Greek
Considering the Romanness of these men leads me to consider the expressions of being Greek: Greekness is another topic that looms large in the discourse that the festivals offer. To be Greek is to be, or to imagine oneself to be, part of a direct tradition in an epoch when the tradition feels threatened. The citizens of Akraiphia rewarded Epameinondas for having revived the traditional (πάτριοι) processions and dances; a couple of decades later, the citizens of Elis, responsible for organizing the games at Olympia, praised a Smyrnaian pancratiast, Tiberius Claudius Rufus, because "he had carefully performed the exercises under the eyes of the *hellanodikai* ("judges of Greekness") according to the traditional custom of our games."[132] It does not matter whether this tradition is genuine or invented: whatever Epameinondas had performed as the traditional rituals and dances was this tradition.

To be Greek means also to assert a privileged cultural background in a world where other traditions – non-Greek and "barbarian" – made their own claims. Like many other Eastern cities in the Imperial age, Antiocheia on the Orontes in Syria had its Olympic games, introduced as the most spectacular hallmark of being Greek; some of these "secondary" Olympic

---

[131] For these men, see Kalinowski (2002) and the studies in Heller and Pont (2012). On Vedius Pollio, Syme (1961).
[132] *SIG³* 1073.20 (after 117 CE).

games had a wide echo in their contemporary world.[133] As we shall see, Libanius had some problems with the way the city had changed the tradition of who was invited to the banquet during this festival, and he did not keep silent about it. But before censuring the Antiocheans, Libanius contrasted their festival with the Elean one that was still felt to be the source of all other games: "Our Olympian Games received so much care that even the Eleans wanted to know our local form and enquired about them."[134] In this respect at least, the Antiocheans were better Greeks than even those for whom Herakles himself had founded the contest.

This same aim of supreme Greekness explains the program of the many musical contests founded during the imperial epoch, such as the one in the Demostheneia of Oinoanda. After the preludes of trumpet-players and heralds and the contests of praise speeches, *encomia*, for both the emperor and the sponsor, there followed performances by flutists (soloists or with a choir), the recitation of comedies and tragedies, finally a citharoedic contest. As Michael Wörrle has shown, the origin of this program – which is far from being confined to Oinoanda but is, with variations, the standard program of musical contests in the Imperial age – lies in the Mouseia of Thespiai, an arch-Greek event that resonates with Hesiod and his Muses.[135] But the Thespian program was much simpler; the imperial contests added not only the encomia as a reference to the imperial umbrella and the local powers, but also had the sequence of comedy – tragedy – citharoedic performance: this does not derive from Thespiai, but from Athens. In some respects, the imperial cities of the Greek East were behaving as if they derived directly from Periklean Athens.

Criticizing festivals

As happens almost anywhere and anytime in human societies, not everybody was happy with this rich display of wealth and lavishness. Some contemporary intellectuals – from Dio and Plutarch in the late first century CE to Porphyry in the late third century CE – had problems with public festivals. Their uneasiness was as much ethical and political as it was theological and religious, and it could feed on philosophical concerns that went as far back as the late sixth century BCE, and that had become

---

[133] See Soler (2006), 37–38. On another case of such Olympia see Parker (2011). We lack a monograph on the Olympia that could stand beside Weir (2004).
[134] Liban. *Or.* 53.2.   [135] Wörrle (1988).

part of Plato's thinking about religion; in this sense these concerns had always been part of the reality of civic cult.[136] This does not imply that the criticism should be understood as originating from a quest for personal religiosity, as constructing "pure" personal religion against tainted public cult. It is no coincidence that the two treatises against animal sacrifice from the period, Porphyry's *On Abstinence* and (Pseudo-)Lucian's *On Sacrifices*, argue out of theological and ethical concerns that go well beyond personal belief. "What the simpleminded people do in festivals and other contacts with the gods," Lucian writes, "and what they pray for and think about them, is such that I am not sure whether anybody is so dim-witted and obtuse that he would not laugh about the silliness of the rituals – although I think that rather than to laugh he should examine whether one could really call these rites pious." In his *On Sacrifices*, Lucian confronts the ungodly thoughts about the gods with the lavishness of sacrifices and rituals: pious thoughts, not lavish rituals are asked for, and the title of the treatise is in some respects a misnomer that hides the more general contestation of the ritual tradition in the name of purity.[137]

This feeling had been current among philosophers and moralists since Heraclitus, and it lived on during the Imperial epoch. Late in the third century CE, Porphyry went as far as to demand the abolition of animal sacrifice altogether. But this did not mean that he therefore wanted to do away with sacrifices and festivals. He was willing to keep them under one condition: "Whoever is about to perform a sacrifice, shall go about it with a pure mind, offering to the gods pleasing gifts, not expensive ones."[138] Philostratus, in his *Life of Apollonius of Tyana*, concurs, following (I think) a tradition that goes back to propaganda of the Asklepieion at Aigai in Kilikia. The wealthy Kilikian who sacrifices "Egyptian bulls and large hogs" contradicts the sound maxim that "we should not go beyond the just means in sacrifices and dedications," and as Apollonius realizes, he does so to overcompensate for his earlier immoral conduct; the Pythagorean sage thus confirms Plato's injunction in his *Laws*, repeated by Cicero, that an impious person should not offer gifts to the gods.[139] The famous Epidaurian temple inscription expresses a similar sentiment:

---

[136] On the moralists see Quet (1981). [137] Luc. *Sacr.* 1. See Graf (2011b) and Belayche (2011).
[138] Porph. *Abst.* 2.19.
[139] Philostrat. *VA* 1.10 (the maxim in 1.11); the same sentiment, although with a less flashy exemplification, in Porph. *Abst.* 2.15–16 after Theophrastus (part of it = F 7 Pötscher), whose story reflects late archaic discussions according to Wehrli (1964), 56. I have argued that the Aigai episodes of *VA* reflect a local sanctuary tradition: Graf (1984–1985). Plato, *Legg.* 4.716B, repeated in Cic. *Legg.* 2.22.

ἁγνὸν χρὴ νάοιο θυωδέος ἐντὸς ἰόντα
ἔμμεναι· ἁγνεία δ'ἐστὶν φρονεῖν ὅσια.

Pure has to be whoever goes into the incense-smelling temple: but purity is to think holy thoughts.

Jan Bremmer has convincingly argued that the epigram originated in late Hellenistic or early Imperial times.[140]

This interest in moral purity resonated with the cities and even with Roman administrators, in many local variations. The tendency to heighten the festive atmosphere through dress and other paraphernalia – Herodes Atticus' white cloaks for the ephebes, for example – should be read in such a key; the same is true for the hexametrical law from first-century CE Kios that gives regulations for the attire of women (barefoot, with pure white robes) in a *kalathos* procession, presumably for Demeter and prescribed by an oracular god.[141] Similar things happened at Andania, at about the same time. Some Imperial cities advertised purity regulations for their sanctuaries, not only for mystery divinities like Dionysos in Smyrna or Men in Attika,[142] or for Asklepios, where direct contact with the god in a dream had always called for heightened purity,[143] but also for city protectors like Athena in Lindos.[144] In the light of this growing awareness of the need for visible purity to express a mental state, the arguments used by Claudius' proconsul (a Roman *pontifex* himself), Paullus Fabius Persicus, to argue against the sale of priesthoods in Ephesos might attest to more than just Roman sensibilities versus Greek lack of principles. A priesthood, he argued, should be given as an honor to the most able candidate, not to the one who would pay the most – the priest represents the divinity, after all, and money should not intrude.[145]

This argument goes together with other attempts at sharpening the borderlines between religion and business that would become much more important only later: this will be the way the Christians will talk, from the moment Christ chased the money-changers and other merchants

---

[140] Bremmer (2002).
[141] *LSAM* 6; the interpretation as an oracle in Nock (1972 [orig. 1958]), 851f.
[142] Dionysos *LSAM* 84 (2nd cent. CE; "Orphic"?); Men *LSCG* 55 (2nd cent. CE).
[143] Epidauros: Porph. *Abst.* 2.19; Cyrene: *LSS* 118.   [144] *LSS* 91 (3rd cent. CE).
[145] *I.Ephes.* 17–19; Paullus' reproach is οὐκ ἐγλέγονται τοὺς ἐπιτηδειοτάτους, ὧν ταῖς κεφαλαῖς ὁ πρέπων ἐπιτεθήσεται στέφανος. "they do not select the most apt to put a wreath on his head," *I. Ephes.* 18B lines 16–18; τῆς παρὰ τοῦ δήμου [τειμῆς ἀεὶ ὁ εἰς αὐτ]ὴν ἐπιτηδειότατος, "the most apt for this honor from the people," *ibid.* c 2–4. The "umfassende Standardisierungsprozess" of religion in the Roman empire that Rüpke (2011), 242 analyzed is thus a partial explanation only (which does not reject his overall analysis); a (somewhat disappointing) discussion of the problem in Buraselis (2008).

out of the Temple, against all traditions, a story which all four Gospels found it necessary to tell.[146] There was some serious blurring of these borders. In 130 CE, the money-changers of Pergamon exacted what they called "festival contributions," a temporary tax for overwork during festivals, and got away with it.[147] The Athenian fishmongers sold fish at an exorbitant price during the Mysteria with their influx of pilgrims and onlookers; this time, Hadrian intervened and stopped the abuse (or entrepreneurship, depending on one's standpoint), one of the many interventions of this emperor in favor of the festival tradition.[148] A century earlier, the Ephesian silver-smiths feared to lose their business if Paul should succeed in intimidating the pious crowds, and only the intervention of a clear-headed magistrate prevented major problems for the traveling apostle.[149] Finally, a close reading of the inscriptions of the Vedii Antonini in second-century CE Ephesos has suggested that the family owed their influence and power in the city not the least to the business ties they had forged with the associations responsible for providing the foodstuffs and other amenities for the big festivals which they organized in various administrative positions.[150]

Given the pessimistic remarks of Dio about Greece's decay, cited at the beginning of this chapter, it appears as a paradox that the orator censures the public display of exceeding wealth, as does his contemporary Plutarch; but the paradox is only superficial. The crisis of the past century might well have sharpened the moralists' perception of overindulgent ostentation, and the recovery that we perceive after Nero's liberation of Greece justified the need for corrective reflection, the more the crowds participated in public over-indulging. If anything, the frequency of the objections suggests that conspicuous spending had moved beyond the courts of the Hellenistic kings to a wider Romanized elite, to men who were often close to the imperial court and whom we would not know if their citizens had not left us long honorary inscriptions. Thus, in an oration that talks about the unchecked pursuit of public recognition, *On Glory*, Dio severely censures the ambition of politicians who were not content with continuing the well-balanced religious traditions but transformed their citizens through their foundations and benefactions into "lovers of songs and dancing and

---

[146] Mark 11:15–18; Matthew 21:21–22; Luke 19:45–46; John 2:14–16.
[147] *IGRom*. 4.352; see de Ligt (1993), 253.
[148] Eleusis: De Ligt (1993), 233. A much more important intervention: Petzl and Schwertheim (2006).
[149] Acts 19:23–40.
[150] Kalinowski (2002), 128–135. This confirms the observation of Dio, *Or*. 35.15–16 on the economic impact of large gatherings; but see de Ligt (1993), 226–228.

drinking and banqueting ... not one man only, but ten thousands or twenty thousands or a hundred thousands."[151] This makes the unchecked quest for glory much more damaging than the unchecked search for bodily pleasures: the latter mostly does damage to one person only, the former to an entire city. If one wants to become a benefactor, one's city would be better served with the sort of building program that Dio, with the help of the emperor, had proposed for Prusa, "in order to better the city and make it more venerable for all."[152]

Even if this is an argument that Dio used in his fight with rivals in the city elite, its tone must have hit a contemporary nerve: the choice – more buildings, not more lavish festivals – is not Dio's alone, as we saw. Conspicuous spending should be an investment in the city's future, not only in one's own career – or: festivals, in the code of Greek moralists, should honor the gods and, at the same time, lead the people to an ethically better way of life. This argument began to lose relevance only after the middle of the second century, when the building boom began to ebb away, and a century later, when the economical and political difficulties made any sponsor a rarity.[153]

Plutarch shares Dio's opinion. He can deplore the contemporary display of conspicuous wealth at the traditional procession of the local Dionysia and contrast this with the ancient simple ways. The past remains the standard for the present, in either direction; but the past is remembered rather selectively. Formerly one used to have, according to Plutarch, "a jug of wine and a vine branch, then someone pulled a he-goat along, someone else followed with a basket of figs, and the phallos came last." Nowadays, we meet instead with conspicuous display, "with gold vessels carried past, precious dress, carriages riding by, and masks."[154] This is not just nostalgia, but a complaint about the moral offense caused by excessive display of wealth. In a more didactic vein, in his address to a young man who wanted to become a politician, the moralist pointed out that festivals were an innocuous occasion for spending only as long as the money was not spent "on exhibitions which excite and nourish the murderous and brutal, or the scurrilous and licentious spirit," with the gladiatorial games as one of its targets, an object of reprehension not only

---

[151] Dio, *Or.* 66.9.
[152] Dio, *Or.* 40, esp. 5 (τὴν πόλιν ἄμεινον κατασκευάζειν καὶ σεμνοτέραν ποιεῖν ἅπασιν) and 8 (with some negative commentaries of his fellow-citizens on his activities).
[153] See Pont (2010); examples of the ongoing boom in Lane Fox (1987), 72–75.
[154] Plut. *De cupiditate divitiarum* 8, 527D (the translation after de Lacy and Einarson in the Loeb edition).

for Roman moralists but for some Greeks as well, once the games had spread to the East.[155] Festivals, in the eyes of moralizing philosophers, are a test for the ethics of a political leader.

With different nuances according to place and society, we find the same ideas throughout the epoch, well beyond the economic nadir of the later third century.[156] An oracle from Didyma, somewhat vaguely dated to the very end of the third century CE, answers the question how one should best worship Apollo. Instead of lavish sacrifices, the god recommends songs: "I enjoy every song,... but especially an old one" – incidentally this again shows how important the singing of hymns has become during the Imperial epoch and explains why a hymn such as the paean to Hygieia, written by the shadowy but presumably early Hellenistic poet Ariphron of Sikyon, was recorded in Epidauros and Athens on two stones from presumably the second century CE, or why in the sanctuary of Diktaian Zeus in modern Palaikastro in eastern Crete a cult hymn, composed perhaps in the fourth century BCE, was again recorded in the third century CE.[157] Although Apollo himself points out that, from early on, his healing power manifested itself through the healing song or incantation, this is only one side of his answer. The other side agrees with the moralists:

> [Νηλεῖδαι], τί μοι] εἰλιπόδων ζατρεφεῖς ἑκατόμβαι
> [λαμπροί τε χρυ]σοῖο βαθυπλούτοιο κολοσσοὶ
> [καὶ χαλκῷ δεί]κηλα καὶ ἀργύρῳ ἀσκηθέντα;
> [οὔ γε μὲν] ἀθάνατοι κτεάνων ἐπιδευέες εἰσὶν.

> "Descendants of Neileus, what shall I do with large hecatombs of cattle, shining statues of rich gold, and images made of bronze and silver? Immortals have no need for possessions!"

These opening lines of the oracle underscore the moralistic urgency of the message; what used to be alternative philosophical theology has by now become much more mainstream.

In a more ascetic vein, the same is still visible in fourth-century Antioch. Like other contemporary cities, Antioch had its own penteteric Olympian games; there, the ruling male citizens gathered at a symposium to which

---

[155] Plut. *Praecepta gerendae reipublicae* 30. 822C. On the gladiators in the East still see Robert (1940). On the criticism, see Barton (1989).
[156] An oracle of Ammon in Cyzicus of about 130 CE that advises against sacrifices belongs to the special circumstances of the Egyptian cults, *StEGO* 08/01/01.
[157] *I.Didyma* 217; see esp. Harder (1956); Peek (1971). On hymns, see more above, nn. 61–66. For Ariphron's hymn, recorded in Epidauros (*IG* iv:1, 132, 2nd cent. CE) and Athens (*IG* ii², 4533, 2nd or 3rd cent. CE), see Furley and Bremer (2001), no. 6.3; the Palaikastro Hymn, *ibid*. no. 1.1.

the agonothetes traditionally invited selected adult citizens. In Libanius' time, invitations began to be extended to selected adolescents as well. Libanius objected to this for ethical reasons: the symposia tended to turn into occasions where adult males could easily woo or even seduce adolescents; he encourages the organizers to return to the previous, more selective and safer custom. The orator couches his protest not in moralistic terms alone, but also in political and religious language: "The discussion is not about banquets, but about the city ... Those not invited to the banquet will hate the agonothetes, but the gods will love the man, since he made the festival more beautiful and pure."[158] A responsible politician has to be able to withstand the often outspoken criticism of the adolescent upper-class males, if this buys the city divine goodwill. As we shall see, the bishops would have applauded the pagan orator.

It is not easy to gauge the effect that these and similar reflections had on the actual festival praxis of the age. In some places, the lavish ritual life continued unabashedly. In the small Pisidian city of Pogla, a third-century assembly voted to honor Aurelius Arteimianos Dilitrianos, their young eponymous magistrate, with the usual statue. During his tenure, he had hosted all citizens and foreigners (δειπνήσαντα τούς τε πολείτας καὶ τοὺς ἐπιδημήσαντας ξένους), and as priest of their local Zeus, he had done the same. But as if he had heard the earlier objections to catering for sensual pleasure, he also contributed money to construction work (εἰς κατασκευὴν ἔργων).[159]

New elements were creeping in, in yet another guise. On the island of Syros, the eponymous *archon* regularly celebrated the vows (*vota*) for the ruling emperor with a sacrifice to Hestia Prytaneia, and sometimes he also celebrated an imperial birthday or the new year's day in a specially lavish way. Honorary decrees for these magistrates stretch from Commodus to Decius, and they present a variety of ways in which the official added splendor to the days. A banquet (δεῖπνον) for the local senate was traditional; but it never went beyond the circle of these eminent citizens. The officials used another way to regale the citizens and "people from the Cyclades staying in town," and sometimes the free women as well: they distributed cash, most often called διανομή, in a well-used term, but sometimes with the almost isolated word σφυρίς, a variant of σπυρίς, "basket," the Greek translation of Latin *sportula*, the present given to

---

[158] Liban. *Or.* 53.27 (οἰήσεται μέν τις περὶ δείπνων εἶναι τὸν λόγον, ἔστι δὲ ὑπὲρ τῆς πόλεως, εἴ τις ὀρθῶς ἐξετάζειν ἐθέλοι), 28 (μισήσουσιν οἱ μὴ φαγόντες τὸν ἀγωνοθέτην. ἀλλ' οἱ θεοὶ τὸν ἄνδρα φιλήσουσι καλλίω πεποιηκότα τὴν ἑορτὴν καὶ καθαρωτέραν).

[159] *IGRom.* 3.407; his cognomen and that of his wife, Aurelia Artemis, give the date.

one's guest.¹⁶⁰ The aristocrats of Syros thus distributed coins not just in the Greek way but also in the Roman, and the local terminology depended on the occasion: as the Roman *sportula*, it was much more generous and combined with a banquet; as the local διανομή, it was much less generous and often without a banquet. During Commodus' birthday celebration in 183 CE, the senators received a banquet and a *sportula* of five denarii while everybody else got a much smaller διανομή of much lesser value; at a later date, during the New Year's celebration, the senators again received a banquet and a *sportula* of six denarii; the day after, they were dined again, but with a διανομή of one denarius only, and the same amount went to the citizens, but without a meal.¹⁶¹

The new times did not just bring the foreign *sportula*, part of the Romanizing elite's new trappings, it also drastically reduced the meals: Syros is not alone in having banquets only for a selected few in the third century. This must also mean that some cities had much less grandiose animal sacrifices, because the sponsors spent their money on other things. A decree from Oinoanda for Marcia Aurelia Polykleia, the wife of one M. Aurelius Artemon – the names suggest that we are after 212 CE – praises her for the sponsorship of a pan-Lycian contest for which she gave money also to be used for a very generous cash distribution (διανομή); but there were no large sacrifices with common meals.¹⁶² In a contemporary epigram from Hadrianoi in Mysia, we find a clear preference for incense-burning over meat, and an honorary epigram from third-century Kyzikos praises a local patron for having enjoyed himself among his fellow citizens with libations, ἐν σπονδαῖσι, without any mention of banquets.¹⁶³ But I hasten to add that this will not become the prevailing norm: as we shall see later, εὐφροσύνη, the "good cheer" of the banquet, will remain the hallmark of euergetism until well into the Christian centuries of the Eastern empire.¹⁶⁴

Conclusions

The traditional festivals in the Greek cities of the imperial East, then, were still a vital part of civic life. They helped to define civic identity in the world of imperial domination, with the emperor as the godlike power in the

---
¹⁶⁰ See *LSJ* s.v. σπυρίς.
¹⁶¹ The series in *IG* xii:5, 663 (Commmodus) to 667 (Decius); σφυρίς in 663.15, 665.4.
¹⁶² *Bulletin de Correspondance Hellénique* 24 (1900), 338 no. 1 (Georges Cousin).
¹⁶³ Hadrianoi: *StEGO* 08/08/03; Kyzikos: *ibid.* 08/01/53; with good commentaries.
¹⁶⁴ See the epilogue, n. 29.

background, and in the foreground, as visible reminders of the faraway power, the wealthy members of the urban elite who all were Roman citizens, often knights or senators, and sometimes former imperial administrators. The festivals gave these benefactors an arena to play their public role, and they helped the cities to define their cultural identity in a world that had not always been Greek, and where the non-Greek cultures were just around the corner.

But they did more. The distinction between festival and daily life had always been a cognitive tool for shaping the distinction between the sacred and the profane: rich food, ample drink, and the splendor of ritual were clear markers of religious time. The festivals of the Imperial epoch, with the heightened splendor of processions and contests and often enough the ampleness of food and drink, interrupted the monotony of daily life and emphasized the festive and even utopian traits. The contestation and debate only demonstrates how common this largesse had become; and as we shall see in the epilogue, the later emperors understood the guarantee of this public happiness as part of their political mission, even in the face of ascetic resistance.

The heightened visuality that characterizes imperial festivals can be understood as serving a similar purpose: the visuality with which we deal is different from the impressive *mis-en-scène* of the Panathenaia or the colorful and exotic pageant performed by Ptolemy Philadelphos during the Dionysia in Alexandria.[165] Although there were a few precedents, it was the Imperial processions that made the gods visible in statues and even in masked priests – a detail lacking in Robin Lane Fox's impressive chapter on "Seeing the Gods" of his book on *Pagans and Christians*.[166] In the same way, they made abstract concepts visible – the institutions of Ephesos through their allegorical images; the divinity in whose honor the festival was performed and who in former times had been present only at the goal of the procession, as the statue that one could see through the open temple doors, or as the main altar to which the prayer summoned the god. And although the emperors were usually incorporated into the civic pantheon and they received their sacrifices alongside the traditional divinities of the festivals, their ontological status was different: this must have worked in the direction of separating out the political from the religious. It was the Christians who set the pace: "Give Caesar what is Caesar's and God what is God's" is not only a compromise between Church and State, it also

---

[165] Callixenus, *FGrH* 267 F 2 (Athen. 5.25–35, 196A–203B). [166] Lane Fox (1987), chapter 4.

conceptualizes the two as two radically different entities. In this respect, then, the imperial festivals should not be underrated. As we will see, the opposition of the Christian apologetics and Fathers helped to shape Christian concepts of sacred and profane, religious and political.

CHAPTER 2

Roman festivals in eastern cities

Introduction

On August 8, 389, the emperor Theodosius I addressed a letter to the prefect of the city of Rome, Caeonius Rufius Albinus, on reforming the legal holidays of the city of Rome, where the emperor was spending the summer. Roman emperors since Augustus had put into effect such reforms, and Theodosius must have been aware of this tradition when he was presenting his best side to the Romans: the festival calendar had a tendency to grow at the expense of the working of the law courts, and good emperors performed the regular pruning and reshaping the calendar needed. Among the days to which Theodosius granted the status of a legal holiday were the Kalendae Ianuariae, Easter, the birthdays of Rome and Constantinople, and "the day which produced the beginning of our imperial power." The letter was reproduced, in its usual abbreviated format, both in the Theodosian Code and the Code of Justinian, adopted in the *Breviarium of Alaric* that reflects early sixth-century Visigothic practice, and translated in the "Imperial Laws" (*Basiliká*) that reflect the adoption of Justinian texts in Greek in the later Eastern Empire.[1] All this means that it kept its binding force as an imperial law after the fifth century not just for the city of Rome but for the entire empire and beyond: just as Easter was an empire-wide holiday, the Kalendae Ianuariae, the two city birthdays, and the Imperial Accession Day must have been celebrated all over the empire, at least in the East, for many centuries.[2]

About two centuries earlier, the rabbis who after the destruction of the Temple were leading the Jews in the Roman province of Syria Palaestina presented their flock with a list of festivals with a very different scope. A

---

[1] *CTh* 2.8.19 (= *Breviarium* 2.8.2); *CJ* 3.12.6; *Basilika* 7.17.23, ed. Scheltema and van der Wal (1955).
[2] More on this below, Chapter 4.

Mishnah in the treatise *Avodah Zarah*, "On Alien Worship," determines which non-Jewish holidays were celebrated in the province and needed to be avoided for business by pious Jews three days in advance.[3] The list poses some questions that I will address below, but a few festivals at least need no explanation – Kalendae, Saturnalia, "the anniversary of the kings," i.e. again the day of accession to imperial power. As Giuseppe Veltri underlined, the ensuing Talmudic discussion would not have been as elaborate as it was if there had not been many Jews who had adopted some of these festivals into their own festival calendar, and if some rabbis, yielding to the power of the factual, had not tried to make them acceptable by reinterpreting them in a Jewish sense.[4]

The two lists, drawn up at a distance of two centuries for two different communities but both valid law for several centuries to come, are interesting on several accounts. Their festivals were originally confined to the city of Rome and, in the case of the Saturnalia or the Parilia, Rome's birthday in the Republican calendar, were thought to derive from king Numa's ordering of the festival calendar at the very beginning of Rome.[5] But both lists show that they were now celebrated outside Rome; and, even more impressively, not in the Latin West but in the Eastern part of the empire, where they remained alive, as Theodosius' text and its reception in the later law codes shows, well into the Christian centuries. The discussions in these lists make us see how the leaders of the two Abrahamic religions tried to adapt to the presence of pagan festivals in their own religious cultures or, in the case of the rabbis, at least in the immediate proximity of their own group, despite the fact that both could not tolerate other gods besides their One God.

There were other festivals as well that moved out from the city to the empire. There were festivals of Numa's calendar, such as the Volcanalia, that were at least celebrated all over the Western empire and again well into Christian times, or the Lupercalia, that still figure in the *Liber caerimoniarum* of the tenth-century emperor Konstantinos VII Porphyrogennetos. There were festivals of more recent origin, such as the Brumalia that survived well into the Byzantine epoch, or the private ritual of the Rosalia, the commemoration of the dead by adorning the graves with roses. Scholarship on all this has been spotty. Some individual festivals have received ample treatment, such as the Brumalia in the Latin Harvard dissertation of 1916 by John R. Crawford, or the *Kalendae Ianuariae*, to

---

[3] *Mishna Avodah Zarah* 1:3.   [4] Veltri (2000).
[5] Still treated as historical by York (1986), following Livy and Plutarch; but see especially Cloud (1979).

which Michel Meslin dedicated a slim monographic treatment in 1970, mostly confined to the pre-Christian West.[6] Others – such as the Rosalia or the Volcanalia – have at least been touched upon by curious scholars.[7]

The overall story of Roman festivals in the Mediterranean East, however, is a story that still waits to be written. The few remarks in Kurt Latte's *Römische Religionsgeschichte* (1960), under the biased heading "Die Auflösung der Römischen Religion," certainly will not do, and the revival of studies on Roman religion that started with the seminal efforts of John Scheid and Mary Beard focused mostly on the religions of Rome and Italy. The one masterly overview, the chapter on "Roman Religion and Roman Empire" in *The Religions of Rome* by Mary Beard, John North, and Simon Price, is limited in scope by the very character of that admirable book, and thus cannot take notice of what still might be byways.[8] The same is true for the two major overviews of the Roman Near East, by Fergus Millar (1993) and by Maurice Sartre (2001/2005), whose authors are more interested in the political than in the religious history of their region.[9] Shorter books on either topic are even more reticent.[10] Nor has the intensive and highly useful work of several research groups on Rome and its empire during the first decade of this century turned to this question.[11] To whoever is in need of data, the edition with commentary of the *Feriale Duranum* by Robert Fink, Allan Hoey, and Walter Snyder (of 1940) still is the best source-book, and the discussions of the calendar of 354, also called after its addressee the Philocalus Calendar, by Henri Stern (1953) and, more restricted, by Michele Salzman (1991), have contributed massively to our knowledge of the late antique calendar; but both studies remain focused on the city of Rome, as they should, without much interest for the provinces, Western or Eastern.

Thus, there are many open questions, and they all concern the mechanisms of religious change. Festivals of the city of Rome and its calendar spread for different reasons and through different carriers throughout the empire. There were the *coloniae*, defined by Gellius as "propagated from the City and having all institutions and laws of the Roman People, not of their own";[12] but there

---

[6] Crawford (1914–1919); Meslin (1970).   [7] Hoey (1937); Kokkinia (1999); Opelt (1970).
[8] Beard, North, and Price (1998), 1: 313–363, esp. 320–339.
[9] Millar (1993), with a chapter on the religious interaction in Syria Palestine, 337–386; Sartre (2001) and (2005).
[10] The most promising short history of Roman religion, Rüpke (2001) ends with Augustan times; his more extensive book of 2011 addresses the Imperial epoch and its calendar, but not our topic.
[11] I mention especially Cancik and Rüpke (1997); de Bloi, Funke, and Hahn (2006); Rüpke (2008b); Auffarth (2009); Blömer, Facella, and Winter (2009).
[12] Gell. 16.13.8 *ex civitate quasi propagatae sunt et iura institutaque omnia populi Romani, non sui arbitrii, habent.*

were few real *deductiones* in the imperial epoch, all for political reasons, such as Corinth (Colonia Laus Iulia Corinthus) under Caesar, Patrai (Colonia Augusta Achaeica Patrensis) under Augustus, or Jerusalem (Colonia Aelia Capitolina) under Hadrian. As Patrai or Corinth show, even in these colonies the religious institutions combined the cults that had remained alive among the original population with the new Roman ones. The honorary colonies of the Greek East, on the other hand, such as Caesarea in Palestine, retained their own traditions. Then, there was the army with their own cult calendar, as demonstrated by as rare a document as the *Feriale Duranum*, which gives an, albeit fragmentary, glimpse into what must have been the overall festival calendar of the army.[13] Those cults could, and did, spread to the population of the garrison cities, and from there perhaps even further out. Finally, there were the Eastern cities themselves that, by their own decision, decided to adopt a festival, or had to decide because the emperors insisted – which brings up the question of the relationship between center and periphery, rulers and ruled, innovation "top-down" and innovation "bottom-up."

Given these complexities, what were the reasons and forces behind the adoption of Roman festivals outside the city of Rome and Italy, especially in the cities of the Greek-speaking East? Were these adoptions connected with the imperial cult either of the army or the city, and were they imposed from above or by the initiative of a city, which is in the last resort of a powerful individual or an equally powerful group that could sway the voting assembly and convince the Roman governor? What were the changes which they underwent under the new conditions of power? And, even more importantly, in the light of the Jewish and Christian reaction to these festivals, how did the Jews of Palestine and the Christians before and after Constantine react to them? How did a few of them survive the Christianization of the empire and the opposition of the Church, or at least of some bishops? How was a pagan festival, dedicated to and often named after a divinity whose sacrifices dominated the day, reconceptualized in a world where sacrifices were prohibited and the old gods had turned into demons to be eschewed and exorcised?

Not all questions can be answered easily, and most resist broad generalizations or at least call for individual case studies before one can attempt a generalization. Developments are not always traceable: the sources on which a study of these festivals has to rely are rather unevenly distributed

---

[13] See Fishwick (1988). An intriguingly isolated celebration is the "festival of Ares," Ἄρεος ἑορτή, on March 1 in a fragmentary calendar in a manuscript in the Bodleian Library (*Catalogus Codicum Astrologicorum Graecorum* IX:1, 137) that Weinstock (1948) assigned to a port city of Asia Minor and understood as "festival for the day when the Roman troops used to be enlisted and discharged" (38).

over time and space. Ovid's *Fasti* and the stone calendars of the late Republic and early Imperial epoch have yielded rich information on the festivals in the city of Rome during the late Republic and the early Augustan period, and antiquarians and grammarians such as Varro or Festus have added additional information. This state of our sources, together with the obsolete belief that "true" Roman religion is best seen in Republican times, is the main reason why the existing treatments of Roman festivals from Hartung (1836) and Wissowa (1912) to Scullard (1981) and Sabbatucci (1988) have confined themselves to the festivals of the late Republican calendar; Dumézil's *Archaic Roman Religion* dies hard, as do Wissowa's less obtrusive constructions.

For the three centuries of Imperial rule after Augustus, information on Roman festivals in Rome and even more so in the rest of the empire is rare to come by, and it depends on chance finds – documents such as the *Avodah Zarah*, whose date precedes the final codification of the Mishna in the third century CE, the *Feriale Duranum* written during the reign of Severus Alexander (222–235), probably in 225–227 CE, or, for the *urbs*, the painted calendar fragments from the excavations under Santa Maria Maggiore in Rome, dated to the third quarter of the third century CE at the latest.[14] These documents are supplemented by chance passages in literary texts of the period, both pagan and Christian.

It is only in the later fourth and earlier fifth centuries when information is again more readily available, for Rome itself through the manuscript calendars of Philocalus (354 CE) and of Polemius Silvius (early fifth century and in part depending on Philocalus), for the Eastern provinces through the writings of Libanius, the polemics of Christian bishops against what they saw as pagan festivals, or the treatise *On the Months* (*De mensibus*) by John Lydos (c.490–560 CE), complemented by references in other writings, from imperial rescripts between Constantine and Theodosius II, collected 438 CE in the Theodosian Code, and Macrobius' *Saturnalia* (in the 420s) to the early Byzantine Chronicles of John Malalas (written after Justinian).[15] Given the character of this information, we can perceive differences between the form a festival took in the late Republican *Urbs* and in an Eastern city in the fourth century, or even in Byzantium in the fifth or sixth centuries. But we are not always able to trace developments, identify the

---

[14] For the calendar of Santa Maria Maggiore, see the excavation report by Magi (1972) and the discussion in Herz (2003), 54, with earlier bibliography.
[15] For Lydus, I have relied on the Teubner edition of Richard Wünsch (1898). See also Bandy (2013); on its serious problems see the review of Anthony Kaldellis, *BMCR* 2014.01.19.

stages of such a development, or understand the forces that brought it about.

This chapter and the next two chapters of this book will address these questions. The present chapter will focus on the festivals in the pre-Constantinian East. Only a few festivals are attested for this epoch, a small number when compared both with the large number of festivals in late Republican Rome and with the much smaller number of festivals that surface again in the later fourth and fifth centuries that I will discuss in the two following chapters. The most interesting and richest evidence comes from Syria Palaestina, not the least as a result of the Rabbinic contestation of non-Jewish festivals, and a key text, the Mishnah on *Avodah Zarah* 1:3, is relatively early, complex, and often overlooked by historians of Roman or Greek religion. A large first part of this chapter thus will deal with the Palestinian evidence, building in some recent work by Nicole Belayche, Emmanuel Friedheim, and, most recently, Stéphanie Binder, whose books all have a somewhat different aim than mine.[16] The nature of the material brings with it that the Palestinian evidence cannot be discussed in isolation; thus, some Roman festivals in the East outside of Palestine will already appear here as well. In a shorter second part, I will discuss what is left on Roman festivals in other places in the Greek East before Constantine.

Roman festivals in Syria Palaestina

Avodah Zarah 1:3

The Mishna on *Avodah Zarah* 1:3 reads (in a tentative translation):[17]

> These are the festivals of the gentiles: Kalendae, Saturnalia, Empowering, the anniversary of the kings, the day of birth, and the day of death.[18]

The list is given in order to more clearly define the Mishnah that precedes (1:1) and that prohibits all business transactions with the "idolaters" on the three days preceding their festivals. Thus, it is not a list of Roman festivals

---

[16] Belayche (2001); Friedheim (2006); Binder (2012).
[17] See Graf (2002) and especially Friedheim (2006), 307–364.
[18] The translation follows, with some changes, the English text in Guggenheimer (2011), 250; see also Kehati (1987), 5; the German translation by Gerd A. Wewers, in: *Übersetzung des Talmud Yerushalmi* IV/7 (Tübingen 1980), 8; and the French by Moïse Schwab, *Le Talmud de Jérusalem* (Paris: Maisonneuve, 1960): "Les jours considérés comme fêtes des païens sont les suivants: les Calendes, les Saturnales, l'anniversaire de l'arrivée au pouvoir, le jour d'installation du souverain, genesis, l'anniversaire de naissance ou de décès"; the disagreement with Guggenheimer's and my text highlights the open questions.

that are prohibited, although in a strict reading this prohibition was implied.

There are some rather elementary questions overshadowing this text. The festival name that I translated as "Empowering" is opaque, and with this comes the problem of whether it is explained or not by the following "anniversary of the kings." As it stands, the text also remains somewhat unclear as to the subjects of "birth" and "death" – are they private individuals or the Roman emperors?

What is obvious is the blatantly Roman character of the list. If proof were needed, the Midrash Rabbah could furnish it.[19] When a non-Jew tried to define himself in opposition to his Jewish interlocutor – in this specific case none other than Rabbi Yohanan ben Zakkai, the founder of the rabbinic tradition[20] – he had the Jews celebrate "Pesah, ʿAṣeret and Sukkot"; whereas his own, non-Jewish festivals were "Kalendae, Saturnalia, and 'Empowering'." If, as is likely, the Midrash depends on Mishnah AZ 1:3, it gives a late antique reading of it. This does not mean that this is the correct meaning: it is indispensable first to try to cope with this immediate problem of reading.

Kalendae and Saturnalia

The Mishnah mentions several festivals or categories of festivals; the exact number depends on whether we regard parts of the list as explications of other parts or not. The first two entries are easily identified, since the text gives them their traditional Latin names in an easy Hebrew transcription, קלנדה (*qlndh*) *Kalendae* and סתרנליעה (*strnlyyh*) *Saturnalia*. *Saturnalia* is an unequivocal Roman festival name; *Kalendae* in this context can only mean another festival, the *Kalendae Ianuariae*, the main festival at the beginning of the Roman year.[21] This is confirmed by the aetiological stories given in the Jerusalem Talmud: they treat the festival without any hesitation as a New Year's festival.[22] The authors of the Mishnah adopted the practice from the Greek realities of Syria Palaestina: Greek texts from the Imperial epoch, both pagan and Christian, most commonly refer to this important festival simply as Καλάνδαι, as if it were an ordinary festival name and not the name of each and every first day of any month. Obviously, the authors of these texts regarded Καλάνδαι as yet another festival name, presumably because it lasted several days and thus could not designate one specific day.

---

[19] *Midrash Rabbah Deuteronymy* 7.7; Liebermann (1964), III; Veltri (2000), 112.
[20] Schäfer (1979).   [21] The hesitations esp. of Hadas-Lebel (1979), 427f. are unfounded.
[22] See Veltri (2000), 117–122.

Furthermore, the calendrical setting given as a rule of thumb by Rav sets the "Kalendae eight days after the winter solstice, Saturnalia eight days before the winter solstice."[23] This rule is not very precise, since the Saturnalia started on December 17, four days before the solstice, and lasted up to seven days under the empire,[24] while the Kalendae at least in the fourth century lasted five days, starting on January 1, ten days after the solstice. But even so, Rav unequivocally again situates the Kalendae in early January, as unequivocally as the aetiological myths narrated in both Talmuds situate it in the deep of winter, shortly after the winter solstice.

Kratesis

The third festival name, קרתסטס or קרתסטם (*qrṭsys* or *qrṭsym*),[25] is a Hebrew loan word from the Greek word κράτησις, an abstract noun meaning "power, empowering, dominion" that is attested since late Hellenistic times.[26] The Hebrew word is attested elsewhere, but never as a festival name;[27] nor are there parallels for such a festival name in our material on Eastern Greek heortology. Thus, it must be a descriptive term. Commentators had to guess as to its meaning, and they made two mutually exclusive suggestions, based on one generally agreed basic fact. There is general acceptance for the idea that we deal with imperial cult, since the following items clearly concern the emperors: thus, the noun must mean "coming into (imperial) power" or "accession to the throne." This is the meaning of the term attested in the Egyptian papyri, where it either refers to Augustus' taking over of Egypt on August 1, 30 BCE, or, in later texts, the general accession of any emperor.[28] This led to the two mutually exclusive explanations of *Kratesis* as either a specific Eastern festival commemorating Augustus' conquest of Egypt, or as a more general festival that celebrated the accession of the ruling emperor.[29] In my mind, there can be no doubt that the latter is meant here. First, there exists no other documentation for the former festival outside the Egyptian papyri, while the lavish celebration

---

[23] Guggenheimer (2011), 253 with n. 92 on the problem that the Yerushalmi has inverted the temporal relationship.

[24] Wissowa (1912), 207 n. 7: three days in the Republic (Macr. *Sat.* 1.10.23), seven already under Domitian (Mart. 14.72; Macr. *Sat.* 1.10.3), while the *feriae* during the festival lasted five days under Domitian (Mart. 4.88.2).

[25] For my purpose, it is irrelevant whether the final letter was -s or -m; see Hadas-Lebel (1979), 431. As often with such words, they are appropriated either in the nominative or, more often, the accusative.

[26] See *LSJ* and Lampe s.vv.   [27] Krauss (1899), 568.

[28] E.g. Euseb. *V.Const.* 1.22 (of Constantine); Chron. Pasch. p. 262 (Commodus).

[29] Celebrating Augustus' conquest of Egypt: Veltri (2000) 127–128 and Friedheim (2006), 337–338 (see also 354–356), who adds the idea that the rabbis extrapolated the festival to every Roman victory (338); imperial accession: Krauss (1899), 568 and Blaufuss (1909).

of the imperial accession (both the actual accession of a new emperor and the recurrent commemoration of Accession Day) is well attested all throughout the empire.[30] Secondly, and crucially, the Egyptian papyri that talk about Augustus' accession never use κράτησις alone, but always κράτησις Καίσαρος, "accession of Caesar (Augustus)": the Greek noun in itself does not refer to the accession of Augustus, but to any ruler's taking of power. Thirdly, the Tosefta to *AZ* 1:3 confirms this reading:

> Kalendae ... Saturnalia, the day on which they took the kingship מלכות (*mlkwt*), 'Empowering', the anniversary of the rulers, day of each ruler.

The passage that precedes 'Empowering' – "the day on which they took the kingship" – is obviously not an explanation of Saturnalia, but of the following unusual term קרתסטם (*qrtsym*): it is a sentence that, as happens often, moved from a marginal gloss into a wrong position inside the sentence.

Besides the story that Adam invented the Kalendae that appropriates the festival for Judaism, the Jerusalem exegesis gives another interesting aetiological story.[31] When Egypt and Rome were at war, they agreed that each army should persuade its commander-in-chief to kill himself; the army whose commander would do so first would have won the war. The Egyptian general flatly declined; the Roman commander, Ianuarius, agreed; this is how the Romans won the war. And because the son of Ianuarius called out for his dying father, the first day of January is called *Kalendae* of January: like Varro and others, the Talmudic narrator derives *Kalendae* from καλεῖν, "to call." And because they mourned him on the second day, January 2 is an infelicitous day, מטלאנט הטממטרא (*melany hymera*) in the Talmud's wording – the correct Hebrew transcription of the Greek rendering (μέλαινα ἡμέρα) of Latin *dies ater*, and a detail that is confirmed for Rome.[32] Later in the debate on the same Mishnah, this story (which is told by Rabbi Yohanan) is understood as pointing to Rome's accession to power in the East with Augustus' victory over Marc Anthony, and thus paralleled by κράτησις. This comment puzzled some of its Jewish listeners who knew that the two festival days, Kalendae and Kratesis, were not the same.

---

[30] Examples in Price (1984), 105, 212f.
[31] The etiologies in Guggenheimer (2011), 251–252; see Schäfer and Hezser (2000), 339–341.
[32] Varro, *De ling. Lat.* 6.29: *dies postridie Kalendas Nonas Idus appellari atri, quod per eos dies nihil novi inciperent* ("the days following the Kalends, Nones and Ides were called black, because on these days they should not begin anything new").

Birthdays and death-days

Whereas the Accession Days by definition concern only the emperors, the birthdays concern also members of the imperial family, especially the emperor's wife; together with accession days, birthdays were the most widespread imperial anniversaries.[33] The next item in our list is (יום) גנוסיטה (*ywm*) *gnwsyh*, another Hebrew transcription of a Greek word, this time of γενόσια, a local form of the more common γενέσια or γενέσιος (ἡμέρα), the birthday of the ruling emperor; a *baraita* explains it with reference to Pharaoh's birthday in Genesis 40:20 and thus guarantees its general meaning.[34] From Augustus onwards, the ruling emperor's birthday was the occasion for an annual or even, after the model of the Greek gods, a monthly celebration both in an entire province and in single cities. Several Greek inscriptions demonstrate this, although none comes from Syria Palaestina. The letter of a governor of Asia under Tiberius described the annual ceremony in the province of Asia: "The choirs from all Asia, gathering at Pergamon at the most holy birthday of Augustus (Σεβαστός) Tiberius Caesar God, perform a task that contributes greatly to the glory of Augustus in hymning the imperial house, offering sacrifices to the August Gods and celebrating festivals and holidays."[35] Often, there were also contests and spectacles on the birthday of the emperor.[36] Such celebrations were not just held in large cities such as Ephesos or Pergamon where Roman officials were likely to stay and participate: the small Cretan town of Lyttos was endowed with a special fund for shows on the birthday of Trajan; on the island of Syros, the chief magistrate, Antaios son of Modestus, invited the local senators to a banquet on Commodus' birthday, doubtless after a sacrifice and vows for the emperor; in tiny Lapethos on Crete, the local priest of Tiberius dedicated a statue to mark the emperor's birthday.[37]

The last two items, "the day of birth and the day of death," caused headaches already for the rabbinic expounders who understood them in two different ways that are not easily reconciled. The Jerusalem Talmud

---

[33] A collection of epigraphical evidence for birthdays, days of accession, and similar days up to 1939 in Snyder (1940).
[34] See Krauss (1899), 180.
[35] *I.Ephes.* 3801; see also the list of expenses for several imperial birthdays, *ibid.* 374.
[36] Price (1984), 105. Perpetua and her fellow martyrs were to die during the games for the birthday of Geta, *Passio Perpetuae* 16.3.
[37] Lyttos: *I.Cret.* I.xviii, 23 (a. 112 CE); Syros: *IG* xii 5.663 (a. 183 CE); Lapethos: *IGRom.* 3.933 = *OGI* 583 (29/30 CE). More in Taeger (1960), *passim*.

gives this explanation: "Day of birth and day of death: up to here, it meant festivals for the community, from here on it means festivals of an individual." This exegesis removes the two last items from the list of public holidays, using precise Latin calendar terminology: we have moved from *feriae publicae* to *feriae singulorum*, the birthdays and funerary celebrations for individuals.[38] In this reading, the end of the Mishnah on *AZ* 1:3 overlaps with the following Mishnah and its list of private festivals, "to cut one's beard or hair, to return from travel, to be released from prison." The Tosefta, however, seems to oppose the anniversary of the emperor to the following "day of each and every emperor," which it defines correctly as *feriae publicae*. The Babylonian Talmud, finally, repeats the wording of the Mishnah, "the day of birth and the day of death," and adds the qualification "deaths of kings"; this again makes them into imperial *feriae publicae*.[39] I prefer to follow this reading. It makes the sequence from 1:3 to 1:4 neater and more orderly – Mishnah 1:3 is focused on public festivals, while the following Mishnah in a new development deals with private celebrations.

If we follow this reading, we deal in this final passage not with the birthday of the reigning emperor – that was dealt with by יום גנוסיה (*ywm gnwsyh*), γενόσια – but with the birthdays of other members of the imperial house. For Rome, these birthdays are well attested in the stone calendars or the Arval Acts; and the army celebrated many of them, according to the *feriale Duranum*.[40] Some of these birthdays were also celebrated outside the Urbs or the army. The province of Asia celebrated Livia's birthday, and a bequest from Gortyn on Crete under Commodus funded among other things celebrations on the birthdays of three members of the imperial family.[41] Another possibility would be to take "the day of birth" as an explication of יום גנוסיה (*ywm gnwsyh*) in the same way the Tosefta had introduced an explication of κράτησις. Even this somewhat unlikely interpretation would still leave us with the imperial memorial day.[42]

In the same way, the "day of death" can only concern a member of the imperial family. The public commemoration of a deceased emperor – presumably on the recurrent day of his funeral – is unheard of. No known calendar mentions such a commemoration, and Ovid in his *Fasti* "almost" left out a reference to Caesar's death: the only festival on that day

---

[38] Underscored by Veltri (2000), 107f.; implicitly, the material treated in *Mishnah AZ* 1:3 and 1:4 seems to acknowledge this system, see below.
[39] Baraita *AZ* 11a.   [40] Fink, Hoey, and Snyder (1940), 182; see also Snyder (1940), *passim*.
[41] *I.Cret.* 4.300; see Price (1984), 105 and below, n. 121.
[42] Thus Blaufuss (1909), 15; Veltri (2000), 129.

was the very relaxed picnic that honored Anna Perenna.⁴³ To commemorate the death of an emperor with a public celebration contradicts the logic of ruler cult. Emperor cult, in the words of Simon Price, "reflects the perception of the permanence and regularity of the empire":⁴⁴ it emphasized this permanence by focusing on the days that set something in motion – the birth of a future emperor, his accession to power, or, on a local level, the arrival (*adventus*) of an emperor in one's city. Nobody commemorated his departure, and nobody commemorated his death; even the actual burial rites of an individual emperor negotiate the tension between individual mortality and the permanence of the institution.⁴⁵ But there were commemorations of death in the imperial house: they did not concern the emperor, but family members who died young and whose death caused so much grief about unfulfilled hope that a public commemoration imposed itself. The stone calendars record two of these deaths, the death of Augustus' grandson Gaius Caesar on February 21 or 22, and that of his brother Lucius Caesar on August 20.⁴⁶ As far as we can see, nothing of this is attested outside Rome, but this might be a source problem. We would know not much about birthdays in the imperial house that were celebrated in Greek cities either, if we had not the one inscription from Gortyn.

The list, then, combines festivals of the imperial cult concerning not just the emperor but other members of his house, with two calendrical festivals, the (new) Kalendae Ianuariae and the (very old) Saturnalia, and it prohibits interaction with the gentiles in the three days preceding these festivals. In the case of the imperial festivals, this is an unequivocal political statement: after the destruction of the Temple by the Romans, orthodox Jews did not participate in celebrations of the imperial power. But how do Saturnalia and Kalendae Ianuariae fit in?

Kalendae Ianuariae and vota

As we shall see in more detail in the next chapter, in several fourth-century sources – mostly Christian polemical sermons, but also in an oration of Libanius – the Kalendae Ianuariae are described as the main festival all over the Roman Empire, from Spain and Gaul in the West to Anatolia and Syria

---

⁴³ Scholarship: Wissowa (1912), 447, 458. Ovid, *Fasti* 3.697–710, introduced with *Praeteriturus eram gladios in principe fixos.*
⁴⁴ Price (1984), 105. ⁴⁵ Ginzburg (1991). ⁴⁶ See Taeger (1960), 130f.

in the East. At that time, its five days of sacrifices, chariot races, and private banquets – lovingly and nostalgically described by Libanius – celebrated and founded the unity of the empire under the emperor (or the two emperors).[47] The calendar date that is present to the Talmudic interpreters – after the winter solstice, when the light becomes longer again – is used as a symbolical expression of the general renewal and, at the same time, the permanence of imperial unity.

Ovid's short description of the public festival in Augustan Rome already set the tone for the centuries to come.[48] After a short prayer to Janus to grant a propitious year to Rome, its leaders, and its people, and after an admonition to his audience to set aside anything divisive and to rest from work, he focuses on the magnificent sacrifice to Jupiter Optimus Maximus on the Capitol. The new consuls sacrifice in the presence of the entire people, all dressed in white, and Jupiter himself looks down upon his world and "sees nothing that is not Roman." The intense visuality of the moment – the brilliance of the white togas and of the sparkling fire on the altar that is reflected by the gold that decorates the temple facade behind it – enhances the imperial message that the event articulates in Ovid's description.

After the first day of the year with its public celebrations, January 2 was a day of rest; to Libanius in the late fourth century, it was a tranquil and serenely festive day for the single households. But as any other day that followed the three named days in the Roman month – Kalends, Nones, Ides – January 2 was regarded, as Varro has it, "as black because one did not begin anything new on these days," even if the notes on the early Imperial stone calendars marked them as *dies fasti*, legal working days.[49] When rabbi Yohanan in his aetiological story described the second day as a "black day," he was aware not only of the opposition between the first day of the year with its festivities and the second with its character as a rest day, but also with its Roman evaluation as *dies ater*.[50]

In Ovid's Rome, the festival of the Kalendae Ianuariae filled one day only, January 1. After Constantine, it lasted significantly longer. The calendar of 354 assigned five days to the festival; similarly in his sermon against the Kalendae, preached in Amasea or Antioch on the festival day of

---

[47] The main texts are Libanius, *Oration* 9 (written after the prohibition of sacrifices by Theodosius) and Asterius of Amaseia, *Homily* 4 (dated January 7, 400).
[48] Ovid, *Fasti* 1.63–88.
[49] Varro, *De ling. Lat.* 6.29 (*dies postridie Kalendas Nonas Idus appellari atri, quod per eos dies nihil novi inciperent*); Festus p. 348 Lindsay; Gellius, *Noctes Atticae* 4.9.5. See Michels (1967), 65f.
[50] Guggenheimer (2011), 252: "The next day they mourn him, a black day."

Epiphany on January 6, 400 CE, bishop Asterius treats January 5 as the last day of the Kalendae. The *Feriale Duranum*, dated between 225 and 227, must have had a one-line entry on January 1 that is now lost; it had nothing on January 2, and recorded on January 3 the usual *vota* for the ruling emperor and the empire with a detailed sacrifice. The calendar does not allow us to conjecture as to whether we already deal with a period of festivities comparable to the city festivals in the later fourth century, or whether in the Dura garrison these were still two unconnected days.[51]

For imperial ideology, January 3 was the main day. It was the day when the *vota publica*, the vows on behalf of the reigning emperor and the empire were formulated. The *vota* were introduced by Augustus in 29 BCE and later turned into a festival that outlasted the Christianization of the empire, as demonstrated by the opposition in canon 62 of the Council in Trullo in the year 692.[52] Outside of Rome, governors, garrisons, and individual cities also offered their *vota* in visible public rituals. Under Trajan, Pliny did so twice as governor of Bithynia; and we just saw how under Severus Alexander the garrison in Dura at the Eastern frontier performed the ritual, as did presumably every army unit in the empire. In the third century, the city of Perge in Pamphylia commemorated the *vota* sacrifices on their coins; the cities of Ptolemais and Cyrene in the Cyrenaica had done so already under Vespasian.[53] Tertullian notes two successive places for the *votorum nuncupatio*, first the center of the army camp, the *principium*, then the Capitolium of the Roman *municipia*: this describes a ritual scenario that must have been valid empire-wide.[54] Governor Pliny duly announced the public performance of the rite to his emperor, who graciously thanked him. Autonomous cities and many Roman colonies documented the performance on inscriptions and coins: it was perceived as an important act to demonstrate solidarity with the emperor and define oneself as part of the empire.

Depending on the performers, the initiative to this ritual could come from the bottom or the top. At least for garrisons such as Dura, the obligation for the rite was imposed from the center, and we can assume

---

[51] The first month preserved in the painted calendar from Santa Maria Maggiore is July: Magi (1972), 24.
[52] Augustus: Cassius Dio 15.19. Trullo: see Nedungatt and Featherstone (1995), 142; the canons did not have any binding character for the emperor.
[53] Pliny: *Epist.* 10.35, 10.100 (two successive years). Dura: Fink, Hoey, and Snyder (1940), 41, col. i.6. Cyrenaica: Reynolds (1962) and (1965). Perge: Weiss (1991). Moesia: Mărghitan and Petolescu (1976).
[54] Tertullian, *De corona militis* 12.3: *Ecce annua votorum nuncupatio : quid uidetur? prima in principiis, secunda in Capitoliis.*

the same for governors such as Pliny and his staff. Autonomous cities might have picked the rite up from the governor performing it in his city rather than from the army; in any case, the initiative must have been entirely theirs.

Given the empire-wide performance of the *vota*, the silence of the Talmud is surprising. Even if the *vota* were not yet the lavish public festival they were later, they must have been performed in some cities of Syria Palaestina, in the garrison cities, such as Legio, or in the seven Roman colonies of which two, Sebaste and Neapolis, were "pagan enclaves" in Samaritan territory.[55] Thoroughly Romanized cities such as Skythopolis/Beth Shean or the long Hellenized cities along the Mediterranean coast could have done the same. On the other hand, the ritual cannot have resonated too well among traditional second-century Jews. But the rabbis must have chosen not to provoke the imperial power in this most vital ritual.

This also means the Kalendae Ianuariae were popular among the population of Palestine not because of its political importance, but for other reasons. The fourth-century Kalendae in the cities of both East and West were a festival of immense sensual enjoyment, with races and gladiatorial games in the circus, and with ample banquets and drinking bouts, dancing, masks, and jesting.[56] All this pleased the people and provoked the ire of the ascetic Christian bishops, who tried to counteract it. In the East Gregory of Nyssa and Asterius of Amaseia chastised their congregation because some of them had preferred the festivities to church-going: "Many" (says an Asterius piqued because his Sunday service on January 1, 400 had remained depleted) "preferred the senseless extravagance and leisure and avoided the meeting in the church."[57] In the West, the more ruthless Augustine prescribed fasting to his flock and kept them all day in the church, regardless of the fun their less obedient family members were having.[58] Although we lack evidence, I feel tempted to assume that the Kalendae Ianuariae in the Palestinian cities of the late second and third centuries already were a similarly enjoyable and tempting affair both for the pagans and for not a few Jews.

The same is true for the imperial days. Accession and birthday were usually commemorated empire-wide, and it has become clear that this had

---

[55] The term is used by Belayche (2001), 171.   [56] See below, Chapter 3 for details.
[57] Asterius, *Hom.* 4.1, Datema (1970), 39; Gregory of Nyssa, *Sermo in diem luminum* (*Opera* 9.221.3–6 and 17–19). On the not uncommon problem of church attendance outside the great church feasts, see Finn (2006), 139–140.
[58] Augustine, *Sermo* 198augm = 26 Dolbeau, par. 7.

been decreed from the imperial center, not chosen by the imperial cities;[59] *ludi* and meals (or, as the Lex Irnitana has it for a *municipium* in Spain, *spectacula ... epulum aut vesceratio*) belonged to the standard events of these days, both highly attractive for the people.[60]

Saturnalia

This also helps to explain the presence of the other festival on this list, the Saturnalia. If we read it as a list of imperial festivals, it would remain isolated: nowhere in the empire were the Saturnalia connected with imperial cult. But we know how attractive the Saturnalia were during all centuries of imperial rule, at least in the city of Rome. They were included in the calendar of 354, and they are the setting of Macrobius' *Saturnalia*, whose dramatic date is set in the 380s.[61] In the calendar of Polemius Silvius, however, December 17 remains only as *feriae servorum*: this might reflect the situation in Gaul rather than in Rome, or a more general replacement of the Saturnalia by a religiously less offensive "Slave Holiday." In the Greek East, at about the same time the Saturnalia were replaced by the Brumalia, as a result of the ecclesiastical condemnation of the festival reflected by John Lydus in Justinian's time.[62]

The festival is more than once attested in pre-Constantinian Syria Palaestina. The Talmud Yerushalmi knows a market fair at Skythopolis/ Beth Shean at the Saturnalia.[63] The Mishnah on *Avodah Zarah* mentions the shops at Beth Shean decorated during a festival, perhaps again the Saturnalia;[64] and the Jerusalem Talmud describes these decorations as myrtle or as "any kind," to which the Babylonian Talmud adds roses and fruit.[65] The rabbinic discussion turns around the question whether these decorations honor the gods – and thus prohibit a visit of the fair because it would be idolatrous – or serve only to attract customers. The fair at Beth Shean has been put together with the Saturnalia that the Feriale Duranum attests for the garrison in Dura and with other texts that show that the festival was popular among the army.[66] Although Scythopolis/ Beth Shean was not a garrison town like Dura-Europos where the camp was almost a part of the city, a major

---

[59] For the West, Fishwick (1987–2005); generally Rüpke (1995), 545f.
[60] *Lex Irnitana*, ed. d'Ors (1986), 10 B 30.
[61] On Macrobius and his *Saturnalia*, Cameron (2011), 230–272.
[62] Lydus, *Mens.* 1.158. More below, Chapter 4.   [63] Belayche (2001), 261.
[64] *Mishnah AZ* 1:4, Guggenheimer (2011), 258.
[65] Yerushalmi: Guggenheimer (2011), 263; Babylonian Talmud on *AZ* 12b,70 "decorated with garlands of roses and myrtle ... with fruit," Cohen (1988).
[66] See Fink, Hoey, and Snyder (1940), 161 with n. 373; add the Vindolanda tablet 301 (*c*.100 CE).

military camp was not far away from Scythopolis.[67] Thus, given the usually close connection between city and army camp, we can assume that the festival and fair in Scythopolis originated with the garrison and over time turned into a city-wide popular event that served also the necessities of the local economy, confirming the key role of the army in spreading Rome's urban cults.[68]

This lengthy history and especially the importance of the festival for the troops can help to explain the inclusion of the Saturnalia in the Mishnah: the rabbinic list gives the festivals celebrated by the non-Jews in the region of Galilee where the Talmud of Jerusalem originated, and in which some Jews took part as well.[69] Tertullian confirms such a reading; what he says about late second-century Africa applies to contemporary Iudaea Palaestina as well. In a chapter in his *De idololatria* in which he castigates the improper and idolatrous way in which Christians share and even appropriate pagan festivals for themselves, he lists Kalendae, Saturnalia, Matronalia, and Bruma, celebrations to which he ascribes gift-giving, play, and banquets as their salient and, to him, offensive characteristics.[70] Be they Christians or Jews, the religious moralists were offended by the same Roman festivals that were cherished by the pagans and by some Jews or Christians around them, and they wanted to draw clear boundaries. We shall see that this remained so up to the councils of Trullo in the East and Braga in the West. There is no need to imagine a communication between the rabbis and Tertullian: they both looked at the Roman festival calendar with a similar attitude, and drew similar conclusions.

Contests, fairs, and festivals

But we have to take a broader look at Palestine in the second to fourth centuries CE in order to fully understand the list in the Mishnah.[71] What had been at various times the Hellenized kingdom of Herod and his successors and then the Provincia Iudaea, was renamed Provincia Syria Palaestina after the Bar Kokhba revolt and became increasingly Romanized. Its many cities,

---

[67] On the camp and its connection with the city see Safrai (1992), 105f., 109.
[68] For Scythopolis/Beth Shean see Lifshitz (1977); Fuks (1982); Belayche (2001), 257–268. "Als Transporteur von Religion ... kann das Heer kaum überschätzt werden," Rüpke (2011), 237.
[69] This is confirmed by the *Midrash Rabbah Deuteronomy* 7.7, Liebermann (1964) 111; Veltri (2000), 112.
[70] Tertullian, *De idololatria* 14.4–6 (more below, Chapter 4). See also *Apologeticum* 42.4 and 5, where the Saturnalia are put together with the Liberalia, the latter also described as an occasion for banquets (*discumbo*).
[71] Masterly overview in Millar (1993), 337–386. See also Goodman (1983), Cotton (1999), and the historical introduction to Belayche (2001).

its theaters, amphitheaters, and Roman baths must have made large stretches of it almost indistinguishable from any urban landscape in the empire, Eastern or Western. Some cities became *coloniae* and, even more frequently, changed their names from Hebrew to Greek or Latin; sometimes they asked for it, as Emmaus did under Elagabal to receive the name of Nicopolis:[72] the imposition of a Latin name from above – as when Jerusalem turned into Colonia Aelia Capitolina – seems not to have been the rule but the exception due to special historical circumstances. This is relevant for the self-perception of these cities: under Caracalla, Scythopolis (Beth Shean, as the Talmud consistently has it) styled itself "sacred and inviolable among the Greek cities of Koile Syria," with emphasis on "Greek city"; this certainly is not imposed from above, but represents the self-definition and the self-consciousness of its citizens.[73]

Festivals were an important part of the life and the self-perception of any ancient city, be it the traditional city festivals or the more recent athletic or musical contests that were added to the calendar, or finally the fairs (πανηγύρεις) that developed around some of these festivals, attracted large crowds, and offered business opportunities to local and traveling merchants alike.[74] In the Imperial epoch, these local festivals that defined a single city went together with the festivals that marked the unity of the empire, especially, but not exclusively, the festivals of the omnipresent imperial cult. They also went together with some of the city festivals of Rome that the *coloniae* took over from the center as part of their Roman self-definition, often following the lead of a garrison. In this somewhat generalizing perspective, the festival calendar of a province like Syria Palaestina must have looked rich and complex. Evidence to demonstrate this richness, however, is scantier than one would wish.[75]

Contests, ἀγῶνες, are well attested for the Palestinian cities and have an attraction and renown that might go much beyond the borders of the province. A decree from Syrian Laodikeia, dated to 121 CE, honors the boxer Aurelius Septimius Irenaeus, a citizen of Laodikeia; in the long list of his victories appear three cities of Syria Palaestina, the maritime cities of Ascalon and Sidon and the inland city of Scythopolis.[76] Another inscription, from Aphrodisias in Caria and dated to 165 CE, honors the pancratiast M. Aelius Aurelius Menander, a citizen of Aphrodisias, who had won many contests, among them at Caesarea on the Sea, where the athletic and

---

[72] Euseb. *Chron.* 2,220; Millar (1993), 375.
[73] *SEG* 37.1531: τῆς ἱερᾶς καὶ ἀσύλου τῶν κατὰ Κοίλην Συρίαν Ἑλληνίδων πόλεων.
[74] An overview in de Ligt (1993). [75] See for a detailed analysis Belayche (2001).
[76] Moretti (1953), no. 85.

musical contests went back to the Hellenization by Herod the Great;[77] at Neapolis in Samaria, a Flavian foundation; at Scythopolis again; and finally, just beyond the borders of the province, at Gaza and at Caesarea Panias at the sources of the river Jordan. The Paneia, the main city contest of Caesarea Panias, appear in two other agonistic inscriptions from the third century, one from Didyma in Ionia, the other from Kos, honoring a citizen of Caesarea.[78] All these contests were part of a regular city festival, centered around the procession and the lavish sacrifice for the divinity celebrated there, like Pan of Caesarea Panias, who had an important sanctuary that remained a pilgrimage center and whom scholars tend to understand as a local Ba'al, without good reasons: to the citizens as well as to the visiting athletes he was just another Greek god Pan, and his pre-Greek past remains impenetrable, and somewhat irrelevant.

The most intriguing cult site, however, is a shrine away from any city, the shrine of Mamre with its sacred terebinth.[79] As late as the early fifth century CE, the cult site attracted pagans (whomever we have to understand by this term), Jews, and Christians to its large annual festival and its market fair. The three groups performed rituals "at the terebinth," each group in its own fashion: at this shrine, three major festivals of three religious groups coincided in time, place, and, to a certain extent, recipient, and they could live together very well, although the rabbis had prohibited participation in this "idolatrous" cult; but they lacked the power to make participation impossible. Fourth-century Christians had this power; but the destruction of the pagan altar and its "idols" and the construction of a Christian basilica ordered by Constantine, after a complaint by his mother-in-law Eutropia, only slowly changed the nature of the worship.[80]

It is much more difficult to get an impression of the festivals which did not have such an international appeal but remained local or regional at best and thus did not leave a big footprint in the epigraphical record. But some glimpses are possible, as the case of Scythopolis shows.

Scythopolis not only had an international contest, it had also a cult of Dionysos that was local but none the less important and visible.[81] Excavations attest to a large town sanctuary and two theaters; from the larger one comes a dedication to the god from Severan times.[82] The

---

[77] Josephus, *Ant.* 16.5.1.   [78] Moretti (1953), no. 72; Robert (1960a), 440–444.
[79] See Kofsky (1998); see also Belayche (2001), 96–104; Burkert (2012), 45–47.
[80] Constantine's letter to the bishops of Palestine: Euseb. *V.Const.* 3.52.
[81] Belayche (2001), 262–267.
[82] The theaters: Applebaum (1978) and Segal (1995) (the larger one was perhaps constructed under Septimius Severus); the inscription: *ZPE* 6 (1970), 6.

Imperial coins of the city figure the child Dionysos with the nymphs: the city, it seems, claimed to be one of the places where the god grew up. There can be no doubt, given all this, that the city had its annual Dionysia, presumably celebrated on quite a large scale, with a procession, a major sacrifice, and scenic performances in the theater, as is usual for Dionysia at this time.

Other cases do not become visible before the Christian contestation of the fourth and fifth centuries, such as the festival of Marnas in Gaza.[83] The indigenous Marnas was the main god, the θεὸς πάτριος of the city that in 243 CE, in a dedication set up in Ostia, styled itself "sacred, inviolate, autonomous, faithful, pious and great."[84] Learned Greeks identified Marnas with Zeus "Born in Crete," Κρηταγενής, for unclear reasons.[85] His main festival must have attracted large crowds; at least in the later fourth century when it had elected to become a *colonia*, like many other cities in Palestine, Gaza featured a chariot race in which a pagan and a Christian *duumvir* ran their horses against each other, according to Jerome, who tells a story of race-track magic and, as a learned writer, compares the horse-race to what happened in the races of the Roman Consualia.[86]

Besides these local festivals there was the large number of festivals that gave religious expression to the unity of the empire, especially when they were connected with the cult of an emperor. It is impossible to draw up a full list of them. There were the standard imperial birthdays and accession days, as we just saw; but every city was free to add an imperial event to its own local festival, as we saw with the τὰ μέγαλα Πτοῖα καὶ Καισηρεῖα in Akraiphia or the blending of Artemis and the imperial house in the Salutaris procession in Ephesos; in all these cases, the initiative is the city's, usually after the initiative of a leading citizen.[87] In addition to these regularly recurring days, there were occasional festivals, especially when the emperor visited a city. In a tradition that went back to the Hellenistic kings, the emperor was received with sacrifices and public feasting; in the later empire, such an *adventus* became a highly formalized ceremony.[88] A standard practice was the burning of incense on small altars in front of the doors of private houses; these altars were usually cut from

---

[83] The evidence on the cult in Belayche (2001), 235–255.
[84] *IG* xiv 926; Sacco (1984), no. 5 (line 7 ἡ πόλις ἡ τῶν Γαζαίων ἱερὰ καὶ ἄσυλος καὶ αὐτόνομος, πιστὴ καὶ εὐσεβής, λαμπρὰ καὶ μεγάλη).
[85] Steph. Byz. s.v. Γάζα, who lists other mythical contacts with Crete.
[86] Hieron. *V. Hilarionis* 11.
[87] Still the best account is Price (1984) and, for the West, the studies in Fishwick (1987–2005).
[88] On the Hellenistic kings see Robert (1966), esp. 186–191 (=*OMS* 7.610–615); for later examples Price (1984), 213.

one single marble block and often show up in the archaeological and epigraphical record, because they were reused for other purposes once the visitor had passed.[89] Already Antiochos Epiphanes incurred the wrath of the Jews by imposing this ritual upon them; but the custom remained, and in the Imperial epoch the rabbis discussed whether Jews could use such small altars as building material once the emperor had left. The answer was affirmative. The discussion shows how many of them were around once the ruler passed, and could be reused as convenient building material.[90]

The rabbis' reactions

The rabbis whose discussions the Jerusalem Talmud reports were aware of at least some of these festivals and fairs, and of the interaction between Jews and non-Jews that they were stimulating. In the discussion of the Mishnah on *Avodah Zarah* 1:4, they mention the fairs in Tyre and Acre (Akko), together with the one "at Botna (בוטנה)," that is at the terebinth tree of Mamre, in a brilliant reading of the text proposed more than a century ago by Wilhelm Bacher.[91] The context of this Mishnah makes it clear that the Mamre fair was as much a fair for non-Jews as the other two that were held in maritime Graeco-Roman cities; the famous later description of the Mamre festival by the church historian Sozomenos confirms this.[92] The rabbis realized that those market-fairs were problematical for Jews who wanted to avoid contact with idolatry: they all were somehow connected with pagan cult. They thus prohibited Jews from doing business at the fair in Mamre, "since it is the most obvious [as to idolatry] among them,"[93] and they pointed out that Diocletian had dedicated the marketplace in Tyre to the genius of his brother Heraclius, which made it belong to the same forbidden category.[94]

There was thus considerable interaction between the inhabitants of the Graeco-Roman cities of Palestine and the Palestinian countryside, despite the different administrative structures of the places and the different ideological and religious backgrounds of the people. In this perspective,

---

[89] Robert (1966).
[90] Antiochos: 1 Macc. 1:55. Altars: *mishna* AZ 4:6, Guggenheimer (2011), 419 ("pedestals of kings"); see Graf (2001). A local case shows how common they must have been: Phokaia, a city with a very meager epigraphical record, still has three small altars, all dedicated to Hadrian, who visited the city presumably during his second Eastern travels in 129 CE, Graf (1985), 423.
[91] Bacher (1909), who understands בוטנה *botna* as a dialectal variation of בוטמא *botma*, "terebinth"; accepted by Kofsky (1998), 20, but not by Guggenheimer (2011), 262, who tries an unconvincing explanation, as did his predecessors.
[92] Sozomen. *Hist. eccl.* 2.4.4; see Belayche (2001), 96–104.   [93] Guggenheimer (2011), 262.
[94] *Ibid*. Heraclius' genius was Herakles, the Melqart of Tyre.

the purely Roman and mostly imperial character of the list in the Mishnah on *Avodah Zarah* 1:3 is striking. The absence of the city festivals cannot be explained with a successful prohibition alone; no prohibition ever has been as successful as this.[95]

A somewhat different approach leads to the same observation. Most of the city festivals must have been accompanied by spectacles of some sort, athletic contests, theatrical performances, horse races; such performances are attested in several cities, and they must have attracted many Jews, as they attracted Christians and provoked Tertullian's *De spectaculis*. One is tempted to explain their absence in the Mishnah with the prohibition of Jewish participation in pagan spectacles that commentators saw expressed in the Jerusalem Talmud's exegesis of the Mishnah on *Avodah Zarah* 1:7 that prohibits the sale of "bears or lions or anything which may cause harm to the public." Bears and lions were the main animals used in gladiatorial *venationes*, and they were as well known in the Greek East as in the Roman West, although they were always viewed as a Roman import.[96] The introduction of these and all the other (Graeco-)Roman spectacles by king Herod the Great was viewed as violently contradicting Jewish traditions; traditional Jews had already reacted in the same way when Antiochos Epiphanes built a Greek gymnasium in Jerusalem.[97] Josephus singles out for special comment the *venationes* that Herod introduced: "Foreigners were astonished at the expense and at the same time entertained by the dangerous spectacle, but to the natives, it meant the destruction of customs held in honor by them."[98] The rabbis who expound the Mishnah in the Jerusalem Talmud concentrated on Roman spectacles: they talked about Roman comedy with its stock characters, and about gladiatorial games whose spectators – "he who sits in the stadion" – are "guilty of bloodshed"; their argument comes close to the Roman moralists' condemnation of these same spectacles.[99] The only statement that can be read as more general is R. Meir's condemnation of everybody who "goes up into the theater: it is prohibited on the count of idolatry," since theaters with their altars of Dionysos are always cult places, and the plays deal with pagan gods and heroes, as Tertullian explained to his Christians.[100] R. Meir would have given the same explanation as his Christian contemporary: from the same premises rooted in a fervent opposition to Roman culture driven both

---

[95] For the difference between the cities and the countryside see Schürer (1973–1979), 2: 85–197.
[96] Still seminal: Robert (1940). There was an import tax on bears: see Symmachus, *Epist.* 5.62.
[97] 1 Macc 1:14.   [98] Josephus, *Ant.* 15.268, 274f.; see Jacobs (1998), 339.
[99] See Jacobs (1998), 333f. For the Roman moralists such as Seneca, *Epist.* 7.4, see Barton (1989).
[100] Tert. *De spect.* 10.

by moral and by religious purism, Jewish and Christian religious leaders arrived at the same conclusions.[101]

The focus on Roman spectacles both in the Mishnah and the Jerusalem commentary might have to do with the origin of these spectacles: they were introduced by Herod the Great, the friend of the Romans. This immediately fed into the anti-Roman bias of the Jerusalem Talmud that is visible even in the rabbis' appropriation of the Kalendae by deriving it from Adam when they realized they had to accept its existence.[102] To judge from Talmudic comments on the behavior of the Roman army, this anti-Roman feeling survived at least into the third century.[103] In the same way, the Mishnah on *Avodah Zarah* 1:3 focuses on the most visible Roman holidays and eclipses all other occasions where a non-Jewish festival might have given rise to contact and business between the communities.

But there might be more. Even if one takes the list as prohibiting Roman festivals only, it is too short. There must have been other Roman festivals, and one immediately springs to mind. The birthday of Rome, the Natalis Urbis or Parilia, was celebrated at least in Rome not just with a solemn sacrifice but with music and dancing comparable to Saturnalia and Kalendae, and it was popular outside the Urbs. Under Commodus, it is attested as a city festival in Gortyn on Crete; *a priori*, other Greek cities, including some of Iudaea Palaestina, could have made it part of their imperial calendar as well.[104] More importantly, the Feriale Duranum lists it: it was an army festival, and the garrisons in Syria Palaestina must have celebrated it as well; and like Saturnalia and Kalendae, it will have attracted some local Jews.[105]

Thus, the list is not simply anti-Roman, it makes a selection even among the Roman festivals; we saw this already in the case of the omitted *vota*. The rabbis must have deliberated long and carefully about what to include and what to exclude, in order to find a compromise between Jewish and Roman interests in a world where commercial interactions were part and parcel of daily life, but carried the risk of contamination through contact with idolatry; such interaction was also often fraught with unhappy political memories. After all, then, why draw up a list at all, and such a short one, when the first Mishnah had stipulated clearly and without ambiguity: "For three days prior to gentile festivals, it is forbidden to trade with them, to lend to them or to borrow items from them, to give or take loans from them, to clear debts or to collect debts from them"? A strict observation of

---

[101] See Jacobs (1998), 337 with the literature cited in his n. 68.   [102] Belayche (2001), 261.
[103] See Oppenheimer (1992), 121–125.   [104] *I.Cret.* 4.300, a. 180/182 CE; see below, n. 121.
[105] Fink, Hoey, and Snyder (1940), 102.

these prohibitions would have excluded many more festivals in the pagan cities of Syria Palaestina from Jewish participation, and its fairs from Jewish visitors. One must assume that there were enough Jews who celebrated these pagan festivals as well, as Jews had participated in Greek festivals under Seleukid rule, and as Jews went to theaters and even sold themselves as gladiators under the emperors.[106] All the more reason for the guardians of a pure religious tradition to point out that at least some of these festivals were festivals of the "idolaters" only and thus out of bounds for traditional Jews.[107]

Out of Palestine

An inscription from Hierapolis (Pammukkale) in Phrygia shows how festivals of different origin in a diaspora community outside of Syria Palaestina interacted; onomastics date the text after 212 CE, the letter forms suggest a date not too far after this. On a sarcophagus, a wealthy couple, P. Aelius Glykon Zeuxianos Aelianus and his wife Aurelia Amia, daughter of Amianos son of Seleukos, had not only inscribed the prohibition to bury anyone except themselves and their children, they added the provision of their funeral bequest.[108] I give the relevant part of this text:

κατέλι- 4
ψεν δὲ καὶ τῇ σεμνοτάτῃ προεδρίᾳ τῶν πορφυροβαφῶν στεφα-
νωτικοῦ (δηνάρια) διακόσια πρὸς τὸ διδόσθαι ἀπὸ τῶν τόκων ἑκάστῳ τὸ
αἱροῦν μη(νὸς) ζ' ἐν τῇ ἑορτῇ τῶν ἀζύμων. ὁμοίως κατέλιπεν καὶ τῷ συνεδρίῳ
τῶν ἀκαιροδαπισ<τ>ῶν στεφανωτοικοῦ (δηνάρια) ἑκατὸν πεντήκοντα, ἅτι- 8
         vacat τινα καὶ αὐτοὶ δώσουσι ἐκ τοῦ τόκου
διαμερίσαντες τὸ ἥμισυ ἐν τῆι ἑορτῆι τῶν καλάνδων,
μη(νὸς) δ' η', καὶ τὸ ἥμισυ ἐν τῆι ἑορτῆι τῆς πεντεκοστῆς.
ταύτης τῆς ἐπιγραφῆς τὸ ἀντίγραφον ἀπε<τέ>θη ἐν τοῖς ἀρχείοις.

> He left behind 200 *denaria* as grave-crowning money to the most holy presidency of the purple-dyers, in order to give each from the interest a share in the seventh month in the festival of Unleavened Bread. Likewise he also left behind 150 *denaria* as grave-crowning money to the association of carpet-weavers, which they too should hand out from the interest, distributing half during the festival of Kalendae on the eighth day of the fourth month and half during the festival of Pentecost. A copy of this inscription is kept in the archives.

---

[106] 1 Macc. 1:43; Jacobs (1998), 340f.
[107] See also Veltri (2000), 122, and Schäfer (2002), 338–342.
[108] Ameling (2004), 414 no. 196; the inscription was known since 1869, but has been re-edited by Ritti (1992–93) and Miranda (1999), 131 no. 23 and 140–145.

The otherwise unknown couple belongs to the city elite, and unlike the wife's family that became Roman only through the *constitutio Antoniana*, the husband's must have obtained Roman citizenship several generations ago, perhaps under Hadrian: Glykon's cognomen Aelianus shows that already his grandfather was an Aelius. If he belongs to a Jewish family, as is likely but not absolutely certain, an intriguing possibility would be to see his father or grandfather as a Hellenized Jewish inhabitant of Aelia Capitolina who emigrated to Hierapolis; but Aelii are so numerous in Hierapolis that this is not very likely.[109] Rather, the Kalendae was part of the cultural identity not only of this couple but of all members of the guild, Jewish or non-Jewish, who were, after all, given money for celebrating it, as they celebrated Pentecost, and who were willing to disregard what the *Avodah Zarah* had stipulated, in the same way as many Jews outside the rabbinic heartland of Iudaea Palaestina were willing to disregard it. By the same token, the Kalendae must also have been part of the cultural identity of all citizens of Hierapolis; in fact, the Kalendae seem more important than any other traditional festival the city might have celebrated, its own traditional New Year festival not excluded.

The way the Kalendae are introduced – not just with its name but its precise date, "on day 8 of the fourth month" – makes clear that the Kalendae Ianuariae did not coincide with the city's traditional New Year festival. The calendar of Hierapolis is unknown, but the numbering of months is attested in other cities of the region; the city's new year must have begun in late September, although not, as in some cities of Asia Minor, on Augustus' birthday, September 23.[110] The exactness of the date should not surprise us: it expresses nothing more than a striving for legal precision in a published document. The inscription gives also the lunar month for Passover, which is the best it can do, since the Kalendae are immovable *feriae stativae*, whereas Passover and Pentecost are movable, and the date of Pentecost depends on the date of Passover.

Conclusions

Whatever the reasons for its short catalog, by singling out these few festivals the Mishnah is a highly valuable and usually overlooked source text for Roman religion in an Eastern province. It is the only testimony for the

---

[109] On the many Aelii in Hierapolis see Ameling (2004), 416.
[110] Samuel (1972), 133 (on numbered months in the region), 174 (on calendars starting September 23). See also Harland (2006).

term κράτησις as referring to a festival of imperial accession. It is also the only unambiguous testimony of Saturnalia in the Greek East outside the army camps, and it is by far the earliest testimony for the festival of Kalendae Ianuariae in the East; at about the time of Rabbah, Tertullian attested to Saturnalia and Kalendae in North Africa.[111] All other testimonies in the East belong to the fourth and fifth centuries (with the exception of the text from Hierapolis in Phrygia and an inscription from second-century Gortyn, to be discussed below), which led to the erroneous assumption that the Kalendae in the East were adopted late.[112] On the contrary, at the time when the Mishnah was formulated not only the specific days of the emperor cult, accession and birthday, but also Kalendae Ianuariae and Saturnalia were already part of an empire-wide system of originally urban festivals of Rome that helped to construct the unity of the empire, and were singled out for protest by those who opposed what they perceived as an unnatural and imposed unity.

After this initial reaction to the daily realities of life under Rome – including the knowledge of minutiae of the Roman calendar, such as the function of a *dies ater* and the opposition between *feriae publicae* and *feriae privatae* – the Palestinian rabbis lost touch with this world during the fourth and fifth centuries. Neither the empire-wide recognition of the Natalis Urbis and the birthday of Constantinople nor the Christian ban on the Saturnalia and the resulting ascent of the Brumalia registered with them. To them, the festivals of the idolaters remained Kalendae, Saturnalia, Accession Day.

Further Roman festivals

The discussion of the Mishnah on *Avodah Zarah* 1:3 had us also look at other Roman festivals outside Syria Palaestina. We saw how the *vota* of January 3 must have been prescribed from the center at least for the *municipia*, the garrisons, and the governors, and how they must have been adopted from there by autonomous cities such as Ptolemais in the Cyrenaica or Perge in Pamphylia; a top-down mechanism thus generated a bottom-up one. We also saw how in the West, in Carthage, Tertullian

---

[111] Tertullian, *De idololatria* 14 (Saturnalia, Kalendae Ianuariae), *Apologeticum* 42.3 (Saturnalia); the *vota publica* in Tertullian, *Apologeticum* 35.7; *De corona* 12.3.
[112] "Certains indices permettent cependant de penser que, dès le Haut-Empire, la fête de Kalendes ... s'est implantée dans l'occident romain": Meslin (1970), 49, who then cites Tertullian and a contemporary mosaic from El Djem in Tunisia; the "orient" was much later. Corrected by Hadas-Lebel (1990), 311f. for Palestine; for the Hierapolis inscription, see note 108.

attested to the performance of several Roman city festivals, the Kalendae Ianuariae, the Saturnalia, the Brumae, the Matronalia, and the Liberalia, all characterized by banquets and other practices that were offensive to the Christian moralist. With the exception of the Mishna and its Kalendae and Saturnalia (and the other Talmudic passages on the Saturnalia), no festival in Tertullian's list is attested in the Greek East before the fourth century.

Lucian and the Saturnalia

The Saturnalia were attested not only in *Avodah Zarah* but also in the calendar of the garrison at Dura-Europos: their celebration was a firm part of the empire-wide festival calendar of the army, and at the other end of the Roman world a letter from Vindolanda, near what would later be Hadrian's Wall in Northern Britain, confirms this.[113] We also saw them accompanied by a market in the autonomous Palestinian city of Scythopolis.[114] If one combines this with Tertullian's information about its importance in Roman Africa, it is not unlikely that the festival had spread from the garrisons to many more autonomous cities in the Greek East as well, not unlike the *vota publica*, whose spread could have brought the celebration of the Kalendae with them, even if the Kalendae Ianuariae were not yet extended to the five days that we know they included in the fourth century (see below).

This popularity of the Saturnalia outside of Rome already in the later part of the second century might help us to understand to whom Lucian addressed his complex and layered *opusculum* Τὰ πρὸς Κρόνον. Although the length of the festival and its calendar setting – seven days during the coldest time of the year – exclude the Greek Kronia that lasted one day and, as far as we can see, took place in late summer, it is still unclear whether he is talking about the Saturnalia in Rome or about Roman Saturnalia as celebrated in a city of the Greek East, and whether he envisaged a Roman audience or a Greek provincial one.[115] A Roman audience is not *a priori* excluded: for a while, his career made Lucian stay in the Roman West and the city of Rome. But an Eastern, Greek audience would be more

---

[113] Vindolanda tablet no. 301 (*c.*100 CE). – For the edition see http://vindolanda.csad.ox.ac.uk/.
[114] Belayche (2001), 261; see above, n. 66.
[115] Seven days: Lucian. *Sat.* 2; already in Republican times according to Nonius and Mommius *ap.* Macrob. *Sat.* 1.10.3f. (who has a discussion on original length of the festival); winter: Lucian. *Sat.* 6; Mommius *ibid*. Versnel's (1993, 89–227) rich chapters on "Kronos and the Kronia" and "Saturnus and the Saturnalia" address the gods and their festival under the aspect of how myth and ritual went together in these cults, but they remain by far the best treatment of both gods.

interesting in the context of my research, of course. However, such an assumption can be considered plausible only if Lucian's text could be shown to contain ritual details that are unknown in our record of the Saturnalia in Rome and thus constitute a local change in an Eastern setting. The absence of such traits in a festival exported by the army from the city of Rome, on the other hand, would not disprove such an assumption, it only would make it unprovable.

The text is far from unambiguous. It begins with a dialogue between Kronos and his priest, then adds two collections of laws on the festival that the priest has been drawing up. It continues with a letter of the priest to Kronos and his answer, and finally another letter from Kronos to the rich and their answer. The presence of a priest of Kronos is not decisive: Saturnus had a temple in Rome, and he must have had a priest even if none is attested; but one can also imagine that a Greek city with an existing cult of Kronos, and such a priest, adopted the Roman Saturnalia. The main topic of the slim work is social justice: Kronos, as the god of the Golden Age with its equal bliss for everybody, takes offense at the asymmetrical gift-giving of the Kronia, where the poor, who cannot really afford it, have to offer presents to the rich, who do not really need them; as a reaction, the god intends to create a modest and temporary redistribution of wealth during his festival. Lucian is not the only author to highlight the social problem in lavish gift-giving as part of the festival culture: we shall see that the Christian opposition to the Kalendae Ianuariae was at least in part based on the very same problem of asymmetrical gift-giving.

In the introductory dialogue, Kronos describes the festival with a wealth of ritual details:[116]

> Mine is a limited monarchy, you see. To begin with, it only lasts a week; that over, I am a private person, just a man in the street. Secondly, during my week the serious is barred; no business allowed. Drinking and being drunk, noise and games and dice, appointing of kings and feasting of slaves, singing naked, clapping of tremulous hands, an occasional ducking of corked faces in icy water: such are the functions over which I preside.

---

[116] Lucian, *Saturnalia* 2: ἐγὼ δ' ἐπὶ ῥητοῖς παραλαμβάνω τὴν δυναστείαν. ἑπτὰ μὲν ἡμερῶν ἡ πᾶσα βασιλεία, καὶ ἢν ἐκπρόθεσμος τούτων γένωμαι, ἰδιώτης εὐθύς εἰμι καί που τοῦ πολλοῦ δήμου εἷς. ἐν αὐταῖς δὲ ταῖς ἑπτὰ σπουδαῖον μὲν οὐδὲν οὐδὲ ἀγοραῖον διοικήσασθαί μοι συγκεχώρηται, πίνειν δὲ καὶ μεθύειν καὶ βοᾶν καὶ παίζειν καὶ κυβεύειν καὶ ἄρχοντας καθιστάναι καὶ τοὺς οἰκέτας εὐωχεῖν καὶ γυμνὸν ᾄδειν καὶ κροτεῖν ὑποτρέμοντα, ἐνίοτε δὲ καὶ ἐς ὕδωρ ψυχρὸν ἐπὶ κεφαλὴν ὠθεῖσθαι, ἀσβόλῳ κεχρισμένον τὸ πρόσωπον, ταῦτα ἐφεῖταί μοι ποιεῖν (translation after H. W. and F. G. Fowler).

Not all these details are present in our information about the Saturnalia in Rome. Drinking, playing dice, and feeding the slaves are well attested; but there is no corroborative evidence for naked dancing (it becomes clear only later that this was a punishment for the loser in a game of dice), shaking the rattle, blackening one's face, and pushing someone into cold water. *Voluptas* and *licentia*, the catchwords for the festival among the Imperial elite, would cover this, but of course these words would cover much more.[117] And the custom to give candles to one's friends that Macrobius explains with a myth sounds somewhat less offensive than the asymmetrical gift exchange that Lucian censures so insistently.[118] On the other hand Martial's list of Saturnalia gifts – from nuts to a boar and a rhinoceros – is definitely more extravagant than Lucian's.

Thus, no detail is really conclusive either way, with one possible exception. Lucian does not mention what irked Seneca, namely that free men put away their toga for a more comfortable garment and were wearing the freedman's *pilleus*.[119] He might have omitted this detail as irrelevant to his main polemical purpose – or it was a custom in the city of Rome only, where the contrast between *togati* and *pilleati* made immediate sense; we have no way to tell how the army dressed up for their Saturnalia. Given the presence of Saturnalia in the Eastern provinces, this then might be significant. Lucian could attest to the transfer of the festival and of many of its customs to the Greek-speaking provinces of the empire, with only few changes and adaptations. The idea is tempting and offers the intriguing possibility of local developments even in the celebration of the Saturnalia by the Roman army.[120]

Parilia aka Natalis Urbis

Between 180 and 182 CE, one Titus Flavius Xenion (his ancestors must have become a Roman citizen under the Flavians, about a century before his time) left in his will the funds to institutionalize eight festival days in the Cretan city of Gortyn. The grateful citizens erected an honorary statue of the donor and summarized the terms of his donation on its base:[121]

---

[117] *Voluptas*: Seneca, *Ep.*18.2 and 3; *licentia*: Plin. *Ep.* 2.17.24 – both shun the festival, and Pliny gets his own *voluptas* from the fact that his study is so remote that the festival's noise cannot reach him.
[118] Candles: Macrob. *Sat.* 1.7.32f.;   [119] Seneca, *Epist.* 18.3; see Martial, 14.1.1.
[120] The highly debated human sacrifice at the Saturnalia in Durostomium in Moesia, according to the *Acta Dasii* is discussed by Versnel (1993), 210–227, who thinks of the possibility of a late development connected with the gladiatorial *munera* at the Saturnalia.
[121] *I.Cret.* 4.300, a. 180/182 CE.

Στηλογρα[φία διανομῶν]
τῶν καταλε[ιφθεισῶν ἐπὶ]
κωδικίλλοις Φλ[α(ουίου) Ξενίωνος]
ἡμερῶν Η   4
πρὸ ΙΑ Καλανδ(ῶν) Μαΐων Ῥώμης γενεθλίῳ,
πρὸ Α Καλανδ(ῶν) Σεπτεμβρίων Κομόδου Αὐ[τοκρ(άτορος) Σεβ(αστοῦ)
γενεθλίῳ],
Νώναις Μαρτίαις κρατήσει Αὐτοκράτορος Ἀντ[ωνείνου θεοῦ]
Σεβ(αστοῦ) καὶ Λουκίλλης Σεβαστῆς γενεθλίῳ,   8
πρὸ ΙΗ Καλανδ(ῶν) Ἰανουαρίων Λουκίου θεοῦ Σεβαστοῦ [γενεθλίῳ],
πρὸ ΙΑ Καλανδ(ῶν) Δεκεμβρίων Φλα(ουίου) Ξενίωνος γεν[εθλίῳ],
Εἰδοῖς Ὀκτωβρίαις Λαμπριοῦς καὶ Ξενοφίλου γεν[εθλίῳ],
πρὸ Ζ Καλανδ(ῶν) Αὐγούστων Ζηνοφίλου γενεθλίῳ,   12
πρὸ Α Καλανδ(ῶν) Αὐγούστων Κλ(αυδίας) Μαρκελλείνης γε[νεθλίῳ].

> Inscriptional version of the distribution left through the will of Flavius Xenon for eight days:
> April 21: for the birthday of Rome
> August 31: for the birthday of the emperor Commodus Augustus
> March 7: for the Accession of the emperor, the divine Antoninus Augustus, and the birthday of Lucilla Augusta
> December 16: for the birthday of the divine Lucius Augustus
> November 21: for the birthday of Flavius Xenon
> October 15: for the birthday of Lamprio and Xenophilos
> July 26: for the birthday of Zenophilos
> July 31: for the birthday of Claudia Marcellina.

The donor financed eight commemorative days, four of them Roman and connected with imperial rule, the other four Greek and connected with his own family. First come the birthday of the city of Rome followed by a series of imperial days, the birthdays of the ruling emperor, Commodus (ruled 180–192), his predecessor and brother Lucius Verus and their sister, Verus' wife Lucilla (executed 182), and the accession day of their father, Marcus Aurelius. The donor must have seen them as the new dynastic family to which he added his own dynasty: his own birthdays and those of four family members; Claudia Marcellina, whose birthday was celebrated on July 31, must have been his wife rather than a daughter-in-law.

A foundation to commemorate one's own birthday or the birthdays of one's family members is not uncommon already in Hellenistic times.[122] A private foundation for the cult of some members of the ruling dynasty and of Rome is less common; the combination of both is even more surprising. We have to assume that Gortyn previously did not possess these imperial

---

[122] An early example: Epikteta on Thera, Wittenburg (1990); more, Schmidt (1908), 47–51.

festivals. Following a pattern we noticed in Chapter 1, it was the initiative of a member of the city elite with double citizenship, Gortynian and Roman, that introduced them to his Greek city, which, like Ephesos, visibly participated in both worlds, being an autonomous city that was also seat of the Roman governor of the Province of Crete. It could also be significant that Commodus was the main recipient of such honors: it is in the reign of Commodus that emperors begin to show a larger presence as benefactors in the autonomous cities in the East, as Dietrich Klose showed in his analysis of the autonomous coinage that attests to games and contests in the Eastern cities of the empire.[123]

In our context, the most intriguing detail is the first item, the celebration of Rome's birthday on April 21. In the Republican and early Imperial stone calendars, this was the date of the festival Parilia, another foundation of king Numa. Varro and the Augustan poets Tibullus and Ovid describe the Parilia as a shepherds' festival, celebrated to purify the flocks and the shepherds.[124] This fits the ideological agenda of an epoch that anchored imperial Rome in its rural past, with Augustus' revival of the Arval Brethren as the most impressive example.[125] The rituals seem to fit this description, although we know their details only through the eyes of these same Augustan writers. But the Menologia Rustica, Farmers' Calendars from the mid-first century CE, confirm these rituals for the later part of April, albeit in the somewhat short and laconic entry "sheeps are purified," *oves lustrant(ur)*: at that epoch, the farmers in the Roman countryside performed these purificatory rituals for their flocks.[126]

This entry in the Menologia Rustica does not hint at the remarkable double, even conflicting character of the festival: it also commemorated the founding of the city of Rome. All the late Republican and early Imperial stone calendars refer both to the Parilia and to the foundation of Rome, *Roma condita*, in their entry on April 21. Already the Fasti Antiates Maiores from the earlier first century BCE do so, which must mean that the festival goes back to the early second century BCE, when Fulvius Nobilior published the ancestor of the preserved calendars.[127] Only one calendar tells us also that "the shepherds' year begins," and only Verrius Flaccus, the antiquarian contemporary of Ovid and Augustus, gives, in his calendar

---

[123] Klose (2004). [124] Varro, *De agricultura* 2.1; Tibull. 2.5.87–100; Ovid, *Fasti* 4.721–862.
[125] Fundamental on the festival: Beard (1987).
[126] See the Menologia Rustica (Colotianum and Vallense) in their April entries, Degrassi (1963), nos. 47 and 48.
[127] Fasti Antiates Maiores: Degrassi (1963), no. 1; Rüpke (1995), 43–44. Fulvius Nobilior: Rüpke (1995), 331–368.

displayed in Praeneste, details of the shepherds' festival that more or less coincide with what the poets tell us.[128] This duplicity of meanings should be given a less evolutionary reading than is usually done; the tension might be inherent from very early on. Romulus and Remus were seen as husbandmen already in our early sources: the shepherds' festival and the founding of the city must have been closely connected. If we follow the lead of Andreas Alföldi and assume that the ideology and reality of warlike bands of husbandmen were important for understanding the history of early Rome, the connection between the two areas is intimate and old; the fact that it was a festival "mainly of the *iuniores*" even in early Augustan times, as Festus has it, points the same way.[129]

On the other hand, the urban ritual must have been more formal than our literary sources with their concentration on bucolic Rome make us believe: the one tantalizing detail, again in a stone calendar, is that "everybody is wearing a wreath."[130] This recalls Hellenistic decrees about how to celebrate a king. When the city of Teos celebrated Antiochos III, the assembly decreed that "everybody in the city should sacrifice and feast in their own house according to their means, and all the people in the city should wear a wreath on this day."[131] Similarly, when the Koans celebrated Ariarathes V of Cappadocia and queen Antiochis, they decided that "the citizens and alien residents and whoever else is staying in the city wears a wreath."[132] Once the Greeks started to celebrate the Roman emperors, they transferred the custom to their cults, as did the Chians in a decree for the birthday of Caligula: "On Panemos 18, all the Chians and every other inhabitant of the city shall wear shining dress and a wreath."[133] Usually, law courts, schools, and shops were closed as well to allow everybody to enjoy the festivities. If this association is correct, by the time of Fulvius Nobilior the Romans must have celebrated the birthday of their city in a similar way

---

[128] Degrassi (1963), no. 17, p. 131: *Pa[r(ilia)* – – –]| *[e]st [*– – –]|*dae qu[*– – –]|*ignes tran[siliunt* – – –]| *principio an[ni pastorici* – – –]|*redigitur.*

[129] Festus 272.3 and 273.1 L.: *Parilibus Romulus urbem condidit, quem diem festum praecipue habebant iuniores.* Alföldi (1974).

[130] *coron[atis omnibus]*, Fasti Esquilini (shortly after 7 BCE?), Degrassi (1963), no. 11, p. 86.

[131] *Anadolu* 1965.36 (*SEG* 27.780 and 28.887), line 24: θύειν δὲ καὶ ἑορτάζειν καὶ τοὺς ἄλους πάντας τοὺς ο[ἰκοῦντας] τὴν πόλιν ἡμῶν ἐν τοῖς ἰδίοις οἴκοις ἑκάστους κατὰ δύν[αμιν· στε]φανηφορεῖν πάντας τοὺς ἐν τῇ πόλει ἐν ἡμέραι ταύτ[η].

[132] *Iscrizioni di Cos* ED5 (= *SEG* 33.675), line 5: [στεφανηφορεῖν] μὲν τὸς πολίτας καὶ τὸς πα[ροίκος καὶ τὸς ἐγ Κῶι ἐ]πιδαμεῦντας.

[133] Robert (1933); the restored text, p. 529 (= *OMS* 1.497), line 5: Χίου[ς μὲν πάντας καὶ τοὺς κατοικοῦ]ντας τ[ὴν πόλι]ν λαμ[πραῖς ἐν ἐσθῆσιν στεφανηφο]ρεῖν ὀκ[τωκαι]δεκάτηι Π[ανήμου]; see also the honors of Sardis for Augustus' son Gaius, *IGRom.* 4.1756.

to how a Hellenistic city celebrated a king: in a vast public display of festivity and joy.[134]

Whatever the exact Republican (pre)history of the Parilia was, they changed name and character during the Imperial epoch. Coins (*aurei* and sesterces) and medals of Hadrian with the genius of the circus on the reverse, dated to the NAT(alis) VRB(is) of 874 AUC, i.e. 121 CE, bear the notice that the emperor for the first time marked this festival with games in the circus, PR(imum) CIRC(enses) CON(stituit); most likely Hadrian changed not only the way the festival was celebrated, but also its name, from the quaint Parilia and its connection with the rustic goddess Pales to the popular "Birthday of Rome."[135] This is also the name used in the Imperial calendars, the Feriale Duranum, Philocalus, and Polemius Silvius; only Polemius Silvius with his typical interest in antiquarian lore adds that the festival was also called "Parilia from the pregnancy of Ilia" (*Parilia dicta de partu Iliae*) – an otherwise unattested etymology which looks back to the birth of Romulus and Remus. Hadrian thus celebrated Rome's birthday not just in the lavish public ritual that recalled the celebration of Hellenistic kings, but added the most popular ritual form of the Imperial age, the chariot race, turning the birthday of Rome into a very visible event. The races did not survive long enough to be noted in the calendar of Philocalus.

But there is also a somewhat different story. Without indicating his source, the learned Athenaeus of Naukratis tells us in his *Deipnosophistae* (written perhaps shortly after Commodus' death in 192 CE), that in former times (πάλαι) the festival was called Parilia, while in his days it was Rhomaia, a major festival for all inhabitants and visitors of the capital; such a wide participation again, like the wreaths worn by all participants, continues the form of Hellenistic royal festivals. According to Athenaeus, the festival was celebrated for τῆς πόλεως Τύχη, for whom Hadrian had built and dedicated a temple.[136] This description turns the goddess into a Hellenizing city goddess, akin to the Tyche of so many eastern cities, especially the Tyche of Antioch. But this is misleading: Athenaeus does not mean a temple of Fortuna Urbis that never existed, he meant the

---

[134] For details, see Chaniotis (1995), and see also Chaniotis (1991).
[135] Strack (1933), 102–105. See Fink, Hoey, and Snyder (1940), 103–106; Beaujeu (1955), 128–136.
[136] Athen. 8.63, 361F ἔτυχεν δὲ οὖσα ἑορτὴ τὰ Παρίλια μὲν πάλαι καλουμένη, νῦν δὲ Ῥωμαῖα, τῇ τῆς πόλεως Τύχῃ ναοῦ καθιδρυμένου ὑπὸ τοῦ πάντα ἀρίστου καὶ μουσικωτάτου βασιλέως Ἀδριανοῦ· ἐκείνην τὴν ἡμέραν κατ'ἐνιαυτὸν ἐπίσημον ἄγουσι πάντες οἱ τὴν Ῥώμην κατοικοῦντες καὶ οἱ ἐνεπιδημοῦντες τῇ πόλει. The date, between 192 and 195, the death of Commodus and his rehabilitation by Septimius Severus, is suggested by Bowie, *DNP* 2.197.

temple of Venus and Roma, *templum Urbis*, dedicated by Hadrian in 121 CE and with its dedication day on April 21, the date of the Parilia.[137]

In Athenaeus' narration, the festival intrudes because of its loud public manifestation ("the sound of flutes, the rattle of cymbals, and the thunder of drums together with singing," αὐλῶν τε βόμβος καὶ κυμβάλων ἦχος ἔτι τε τυμπάνων κτύπος μετὰ ᾠδῆς) that interrupts the discussions of the learned men in the house of P. Livius Larensius in Rome; and since one of the discussants, the orator Ulpianos of Tyre, does not know what is going on, he is given an explanation. (This also qualifies Ulpianos as a foreigner with limited experience of Roman realities and argues against his identification with the famous jurist who was executed in 228, which has some relevance for the dramatic date.) More to the point, this explanation shows that the festival must at this point in time, in the 190s, be specifically Roman and perhaps relatively new. The description fits with what we learned from Hadrian's coins: by the mid-second century, the quaint shepherds' festival in which Tibullus and Ovid jumped over bonfires made from burning beanstalks had turned into something very different, a raucous city festival with a sacrifice to Venus and Roma (and presumably Fortuna Urbis), chariot races in the Circus Maximus and public dancing in the city streets. Rhomaia as the festival name is somewhat surprising: I suspect that Athenaeus' outside perspective made him, consciously rather than by mistake, use a name for a festival celebrating Rome that was well attested in the Greek world since late Hellenistic times but not at home in the celebrated city itself.[138]

The changes that Hadrian (if it was him) brought to the traditional festival were momentous, and resonated with the later development of city festivals. Its main elements were the circus performance and the city-wide street dancing, combined with lavish eating and drinking for everybody who at this point in time was living in the city, regardless of whether they were citizens or not. In later centuries, eating, drinking, and dancing in the city streets will be praised as an imperial contribution to *laetitia populi*, and Hadrian must have such an entertainment in mind; it persisted through the centuries, despite the Christian bishops who attacked it as expression of *licentia*, immorality that did not become a true Christian. The circus games belonged to the same popular entertainment and were equally attacked by some bishops; at the same time, the games were the very moment when the

---

[137] The dedication in Cassius Dio 69.4.5; the name *templum Urbis* in *Hist. Aug. Hadrian* 19.12 and Ammian. 16.10.14. See Wissowa (1912), 340; Steinby (1993–2000), 5: 121–123.

[138] On the festival Rhomaia or rather Ῥωμαῖα see Mellor (1975).

emperor and his city were united in the same place and where the emperor could directly see, hear, and feel the mood of his people. Over the centuries – and not the least in Byzantium – this would turn into a major tool of governance.[139]

Nobody gives a reason why Hadrian changed the name. I suspect it to be the result of his imperial perspective that firmly looked towards the East: the new name made it much easier to export the festival from the Urbs to the Empire. This fits an emperor who was famous for the introduction of (agonistic) festivals in many cities of the East: by the last count, he founded twenty-one such festivals in the Greek world.[140] The Cretan bequest from which this discussion started is about contemporary with Athenaeus and attests to such an export, initiated by a leading citizen of Gortyn who was also a Roman citizen. Outside Rome, the name Parilia with its reference to the rural goddess Pales must have been opaque, whereas the descriptive Natalis Urbis or its Greek translation Γενέθλιος Ῥώμης made obvious sense. Even inside the city, not everyone remembered the shadowy Pales behind the festival name, and the dissimilation from *Palilia to Parilia did not help. As Festus tells us, already late Republican grammarians were deriving the festival name not only correctly from the goddess, but also from *parere*, "to give birth," in this case of lambing sheep: the grammarians were aware of the pastoral connotations of the ritual.[141] The learned author who was the source of Polemius Silvius' calendar transferred this latter derivation from sheep to Ilia/Rhea Silvia because he wanted to make sense of the second element in Par-ilia. And since the corrective connection with farming that had been available to Festus must have long disappeared from collective memory, the only aetiology available connected it with Romulus' foundation of the city, and hence with his unhappy mother.

An agonistic festival: the Capitolia

The Capitolia, the agonistic festival with which, in the words of Louis Robert, "Rome introduced itself into the Greek world of agonistics and became one of its capital cities," presents the intriguing and unique

---

[139] On the circus and imperial government see Arena (2010) as well as the older works of Yavetz (1969) and Levêque (1984).
[140] Boatwright (2000), 99; see Gouw (2008), 97.
[141] Both etymologies in Festus s.v. Pales (248.18 L.): *Pales dicebatur dea pastorum, cuius festa Palilia dicebantur, vel, ut alii volunt, Parilia, quod pro partu pecoris eidem sacra fiebant*. The form Palilia is a grammarian's reconstruction and not attested outside Festus (and in some manuscripts on Tibull. 2.7.87, according to the edition of Muretus, Venice 1562; see the app. crit. in G. Luck's Teubneriana).

problem of a festival invented for Rome in a Greek mood and later exported back to the Greek world.[142] Both the festival in Rome and its reception in a few Eastern cities are relatively well researched, and I can be brief.[143]

In 86 CE, Domitian founded the Capitolia, doubtless inspired by the ephemeral Neronia, the first contest in Rome after a Greek model, which scandalized traditionalists and failed because of the idiosyncrasies of its founder.[144] Domitian, Suetonius tells us,

> also established a quinquennial contest in honor of Jupiter Capitolinus, of a threefold character, comprising music, horsemanship, and gymnastics, and with considerably more prizes than are awarded nowadays. For there were competitions in prose declamation, both in Greek and in Latin; and in addition to those of the lyre-players, between choruses of such players and in the lyra alone, without singing, while in the stadium there were races even between girls.[145]

Domitian was presiding, fittingly dressed *more Graeco*: the tripartite structure replicated the Greek structure of ἀγὼν μουσικός, γυμνικός, ἱππικός, as Suetonius explained when he introduced the Neronia. The girls' races, which were soon abolished, must have followed the model of the girls' races in Olympia, just as Nero had the Vestal Virgins assist his games as spectators "because at Olympia the priestesses of Ceres were allowed the same privileges," and just as the naming after Jupiter Capitolinus echoed the Greek name after Zeus Olympios, the supreme god of Greece.[146] The formula proved highly successful, and the Roman games soon became the fifth most important stop on the athletic circuit, after the classical four, Olympia, Pythia, Nemea, and Isthmia, with some tweaking of the disciplines between Domitian's founding and Suetonius' report.[147]

---

[142] Robert (1970), 8.   [143] See Friedländer (1921), Lana (1952), and especially Caldelli (1993).

[144] Suetonius, *Nero* 12.3 *instituit et quinquennale certamen primus omnium Romae more Graeco triplex, musicum gymnicum equestre* ("he was likewise the first to establish at Rome a quinquennial contest in three parts, after the Greek fashion, that is in music, gymnastics, and horsemanship"); the Roman reactions, Tac. *Ann.* 14.20 *ad morem Graeci certaminis, varia fama ut cuncta ferme nova* ("in the way of a Greek contest, with mixed reputation, as most innovations").

[145] Suet. *Domit.* 4.4: *instituit et quinquennale certamen Capitolino Ioui triplex, musicum equestre gymnicum, et aliquanto plurium quam nunc est coronatorum. certabant enim et prosa oratione Graece Latineque ac praeter citharoedos chorocitharistae quoque et psilocitharistae, in stadio uero cursu etiam uirgines.* (Translation after J. C. Rolfe.) The wording echoes his passage on the Neronia. Censor. *De die natali* 18.15 gives the date, *duodecimo eius et Ser. Cornelii Dolabelli cos.*, that is 86 CE.

[146] Suet. *Nero* 12.4 *quia Olympiae quoque Cereris sacerdotibus spectare conceditur*. On the name, Tert. *De spect.* 11.1 *Olympia Ioui, quae sunt Romae Capitolina*.

[147] Friedländer (1921), 279.

In the Severan Age, coins allow us a glimpse of the export of these Roman games to the East, mostly to two clusters of towns, one cluster in Caria, the other one in northern Syria. Inscriptions attest the festival as ἀγών Σεουηρεῖος Αὐγουστεῖος Καπετώλιος πενταετηρικός πολειτικός in Olbasa in Pisidia. In 275, a letter from Aurelian to Oxyrrhynchos attests it in this city, as a contest in which the Dionysiac artists were involved. In an appendix of his study on the festivals of eastern Kilikia, Ruprecht Ziegler has collected and interpreted this material.[148] Ziegler was mainly interested in the Syrian cluster; he was able to show that Laodikeia must have received the status of a colony of *ius Italicum* and the Σωτήρια Καπετώλια ἰσοκαπετώλια from Septimius Severus in 197/198, in a complex move as consequence of the city's siding with Septimius Severus in his war with Pescennius Niger and, among other things, in order to counterbalance the famous Olympia in neighboring Antioch; Heliopolis/Baalbek, Tyrus, and Sidon received comparable rewards under the emperor Elagabal. The adoption of this very Roman festival thus was a top-down move initiated in the capital, in a very specific political situation in which the emperor wanted to grant a favor to a city. Unlike festivals such as the Kalendae or Saturnalia, games brought not just entertainment and relaxation but international fame and with it money to a city that could organize them.

The second local cluster concerns the Carian cities Aphrodisias and Antiochia, both attested by coins only. The circumstances and the chronology are much less clear; but here too one has to assume that it was an emperor who granted the *agon* to a city, this time an independent city such as Aphrodisias.[149] The same haziness surrounds the ἀγών ἱερός εἰσελαστικός οἰκουμενικός πενταεηρικός σκηνικός γυμνικός ἱππικός ἰσοκαπιτώλιος Καπετωλίων in the letter of Aurelian to Oxyrrhynchos. But the contest has a very elevated position and is important for the Dionysiac artists; it must be the result of imperial beneficence rather than city initiative.[150]

Olbasa in Pisidia presents a clearer case, and it is quite different. The city was founded by Augustus as *colonia Iulia Augusta Olbasena* and shared as such its main cults with Rome; an inscription of Hadrianic date mentions the priest of Zeus Kapetolios and Hera Kapetolia.[151] I assume that the city celebrated a penteric contest open only to its citizens (πολιτικός) in order

---

[148] Ziegler (1985), 147–151.
[149] Ziegler (1985), 147 adds a third unknown Carian city; but here, the contest is called Κωμμόδεια ἰσοκαπετώλια, Moretti (1953), no. 87.
[150] *Berliner Griechische Urkunden* 4.1074, a file about the imperial privileges for the Dionysiac artists.
[151] *IGRom.* 3.415.

to honor its illustrious founder; it was and remained a local affair which the city instituted, to express their civic pride, but without any ambitions for wider international fame.[152] This is why this contest never appears on the coins of the town, perhaps the most important tool of civic self-promotion in the Empire.[153] In the four inscriptions that all were inscribed on the bases of victorious citizens, the contest is either called ἀγὼν Αὐγουστεῖος Καπετώλιος or ἀγὼν Σεουηρεῖος Αὐγουστεῖος Καπετώλιος – *certamen (Severium) Augusteum Capitolium*, if one wanted to Latinize it.[154] The development of the complex name is not entirely clear; I imagine that the city named its contest originally *Augustea Capitolia* by combining its own Roman name, Augusta Olbasena, with the famous Roman contest founded by Domitian, but without attempting any over-local cachet, and included Septimius Severus at a later stage.[155] But this is entirely conjectural, even if an initiative by the city seems most likely.

Conclusions

The festivals connected with the imperial cult aside, there were at least three festivals of the city of Rome that were adopted in the Greek East between the first and the third centuries CE – the Saturnalia, whose institution, in Roman belief, preceded the reform of the calendar by Numa, and which is attested in Iudaea Palaestina and perhaps also in Lucian's complex treatise Πρὸς Κρόνον, a pamphlet on social justice; the Parilia in their new, Hadrianic form as *Natalis Urbis* attested in Gortyn; and the Kalendae Ianuariae, perhaps already in their developed form that combined the sacrifice and festivities of January 1 with the *vota* for the emperor on January 3, again in Iudaea Palaestina and in Hierapolis in Phrygia, perhaps as a public festival or as a private export from Palestine. They shared the form of being joyous, sensuous, and even boisterous occasions for freedom, enjoyment, and even uninhibited behavior, drinking, dancing, and singing, and they involved the entire city population, including Jews and Christians. This made them provoke hostility from the guardians of orthodoxy, the rabbis and the Church fathers: to the feeling of joy and *communitas* (to use a term whose theoretical underpinning has become rather unfashionable),[156] they opposed some of the moralistic

---

[152] Jüthner (1902), 289 connects the double title with the Augusteia founded by Augustus in Naples and introduced to Rome by Domitian. This is possible, but not necessary.
[153] Ziegler (1985), 147 n. 7.   [154] *IGRom.* 3.411–413.   [155] Ziegler (1985), 147.
[156] Originally coined by Turner (1969); for critical voices on this approach, see esp. Jules-Rosette (1994) and D'Agostino (2001).

arguments made already by pagan moralists such as Seneca and, more urgently, the need to erect boundaries between the true believers and the pagans, turning these festivals into a battleground of ideologies.[157]

In all three cases, we can at least formulate a hypothesis on the agency behind the spread of the festival. The *Natalis Urbis* in Gortyn was part of a foundation established under Commodus by a local grandee with double citizenship, Gortynian and Roman. Since the cults established by the foundation concerned both the imperial house and the founder's family, the donor intended to express the double allegiance he felt bound to; and since the assembly of Gortyn voted to accept the donation and institutionalize the cults, the city shared in this double allegiance. Not unlike what Vibius Salutaris had achieved in his donation for a splendid procession in Ephesos, the Gortynian donation juxtaposed the local polis and the city of Rome with its imperial house.[158] This, then, was a private initiative that a Greek city accepted and institutionalized: provincial elites gave themselves a touch of Romanness by adopting Roman festivals, and extended this to their cities. The combination of Natalis Urbis and emperor cult, however, might follow a form set in the capital: a century after the Cretan foundation, the Natalis Urbis celebrated at the imperial court of Trier was combined with a formal praise oration to the emperor Maximianus.[159] The vagaries of our documentation make it impossible to decide whether the donor followed a model he had come to learn in Rome or in an Eastern city.

A similar, although more complex combination of imperial cult, Eastern local elites, and Roman festivals is visible in Pergamon, and shows another side of the mechanism of how these festivals migrated from Rome to the Eastern provinces. An altar, dedicated by the *hymnodoi* of the imperial cult at the time of Hadrian, lists the donations that the three leading officials, the president (εὔκοσμος), the priest, and the secretary, were obliged to make on the main festivals with which they were concerned.[160] These *hymnodoi* were a prestigious and long-lived provincial association, founded under Augustus to sing hymns in the emperor's praise, and its members were leading provincials, many of

---

[157] On some of the theoretical reflections see Belayche (2007).
[158] On Salutaris: above, Chapter 1.
[159] As the unknown orator himself states, *Panegyricus Maximiani* (*Panegyrici Latini* no. 10 Minors), 1.
[160] *IvP* 2.347. Main discussions in Robert (1960b), 340–342 = *OMS* 2.856–858 ("une association romanisée et romanisante" ... "une coutume venue de Rome," 342) and Price (1984), 90; a (partial) translation in Beard, North, and Price (1998), 2: 255–256; absent from Meslin (1970), who focuses on the West, and on literary texts.

them with Roman citizenship; in about 44 CE, the proconsul Paullus Fabius Persicus was careful not to step on their privileges when he reorganized the musical performances in the festivals of Ephesos.[161] The festivals mentioned in the Pergamene text were not unexpectedly those of the imperial house, namely the birthdays of Augustus, Livia, and other members of the imperial house, and the imperial mysteries; but they also celebrated the Rosalia to remember the deceased members of the association, and finally the Kalendae Ianuariae, the one festival that, as we have seen, since the days of Augustus expressed the belonging to the political and religious world of Rome in its purest form – not in the calendarical form of the New Year (the New Year of the province of Asia started on Augustus' birthday, September 23, the first day of their "month of Caesar," Kaisarion), but as a celebration of Rome and its order, very much in the sense given to it in Ovid's description of the day as *nil nisi Romanum*, but by now with an emphasis on the ruling house, whose members often entered their consulship on this day.[162] I thus agree with Louis Robert's characterization of the association as "romanisée et romanisante"; at the same time, however, this Romanness in Pergamon paved the way for these festivals to be embraced more widely by Greek cities.

Other festivals must have spread from Roman garrisons to the cities near by – not just in Syria-Palestine and other Eastern provinces, but also in Tertullian's Carthage. This is most certainly the case for the Saturnalia that, in Scythopolis, were accompanied by a local fair that was the meeting ground of soldiers, local pagans, and local Jews: in order to establish a fair, the city needed the permission of the Roman authorities, thus the assembly had to make a decision and take a vote on whether to accept the festival that went with it or not. In the case of the Kalendae, it is more difficult to perceive a mechanism of distribution. Coloniae as well as garrisons celebrated it, together with the *vota* of January 3; this invited imitation in other cities. And perhaps it was the *vota* that brought the Kalendae with it as well: even if the festival had not yet reached its complex length of five days, the two events were closely related to each other. Like the Kalendae, the *vota* were performed by the garrison, the provincial governor in his own administrative seat, and the political authorities of all *coloniae* and *municipia*, and they were adopted by autonomous cities, again to give expression

---

[161] *I.Ephes.* 17 lines 56–61 and 18D lines 10–19; see above, Chapter 1, nn. 58–59.
[162] Far from being an "alien date" (Price 1984, 90), the Kalendae Ianuariae thus are crucial for local imperial ideology.

to their Roman allegiance. Like the Saturnalia, the joyful celebrations of January 1 and presumably 3 with, at least in the fourth century, its games and races, attracted the urban crowds and made the festival desirable. But unlike in the case of the Saturnalia, the political significance of the central ritual act helped to establish the festival and anchored it in the local polis calendar. But even then, the establishment of the festival in an autonomous city was a bottom-up affair in which the periphery responded to the center and not the other way round.

PART II

Roman festivals in the Greek East after Constantine

Introduction

As it will turn out, the information on Roman festivals in the Greek East is much richer when we turn to the period after Constantine. The main reason for this seeming paradox is the contestation of some of these festivals by the Christian church as remnants of paganism that had to be removed, and, simultaneously, the tenacity with which both the emperors and the population of the Eastern (and, in some cases, Western) Empire were holding on to them, each for very different reasons. For the inhabitants of the empire, regardless of their religious affiliation, these festivals were welcome occasions for entertainment and relaxation, as Emmanuel Soler in a rich monograph has shown for fourth-century Antioch;[1] this also explains why the Kalendae Ianuariae in varying forms survived in medieval Eastern North Africa. For the emperors, it was more complicated. On the one hand, a good emperor understood himself as a guardian of popular happiness; this might have helped him to defend some of these holidays against over-eager ecclesiastical pressure. On the other hand, some of these festivals maintained the link with imperial ideology and with the construction of an empire-wide culture that had already developed during the pre-Constantinian centuries, which again called for imperial protection.

In the following chapters, I will describe and analyze these festivals – the Lupercalia, the Brumalia, the Kalendae Ianuariae – and the mechanism that helped them survive. But first, I will have a look at the reform of the legal calendar that the emperor Theodosius I enacted in 398, when he spent a short summer in Rome. One of the most important activities of an emperor was to decide on legal problems; the resultant laws would often outlast the individual reign, and often the Roman empire. One of the main means of protecting a holiday in Rome was to accept it into the legal

[1] Soler (2006); see also Sandwell (2007).

calendar: the fact that during certain holidays the law courts were closed was as momentous as the fact that during other days spectacles were forbidden. Theodosius' reform was even more momentous because the relevant letter to the prefect of Rome became empire-wide law and was received in the code that Theodosius II issued in 439 and from there in several other codes in West and East. It is thus urgent to have a closer look at details of this law, its genesis and its reception into later law codes. Only then do I feel ready to turn to some of the festivals and their contested performance in the Eastern Empire – first in the fourth century, then in the following centuries, during which some festivals gained an undisputed acceptance while others remained the object of ecclesiastical attack and protest.

CHAPTER 3

Theodosius' reform of the legal calendar

The imperial rescript

On August 8, 389, the emperor Theodosius I signed a letter in Rome – technically a rescript, an answer to a question from an administrator – addressed to Albinus, the *praefectus urbi* of Rome. This is the text as excerpted in the Theodosian Code:[2]

> Imppp. Valentinianus, Theodosius et Arcadius aaa. Albino pf. U.
> Omnes dies iubemus esse iuridicos. illos tantum manere feriarum dies fas erit, quos geminis mensibus ad requiem laboris indulgentior annus accepit, aestivis fervoribus mitigandis et autumnis foetibus decerpendis.
> Kalendarum quoque Ianuariarum consuetos dies otio mancipamus.
> His adiicimus natalitios dies urbium maximarum, Romae atque Constantinopolis, quibus debent iura deferre, quia et ab ipsis nata sunt.
> Sacros quoque paschae dies, qui septeno vel praecedunt numero vel sequuntur, in eadem observatione numeramus, nec non et dies solis, qui repetito in se calculo revolvuntur.
> Parem necesse est haberi reverentiam nostris etiam diebus, qui vel lucis auspicia vel ortus imperii protulerunt.
> Dat. vii. id. aug. Romae, Timasio et Promoto coss.
>
> The emperors Valentinian, Theodosius and Arcadius Augusti to Albinus, the City Prefect.
> We order that all days shall be court days. Only those days shall remain as days of vacation which each year, for a period of two months, indulgently give rest from labor, in order to mitigate the summer heat and to gather the autumnal fruits.
> We also give over to leisure the customary days of the Kalendae Ianuariae (or: at the beginning of each January).[3]

---

[2] *CTh* 2.8.19; translation after Pharr (1952), 44.
[3] Pharr (1952), 44 translates "the Kalends of January (January 1) as a customary rest day." This is erroneous because in the late fourth century the *Kalendae Ianuariae* lasted several days, as the Greek translator in the *Basilika* 7.13.23.1 understood: καὶ ἐν Ἰανουαρίωι δὲ μηνὶ αἱ συνήθεις ἡμέραι ἔστωσαν ἄπρακτοι.

We add to these the birthdays of the great cities of Rome and Constantinople, to which the legal proceedings should pay deference because they owe their origin to them.

We also add the holy Pascal days, seven preceding and seven succeeding Easter, and also the Sundays which return at regular intervals.

An equal reverence shall be paid to our days which brought forth the auspicious beginning of our life and the onset of our reign.

Given in Rome on the seventh day before the Ides of August, during the consulate of Timasius and Promotus.

In a somewhat longer form the rescript also appears in the Justinian Code and, with some expansions, in the *interpretatio* that follows the Theodosian text in the *Breviarium of Alaric* that reflects early sixth-century practice in Visigothic Gaul; finally, a Greek translation among the "Imperial Laws" (*Basiliká*) demonstrates the adoption of Justinian texts for the later Eastern Empire.[4] This multiple reception shows how important this text became in the legislation of the centuries after Theodosius I. With the exception of Jacques Godefroy's (Gothofredus) splendid seventeenth-century commentary on the Theodosian Code, these texts have never been closely analyzed, and certainly not as to their importance for the history of pagan and Christian festivals in late antiquity, to the survival and reinterpretation of old Roman festivals, and their relationship to the new Christian holidays.[5] In what follows, I will try to understand the function of the original text as well as the import of its inclusion in the two imperial codes and the role it played in the history of Roman festivals in the later Roman Empire.[6]

---

[4] *CTh* 2.8.19 = *Breviarium* 2.8.2; *CJ* 3.12.6; Basilika 7.17.23, ed. Scheltema and van der Wal (1955).

[5] I used the commentary in the edition of Daniel Ritter (Leipzig: Weidmann, 1736–1745; a somewhat later edition, Mantua and Venice: Franciscus Pitterius, 1740–1746), with its full title *Codex Theodosianus cum perpetuis commentariis Jacobi Gothofredi, viri senatorii et iurisconsulti superioris seculi eximii. Praemittuntur chronologia accuratior chronicon historicum et prolegomena subiiciuntur notitia dignitatum, prosopographia, topographia index rerum et glossarium nomicum. Opus posthumum div(inum) in foro et schola desideratum recognitum et ordinatum ad usum codicis Justinianei opera et studio Antonii Marvillii, antecessoris primicerii in universitate Valentina. Editio nova in VI tomos digesta, collata cum antiquissimo codice Wurceburgensi, emendata variorumque observationibus aucta, quibus adjecit suas Joan(nes) Dan(ielus) Ritter, P.P.*

On Jacques Godefroy (1587–1652), professor of law in Geneva and son of Denys Godefroy (1549 – 1622), a Hugenot courtier of the King of France turned professor in Geneva when he had to leave France, see Schmidlin and Dufour (1991).

[6] The text has not been much discussed; a very short account (in the framework of a discussion of the "abolition of pagan festivals") in di Berardino (2005), 112; an earlier version of parts of this chapter in Graf (2014).

Theodosius as law-giver in summer 389

Recent research on the Theodosian Code has emphasized the importance of the original cause for the imperial rescript that very often is a reaction to a local problem on which a local functionary had sought information and guidance from the imperial center; the template is Pliny's letter to the emperor Trajan on the Christians in Bithynia and the short imperial answer that was to guide the procedures against the Christians in later times. Fergus Millar has made this into a central tenet in his book on Theodosius II.[7] However, as our text will show, things might be somewhat more complex, and an emperor sometimes less reactive.

On August 8, 389, Theodosius I had been in Rome for about two months.[8] He came from Milan, where he was residing in order to deal with the affairs of the West after his victorious campaign against the ursurper Magnus Maximus that ended with Maximus' death near Aquileia on August 28, 388. To judge from the preserved letter dates, Theodosius arrived in Rome at some time between May 5 (*CTh* 8.4.16, written in Milan) and June 17 (*CTh* 16.5.18, written in Rome); on September 6, he was again on his way back to Milan (*CTh* 9.3.5, written in Forum Flaminii in Umbria). The Roman aristocrats, eager to please him after they had backed Maximus, now dead and maligned as a *tyrannus*, "usurper," accorded him all the honors they felt necessary in order to gain his benevolence, including a triumphal procession, as they had accorded to Constantine and Constantius II – although technically, as Augusto Fraschetti has insisted, this was not a *triumphus* but an *adventus*, because no emperor since Constantine would sacrifice to Jupiter Optimus Maximus on the Capitol and deposit his victory crown in the lap of Jupiter's image.[9] As custom demanded, a famous orator addressed a panegyric to him: Latinius Drepanius Pacatus, orator and Christian poet from Gaul, delivered it in a meeting of the senate, to blot out the memory of Symmachus'

---

[7] See Matthews (2000) and Millar (2006).
[8] On Rome and fourth-century emperors, Van Dam (2007), 73–78 (75 on Theodosius); more in Graf (2014).
[9] Sozomen. *Hist. eccl.* 7.14 ἐπινικίαν πομπὴν ἐπετέλεσε. On the triumphal procession and its transformations in late antiquity see McCormick (1986), 34–36; Fraschetti (1999), 47–63; but see Constantine Porphyrogennetos, *De insidiis* 74 (p. 114 de Boor) on Constantius II; Synes. *Ep.* 40, a letter to one Uranius accompanying the gift of a horse for hunting and "the Libyan Triumph" – not Uranius', if he rides in it, but an otherwise unattested victory celebration.

panegyric for Maximus that must have been as embarrassing for the senate as it was depressing and costly for its author.[10]

To judge from the letters preserved in the Theodosian Code, the emperor used his time in Rome not just to win over the senatorial aristocracy and to be won over by them, or as the church historians claim, to clean up moral scandals in Rome (Socrates) or "to re-order" (εὖ διέθηκε) the Church of Italy, thus proving his orthodoxy (Sozomenos).[11] During his summer in the City, he also addressed a series of mostly legal questions that in part found their way into the Theodosian Code.[12] The Code preserves excerpts from ten letters written in Rome during the summer of 389, eight of them addressed to the City Prefect Albinus and two to Proculus, prefect of the city of Constantinople, about administrative problems of that city – somewhat surprising, as this would have been Arcadius' domain, and the Constantinopolitan prefect should have consulted him and not Arcadius' father Theodosius: obviously, Theodosius was not just re-ordering Italy but also thinking of his final return to Constantinople, and the young prefect whom Theodosius installed before he left for the West was aware where the real power was residing.[13]

Among the many important Albini of the period, Albinus *praefectus urbi* is Caeionius Rufius Albinus, an aristocrat from one of the most important Roman houses of the fourth century.[14] He is not only attested by the imperial letters in the Code, but also by four statue bases from the Roman Forum that honor the three rulers of the time, Valentinian II, Theodosius, and Arcadius, and Theodosius' mother Thermantia; the inscriptions on the bases give his full name and rank.[15] Thus, Caeionius Rufius Albinus, whom we also know as an interlocutor in Macrobius' *Saturnalia*, must have entered his office not too long before Theodosius' visit, installed after the troubles

---

[10] Pacatus' panegyric: *Panegyrici Latini* no. 2, see also Nixon (1987); on the poetry of Drepanius see Turcan-Verkerk (2003). Nobody had an interest in preserving Symmachus' panegyric; on its history and Symmachus' recovery from its consequences under Theodosius see Sogno (2006), 68–76 (based on his letters): the panegyric was "an unwelcome consequence of having powerful friends at court" (68).

[11] Sozomen. *Hist. eccl.* 7.14 says that he reorganized the Italian Church after the death of Justina, the mother of Valentinian II and the most assertive Arianic Christian at his Milan court.

[12] Socrates, *Hist. eccl.* 5.18.1 only talks about Theodosius' generosity towards the city of Rome, and how he cleaned the city up from moral offenses, with two somewhat anecdotal stories in order to explain two laws that stress his moral probity, 5.18.3–12; see Errington (1997), 45.

[13] *CTh* 14.17.9 and 15.1.25; for the "correct" procedure see *CTh* 9.21.9 of June 26, written in Constantinople and addressed to the *comes sacrarum largitionum*, Tatianus, on punishing the *cataractae*, producers of fake coins: the Greek term points to an Eastern problem. I omit *CTh* 4.22.3 and 8.4.17 because their dates cannot be correct.

[14] Chastagnol (1962), 233–236; *PLRE* 1.37–38. See also the detailed portrait by Liénart (1934).

[15] *CIL* 6.3791a = 31413, 36959, 3791b = 31414 (*ILS* 789), 36960 (*ILS* 8950).

with Maximus because he was reliable, as were the many other members of the family who served in this function, and presumably because he had kept some distance from Maximus, as had other aristocrats such as Ausonius.[16] He stayed in office for about two years: the letters in the Code range from June 17, 389 to February 24, 391, and the first letter we have to his successor, Faltonius Probus Alypius, is dated June 12, 391. The inscriptions make a not very subtle point by addressing each of the three emperors as *extinctor tyrannorum ac publicae securitatis auctor*, a title that in reality only Theodosius could claim, the hyperbolic *tyranni* being in reality only the one just executed by the angry soldiers. The emperor himself had used the term in a letter from January 14, 389:[17] the statues must have been erected in the year of the imperial visit, most likely in the emperor's presence. One wonders what the signal honor of Thermantia really means: after all, Valentinian's mother Justina, a victim of the deposed tyrant, had died in late 388 or early 389, presumably at about the same time as Thermantia, and could have been honored in the same way. Political reasons must have been more important than the fact that Justina was Arianic while Thermantia was Catholic: the inscription styles her not just as Theodosius' mother, but also as grandmother of Arcadius and Honorius "who by the excellence of her nature has augmented the divine lineage," *praestantia indolis suae augenti divinam prosapiam*. The new prefect clearly perceived Theodosius' dynastic intentions and realized that the future lay not with the young Valentian, who nominally was still the Augustus of the West, but with the even younger Honorius, both present in the city that summer; any assumption that we might have lost a fifth inscription is baseless.

Whatever else Theodosius did in Rome during the summer of 389, he also had a busy time as a law-giver; the letters, signed by Theodosius in Rome and addressed to Albinus, are a unique documentation of imperial activity in a short arch of time and under conditions we know well. I give a list:

June 17, on the Manichaeans and their expulsion especially from Rome, *CTh* 16.5.18

July 25, on the appeal in litigation arising from Imperial moneys, *CTh* 11.30.49

August 8, on legal holidays in Rome, *CTh* 2.8.19

---

[16] On the two Albini in the *Saturnalia*, our Caeionius Rufius Albinus (praef. urbi 389–391) and Caecina Decius Albinus (praef. urbi 402), see Cameron (2011), 233–235. On the family, "one of the great houses of the fourth century" (Cameron 2011, 138), founded by the homonymous consul of 314 and praefectus urbi 313–315, see Weber, R. (1989).

[17] *CTh* 15.14 (written in Milan), a letter addressed to the praetorian prefect of Gaul in which he was cleaning the legal system of remnants of the period of Maximus.

August 16, on trials of magic, *CTh* 9.16.11

August 16, on the compulsory service as *mancipes*, supervisors, *CTh* 12.16.1

August 18, on restoring the grazing rights of swine herders, *CTh* 14.4.5

August 25, on restoring the privileges of pork-butchers granted by Gratian, *CTh* 14.4.6

August 28, on water rights of individuals, *CTh* 15.2.5

With the exception of the first, all these texts have to do with the administration of the city of Rome, in a clear order – first and foremost legal proceedings, then matters of supply.[18] Again with the exception of the first, they were all written in a short period of about five weeks, between July 25 and August 28, in the later part of Theodosius' stay in Rome, and at a time in *ferragosto* when most other business must have come to a halt because of the summer heat. This looks deliberate: the letters are unlikely to deal with chance matters that passed the desk of the city prefect and needed imperial advice, they appear consciously selected by Theodosius in close collaboration with Albinus. Theodosius had a keen interest in legal matters, even in the cases when he had only to react to a prefect's queries. Albinus, in turn, as we learn from the four Roman inscriptions, had been *vice sacra iudicans*, an extraordinary magistrate charged by the emperor to represent him (or his governor) in either Asia or Africa: Theodosius thus must have been aware of Albinus' impressive knowledge and reliability in matters of the law, and decided to make use of it.[19] Once Theodosius left Rome, the interchange between emperor and prefect almost ceased: he only sent two more letters to him, on different topics on which Albinus must have needed an imperial input.[20]

But Theodosius' interest in the law and his use of Albinus' knowledge and experience is only part of the picture. Theodosius' legal activities must have had the aim of impressing upon the Romans his good intentions and care for the city. When he arrived, he was to them first and foremost yet another powerful army commander who had taken over the West and who had just deposed the earlier dynasty of which the young Valentinian II was the last and weakest member. Theodosius thus needed to appear as a good emperor and protector of Rome. To care for meat and water supply was useful: a good emperor cared for the bodily needs of his subjects. But a good emperor cared even more for the orderly functioning of the legal

---

[18] The letters on matters of Constantinople fall in between these dates and treat of different topics: on July 17 *CTh* 15.1.25 on the protection of public buildings in Constantinople and on July 26 *CTh* 14.17.9 on the *annona* to minor functionaries in Constantinople.

[19] See Liétard (1934), 61f., after Mommsen and Seeck.

[20] *CTh* 9.10.4 (March 6, 390: *Ad legem Iuliam de vi*) and 15.1.27 (April 4, 390: *De operibus publicis*).

system; even Claudius was lauded for this, as was Marcus Aurelius, and Constantine left his clear mark in the body of laws.[21]

In this respect, Theodosius' letter on the trials against magicians is perhaps the most instructive among the preserved Roman rescripts.[22] The persecution of sorcery (*maleficium* or *magia*) has a long history in Roman law. Before the troubled third century, trials that focused on sorcery as the sole crime remained extremely rare, and conscientious emperors did not pursue such an accusation. The reason lay with the nature of the relevant laws, a clause in the Law of the Twelve Tablets that persecuted sorcery that damaged property rights, and the *lex Cornelia de sicariis et veneficis* that was mainly concerned with homicide but could also deal with sorcery that infringed upon the bodily integrity of a free person; neither of these laws isolated sorcery as a special act, which must have discouraged legal action.[23] Constantine put the prosecution of sorcery onto a new legal footing by allowing the prosecution of people who used magic (*magicis accincti artibus*) against the bodily or sexual integrity of free persons, but he excepted healing and weather magic from prosecution and punishment, and he separated it radically from astronomy or divination. This made harmful sorcery a criminal act that was much more clearly defined than before. Not surprisingly, later emperors – especially Constantius II – muddied the waters again.[24]

Theodosius concentrated on a very real detail: a person suspected of sorcery and apprehended on that charge had immediately to stand public trial instead of being imprisoned for an undetermined time. The rhetorical flourishes of the passage that qualifies a "person polluted by the taint of sorcery" (*maleficiorum labe pollutum*) as a "common enemy" (*communem hostem*) underlines the seriousness of the problem, as the emperor explained in what follows. Many people, he pointed out, were apprehended as sorcerers and killed while they awaited trial; one has to think that among these defendants, there was both an unusually high death rate from torture and other suspicious deaths. Thus, the suspicion arose that these deaths had nothing to do with justice, but on the contrary helped guilty people. By killing an accused person before the interrogations and the trial, one could prevent him from naming accomplices, especially

---

[21] On Claudius see Suet. *Claud.* 14, Dio 60.4.3; in Sen. *Apoc.* 7.4, Claudius claims *ius dicebam totis diebus mense Iulio et Augusto*, and his Apollo predicts of Nero *legum silentia rumpet, Apoc.* 4.1 v. 23. On Marcus Aurelius, HA Capitolinus, *Marcus Antoninus* 10.10. On Constantine, Eusebius, *Vita Constantini* 4.26–28 with the comments of Cameron and Hall (1999). More below, n. 32.
[22] *CTh* 9.16.11.   [23] See Liebs (1997) and Castello (1991).
[24] Constantine: *CTh* 9.16.3 (May 23, 321/24 or 317/19); Constantius II: 9.16.4–6; Valentinian I: 9.16.7.

oneself and one's friends; or the accusation of sorcery was abused to get rid of an otherwise innocent personal enemy who would handily die under torture and never stand trial.

The letter especially addresses the problem of charioteers (*quisquam ex agitatoribus*). Sorcery in connection with the chariot races was rampant, and charioteers or their backers commonly hired ritual specialists to perform the binding spells whose lengthy and somewhat grisly texts call death and injury upon both the rival horses and their charioteers; we still possess a considerable number of these spells, and they were usually found in the excavations of an ancient circus.[25] The ritual survived well beyond the time of Theodosius I: his letter was taken over into Justinian's Code (*CJ* 9.18.9), because it remained relevant to Byzantine society – with a gloss explaining the uncommon word *agitator*, "charioteer" by the more usual *auriga* to a readership whose Latin was only their second language.[26] At about the same time that the text was included in the Code of Justinian, Theoderic's chancellor Cassiodorus was aware that very successful charioteers were running the risk of being suspected of magic, and sometimes were guilty of it.[27]

We cannot know whether Theodosius was himself directly aware of the problem in Rome. More likely, it is one of the things to which a conscientious Urban Prefect would be drawing the emperor's attention; he would even suggest the solution that the imperial letter would then prescribe. But Theodosius must have seen the possibilities that this offered him: although a Christian and thus sharing the Christian rejection of sorcery, like Constantine he put a fair trial above any ideologically motivated prosecution of sorcery at all costs, unlike some of his predecessors.[28]

The one seeming exception in the catalog of Theodosius' legal work in Summer 389 is the constitution that bans the Manichaeans "from the entire world, but especially from this city" (*ex omni quidem orbe terrarum, sed quam maxime de hac urbe pellantur*): it does not fit into the topic of the later Roman decisions, and it is considerably earlier, written shortly after the emperor's arrival in Rome. At the time, the Roman Manichaeans must

---

[25] A general survey in Pavis d'Escurac (1987); a good sample in Gager (1992), 53–74.
[26] On the problems of bilingual communication in the late antique state see Millar (2006), 20–25, 88–92.
[27] Cassiodor. *Variae* 3.51.2: *frequentia palmarum eum faciebat dici maleficum, inter quos magnum praeconium videtur esse ad talia crimina pervenire. necesse est enim ad perversitatem magicam referri, quando victoria equorum meritis non potest applicari*. See Lee-Stecum (2006), 226.
[28] See also Sandwell (2005).

Theodosius' reform of the legal calendar 113

have been numerous and well integrated, despite papal opposition.[29] They famously hosted Augustine before the then prefect Symmachus had him sent to Milan as professor of rhetoric in 382: Symmachus at least had no problems with a professor who was a Manichaean. But if he had hoped to use him as a counterweight to Ambrose's stubborn and fierce Christian orthodoxy, he underrated both Ambrose's charisma and Augustine's intense spiritual quest. On the Christian side, the rejection of Manicheans had reached a new peak a few years earlier, when in 381 and 382 Theodosius and Gratian had signed two constitutions issued in Constantinople against Manichaeans in the East.[30]

A pagan intellectual such as the prefect Albinus should *prima facie* have no problems with the Manichaeans, but he must have been aware of the two constitutions, and it might well have been his initiative to ask Theodosius personally whether and how they were to be applied in his city. It would have given him the occasion to show his loyalty to the emperor, to present Theodosius with a case to make a programmatic statement, and even to test the loyalty of Rome's ruling class.[31] It is also possible that either the prefect or the emperor was in turn alerted by the bishop of Rome, Siricius (385–399), whom the *Liber Pontificalis* connects with the prosecution of Roman Manichaeans: he is said to have exiled them (which would have been the prefect's business, not the bishop's, and so is highly unlikely), and to have severely restricted their conversion to Christianity (which he could do): this points to a surge of conversions as the natural reaction to an Imperial expulsion order.[32] In this reading, rather than being an exception, this early rescript confirms how the Roman legislation of summer 389 was the work of a close collaboration between emperor and prefect, and served Theodosius' programmatic ends. This is equally true for the law on the festivals (*CTh* 2.8.19), whose text I quoted in full at the beginning of this chapter, and to which I now turn.

---

[29] Already pope Miltiades (310/11–314) went against them, *Liber pontificalis* 32 (*MGH Scriptores: Gesta Pontificum Romanorum* 1, p. 46 Mommsen): *et inventi sunt Manichaei in urbe ab eodem*.
[30] *CTh* 16.5.7, to the *praefectus praetorio* (of Oriens), and 16.5.9, to Florus, his successor. On Florus see *PLRE* 1.367 s.v. Florus 1; on his predecessor, Flavius Neoterius, *PLRE* 1.623.
[31] It is likely that Sozomenus' remark that Theodosius εὖ διέθηκε the Italian Church refers to this as well, *Hist. eccl.* 7.14.
[32] *Liber pontificalis* 40 (*MGH Scriptores: Gesta Pontificum Romanorum* 1, p. 86): *Hic invenit Manichaeos in urbe, quos etiam exilio deportavit; et hoc constituit, ut, si quis conversus de Manichaeis rediret ad ecclesiam nullatenus communicaretur, nisi tantum religatione monasterii die vitae suae teneretur obnoxius*. "He found Manichaeans in the city whom he had sent into exile; and he decreed if someone among the Manichaeans should return to the Church, that he should not take communion except if he were relegated to a monastery to end his days there in guilt."

Theodosius' reform of the legal calendar of the City of Rome

The preface of *CTh* 2.8.19 gives the overall intent of the imperial will: "We order that all days shall be court days." Exceptions to this general rule follow, and they are clearly marked as such. In the list of exceptions, one is tempted to see an opposition between state and church: at a first glance, the text seems to combine traditional Roman state festivals with new Christian ones. But this view distorts and simplifies what the text is really about. There are the *feriae* dictated by the necessities of climate and agriculture, during the summer heat and the Fall harvest; there are the days during the festival period of the *Kalendae Ianuariae* that Theodosius calls "customary" (*consuetos*), and that he groups together with the Foundation Days of Rome and Constantinople as holidays in the political calendar; there are the birthdays and accession days of the three rulers who are mentioned at the beginning (*nostris diebus*), although the writer of the text was Theodosius alone, since the letter was written in Rome and for Rome. Finally, there are the Christian holidays, the Sundays and Easter with the seven preceding and following days. This Christian list is surprisingly short; later law codes in East and West expanded it, as we shall see.

Jacques Godefroy has already pointed out that it was an ongoing concern of the emperors, from Augustus to Marcus Aurelius, to clean up the legal calendar from the accretion of holidays, in order to have enough working days for the impending legal business:[33] to take good care of the legal system was a sign of a good emperor.[34] The accretion was due to an ever growing number of honorary days for emperors and their relatives – yet another birthday, accession day, victory, or arrival in a city, decreed not necessarily by an emperor but by an all too obsequious senate or, outside

---

[33] Godefroy (1736–1745), 141. Augustus: Suet. *Aug.* 32.2 *ne quod autem maleficium negotiumve inpunitate vel mora elaberetur, triginta amplius dies, qui honoraris ludibus occupabantur, actui rerum accomodavit*, "that crimes might not escape punishment, nor business be neglected by delay, he ordered the courts to sit during the thirty days which were spent in celebrating honorary games" (translation by Alexander Thomson and T. Forester). We thus do not have an overall number of business days. Claudius was in the tribunal *etiam suis suorumque diebus, nonnumquam festis quoque antiquitus et religiosis*, Suet. *Claud.* 14, see Dio 60.4.3, and he did away with the break between summer and winter term but seems to have added the break days at the end of the year, which Galba turned into business days as well: Suet. *Galba* 14.3, cf. Sen. *Apocol.* 7.4. Marcus Aurelius: HA Capitolinus, *Marcus Antoninus* 10.10 *iudiciariae rei singularem diligentiam adhibuit; fastis dies iudiciarios addidit, ita ut ducentos triginta dies annuos rebus agendis litibusque disceptandis constituere*, "To the administration of justice he gave singular care. He added court-days to the calendar until he had set 230 days for the pleading of cases and judging of suits" (translation: David Magie, Loeb).

[34] See the passages on Claudius and Marcus Aurelius in the preceding note; in Sen. *Apoc.* 7.4, Claudius claims *ius dicebam totis diebus mense Iulio et Augusto*, and his Apollo predicts of Nero *legum silentia rumpet, Apoc.* 4.1 v. 23.

Theodosius' reform of the legal calendar 115

Rome, by any city body or local administrator. This explains why Constantine, another emperor with a keen sense for the law, insisted on the imperial monopoly for determining festival days: no administrator should institute *feriae* nor call them *imperiales* – presumably to prevent abuse by adulation.[35] This possibility of abuse was inherent in the imperial system since its foundation, and already Augustus had declared all honorary days as legal business days, from his insight into the problems that an unrestricted growth would create.[36] Once the law became the almost exclusive monopoly of the Urban Prefect, as was the case in the fourth century, the encroachment of holidays must have been even worse, and even more in need of control and pruning.[37] This explains why the text as we have it begins with a bald command: *omnes dies iubemus esse iuridicos.*

The exceptions in our text aim at a compromise between the needs of the law courts, on the one hand, and those of the emperor, the bishops, and the people of Rome on the other hand. In the case of the "customary" five days at the beginning of the year, *Kalendarum Ianuariarum consuetos dies*, Thedosius' formulation hides the fact that before his regulation, January 1 was at least a token day of work, *F(astus)* in the Julio-Claudian calendars. In the later fourth century, it must have become an informal holiday, otherwise Valentinian and Valens would not have had to order the praetors to start their office on January 1, at the peril of punishment for non-compliance.[38] Theodosius thus clarifies a somewhat murky situation. In the early third century, December 31 was also a day without legal business; it is unclear whether Theodosius included it in the "traditional days of the Kalendae of January," but it is likely, given that this still survives in the *Basilika*.[39] In summer and autumn, Theodosius decreed two periods of legal holidays *ad requiem laboris*, "to rest from work." Although the early stone calendars bear no trace of a seasonal arrangement of such holidays, indications of the influence of climate conditions over the law courts go back at least to the first century CE. In Seneca's caricature, Claudius

---

[35] *CJ* 3.12.3 (April 13, 323): *A nullo iudice praesumi decet, ut auctoritate sua ferias aliquas condat. nec enim imperiales ferias vocari oportet, quas administrator edixerit, ac per hoc, si nomine eximuntur, etiam fructu carebunt*, "No judge must presume to establish holidays by his authority. Such days, ordered by a governor (administrator) should not be called imperial holidays, and they, being deprived of that name, also lack the advantage thereof" (translation: Fred Blume, www.uwyo.edu/lawlib/blume-justinian).
[36] Augustus: Suet. *Aug.* 32.2. Characteristically, Claudius personally lived up to this, Suet. *Claud.* 14.
[37] On this development see Chastagnol (1960), 84–136.
[38] *CTh* 6.4.20 (Valentinian I and Valens to the *praetor urbanus* Clearchus; May 8, 372).
[39] Ulpian: *Digest.* 2.12.5 (Ulpianus libro 62 *Ad edictum: Pridie Kalendas Ianuarias magistratus neque ius dicere, sed nec sui potestatem facere consuerunt); Basilika* 7.17.5.

bragged that he sat in court even during July and August: this makes sense only if it was unusual.[40] Under the Flavians, Statius admonished an orator that the harvest season had emptied the forum and legal strife was pausing, so he should go slowly as well.[41] It is unclear how formalized this pause was; Statius' admonitions leave room for some legal work, and the Younger Pliny still attended to some form of legal proceedings during the summer break.[42] The first formalization of which we hear goes back to Marcus Aurelius. In a speech to the senate, snippets of which are preserved in the *Digest*, he outlined a major reform of legal procedures.[43] He extended the business year to 230 days and at the same time proposed two months during summer and fall harvest when a praetor should summon nobody to a trial; only exceptions due to the urgency of the matter were possible. Given the climate differences in an empire that stretched from North Africa to Holland and from Britain to Syria and Egypt, in the provinces the governors could determine the exact time of the two breaks according to local customs and needs. It was to this reform that Theodosius looked back in his order to allot a month each to either break.[44]

Another age-old tradition is to halt the courts for the anniversaries of the two ruling cities and the birthdays and accession days of the ruling emperors; we saw how the Palestinian rabbis counted birthdays and accession days among the "festivals of the idolaters."[45] But in both cases this tradition underwent some changes. According to the calendar of Philocalus, the Anniversary of Rome, the former Parilia, was still celebrated in the year 354. This calendar with its focus on Rome registers only the Natalis Urbis on April 21, but not the corresponding day, May 11, for Constantinople; neither does, almost a century later, the text of Polemius Silvius.[46] Theodosius' transmitted text, destined for Rome, must mean

---

[40] Sen. *Apoc.* 7.4.
[41] Stat. *Silv.* 4.4.39–42; see also Plin. *Ep.* 8.21.2 (next note) and Gell. 9.15.1 (*cum Antonio Iuliano rhetore per feriarum tempus aestivarum decedere ex urbis aestu volentes Neapolim concesseramus*).
[42] Plin. *Ep.* 8.21.2: he talks about *Iulio mense quo maxime lites interquiescunt*, but still might go to court sometimes in the early morning.
[43] Ulpian, *Digest.* 2.12.1, *oratione divi Marci* (from book 4 *De omnibus tribunalibus*), 2.12.2 *eadem oratione... in senatu habita* (from book 5 *Ad edictum*).
[44] The text has *geminis mensibus*, an ambiguous phrase that the interpretatio understood as two months for each break; this, however, is not borne out by the dates the text specifies, with the *feriae messivae* from June 25 to August 1, and the *Vindemniae* from August 23 to October 15. The Greek text in *Basilika* 7.17.23 that translates *CJ* 3.12.6, has the more likely "two months," οἱ δὲ δύο μῆνες, one for each break; see also *ibid.* 7.17.21 ἐν τοῖς δύο μησὶν τῶν ἀπράκτων.
[45] *Avodah Zarah* 1:3, above Chapter 2.
[46] Polemius Silvius on April 21 has *Natalis Urbis Romae, Parilia dicta de partu Iliae*, reproducing Filocalus' dry *Natalis Urbis*, but then explaining *Urbs* and adding antiquarian information on its earlier name and its etymology.

that the Romans also celebrated the birthday of Constantinople, if this is not an interpolation by the editors of the Code; if this really is what the emperor wrote, the former Westerner Theodosius wanted to underline the unity of the empire and the role Constantinople had to play in this. This would correspond to his decision about a decade earlier, after his accession in the middle of a Gothic war, to abandon Thessalonica despite its strategic usefulness and to set up his permanent court in Constantine's city.[47]

On the other hand, two honorary days for each reigning emperor look rather austere. In the calendar of 354, each consecrated emperor from C. Iulius Caesar to Diocletian had his anniversary celebrated, and the emperors of the ruling Constantinian dynasty, from Constantius Chlorus onward, had at least two days, the physical birthday and the day of their accession to Caesarship. All in all, in the year 354 the Romans celebrated twenty-six memorial days for the birthdays alone, some of them marked by circus games, and six additional days for events of the Constantinian dynasty, these all with somewhat elusive *ludi votivi*.[48]

To these days, determined on the one hand by the necessities of the climate in an agrarian society, on the other hand by political considerations – the Kalendae with the *vota* as main event no less than the honorary days of the ruling emperors and the birthdays of the two imperial cities – Theodosius added specific Christian days: the Sundays, and the two weeks around Easter.

Easter, as the oldest and most sacred Christian festival, should not surprise us.[49] Its impressive splendor is perhaps best captured by the lady Egeria, who shortly before Theodosius' Roman summer had lived in Jerusalem, from Easter 381 to Easter 384, and has left us a detailed description.[50] At about the same time, imperial legislation becomes visible. Since the reign of Valentinian I in the West, the festival had been marked by an amnesty for minor criminals; in 381 and again in 385, Valentinian II (or whoever inspired the boy emperor at this point) confirmed the amnesty for Italy, although the list of exceptions was somewhat expanded.[51] In a letter written in 380 in Thessalonica and addressed to the *vicarius* of Macedonia, Theodosius declared Easter and the two weeks around it as free from public and private legal business; perhaps this was, as other decisions on Church

---

[47] See Errington (1997).   [48] See Stern (1953), 33 (for the gap), 70–88 (for the imperial days).
[49] For an overview of its ancient history see Bradshaw and Johnson (2011), 39–68.
[50] Egeria, *Peregrinatio* 27–40. For a short analysis of the Jerusalem holiday period, see Baldovin (1989), 39–41.
[51] Valentinian I: *CTh* 9.38.3 (Rome, May 5, 367 [369]). Valentinian II and Theodosius: 380/381 *Const. Sirm.* 7 and *CTh* 9.38.6 (Rome, July 4, 381). Theodosius: *CTh*. 9.38.8 (Milan, 385).

matters made in these early days in Thessalonica, suggested by Acholios, the bishop of Thessalonica.[52] We have no document before our 389 Roman constitution that Theodosius wanted this rule applied elsewhere as well; in 392, he applied it to the entire Oriens, but again we lack documentation for an even wider application, although it must have been extended empire-wide.[53]

In a reform that strives for as many legal days as possible, the seven days before and seven days after Easter are striking and made some scholars see a clear Christian bias in the law.[54] The seven before Easter reflect the Holy Week, which we know best for Jerusalem, thanks to Egeria's detailed description of this *septimana maior*, "Great Week."[55] Once regarded as a Jerusalem invention that spread to the rest of Christianity in post-Nicene times, the Holy Week has been shown in recent research to have a more complex origin; but research has focused mainly on the East.[56] Thus, it needs to be underlined that Theodosius' law meant that well before 389, Holy Week was observed in whatever form in Rome as well – in a liturgical form that was strong enough that Theodosius agreed to accept it. The same is true for the week after Easter, the Easter Octave: Theodosius' rule agrees with the special emphasis put on this week in the period that leads from Easter to Pentecost, and it again shows that the Roman liturgy had it fully integrated.[57] This agrees with Egeria's observation that "the eight days of Easter they attend in the same way as we do": there is no big variation between East and West, or Jerusalem and Rome.[58]

Sundays were freed from litigation already by Constantine, with manumission and emancipation as the only permitted legal acts.[59] The law courts were slow to react; Theodosius or Gratian repeated the prohibition on November 3, 386, making any break a sacrilege – not, presumably, for a pagan who was not bound by any rule to observe Sunday, but for a Christian; already before that, in 368 Valentinian I had made it illegal to

---

[52] *CTh* 9.35.4 (Thessalonica, March 27, 380). On another constitution inspired by Acholius, see Errington (1997), 37.
[53] *CTh* 2.8.21 (May 27, 392, to the praetorian prefect of Oriens).
[54] "Concessioni per i christiani": P. Siniscalco, in Gaudemet, Siniscalco, and Falchi (2000), 116.
[55] Egeria, *Peregrinatio* 30.1–38.1.
[56] Overview in Bradshaw (2002), 185–187; Bradshaw and Johnson (2011), 114–119.
[57] See Bradshaw (2002), 182.
[58] Egeria, *Peregrinatio* 39.1 *Octo autem illi dies paschae sic attenduntur quemadmodum et nos*. (I adopt Wistrand's *octo* instead of *sero* of most manuscripts.)
[59] Constantine prohibited legal business and work in the cities on Sundays, but allowed agricultural work because its success depended on the weather, *CJ* 3.12.2 (March 5, 321); almost four months later, he reiterated the prohibition of legal business but allowed emancipation and manumission, *CTh* 2.8.1 (July 3, 321).

prosecute a Christian for taxes on a Sunday.[60] In the early fifth century, the holiness of Sunday, Easter, and other main Christian festivals was further increased by a series of prohibitions that concerned theatrical and other spectacles.[61] The most elaborate constitution is a letter that Theodosius II addressed in 425 to the praetorian prefect of Oriens: it added the "commemoration of the apostolic passion" to the list of sacred days without spectacles.[62] The "apostolic passion" must be that of Peter and Paul, whose arrival in Rome and passion the writer of the Philocalus calendar specifically marked in his list of consuls, as he marked the birth and passion of Christ.[63]

When one tries to assess Theodosius' intention and achievement in the constitution on legal holidays of Rome, one has to stress the judicious mixture of traditionality and innovation that characterizes his reform. By retaining the Kalendae and, if anything, reinforcing its role by making every day of the festival a legal holiday, Theodosius built on existing custom and simply cleared up ambiguities. He did the same by formalizing the two large pauses in summer and autumn and by selecting among the honorary days. Out of more than twenty-six such days attested in the calendar of 354, only the four physical and institutional birthdays of the two Augusti were considered legal holidays. This assumes that both Rome and Constantinople celebrated both Augusti; given the insistence with which the imperial letters always name all Augusti, this is highly probable.

---

[60] Imp(eratores) Gratianus, Valentinianus et Theodosiis A(ugusti), *CTh* 2.8.18 (Aquileia, November 3, 386); Valentinian I: *CTh* 8.1.1 (Trier, April 21, 368); see also 11.7.10. See di Berardino (2005), 102–104.

[61] Quadragesima, Easter, Christmas, and Epiphany: *CTh* 2.8.24 (Ravenna, February 4, 405?); for the longer list in *CTh* 15.5.5 see next note. Sundays alone: *CTh* 2.8.20 (Constantinople, April 17, 392: circus games allowed on a Sunday when it is an imperial birthday); 2.8.23 (Constantinople, August 27, 399: circus games, theatrical performances, and chariot races allowed on a Sunday when it is an imperial birthday); 2.8.25 (Ravenna, April 1, 409: no exceptions at all to the Sunday prohibition).

[62] *CTh*.15.5.5 (Constantinople, February 1. 425): *Dominico, qui septimanae totius primus est dies, et natali adque epifaniorum christi, paschae etiam et quinquagesimae diebus, quamdiu caelestis lumen lavacri imitantia novam sancti baptismatis lucem vestimenta testantur, quo tempore et commemoratio apostolicae passionis totius christianitatis magistrae a cunctis iure celebratur*, "On the Lord's day, which is the first day of the whole week; on the birthday and epiphany of Christ; and on the days of Easter and Pentecost, as long as the vestments that imitate the light of the heavenly font testify to the new light of baptism [i.e. the white robes of the newly baptized]; and the time when the commemoration of the apostolic passion, the teacher of all Christianity, is duly celebrated by all." – The identical addition of the apostles in the text of Theodosius' calendar reform in *CJ* 3.12.6 (*quo tempore commemoratio apostolicae passionis totius christianitatis magistrae a cunctis iure celebratur*), presumably introduced by the editors of *CJ* after the catalog of Theodosius II.

[63] Christ's birth: Caesare et Paulo coss. (year 1 p.C.n.; *Chronica Minora, MGH Scriptores: Auct. Ant.* 9, p. 56 Mommsen), passion: Gemino et Gemino coss. (year 27 p.C.n., p. 57 Mommsen). – Peter and Paul: arrival in Rome Galba et Sulla coss. (year 33: *his consulibus Petrus and Paulus ad urbem venerunt agere episcopatum*; p. 57 Mommsen); passion coss. Nerone Caesare et Vetere (year 55: *his consulibus passi sunt Petrus et Paulus iii Kal. Iul.*; p. 57 Mommsen).

At any rate, this selection was radical, although less radical than Augustus', who declared all honorary days as legal business days. Such a zero solution was impractical and undesirable; Augustus' solution was quickly forgotten, if the unconventional Claudius is specifically remembered as following the rule of the law.[64] Obviously, other forces were stronger than administrative rationality: ambition and adulation under bad emperors, but also – and perhaps especially in Theodosius' troubled time – the need to make the unity of the empire under its ruling family felt to all inhabitants by means of the splendor, joy, and relaxation of a festive day. An innovation that worked in the same way to counteract the centrifugal forces so recently seen at work in Maximus' ascendance was the celebration of the Foundation Day of Constantinople in Rome, provided that this is not an interpolation by the committee of the Theodosian Code into Theodosius' original law.

This does not mean that any other honorary day was abolished; such a day simply did not qualify as a legal holiday, regardless whether it was celebrated with games or not. We have no good reason to doubt that these other days were retained in some form or other. Positive proof, however, does not exist: they certainly appear in the fifth-century manuscript calendar of Polemius Silvius, but this is an antiquarian document based on the Calendar of 354 and does not necessarily tell us anything about contemporary Rome or Constantinople.

Then there is Christianization, both quiet and overt; but in either case, it stays away from radical solutions. By declaring the fourteen days around Easter and all Sundays legal holidays on the same level as the seasonal holidays, the Kalendae Ianuariae, and the four honorary days, Theodosius made these Christian days relevant for all inhabitants of the city, not just for the Christians: except for very urgent cases, there were no legal services available on these days even to pagans, regardless whether the law officers were Christians or pagans. On the other hand, even a pagan traditionalist would have to go to court on one of the hallowed festival days that were thought to go back to king Numa, if he was summoned. In this respect, Theodosius' constitution was a firm step towards Christianizing the city of Rome, and the pagan prefect had no choice but to go along.

Still, Theodosius was somewhat conservative in counting only Easter and the Sundays as non-business days, not the other important Christian festivals, Pentecost and Nativity (that is Christmas or Epiphany).[65] In the early third century, Origen had listed Sundays and Saturdays, Easter and

---

[64] Suet. *Claud.* 14.
[65] On Christmas and Epiphany see Bradshaw and Johnson (2011), 123–157; Bradshaw (2002), 187–190.

Pentecost as the Christian equivalents to pagan city-wide festivals (ἑορταὶ δημοτελεῖς); for the fourth-century East, Easter, Pentecost, and Epiphany were the major Christian holidays, as the so-called canons of Athanasius attest for late fourth- or early fifth-century Egypt and as Egeria's *Itinerary* confirms for Jerusalem already in the 380s; in both places, by the way, Christmas is absent.[66] Augustine's sermons on Christmas and Epiphany demonstrate that in the West these two festivals together had a very high status at least in the early fifth century, with Christmas somewhat more important than Epiphany, it seems. There has been a modern scholarly debate about when exactly these two festivals were adopted in the West: testimonies for both become more numerous after the mid-fourth century only, although Christmas might be attested somewhat earlier and is mentioned in the calendar of 354.[67] Whatever the answers in this discussion, it is clear that in Rome of 389, Christmas and Epiphany were less firmly entrenched than Easter was: this must have allowed Theodosius and Albinus to omit them, as they omitted even honorary days of the dynasty of Constantine, in order to achieve their goal of pruning down the holidays. It also suggests that the bishop of Rome had less influence on the choice of days than the Urban Prefect – which should not surprise us in a legal matter.

Pentecost was omitted from the list, one could argue, because it fell on a Sunday anyway; it was well established already in Origen's Egypt and Tertullian's Africa.[68] But Easter, always on a Sunday as well, is named. Thus, it remains remarkable that Pentecost is not, and the redactors of the later codes felt a need to amend this: this underlines how little influence on Theodosius or Albinus the bishop of Rome had in this matter. The absence of the festival of Peter and Paul, the quintessential Roman saints, confirms this even more drastically. Again, they were added in Justinian's Code, in a

---

[66] Origen, *C. Cels.* 8.22 τὰ περὶ τῶν παρ' ἡμῖν κυριακῶν ἢ παρασκευῶν ἢ τοῦ Πάσχα ἢ τῆς Πεντηκοστῆς δι' ἡμερῶν γινόμενα. Egeria: *Itinerarium* 25–26 (Epiphany; fragmentary), 30–40 (Easter), 43 (Pentecost); she adds the Encaenia, the consecration festival of the Golgotha church, 48. See esp. Baldovin (1989). The Canons of (Pseudo-)Athanasius: canon 16, Riedel and Crum (1904), 26f.(Arabic), and canon 66, Riedel and Crum, 43 (Arabic) and 131 (Coptic); on date and authenticity see W. Riedel, in Riedel and Crum (1904), xii/xxvi (Athanasius, around 364 CE), *contra* René-Georges Coquin, "Canons of Pseudo-Athanasius", *Copt. Enc.* 2.458 ("The great Saint Athanasius cannot have been its author"; date: before mid-fifth century CE).

[67] See the debate between Usener (1911) and Botte (1932). More in Förster (2007), 25–55 (history of scholarship), 219–262 (Italy, with Rome 244–260); see also Bradshaw and Johnson (2011), 123–130. Calendar of 354: not in the monthly entries of the festival calendar, but in the *fasti consulares* (Mommsen, *MGH*, 56) and the *feriale* of the Roman church (Mommsen, *MGH*, 71).

[68] Origen, *C. Cels.* 8.22 (Easter, Pentecost, and Sunday are the most important Christian festivals); Tert. *De baptismo* 19.2 (in a discussion of the most apt days for baptism). See Bradshaw and Johnson (2011), 69–74; Bradshaw (2002), 182–183.

wording that is identical to one used by Theodosius II in a letter of 425 – if they had been already in Theodosius' original letter, the Theodosian Code would doubtless have preserved them.[69]

The most radical intervention was to omit all the great festival days of pagan Rome; but it goes almost without saying that a Christian emperor could not do otherwise. Theodosius acted by quiet omission, and it was left to his son Arcadius to formulate the principle, in a constitution addressed on July 3, 395, to the *corrector Paphlagoniae*: "We remind you that we have in the past enjoined that the regular superstitious days of the pagans should not be counted as legal holidays."[70] Rather than to assume that this refers to an earlier but lost constitution of Arcadius, I think that Arcadius refers back to the decree of 389 that, after all, was signed by him as well, as it was by the younger Valentinian. In another situation and environment, Arcadius felt able to spell out what his father diplomatically passed under silence.[71] None of the days in Theodosius' calendar contradicts Arcadius' definition as *sollemnis paganorum superstitionis dies*. The former Parilia were renamed Natalis Urbis already in the second century CE, as we saw, and the somewhat shady goddess Pales was supplanted by a neutral description; with the exception of the antiquarian Polemius Silvius, nobody in the fourth century remembered the old name.[72] Only the Kalendae Ianuariae could be perceived as retaining the name of a "pagan superstitious holiday"; after all, they preserved the name of a Roman god, Janus, and some Christians made the argument and sometimes succeeded, as we shall see. But with Ianuarius being a month name, as innocent (or not) as Martius or Aprilis (provided we believe Ovid's derivation from Aphrodite), the argument sounds somewhat specious, and the more common name of the festival, Kalendae/Καλάνδαι, has no idolatrous overtones at all. Already the Palestinian rabbis had forgotten Janus and told instead the story of general Ianuarius, the founder of the festival.

With all these changes, Theodosius' reform succeeded – as already Jacques Godefroy figured out – in reserving 240 business days per year, ten more than Marcus Aurelius had done; this was quite an achievement.[73]

---

[69] CJ 3.12.6 (*quo tempore commemoratio apostolicae passionis totius christianitatis magistrae a cunctis iure celebratur*); for the parallel see CTh 15.5.5 (February 1, 425), on the prohibition of spectacles.
[70] *Sollemnes paganorum superstitionis dies inter feriatos non haberi olim lege reminiscimur imperasse*: CTh 2.8.22 (July 3, 395, Constantinople).
[71] But see Pharr (1952), 45 n. 15 ("not extant").
[72] Polemius Silvius notes on April 21 *natalis Urbis Romae, Parilia dicta de partu Iliae*; Philocalus has only *Natalis Urbis*.
[73] Marcus Aurelius: HA Capitolinus, *Marcus Antoninus* 10.10; Godefroy (1736–1745), 141. Contemporary Italy could learn a lot from Theodosius and Albinus.

It should not surprise that twenty years later Honorius granted the Jews the privilege not to appear in court during Sabbath; there were enough business days available otherwise.[74]

The reception of Theodosius' text

The preceding argumentation presupposes that the text in the Theodosian Code preserves Theodosius' constitution in an almost documentary form, excerpted from a larger document but with no vital changes and omissions, and that in the eyes of the editors of the Code, it was not just a document for Rome but a text "with edictal force or of general application" (*edictorum viribus aut sacra generalitate subnixas*).[75] This corresponds to the way the Code is perceived nowadays, after John Matthews' authoritative work – as an edited collection of legal documents issued by the emperors since Constantine that were to give empire-wide guidance to the practice of law.[76] Which means that the reform of the legal calendar of Rome, elaborated in Summer 389 by Theodosius I together with the prefect of Rome, Albinus, and with the emperor's *consistorium*, was, in the eyes of the committee that edited the Theodosian Code, to be applied throughout the empire. We have no way to tell whether this is a new development, or whether the text – for which the history of its writing is ample confirmation – had been applied more widely already by earlier emperors (mainly, of course, by Theodosius I, its author), despite its narrow local origin, or whether it remained, in the words of Theodosius II, "given to be valid or published in certain provinces or places" (*in certis provinciis seu locis valere aut proponi iussae*). Matthews has shown that this local or regional validity should not be read in opposition to the demand for general validity (*generalitas*), since *generalitas* was created by the source of the law, the emperor, regardless its local application.[77] Whatever its original validity, then, the inclusion in the Theodosian Code made it valid empire-wide, and the changes in Justinian's version will prove the point.

There were later texts, not just Justinian's, all with variations that are the result of the continuing use. The first in chronological order is the interpretation that the editors of the first Visigoth Code, the *Breviarium* of Alaric, added to the text which they took over from the Theodosian Code

---

[74] *CTh* 2.8.26 (July 26, 409); *Breviarium* 2.8.3; *CJ* 1.9.13.
[75] See the initial law of 429, *CTh* 1.1.1; the law of 435, cited in the minutes of the senate meeting in 438, *CTh* 1.1.5, summarizes this as *omnes edictales generalesque constitutiones*.
[76] See Matthews (2000). [77] The phrase, *CTh* 1.1.5 (law of 435); see Matthews 2000, 65–68.

and which king Alaric published in 506.[78] Next is the text in the Code of Justinian, issued between 529 and 534, that confirms the ongoing empire-wide importance of Theodosius' reform.[79] There is another Visigoth transformation in the *Liber Iudiciorum*, the fusion of Roman and Visigoth legal traditions of about 654;[80] there is finally a Greek adaptation of Justinian's text in the *Basilika*, the collection of imperial laws adapted for the emperor Leo the Wise (886–912).[81] All these texts were written, as was

---

[78] *CTh* 2.8.19, interpretatio: *Causas per anni spatium omnibus diebus secundum leges audiri praecipimus.* 1. *Et licet lex quattuor menses ad fructus colligendos indulserit, sed ita pro provinciarum qualitate et pro praesentia dominorum credidimus faciendum, ut a die VIII Kalendarum Iuliarum usque in Kalendas Augusti Messivae feriae concedantur, et de Kalendis Augusti usque in X Kalendas Septembris agendarum causarum licentia tribuatur; a X autem Kalendis Septembris usque in Idus Octobri Vindemiales feriae concedantur.* 2. *Dies etiam dominicarum, qui feriati sunt, ab audiendis negotiis vel exigendis debitis sequestramus.* 3. *Sanctos etiam Paschae dies, id est septem qui antecedunt, et septem qui sequuntur, nec non et dies natalis Domini Nostri vel Epiphaniae sine forensi strepitu volumus celebrari.* 4. *Natalem etiam principis vel initium regni pari reverentia convenit observatio.*

"We decree that on every day throughout the year legal cases should be heard according to the laws. [1] Although the law frees four months to bring in the harvest, we think that one should proceed according to the peculiarities of the provinces and the presence of the land-owners that Harvest Vacations should be granted from June 24 to August 1 and that legal actions should be permitted from August 1 until August 23; and one should grant Vintage Holidays from August 23 to October 15. [2] We also free the Sundays, that are holidays, from doing legal business or from collecting debts. [3] We also want to celebrate without the noise of the law courts the sacred Easter days, that is the seven days that precede and the seven days that follow Easter, and also the day of the birth of our Lord and Epiphany. [4] It also is fitting to observe with similar reverence the birthday of the ruler and the beginning of his rule." Mommsen's edition of *CTh* prints also the Visigothic interpretations; on them see Conrat (1903) and Gaudemet (1965).

[79] *CJ* 3.12.6; changes against *CTh* 2.8.18 are in bold and not italicized: *Imperatores Valentinianus, Theodosius, Arcadius. Omnes dies iubemus esse iuridicos.* 1. *Illos tantum manere feriarum dies fas erit, quos geminis mensibus ad requiem laboris indulgentior annus accepit aestivis fervoribus mitigandis et autumnis fetibus decerpendis.* 2. *Kalendarum quoque Ianuarium consuetos dies otio mancipamus.* 3. *His adicimus natalicios dies urbium maximarum Romae atque Constantinopolis, quibus debent iura differri, quin et ab ipsis nata sunt, sacros quoque Paschae dies, qui septeno vel praecedunt numero vel sequuntur,* dies etiam natalis atque Epiphaniorum Christi et quo tempore commemoratio apostolicae passionis totius christianitatis magistra a cunctis iure celebratur: in quibus etiam praedictis sanctissimis diebus neque spectaculorum copiam reseramus. 4. *In eadem observatione numeramus et dies solis, quos dominicos rite dixere maiores, qui repetito in se calculo revolvuntur.* 5. *Parem necesse est habere reverentiam,* ut ne apud ipsos arbitros vel a iudicibus flagitatos vel sponte delectos ulla sit agnitio iurgiorum, nostris etiam diebus, *qui vel lucis auspicia vel ortus imperii protulerunt.* 6. **In quindecim autem paschalibus diebus compulsio et annonariae functionis et omnium publicorum privatorumque debitorum differatur exactio.**

[80] *Liber iudiciorum* (*Lex Visigothorum*) 2.1.12, in Zeumer (1902), 69–70. The history of Visigoth codification is complex: the first codification, by Theoderic's son Euric (ruled 466–485), concerned only the Visigoth laws; a second codification, under Euric's son Alaric, made the Roman tradition available to the Visigoths and resulted in the *Breviarium* of Alaric (506 CE); the third codification, under king Chindaswint (Chindasvindus) and his son Recesswint (Recessvindus), fused both traditions in the *Liber Iudiciorum* or *Lex Visigothorum* of c.654. See Zeumer (1902), xiii–xvi.

[81] *Basilika* 7.17.23, ed. Scheltema and van der Wal (1955); I changed the paragraph numbers in order to align them with the Latin texts.

Πᾶσα ἡμέρα ἔμπρακτος ἔστω. 1. οἱ δὲ δύο μῆνες καθ᾽ἕκαστον ἔτος πρὸς ἀνάπαυσιν τοῦ καμάτου συγκεχώρηνται, τουτέστιν ὁ τῶν θεριστικῶν καὶ ὁ τρυγητικῶν. 2. καὶ ἐν Ἰανουαρίωι δὲ μηνὶ συνήθεις

the original constitution, in order to give guidelines and instructions for the practice of law. The various changes, additions, and omissions in the texts demonstrate how the editors sought to make it clear how a text written on August 8, 389 for the city of Rome remained relevant for other places and other epochs, but they also throw Theodosius' intentions into relief.

The *interpretatio*, intended for the Roman inhabitants of the Visigothic reign of Alaric II (reigned 484–507), gives precise dates for the summer and fall breaks and justifies this with the uniform climate in the area concerned, southwestern France – Aquitaine, Languedoc, and Roussillon – and parts of western Spain. It omits the birthdays of Rome and Constantinople, which would make not much sense in a kingdom that contained neither city nor felt any obligation towards them, but it preserves the royal days, albeit restricted to the one *princeps* with whom the subject of the Visigothic king dealt – incidentally, this confirms that the interpreter understood Theodosius' provision as dealing only with the active rulers, not their predecessors. It also omits the "traditional days of the Kalendae" and expands the list of Christian festivals by adding "the birthday of our Lord and Epiphany," *dies natalis Domini nostri vel Epiphaniae.* The later Visigothic code, the *Liber Iudiciorum,* is even more expansive on the harvest holidays and even gives different dates for the province of Carthage with its African climate. The days of the Kalendae are again omitted, which confirms that their omission in the *Breviarium* was intentional; in their stead, the Christian festival list is even longer and comprises Nativity, Circumcision, Epiphany, Ascension, and Pentecost – that is,

ἡμέραι ἔστωσαν ἄπρακτοι· 3. καὶ αἱ γενεθλιακὴ ἑτέρας Ῥώμης ἡμέρα· χρὴ δὲ γὰρ ἐν τοῖς δύο τούτοις γενεθλιακοῖς ἀργεῖν τὰ δικαστήρια ὡς ἐκ τῶν δύο πόλεων ἐπινοηθέντα. 4. καὶ αἱ ἑπτὰ δὲ πρὸ τοῦ πάσχα ἡμέραι καὶ αἱ ἑπτὰ μετὰ τὰ πάσχα, καὶ αἱ τοῦ γενεθλίου τοῦ σωτηρος ἡμῶν καὶ αἱ τῶν ἐπιφανίων, καὶ ὅτε μνήμη τοῦ πάθους τῶν ἁγίων ἀποστόλων γίνεται, ἄπρακτοι ἔστωσαν καὶ μηδεμία θέα ἐπιτελείσθω. 5. καὶ τὴν κυριακὴν δὲ ὁμοίως ταύταις ταῖς ἡμέραις προσήκει τιμᾶσθαι, καὶ μηδὲ παρὰ τοῖς ἄρχουσιν ἢ χαμαιδικασταῖς ἢ παρ' ἑτέροις δικασταῖς ὑπόθεσις γυμναζέσθω. 6. καὶ ἡ ἡμέρα δὲ ἡ γενεθλιακὴ τοῦ βασιλέως, ἢ καθ' ἣν ἀνηγορεύθη βασιλεύς, ἄπρακτος ἔστω. 7. ἐν δὲ ταῖς δεκαπέντε πασχαλίαις ἡμέραις μηδὲ περὶ δημοσίων συντελειῶν μηδὲ περὶ ἰδιωτικῶν χρεῶν ὑπόμνησις προσαγέσθω τινί.

"Every day shall be a day for legal action. [1] Every year, two months shall be given to recover from hard work, namely the summer month and the vintage month. [2] In January, the usual days shall be without legal action. [3] Equally the birth day of both Romes; on those two birth days the law courts shall pause because they originated from the two cities. [4] Equally shall be without legal action and without spectacles the seven days before Easter and the seven days after Easter, and the days of the birth of our savior and the days of epiphany, and when one remembers the passion of the holy apostles. [5] And one should honor the Sundays in the same way as these days, and there shall be no case acted before the rulers or the petty judges or the other judges. [6] And the birthday of the king or the day when the king was installed, shall be without legal action. [7] In the fifteen Easter days nobody shall receive a notice either of public tax debts or private debts."

among other things, a series of holy days from December 25 through January 1 to January 6: there was thus no room for the Kalendae.

Unlike the later Western texts, the version of Justinian's committee and the translation of its text in the *Basilika* do not omit the days of the Kalendae. That the originally Roman Kalendae Ianuariae remained a legal holiday in the Byzantine empire but disappeared from the Western, Visigothic calendars is a paradox that needs explanation; we shall come back to this in the next chapter. On the other hand, Justinian did add some Christian festivals. As in all versions after Theodosius, Christmas and Epiphany are added; he also adds two other festivals, the days of the "apostolic passions," that is of Peter and Paul: these festivals made sense in the liturgies of New Rome (as they would have done in Old Rome, in whose legal calendar they do not appear), but they would have been without interest in Visigothic Gaul, to which neither Peter nor Paul ever had travelled. None of this is in the excerpt in the code of Theodosius II from 439, nor does it come from Theodosius' original text, where the inclusion of Peter and Paul would contradict Theodosius' aim of finding a good balance between church and state festivals; it all looks like expansions in Justinian's age.

Justinian's editorial committee also added two details that transcended the unity of purpose of the law that Theodosius I had announced in its introductory sentence, to allow as few legal holidays as possible. The text of the new committee prohibits spectacles on the Christian holidays and gives instructions not to collect taxes or to recover debts during the two weeks around Easter. This latter double provision derives from the same intention for clemency that motivated the Easter amnesty for most crimes, except the most heinous ones, pronounced the first time by Valentinian I, Valens, and Gratian in 367 or 369, and several times modified after that.[82] The former is an interpolation from a group of earlier laws that concentrated on the holiness of the Christian holidays; we have them as excerpts in the Theodosian Code, with a constitution of Theodosius II on February 1, 425 as the most recent text, and they clearly suggest that the document of Theodosius I did not contain any such provision; it would also have exceeded the unity of purpose – to restrict the number of legal holidays – expressed in its first sentence. When Justinian's committee made its

---

[82] *CTh* 9.38.2–9; 9.38.9 (= *CJ* 1.4.3) was written in 385 to Neoterius, *praefectus praetorio* of the East and signed by Gratian, Valentinian (II), and Theodosius, who as Augustus of the East was the real author; it grants amnesty during Easter to all criminals except those imprisoned for sacrilege, adultery, incest, rape, murder, high treason, and further the *venefici, malefici*, counterfeiters of money, and those who disturbed the peace of the dead.

addition, it introduced part of the wording of this constitution of Theodosius II on the prohibitions of spectacles – the phrase *quo tempore commemoratio apostolicae passionis totius christianitatis magistrae a cunctis iure celebratur*, identical in both texts – into the constitution of Theodosius I on legal holidays, a clear case of the nowadays somewhat contested concept of interpolations in the texts of the Code of Justinian.[83]

The reception and adaptation of Theodosius' ruling on legal holidays for the city of Rome into the law codes for the Later Roman Empire of Theodosius II and Justinian, the Visigothic kingdom of Southern France, Spain, and, at a later stage, North Africa, and the Byzantine Empire of Leo the Wise not only proves how well balanced and useful this ruling – the final one in a long series of imperial attempts to clean the legal calendar of encroaching holidays – was in the eyes of later rulers, it also justified and protected the days it defined as legal holidays. This includes – except among the Visigoths – the "traditional days" of the Kalendae Ianuariae or, as the text in the *Basilika* rephrases, "the usual days in the month of January," aptly omitting what could be read as the festival name. It also includes – at least for Theodosius II and Justinian – the birthdays of Rome and Constantinople (with the same omission of a more specific festival name); Leo's version narrows the celebration down to "the birthday of the Other Rome" – the first Rome having become irrelevant and far away for ninth-century Byzantium. But whatever the careful language was, it meant that the descendants of the Parilia and the Kalendae Ianuariae were surviving and received imperial protection in the cities of the shrinking Roman Empire on a level comparable with Easter and the Christian Sunday, centuries after Ovid in his *Fasti* had described the Augustan Kalendae and Parilia. Theodosius' attempt to gain the respect of the Roman elite during a few weeks in Summer 389 had unforeseen and important long-term consequences in the festival calendar.

---

[83] *CTh* 15.5.5 (Theodosius II on February 1, 425); the phrase expands a constitution of Honorius from February 4, 405 (*CTh*. 2.8.24) prohibiting spectacles on Sundays, Easter, Christmas, and Epiphany, by adding the days of Peter and Paul. On interpolation by Justinian's committee (in this case into the Digest) see Johnston (1989); our case qualifies as intentional interpolation in order to bring an earlier text up to the needs of the present.

CHAPTER 4

Contested festivals in the fourth century

The Christian contestation of the Kalendae Ianuariae

At about the time of Theodosius' Roman ruling, two of the most influential Christian preachers and theologians were preaching against the Kalendae Ianuariae: John Chrysostom in Antioch, at some time between his ordination in 386 and his installation as bishop of Constantinople in 397, and Augustine in Carthage in 403. In between, in a sermon of January 6, 400, Asterius, bishop of Amaseia, was attacking the same festival. Other Christian sermons on the topic might be lost. It is tempting to understand these sermons as a protest of the bishops against the imperial decision of 389. In 392 or 393, the pagan orator Libanius talked in Antioch to his students on the Kalendae; this might well be a reaction to John Chrysostom's sermon and underscores the momentousness of Theodosius' decision. In this chapter I will analyze these four public addresses (the three sermons and the one talk) as almost contemporary voices in a debate on a major festival of the Roman tradition.[1]

Libanius on the Kalendae Ianuariae in Antioch

Late in his career, the orator Libanius pronounced in front of his students (9.4: ὦ νέοι) what he called an *enkomion* on the Kalendae. Speaking on the very first festival day, he began with an apology: although praise is a way to honor the gods, "and it is a powerful divinity that this festival is celebrating", he never before had publicly

---

[1] On the realia see Meslin (1970), 51–93, on the Christian criticism the somewhat disappointing remarks on "la critique chrétienne," 95–118; on the wider Christian contestation of pagan festivals still see the overview of Harl (1981), who convincingly argues for taking the episcopal voices seriously: they are not just rhetoric but are a serious redefinition of what a festival is ("vise une réalité," 126).
  An earlier version of this chapter was published as Graf (2011a).

praised the festival.² He understands this praise as an obligation that he has to fulfill before his death: "Better to die when one has fulfilled all one's obligations instead of leaving them behind unfulfilled."³ This helps to date the oration: Libanius died in 393 CE, the speech should not be much earlier.⁴ Towards its end, he refers to an imperial command that set an end to sacrifices – although sacrifices were prohibited several times during the fourth century, and Libanius in his *Pro Templis* refers to an earlier prohibition by Valens and Valentinian that Theodosius endorsed, it is not unlikely that he means Theodosius' general prohibition of pagan sacrifices, dated on February 21, 391 CE.⁵ Unlike the closing of the temples, to which Libanius reacted with a speech that has not given up all hope (translated into Latin by Jacques Godefroy, who in his Calvinist, iconoclast Geneva was interested in the late antique confrontation between Christianity and traditional religion), the absence of sacrifices in the *Kalendae* appears final and irrevocable.⁶ If Libanius reacted quickly, he talked to his students on January 1, 392; otherwise, he had one more January left in his life.

Although he claims that he never gave a formal praise of the festival, he already once before spoke and wrote about the Kalendae, in a somewhat pedantic exercise (*progymnasma*) on the festival.⁷ There, he started out with stressing the uniqueness of the Kalendae. Humans love festivals, "because they absolve them from labor and sweat and allow them to play, eat plentifully and live as agreeably as possible,"⁸ and therefore there are

---

² Liban. *Or.* 9.1: Ἡ μὲν οὖν ἑορτὴ καὶ αὐτὴ προσάγει τὸ αὐτῆς εὖ ποιήσουσα ἡμᾶς, ἡμεῖς δὲ οὔπω πρότερον αὐτῇ πεποιήκαμεν ἐγκώμιον, καὶ ταῦτα εἰδότες, ὅτι τιμὴ μὲν τοῦτο καὶ αὐτοῖς τοῖς δαίμοσιν ὧν ἑορταί, δαίμονος δὲ μεγάλου τήνδε εἶναι συμβαίνει τὴν ἑορτήν. "The festival itself shows its power by making us well, but we never before have composed its praise, although we know that this is an honor also to the divinities to whom the festivals belong, but it happens that this festival here belongs to a great divinity."
³ *Ibid.* 3: βέλτιον γὰρ ἀποδόντας τελευτᾶν τὸν βίον ἢ ὀφείλοντας.
⁴ On the dating problems see Petit (1956).
⁵ The earlier prohibition, Liban. *Or.* 30.7; on its date, a. 386, see Petit (1956). The law of 392, *CTh* 16.10.10.
⁶ On the closing of the temples: Liban. *Or.* 30. The Latin version *Libanii Antiocheni de templis Gentilium non exscindendis ad Theodosium Magnum Imperatorem oratio*, [Geneva] 1634, with an ample commentary; another book of Godefroy on Christians and pagans in late antiquity is his *De statu paganorum sub christianis imperatoribus seu commentarius ad titulum X de paganis libri XVI codicis Theodosiani auctore Iacobo Gothofredo* (Leipzig: G. Vögelin, 1616). Reformation and Counter-Reformation (with their very direct impact on Godefroy father and son) certainly is the subtext underlying this interest of Godefroy *fils*, at the time actively engaged in Geneva's politics.
⁷ Προγύμνασμα περὶ καλανδῶν, *Prog.* 12.5.
⁸ *Prog.* 12.5.1 Τὰς ἑορτὰς οἱ ἄνθρωποι φιλοῦσιν, ὅτι αὐτοὺς ἀπαλλάττουσι μὲν πόνων τε καὶ ἱδρώτων, παρέχουσι δὲ παίζειν καὶ εὐωχεῖσθαι καὶ ὡς ἥδιστα διάγειν.

many festivals on all levels of society, from the family to the nation – but only the Kalendae are celebrated in the entire Roman empire.[9] He then walks his audience through the festival, from the preparation through the festival days with their specific activities to the moment when all is over and people begin to look forward to the next Kalendae.

Unlike this descriptive and ecphrastic earlier piece, the later praise speech is very selective with details. Like its predecessor, it begins with the ubiquity of the festival, in an almost cosmic view that recalls Ovid's statement that on this day Jupiter sees *nil nisi Romanum*:[10]

> This festival is performed wherever the Roman Empire rules, and everyone is excited and rejoices and is happy: . . . it flourishes in all plains, on all hills, on all mountain tops, on lakes and rivers, wherever ships sail; and you could find it even on the sea if the season would not be too inclement for maritime travel.[11]

Even if this is rhetorical exaggeration, it shows how widespread the celebration was at the end of the fourth century, and it explains why later codes of law adopted Theodosius' ruling of August 8, 389 that originally was destined solely for Rome.

He then focuses on a few reasons for praise. First comes its lavishness and generosity (6–10): "Everywhere one drinks, eats and laughs, excessively in rich houses, better than usual in poor ones, as if we all were Sybarites; a craze for spending has taken hold of all.[12] . . . If one said that this is the sweetest time of the year, one would not miss the mark."[13] Then follows the atmosphere of a festival that has removed all fear and anxieties (11–13), where students do not have to fear their teachers nor the teachers their students or the slaves their masters, where trials are stopped and prison inmates feel at peace, and where even fathers cease to grieve for their dead sons. This creates a feeling of joyous harmony even among people who were at odds with each other: "It reconciles citizen with citizen, child with child and woman with woman, and it brings together those who in a family

---

[9] *Prog.* 12.5.2 μίαν δὲ οἶδα κοινὴν ἁπάντων ὁπόσοι ζῶσιν ὑπὸ τὴν Ῥωμαίων ἀρχήν.
[10] Ovid, *Fasti* 1.86.
[11] Libanius, *Or.* 9.4 Ταύτην τὴν ἑορτὴν εὕροιτ' ἄν, ὦ νέοι, τεταμένην ἐφ' ἅπαν ὅσον ἡ Ῥωμαίων ἀρχὴ τέταται, καὶ κινεῖταί τε ἕκαστος καὶ χαίρει καὶ γέγηθε . . . [5] ἀνθεῖ δὲ ἐν ἅπασι μὲν ἡ ἑορτὴ πεδίοις, ἐν ἅπασι δὲ γηλόφοις, ἐν ἅπασι δὲ ὄρεσι καὶ λίμναις καὶ ποταμοῖς, ἐν οἷς πλοῖά τε καὶ πλέοντες, καὶ ἐν τῇ θαλάττῃ δ' ἄν, εἰ μὴ ἄπλους ἦν ὑπὸ τῆς ὥρας ἡ θάλαττα.
[12] Liban. *Or.* 9.6: πανταχοῦ δὲ πότοι καὶ τράπεζαι Συβαριτικαὶ καὶ γέλωτες. αἱ μὲν τῶν εὐδαιμόνων τοιαῦται, τῆς εἰωθυίας δὲ καὶ ἡ τοῦ πένητος ἀμείνων. ἔρως γάρ τις λαμβάνει τοὺς ἀνθρώπους δαπάνης.
[13] *Or.* 9.10 τοῦτό γε ἔτους τὸ ἥδιστον εἶναι λέγων τις οὐκ ἂν ἁμάρτοι.

have moved apart: they come to an understanding and utter only one word, 'festival', even if before they despised each other."[14]

Then Libanius returns to the general generosity of the Kalendae. The festival "becomes a teacher of men not to cling excessively to gold but to let it go and put it onto the hands of others: even the emperor is taught this lesson by the festival."[15] This sets the stage for the last item: the festival is adored by teachers because they get their payment, with a reminder that, after all, the students get back the best education possible. This then is also a piece of self-promotion for the teacher who needs that remuneration: one hopes that it was as generous as the festival's atmosphere suggested.

The final paragraph turns to the consuls who leave and enter office on the first of January – and to a somewhat melancholy memory of past glory: "The altars of the gods do not have everything they had before, because the law hinders it: before this hindrance, this inception of the year used to give us much fire, much blood, and much smoke that was raising to the sky from many altars everywhere: in this festival, even the gods received a splendid meal."[16] Now, after Theodosius' prohibition, the gods – mentioned at the very beginning of the speech as participants – are excluded from the festivities.

One should not underrate the force of this image that closes the encomium. Its elements are traditional: fire on all altars, the rising smoke or rather, as Libanius has it, κνίση, the mixture of wood smoke, burning meat, and evaporating wine, with incense freely added. Throughout antiquity, it was well understood that a festival was the more splendid the more animals were slaughtered, burnt, and eaten. As we saw in the first chapter, honorary decrees praised local officials for the lavish public banquets after the sacrifices that marked their entry into office, and the same conception still reverberates in late antique Christian authors such as Choricius of Gaza, who insists on the lavish banquets that turn a saint's festival into a laudable event.[17] It was less often spelled out that the sacrifice did not only feed the humans, however much they enjoyed free meat and wine, but also

---

[14] *Or.* 9.14–15 διήλλαξε δὲ καὶ πολίτη πολίτην καὶ ξένῳ ξένον καὶ παῖδα παιδὶ καὶ γυναῖκα γυναικὶ τά τε ἐν ταῖς συγγενείαις διεστηκότα συνέστησε τῶν εἰς διαλλαγὰς ἀγόντων τοῦτο μόνον λεγόντων, τὴν ἑορτήν, τῶν ἄλλων σφίσι τῶν πρότερον καταπεφρονημένων.

[15] *Or.* 9.15 διδάσκαλος ἀνθρώποις γίνεται τοῦ μὴ σφόδρα ἔχεσθαι χρυσίου, προΐεσθαι δὲ καὶ εἰς ἄλλων ἐντιθέναι δεξιάς. παιδεύεται δὲ ταύτην τὴν παιδείαν ὑπ' αὐτῆς καὶ βασιλεύς.

[16] *Or.*9.18 βωμοί τε θεῶν νῦν μὲν οὐ πάντα ἔχουσι τὰ πρόσθεν νόμου κεκωλυκότος, πρὸ δέ γε τοῦ κωλύματος ἥδε ἡ νουμηνία πολὺ μὲν πῦρ, πολὺ δὲ αἷμα, πολλὴν δὲ ἐποίει κνῖσσαν ἀπὸ παντὸς χωρίου πρὸς τὸν οὐρανὸν ἀνιοῦσαν, ὥστε καὶ τοῖς θεοῖς εἶναι λαμπρὰν ἐν τῇ ἑορτῇ τὴν δαῖτα.

[17] Choricius, *Oratio* 1 (*Laudatio Prima Marciani Episcopi*), intr. 1–5, esp. 4f. (p. 2 Foerster and Richtsteig). See Litsas (1982) and Hevelone-Harper (2005), 81–83.

the gods; in a comic parody of this ideology, however, eight centuries before Libanius, Aristophanes had made fun of it when his birds were blocking the κνίση from rising to heaven, to starve the gods into submission. For the inhabitants of the Roman Empire, the Kalendae were the one occasion that permitted excessive consumption in the middle of a season where otherwise one was living rather poorly from whatever one had put aside in summer and autumn.

Libanius' praise thus has an agenda. The festival's lavishness, generosity, and atmosphere of civic and private concord are praised against the backdrop of a world where traditions were disappearing because of partisan ideologies and lack of tolerance. All the more important it was to save what could be saved, including this occasion of world-wide joy.

The Kalendae of January had always been an important festival in the Roman calendar, first in the city of Rome, then in many cities of the empire. And since these cities at least in the East followed their local calendars, which usually put the New Year at a very different place, the name Kalendae (Ianuariae) changed from its calendrical meaning of January 1, as the official New Year's day of the city of Rome, to the name of a festival that was added to any city's calendar and its local New Year's day and became in the Greek world simply Καλάνδαι. At the same time, it was extended from the first day of the year, *Kalendae Ianuariae*, to four or five days. The inauguration of the consuls and, in a pagan context in which the Christian emperors since Constantine did not participate any more, the sacrifice to Jupiter Optimus Maximus still marked the first day, at least in the capital cities of the Empire, but with the emperor becoming somewhat more important than the changing consuls. The second day was confined to the private houses, with carnivalesque inversions: masters and slaves played dice (forbidden on other days) and dined together, or the masters even served their slaves, in an even more carnivalesque mood. The emperor and his house became highly visible on the third day, with the *vota*, the public vows for emperor and empire; over time, this turned into its own festival day, *Vota* or Βότα.[18] The rest of the day was given over to chariot races. These races grew in importance and took place also on the fourth and fifth days, and other rites were added locally – complex gift giving (*strenae*)

---

[18] Surprisingly, Libanius, *Prog.* 12.5.13 does not mention the *Vota* but concentrates on the horse races of the day. The Greek form is found e.g. in canon 62 of the Council in Trullo, wrongly understood as "feasts in honor of Pan, the god of the inhabitants in the Peloponnesos" by Constantelos (1970), 24, reprinted in Constantelos (1998), 164; his main argument is based on this erroneous assumption that goes back to Du Cange.

as another rite to affirm social roles, the performance of satiric songs, or masked parades through the city street.

At the same time as its carnival, races, and banquets made it a favorite of the urban crowds, the festival expressed the unity of the empire under the emperor and his house, thanks to the importance of the *vota*: it thus turned into perhaps the most important and most popular calendrical vehicle of imperial ideology. This is why the "mighty daimon," μέγας δαίμων, whom Libanius evoked at the beginning of his address could be either Jupiter or the emperor or both at the same time: unlike θεός with its clear meaning that could only designate a god or the dead and divinized emperor, the Homeric δαίμων remains vaguer and designates any being larger than an ordinary human.

Antioch and its Kalendae had already once become important in the fourth century. In July 362, Julian arrived in the city with his court, preparing his fateful campaign against the East; for over half a year, Antioch turned into the hub of the empire. It was here that Julian celebrated the Kalendae Ianuariae of 363, with the inauguration of the new consuls, the horse races, and the ample celebrations that we know from Libanius – and the intriguing incident of the *Misopogon*.[19] On January 1, his teacher Libanius performed the panegyric on the emperor; Julian was so impressed that (as Libanius reports in his autobiography) "he jumped up from his throne, threw out his arms, widely opening his cloak" – a loss of imperial restraint that "narrow-minded critics" (τὶς τῶν ἀγγάρων) might well have censured. "But," asked the flattered Libanius, "what is more regal than if a king lets his soul soar to the sky through the beauty of an oration?"[20]

The amplitude of the performance had its political reasons: it was part of Julian's restoration of pagan traditions. The Kalendae with their emphasis on traditions that went back to the Roman Republic were vital to this project, and its ample sacrifice to Jupiter Optimus Maximus emphasized this tradition. The celebration of the Kalendae had even become more important, and the emperor perhaps even somewhat desperate, after the first major act of restoration in Antioch met with disaster. The formerly splendid temple of Apollo in Daphne which Julian visited immediately after his arrival and which he was lavishly restoring burnt down in the autumn of 362, visibly and cruelly setting back Julian's program.

---

[19] See Gleason (1986); Hawkins (2011).
[20] Liban. *Or.* 1 (*Autobiography*), 129 τί γὰρ δὴ βασιλικώτωερον τοῦ βασιλέως ψυχὴν πρὸς κάλλη λόγων ἀνίστασθαι;

John Chrysostom on the Kalendae Ianuariae in Antioch

We cannot know whether John Chrysostom was in the audience on January 1, 363, when Libanius held his panegyric on Julian. It is possible: the performance was public, the crowd was huge (Libanius talks hyperbolically of an audience of ten thousand, μύριοι), and as the son of a leading citizen John must have been old enough to be brought along by his father.[21]

However that may be, as a Christian priest John Chrysostom was among those who fiercely attacked the celebration of the Kalendae. John delivered what is the earliest preserved among the sermons against the Kalendae: he spoke when he still was a priest, in place of his absent bishop Flavianus. He had become priest in 386; this dates the sermon between January 1, 387 and the year 398, when he was promoted to the see of Constantinople. I think that the sermon is somewhat later than 387: the bishop of Antioch would hardly have asked a newly consecrated priest to stand in for him on this important day, however prominent by rank and talent he was.

After a short praise of the absent bishop and a somewhat longer one of the apostle Paul, the preacher immediately talks business, and he sounds aggressive, even shrill. "We are fighting a war, not against the Amalekites, not against other foreign attackers, but against the demons who parade through the market place!"[22] John then launches into a long, aggressively demonizing description of what he sees happen in the city around him: "The devilish all-night celebrations that are held today, the jests and songs of blame and censure, the nocturnal dancing and this entire ridiculous comedy: all this keeps our city in a stronger and crueller captivity than any outside enemy would do."[23] And what happens inside the taverns is even worse than what he sees happening outside – men and women drink together, lavishly and lasciviously, and regard it as a good omen for the coming year: the opulence of the first day guarantees the opulence of the entire year.

This leads to the first basic distinction between Christians and pagans. Christians do not care for the characters of single days, and Christians do not mark single days through festivals: if, as Paul wrote, the true festival is performed with "the unleavened bread which is sincerity and

---

[21] Liban. *Or.* 1.127. John was a member of Antioch's elite, γένος τῶν εὐπτρίδων, according to Sozomen. *Hist. eccl.* 8.2.
[22] John Chrysostom, *Hom. in Kalendas* 1 (*PG* 48, 954): ἡμῖν πόλεμος συνέστηκε νῦν ... δαιμόνων πομπευσάντων ἐπὶ τῆς ἀγορᾶς.
[23] *Ibid.* 1.954 αἱ γὰρ διαβολικαὶ παννυχίδες αἱ γινόμεναι τήμερον καὶ τὰ σκώμματα καὶ αἱ λοιδορίαι καὶ αἱ χορεῖαι αἱ νυκτεριναὶ καὶ ἡ καταγέλαστος αὕτη κωμωιδία. παντὸς πολεμίου χαλεπώτερον τὴν πόλιν ἡμῶν ἐξηιχμαλτώτισαν.

truth,"[24] for a Christian each day is a festival day, and there is no need for other festivals. "A Christian should not celebrate months or new moons or Sundays, but he celebrates a festival each day ... To observe specific days is not Christian philosophy, but pagan error."[25] If taken seriously, this rejects any Christian holiday, Sunday or Easter included: there is no room for festivals anymore in Christianity. Although this sounds like the unrealistic dream of an ascetic ideologue, it is far from being innocent politically, given the eminent political role of the Kalendae of January.

John, however, does not spend much time on this dangerous topic but returns to his main argument, the Kalendae. Their rites are child's play; a true Christian does not participate in them. "Do not kindle a visible light on the forum, but a spiritual light in your heart ...; do not crown the door of your house, but live in a way that Christ will crown you with the crown of virtue."[26] The rites of the Kalendae – the candles on the market place, the greeneries around one's house door – are allegorized and spiritualized in a movement that recalls the spiritualization of Catholic ritualism that will be characteristic of Protestantism. It even turns into an anticelebration: the true Christian shall stay home and feed the poor. "When you hear the noise and perceive the wantonness and the processions of the demons, when the agora is filled with bad and loose people, stay home and keep away from chaos!"[27] Non-participation is the only possible attitude for a good Christian, and not just in the face of sinful behavior. To burn candles, to have a good dinner and adorn one's door is as bad and as forbidden as any other bad behavior. Under the surface of a moralizing argument, we easily perceive a generalized resistance against any form of pagan ceremonialism. This has as many political implications as it has religious ones.

Twice now, the preacher has talked about a procession of demons through the agora. This is more than rhetorical hyperbole of the sort that labels the festival in general as a ἑορτὴ διαβολική: it targets a specific ritual detail. In several cities, we hear of the use of masks at the Kalendae. In the West, they are "stags, old women, and other monsters" (*cervuli, anniculae*

---

[24] 1 Cor. 5:8.
[25] John Chrysostom, *Hom. in Kalendas* 3.956 τὸν γὰρ Χριστιανὸν οὐχὶ μῆνας οὐδὲ νουμηνίας οὐδὲ κυριακὰς ἑορτάζειν χρῆ, ἀλλὰ διὰ παντὸς τοῦ βίου τὴν αὐτῶι πρέπουσαν ἑορτὴν ἄγειν. ... τὸ παρατηρεῖν ἡμέρας οὐ Χριστιανικῆς φιλοσοφίας, ἀλλ' Ἑλληνικῆς πλάνης ἐστίν.
[26] *Ibid.* 3.957 μὴ τοίνυν ἐπὶ τῆς ἀγορᾶς ἀνακαύσηις πῦρ αἰθητὸν ἀλλ' ἐπὶ τῆς διανοίας ἄναψον φῶς πνευματικόν ... μὴ τὴν θύραν τῆς οἰκίας στεφανώσηις, ἀλλὰ τοιαύτην ἐπίδειξαι πολιτείαν ὥστε τὸν τῆς διακοσύνης στέφανον σῆι κεφαλῆι παρὰ τῆς τοῦ Χριστοῦ δέξασθαι χειρός.
[27] *Ibid.* ὅταν ἀκούσηι θορύβους, ἀταξίας καὶ πομπὰς διαβολικὰς πονηρῶν ἀνθρώπων καὶ ἀκολάστων τὴν ἀγορὰν πεπληρωμένην οἴκοι μένε καὶ τῆς ταραχῆς ἀπαλλάτηις ταύτης.

et alia monstra), in the East (but also in Ravenna, the Imperial city) masks of the gods: Janus and Saturnus in Philadelphia in Lydia, a *pompa daemonum* in Ravenna and Antioch, with the masks of Saturnus, Hercules, Diana, and Vulcanus.[28] The council in Trullo in 692 still attacks the "dances and initiations in the name of what the Greeks wrongly call gods, done by men and women and performed in an ancient way that is alien to Christian life," although the council connects them not with the Kalendae only but with any use of masks, including those used on stage.[29] As the presence of Saturnus shows, the masks at the Kalendae continue those attested in earlier times at the Saturnalia. The opulence and sensuality of the Kalendae was bad enough, the appearance of pagan gods pushed the bishops over the edge.

John's disapproval and rejection of the rituals makes him insist that his flock commits itself to what amounts to civil disobedience. But as if this were too hot a topic, he quickly generalizes all this: Christians do not make small talk during their social interactions, they talk about their φιλοσοφία, their doctrines, and they do not keep quiet when they see things that contradict their philosophy. And if by doing so they make enemies, they would do it in the name of God. And – now the sermon turns ugly – in God's name they are even allowed to use the sword, as the Biblical story of Phinehas shows: "What he did," says John, "was murder, but it was a punishment that turned into salvation for all who were on their way to disaster."[30] If we take this seriously, it is much more than just instigation to civil disobedience: it preaches armed resistance in the name of religious purity. The story of Phinehas legitimated violence against other Jews who did not observe the strict boundaries towards non-Jews: by killing a fellow Israelite who slept with a Midanite woman, Phinehas "made expiation for the Israelites" and prevented Jahweh from destroying all Israelites in a plague (but only after it had already killed "twenty-four thousand").[31] It is somewhat surprising that this comes from the same preacher who must remember what happened in 387 when an angry crowd attacked imperial images and when Theodosius punished the city.[32] A well-meaning

---

[28] Caesarius of Arles, *Sermo* 193, see Arbesmann (1979); Lydus, *Mens.* 4,2; Petrus Chrysologus (earlier Caesarius of Arles), *Sermo de Pythonibus, PL* 65.37.

[29] Trullo, canon 62 (τὰς ὀνόματι τῶν παρ' Ἕλλησι ψευδῶς ὀνομασθέντων θεῶν ἢ ἐξ ἀνδρῶν ἢ γυναικῶν γινομένας ὀρχήσεις καὶ τελετάς, κατά τι ἔθος παλαιὸν καὶ ἀλλότριον τοῦ τῶν χριστιανῶν βίου), Nedungatt and Featherstone (1995), 142–144. See Trombley (1978).

[30] John Chrysostom, *Hom. in Kalendas* 6.961f.: τὸ μὲν γινόμενον φόνος ἦν, τὸ δὲ κατορθούμενον ἐξ ἐκείνου σωτηρία τῶν ἀπολλυμένων πάντων.

[31] *Numeri* 25:1–15; see Collins (2003), 12–13 against unjustified attempts to downplay the violence.

[32] Liban. *Or.* 19.15, 20.3, 22.5.

interpreter might doubt whether John wanted to take Phinehas' actions as a literal example; but even so, there is no doubt whatsoever that John abhorred the rites of the Kalendae, and not just the lewd dances and songs in the taverns and the masks of the gods on the agora. His aim was to keep away his Christians from any participation in the festival, and even to convince the pagans to do the same.

From sermon to encomium?

Libanius' oration on the Kalendae and John Chrysostom's sermon against the festival are about contemporary; it is tempting to connect the two. Neither text reacts directly to the other: John Chrysostom attacks a festival that lured many of his Christians away from church, that offended his ascetic ethics, and that expressed pure idolatry. Libanius claims to make up late in his life for an omission, the praise of the Kalendae, but with the hidden agenda to praise a festival that has become the target of Christian aggression. In this context, the insistence on civic harmony that transcends the male citizens – "it also reconciles citizen with citizen, child with child and woman with woman, and it brings together who in a family has fallen apart" – could be read as an implicit answer to John's belligerent separatism. It is thus tempting to see Libanius as reacting to John, the pagan to the Christian, in the same way as the pagan Libanius reacted to the Christian closing of the temples, but also in the way the mild professor reacted to his strident but very gifted student. Libanius did not simply object to John's Christian faith, as Sozomen claims, but to his lack of moderation; that he was a Christian was no problem for Libanius, but lack of moderation had also made him, at the time of Julian, admonish a too intransigent pagan administrator.[33]

There is, however, no clear echo of one text in the other; rather, they represent two radically different ways of looking at the same traditional event, one that of a somewhat nostalgic pagan who regrets the disappearance of the sacrifices, the other of a belligerent Christian ascetic. This does not argue against my feeling that Libanius reacted to John; the two media, the sermon and the formal encomium, are simply too different from each other. Still, it is conceivable that both react to Theodosius' endorsement of

---

[33] Sozomen. *Hist. eccl.* 8.2: shortly before his death, his friends asked whom he would recommend as his successor, and he answered: "John, if the Christians had not hijacked him" (εἰ μὴ Χριστιανοὶ τοῦτον ἐσύλησεν); for the too harsh administrator, one Alexander, see *Epist.* 811 and 1351. See Maxwell (2006), 60 (Libanius and John); Cribiore (2013), 154–160 (Libanius' moderate paganism).

the Kalendae in his Roman decree, provided that the decree had become empire-wide policy as soon as the emperor returned to Constantinople.

Asterius of Amaseia on the Kalendae Ianuariae

A third homily, performed not a decade after Libanius' praise, expands this perspective. It is the Homily on Epiphany, addressed to a local congregation on January 6 of 400 CE by Asterius, bishop of Amaseia, in this city in the mountains above the Black Sea coast where he resided as bishop between *c.*380/390 and 420/425.[34]

In his homily, the bishop of Amaseia censured his congregation for their absenteeism from the last Sunday's sermon on January 1, the first day of the Kalendae. As in other places the festival "of the rabble outside," τοῦ ἔξωθεν συρφετοῦ – the celebrating pagans and the "false" Christians who were following them – held more attraction than the bishop's office.[35] In order to heal his erring congregation, Asterius intends to show them the true character of the pagan festival. At the center of this λόγος κατηγορικός, "public accusation" (thus its title in the manuscripts) is the rejection of the claim that the festival creates happy harmony:[36]

> Of a general feast, this, then, should be the rule and law: ... that the happiness be common to all, not that a part enjoy themselves and the rest be left in dejection and pain – this is characteristic of war rather than of a feast. ... I see only a few making merry, while the mass of the people are melancholy, even though they try to conceal their dejection by a cheerful demeanor.

The underlying definition of a festival – a communal event full of merriment and happiness – is traditional in ancient cultures, Christian as well as pagan: we saw how Libanius claimed exactly this character for the Kalendae. The rift between the many and the few that breaks up the festival's communality is due, Asterius claims, to the fact that the festival clings to material goods in a way that is far from being generous and thus cannot satisfy many. Its custom of gift-giving favors only the very rich at

---

[34] Datema (1970), xvii–xxv.
[35] For another case (Gregory of Nyssa) see Datema (1970), 228. In 398, the African bishops decided to excommunicate whoever preferred spectacles to the mass, Mansi III 958 can. 88 (*qui die solenni praetermisso solenni ecclesiae conventu ad spectacula vadit, excommunicetur*); in 401, they decided to petition the emperors to ban spectacles on Sundays and all other Christian holidays, Munier (1974), 137; Arcadius and Honorius prohibited spectacles on Sundays in 399, *CTh* 2.8.23, and they added Quadragesima, Easter, Christmas, and Epiphany in 405, *CTh* 2.8.24 (dated 400).
[36] Asterius, *Hom.* 4.2; translation after Anderson and Goodspeed (1904).

the upper end of the gift-giving chain and tempts the less affluent into making debts to pay for the presents they are expected to give their betters, in the typical reciprocality of ceremonial gift-giving.[37] The begging by vagrants and stage artists (ἀγύρται καὶ οἱ τῆς ὀρχήστρας θαυματοποιοί) is so insistent that whoever is able to do so shuns the city; and it even turns small children into money-grubbing extortionists who ask for a richer gift when they hand you their "newfangled presents, apples covered with silver tinsel."[38] Far from uniting the city in the common purpose of merriment, the festival makes a few enjoy themselves and leaves the rest in dejection and pain: "this is characteristic of war rather than of a feast."[39] After this central exposition (3–6), he adds three details – the dissolute way in which the soldiers celebrate the festival, by cross-dressing and making fun "of the laws and the government of which they have been appointed guardians";[40] the egotistic expenses of magistrates in order to gain fame and status; and the fate of a few recent consuls who entered office during this festival and who came to a bad end. The sermon ends with the swift ascent and downfall of these men: "Are not these political eminences like visions of baseless dreams, delighting for a little, then fleeting away, blooming and withering?"[41]

In his 1911 doctoral dissertation, Max Schmid suggested that Asterius' homily was "an ironic reaction to Libanius."[42] This is a seductive assessment. The structure and the main arguments of Asterius' homily are entirely determined by Libanius' encomium. To Libanius' praise of generosity and general happiness, Asterius answers with his accusation of class division and overwhelming unhappiness, both due to the custom of ceremonial gift-giving; to his picture of generous aristocrats, Asterius opposes the magistrates who spend their money on presents in order to gain personal fame and influence; and against Libanius' final image of the consuls entering office, Asterius puts the narration of the dire fate of several recent consuls.

Still, Schmid's assessment is too narrow: the homily is more than a clever exercise in intertextuality. It has an immediate rhetorical and a long-term polemical goal. Asterius' immediate reason for the homily is to teach his

---

[37] On this see Hénaff (2013). [38] Ibid. 6.1 δῶρα ... καινά, ὀπώρας ἀργυρίωι καθηλωμένας.
[39] Asterius, Hom. 4.2.1 μέρος μὲν ἥδεσθαι, τὸ δὲ λειπόμενον ἐν λύπῃ καὶ κατηφείᾳ διάγειν· τοῦτο γὰρ πολέμου μᾶλλον ἢ ἑορτῆς ἐξαίρετον.
[40] Ibid. 7.1 μανθάνουσιν ... παιδιὰν κατὰ τῶν νόμων καὶ τῆς ἀρχῆς ἧς ἐτάχθησαν φύλακες.
[41] Ibid. 9.5 ἆρα οὖς ... οὐ πάντα ... φάσματά ἐστιν τὰ ἀξιώματα ἀνυποστάντων ὀνείρων, τέρψαντα πρὸς ὀλίγον, εἶτα παραδραμόντα, ἀνθήσαντα καὶ μαρανθέντα;
[42] Schmid (1911), 43–44.

Epiphany congregation that they should not repeat what they did last Sunday, to prefer the Kalendae over the Christian mass. If he decided to do so by refuting Libanius' encomium, he did it with a publication of his sermon in mind, to reach a much wider audience: Amaseia is too far away from Antioch for a member of his congregation to have been able to hear Libanius speaking. Some might have read it, since speeches went into circulation – but so did sermons, and Asterius must have intended a quick publication of his text in order to attack and refute Libanius' defense of the Kalendae.[43]

Augustine on the Kalendae Ianuariae

We thus have a body of almost contemporary texts on the Kalendae that center on Antioch: Libanius' encomium of January 1, 392 or 393, addressed to his students; John Chrysostom's sermon that he performed on a January 1 between the years 387 and 398; and Asterius' homily of January 6, 400, with Asterius reacting to Libanius, and Libanius most probably reacting to John Chrysostom. Before entering into a discussion on what this means, I would like to add yet another sermon, the one preached by Augustine in Carthage during the Kalendae Ianuariae presumably of 404.[44]

Although small parts of this sermon have been known to scholars all along, the entire sermon has been found relatively recently in an overlooked manuscript in Germany. In 1990, the *Stadtbibliothek* (City Library) of Mainz published a new and thorough catalogue – so thorough and detailed that in the same year, François Dolbeau could announce the discovery, in a fifteenth-century manuscript of sermons that had belonged to the local Carthusian monastery, of no less then twenty-six sermons of

---

[43] Asterius might also echo Libanius' earlier progymnasma: Liban. *Prog.* 12.5.7 καὶ τὸ δέξασθαι φερόμενον παρώσαντα τὸν πέλας ἥδιστόν τε καὶ χαίρουσιν ἐνταῦθα καταπατούμενοι :: Asterius, *Hom.* 4.2 πάντα δὲ θορύβου γέμοντα καὶ ταραχῆς, καὶ τὸ πλῆθος πρὸς ἑαυτῷ εἰκῆ ὠθιζόμενον.

[44] *Sermo* 198augm = 26 Dolbeau. The new sermons are numbered either by insertion into the continuous list of the Maurist edition (198augm) or by their number in a list of all the sermons Dolbeau edited. This is confusing when using the edition of Dolbeau (1996) that gives the provisional number he assigned them in his first publication; for a concordance Dolbeau (1996), 643–644. On the year, Dolbeau (1996), 353. Dolbeau (1996), 353 assumed without discussion that Augustine was preaching on January 1. This is not a given, since the festival lasted four or five days, and the day hinges on 26.2. If we follow Libanius' ecphrasis (*Progym.* 12.5) as a guide, the *strenae* (δῶρα) were specific for January 1, playing the dice for January 2 and 3. Augustine's text confirms January 1 only if we connect *hodie* with the first future participle alone; or then Carthage had different customs, or (less likely) Augustine conflated the single acts. The day need not be Sunday, and in 404, Sunday was January 3; see Bickerman (1933), 61. If Augustine preached on January 1, African Christianity marked the New Year with an Office but did not participate in the city festival.

Augustine which were known either by title only from the bibliography Augustine's disciple Possidius had drawn up and from an inventory of the nearby library of the monastery of Lorsch, or from the few fragments contained in John the Deacon, Bede, and Florus.[45] Dolbeau immediately began to publish these texts, each with a short introduction, a full critical apparatus and some explanatory notes in the relevant periodicals, and collected these single publications into an edition that appeared in 1996.[46]

The sermon that is relevant here has the number 26 in Dolbeau's collection and 198*augm* in the all-inclusive list of Augustine's sermons.[47] Fragments of it had been already known: a very abridged version of its beginning was listed as Augustine's sermon 198 "On the Kalends of January" (which some scholars attributed to Caesarius of Arles[48]); from other small fragments of the same sermon, cited by Bede and John the Deacon, the *Patrologia* had reconstructed two further sermons, nos. 197 and 198A. It is now obvious that these pieces all belong to the one long sermon, without any doubt written by Augustine and performed in Carthage "for over two and a half hours," in Peter Brown's estimate.[49]

Augustine starts out from the immediate circumstances:

> We remind you, beloved ones, since we see that you have come together as if for a celebration and have assembled at this hour and in this place more numerous than usually, to recall again and again what you just have been singing.[50]

What they had been singing was Psalm 105 (106), from which Augustine cites just the final prayer of Israel: "Save us, o Lord our God, and gather us from among the heathen, to give thanks unto thy holy name."[51] The occasion was the festival of the Kalendae, to which Augustine immediately applies the Psalm verse:[52]

---

[45] See the announcement by Dolbeau (1990), 355–359, and the paper by Verbraken (1974).
[46] Dolbeau (1996).
[47] See the list in *Revue des Études Augustiniennes* 38 (1992), 389–391. The sermon in Dolbeau (1992) and (1996), no. 10, 345–417. An English translation in Hill (1997), 180–237; a critical edition with a German translation, notes, and rich introduction in Drobner (2010), 107–318.
[48] E.g. Meslin (1970), 103, 113.
[49] Brown (1996), 46. On the sermon and the Kalendae see especially Scheid (1998).
[50] *Admonemus caritatem vestram, quoniam vos quasi sollemniter convenisse conspicimus et ad hanc horam atque ad hunc locum solito frequentius congregatos, ut etiam atque etiam memineritis quod modo cantabatis.*
[51] *Salva nos, domine deus noster, et congrega nos de gentibus, ut confiteamur nomini sancto tuo*, Psalm 105 (106):47 = *Sermo* 26.1–2.
[52] *Sermo* 26.1: *Et modo si sollemnitas gentium quae fit hodierno die in laetitia saeculari atque carnali, in strepitu vanissimarum turpissimarumque cantionum, in celebratione ipsius falsae festivitatis, si ea quae agunt hodie gentes non vos delectant, congregamini de gentibus.*

> And if the festivities of the heathen that take place today in secular and carnal joyfulness, in the din of the most empty and reprehensible songs, in the celebration of the very wrong festival, if what the heathen do today does not please you: then you are gathered from among the heathen.

The contrast is stark: the Christians have gathered "as if" for their own celebration, singing their sacred psalms, whereas the pagans outside celebrate the wrong festival amidst the most irreverent songs.

In what follows, Augustine develops this contrast. He does so first by discouraging any Christian from participating in any form in the pagan entertainment:[53]

> Today you are about to exchange gifts with a heathen, to play dice with a heathen, to get yourself drunk with a heathen: how do you believe something different, hope something different, love something different? How can you sing without wincing: "Save us, o Lord our God, and gather us from among the heathen"?

As in John Chrysostom's Antioch and Asterius' Amaseia, Christians were tempted to participate in the celebration, from the most innocent gift-giving (*strenae*) to the most reprehensible drunkenness. It is alone the gift-giving that makes Augustine pause. To give is not bad in itself, and not to give might be reprehensible, but Christians replace the *strenae* with something better: "They give gifts, we give alms." Chrysostom had advised the same. Christians perform their own form of ritual gift-giving; to participate even in a detail of the pagan rite would be to fall into idolatry, to sacrifice, as Paul said, to demons, not to God.[54]

Another psalm verse brings up the second theme of the introduction, humility and fasting: "My clothing was sack cloth; I humbled my soul with fasting."[55] To give alms is one answer to the pagan ceremonies, to fast is the other. In a double sense that Augustine now explores, fasting can mean to abstain from the pagan amusement, but also to abstain from food during this day in order to extinguish any desire of participating in the pagan festival. In a remarkable passage, Augustine signals that he is aware how this will affect his congregation:[56] "The father wishes to fast, the son not, or

---

[53] Sermo 26.2: *acturus es hodie celebrationem strenarum cum pagano, lusurus alea cum pagano, inebriaturus es te cum pagano: quomodo aliud credis, aliud speras, aliud amas? quomodo salva fronte cantas: salva nos, domine deus noster, et congrega nos de gentibus?* On the relevance of this sentence for the exact date see above, n. 44.
[54] 1 Cor. 10:20, cited in para. 3 (line 48 Dolbeau).
[55] *Induebam me sacco et humiliabam in ieiunio animam meam*, Psalm 34 (35):13.
[56] Sermo 26.7 (line 166): *vult pater ieiunare, non vult filius, aut vult filius, non vult pater; aut vult maritus, non vult mulier, aut vult illa et ille non vult.*

the son wishes and the father not; or the husband wishes, not his wife, or she wishes and he does not." Some families contain both Christians and pagans, as Augustine's own family did. In other families, although fully Christian, not everybody was prepared to renounce the merriment of the festival, even if Augustine's congregation was not as given to absenteeism as the one of Asterius on Sunday, January 1, 400 – but then he was the famous guest speaker; and he does not tell us how full his church was, or how his crowd reacted to his demands.[57] The bishop's demand to refrain from participation introduced tensions into those very families. Augustine will confirm this later in the sermon: "I wish it were only the pagans that would cause us grief!" "So-called Christians" need to mend their ways as well.[58]

Thus, Augustine had several problems with the Kalendae. One is gift-giving. Although he does not underline the lack of reciprocity and the excesses, his criticism joins that of Asterius; but unlike the bishop of Amaseia, Augustine comes up with a positive reaction: *Da eleemosynam!*[59] Alms-giving was a continuous concern of Christian preachers, and his sermon on the Kalendae joins a large number of other sermons, and not just by Augustine, as Richard Finn showed, that promoted Christian alms-giving.[60] I will have to return to it.

The other one is the temptation of food, drink, and merriment: to this, he opposes fasting, not just in the figurative sense of abstention from the festival, but as literal abstention from food in an act of contrition. He admonishes his congregation to pray for those who participate in the festivities and at the same time to fast, in order to make the prayer acceptable to God.[61] Underlying all this is the theologian's identification of the festival as idolatrous, given to the pagan *daemonia*, and the conviction that to celebrate together with a pagan would turn a Christian into a pagan and idolater as well – we are far from Paul's relaxed view when in Corinth.[62] Although Augustine's admonition to his Christians to keep away from the pagans is less shrill than John Chrysostom's exhortation to do battle, the overall goal is the same. The harmony of a festival that unites "citizen with citizen, child with child, woman with woman," praised by

---

[57] On one such reaction, mirrored in sermon 2 Dolbeau (= *sermo* 359B in the traditional numbering), see Brown (2012), 340–341.
[58] *Sermo* 26.9 (line 201) *utinam solos paganos plangeremus! ... ut qui vocantur Christiani corrigi mereantur*.
[59] *Sermo* 26.8 (line 176).
[60] Finn (2006), 147–155; for alternatives in early Byzantine culture, see Caner (2013).
[61] *Sermo* 26.8 (line 175) *ora pro illo; ut autem oratio tua exaudiatur, ieiuna pro illo et da eleemosynam*.
[62] 1 Cor. 10:25–27.

Libanius, yields place to separation without compromise. If Augustine preached, as is most likely, in a year when January 1 was not a Sunday, the separation is even more pronounced:[63] as if it were a Sunday, the Carthaginian Christians marked the New Year with an office celebrated by the most famous bishop of Africa, and kept away from the city festival.

The rest of the sermon continues the same topic, but moves away from the immediate circumstances of the calendar to image worship and theurgy; this might reflect contemporary problems in Carthage as well, but does not concern us here.

Other Western Kalendae sermons

In the corpus of preserved Latin sermons, there are three more texts that concern the Kalendae. One is ascribed to Petrus Chrysologus, bishop of Ravenna from c.433 to his death in c.450, the second to Maximus, bishop of Turin (died between 408 and 423), the third has been transmitted either in the corpus of Ambrose of Milan (but does not fit his style or times) or again in that of Maximus (where it might fit somewhat better). Petrus' sermon is rather vague on the festival, the other two contain ritual details that resonate with what we know from the East: cross-dressing and masks in the genuine Maximus, dancing and excessive eating and drinking in pseudo-Ambrosius. All three sermons are again from the early fifth century (Petrus', the most vague, might also be the latest), and although they do not contribute new information, they fit into the chronological bracket we deal with, and its insistence on censuring the Christian participation in the Kalendae.

Contested Kalendae

The texts just discussed stretch over a period of less than fifteen years. Libanius' speech of 392 or 393 is answered by Asterius' sermon in 400, Augustine's followed in 403, the three other sermons are not much later, except the Chrysologus sermon; the most uncertain date is that of John Chrysostom's sermon which he must have given between 387 and 398. Above, I have argued that Libanius' speech is best understood as a reaction to John's attack on the festival, by setting its harmony and its other social benefits against John's declaration of war. Augustine shares only a few arguments with John Chrysostom, especially the transformation of *strenae*

---

[63] On the Sundays see Bickerman (1933), 61.

into the Christian form of gift-giving, alms-giving, and the radical refusal of participation, which Augustine turns into the command of fasting on a festival that was characterized by lavishness. Augustine's overall aim, however, is somewhat different: although he spoke on January 1, as did John and Libanius, the admonition to his Christians not to participate in the celebration is embedded in a more general discourse on how Christians distinguish themselves from pagans – by not repeating trivial rites current in the pagan world, such as kissing the columns at the church door, by not worshipping images, by not listening to the lure of theurgists (whom one senses were active in Augustine's Carthage) but accepting Christ as the mediator between this world and God.[64] Far from being concerned only with one festival, Augustine understood the debate to be part of his ongoing concern to give orthodox, Catholic Christianity much sharper borders and outlines than it had at present; the later Latin sermons follow this same agenda.

The proliferation of texts about the Kalendae Ianuariae at this point in time is remarkable, and it is difficult not to suspect a connection with Theodosius' letter to Albinus on the legal calendar of Rome that endorsed not only Easter, but also the Kalendae Ianuariae. This context explains the protest of two of the most prominent and outspoken bishops of the time, John Chrysostom and Augustine, and it explains the defense by the most famous contemporary pagan orator; Libanius must have been surprised and pleased by the decision of an emperor whom he knew to be not very friendly towards many other aspects of the Hellenic tradition, and who had just prohibited all sacrifices. The orator had already once defended threatened pagan institutions, in the *Pro Templis* of about 386, a speech that was formally addressed to the emperor but that he sent to leading pagans at the court, in the hope of obtaining their powerful backing for his cause.[65]

This scenario presumes that a wider application of Theodosius' text, written for Rome, happened shortly after its promulgation in Rome in August 389. This is very plausible. Presumably from the start the text was written for an empire-wide application, even if seemingly addressed to Rome only: imperial pronouncements can be general even then, and this is

---

[64] Kissing the columns is addressed in para. 10 (line 231) *imperiti pagani faciunt hoc, ut idolum tamquam idolum adorent, quomodo faciunt et vestri qui adorant columnas in ecclesia*, and repeated in para. 16 (line 381) *nos in Christo publice praedicamus, ne columnae vel lapides aedificiorum in locis sanctis vel etiam picturae adorentur*. See Brown (1998). Theurgists are implied in para. 37 (line 866) by the people who "want to purify themselves with rites" (*purgari sacris*) that involve demons and must be identical with *chaldaica aut magica sacra* in line 863.
[65] Petit (1951) dates *Pro Templis* to 386, see also Petit (1956), 507.

certainly how both Code Committees, the one under Theodosius II and the one under Justinian, read the text.[66] Theodosius strengthened the celebration of the Kalendae Ianuariae for the same reason that he strengthened the celebration of the imperial birthdays, accession days, and the birthdays of Rome and Constantinople by making them legal holidays: to protect festivals that promoted the unity of the empire and the symbolic presence of its rulers. The Kalendae Ianuariae with its *vota* on January 3 was crucial to this enterprise; and the festival could become acceptable to Christians as well as pagans, given that it was not necessarily addressed to a pagan divinity. This might explain why John Chrysostom and Augustine vehemently insist on the pagan character of the festival, even after the abolition of the city sacrifice of January 1, with an argumentation – "it is pagan because it is celebrated by pagans" – that is circular and did not really convince people, given the many Christians who participated. Christian orators therefore had to adduce other arguments, of a moralistic and ascetic order, to remain convincing.

Councils and emperors

Heathen Kalendae

In order to get a better understanding of the background of this debate, it is necessary to widen the perspective and to include the discussions that Christian leaders had at their synods and councils. The material is not always easily available: the most comprehensive collection still is the *Sacrorum Conciliorum Nova et Amplissima Collectio* which was initiated by the archbishop of Lucca, Gian Domenico Mansi (1692–1769) and published in a revised edition in Florence after 1759.[67] In the last decades, a few regional collections have appeared in good editions, but much remains to be done: Mansi's vast collection, far from reliable and without an index or a searchable electronic edition, still remains a major source.[68]

---

[66] Matthews (2000), 16–18, 65–70.
[67] On Mansi see Fabrizio Venni, in *Dizionario Biografico degli Italiani* 69 (2007); he left an autobiographical poem in Latin, *Carmen elegiacum de vita sua,* written 1762, published by Aldo Marsili (Lucca: Paccini, 1984). The acts of the early ecumenical councils have been republished by Eduard Schwartz and Johannes Straub after 1914, but they are less informative on the local contestation than those of the regional synods and councils: as far as we can see, it was only at regional synods and councils that the Kalendae were discussed.
[68] For the late antique councils in Gaul and Africa see Munier (1963) and de Clercq (1963) on Gaul, Munier (1974) on Africa; for the later councils of Gaul see Massen (1893) and Wermighoff (1906/1908).

Contested festivals in the fourth century

When compared to the discussion we just witnessed, the documentation in West and East is late. In the Latin West, the documentation starts either with a council in Tours in 567 or a synod in Autun that is dated only between 561 and 605. Canon 1 of the Autun proceedings prohibited masks and *strenae* at the festival.[69] In the prolix canon 23 of the Council of Tours, the assembled bishops more generally censured the Kalendae as the festival of a pagan god whom they then debunked with an euhemeristic argument: "Janus was a pagan man, a king, but he could not be a god."[70] In the East, the key text is canon 62 of the council in Trullo in 692.[71] The council cracked down on a wide variety of entertainments that were perceived as pagan, including "the so-called Kalendae and also the so-called *vota* and the so-called Brumalia, as well as the feast that is celebrated on the first day of the month of March." The distinction between Kalendae and *vota* must mean that the Byzantine bishops, somewhat unusually and in contrast to their colleagues in Merovingian France, perceived the merriment of January 1 as distinct from that of January 3, not as part of a larger festival cycle that occupied the first four or five days of the year. Most of the offending behavior – public dancing, cross-dressing, the wearing of masks – was already chastised in Asterius' homily almost two hundred years before.

But there is a piece of information on such customs that might attest to them at the same epoch or even earlier, either in then Suebian Galicia or in the Byzantine East, or both. The report of the Second Council of Braga on June 1, 572 is followed by a collection of canons ascribed to Martin, metropolitan bishop of Braga in Galicia, and addressed to bishop Nitigisius, the metropolitan of the neighboring church province of Lugo; the canons claims to be translations from the Oriental Fathers, although some have no parallels in the East, and there is no reasonable doubt about the authorship of Martin.[72] Canon 73 deals with the Kalendae:[73]

> It is prohibited to celebrate the day of the Kalendae and to do nothing during a pagan leisure period, or to crown one's house with laurel and green boughs: this entire behavior is pagan.

---

[69] Canon 1: *Non licet kalendis Ianuarii vetulo aut cervolo facere vel streneas diabolicas observare, sed in ipsa die sic omnia beneficia tribuantur, sicut et reliquis diebus.* Massen (1893), 179; de Clercq (1963), 265.

[70] Canon 23: *Enimvero quoniam cognovimus nonnullos inveniri sequipedas erroris antiqui, qui Kalendas Ianuarii colunt, cum Ianus homo gentilis fuerit, rex quidem, sed esse deus non potuit: quisquis ergo unum Deum Patrem regnantem cum Filio et Spiritu Sancto credit, non potest integer Christianus dici, qui super hoc aliqua de gentilitate custodit.* Massen (1893), 133; De Clercq (1963), 191.

[71] See Nedungatt and Featherstone (1995), 142–144.   [72] See Barlow (1950), 84–87, 123–144.

[73] *Non liceat agere diem Kalendarum et otiis vacare gentilibus neque lauro aut viriditate arborum cingere domos. omnis haec observatio paganissima est.* See Barlow (1950), 123–144.

The text finds no earlier correspondence in any Eastern canon; but Martin's claim might still be correct. As importantly, these canons must have been translated – and, as the translator insists, more correctly than in earlier translations (that are lost to us) – because they were seen as relevant for their communities by the local bishops.[74] His one preserved sermon, *De correctione rusticorum*, helps to bolster this claim. Martin describes as current practice among his own peasants in Braga "to observe the Vulcanalia and Kalendae, to adorn the table and to put laurel out" (*Vulcanalia et Kalendas observare, mensas ornare, et lauros ponere*), and disapproves of it as a regress into pure paganism and idolatry.[75] The combination of the translated canon and the detail from the sermon point to a real problem in the local churches, even if sometimes such details in a sermon might be shaped by the learned preacher's wider reading. Our text comes barely a decade after the council of Tours, but precedes the council in Trullo by a century; if we believe the claim of a Greek origin for the canon, the bishops in Trullo recycled earlier misgivings that in the past had as little effect as their own canon would have in the future.[76]

The Gallic bishops assembled in 567 in a council in Tours were in turn aware that their resistance to the Kalendae had a long history. Canon 18 "On Fasting" treats the "ancient custom, begun by the monks" (*antiqua a monachis instituta*) and gives as its most complex application the customs in the festival period between Christmas and Epiphany that go back to *patres nostri*:

> Every day between Christmas and Epiphany is a festival day, and they all will have banquets except during those three days where our ancestors, to stamp out the pagan habit, decided to have private offices during the Kalendae Ianuariae – to sing in the church and at the eighth hour celebrate the Mass of Circumcision to God on the very first day of January.[77]

---

[74] Barlow (1950), 87: "It must be granted that St. Martin would have selected canons which were still applicable in his time and which he felt would answer specific problems."

[75] De corr. 16, with the conclusion *ecce ista omnia post abrenuntiationem diaboli, post baptismum facitis et, ad culturam daemonum et ad mala idolorum opera redeuntes, fidem vestram transistis et pactum quod fecistis cum deo disrupistis* ("look, you do all this after your renunciation of the devil and your baptism, and you have transgressed on your faith and rescinded the pact you made with God when you turned back to the worship of demons and the bad acts of idols"). There is no good reason to assume that the sermon was influenced by Augustine's on the Kalendae, as scholars believed before the Mainz manuscript was published.

[76] See Kaldellis (2011), who argues that the authors of the Trullo canon were radical conservatives out of touch with reality.

[77] Concilium Turonense, *Canon* 18 = de Clerq (1963) 182: *Quia inter natale Domini et Epifania omni die festivitates sunt, idemque prandebunt excepto triduum illud quod at calcandam gentilium consuetudinem patres nostri statuerunt privatas in Kalendis Ianuariis fieri letanias, ut in ecclesia psalletur et ora octava in ipsis Kalendis circumcissionis missa Deo propitio celebretur* (in the Western Church, January 1 was also the day of Christ's circumcision); see also Massen (1893) 126.

Contested festivals in the fourth century 149

Isidore of Seville confirms this custom and its reason in his treatise *On Church Offices*: "The Church began fasting during the Kalends of January, because of the pagan error."[78] He adds an ample description of the rituals performed by the pagans that ranges from masks to ecstatic dancing and reiterates that the church leaders instituted a world-wide fast "throughout all the churches" against the sin of this debauchery; the claim that this fasting was adopted by all the churches confirms the hostility of all the different Christian groups in East and West.[79] The Fourth Council of Toledo, held in 633 when Isidore was still in office, concurs and gives details of what was allowed: "fish and cabbage, like during Lent . . .; some do not drink wine."[80] The insistence on this fast suggests that its cause, the ubiquity of the rites of the Kalendae Ianuariae, had not yet disappeared, confirming the complaint of Martin of Braga, Nitigisius of Lugo, or their colleagues in Tours, Autun, and Byzantium.[81] We cannot know whether

---

[78] Isidore, *De ecclesiasticis officiis* 1.41 (PL 83.774D): *Ieiunium Kalendarum Ianuariarum propter errorem gentilitatis instituit Ecclesia. Ianus enim quidam princeps paganorum fuit, a quo nomen mensis Januarii nuncupatur, quem imperiti homines veluti deum colentes in religione honoris posteris tradiderunt, diemque ipsum scenis et luxuriae sacraverunt.* "The Church began fasting during the Kalends of January, because of the pagan error. Janus was a prince of the heathen after whom the month January is named; unenlightened people worshiped him like a god, transmitted it as religious form of honor to posterity and sanctified it as a day of spectacles and luxury."

[79] Ibid. 2–3 (775AB): *Tunc enim miseri homines, et quod peius est, etiam fideles, sumentes species monstruosas, in ferarum habitu tranformantur: alii, femineo gestu demutati, virilem vultum effeminant; nonnulli etiam de fanatica adhuc consuetudine quibusdam ipso die observationum auguriis profanantur; perstrepunt omnia saltantium pedibus, tripudiantium plausibus, quodque est turpius nefas, nexis inter se utriusque sexus choris, inops animi, furens vino, turba miscetur. proinde ergo sancti patres considerantes maximam partem generis humani eodem die huiusmodi sacrilegiis ac luxuriis inservire, statuerunt in universo mundo per omnes ecclesias publicum ieiunium, per quod agnoscerent homines in tantum se prave agere, ut pro eorum peccatis necesse esset omnibus ecclesiis ieiunare.*

"At that time pitiable people and, much worse, even believers adopted monstrous shapes and turned into the forms of animals; others changed themselves through feminine behavior and emasculated their manly appearance; some polluted themselves also with the still-extant pagan custom of observing auguries on this very day. Everything resounds from the feet of the dancers, the clapping of the gambolers; and what is much worse they combine choruses of both genders and mix as a crowd that has lost its mind and raves in drunkenness. Therefore when our Sacred Fathers realized that a very large part of humanity was on the same day paying service to sacrilege and debauchery, they decreed general fasting in the entire world and throughout all churches, through which humanity should gain the insight that they were behaving so badly, that it was necessary in all churches to fast for their sins."

[80] Quartum Concilium Toletanum, canon 11: *Kalendis Ianuariis, quae propter errorem gentilitatis aguntur . . . etiam praeter piscem et olus sicut in illis XL diebus ceteris carnibus abstinetur et a quibusdam etiam nec vinum bibitur.*

[81] Or, for that matter, the prohibitions on which, in the early eleventh century, Burchard, bishop of Worms 1000–1025, insisted in his collection of canonical law, the *Decretum*: see in the catalog of short questions a bishop asks when opening a synod in book 1.94 question 50 (*PL* 140.577D) and the lengthy description in book 10 (*De incantatoribus et auguribus*), 35 and 36 (*PL* 140.835D) and finally several entries in book 19 (*Corrector*), *PL* 140.960D–961A and 965D = Wasserschleben (1851), 643 no. 53a; 649 no. 87. An English translation: Shinners (2007), 442–456.

this insistence on fasting during the Kalendae Ianuariae, confined to the West and for the first time attested in Augustine's sermon, goes back to an invention of the bishop of Hippo (Isidore's ascription to *nostri Sancti Patres* would certainly fit) or whether it pre-dates Augustine as a radical, ascetic, and monastic answer to the pagan festivities. What is clear, on the other hand, is that Christians perceived fasting as somber and thus kept it strictly away from their own joyous festivals.[82]

However we answer this last question, we perceive two spikes of Church resistance against the Kalendae, the first in several sermons in East and West between *c*.390 and *c*.420, the second in canons of regional synods between Autun (after 561) and Tours (567) in the West and Trullo (692) in the East, with Martin of Braga referring to an Eastern canon pre-dating Trullo but also presumably applying it to the Galician church; a few other existing festivals – Vota, Brumalia, and Matronalia in the East, Vulcanalia in the West – were attacked as pagan as well.

I read the first spike as an episcopal reaction to Theodosius' official endorsement of the Kalendae in Summer 389. The second spike, at least in its Western version, ties in with our earlier observation that the Visigoth versions of Theodosius' law, Alaric's *Breviarium* of 506 and the *Liber Iudiciorum* of about 563, omitted the Kalendae Ianuariae from their list of legal holidays.[83] The Visigoth kings formulated their law codes with the approbation and collaboration of the Church, be it Arian or Catholic: before the Arian Visigoths had turned Catholic, Alaric assembled his collection *adhibitis sacerdotibus ac nobilibus viris*, "with the collaboration of priests and noblemen" of Southern Gaul, and subjected the collection to the approval of the bishops and leading men of his kingdom, *venerabilium episcoporum vel electorum provincialium nostrorum adsensus*; after the conversion to Catholicism, Recesswint presented the *Liber* to the Council of Toledo of 653 and expected the bishop's approval.[84] It was the bishops of the Visigoth kingdom who deleted the Kalendae from Theodosius' list of legal holidays, despite its popularity among the locals.

This is confirmed by laws of the Burgundian kings that were codified shortly before Alaric's *Breviarium*, between 500 and 506. In their title on

---

[82] Dihle (1992), 326–327, with a list of Christian texts, 327 n. 28.
[83] Interpretatio of *CTh* 2.8.19 and *Liber iudiciorum* (*Lex Visigothorum*) 2.1.12, in Zeumer (1902), 69–70; see Chapter 3, nn. 77 and 79.
[84] Alaric: see his dedicatory letter, edited in Zeumer (1902), 465f., and in Mommsen's *Prolegomena* to *CTh* (Berlin: Weidmann, 1905), xxxiii; on the procedure Gaudemet (1965), 10. King Recesswint: Zeumer (1902), 472; similarly, king Erwic presented his revision to the Council of Toledo of 681, Zeumer (1902), 475.

legal actions, they show a similarly purely Christian list of legal holidays: legal action is prohibited "during the grain and wine harvest holidays, the fifteen days of Easter and the seven of Christmas, also on all Sundays and the days of Epiphany and Pentecost."[85] Shortly before Alaric's code was written down, the Burgundian law-givers came to the same conclusion as those of Alaric, to omit the "pagan" Kalendae: the pressure of the bishops is obvious. We do not know whether the Suevian rulers of Galicia did the same; we saw the opposition of their bishops, but their rule might not have lasted long enough to motivate a king to create a code of law.

Ironically enough, the Christian rejection of the Kalendae as a pagan relic had a lasting impact on the reception of Theodosius' law by the "barbarian" Germanic kings, while the Christian Byzantine emperors, starting with Theodosius I, all turned a deaf ear to the complaints of their bishops. The collapse of the legal traditions in the West opened an occasion for the learned bishops to influence the law, and the conquering upstarts proved to be more obedient to the Church than the true Romans: after all, being conquerors and usurpers, they knew about the need for powerful native allies.[86]

But there is a wider background of fourth-century Christian resistance to pagan festivals, to which we have to turn now.

The fight of the African church against pagan festivals

The bishops who attacked traditional pagan festivals had three aims, one more ambitious than the other two. First, they prohibited the participation of Christians together with pagans in pagan city festivals; second, they banned the adoption and celebration of such festivals by Christians even when only Christians were present; third, and most ambitiously, they wanted to eradicate all these traces of paganism from the face of the world. This last goal is relatively new and a radical consequence of the

---

[85] *Lex Romana Burgundionum* (500–506 CE), ed. Rudolph von Salis, MGH Leges: Leges nationum Germanicarum 2.1 (Hannover: Hahn, 1892), 136, tit. 11.5: *Messinis vero feriis et vindimialibus, paschalibus etiam xv diebus et natalis domini septem, dominicis etiam diebus ceterisque epiphaniae et quinquagissime nulla prorsus sunt litigia commovenda.* "No legal action can be set in motion during the grain and wine harvest holidays, the fifteen days of Easter and the seven of Christmas, also on all Sundays and the days of Epiphany and Pentecost."

[86] On the collapse of the law in the West see already the complaint of Valentinian III in 451 on the state of the law in Italy, *Novellae Valentinianae* 32.6 *causidicos et iudices defuisse hodieque gnaros iuris et legum aut raro aut minime repperiri*, "advocates and judges are lacking, and experts of jurisprudence and the laws are found rarely today or not at all." It must have been worse in Gaul and Spain, overrun by German conquerors.

new status of the church after Constantine, the first two pre-date Constantine, as Tertullian demonstrates. In his *De idololatria,* he censured both the participation of Christians in popular pagan festivals, Saturnalia and Kalendae Ianuariae, and the adoption by Christians of *Saturnalia et Ianuariae et Brumae et Matronales,* private festivals celebrated in the single households with banquets and presents but, presumably, often without pagan participation.[87]

The censure of Tertullian and other Christian leaders did not help much, it seems. A century later, in 304 or 308, the council of Eliberi in Spain promulgated several canons against the participation of Christians in pagan festivals, among other things forbidding any Christian "to walk like a pagan up to the image of Jupiter on the Capitol in order to sacrifice and to view the image."[88] With this formulation, the bishops take a wider aim than just at the Kalendae with their processions and sacrifices to Jupiter Optimus Maximus, both in Rome and in any *colonia*. But it certainly made this central act of the Kalendae Ianuariae impossible – and a similar preoccupation must be behind the quiet refusal of Constantine ever to perform the New Year sacrifice to Jupiter Optimus Maximus in Rome.[89] Things were not much different in the East. In 314 the council of Ancyra not only prohibited Christian participation in pagan sacrifices, but forbade Christians to sit together with pagans during festive banquets, even if they would bring along their own food and not eat from sacrificial meat; this is much less open-minded than Paul's recommendations to the Corinthians.[90] The council of Laodikeia in 364 repeated the prohibition: "A Christian may not celebrate a festival together with pagans and participate in their godlessness."[91]

Most of the discussions surrounding these prohibitions are lost; canon 18 of the synod of Tours, discussed earlier in this chapter, is unusually prolix in explaining the reasons for fasting during the Kalendae Ianuariae from the rejection of pagan feasting "by our fathers."[92] There is a somewhat more elaborate documentation for early fifth-century Africa, thanks to a collection of local and regional councils held in 419 under Aurelius, the

---

[87] *De idololatria* 14.4 and 7.
[88] Concilium Eliberitanum, can. 59 (Mansi 2.15): *prohibendum ne quis Christianus ut gentilis ad idolum Capitolii causa sacrificandi ascendat et videat.*
[89] See Fraschetti (1999), 7–31.
[90] Ancara, Canon 7 (Mansi 2.516): *de iis qui in festo ethnico in loco gentilibus deputato convivati sunt et proprios cibos attulerunt et comederunt,* "on those who in a pagan festival sit banqueted in a place reserved for pagans but have brought their own food and eaten it."
[91] Canon 39 (Mansi 2.570) *non oportet cum gentibus festum agere et eorum impietati communicare.*
[92] Concilium Turonense, *Canon* 18 = de Clerq (1963), 182.

Contested festivals in the fourth century 153

powerful and long-serving bishop of Carthage, in office from 391 to his death around 430.[93] Although the problem of the Donatists and the organization of the church took up most of the discussion of the assembled bishops, a few times they also discussed what to do about the remnants of paganism.

The council of Carthage on June 16, 401 discussed and decided on a long list of requests to the emperors. Two concern paganism. Canon 58 dealt with statues and temples and asked the emperors to decree that the statues throughout the province should be "cut away" and to destroy all "temples that had no ornamental function since they were built on the countryside or in a hidden spot" in the cities together with the images.[94] Canon 60 dealt with festivals, banquets, and dances:

> One has also to petition the following: since in many places, there are still banquets for the gods that contravene imperial prohibitions and are based on pagan error, so that Christians are still forced by pagans to participate (which is a new persecution in the era of the Christian emperors), they should prohibit this and punish it with a fine on the cities and the estates, especially since they do not hesitate to celebrate in this way even the birthdays of the martyrs, even in sacred places. On these days also (to say this makes us feel ashamed), they perform most scandalous dances in city quarters and on the streets: their lawless lasciviousness attacks the honor of matrons and the feelings of uncounted women who piously came to participate in this most holy day and almost forbids access to holy religion.[95]

Christians did not just participate in pagan festivals, they imported pagan ritual forms into the festivals that were held at the graves of their martyrs and in their churches: the coexistence of different forms of religion created influences from both sides, and "syncretism" would remain an ongoing

---

[93] The texts collected in Munier (1974).
[94] Canon 58 (Mansi 3.766): *Instant etiam aliae necessitates religiosis imperatoribus postulandae, ut reliquias idolorum per omnem Africam iubeant penitus amputari; nam plerisque in locis maritimis atque possessionibus diversis adhuc erroris istius iniquitas viget. ut praecipiantur et ipsas deleri et templa eorum, quae in agris vel in locis abditis constituta nullo ornamento sunt iubeantur omnino destrui.*

"Also other urgent causes suggest asking the most pious emperors to order that the remnants of idols throughout Africa should be removed, since in several coastal regions and private estates the wrongness of this error still persists. They should order these remnants to be removed and command their temples, which have no ornamental function since they were built on the countryside or in a hidden spot, to be destroyed."

[95] Canon 60 (Mansi 3.766): *illud etiam petendum, ut quoniam contra praecepta divina convivia multis in locis exercentur, quae ab errore gentili attracta sunt, ita ut nunc a paganis Christiani ad haec celebranda cogantur; ex qua re temporibus Christianorum imperatorum persecutio altera fieri occulte videatur: vetari talia iubeant et de civitatibus et de possessionibus imposita poena prohibere: maxime cum etiam in natalibus beatissimorum martyrum per nonnullas civitates et in ipsis locis sacris talia committere non reformident. quibus diebus etiam, quos pudoris est dicere, saltationes sceleratissimas per vicos et plateas exerceant, ut matronalis honor et innumerabilium feminarum pudor devote venientium ad sacratissimum diem iniuriis lascivientibus appetatur; ut etiam ipsius sanctae religionis pene fugiatur accessus.*

concern of the church for many centuries.[96] Often enough, the necessity to articulate oneself as part of an urban community was stronger than the resistance of those bishops who were drawing hard and fast borderlines between Christians and pagans, as they did also between true Christians and heretics, or between Christians and Jews.

The two petitions were part of a larger bundle of six requests to the emperor, two on questions of episcopal jurisdiction, two more on other problems raised by a society that remained pagan in many aspects of its life: a request to ban spectacles on Sundays, on martyrs' holidays, and at Easter, when the circus proved more attractive than the church; and another request not to force converted actors to act again. The emperor addressed must have been Honorius; and since the assembly had already decided to send envoys to the bishops of Milan and Rome on a problem with the Donatists, the same envoys were to carry these petitions to the imperial court.[97] Two months later, at a meeting in Carthage on September 9, 401, the bishops added the further petition that "all remnants of idolatry should be absolutely destroyed, not only in images but also those in specific places such as groves and trees"[98] – a manifestly more radical request than the earlier one that had only asked for the destruction of images and outlying temples that could contribute nothing to the beauty of a city.

Two years earlier, two rescripts from Honorius to the proconsul of Africa had already addressed similar questions, but in a somewhat more open-minded way than what the bishops wanted. Both are dated August 20, 399; they are either two answers to earlier requests by the African bishops signed on the same day or parts of a more complex answer that the editors of the Theodosian Code split into two laws. One of them prohibits the destruction of temples, provided they were "empty of illicit things," forbids any attempt at sacrifice, and orders the removal of the images without causing an uproar.[99] The order to preserve temples concurs

---

[96] The fight of the Catholic church against imports from pre-conversion native religions is where the term originated. On the problems see Berner (1979).
[97] At the council of August 24, 403, the envoys to Italy reported back, Mansi 3.787.
[98] Canon 84 (Mansi 3.784): *ut reliquiae idololatriae non solum in simulacris sed et in quibuscumque locis vel lucis vel arboribus omni modo deleantur.* The clumsy syntax thus is theirs.
[99] CTh 16.10.18 *Imperatores Honorius et Arcadius Augusti Apollodoro proconsuli Africae. Aedes illicitis rebus vacuas nostrarum beneficio sanctionum ne quis conetur evertere. Decernimus enim, ut aedificiorum quidem sit integer status, si quis vero in sacrificio fuerit deprehensus, in eum legibus vindicetur, depositis sub officio idolis disceptatione habita, quibus etiam nunc patuerit cultum vanae superstitionis impendi.* "No man by the benefit of our sanctions shall attempt to destroy temples which are empty of illicit things. For we decree that the condition of the buildings shall remain unimpaired. But if any person should be apprehended while performing a sacrifice, he shall be punished according to the laws, and idols shall be taken down under the direction of the governor's staff after an investigation has been

Contested festivals in the fourth century

with an earlier rescript of Theodosius I to the military commander of Osroene on a specific temple, presumably in Edessa: it should be left open "for the common use of the people," and "all celebrations of festivities" (*omni votorum celebritate servata*) should be respected as long as nobody performed a sacrifice.[100] Far from being radical, the emperor – to whom Libanius at about the same time had addressed his oration "For the Temples" – insisted on the preservation of traditional festivals together with their settings, the temples, now without idolatrous images and burning animal parts. This goes together with the compromise for which Libanius was praising Theodosius in his "For the Temples," to allow the burning of incense on the altars, as long as this would not lead to sacrifice.[101] The compromise is rather curious since it works only if incense burning is not viewed as an act of worship for a specific divinity, which would be idolatry, but as a general sign of festivity.

The other rescript also insists on the celebration of public festivals, as long as they do not contain sacrifices:[102]

> Just as we have already abolished profane rites by a salutary law, so we do not allow the festal assemblies of citizens and the common pleasure of all to be abolished. Hence we decree that, according to ancient custom, amusements shall be furnished to the people, but without any sacrifice or any accursed superstition, and they shall be allowed to attend festal banquets whenever public desire so demands.

---

held, since it is evident that even now the worship of a vain superstition is paid to the idols." (Translation after Pharr 1952.)

[100] *CTh* 16.10.8 (November 30, 382). The reception of this very specific text in the Code must mean that the editors regarded it as still relevant. The relevant text:

Aedem olim frequentiae dedicatam coetui et iam populo quoque communem, in qua simulacra feruntur posita artis pretio quam divinitate metienda iugiter patere publici consilii auctoritate decernimus . . . ut conventu urbis et frequenti coetu videatur, experientia tua omni votorum celebritate servata auctoritate nostri ita patere templum permittat oraculi, ne illic prohibitorum usus sacrificiorum huius occasione aditus permissus esse credatur.

"We decree that the temple shall continually be open that was formerly dedicated to the meeting of throngs of people and now still serves for the common use of the people, and in which images are reported to have been placed which must be measured by the value of their art rather than by their divinity . . . In order that this temple might be seen by the assembled city population and by frequent crowds, your experience shall preserve all celebrations of festivities, by the authority of our own divine imperial response you shall permit the temple to be open, but in such a way that the performance of sacrifices forbidden therein may not be thought to be permitted under the pretext of such access to the temple." (Translation after Pharr 1952.)

[101] Liban. *Or.* 30.7.

[102] *CTh* 16.10.17 = *CJ* 1.11.4: *Idem A(ugusti) Apollodoro proconsuli Africae. Ut profanos ritus iam salubri lege submovimus, ita festos conventus civium et communem omnium laetitiam non patimur submoveri. Unde absque ullo sacrificio atque ulla superstitione damnabili exhiberi populo voluptates secundum veterem consuetudinem, iniri etiam festa convivia, si quando exigunt publica vota, decernimus.* (Translation after Pharr 1952.)

This is a clear rejection of the episcopal request to prohibit festivals, and it takes no position on the question whether pagans and Christians should be allowed to celebrate together; sacrifices are prohibited, and this removes the one theologically cogent argument against public festivities. Just as in Edessa twenty years earlier, tradition (*vetus consuetudo*) and public desire (*vota*) are still the guidelines for the emperor. And they would remain so: this very same decree was reproduced also in the Justinian Code (*CJ* 1.11.4).

The request for the abolition of rural sanctuaries, on the other hand, was already met in 399 by a rescript of Arcadius to his praetorian prefect Eutychianos, which ordered the quiet and discreet destruction of all temples on the countryside in order to remove the material basis for superstition.[103] It looks as if the bishops at their meeting of June 401 were not yet aware of this, but were informed of it not much later and asked at their September meeting also for the abolition of sacred groves and trees.

Their decision in favor of new petitions at the June meeting shows how unhappy the bishops were with the earlier imperial answers, and that they decided not to give up. It seems to have worked out. Six years later, on November 25, 407 Honorius signed a constitution that covered both the Donatist question and the problems of paganism.[104] A part of it was adapted in the Theodosian Code as a text on images and temples that corrected older policies, another part as a text on the Donatists. This must be the somewhat belated imperial reaction to the requests of June and September 401 rather than to later petitions of a similar content. A comparison of the episcopal requests and the imperial rescripts shows how far the emperor was willing to give in to the bishops of Africa and with it to set new law for the empire.

On June 16, 401, the bishops had asked for the removal of all *idola*, pagan cult statues, that were still left in remote areas along the coast and on the estates (*reliquias idolorum per omnem Africam iubeant penitus amputari*), and to destroy the shrines in these areas, since they had not even an aesthetic function (*templa eorum, quae in agris vel in locis abditis constituta nullo ornamento sunt iubeantur omnino destrui*). Honorius ordered his praetorian prefect to remove images that "received or still receive pagan cult" (*simulacra ... quae aliquem ritum vel acceperunt vel accipiunt*

---

[103] *CTh* 16.10.16 *Impp. Arcadius et Honorius a(ugusti) ad Eutychianum praefectum praetorio. Si qua in agris templa sunt, sine turba ac tumultu diruantur. His enim deiectis atque sublatis omnis superstitioni materia consumetur.*

[104] *Const. Sirm.* 12; see *CTh* 16.10.19 on images and temples, and 16.5.43 on the Donatists. See Matthews (2000), 147–151 for a close analysis of the relationship among the three texts.

paganorum), but to preserve the temple buildings themselves "in cities and towns and outside towns" (*aedificia ipsa templorum, quae in civitatibus vel oppidis vel extra oppida sunt*); and to destroy altars and shrines (*templa*) on private estates, but to preserve the temples on imperial estates for common use, provided that they were not used for sacrifices. He also offered a ruling on public banquets that sounds deliberately ambiguous but nevertheless points to a conflict between imperial and ecclesiastical powers:

> It is entirely prohibited to hold banquets or to perform any celebration in honor of a sacrilegious rite in a polluted place. We confer upon the bishops of these places the right of ecclesiastical execution to prohibit these very things; and we impose upon the judges a fine of twenty gold pounds, and the same upon their office staff, if these rulings should be neglected by their connivance.[105]

The emperor did not prohibit every public festival and banquet, but only those that were "honoring sacrilegious rites" and were connected with "polluted places." It is obvious that the former term means the forbidden sacrifices, while the latter must refer to pagan temples that still contained divine images: in the imperial letters of the late fourth and early fifth century, *funestus* is associated with terribly wrong religion or politics.[106] Thus, the emperor did not abolish or correct earlier rulings, although his language was more emotional and much less clear than in the letter to the proconsul of Africa of August 20, 399; but by handing over the power to prohibit such actions to the local bishops and threatening non-complying judges with heavy fines, the emperor gave the bishops a certain latitude to decide for themselves how far they would want to go. This explains why only some bishops connected the Kalendae with the pagan god Janus (as the bishops assembled in Tours or Seville had done) and stressed the cross-dressing and lewd dances in the hope of remaining inside the framework of the law when trying to outlaw the Kalendae. It also shows how much resistance the bishops met even among the local functionaries in their repression of paganism. Overall, in the question of public festivals the emperor did not surrender to the African bishops. But they had at least the

---

[105] *CTh* 16.10.19: *Non liceat omnino in honorem sacrilegi ritus funestioribus locis exercere convivia vel quicquam sollemnitatis agitare. Episcopis quoque locorum haec ipsa prohibendi ecclesiasticae manus tribuimus facultatem; iudices autem viginti librarum auri poena constringimus et pari forma officia eorum, si haec eorum fuerint dissimulatione neglecta.*

[106] *CTh* 16.16.7 (Theodosius II, a. 413): *nefarios eunomianorum coetus ac funesta conventicula*; 16.5.19 (Theodosius I, a. 389): *sub cuiuslibet haeresis sive erroris nomine constituti ex funestis conciliabulis*; 15.14.9 (Honorius, 398): *funestorum tantum consulum nomina iubemus aboleri* (the consuls elected by the tyrant Eugenius).

satisfaction that on June 7, 408, a week before the bishops met at their council of June 16, the proconsul Porphyrius had the imperial text posted on the forum of Carthage as part of his own proconsular edict.[107] Which does not mean that they gave up: in that very meeting they reconfirmed the mandate of Fortunatius for an embassy *contra paganos et haereticos*.

Thanks to the way in which legal documents and the acts of the African councils under bishop Aurelius intersect, we are able to see the interplay of forces and some of the moves on both sides – the relentless pressure of the bishops on the emperor's court and the way the emperors did not yield much real territory but reacted mostly with symbolic and rhetorical gestures. Given this interplay, it becomes much more likely that the sermons against the Kalendae after 389 really were triggered by Theodosius' legitimization of the Kalendae that went against the church agenda: turning them into a legal holiday period assured the city-wide participation in the revelries of pagans, Christians, and Jews and blurred the borderlines the bishops had been trying hard to draw for at least a century.

The same interplay, but with a different outcome, has been visible in the reception of Theodosius' law among the Burgundian and Wisigothic kings of Gaul and Spain: there too the acts of the council and a sermon, this time that of Martin of Braga, show the continuous pressure of the bishops against the pagan remnant which they consider the Kalendae Ianuariae to be. Here, they succeeded, at least partially: the official law calendar omitted the Kalendae Ianuariae; private customs, however, were not eradicated easily.[108]

What was at stake for either side? For the more radical bishops, it was the purity of their faith and their agenda, articulated already at the first Nicene Council, to enforce strong definitions of Christianity in the face of all other religions. This came at the price of a sharp separation between pagans, Christians, and Jews inside the same community, be it town, province, or

---

[107] This is the regular way of publication, see Matthews (2000), 186. On the council of June 16, 408, see Mansi 3.810.

[108] For some instances of survival of the Kalendae, see Brown (1996), 46 (East), 81 (Britons), 102 (Christianization in Spain). In the early eleventh century, the *Decretum* of Burchard of Worms still attests to observations of the Kalendae: general remarks in 1.94 (*PL* 140.577D: *est aliquis qui in Kalend. Ianuarii aliquid fecerat, quod a paganis inventum est*, "Is there someone who did something … that the heathens invented?"); 10.15–16 (PL 140.835D), with a list of rites at the Kalendae (greeneries, banquets, dancing on the streets); 19 (*PL* 140.960CD = Wasserschleben 1851, 643 no. 53a) with another list that combines traditional rites (banquets, dancing on the streets) with unusual (and thus more recent?) divination rites; *ibid*. (*PL* 140.965B = Wasserschleben 1851, 649 no. 87), the traditional Western masks (*cervulus aut vetula* [*vegula* mss, *in vehiculo* coni. Wasserschleben]), on which see Meslin (1970), 81–83 and often.

empire. The bishops were aware of this: we saw how Augustine pressed for a "pure" celebration of the Kalendae Ianuariae although he fully realized that he was creating rifts even within single families. But clear boundaries were more important, and an earlier affair, fought in 395 by the then still priest of Hippo, highlights how important these clear boundaries were to him.

For decades already, the Christians of Hippo had celebrated a festival for their local saint, Leontius, in a celebration that was happy, relaxed, and rather alcoholic; tellingly, the locals called it *Laetitia*. Augustine tried to prohibit it, against the vociferous and tenacious resistance of many parishioners, and succeeded only after a prolonged struggle around Ascension of 395, with two sermons (the first not very well attended) and a long public discussion. He finally convinced the opponents with the argument that these banquets were a compromise between the Church and the needs of the recently converted Christian masses for entertainment; it was now time to do away with what on all accounts was still paganism; the *ecclesiae transmarinae*, those in Italy or the East, had done so long ago. One can reasonably doubt both Augustine's reference to less backward churches and his reconstruction of Christian ritual innovation after Constantine: what matters is his perception, shared with other African bishops, that certain features of Christian public festivals were pagan and needed to be eliminated.[109]

For the emperors, such a demarcation was unacceptable. The emperor stood for the harmony, peace, and happiness of all inhabitants of the empire, Christians, pagans, and Jews alike. Actions against pagan monuments were also actions against the tradition of the empire and would provoke resistance and anger: this explains the moderation and circumspection with which temples and statues were treated — and which could include imperial patronage for the restoration of the sanctuary of Isis in Ostia under Gratian, Valens, and Valentinian.[110] The festivals were part of the same tradition, and they gave the people an occasion to seek happiness and relaxation; once the sacrifices and prayers to the demons of old were removed, nothing should prevent their celebration, provided they did not provoke the other groups. In 408, Theodosius II guaranteed the Jewish performance of Purim, together with all other Jewish festivals, if the Jews would stop burning a figurine of Haman on a cross, which had led to

---

[109] Augustine, *Ep.* 29; see Lancel (1999), 227–229; the compromise: Origen, *Contra Celsum* 8.21–23, see Dihle (1992), 328–329.
[110] Alföldi (1937); see the contemporary Ausonius for the Roman festival of Isis, *Ecl.* 24.25–26. This is not "pagan revivalism," but consistent imperial policy; see Boin (2010).

Christian protests: all religious traditions had their rights.[111] Some festivals also gave a festive expression to the political order in which every city was connected, in the last instance, with the ruling emperor, wherever he happened to reside. The Kalendae were understood as a festival of several days that included the *vota* and thus firmly belonged to this category. They were necessary; no bishop should touch them.

And then there was the people; we mostly hear only indirectly of them, in the often angry descriptions of their doings. For all we can see, they wanted the joys, splendor, and exhilaration of the festivals. Amasius realized this the hard way when they stayed away from his sermon on January 1. But I doubt whether he was the only preacher who had this problem; even the brilliant Augustine might not have filled his Carthaginian church. He does not say so, but behind the screen of his well-turned words we hear the happy shouts of the crowd outside, including family members of his congregation. The emperors were more aware of this, and sometimes could be explicit. When Honorius declared that he did not want to suppress popular enjoyment (*laetitia*) but insisted on giving to the people an occasion for pleasure according to tradition (*exhiberi populo voluptates secundum veterem consuetudinem*), not all bishops must have been happy, neither about the imperial permission for *voluptas* nor about the reference to *vetus consuetudo*.

The one thing that is curiously underplayed is social concerns. Festivals, after all, were conspicuous displays of wealth, private wealth as much as imperial wealth. When, a few centuries earlier, Salutaris had his thirty-nine gold and silver images carried through Ephesos, he did not only add to his city's splendor, he demonstrated his own generous wealth, as did, on a village level, P. Aelius Menecrates in Lydian Almoura, who donated a silver basket for the procession of Demeter.[112] But more importantly, wealth bought sacrifices and the ensuing banquets. Epameinondas of Akraiphia was far from being the sole benefactor who fed his city at a festival – and

---

[111] *CTh* 16.8.18: *Impp. Honorius et Theodosius aa. Anthemio praefecto praetorio. Iudaeos quodam festivitatis suae sollemni Aman ad poenae quondam recordationem incendere et sanctae crucis adsimulatam speciem in contemptum christianae fidei sacrilega mente exurere provinciarum rectores prohibeant, ne iocis suis fidei nostrae signum inmisceant, sed ritus suos citra contemptum Christianae legis retineant, amissuri sine dubio permissa hactenus, nisi ab illicitis temperaverint.* See also *CTh* 16.8.21 (412 CE). The cross in the story is a late Christian import: the LXX text of Esther has simply ξύλον, "wood," whereas the Vulgate oscillates between *trabes* (Esther 5.14), *lignum* (7.9), the technical *patibulum* (7.10), and *crux* (5.14); fourth-century authors use *crux*, e.g. Sulpic. Sever. *Chron.* 2.13 or Hieron. *In Galat. commentar.* 2, p. 362B; Euagrius, *Altercatio legis inter Theophilum Christianum et Simonem Iudaeum* p. 1147AB compares Haman and Christ.

[112] Ephesos: *I.Ephes.* 27, with Rogers (1991); Almoura: H. W. Pleket, *Talanta* 2 (1970), 61 no. 4; see above, Chapter 1.

stimulated the local economy by doing so: he bought sacrificial animals in large numbers, but also fire-wood, flour, and wine (provided that his own estate did not provide this); and he gave work to the craftsmen who used the resulting hides, the local fullers and leather-workers. Although epigraphical texts that praise a local benefactor for his lavish banquets become rare after the second century CE, we have no reason to think that the practice ceased: the abolition of animal sacrifice as part of a local festival also meant the abolition of an occasion where the wealthy could display their generosity, and where the inhabitants of a city, be they citizens or not, rich or poor, could enjoy a lavish meal. It is true that during the centuries of Roman imperial power, the Roman habit of distributing presents – *strenae* and *sportulae* – had also entered the Eastern cities: we saw how the horse-racing grandees of Antioch, on their way to the temple on January 1, generously were throwing *aurei* to the crowds, who picked them up eagerly. Others in other towns must have done the same, although they remain invisible to us.

When the bishops criticize the gift-giving habits of the Kalendae, they thus distort the reality: it must have been far from being as asymmetrical as Asterius or Augustine claimed. What had disappeared with the abolition of sacrifices were the lavish banquets. Even Augustine must have seen that fasting was not the perfect answer, even if the Western church insisted on fasting during the Kalendae for several centuries to come. At their own festivals, the bishops acted as generously as the pagan rich had.[113] In Egypt, the canons of Athanasius provided for distributions on Sundays, at Easter, Pentecost, and Epiphany, this last festival taking up the role of the generous Kalendae; in Africa, Augustine marked even the anniversaries of his ordination as bishop with distributions to the poor (*compauperes nostri*).[114] What had changed from pagan Kalendae to Christian festival was the recipients of such largesse, and the source for it. The means now came from the donations of the rich, the alms that not only Augustine insisted upon, and it did not indiscriminately go to everybody, or everybody who was able-bodied enough to pick up an *aureus* in a throng of bystanders: it went to the Christian *pauperes*, the not so rich part of the townspeople. In a changing society, splendidly analyzed by Peter Brown, the Christian church did not just step into the role of the wealthy, it reshaped their

---

[113] See Finn (2006), 78–82.
[114] Egypt: Canon 16 in Riedel and Crum (1904), 27 (Arabic version) ("The great Saint Athanasius cannot have been its author," René-Georges Coquin, "Canons of Pseudo-Athanasius", *Copt. Enc.* 2.458, who dates the text before mid-fifth century CE). Africa: Aug. *Serm.* 339.4; see Lambot (1950), 115.

role (and by doing so it reshaped its own role) by channeling the redistribution of wealth.[115] The bishops might argue against festivals such as the Kalendae mainly in religious and ethical terms; but underneath was also a question of power and influence, to be gained through the gratitude of the urban crowds.

Thus, these positions were not easily reconciled. At least the more radical bishops pressed for more, later councils repeated the earlier demands, and individual bishops, not least the powerful bishop of Rome, took action of their own; but only in the kingdoms of the Germanic conquerors could the bishops step into the role of law-givers and frame the laws according to their interests. Inside the empire, Augustine in his old age had learned not to expect too much from the State, despite some "rash claims" about the usefulness of the imperial government.[116] The emperors in turn tried not to yield too much ground and, during the following centuries, found new ways of appearing to compromise while holding on to their own agenda; Justinian's declaration that he felt obliged only by the canons of the first four ecumenical councils sounds like a defense against all too importunate bishops.[117] Unlike many bishops, who were trained and attuned to manipulate the souls according to their own doctrine, the emperors had learnt that one neglected the desires of the population at one's own peril: revolts were not uncommon in the cities of the empire. This must account for the survival of the Kalendae in the East, their Christianization, and their persistence among the Roman (but in no way pagan) subjects of the barbarian kings who succeeded the imperial governors in Gaul and Spain.[118]

---

[115] Brown (2012). As Possidius explained in his *Life of Augustine* 23.1: 23 *Compauperum vero semper memor erat, eisque inde erogabat, unde et sibi suisque omnibus secum habitantibus; hoc est, vel ex reditibus possessionum ecclesiae vel etiam ex oblationibus fidelium*, "He always thought of the poor and gave them from the same sources that he used for himself and his entire household, that is either the income of the church possessions or also from the donations of the believers." This is also the topic of the new sermon Erfurt 4 (= 350 F), Schiller, Weber, and Weidmann (2009), 189–200.
[116] Brown (1967), 338.   [117] Justinian, *Novella* 131.1.
[118] For instances of this persistence see below, Chapter 8.

CHAPTER 5

The Lupercalia from Augustus to Constantine Porphyrogennetos

Augustus and the Lupercalia in the Imperial age

Like many other festivals of the city of Rome, the Lupercalia become almost invisible to modern scholarship during the first three Imperial centuries; modern reconstructions and debates are mainly based on the rich documentation of late Republican and Augustan times, in Dionysius of Halicarnassus, Livy, and, unsurpassed in richness, Ovid.[1] Only their special social cachet caused the *luperci* and their rites to leave a trace in our documentation for the imperial epoch. Theirs was the only priestly *sodalitas* that Augustus reserved for the knights, whereas all other *sodalitates* became the privilege of the senatorial aristocracy, most prominently the Arval Brethren. While, in his reforms, Augustus allocated the concern for bread and agrarian fertility to the ruling aristocrats who, together with the emperor, made up the twelve Brethren, the equally vital but much more slippery and titillating concern for human and animal fertility was removed at arm's length to adolescent equestrian *luperci*; this distance between the toga-wearing Brethren, solemnly handling "dry and green wheat and bread decorated with laurel" and the almost naked *luperci* with their whips not only echoed Cicero's disdain for the savage and uncouth *luperci* but determined a distance from the heart of power that was still felt in tenth-century Byzantium, as we shall see.[2] Still, to be made a *lupercus* turned into a highly coveted status symbol of "near-aristocracy" that was publicly marked with the statue of the new *lupercus* already in Julio-Claudian times – a new habit of this age, as the Elder Pliny tells us, himself of an equestrian background.[3]

---

[1] A summary in Scullard (1981), 76–78; see also Scholz (1981); Ulf (1982), and Carafa (2006).
[2] *Fruges aridas et virides contigerunt et panes laureatos*, Scheid (1998), no. 100 a. 7 and often; Cic. *Pro Caelio* 26 *fera quaedam sodalitas et plane pastoricia atque agrestis*, "some savage association of herdsmen and rustics."
[3] Plin. *Nat.*34.18: Among the Roman innovations in the iconography of statues *Lupercorum habitu tam noviciae sunt quam quae nuper prodiere paenulis indutae*; see Veyne (1960), 105. On the transformation of the Lupercalia between Caesar and Augustus see Ferriès (2009).

Inscriptions from both Rome and the provinces show how to be selected a *lupercus* in Rome was viewed as an important early step of an equestrian *cursus honorum; sacris lupercalibus functo*, "to have performed one's duty as a *lupercus*" remained a major career step through most of the Imperial age.[4] The last *lupercus* whose name we know is one L. Crepereius Rogatus, *vir clarissimus*, a member of the senatorial elite of the earlier fourth century; he must have been a young man when Diocletian came to power.[5] A *vir clarissimus* being a *lupercus* is a novelty: throughout most of the Imperial age, Augustus' assignation of the priesthood to the knights remained valid. Valerius Maximus defined the Lupercalia not just as an event of the *ordo equestris*, but when *equestris ordinis iuventus* becomes visible (*spectaculum*) to the city, and Paul Veyne aptly characterized the participation in the rituals of the Lupercalia and the *transvectio equitum* as the initiation ritual of the young *equites* of the Empire.[6]

The pride and self-consciousness of these equestrian *luperci* allow us to glimpse a few details of their ritual. In a grave inscription from mid-Imperial Rome, the deceased, M. Ulpius Maximus, is described by his wife as *eques Romanus, qui et lupercus cucurrit*: the race through central Rome was still the most memorable detail.[7] Not even the dress-code had changed much since Ovid's characterization (and saucy explanation) as *nudi luperci*.[8] An image on the second-century grave altar of Ti. Claudius Liberalis, a young knight from Tibur who died at the age of sixteen, depicted him with a naked upper-body and a tight-fitting piece of fabric wrapped around his lower belly and upper thighs, starting well below the navel and folded in the shape of bermuda-shorts that allow the thighs to move freely. Compared even with the *trabea equestris*, the knee-long equestrian tunic that the same young man is wearing on the image of the *transvectio*, such an artful draping of one's lower body must have felt rather nude, even precarious – like publicly wearing only boxer shorts instead of a

---

[4] For the attested *Luperci* see Rüpke (2005); a revised English edition (2008a); see also Scheid and Granino Cecere (1999). *Sacris lupercalibus functo* in two contemporary inscriptions from third-century Mauretania, Rüpke (2008a), nos. 2206 and 2257; on the interpretation, *ibid.* p. 771 on no. 2257.
[5] For the last *luperci*, Scheid and Granino Cecere (1999), 85; for the slow eclipse of the knights during the Constantinian dynasty see Lepelley (1999).
[6] Val. Max. 2.2.9; Veyne (1960); North and McLynn (2008), 178.
[7] *CIL* 6.2160 = *ILS* 4947; see Rüpke (2008a), no. 3321.
[8] Ovid, *Fasti* 2.267, the myth 2.283–358. *nudi luperci* also in Varro, *De ling. Lat.* 6.34, Livy 1.5.3, and Verg. *Aen.* 8.663; γυμνούς Tubero in D.H. *Ant. Rom.* 1.80.1. Christian authors repeat this, see Prud. *Adv. Symm.* 816; Rufin. *Apologia* 2; Gelasius, *Ep.* (PL 59.113D); see also Serv. Dan. *ad Aen.* 8.343: *hodieque nudi currunt.* Justin 43.1.7 describes the statue of Lupercus set up by Euander similarly as *nudum caprina pelle amictum*.

The Lupercalia

business suit or a uniform.[9] This outfit made him look and feel only slightly more dressed than the loincloth cut from the hide of a sacrificial goat that Aelius Tubero in the thirties BCE imagined Euander's young men to wear when they were celebrating their archaic, pre-foundation Lupercalia.[10] But it still must qualify as *nudus*: *nudus* does not always mean "stark naked" but only "having one's main garment removed."[11] This is what the aetiological story implies: the young herdsmen shed their garments the better to pursue the cattle thieves.[12] The description of the famous statue of Pan Lupercus in Pompeius Trogus agrees: the image is "naked and wrapped in a goat skin ... and in this dress today one runs in Rome at the Lupercalia."[13] Other images of the Imperial epoch concur: with one exception, all the images show the *luperci* in this shorts-like dress.[14] When both Ovid and the Christian writers stress the nudity, they have their own reasons: for Ovid, the eroticism adds to the fascination of the rite, for the Christians it heightens its scandal.

The festival remained popular beyond the reign of Constantine and is noted in the Menologia and the calendars of Philocalus in 354 CE and of Polemius Silvius. But we lack details, and the entry of the otherwise antiquarian-minded Polemius is curiously short, almost abrasive. The contemporary Christian polemics equally demonstrate not much more than that the festival was still performed. Again the texts do not give many details; and even if there are some, one might distrust their reliability. A text such as Prudentius' *Against Symmachus* that lists the *luperci* among the performers of traditional Roman festivals and describes "the whips and the running of the naked young men at the Lupercalia" might owe more to learned literature, such as Ovid's *Fasti*, than to the observation of the custom in his own century.[15] Still, Symmachus

---

[9] See Veyne (1960), 104, with fig. 9 ("presque nu, vêtu d'un simple pagne"); a second monument, 105 with fig. 8.3; see also Tortorella (2000) and North and McLynn (2008), 178, with tab. III; their term "kilt" is quite misleading, since a kilt starts rather higher up on the body.

[10] Tubero frg. 3 Peter (= D.H. *Ant. Rom.* 1.80.1), describing Euander's men celebrating the Lupercalia γυμνοὺς ὑπεζωσμένους τὴν αἰδῶ ταῖς δοραῖς τῶν νεοθύτων "naked but their genitals clothed in the hides of the newly sacrificed goats"; both Ovid, *Fasti* 5.101 (*cinctuti Luperci*, "L. in athletic shorts" – in contrast to the *nudi Luperci* of *Fasti* 2, *passim*; see also Val. Max. 2.2.9 *cincti*) and Plut. *Rom.* 21.5 (περιζώματα) echo ὑπεζωσμένους but do not necessarily imply the most skimpy dress; Wiseman (1995), 82 overstates Augustus' concern for modesty.

[11] See *OLD* s.v.   [12] The aetiology from Livy 1.5.3 to Serv. *ad Aen.* 8.663.

[13] Iustin. 43.1.7 *ipsum dei simulacrum nudum caprina pelle amictum est quo habitu nunc Romae Lupercalibus decurritur*.

[14] Tortorella (2000); the exception (*ibid*. 251) is a fragment of a Campana tile from the area of the house of Livia.

[15] Prud. *Adv. Symm.* 816–817 *iamque lupercales ferulae, nudique petuntur | discursus iuvenum; nudorum lupercal*; also in Rufin. *Apologia* 2. McLynn (2008), 168f. refers to two fourth-century images, one

presents the pagan elite of the late fourth century as eager sponsors of the ritual. At least the nudity remains well attested, and Donatus (Servius Danielis) observed it in his own epoch, the mid-fourth century, as did a dismayed pope Gelasius at the end of the fifth.[16]

Thus, the festival survived the Christianization of the empire and the prohibition of pagan sacrifices. The sacrifices of a dog and of a billy-goat (*caper*), both attested only because of Plutarch's love for weird learning, seem to have been a less visible part of the ritual that preceded the course of the *luperci*: these quaint rites could obviously be given up without an essential feeling of loss (except presumably among some conservatives and antiquarians), since it was the visible public performance, the nude running and whipping on a predetermined route along the old core of Rome and its sexually flavored excitement, that mattered more than precise ritual conservatism.[17]

More than a century after Symmachus, the Lupercalia famously provoked the ire of pope Gelasius (492–496 CE), who addressed an angry pamphlet to its aristocratic Christian defenders in Rome.[18] We don't know whether he succeeded in abolishing it, whether he was serious at all or whether he just wanted to test the waters, or if such a prohibition would have outlasted his papacy. Modern scholars have usually expressed their surprise at the long survival of the Lupercalia and added a final Christian transformation: until recently it was accepted without any doubt that it turned into the festival of *Purificatio Mariae*, Germany's *Mariae Lichtmess*, on February 2.[19] None of the moderns, however, has equalled the eloquence of the first scholar who expressed his surprise, the

---

from Africa and the other from Rome, that show modestly attired Luperci who whip a rather immodest woman.

[16] Serv. Dan. *ad Aen.* 8.343: *hodieque nudi currunt*; see Murgia (2003), 53; Pellizani (2003), 129. Gelasius, *Ep.* (*PL* 59.113D): *ipsi cum amiculo nudi discurrite*, which the addressees refuse to do. Murgia (2003) argues from the past tenses in Serv. *ad Aen.* 8.663 (*consuetudo permansit ut nudi Lupercalia celebrarent*), that in Servius' own time (early fifth century), the rite was abolished; but given Gelasius' letter, this must have been temporary at best, and the perfect can also be understood as resultative: see Pellizani (2003), 129.

[17] On the sacrifices: Plut. *QRom.* 68 and 111 (dog), Ovid, *Fasti* 2.445 (its hide is made into the whips; the same in Festus s.v. *creppos*, p. 49.18 Lindsay, and Plut. *Rom.* 21.6, 32c where the sacrifice of αἶγες is part of the initiation of the Luperci), Val. Max. 2.2.9, Serv. *Aen.* 8.343 (*caper*). The route of the *luperci* is contested: against an older opinion that, under the influence of folklore models, understood it as a circular lustration of the Palatine, Michels (1953) argued for a somewhat aimless running around; since then, the quest for a clear route has not stopped, see e.g. Munzi (1994) or Valli (2007).

[18] *CIL* 6.37911a = 31413, 36959, 37911b = 31414 (*ILS* 789), 36960 (*ILS* 8950).

[19] Rejected by Schäublin (1995).

learned and garrulous cardinal Cesare Baroni (1538–1607) in his *Annales Ecclesiastici*.[20]

> Who would believe that after the many edicts that Christian emperors so often directed against idolatry, and after the zeal with which the Holy Popes wanted to eradicate it, the Lupercalia, brought to Italy before Rome's foundation, still survived in the City in the times of pope Gelasius? And who would not be astonished that it was adopted by Christians?

In order to make his point, Baronius added the text of Gelasius' letter after a manuscript in the Vatican, with a few necessary corrections and some short and pertinent comments. This *editio princeps*, triggered by his surprised indignation (or so he says), remains the one great and lasting service Baronius did to our knowledge of the late antique Lupercalia. Later scholars did not pay him back well: instead of recognizing his merit, they preferred to credit him with the idea that Gelasius abolished the Lupercalia and replaced it with the Christian festival of *Purgatio Mariae*. This is doubly wrong. Neither did Gelasius (or anybody else) replace the Lupercalia with a festival of Mary, as Christoph Schäublin has demonstrated, after a few earlier skeptical scholars;[21] nor does this wrong-headed idea go back to the learned Baronius: already the abbé Migne pointed this out in one of his learned footnotes that nobody seems to read. Although I am unable to tell where the idea comes from, I reiterate Migne's observation that it is not to be found anywhere in Baronius' ample writings.[22] And as to unjustly overlooked earlier scholars: none other than the splendidly learned Benedictine scholar, Hugo Menardus (Nicolas-Hugues Ménard) rejected the same connection in his 1642 notes on Gregory the Great's *Liber Sacramentorum*, reprinted by the abbé Migne, and more sensibly derived the Christian ritual instead from pagan rituals during the month of February.[23] Again this has remained without any resonance in nineteenth- and twentieth-century scholarship.

---

[20] Edited in twelve volumes, 1588–1609. I cite the Paris edition of 1867, ed. by Augustin Theiner, vol. 8, p. 569: *Quis credere possit, post tot Christianorum imperatorum edicta adversus idololatriam saepissime lata, postque sanctorum Pontificum ad eamdem extirpandam adhibita studia, viguisse tamen adhunc Roma ad Gelasii tempora, quae fuere ante exordium Urbis allata in Italiam Lupercalia? Et quis satis digne admirari queat, eadem quoque recepta ab hominibus Christianis?*

[21] Schäublin (1995); among the skeptics, he cites Dölger, and he could also have cited Usener (1911/1969), 311–312.

[22] Baronius looms somewhat large in Green (1931), who must echo Fowler (1899), 321; Migne's rejection in *PL* 85.691, without a source other than *alii* (but not Baronius).

[23] *Quare hujus solemnitatis celebrandae viam non aperuit Gelasius papa, cum Lupercalia sustulit*, *PL* 78.299A; his own theory is based upon Ildephonsus of Toledo (died 667 CE), who in his *Sermo X in Purificatione Sanctae Mariae* claims that the Christian candle-light processions on this holiday were transformed from the pagan purifications rituals for the god Februus, without, however, mentioning the Lupercalia (*PL* 96.277AB).

Whatever happened in the Roman West, in the Greek East the festival survived even longer. It is attested in a long description in the *Book of Ceremonies* by the emperor Constantine VII Porphyrogennetos (born in 905, ruled 913–959) among the rites that demand the emperor's attention.[24] But neither here nor in Gelasius' description does the festival look very much like its namesake in Caesar's or Ovid's time.

Pope Gelasius and the Lupercalia in late-fifth-century Rome

Gelasius' small pamphlet with the long title "Against the Senator Andromachus and the Other Romans Who Decided to Perform the Lupercalia According to the Ancient Custom" (*Gelasius Papa I adversus Andromachum senatorem ceterosque Romanos qui Lupercalia secundum morem pristinum colenda constituebant*) is an interesting mixture of polemics and defensiveness.[25] It is unclear whether the title, present already in the oldest manuscript, an eleventh-century *Vaticanus*, goes back to Gelasius' time or was added later.[26] But even if it is not authentic, the title still must contain contemporary information: the name of Andromachus does not appear in the text itself, but it perfectly fits the time. One Andromachus was a leading Roman aristocrat of the late fifth century, in 489 *magister officiorum* of king Odoacer and his ambassador to Byzantium, for which mission he received additional instructions from Gelasius.[27] At the time of the letter, he was perhaps Urban Prefect, which would explain why Gelasius addressed his pamphlet mainly to him.

The structure and many details of the short treatise remain somewhat opaque. As a text with an immediate political aim, it reflects a specific situation and alludes to specific arguments that were perfectly clear to contemporary readers, but are somewhat lost on us. In a paper published in 2008, Neil McLynn has given the entire text a very close reading in order to reconstruct why it was published; this has considerably helped its historical understanding.[28]

---

[24] Constantine Porphyrogennetos, *Liber caerimoniarum* 1.82 ed. Vogt, 2:1, 164–168, and his commentary in 2:2, 172–177. An English translation and short commentary by Moffatt and Tall (2012).
[25] The most recent edition is Pomarès (1959) whom I cite with his paragraphs (which follow Günther 1895) and page numbers. See also *PL* 59.110–116 (after the edition by Philippe Labé, Paris 1671); *Gelasius, Tractatus* 6, in Thiel (1868), 598–607; *Collectio Avellana* 100, in Günther (1895), 453–464.
[26] On the manuscripts of the *collectio Avellana* see Pomarès (1959), 150–153.
[27] *PLRE* 2.89 (the *magister officiorum*, "perhaps identical" with Gelasius' addressee); the instructions from Gelasius in his *Ep.* 10 (= Thiel [1868], *Ep. pont.* 1.346).
[28] McLynn (2008), who succeeds in setting right several assumptions in what was for some time the leading monograph on the text, Holleman (1974). See also the short sketch in Brown (1988), 430 and Valli (2007).

The Lupercalia 169

The papal pamphlet begins with an attack on people who "sit at home knowing nothing" but publicly accuse others without checking their facts, just to slander them, *studio cacologiae*. The somewhat precious Greek word, at home in Classical Greek texts of the fifth and fourth centuries BCE, but also in some Christian writers, but basically unknown in Latin texts, might well be a calculated jibe at the Roman aristocrats with their pride in their Eastern connections: the pope too knew his Greek, Classical or Ecclesiastical.[29] However this may be, the tensions between the pope and the aristocrats are obvious, and they are not exactly unusual at this time.[30] They accused him, Gelasius says, of doing nothing against bad behavior inside the church. But these people, he goes on, would not realize that there is not only corporeal adultery that needs punishment, but also spiritual adultery, which is much worse since it opens the mind to the devil. This spiritual adultery consists in the fact that, although Christians, these people "do not abhor, do not reject, do not fear to claim" that not to have worshiped the god Februarius has led the Romans to disease. The rhetoric shows what made the writer angry.

The strangely isolated god Februarius calls for a short detour and even a conjecture on the text.[31] Roman antiquarians since Varro and Festus derived the month name Februarius from *februare*, "to purify" and *februa*, "means or rites of purification." The last to do so was Augustine, who defined the *februa* as *sacra Lupercorum*: he knew his Varro inside-out.[32] Not many years later, exaggerated theism took over. Macrobius derived the month from a god Februus *lustrationum potens*; mediated through Isidore's *Origines* and Bede's *De temporum liber* (who cites Macrobius verbatim), this became the standard derivation of the month name in the Latin West.[33] However, Macrobius usually does not invent things like this.

---

[29] The Classical κακολογία (since Hdt. 7.237) is in Latin attested only in Jerome's commentary *In epist. ad Rom.* (PL 30.649C) and in two very learned Medieval authors, the twelfth-century French theologian Petrus Comestor, who in a sermon to his students plays with *paralogia, scenologia, physiologia, theologia, cacologia* (PL 198.1732A) and the ninth-century monk in St. Gall, Walahfrid Strabo, who in his commentary on *Num.* has the (Pindaric and Aristotelian) adjective *cacologus* (PL 113.401C); thus, the word is as unusual and preciously learned as the *deus Februarius* whom Gelasius invokes later. On the other hand, many Greek Christian writers use it, such as Origen, Athanasius, John Chrysostom and his student Palladius, Epiphanius of Salamis, Basilius of Caesarea or Cyril of Alexandria, albeit not very often; but it would be available to a learned Western cleric.

[30] See Sessa (2012), 209–212 ("mistrusting the bishop"); the Lupercalia affair on p. 211.

[31] The god in *Epist.* 3, p. 164 Pomarès: *quia daemonia non colantur et deo Februario non litetur*.

[32] On *februare, februa*, Lupercalia, and February see Varro, *De ling. Lat.* 6.13, 34; Festus s.v. Februarius, p. 75 L.; Ovid, *Fasti* 2.19 etc.

[33] Macrob. *Sat.* 1.13.3 (another argument for the late date of Macrobius); Isidore, *Orig.* 5.33.4; Bede, *De temporum liber* 12 (PL 90.351C).

The inventor of the god Februus might be an otherwise unknown Anysius who, in his work *On Months* cited by John Lydus, derived the month name from the Etruscan god Φεβροῦος ὁ καταχθόνιος.[34] It is not easy to date Anysius, but the personal name is not attested before the Antonines,[35] and his etruscological interests recall the work of Cornelius Labeo, who belongs to the late third century CE, and whom John Lydus cited several times.[36] Likely, Anysius arrived in Lydus through Labeo; but one cannot be certain, and Anysius could be later. But whatever the answer to this is, for Gelasius' text it matters only that a god Februarius is unattested, a god Februus well known to Latin Christians after Macrobius: this argues strongly for reading Februus and not Februarius in Gelasius. A distracted (or speculative) scribe might easily slip up on Februus and replace it with the month name Februarius; and in a tradition based on one single manuscript of which all other manuscripts are either direct or indirect copies, such a slip leaves no trace. (It is worthwhile noticing how gods seem to proliferate in learned theories once polytheism had run its course.)

To come back to the letter. The strange idea of spiritual adultery hides the very real misbehavior not punished by the pope but censured by some among Rome's aristocrats: adultery by a member of the clergy. To be called morally idle and lax in a matter of sexual ethics close to home obviously needles a pope who, as much as any of his predecessors, claimed moral authority in private sexual behavior. It provoked his counterattack against the defenders of "pagan behavior": why would a professed and baptized Christian want to worship the god Februus in order to gain protection?[37] (Which shows that the Lupercalia was not just defended by a "pagan faction" of the senate, as earlier scholars argued, relying on the rather problematical concept of entrenched religious partisanship in post-Constantinian Rome.[38])

---

[34] In Lydus, *Mens.* 4.25.
[35] *PLRE* contains several Anysii; most of them are Easterners, and none looks like a writer (1.79f.: three names, the most promising Anysius 2, presumably a jurist known from Libanius' letters; 2.108 has four, the only Westerner being Anysius Marcellus Maximus "ex tribunis," *CIL* 5.1652); the earliest seems an Anysios in Thyateira, *SEG* 26 (2006), 1353.
[36] On Labeo see Mastandrea (1979) and Briquel (1997), 119–137; on Anysios: Mass (1992), 62 (who mistakenly calls him Anysias).
[37] Gelasius, *C. Luperc.* 3, p. 164 Pomarès: *Quomodo autem non <in> hanc partem recidit qui cum se Christianum videri velit et profiteatur et dicat, palam tamen publiceque praedicare non horreat, non refugiat, non pavescat, ideo morbos gigni quia daemonia non colantur, et deo Februario non litetur?*
[38] Markus (1990), 131–5, esp. 133 ("the end of partnership between the papacy and the Christian aristocracy"). See Cameron (2011), *passim* for counter-arguments.

The Lupercalia

But Gelasius does not spend much time with this question: it is rather well-worn by now, although it still can raise anti-pagan instincts – which was what he wanted. What had always mattered much more than the divinity presiding over the Lupercalia was the ritual race and the flogging of female bystanders.[39] Gelasius concentrates most of his energies on refuting the accusation that by abolishing the rite he removed an instrument of supernatural protection from the city. This argument must have loomed large in a recent debate, where it was used by Andromachus and other Roman aristocrats – by now presumably all members of the Catholic Church – to defend the ritual.[40] It is probable that at some point in the recent past, the ritual had been suspended, but it was revived recently. It must have been when defending this resumption that Andromachus argued that its suspension had caused disease.

The arguments on both sides need some thought. Relying on Livy, the pope singles out *sterilitas feminarum*, and rejects the arguments of the senators who had argued (as Gelasius reports), that the omission of the Lupercalia caused pandemics (*morbos*). When he then tells them that the omission of the Lupercalia cannot have been responsible for the present calamities, he presents a longer list, *pestis, sterilitas (terrarum), bellorum tempestas*;[41] and when he argues *e contrario* against them, he claims that the obvious and aggravating prosperity of the East was possible without Lupercalia (*oriens omnium rerum copiis exuberat et abundat*, 23). The senators thus must have argued that the Lupercalia guaranteed prosperity and protected against illness, bad harvests, and war; they never mentioned female fertility. This was too closely associated with the embarrassing sexuality of naked young men beating young women: the senators curtailed and desexualized the earlier interpretations that went as far back as Varro and that claimed that the rite of the Luperci was a purification ritual that guaranteed human fertility.[42] There is an interesting parallel to this

---

[39] In all Republican and early Augustan texts, the god of the Lupercalia, if he is mentioned, is usually Pan/Faunus; see Wiseman (1995), who puts too much emphasis on the question to which divinity the Lupercalia was dedicated. Fest. s.v. Februarius, p. 75 Lindsay is alone to mention Juno Sospita, and Lydus, *Mens.* 4.25 cites one Anysios, who connected the Luperci with an agricultural ritual for the Etruscan underworld god Februus.

[40] Gelasius, *Ep.* 10.7 (Thiel).

[41] Gelasius, *C. Luperc.* 13, p. 172 Pomarès; see also 21, p. 178 *de siccitate, de grandine, de turbinibus, de tempestatibus variisque cladibus* as results of present-day behavior; and 25a, p. 182: Alaric's capture of Rome and the civil war between Anthemius and Ricimer.

[42] See Varro, *De ling. Lat.* 6.3.13, 6.4.34, ant. F 76 Cardauns; Festus s.v. Februarius, p. 75 Lindsay; Ovid, *Fasti* 2.425–452 and 5.101f. (*luperci ... lustrant*); Plut. *Rom.* 21.4 (καθάρσιος, see 21.10), 21.7 (female fertility). Purification alone: D.H. *Ant. Rom.* 1.80.1 (= Tubero F 3 Peter) and Censor. *De die*

change in a notice in John Lydus' *On the Months*: in his entry on February, he tells that the Etruscan underworld god Februus "was worshiped by the Luperci so that he might produce the harvest" (θεραπεύεσθαι δὲ πρὸς τῶν Λουπερκῶν ὑπὲρ ἐπιδόσεως καρπῶν), and he gives as his source the already mentioned treatise of Anysius, *On the Months*.[43] The god Februus in John echoes *deus tuus Februarius* (or, in my reading, Februus) in Gelasius; John's alleged stimulation of the harvest echoes one of the reasons that Gelasius rejects, *sterilitas terrarum*.[44] One wonders whether Gelasius' opponents still were reading Anysius, or at least Cornelius Labeo. In what feels like a battle of antiquarians, the pope instead cites Livy's now lost second decade for the reason given in most other sources, *sterilitas mulierum*; Livy's authority must have come in handy.[45]

But the Lupercalia in Andromachus' time was not the festival of the late Republic, as Gelasius is not slow to point out:[46]

> At the epoch of your ancestors, the noblemen themselves were running, and the ladies were beaten, their bodies exposed to the public. Thus, originally you yourselves were involved in the Lupercalia. It would have been enough to do nothing instead of celebrating the rite in a bad way – but although you thought that the cult was venerable and would bring wholesomeness, you moved it down to people that are vile and common, abject and of the lowest order.

Gelasius projects his contemporary Lupercalia, where women let themselves be beaten on their naked bodies, into the past, where, as Plutarch tells us, noble ladies just stretched out their hand, like Victorian schoolboys; but he has at least done some antiquarian homework. From his sources he knows that the Republican and Augustan *luperci* were members of the aristocracy (Marc Anthony's performance as a *lupercus* was still

---

natali 22.15; *sterilitas* and *puellae* Serv. Dan. *ad Aen.* 8.343 (*nonnulli ... dicunt*). The two interpretations, purification and fertility, are not mutually exclusive: see Valli (2007), 123–125.
[43] Lydus, *Mens.* 4.25; the notice escaped the attention of Wiseman (1995).
[44] On *deus Februus* instead of the transmitted *deus Februarius* in *Epist.* 3, p. 164 Pomarès see above, n. 31. *Sterilitas* (presumably of the fields): Gelasius, *C. Luperc.* 13, p. 172 Pomarès.
[45] Gelasius, *C. Luperc.* 12, p. 170 Pomarès: *Lupercalia autem propter quid instituta sunt, quantum ad ipsius superstitionis commenta respectant, Livius in secunda decade loquitur* (= Livy, frg. 36 Weissenborn). *Nec propter morbos inhibendos instituta commemorat, sed propter sterilitatem, ut ei videtur, mulierum, quae tunc acciderat, exigendam.*
[46] Ibid. 16, p.174: *apud illos enim nobiles ipsi currebant, et matronae nudato publice corpore vapulabant. vos ergo primi in Lupercalia commisistis; satius fuerat non agere quam ea cum iniuria celebrare; sed deduxistis venerandum vobis cultum, et salutiferum quem putatis, ad viles trivialesque personas, abiectos et infimos.*

The Lupercalia 173

remembered in late antiquity[47]), and he is aware of the sexuality of the rite that his opponents tried to obscure.[48] In Gelasius' time, however, the course with the whip must have turned into a general spectacle, performed, as McLynn suggested, by professional actors, with nude actresses replacing the noblewomen; the defamation of actors as "vile" and "abject" is a standard Christian evaluation that denigrates not just the actors but also the rite, not unlike Cicero's remark on the savage character of the *luperci* of his own time was intended to undermine a witness of his opponent.[49] The reasons for this recent change are obvious. Gelasius somewhat underhandedly suggests that the aristocrats were ashamed to run themselves in a somewhat embarrassing costume, and he might well be right. As the debate on the meaning of the rite suggests, its defenders were at pains to remove the sexual connotations.[50] In an age, furthermore, whose aristocratic dress codes had become much more elaborate and, at the same time, exclusive, nudity must have sat better with actors and entertainers. But despite the social background of the actual performers, the Lupercalia remained firmly a concern of the Roman aristocrats, who acted as *Lupercaliorum patroni*.

The second contemporary detail comes towards the end. Gelasius calls his aristocratic opponents not just "protectors of the Lupercalia," but also "defenders of reprehensible songs" (*cantilenarum turpium defensores*). He clarifies quickly what he means – not bawdy or lascivious songs, but songs that make morally problematical behavior, sexual and otherwise (*obscenitates et flagitia*), known to a larger public, "publicizing the misdeeds of each and everybody" (*facinora uniuscuiusque vulgando*). It is the sort of songs that participants in the Basel carnival ("Fasnacht") are deeply familiar with: the "Schnitzelbänke" (lampoons) that make fun of anyone among the city elite (and sometimes well beyond it) whose behavior does not fit the moral or behavioral standards expected from a person of his or her standing; the same corrective lampooning already inspired the parabasis of Old Comedy, as Thomas Gelzer, scion of an old Basel Family, once pointed out.[51] It was this lampooning to which Gelasius must have obliquely referred already in his introductory remark on the aristocratic

---

[47] E.g. in Dio 44.11.2 or in Cassiodorus' *Chronicle* (*PL* 69,1226B).
[48] But that was already clear to Cic. *Philip.* 13.31.
[49] Cic. *Pro Caelio* 26 *fera quaedam sodalitas*. The interesting problem is that both the accuser Balbus and the defendant Caelius were *luperci*.
[50] On nudity in late fourth-century Antioch see Brown (1988), 315–317. As a public spectacle, the Lupercalia cannot have been performed anymore on February 15 because this date could have already been inside the Lent period, when spectacles were prohibited; see below on the date in Byzantium.
[51] Gelzer (1992).

penchant for *cacologia*: although the real singers were the performing actors on the street, the inspiration for their texts – and perhaps their very texts, if again the Basel *Fasnacht* is a model – come from the aristocratic *patroni* who from the comfort of their houses embarked with relish on the *cacologia* of the lampoons.

This allows a reconstruction of the events in Gelasius' Rome. Early in his papacy, the Roman aristocrats, with Andromachus as their speaker, wanted to revive the Lupercalia that had been dormant for some time. With the argument that their dormancy had catastrophic consequences, they argued from a recent outbreak of a pandemic, and more generally from the festival's role as securing prosperity and good harvests. Since the age when successful knights were very proud of having served as *luperci*, the city elite had felt responsible for them; the last *lupercus*, we remember, was a *vir clarissimus* who died perhaps under Constantine, and even if he did not get the details right, Prudentius must have realized who was behind the Lupercalia when he brought it up in his poem against Symmachus. The aristocracy remained *Lupercalium patroni* under Gelasius, although they performed no more themselves. Their intention to bring the rite back must have led to some discussion with the pope, who could not have been overjoyed at the idea and who must have had theological problems with Andromachus' argument; but behind this argument was the same intention that the emperors had all along, not to touch those festivals that provided entertainment and happiness to the people. But when it was pointed out to him that none of his predecessors had succeeded in making the emperors prohibit the rite, he let it pass; being already embroiled in battles with the emperor and the patriarch of Constantinople on the status of the papacy, Gelasius had bigger fish to fry.[52] So the Lupercalia came back. But then, at a celebration to which the pamphlet reacts and that must have been very recent, someone had the bad idea to lampoon an adulterous priest and, implicitly or explicitly, his protector, the "morally lax" pope Gelasius.[53] Laxity of sexual mores sometimes became an issue among contemporary popes: pope Symmachus, who took the chair of Peter two years after Gelasius' death and the short papacy of Anastasius, was lampooned for his relationship with a courtesan with the speaking name Conditaria, "Spicy."[54] The

---

[52] See Ullmann (1962), 15–27, and *passim*.
[53] McLynn (2008), 171 suggests that the pope had heard of plans to lampoon him which made him react with the pamphlet; but the arguments of the lampoons are usually kept secret before their very performance, and the papal indignation makes more sense if he was taken by surprise.
[54] Chadwick (1981), 32.

lampooning broke the truce between papacy and *urbs*, and the pope made it very clear that in order not to appear morally lax he had to attack the Lupercalia and to excommunicate Andromachus, and that he would not forgive any Christian who would perform the ritual:[55]

> As far as I am concerned, no baptized Christian shall perform this: only the pagans, whose rite it is, shall follow it through. I have decided to pronounce formally that the ceremony is doubtless dangerous and damaging to Christians.

This sounds final, except that the last word in these matters was not the pope's. Given the imperial protection of these rituals and the ties of Andromachus to the new (although short-lived) Gothic ruler, Gelasius might have succeeded as little as his predecessors in permanently banning the festival.[56]

Constantine Porphyrogennetos and the Lupercalia in tenth-century Constantinople

In his rejection of a link between Lupercalia and prosperity, Gelasius makes a bold claim: "Why is the East prosperous and plentiful in everything, yet it has never performed the Lupercalia nor does it perform it now?"[57] Given that a form of the festival was celebrated in tenth-century Constantinople, the statement is surprising: would not the tenth-century form most likely derive from an earlier festival celebrated in the city, in the same way as the middle-Byzantine Kalendae and Brumalia (on which more below) continued the respective city festivals introduced by Constantine into his new Rome? It might be that Gelasius never was in Constantinople and so did not know, or that in his eagerness he overlooked the existence of the ritual in Constantinople. Either possibility is more likely if it already had radically changed its ritual form from the one it had in Rome to something attested five centuries later; Gelasius' invective would then constitute a terminus ante quem for such a change.

---

[55] Gelasius, *C. Luperc.* 30, p. 186 Pomarès: *quod ad me pertinet, nullus baptizatus, nullus Christianus hoc celebret, et soli hoc pagani, quorum ritus est, exsequantur. me pronuntiare convenit Christianis ista perniciosa et funesta indubitanter existere.*
[56] Or did he see Odoacer's demise in 494 as his chance? If so, nothing in the pamphlet points to this.
[57] Gelasius, *C. Luperc.* 23, p. 180 Pomarès: *cur nunc oriens omnium rerum copiis exuberat et abundat, qui nec celebravit unquam Lupercalia, nec celebrat?*

The ritual

Our only source for Lupercalia in medieval Constantinople is the *Book of Ceremonies* (*De cerimoniis aulae Byzantinae*), compiled by the emperor Constantine VII Porphyrogennetos (ruled 919 to 959) as part of his attempt to preserve the imperial traditions. The Lupercalia appears in the section that describes imperial presence in the circus, in this case at the "meat-market horse race that is called of the Lupercalion," περὶ τοῦ μακελλαρικοῦ ἱπποδρομίου τοῦ λεγομένου Λουπερκαλ(ίου).[58] As always in this text, the ceremonies are described from the perspective of those who have to perform: the emperor and his main courtiers – foremost the Head Chamberlain (πραιπόσιτος) and the Master of Ceremonies (ὁ τῆς καταστάσεως) – are the main actors and addressees. Other groups and actors appear only marginally, and the city populace becomes important only in its relationship to the emperor, as a source of acclamations.

The textual history of the *Liber caerimoniarum* is complex and layered, with materials from different sources and learned later additions. This shall not concern us here. Although some of the details for the Lupercalia race mostly come not from the court, but from the city archives, and not all are consistent as to whether the celebration assumes one or two emperors (which changed during Constantine's rule, from monarchy to dyarchy and back), these inconsistencies do not affect my argument.[59]

The μακελλαρικὸν ἱπποδρόμιον is the "Carnival's Race": it is the last race before the forty days of Lent, when meat was prohibited, as were circus games and other spectacles. This ties the date of the race to the date of Easter.[60] Lent began on Sunday Quadragesima, which could be as early as February 8, a week (by now an accepted unit of time) before the traditional date of the Lupercalia: since a circus race could neither happen during Lent nor, incidentally, on a Sunday – Sundays were freed from any spectacle by a decree of Honorius and Theodosius II in 409, the seven days of Quadragesima and Easter already by 405 – the Lupercalia in Constantinople must have lost its immovable date of February 15 in favor

---

[58] Constantine Porphyrogennetos, *Liber caerimoniarum* 1.82, pp. 164–168 ed. Vogt = 1.73, pp. 364–369 Reiske; see the commentary in Vogt (1935–1940), 2.2: 172–177 (see also the notes in Reiske [1829–1830], 344–345). A reproduction of Reiske's text with an English translation and very short notes: Moffatt and Tall (2012). See Duval (1976) and (1977).

[59] In his edition, Albert Vogt argued that Constantine's research must cover the past two centuries, since Constantine V (ruled 741–775), Vogt (1935–1940), 2.1: xx.

[60] On the date see Grumel (1936).

of a movable date somewhere in February, on one of the last weekdays before Sunday Quadragesima.[61]

The introductory paragraph of the long description in the *Liber caerimoniarum* deals with the formal announcement of the race.[62]

> One day before the race, the *praepositus* goes to the emperor and reminds him to order that the race be held, and when he has received the agreement to hold it, he goes, calls the Master of Ceremonies and sends him to the heads of the demes and the city administration to tell them that the race will be held.

Being an "ordinary race" (ἱππικὸν παγανόν),[63] it is organized by the city and not by the emperor; given its mobile date, all the people involved – on the court and the city side – have to be informed of its impending performance (even if preparations must have started much earlier).

On the day of the race itself, the emperor is being prepared for his public appearance in the circus. In a complex movement, he first walks from the palace to the dining room in the circus, where the patricians and the soldiers greet him by prostration. He then proceeds to the throne lodge (κάθισμα) in the circus; there, he receives the acclamations of his people, greets them, and gives the sign for starting the race. After the first three races, the ceremony that is special to this day commences:[64]

> When three races have been held, after the third race, on a command, the *actuarius* gives a sign with his hand, holding a napkin, to the city

---

[61] Sundays: *CTh* 2.8.25 (extending an earlier prohibition, *CTh* 2.8.23 of 399 also to imperial birthdays); Quadragesima and Easter: *CTh* 2.8.24 (mistakenly dated to 400, the first consulship of Stilicho).

[62] p. 164.3 Vogt (p. 362.9 Reiske): Εἰσέρχεται πρὸ μιᾶς ἡμέρας τοῦ αὐτοῦ ἱπποδρομίου ὁ πραιπόσιτος πρὸς τὸν βασιλέα, ὑπομιμνήσκων αὐτόν, εἰ κελεύει ἀχθῆναι τὸ αὐτὸ ἱπποδρόμιον, καὶ λαβὼν παρὰ τοῦ βασιλέως συγκατάθεσιν πρὸς τὸ ἄγεσθαι αὐτό, ἐξέρχεται, καὶ προσκαλεσάμενος τὸν τῆς καταστάσεως, ἀποστέλλει αὐτὸν πρὸς τοὺς δημάρχους καὶ τὸ πολίτευμα, εἰπεῖν πρὸς αὐτούς, ὡς ὅτι ἄγεται ἱπποδρόμιον. All translations from *Lib. caer.* are my own; but see also Moffat and Tall (2012), 364.

[63] On the possible meanings of παγανός see Vogt (1935–1940), 2.2: 173.

[64] p. 165.22 Vogt (p. 366.4 Reiske): καὶ ἀχθέντων τῶν τριῶν βαΐων, ἀπὸ τοῦ τρίτου βαΐου νεύει ὁ ἀκτουάριος ἀπὸ κελεύσεως μετὰ τῆς χειρὸς αὐτοῦ, κρατῶν ἐγχείριον, τὸ πολίτευμα, καὶ ἀποκινεῖ ἐκ τοῦ Διϊππίου διὰ δύο. ἐλθόντος δὲ ἕως τὰ κριτάρια, ἄρχονται λέγειν ἀντιφωνικῶς, τὸ μὲν ἓν μέρος· "Ἴδε τὸ ἔαρ τὸ καλὸν πάλιν ἐπανατέλλει," τὸ δὲ ἕτερον μέρος· "φέρον ὑγίειαν καὶ χαρὰν καὶ τὴν εὐημερίαν," καὶ τὰ λοιπά, καθὼς ἡ συνήθεια ἔχει. καὶ κατελθόντες μέχρι τῶν Πρασίνων καμπτοῦ, ἐνοῦνται ἀμφότεροι, καὶ λέγουσιν ἀπελατικοὺς τρεῖς μέχρι τοῦ Καθίσματος· κατέρχεται δὲ καὶ ὁ ὕπαρχος πόλεως ἀπὸ κελεύσεως, καὶ ἑνοῦται τῷ πολιτεύματι εἰς τὸν Χαλκόν, συνεισερχόμενος αὐτοῖς μέχρι τοῦ στάματος, καὶ ποιοῦσι προσκύνησιν ἅπαντες ἐν τῷ στάματι. καὶ εἶθ' οὕτως ἵσταται ὁ νεανίσκος ἐν τῷ δεξιῷ μέρει τοῦ ὑπάρχου, εὐφημῶν καὶ λέγων οὕτως· "Ὁ βοηθῶν τοὺς δεσπότας." ὁ λαός· "Εἷς ὁ Θεός," καὶ τὰ ἑξῆς, καθὼς ἡ συνήθεια ἔχει. καὶ ἀνέρχονται ἐπὶ τὰς θύρας εὐφημοῦντες τὸν βασιλέα, λέγοντες καὶ τοῦτο· "Ναί, Κύριε, πολλὰ αὐτῶν τὰ ἔτη." καὶ ἐξέρχονται. ὁ δὲ ὕπαρχος λαβὼν νεῦμα ἀπὸ κελεύσεως παρὰ τοῦ ἀκτουαρίου, εὐθέως ἀπὸ τοῦ στάματος ἀνέρχεται, ὅθεν κατῆλθεν καὶ μετὰ ταῦτα τελεῖται τὸ τέταρτον βαΐον. See Moffat and Tall (2012), 366.

administration; they move from the *diippion* in two groups. When both groups arrive at the tribunals, they begin to pronounce an antiphony, one group saying: "Beautiful Spring returns again," the other: "Bringing health, joy and prosperity" and all the rest, as is custom. They walk up to the field of the Greens, reunite there and utter three acclamations (ἀπελατικούς) towards the Throne Lodge. On an order, the City Prefect descends, joins the city administration at the place called Chalkos, and they walk together to the *stama*; there, they all make a deep reverence. Then, the Young Man at the side of the Prefect utters an acclamation and says: "He Who protects the rulers", and the people: "God is One", and all the rest, as is custom. And they walk up to the doors, acclaiming the emperor, and saying: "Verily, Lord, many years for him," and they exit. The Prefect, after a command and on a nod from the *actuarius*, exits quickly from the *stama* to where he went, and then the fourth race is run.

In the perspective of the *Liber*, what counts is not the races but the carefully choreographed movements of groups or individuals, and the acclamations and hymns they offer to the emperor. The main hymn praises spring: we are dealing with a spring ritual, even if mid-February might feel early for spring in Constantinople.[65] But one should keep in mind that at least in the ritual Roman calendar, March 1 was equally read as a New Year's festival, celebrated with the first green leaves.[66]

After the spring hymn and its antiphonic response that connects the new season with "health, joy, and prosperity," a young man (νεανίσκος) appears at the side of the Urban Prefect and starts an invocation to God as the protector of Kings: in the new season (or new year) that now begins the emperor is in need of divine protection, and of "many years for him." The text does not explain who the young man is and who invited him to his role; we see him simply standing there, playing his part in the liturgy. Given the text's perspective, which describes the ceremony through the eyes of the emperor, this means that the election of the young man lies outside the emperor's responsibility: it must have been the city administration, not the court, that selected him for his role. This explains why he is paired with the Urban Prefect, on whose side he (suddenly) stands. From the list of recipients of distributions for this race, we learn that at least as to remuneration for his services, he was regarded as part of the leading

---

[65] See Grumel (1936), 431–2. Modern average temperatures for Istanbul are identical for January and February (5.5°C), somewhat below the March average (7°C).
[66] Ovid, *Fasti* 3.139 *frondes sunt in honore novae*; in his interview with Janus, Ovid had been perplexed why the new year would not begin in spring, *Fast.* 1.149–160. See Feeney (2007), 204–205 on the question of when the Roman year should "really" begin.

The Lupercalia 179

hippodrome personnel, like the *actuarius* or the faction leaders and charioteers.[67]

In the afternoon, after the emperor returned to his lodge from his lunch, other races were added:[68]

> When three races have been held, in the fourth race the charioteers dismount after the fifth turn in the curve of the Greens: they run, riding each other until the *stama*. And they receive the prizes as in the first afternoon round. This happens every year, that they run a foot race in order to close the racing year.

This confirms the character of the Lupercalia Race as marking the end of an annual cycle and the beginning of a new one whose future bliss one hoped to gain through the praise of spring and the invocation of God on behalf of the emperor. To replace a horse race with a foot race of the charioteers riding each other is a somewhat scurrilous inversion of the normal procedure, in line with the innumerable rites of inversion that mark the New Year in many cultures around the globe. The charioteers, all-powerful and coveted in Byzantine society, are demoted to playing the role of their horses: this recalls the female cross-dressing of the military in many Kalendae festivals in East and West, or the slaves being served by their masters at the Saturnalia in Rome. Given the importance of the circus as a space of social symbolism in Byzantine society, it should not surprise us that it was here that its main actors, the charioteers, re-enacted the inversion, in the same way as in the third and fourth centuries in other towns it was the market-place that saw the cross-dressing of the soldiers who were at that epoch the main expression of power, albeit at the time with more sinister consequences. Armies win thrones, charioteers rarely do.

Distant ritual memories

Where is the traditional Roman Lupercalia in all this? Scholars have pointed to two details as transformed memories of the old ritual: the young man and the running charioteers.

The young man (ὁ νεανίσκος) is not part of the court but belongs to the leading hippodrome personnel; he might well be a young nobleman, acting on behalf of his city. This resonates with what we know about the *luperci* of

---

[67] *Liber caerimoniarum* 2.55, p. 799 Reiske; see Vogt (1935–1940), 2.2: 174.
[68] p. 166.15 Vogt (p. 367.3 Reiske): Καὶ ἀχθέντων τῶν τριῶν βαΐων, ἐν τῷ τετάρτῳ βαΐῳ ἀπὸ πέμπτης τάβλας κατέρχονται οἱ δ ἡνίοχοι ἐν τῷ τοῦ Πρασίνου καμπτῷ, καὶ τρέχουσιν ἡνιοχοῦντες ἀλλήλους μέχρι τοῦ στάματος, καὶ λαμβάνουσιν τὰ ἔπαθλα, ὡς ἐπὶ πρώτου βαΐου τῆς δειλινῆς. Τοῦτο δὲ τὸ ἐτήσιον γίνεται, ἤγουν τοῦ τρέχειν αὐτοὺς πεζούς, διὰ τὸ συγκλεῖσαι τὰ ἱπποδρόμια τοῦ χρόνου. See Moffat and Tall (2012), 367.

the Imperial age. During these centuries, the *luperci* were always equestrian *adolescentes* above the age of sixteen who represented the festival and whose images could be seen in the city of Rome and, after Constantine, perhaps also in Constantinople. When reshaping the Lupercalia, Augustus had insisted on age limits. He forbade the selection of *imberbi*, beardless youngsters, presumably for moral reasons, but he must also have insisted on their status as young men, perhaps in the light of Marc Anthony who still was running – naked – at age 38, on February 14, 44 BCE.[69] Valerius Maximus had described the ritual as the spectacle of the *iuventus equestris ordinis*, and to Prudentius, it was still the *nudi discursus iuvenum*, "the naked races of young men," even if this description owes more to the author's learning than to his actual observation.[70] The funerary altar of a young *lupercus*, whose parents must have been proud of his role, gave his age as sixteen years.[71] Thus a young man, a νεανίσκος, is an easy transformation for the most visible actor of the Lupercalia throughout the Imperial centuries. At the same time, such a young performer is an apt symbol for the new year that was about to come back, and the hopes connected with it. The fact that he was connected not with the emperor but with the city prefect looks like the Byzantine variation of the distance between the luperci and the center of power that characterized the uncouth *luperci* in Cicero's Rome, the equestrian *luperci* in Augustus' reform, and the actors who played them in Gelasius' time.

Although running was emblematic enough of the *luperci* to become the quasi-technical term for participation, from Ovid's repeated use of the verb *currere* to Prudentius' *discursus*, the foot race of the charioteers is less easily derived from this rite.[72] But it is possible to combine running young men and the circus already in Rome. Andrea Carandini, the most knowledgeable expert on Roman topography, observed that in the complex topography of late Republican and Imperial Rome the *lupercal* on the West slope of the Palatine could only be accessed through the Circus Maximus: the extended Circus structure blocked any other access.[73] If this is correct, then at the beginning and the end of each Lupercalia race naked young men were running through the Roman Circus. As to Constantinople,

---

[69] See North (2008).
[70] Val. Max. 2.2.9; Prud. *Adv. Symm.* 816f., with the standard epithet since Varro, *De ling. Lat.* 6.34; Livy 1.5.3 and Verg. *Aen.* 8.663.
[71] *Lupercalibus vetuit currere imberbes*, Suet. *Aug.* 31.4; on the young Ti. Claudius Liberalis (*CIL* 6.3512 = 14.3624) see above, n. 9.
[72] Ovid, *Fasti* 283–288; Suet. *Aug.* 31.4; *CIL* 6.2160 = *ILS* 4947; *discursus iuvenum*, Prud. *Adv. Symm.* 816f.
[73] Carandini (2008), 12–18.

Massimiliano Munzi suggested that the statue of the she-wolf with the twins in the Hippodrome, attested in Niketas Choniatas when it fell victim to Crusader greed, was not just a symbol of the New Rome: as in Rome the statue since mid-Republican times marked the *lupercal*, Munzi took its presence in the Hippodrome as a very concrete indication that the *lupercal* in Constantinople was as closely connected with the Hippodrome as it was with the Circus Maximus in Rome.[74] One of Carandini's students, Daniela Bruno, developed this idea and suggested that in Constantine's city, in imitation of the tight Roman topography, it was accessed through a door in the *kathisma*.[75] This combination of *lupercal*, Hippodrome, and *kathisma*, then, would preserve the association of the circus with running young men in Constantinople as well. After the abolition of the naked race of the *luperci*, the foot race of the charioteers would at least preserve its memory.

If one holds this to be too imaginative, one can also think that it was not the foot race of the charioteers that was a transformation of the running *luperci* but the chariot race as such. Unlike any other festivals, the Roman Lupercalia was not marked by horse races in the fourth-century calendar of the *urbs* (this would explain why the *luperci* could run through the Circus Maximus without mortal danger): neither Philocalus nor Polemius Silvius note them. Thus, it might well have been the later Byzantine transformation of the festival into the last horse race before the fasting season that turned a foot-race around the Palatine into yet another set of races in the circus of Byzantium with its deep infatuation with chariot races. And if the final chariot race of the year had to be closed with a ritual inversion, it was almost inevitable to have the charioteers run instead of their steeds, with or without the memory of the running *luperci*.

Transformations of a festival

The scant information on the Lupercalia during the first centuries of the Imperial age does not permit the reconstruction of an unbroken and transparent history of the festival. This is not different than the rest of the festival calendar, where usually the late Republican and Augustan phases are very well documented whereas the centuries after that remain almost dark. There may not have been many changes anyway. Even under Diocletian, the *luperci* still came from the equestrian order, and they were

---

[74] Munzi (1994), 353–354; see Nicetas Choniatas, *De signis* 7, p. 860 Bekker.
[75] In Carandini (2008), 18–20.

young men; in the calendar of 354, the festival date was still February 15 (here as often, Polemius Silvius cannot qualify as independent evidence), and a race of nude (or rather scantily clad) young men remained the salient characteristic of the festival for Donatus and Prudentius in the later fourth and Servius in the early fifth century; in the age of Justinian, John Lydus still knows of the *luperci*, although only indirectly.[76]

As far as we can see, the form of the festival remained surprisingly close to its reformulation under Augustus that to us appears to have been mainly a reform of who would participate, namely young knights; it seems that no major change took place in Imperial times.[77] The most enigmatic rite, which involves "two young men of noble origin" (μειράκια δύω ἀπὸ γένους), is known to us only through Plutarch, who must follow a pre-Augustan Roman antiquarian, most likely Varro; one has to assume that here, too, knights replaced the aristocrats, if the rite survived at all as the token initiation of the new *luperci*.[78] Nor do we have indications that at first the transfer to Constantinople after 324 changed anything. Such a transfer is not attested, but we have to assume it both because the festival still existed in the tenth century and because of the general assumption that Constantine's New Rome also adopted Rome's festival calendar, especially a festival with Romulean connotations as strong as the Lupercalia had; and we saw that the statue of the she-wolf with the twins could be read as an indication that in New Rome the Hippodrome was close to the *lupercal*.[79] We have no indication as to the time or the authors and motives of the transfer, but it most likely goes back to the early days of the New Rome with its emulation of the older city.

The major changes happened after Constantine. There must have been two locally and temporarily separated reformulations, one in Rome in the fifth century, another one in Constantinople at an unknown date. Both tried to adapt a very popular festival to a Christian empire.

In Rome, the *luperci* and their performance remained at the center of the action, supplemented by lampoons; but the performers were no longer knights or aristocrats but professional actors. The senatorial defenders of the festival also attempted a partial reinterpretation of the festival's meaning that we perceive only in Gelasius' reaction to it. The festival always had

---

[76] Lydus, *Mens.* 4.25, citing the otherwise unknown Anysius.
[77] See the permanence of the iconography between Augustus and the third century CE, Tortorella (2000).
[78] Plut. *Rom.* 21.6. On the initiatory background (but with a different reading) see Ulf (1982) and Bremmer (1987).
[79] Munzi (1994), 351, 353–354; Carandini (2008), 18–20.

The Lupercalia

two meanings that in the eyes of some ancient authors were not incompatible: at least Festus, Ovid, and Plutarch combined the meaning of a purification ritual with that of a ritual that served to provoke fertility in young women.[80] Later authors such as the unknown source Gelasius is relying on replaced the overall aim of helping female fertility and the concomitant sexualized atmosphere with healing, prosperity, and agrarian fertility: the open sexuality must have offended new sensibilities, and the reinterpretation could build on the understanding of the festival as a cathartic rite that is already attested in late Republican times.

In Constantinople, the festival that we perceive in the *Liber caerimoniarum* lost all these traits, became tied to the Circus and the emperor, and turned into a seasonal ritual that enacted the transition from winter to spring. The shadowy Anysius can show how such a seasonal reading might go back to pre-Constantinian Rome; but it became vital once the ritual needed to be kept because as a ritual of the hippodrome it was closely connected with the emperor but had to be reformulated because of its offensive sexuality.[81] We cannot tell whether outside the courtly world there were also more wordly entertainments: there is no Byzantine text on the Lupercalia outside the *Liber caerimoniarum*. The humorless bishops who assembled in the Trullo in 692 offered, in their canon 62, a long list of bad ritual behavior during Kalendae, Vota, Brumalia, and other unnamed popular festivals, but they did not mention the Lupercalia: at the time, the reformulated festival was either confined to the imperial court and therefore taboo for the bishops, or it was temporarily suspended.

In Byzantium, as we saw, the date moved from its fixed position on February 15 to a movable weekday before the beginning of Lent on Sunday Quadragesima; this was the consequence of a focus on horse races, which were prohibited on Sundays and during Lent. It might be that this had happened also in Gelasius' Rome, as part of the adaptation of the festival to the Christian calendar. Although in Rome the Lupercalia did not contain horse races, it is not easily conceivable that any pope would have tolerated the mass entertainment of the Lupercalia on a Sunday or during Lent, even if he allowed the ritual to take place. Thus, a movable date in early February, coordinated with and dependent on the Easter date, would have imposed itself here as well.

---

[80] Festus s.v. Februarius, p. 76 (*mulieres februabantur*); Ovid, *Fasti* 2. 425–452, 5.101f.; Plut. *Rom.* 21.4 (καθάρσια, cp. 10), 7 (young women).
[81] Anysius ap. Lydus, *Mens.* 4.25.

CHAPTER 6

John Malalas and ritual aetiology

Introduction

Festivals are not only performed, their performance is also explained and legitimated by aetiological myths. As scholars of Greek festivals we have been trained to pay attention to the aetiological stories that are told about them in literature, from the Homeric Hymns and the tragedians to Pausanias and beyond. The same is true for Roman festivals, and Ovid has dutifully collected many of these stories in his *Fasti*. But can we make the same claim for the festivals in post-Constantinian times and for the Byzantine authors who might propose such aetiologies? In this chapter, I will answer this question in the affirmative, and I will look at one specific author to do so, an author whose work was crucially important for later Byzantine historians.

The Chronicle (*Chronographia*) that one John of Antioch, nicknamed ὁ ῥήτωρ "the Orator" or, more commonly, with the Hellenized Syrian word for "orator", Malalas, began to write under Justinian and finished some time after the death of his emperor, still remains to be explored in many respects, even after two fundamental collections of scholarly studies and the impressive edition by the late and learned Johannes Thurn that replaced the 1837 edition by Dindorf.[1] In its seventh book, the author treats the foundation and ascent of Rome, with a series of stories that focus mainly on Rhomos, as he calls Romulus in a Greek tradition that goes back to the fourth century BCE.[2] The stories deal mostly with the foundation of Roman institutions:[3] Rhomos built the first temple of Mars; renamed the first month of the year from the

---

[1] See Agusta-Boularot, Beaucamp, Bernardi, and Caire (2006); Jeffreys (1990b). The edition: Thurn (2000); an English translation, based on Dindorf's edition that in turn was closely based on Chilmead's edition of 1691, was published by Jeffreys, Jeffreys, Scott et al. (1986).
[2] Hellanicus, *FGrH* 4 F 84; most Greek writers follow this tradition, not the least Strabo, Dionysius of Halicarnassus, and Plutarch.
[3] See Scott (1990).

unimaginative *Primus* to *Martius* in honor of his father Mars; founded, among other things, the festivals Brumalia and *Martis in Campo*; and introduced the horse races with their four color-coded factions, the greens, reds, blues, and whites, and the fights between the fans of these factions – already Rhomos, like the emperors contemporary with Malalas, used the tensions between the factions as subtle tools of government.[4] Other aetiological stories concern the month name Februarius and the sacrifices during this month, all attributed to Manlius Capitolinus, and a festival called Consilia founded by M. Iunius Brutus.[5] Often, these stories sound so strange that they have incurred the distrust and disdain of scholars used to Greek and Roman mythology, if they ever took notice of them.[6] But they deserve more attention than they have received up to now. In this context, I will concentrate on the festivals Brumalia and Consilia, after an introductory analysis of a different story that belongs to the same context, but does not explain a festival; it does however illustrate the mechanisms of Malalas' aetiologies in a very clear way.

Rhomos and double kingship

After the murder of his brother that accompanied the foundation of Rome (Malalas tells us), the new city suffered heavily from civilian unrest. The new king sought advice from the god in Delphi; the Pythia ordered him to share the power with his brother. This advice was difficult to follow: how do you share power with a dead person, worse with a person whom you yourself killed? Rhomos found a way by founding three institutions. He made a golden image of Remus and put it on a second throne, next to his own; in all his official pronouncements, he made use of the first person plural, as if these pronouncements came from both of them; and he sent golden portrait busts of his brother together with those of himself to all the cities of his empire.[7]

This story is not attested before Malalas, but it founded its own narrative tradition in later Byzantine chronicles.[8] But a century earlier, Servius had

---

[4] *Chron.* 7.5 εἶχεν αὐτοὺς εὐμενεῖς καὶ ἐναντιουμένους τῶι σκόπωι τῶν ἐναντίων αὐτοῦ.
[5] February *Chron.* 7.10–12; Consilia, *Chron.* 7.9.
[6] See the overview in Walt (1997), 292–293, who calls them *künstliche Aitia*; this presupposes an eighteenth- and nineteenth-century opposition between "artificial" and "natural" myth. The otherwise well-informed dissertation of Hörling (1980) looks only at Greek myths.
[7] *Chron.* 7.2.
[8] It also influenced later stories about Constantine: see Dagron (1984), 93–97 on Constantine's dedication of a statue in order to do penance for the murder of his son Crispus.

told a similar story, without indicating his source.⁹ After the murder of Remus (Servius narrated), Rome suffered from a plague (*pestilentia*). An oracle ordered Romulus to placate Remus' ghost: this was perhaps the obvious answer, and certainly less paradoxical than the oracular answer in Malalas. But unlike what we (and any pagan Greek or Roman) would have expected, Romulus did not perform sacrifices and purification rites, he rather addressed Remus' ghost in a more direct way: every time when he set out on official business, he put an empty *sella curulis* with a sceptre, a crown, and all other regalia next to his own. This placated Remus' ghost, the plague disappeared, and Romulus preserved this custom during the rest of his reign. Philippe Bruggisser has shown how the Servian story reflected the system of two Augusti that was tried out by the Antonines, systematized during the tetrarchy with its clear separation between an Eastern and a Western half of the Empire, and given permanence in 395 when the two sons of Theodosius I, Arcadius and Honorius, split the empire between themselves.¹⁰ Bruggisser did not address the question whether the story was an invention of Servius or an earlier author, nor was he interested in the details and mechanics of its narrative. Instead, he underlined how the late Republican and early Imperial myth of the twins Romulus and Remus was adapted to the institutional realities of the late fourth and early fifth centuries. This is correct, but can be extended.

The strange turn the story takes – the plague leads to a new custom instead of the expected and traditional ritual purification – argues for an origin with Servius, or certainly not before Theodosius' prohibition of sacrifices in Servius' youth. The new Christian world had no use for purification sacrifices – not, as anti-Christian propaganda had it, because baptism healed even the worst sins (an idea as old as Julian), but because traditional propitiation needed animal sacrifice.¹¹ But the Christian world still needed aetiological stories for new imperial customs, and since Romulus, the first Roman king, in the words of Gilbert Dagron,

---

⁹ Serv. *Aen*. 1.276 EXCIPIET GENTEM *Remo scilicet interempto, post cuius mortem natam constat pestilentiam; unde consulta oracula dixerunt placandos esse manes fratris extincti; ob quam rem sella curulis cum sceptro et corona et ceteris regni insignibus semper iuxta sancientem aliquid Romulum ponebatur, ut pariter imperare viderentur.* "HE WILL TAKE OVER THE PEOPLE, that is after the murder of Remus, after whose death a plague rose, as we are told; when consulted, the oracles said one should propitiate the ghost of the dead brother; therefore a *sella curulis* with a scepter, a crown and the other royal insignia was always put next to Romulus, when he did official business so that they seemed to rule together." See Bruggisser (1987), 136–138; Pellizzari (2003), 90.
¹⁰ Bruggisser (1987), 136–138.
¹¹ See the story on Constantine's baptism in Zosim. 2.19, with the rich commentary of Paschoud (1971); see also the commentary in his Budé edition, n. 39, pp. 219–224.

"is the prototype for the Byzantine emperor," the story is built around him.[12]

Malalas' story shares with Servius not only the aetiological concern and the main actor, Romulus, but also the narrative structure. Both stories start out with the foundational fratricide. Remus' death is a transgression that leads to supernatural punishment through a plague (in Servius) or civil war (in Malalas) – Servius' narration, which leads from transgression to plague to healing, follows a traditional story pattern, Malalas' civil war is more surprising and recalls, if anything, Horace's *Epode* 16. In both cases, the catastrophe triggers an oracle whose advice the new king follows in a rather ingenious way. As a narrative device, all this is as old as the first book of the *Iliad*.[13] A subgroup of the story pattern has an oracular advice that needs ingenuity because it seems almost impossible to realize: the best-known example is the Wooden Wall oracle in Herodotus.[14]

Details of the two stories, however, differ radically. The differences are tied to the aetiological concerns, and these again are tied to the historical moment in which the story was shaped. Servius' story reflects a detail of imperial protocol in the later fourth century where the second, absent Augustus used to be represented by an empty curulian seat: in the official representation of the power structure, the two Augusti were always thought together, "so that they seemed to rule together" (Servius). In the same way, the constitutions and rescripts in the Theodosian Code consistently are signed by both or, if applicable, all three Augusti in order of seniority every time when more than one Augustus ruled the empire, although it was usually only one of them for whose area the rescript was destined and with whom the original decision originated; and often the place of signing and sometimes a detail in the text give this fact away. This argues for Servius as the inventor of the story, after the two sons of Theodosius had split the empire. We saw that a similar conclusion can be drawn from the fact that it is not a purification ritual that heals Romulus' problem.

Malalas is more intriguing. Although his story is comparable, he explains a very different custom, a detail of imperial style: the consistent use of the *pluralis maiestatis*. Although this plural was sometimes used already in the letters of Hellenistic kings and earlier emperors, it happened in an inconsistent manner, and only Gordian III (238–244) formalized the habit. The plural made sense in a reign with several Augusti; but it must have seemed

---

[12] Dagron (1974), 341–344; the citation 342: "le premier roi Romain est le protoype des empereurs byzantins."
[13] See on this narrative scenario Burkert (1994), 24 (again in 2011, 266).
[14] Hdt. 7.141.3–4; all the sources in Fontenrose (1978), 316, Q147.

strange enough under the monarchy of Justinian to trigger an aetiological story. The other detail in Malalas, the dispatch of double portraits, must have been aetiological in origin as well; it was a firm custom of the emperors since the Julio-Claudians to send images of themselves to select cities. Again, a double portrait made sense in the later fourth and early fifth century, under the system of two Augusti, but it could not occur anymore under Justinian's monarchy: this is why this time Malalas does not explain the detail from contemporary imperial protocol.[15] This implies that he retells a story that was invented for the earlier political system at some point between Servius and Malalas, and adapted it to his own circumstances, all the while retaining elements that had lost their functionality.

Another observation leads to the same chronological conclusion. When Gilbert Dagron analyzed the stories in the Byzantine *Parastaseis* (eighth century) about how Constantine killed his homonymous son and did repentance by making a gilded silver statue of his victim and performing a supplication ritual in front of it, Dagron understood this as an echo of the story from Malalas, with Constantine the founder of the new Rome mirroring Romulus the founder of the first city, on the background of the widespread folktale motif that a murder victim could be reconstituted by a statue.[16] If this is correct, the story as such has no need for Romulus' sending out two busts, one of himself and one of Remus, nor does the story in the *Parastaseis* have more than one single statue, the one of the victim that the murderer worships to be atoned. The reduplication of the images is due solely to the imperial protocol before Justinian, with its two Augusti; in Malalas' own time, such a reduplication had lost its meaning.

Thus, even if Malalas' early Roman stories are relevant for Constantinople at the age of Justinian, not all have been invented by Malalas: an adaptation of an earlier story is always possible. And a few stories have a wider validity than just for Justinian's Byzantium. The *aitia* for the month names Februarius and Martius are valid wherever the Roman calendar was valid; they still might have been invented by Malalas, however. A small number is valid only for the city of Rome, especially the cluster of *aitia* connected with Mars:[17] Rhomos built his first temple, named the first month Martius in the honor of his divine father, and introduced a festival with horse races at the beginning of his month, calling it *Martis in campo* (Μάρτις ἐν κάμπωι). This name is descriptive either of the temple or the festival; the calendar of Polemius

---

[15] In the stories about Constantine and Crispus, told in the much later Byzantine *Patria*, we always deal with a single image only.
[16] Dagron (1984), 93–97.   [17] Malalas, *Chron.* 7.3.

Silvius notes it as Natalis Martis, with circus games, and the games seem to have survived for several centuries.[18] In this case, it is possible or even plausible that Malalas had heard of them from friends or colleagues who had business in Rome, if it was his own invention.

Romulus and the Brumalia

The analysis of the Romulus (resp. Rhomos) and Remus story shows that John Malalas tells a story from Rome's foundational past in order to give an aetiology for a custom in his own time, under the reign of Justinian; even when he adapted a pre-existing story to his own needs, he was aware of the aetiology and omitted in his explanation details that did not fit anymore. His narration unfolds before a background of traditional story-telling, visible both in the motif of the statue that replaces a murdered person and in the well-established pattern that leads from transgression through supernatural punishment to human foundational reaction, a pattern which we know from countless aetiological myths and that finds its root in living reality as early as the Plague Prayers of the Hittite king Mursilis and as late as the Phrygian confession stelai. It is not easy to determine how much Malalas himself relies on oral traditions that must have existed and also fed into the stories in the *Patria*, as Gilbert Dagron showed, and how much he himself invented; but this is irrelevant in our context.[19] What matters much more is the insight that Malalas' stories can help to reconstruct and understand customs and institutions of his own time.[20] This is relevant for my own narrative, about festivals.

Malalas' chapter on Rhomos and Rhemus does not follow chronology but focuses on Rhomos' deeds and achievements, with the fratricide, as the foundational event of his kingship (7.2), narrated well before the birth story (with a she-wolf rationalized as cow-girl) and the upbringing by Faustulus and his wife "She-wolf" (Λυκαίνα) (7.7). This leads to the Brumalia:[21]

---

[18] See Salzman (1991), 126 and, as to its survival, 239 n. 27 (still attested by Atto of Vercelli, *Sermo III in festo Octavae Domini* in the seventh century).
[19] See Dagron (1984) for the *Patria*.
[20] For the Brumalia, the case in question, see Bernardi (2006).
[21] *Chron.* 7.7 (p. 137.68 Thurn): τούτου οὖν ἕνεκεν ὁ Ῥῶμος ἐπενόησε τὸ λεγόμενα Βρουμάλια, εἰρηκώς, φησίν, ἀναγκαῖον εἶναι τὸ τρέφειν τὸν κατὰ καιρὸν βασιλέα τὴν ἑαυτοῦ σύγκλητον πᾶσαν καὶ τοὺς ἐν ἀξίαι καὶ πάσας τὰς ἔνδον τοῦ παλατίου οὔσας στρατιᾶς ὡς ἐντίμους ἐν καιρῶι τοῦ χειμῶνος, ὅτε τὰ πολεμικὰ ἔνδοσιν ἔχει. καὶ ἤρξατο πρώτους καλεῖν καὶ τρέφειν τοὺς ἀπὸ τοῦ ἄλφα ἔχοντας τὸ ὄνομα, καὶ λοιπὸν ἀκολούθως ἕως τοῦ τελευταίου γράμματος, κελεύσας καὶ τὴν ἑαυτοῦ σύγκλητον θρέψαι τῶι αὐτῶι σχήματι. καὶ ἔθρεψαν καὶ αὐτοὶ τὸν στρατὸν ἅπαντα καὶ οὓς ἐβούλοντο. οἱ οὖν ἑκάστου ἀριθμοῦ πανδοῦροι ἀπὸ ἑσπέρας ἀπιόντες εἰς τοὺς οἴκους τῶν

> Therefore Romulus invented what is called the Brumalia, telling (it is said) that the emperor at the time needed to host his entire senate, all persons of high standing, and the soldiers inside the palace as honored guests during the winter when war was at rest. And he began to call and feed first those whose name began with an A, and so forth down to the final letter; and he ordered his own senators to be hosts in the same manner. They fed the entire army and whomever they wanted. And every evening the musicians of each unit went to the houses of those who had invited them to a meal on the following day and played in order to make it known to the person that they would eat there the next day. This custom of the Brumalia has remained in the Roman state up to the present.

Malalas then explains what this has to do with Romulus' strange upbringing.[22]

> Rhomos did this because he wanted to erase the arrogance towards him: the Romans who were his adversaries hated and taunted him, saying that as someone whom they could mock he should not be king, since he and his brother were fed by other people until they grew up and became kings.

The "other people" who fed him were Faustulus and his wife Lykaina, and this turned into a major problem for the twins, because, as Malalas explains,[23]

> among the Romans and in general among the people of old to be fed by other people was regarded as shameful: this is why in the so-called "symposia among friends" each participant brought with him his own food and drink and it was made available to every participant.

This leads to an etymology of the festival name:[24]

> He named the meal in Latin *bromalium* (βρωμάλιουμ), that is to be fed by others, as the most wise Roman historian Licinius explained.

The custom that during a period of twenty-four days the emperor and his entire nobility feed a large group of people is explained as a measure of

---

καλεσάντων αὐτοὺς ἐπ' ἀρίστωι εἰ τὴν ἑξῆς ἤλουν πρὸς τὸ γνῶναι ἐκεῖνον, ὅτι παρ' αὐτῶι τρέφονται αὔριον. καὶ κατέσχε τὸ ἔθος τῶν Βρουμαλίων ἐν τῆι Ῥωμαίων πολιτείαι ἕως τῆς νῦν.

[22] 7.7 (p. 138.81 Thurn): τοῦτο δὲ ἐποίησεν ὁ αὐτὸς Ῥῶμος θέλων ἐξαλεῖψαι τὴν ἑαυτοῦ ὕβριν, ὅτι οἱ Ῥωμαῖοι ἐχθροὶ αὐτοῦ ὄντες καὶ μισοῦντες αὐτὸν καὶ λοιδοροῦντες ἔλεγον, ὅτι οὐκ ἐχρῆν αὐτὸν βασιλεῦσαι ἐνυβρισμένον ὄντα, διότι ἐξ ἀλλοτρίων ἐτροφήσαν οἱ δύο ἀφελφοί, ἕως οὗ τελείας ἡλικίας ἐγένοντο καὶ ἐβασίλευσαν, σημαίνοντες ὅτι τοῦ Φαυστόλου τοῦ γεωργοῦ καὶ τῆς γυναικὸς αὐτοῦ Λυκαίνη ἐτράφησαν ἐκ ἀλλοτρίων ἐθίοντες, ὡς προγέγραπται.

[23] 7.7 (p. 138.86 Thurn): ὄνειδος γὰρ ὑπῆρχε παρὰ Ῥωμαίοις καὶ πᾶσι τοῖς ἀρχαίοις ποτὲ τὸ ἐκ τῶν ἀλλοτρίων τρέφεσθαί τινα· ὅθεν καὶ ἐν τοῖς συμποσίοις τοῖς λεγομένοις φιλικοῖς ἕκαστος τῶν συνερχομένων εἰς τὸ συμπόσιον τὸ ἴδιον αὐτοῦ βρῶμα καὶ πόμα μεθ' ἑαυτοῦ κομίζει, καὶ εἰς τὸ κοινὸν πάντα παρατίθεται.

[24] 7.7 (p. 138.93 Thurn): καλέσας καὶ τὸ ὄνομα τοῦ ἀρίστου ῥωμαϊστὶ βρωμάλιουμ, ὅ ἐστιν τραφῆναι ἐκ τῶν ἀλλοτρίων, καθὼς ὁ σοφώτατος Λικίννιος ὁ Ῥωμαίων χρονογράφος ἐξέθετο.

social compensation. In order to convince his fellow Romans that he was not the poor and despicable person who lacked the means to feed himself but a real king, Rhomos introduced the overly generous custom that he would for almost an entire month feed a large number of people, organized according to the alphabet: he would thus honor "his entire senate, every other outstanding person, and his personal guard." Each day, all the guests would have names beginning with the same letter, and the invitations would run from alpha on November 24 to omega on December 17. The archaic mind-set that read the inability to feed oneself as shameful is explained from the ancient custom of the συμπόσιον φιλικόν or *eranos* to which each participant contributes a share: the *eranos* is the counter-model to the Brumalia dinners. This act of generosity, invented by Rhomos to prove that he had vast means at his disposal and could shame his opponents, was then extended by royal order to all senators – a move that remains unexplained by Malalas but could be read as demonstration of Rhomos' power and thus again as a measure to shame his opponents into obedience.

The element of coercion that can be felt in the aetiology is also visible in the explanation that Malalas gives of the custom that the military musicians announced themselves already on the eve of the banquet, as if the host could have forgotten his duty and needed to be reminded of it. The etymology, finally, deriving Brumalia "from the Latin brōm-alia," means that Malalas combines the Greek βρῶμα with *alius* and reads it in an almost cynical way. Nothing would have prevented him from reading the two components in the inverse and more natural way as "to feed others": once again, Rhomos' hurt pride seems to be the main motive. In a way, then, Malalas' aetiology testifies to the undercurrent of unease – perhaps more among the aristocracy than at the court – about the ongoing and costly custom.

The "most wise Roman historian Licinius," whom Malalas cites as his source for the etymology at the end of his chapter, is Cicero's contemporary Licinius Macer.[25] He is responsible only for a part of the story, and certainly not for the aetiology and etymology of Brumalia that did not exist in his time. In a fragment of his *Historia*, Licinius tells how Acca Larentia, the poor herdsman's wife who brought up the twins, later married a rich Tuscan, inherited his fortune and made Romulus her heir, who out of gratitude instituted *parentalia*, rites at her grave in her memory; it is one of the competing aetiological stories to explain the festival of the Larentalia.[26]

---

[25] On him see Wilhelm Kierdorf, *DNP* 7.167–168; Walt (1997).
[26] Licinius, *Historia* F 1 Peter (= Macrob. *Sat.* 1.10.17); Walt (1997), 197 F 2, see 196 F 1; other stories with the same aetiological aim in Cato, *Origines* F 16 Peter and Valerius Antias, *Annales* F 1 Peter. See Bernardi (2006), 64.

The Larentalia were celebrated on December 23, close enough to the Brumalia to make Malalas feel justified in connecting the Brumalia with Romulus and refer to Licinius Macer as his source, through whatever intermediate authors he had that information.[27]

There is a problem with Malalas' description of the proceedings, however. His Rhomos held twenty-four banquets, each for guests whose names began with the same letter, and he made his senators do the same; he also made his musicians visit the next host on the eve of the banquet to make it known who the host would be. This, however, does not agree with what we know about the Brumalia in Constantinople and elsewhere. Several times, the festival is named after someone – "the Brumalia of Justinian," "the Brumalia of the grammarian Kollouthos," "the Brumalia of our mighty lord Apion," "the Brumalia of the Lords," that is the Augusti Leo and Alexander and the Augusta Zone. In this nomenclature the naming person is the host, and host of only one party; and as one would expect, Apion's Brumalia is held on the first day, November 24.[28] For the same reason, the single banquet could be called with the singular, τὸ βρουμάλιον: we have a description of the lavish *brumalium* of the emperor, Constantine Porphyrogennetos.[29] Malalas' inversion of the proceedings in his aetiology stresses Romulus' potlatch-like generosity with which he reacted to the slur – and it helps to illustrate the equally potlatch-like perception of the festival in his time.

As we shall see below, the Brumalia were unknown in the Latin West; the one-day festival of November 24, the Bruma out of which the later custom must have developed in the East, is not attested before the late second century, in Apuleius and Tertullian.[30] The Ῥωμαίων πολιτεία of which Malalas talked is again Justinian's state, not Romulus' early Rome.

Brutus and the Consilia

Another aetiological story is not connected with Rhomos/Romulus the first king but with Brutus, the first consul of Rome, and it concerns an enigmatic and otherwise unattested festival, the Consilia.[31] When he

---

[27] See the discussion of earlier theories (Servius; Julius Africanus) in Walt (1997), 292–297.
[28] Justinian: Choricius, *Or.* 13; Kollouthos: Georgius Grammaticus, *Poem* 9, in: Ciccolella (2000), 180–262; Apion: *POxy.* 24.2480, line 37.
[29] *Theophanes Continuatus: Const.* 15, p. 456 Bekker.
[30] Apuleius cited by Cassianus Bassus, *Geoponica* 1.1.9 ed. H. Beckh (Leipzig: Teubner, 1895), 6; Tert. *Idol.* 14.6.
[31] Malalas, *Chron.* 7.9 (p. 139–140 Thurn).

recounts the expulsion of the last Roman king, Tarquinius Superbus, and the events that accompany and follow it, John Malalas is not interested in the creation of republican institutions for which he must have had no more interest or understanding than any other subject of Justinian; the way the first period of Roman kingship ended cannot be relevant in Justinian's time, but there might be institutions in Justinian's time that can be tied back to a great Roman such as Brutus. Accordingly, Malalas' main focus is on the aetiological role of Brutus' actions for institutions that fit into Justinian's time, and on the human drama of Brutus' life.

He tells a complex story that centers on the treason of Brutus' son, who was a friend of Tarquinius' son Arruns: the younger Brutus agreed to open the city to Tarquinius and to kill his own father. Brutus' slave Vindicius learned of this and told his master; Brutus arrested his son, interrogated him publicly on the forum, and, when he confessed, killed him without much ado (the verb ἐφόνευσε used by Malalas perhaps expresses his disapproval). The senate, unconcerned by this open act of paternal violence, immediately made Brutus and Collatinus the first consuls and sent a letter to Tarquinius' soldiers asking them to change sides; the soldiers obeyed without hesitation. Brutus then decided to reward his slave publicly: he founded a festival day in honor of Justice, Δίκη, over which he himself presided, sitting on the rostra; he sat his slave next to himself, slapped his cheek three times and pronounced him a free man, then put his own ring on the slave's hand and conferred on him the dignity and some of the income of a *comes*. He called this festival day *Consilia* (which Malalas translated as περιοχῆς ἡμέρα, doubly enigmatically because neither the reason for the translation nor its meaning are immediately clear from the context), and decreed that henceforth the consular magistrates of all provinces should celebrate it as a festival of Justice to honor outstanding slaves. This still happened in his day, as the historian tells us.

In many respects, Malalas' account is close to Livy's story on the expulsion of the Tarquins and the creation of the Republic despite the resistance of young Roman noblemen; it even shares the name of the slave, Vindicius, with Livy, and Malalas refers to Λίβιος ὁ σοφός as his main source.[32] The few scholars who worked on this passage have refused to believe that he read Livy. This might be too radical: as an orator with a legal training, Malalas must have had at least a practical knowledge of Latin, and Livy was still read in his time, at least in excerpts or epitomes, and in the early fifth century the Symmachi were busy with his text; even if the three

---

[32] Livy 1.57–60.

Livy fragments from Egypt pre-date Malalas by two centuries, in some form or other a text might have been available in the East.[33] However that may be, Malalas follows Livy's account in its main outlines. At the same time, he adds considerable drama: the murderous plan against Brutus is conceived and organized by his son alone, not by a group of young aristocrats; as soon as Vindicius informs the older Brutus, the father arrests his son, confronts him on the Forum, and kills him upon his confession. The main story is told much more tersely than in Livy; Malalas' narrative slows down only when he comes to the details of how Brutus manumitted Vindicius at the Consilia. This is his main interest in the story and his main innovation, besides the detail that the Senate immediately made the army switch loyalties, a detail that reflects late antique experience where imperial power was based on the loyalty of the armed forces alone.

There is no scholarly discussion of this aetiological myth for an otherwise unattested festival Κονσίλια, *Consilia*, simply because the editors of Malalas did not believe in their text. In his masterly edition, Dindorf suspected that Malalas meant the *Consualia*, which tradition then must have "normalized" to *Consilia* (after all, most ancient sources connect the god Consus with *consilium*); this has become a certainty with more recent scholars, and even Thurn's edition refers back to Dindorf.[34] But this suggestion is highly unlikely. The Consualia was famous for its horse races and still mentioned alone for this by Jerome in the story of the horse races in the local cult of Marnas in Gaza.[35] More importantly, in the entire literary record the festival is used by Romulus as a pretext to invite the Sabines with their wives and daughters; it was either founded before Romulus or invented by him for this very purpose.[36] This history of deceit in order to gain sexual gratification was the reason why Christian authors would reject the festival as embodiment of pagan immorality.[37] Nor is it likely that the festival was still celebrated in the sixth century. John Lydus, Malalas' contemporary, points out that "the ancients called the horse-races Consualia," which must mean that the festival was unknown in

---

[33] See on the papyri Funari (2011), with the problematic thesis of a late Eastern revival of Livy, 39–48.

[34] *Consualia in mente habuisse videtur*, Dindorf (1831), 183, who also refers to the Slavic translation Konusulia that, however, is as likely a mistake as a distorted memory of *Consualia*. For recent scholars, see e.g. Croke (1990), 7, "Consilia (= Consualia)," or Jeffreys (1990b), 60. For Consus and *consilium*: Varro, *Rer. ant. div.* frg. 140 Cardauns; Festus 36.19 Lindsay.

[35] Jerome, *Vita Hilarionis* 11.

[36] Varro, *De ling. Lat.* 6.20; Cic. *Rep.* 2.12; D.H. *Ant. Rom.* 1.33.1–3 (the Arcadian foundation of the Consualia), 2.31.2–3 (Romulus' decision to abduct the Sabine women); Liv. 1.9.6 (Romulus' invention); Ovid, *Fasti* 3.199; Festus 41 L.; Plut. *Rom.* 14.3. See Scholz (1993) and Bernstein (1997).

[37] See Tert. *De spect.* 5.5–6; Cyprian, *Quod idola dei non sint* 4 (*deum fraudis*); Novatian. *De spectaculis* 4. 4.

Justinian's Byzantium, perhaps had never made it from Old Rome to New Rome because it was closely tied to a landmark in the Circus Maximus.[38] Malalas' Consilia, on the other hand, is clearly defined: Malalas does not mention horse races, the Consilia are a festival day of reversal whose main event was the solemn manumission of slaves either by their masters or, more plausibly, by the consular governor of a province. And where Roman writers from Varro to Augustine had connected *Consus*, the divine recipient of the Consualia, with *consilium*, Malalas connects the festival name *Consilia* with the word *consul*: it was the first consul, Brutus, who instituted the festival day, and it was, in Malalas' words, "the consular rulers of the provinces," οἱ ὑπατικοὶ ἄρχοντες τῶν ἐπαρχιῶν, who performed the rite.[39]

This leads to the details of Malalas' description. They all have to do with the manumission of a slave; this invites us to have a look at the laws and legal customs involved. According to the Roman jurists, there existed in Imperial Roman society two basic ways of formally setting free a slave: after the owner's death through one's testament (*testamento*), or during the lifetime of the owner in a legal proceeding, through the act of *vindicta*; the law texts on the *vindicta* – based on the lex Aelia Sentia of 4 CE – insist on the merits of the slave that had to be approved by a magistrate.[40] Paulus, in his commentary on the lex Aelia Sentia, lists typical reasons for manumission during the lifetime of the owner, such as "when the slave helped his master in a battle, protected him against robbers, nursed him when he was sick, revealed plots against him," this last cause fitting Vindicius so directly that it has been suggested that the person of Vindicius was invented to justify the *manumissio vindicta*.[41]

With the change of legal procedures and the rise of the magistrate's *consilium* during Imperial times, the *manumissio vindicta* became a *manumissio apud consilium*; the *consilium* was a body of advisors to a magistrate, be it the emperor in Rome or any chief magistrate of a province. In the provinces, the manumission took place on the last day of the provincial *conventus*, the period when the governor sat in court. The institutional

---

[38] Κωνσουάλια τὰ ἱπποδρόμια καλοῦσιν οἱ ἀρχαῖοι, Lydus, *Mag.* 1.30, p. 46 Bandy.
[39] Consus *deus consilii*: Varro, *Rer. ant. div.* frg. 140 Cardauns; Festus 36.19 Lindsay; see also Plut. *Rom.* 14.3 (τὸν θεὸν Κῶνσον . . . βουλαῖον ὄντα, κωνσίλιον γὰρ ἔτι νῦν τὸ συμβούλιον); Tert. *Ad nationes* 2.11, *De spect.* 5.5 (*Conso dicaverit deo ut volunt consili*); Arnob. *Adversus nationes* 3.23.2; Aug. *De civ. D.* 4.11; Auson. *Eclog.* 23.16. Only Lydus, *Mag.* 1.30, p. 46 Bandy combines Consus, *consilium*, and *consul*.
[40] See Rotondi (1912), 455, a. 757/54. *Post causam ab iudicibus probatam, CJ* 7.1.1; *apud consilium iusta causa manumissionis adprobata*, Gaius, *Sent.* 6.18.
[41] Digest. 40.2.15.1 *quod dominum in proelio adiuvaverit, contra latrones tuitus sit, quod aegrum sanaverit, quod insidias detexerit*; on Vindicius, Gottfried Schiemann, *DNP* 12.230.

changes in the *manumissio vindicta* also seem to have affected the legal ritual: in its earlier form, the legal action called *vindicatio* was performed by a *lictor* touching the slave with a rod (*festuca*), as he touched every other object that underwent the *vindicatio*. At some point during the Imperial epoch, this was changed, and the presiding magistrate now slapped the cheek of the slave. In our texts, this is sometimes simply alluded to as *alapa*, "smack"; a few late texts, however, are more outspoken, such as Claudian's image that "the cheeks reddened into a citizen's," *in civem rubuere genae*.[42] This change in the legal ritual marked a new distinction between a manumitted slave and a vindicated object: at some point, the law insisted on the humanity of a slave, to the extent that some jurists were even concerned that a too strong *alapa* would cause an injury.[43] But manumission did not turn a *libertus* into an *ingenuus*, a free-born Roman citizen, in at least one respect: unlike the free-born Roman, the freedman could not hold public office. At least in Imperial times, this could be healed through a provision in the lex Iulia et Papia, laws originally written for a very different purpose: the emperor conferred the *ius anulorum aureorum* on an exceptional slave, which made him in most respects equal to a free-born citizen and offered him the possibility of public office.[44]

A close parallel to Malalas' description of Brutus' action at the new Consilia comes from the end of the *panegyricus* (*Carmen* 2) that Sidonius Apollinaris wrote in 468 on the second consulship of the (Western) Augustus Anthemius. The poem is set on the Kalends of January, when the new consul was accessing his office (one does well to recall that the Kalendae Ianuariae in late antiquity had developed into a festival of several days). It ends with an address to the new consul and emperor:[45]

---

[42] Claudian, *De quarto cons. Honor.* 614–61. See the material in Nisbet (1918), 6 (Malalas escaped his notice).

[43] *CJ* 8. 48. 6 *iniuriosa rhapismata*; see also Iust. *Novell*. 81 *praef.* (*si emancipationis actio dudum quidem et per eas quae nuncupantur legis actiones facta cum iniuriis et alapis liberabat eos huiusmodi vinculis*... "if an act of emancipation which formerly, at the time of the *legis actio*, took place through insult and blows, liberated them from such bonds... " [translation Frederick Blume]).

[44] *Digest*. 40.10.5 (*Paulus libro nono ad legem Iuliam et Papiam*): *Is, qui ius anulorum impetravit, ut ingenuus habeatur* ("he who gained the *ius anulorum* should be regarded as a free-born"); 40.10.6 (*Ulpianus libro primo ad legem Iuliam et Papiam*): *Libertinus si ius anulorum impetraverit, quamvis iura ingenuitatis salvo iure patroni nactus sit, tamen ingenuus intellegitur* ("When a freed-man has gained the *ius anulorum*, he should be regarded as a free-born man, even when he gained the rights of a free-born when the right of his *patronus* was not invalidated"). See also *CJ* 6.8.2 *aureorum usus anulorum beneficio principali tributus libertinitatis; Digest*. 38.2 *etiamsi ius anulorum consecutus sit libertus a principe*. On some key aspects of the Lex Iulia et Papia see McGinn (1998), 70–139 (none of them relevant here).

[45] Sidonius Apollinaris, *Carmen* 2.544–548 (my translation).

> nam modo nos iam festa vocant, et ad Ulpia poscunt
> te fora, donabis quos libertate, Quirites,   545
> quorum gaudentes exceptant verbera malae.
> perge, pater patriae, felix atque omine fausto
> captivos vincture novos absolve vetustos.

> Already the festivities call me, and the Roman citizens to whom you will give freedom ask you for the Forum Ulpium: their cheeks will gladly receive the blows. Go ahead, Father of the Fatherland, with Luck and a Happy Omen: you who will put new captives in bonds, free the old ones!

Whereas the poet will participate in the general festivities of the Kalendae, the new consul and emperor will be the main actor in the ceremony of manumission performed in the Forum of Trajan, whose most memorable act is the emperor forcefully slapping the future Roman citizen – which in Rome happened "on fixed days" since the *urbs*, unlike the provinces, did not know or need the institution of the provincial *conventus*.[46]

It is immediately obvious how closely Malalas models his story on these details that were enacted less than a century before he wrote. Vindicius is set free by his own living owner, who is a presiding magistrate; the manumission is based on obvious merits of the slave, and it is followed by Brutus conferring upon him his own ring, the symbol of his own citizen status and thus the equivalent of the *ius anulorum aureorum*; this enhanced status then allows Brutus to make Vindicius a *comes*, giving him a high office with its concomitant income. There was a discussion among jurists about whether a magistrate or a council member could propose the manumission of his own slave, as Brutus did; at least the jurist Salvius Iulianus (born *c.*100 CE) thought this possible, did so when he was praetor and consul, and cited as a precedent his own teacher Iavolenus Priscus; Malalas' story confirms this – a fact overlooked by legal scholars, who usually do not read Byzantine historians.[47] The aetiological aim becomes

---

[46] Gaius, *Sent.* 7.20 (*idque fit ultimo die conventus; sed Romae certis diebus apud consilium manumittuntur*, "this happened on the last day of the *conventus*; but in Rome manumission was performed on fixed days at the *consilium*"; the Roman *consilium* consisted according to the same passage of five knights). See Sguaitamatti (2012), 41–45.

[47] *Digest* 40.2.5: *An apud se manumittere possit is qui consilium praebeat, saepe quaesitum est. Ego, qui meminissem Iavolenum praeceptorem meum et in Africa et in Syria servos suos manumisisse, cum consilium praeberet, exemplum eius secutus et in praetura et consulatu meo quosdam ex servis meis vindicta liberavi et quibusdam praetoribus consulentibus me idem suasi.* "Whether one may manumit in one's own court, providing a council, is a question often asked. For my part, since I remembered that my teacher, Javolenus, had manumitted his slaves both in Africa and in Syria, when providing a council, I followed his example in my own praetorship and consulship and freed some of my own slaves *vindicta* and persuaded some of my own praetors who asked my advice to do the same." Translation: Watson (1998).

even more visible in the utterly anachronistic recommendation of Brutus, acting now more like an emperor than a consul, that in the future all heads of provinces should honor deserving slaves, and should do so by instituting the day *Consilia*. The same aim appears also in the overall development of the story: the manumission of Vindicius takes place on the last day of what has begun with a public trial on the Forum, directed by the first consul Brutus against his son, just as the manumission *apud consilium* takes place on the last day of the provincial *conventus*. And finally the date of the story – the beginning of the new Republic – recalls the Kalendae Ianuariae, the New Year festival on which Sidonius had described the actions of Anthemius.

In other words: Malalas follows the traditional story of Brutus' accession to power that includes the intrigues of Tarquinius Superbus and the help of the aetiologically named slave Vindicius. But he gives it a distinctive late antique flavor and turns the events into a double aition. Implicitly the story is a charter myth for the way in which in late antiquity Romans freed their deserving slaves by slapping their faces three times and giving them the citizen's ring; explicitly Malalas explains the otherwise unattested day *Consilia* with its honors conveyed to slaves on the final day of the provincial *conventus*. This day had its name not, as Malalas implies, from the presence of the consul but from that of the magistrate's *consilium*, who advised on the justification of these manumissions (although the presiding magistrate himself must have been a former consul, a *vir consularis*). Malalas, the legally trained "Orator," must have known the *consilia* well from his own home town Antioch, the residence of the provincial governor of Syria Prima, and in all likelihood he was more than once a member of such a *consilium* that "in the provinces consisted of twenty assessors who were Roman citizens."[48]

The festival name *Consilia* could thus be translated as "Day of the Committees." This still leaves unexplained what Malalas meant with his Greek form of the festival name, περιοχῆς ἡμέρα. Its explanation must be connected with the strong consular coloring of the day in Malalas – not in some irrational vagary of an early Byzantine etymologist, but in a rational connection; after all, Malalas derived the day's name not from *consilia* but from *consul*. Greeks, as John Lydus explained, called the consuls "ὕπατοι that is 'high and great,' ὑψηλοὺς καὶ μεγάλους."[49] A synonymous term of

---

[48] Gaius, *Sent.* 7.20: *in provinciis autem viginti recuperatorum civium Romanorum*. On Malalas and Antioch see Scott (1990a), 70.
[49] Lydus, *Mag.* ed. Bandy, p. 46.3.

"high and great" is περίοχος, "superior, preeminent": I suggest that this is the reason why Malalas associates *Consilia* with περιοχή and calls it "Day of Excellence."[50]

But why did Malalas choose Brutus and not, as in most other aitia of his seventh book, Romulus, who as the first Roman king would have been a natural model for the Byzantine emperor, his distant successor? Brutus as the founder of the Republic should not have interested Malalas much, given his general disregard of democratic institutions.[51] Two reasons offer themselves, and they are connected. On the one hand, Brutus is the first consul, and in terms of the law it is not the emperor *qua* emperor, it is the consul or the consular magistrate who is responsible for the *manumissio apud consilium*, as Sidonius' poem shows. On the other hand, the firm connection of Brutus with freedom has now been turned away from the democratic freedom of citizens – which is irrelevant to the subjects of the emperor – towards the freedom of slaves from their social condition. Both aspects make perfect sense under Justinian; in fact this was perhaps the only aetiology in which Brutus still could make sense in Justinian's monarchy.

Conclusions

It is by now obvious how Brutus' story serves as an aetiological myth for a legal and social institution of the later Imperial epoch. This is all the more intriguing as the form which this institution had taken in late antiquity was an innovation that replaced the former *manumissio vindicta* with its *festuca*-wielding lictor; like any aetiological myth, this one serves (in Malinowskian terms) as a charter for this new institution, giving not just a reason for its specific form, but lending it also high antiquity, legitimacy, and dignity. If Malalas invented the story himself – and nothing prevents us from assuming this, although it cannot be proven – he adapted an age-old story that he himself connected with the impressively-sounding "Livy the Wise" to the exigencies of a new age and its invented traditions, in the same way as – to give just one example – not long after 27 BCE an unknown Roman invented the aetiological story for the Augustan restoration of the Arval Brethren by reshaping the age-old story of Romulus and his foster-parents Faustulus and Acca Larentia.[52]

---

[50] See *LSJ ad voc.*
[51] See esp. Jeffreys (1979), esp. 206f.; Scott (1981), 68 and Scott (1990b), 150.
[52] Scheid (1975), 352–363; the same model is used by Bremmer (1993).

The same is true for the other two aetiological stories analyzed in this chapter, which both used Romulus or rather Rhomos as a model for imperial institutions of Malalas' own time and by doing so reshaped the traditional story. In the aition for the Brumalia, like in the one for the Consilia, Malalas refers to another famous historian of Republican Rome, "the wise Licinius," to legitimize his story, although there it was only a detail that really went back to Licinius Macer and not, as with Brutus and Livy, the entire outline of the story. Thus, he might be unreliable as to his sources, but not in his aim as a historian: far from being a fantasizing liar, John Malalas still followed what Greek and Roman historians regarded as their main vocation, to explain the present from the past, even if with him this turned into an explanation of the past from the present – a not uncommon fate for any historian. And it shows how vibrant the festival culture and its need for invented traditions remained in the age of Justinian. A closer look at the history of the Brumalia will confirm the importance of this festival in Byzantine society.

CHAPTER 7

The Brumalia

The Brumalia are attested only in Byzantium. But at least after the study of John Crawford it is clear that there was a festival in the Latin West that Crawford understood as its predecessor (and that scholars sometimes even confuse with it), the Bruma, attested mainly but not only in Tertullian.[1] This chapter first looks at the Bruma to understand its character and history, then studies the Brumalia in its Byzantine context.

The Bruma in the Latin West

The main attestations for the Bruma come from Tertullian's *De idololatria*, a treatise with a somewhat controversial but most likely pre-Montanist, that is pre-208 CE date.[2] In a chapter that insists on the almost unavoidable *idololatria* of even the most deeply Christian schoolteacher, who, after all, will have to teach literature full of "names, genealogies, myths" (*nomina, genealogias, fabulas* 10.1) of the pagan gods, he adduces as one of his additional arguments that a schoolmaster's pay-day was tied to certain festivals, among others the Bruma and Cara Cognatio.[3] To Tertullian, the festival – whose name here is a feminine singular, the noun *bruma* "the shortest day, Winter solstice, winter" – is thus just one of the many Roman city festivals; it shares the important social function of gift-giving with the Cara Cognatio, a family banquet on February 22.

In a later and longer argument that is crucial for the question of how Christians and non-Christians could live together in the same city, Tertullian argues not only against any participation of Christians in pagan festivals "in dress or food or any other kind of their entertainment"

---

[1] Crawford (1914–1919); see also Mazza (2005).
[2] See the discussion in Waszink and van Weiden (1987), 10–13, who opt for a time between 198 and 208, most likely between 203 and 206 CE.
[3] Tert. *Idol.* 10.3 *Brumae et Carae Cognationis honoraria exigenda omnia*.

(*sive habitu sive victu vel quo alio genere laetitiae earum* 14.2), but also against the performance of these festivals in a purely Christian context:

> By us, to whom Sabbaths are strange and the new moons and festivals formerly beloved by God, the Saturnalia and New-year's Festival and Brumae and Matronalia are frequented; presents come and go and New-year's gifts, games join their noise, and banquets join their din.[4]

Although Christians do not perform any Jewish festival, they still cling to the more entertaining and socially relevant pagan festivals, the Saturnalia, Kalendae Ianuariae, Brumae (here in the plural), and Matronalia with their conviviality, entertainment, and gift exchange. The passage shows how Christians in Carthage (and presumably elsewhere) tried to adapt their culture to the exigencies of Christianity without losing too many social traditions. In a Christian context, they performed these festivals as mere social banqueting and gift-giving; they might have avoided inviting any of their pagan or Jewish neighbors and friends, but they were clinging to the festivals because of their social importance, because of the socially important ties forged by invitations to banquets and by gift-exchange. Each of these festivals could be performed without a private animal sacrifice: there were public sacrifices such as the sacrifice to Jupiter Optimus Maximus at the Kalendae Ianuariae on the Capitol or to Juno Lucina on her altar at the Matronalia, but that was not what mattered for the single households, and Christians could stay away from the public sacrifices, if they so chose, but they could not break the family and neighborhood ties that easily. The Kalendae were a day of individual gift-giving, as were Saturnalia and Matronalia – one offered small take-home gifts, *apophoreta*, to one's guests at the Saturnalia (Martial could fill an entire book with short poems that went together with these *apophoreta*) and more substantial presents to one's wife at the Matronalia.

Gift-giving had high social relevance and was closely observed by one's peers: Vespasian is singled out by Suetonius for having given *apophoreta* to the men at the Saturnalia, to the women at the Matronalia, "but not even this wiped out his old reputation of greediness"; his penny-pinching was famous.[5] Kalendae, Saturnalia, and Matronalia were also days of special banquets; the Saturnalia and the Matronalia were mentioned together as

---

[4] Ibid. 14.6: *nobis, quibus sabbata extranea sunt et numeniae et feriae a deo aliquando dilectae, Saturnalia et Ianuariae et Brumae et Matronales frequentantur, munera commeant et strenae, consonant lusus, convivia constrepunt.* (Translation after S. Thelwall, *Library of the Ante-Nicene Fathers*.)
[5] Suet. *Vesp.* 19.1: *dabat sicut Saturnalibus viris apophoreta, ita per Kal. Mart. feminis. et tamen ne sic quidem pristina cupiditatis infamia caruit.*

the festivals where the slaves were dined by their owners, by the master on the Saturnalia, by the lady on the Matronalia.[6] The Bruma or Brumae, then, must fit into this same atmosphere of lavish banquets and gift-giving; this explains why it was one of the days when teachers could expect remuneration.

Tertullian does not give a date for the festival. Latin *bruma*, shortened from *brevissima*, is the technical term for the winter solstice, usually dated in Rome around December 25.[7] The two late manuscript calendars propose a date for the festival, incidentally confirming that the Bruma were not a local Carthaginian affair but celebrated in fourth-century Rome as well: both assign the festival to November 24, a month before the winter solstice. Two notices in the Greek *Geoponica*, a Byzantine collection of earlier agricultural lore, confirm this festival date, and help identify other possible late second-century references. A short notice does not give much more than the date; it is cited after Florentius, a writer of Severan times and thus a contemporary of Tertullian.[8] A longer notice calls it "the festival day that the Romans call Bruma," and informs us that "according to Democritus and Apuleius" the weather on this day will foretell the weather during the entire winter.[9]

The bulk of the *Geoponica* goes back to Cassianus Bassus, whom most recent scholars date to the sixth century; the intriguing question is how far back the information really goes that Bassus ascribes to Democritus and Apuleius.[10] In the case of Apuleius – whom the *Geoponica* cite not infrequently – René Martin has argued for an otherwise lost but genuine work on rural magic and divination; it is also cited in the *De re rustica* of Palladius, whom the honorific *vir illustris* dates to Constantine's time or later.[11] I concur, although the argument for a genuine work of Apuleius is based on its content and could as well work the other way round, given

---

[6] Banquets: Macr. *Sat.* 1.12.7 (on March 1) *servis cenae adponebant matronae, ut domini Saturnalibus*; the same, Lydus, *Mens.* 3.22, p. 61.18 Wünsch, see Wissowa (1912), 185 n. 7.
[7] Plin. *Nat.* 18.220–223, the date in 221: *a.d. VIII kal. Ian. fere*, "about December 25."
[8] Cassianus Bassus, *Geoponica* 1.1.9 ed. H. Beckh (Leipzig: Teubner, 1895), 6; Crawford (1914–1919), 366.
[9] Cassianus Bassus, *Geoponica* 1.5.3–4, p. 10 ed. Beckh; Crawford (1914–1919), 366: Δημόκριτος δὲ καὶ Ἀπουλήϊός φασι τοσοῦτον χρὴ προσδοκᾶιν ἔσεσθαι τὸν χειμῶνα ὁποία ἔσται ἡ ἡμέρα τῆς ἑορτῆς, ἣν οἱ Ῥωμαῖοι Βροῦμα καλοῦσι, τουτέστι ἡ τετάρτη ἑκὰς τοῦ Δίου μηνὸς ἢ Νοεμβρίου: "Democritus and Apuleius tell that one should expect the winter to be such as the day of the festival that the Romans call Bruma, i.e. the 24th day of the month Dios or November." Although οἱ Ῥωμαῖοι in a Byzantine text can mean "we Byzantines," I read it as pointing to Rome, given the different name the festival had in Byzantium.
[10] A discussion and survey in Georgidou (1990), 20.
[11] Palladius, *De agri cultura* 1.35.9 (the date after *DNP* s.v. Palladius); see Martin (1972).

Apuleius' later reputation as magician. As to Democritus, whom Palladius and Cassianus Bassus cite several times as well, Martin argued for an apocryphal treatise read by another writer on agriculture, the treatise Περὶ ἀντιπάθων cited in Columella.[12]

This would bring down the date of the Bruma well into the Flavian epoch. But things are more complex than this. John Crawford has pointed out that the notice in the *Geoponica* recalls a passage in Pliny's encyclopedia where he cites Democritus for the information that the weather at *bruma* predicts the weather of the entire winter.[13] Pliny means the winter solstice, the "real" *bruma* in December, and not the November festival of which there is no trace in first-century sources: among the Julio-Claudian stone calendars, only the Fasti Maffeiani preserve the dates of late November, but it does not record the Bruma, and nor do the *Menologia rustica*, which are complete and about contemporary with Pliny.[14] Thus, either the belief was transferred from the winter solstice to the homonymous Bruma festival, or a later writer such as Apuleius transferred it erroneously: whatever the answer, the *Geoponica* attest the Roman Bruma festival at the earliest in Apuleius' lifetime, a generation before Tertullian. This dates the innovation at some point between Pliny and Apuleius.

There is a link between the winter solstice and November 24. A calendar that John Lydus in his *De ostentis* claims to have "literally translated" from the calendar of Clodius "the Etruscan" correlates November 24 as "prelude to the winter solstice" with December 23 as the day when "the *bruma*, that is the winter solstice, is full."[15] The same set of data, in a somewhat different formulation, is preserved in a very similar calendar in a fourteenth-century manuscript in the Vatican Library, but ascribed not to Clodius but to Hermes Trismegistos.[16] While the editor of John Lydus, Curt Wachsmuth, identified Clodius ὁ Τοῦσκος with Clodius Tuscus, a very shadowy grammarian of Augustan date, Lorenzo Bianchi declared him as an invention of Lydus, for the one reason that similar calendars are transmitted outside the tradition of Lydus' *De ostentis*; one of them is the calendar of Hermes Trismegistos.[17] But the formulation ἡ βροῦμα, οἱονεὶ ἡ χειμερινὴ τροπή

---

[12] Columella, *De re rustica* 11.3.64; see Martin (1972), 250.
[13] Plin. *Nat.* 18.231; Crawford (1914–1919), 366.
[14] The Fasti Maffeiani are dated by Torrelli (1992), 84 n. 7 to 8 CE at the earliest.
[15] Lydus, *De ostentis* 69 (προοίμια τῆς χειμερινῆς τροπῆς); 70 (συμπληροῦται ἡ βροῦμα, οἱονεὶ ἡ χειμερινὴ τροπή). The date, two days earlier than in Plin. *Nat.* 18.220, explains Pliny's hesitations in 221 (*a.d. VIII kal. Ian. fere*, "about December 25").
[16] Vaticanus graecus 1056, edited by Bianchi (1914).
[17] Wachsmuth (1897), in the introduction of his edition of Lydus, *De ostentis*; Bianchi (1914). See *DNP* 3.42 and Domenici (2007), 151 n. 120 (both are too vague).

feels like a gloss by Lydus translating the Latin word *bruma*; thus, one should not doubt his claim that he translated a Latin text even if a later manuscript ascribed it much more grandiloquently to Hermes Trismegistos.[18] I feel less confident about the real authorship of Clodius the Etruscan. Etruscan lore appealed to John the Lydian, who believed in an old connection between Lydia and Etruria and whose epoch believed in the excellence of Etruscan divinatory lore.[19] The name Clodius Tuscus might well have been enough to make him take the Augustan grammarian as a venerable Etruscan; Tuscus is rare but not inexistent as a cognomen.[20]

But the question of whether these calendars have a distinct and knowable author is not very relevant here. More important is the insight that November 24 and December 23 are correlated in solar astronomy, November 24 as the day when the sun visibly enters the hibernal downward slide, and December 23 as its nadir, the winter solstice: this explains why at some point in time November 24 became the festival Bruma as the prelude to the real *bruma*, preparing for the dark period with ample food and generous hospitality. It is unclear whether these calendars themselves also imply the festival, or whether they belong to the first century that precedes the institution of the Bruma festival in the second: none of them gives festival names. Nor does the astronomical information exclude the possibility that the festival might have originated in the countryside as a festival to mark the end of the harvest season and the onset of winter: this at least was the understanding of the eleventh-century historian Georgios Kedrenos, who explained that the later Brumalia festival came from "the farmers who, resting after their work on the fields, fed each other in turns after their respective names in banquets and leisure-time."[21] This is an aetiological story and as such historically unreliable, not unlike the story that explains the U.S. festival of Thanksgiving, which sits at about the same point in time. Thanksgiving, like Bruma, might well feed on the same two roots, agriculture with its care for the human belly and the solar cycle; astronomy, after all, can mirror more general perceptions of the seasonal cycle. At some point, however, the hypothetical agrarian Bruma must have

---

[18] Wachsmuth (1897), 157 n. 2.
[19] Lydians and Etruscans: e.g. Lydus, *Mens.* 37 p. 16 Wünsch, an opinion that had Herodotus' authority. See Bianchi (1914), 15; on John Lydus and Etruscan lore also Briquel (1997), 199–200.
[20] Examples in *ILS* 4.250.
[21] Georgius Cedrenus, *Compendium* vol. 1, p. 259 Bekker: ἐπετέλεσε [sc. Romulus] δὲ καὶ τὰ καλούμενα βρουμάλια, καθάπερ οἱ γεωργοὶ μετὰ τὴν γηπονίαν ἀναπαυόμενοι ἀμοιβαδὸν ἑαυτοὺς ἀπέτρεφον πανηγυρίζοντες καὶ ἀγραυλοῦντες ἐπὶ τοῖς ἀλλήλων ὀνόμασιν.

gained urban status, in order to become one of the festivals at which the teachers expected their salaries.

A medieval continuation

Whenever the *Bruma* was created, it survived in the Latin West well into the Middle Ages. The council of Rome that pope Zachary organized in 743 or 744 contains a canon that tried to prohibit it:[22]

> No-one should dare to celebrate the January Kalends and the Broma [*sic*] in a pagan rite, or to prepare tables with meals in [private] houses, nor to organize singing and dancing on streets and squares: this is the greatest injustice in God's eyes; be it cursed!

The combination is interesting. The Bruma, like the Kalendae, were still the occasion of exuberant festivities in private banquets or public dancing and singing that centuries of Christianization had not fully eradicated – at least in the eyes of the severe clerics who legislated against them. The canon might be the papal reaction to a complaint to the pope that Boniface, the apostle of the Germans, made in a letter of 742 about the bad example that the exuberant Kalendae on Rome's streets set for the visiting Germans that Boniface had recently baptized and weaned off their heathen sensuality; the valiant monk and saint-to-be was pretty frustrated about what his converts brought back from their pilgrimage to the Eternal City.[23] The Bruma did not appear in Boniface's letter, which, however, concerned other comparable events; the Bruma might have escaped the censorial notice because it remained an indoor affair.

Shortly after this, Charlemagne and his son Pippin outlawed those "depraved people" who "worshipped those who were holding the Bruma" (*brumaticos*): the custom is mentioned together with the lighting of candles and making vows for the sake of people, and the use of magically adulterated communion bread.[24] Not all the details are clear, but they are consistent with the interpretation of the Bruma as a household event.

---

[22] Canon 9 (Mansi 12.384): *ut nullus Kalendas Ianuarias et Broma ritu paganorum colere praesumpserit aut mensas cum dapibus in domibus praeparare, ut per vicos et plateas cantationes et choros ducere, quod maxima iniquitas est coram Deo: anathema sit.*

[23] Boniface, *Ep*. 50 (*MGH Epistolae: Epistolae Selectae* 1, p. 301, 8–16) = *Ep*. 49 (*PL* 89.747A).

[24] *Capitulum Caroli Magni et Pippini filii*, in: Alfred Boretius, ed., *Capitularia Regum Francorum* 1 (*MGH Leges*) (Hannover: Hahn, 1883), 202, no. 96.3 (date between 790 and 800): *De pravos illos homines qui brunaticus* [i.e. *brumaticos*] *colunt et de hominibus suis subtus maida cerias incendunt et votos vovent: ad tale vero iniquitas eos removere faciant unusquisque; nisi voluerint ad ecclesiam panem offerre, simpliciter offerant, non cum aliqua de ipsa iniqua commixtione.* ("On the depraved people who worship those who hold the Bruma, light *maida* candles underneath their people, and make

Unlike in the case of the Roman canon that I am tempted to read as a case of unbroken continuity with the earlier Roman festival, here it is conceivable that a local Germanic or Celtic ritual was hiding under the Roman name.[25] But even then, the use of the festival name proves that the originally pagan festival was still remembered, even if only by the learned clerics who advised the king.

Eastern sensibilities: the Heliodysia

To sum up, then, before Constantine the *Bruma* appeared mainly as a household affair with banquets and gift-giving but no attested outward manifestation in the streets, and it marked the point when the sun entered its final downward slope towards the winter solstice. It was at home in Rome as well as in other Western cities, at least in colonies such as the Colonia Iulia Carthago: this argues for a transfer of the Bruma also to Constantine's New Rome. At some point in time, the one-day Western Bruma was transformed there into the twenty-three-days-long Brumalia. We can at least formulate a hypothesis as to how this happened.

An additional punctilio imposes itself. An otherwise unknown winter festival echoes the Bruma in a suggestive way. In a Greek calendar from a fourteenth-century Baroccianus in the Bodleian Library, November 22 is marked as Ἡλιοδυσία – obviously not the winter solstice but a point when the downwards movement became visible, comparable to Clodius the Etruscan's "prelude to the winter solstice," but two days earlier.[26] The calendar combines festivals of different origin, the Egyptian New Year, the Isiac Ploiaphesia, and even an Ἄρεος ἑορτή on March 1 which must be a festival of a Roman garrison; partly because of this, Stefan Weinstock argued that the underlying calendar with its eclectic festivals belonged to an Anatolian port city and was compiled in about 15 BCE.[27] The *Heliodysia* must be an Eastern festival that we cannot place anymore; but it shows how somewhere in the East a date in late November was perceived as the starting point of the sun's downward slope, comparable to the Western

---

vows: everyone should remove them from such misdeeds. And if they want to offer bread in the church, they should offer it pure and not with some illegal admixture in it.") Not everything is clear, as the editor in *MGH* remarked (*quales sane sint superstitiones non omnino liquet*); on the communion bread see also canon 5 of the German Council of 743, Mansi 12.365ff. (*hostias immolatitias quas stulti homines iuxta ecclesias ritu pagano faciunt*).

[25] The editor in *MGH* suggested "Iulfest."
[26] Codex Baroccianus 131, *fol.* 134 and 134ᵛ; see *Catalogus codicum astrologicorum Graecorum* 9:1 (1951), 137. See Mazza (2005), 164.
[27] Weinstock (1948); and see Weinstock (1964), 394.

Bruma festival. The Brumalia, then, could rely not only on Western but also on Eastern perceptions.

The Brumalia in Constantinople

We saw how John Malalas explained the festival in his time, under Justinian, as an invention of Romulus in order to defend himself against the stigma of low origins and the envy of the Roman aristocrats. A very different and rather more complex account of the same Brumalia is given by Malalas' contemporary, the learned administrator John Lydus, in his work *On the Months*.[28] The preserved but fragmentary text talks about the Brumalia not in the chapter on November, where we would expect it, but on December; in November, Lydus only records that for the Romans the season of leisure lasted "from November 15 and during the entire month of December, and they spent this leisure-time exclusively with festivities because of the shortness of the days."[29] After having noted horse races on December 5 (4.156, a fragment) and presented a lexicographical excursus on the term διπούνδιοι for "recruits" (4.157), he embarks on a long paragraph on the Brumalia (4.158) – at a place where, in the calendrical order that Lydus follows as his template in book 4, one would expect a discussion of the Saturnalia of December 17. He starts from a tripartite social structure for ancient Rome (his own, not Dumézil's), with citizen soldiers, farmers, and hunters, then ties this to the calendar. Farmers and soldiers cannot exercise their profession during the cold weather and the short days of midwinter: "This is why they called the season in their own language *bruma*, that is 'short day', and Brumalia, that is 'winter festival'."[30] The mention of the Brumalia serves as a transition to the seasonal customs of midwinter:

> Being inactive during this time until the winter solstice, the Romans had formal visits towards night-time, shouting a greeting to each other and saying in their native language *vives annos*, that is "live long."[31]

---

[28] *Mens.* 4.158. On John Lydus see esp. Maas (1992); this passage, 64–66.

[29] Lydus, *Mens.* 4.151 (preserved not in the main manuscript tradition, but only in a fourteenth-century Greek manuscript in Berlin, Wünsch's *Hamiltonianus*): ἀπὸ δὲ τῆς πεντεκαιδεκάτης τοῦ Νοεμβρίου μέχρις ὅλου τοῦ Δεκεμβρίου ἤργουν οἱ Ῥωμαῖοι, ἐν μόναις εὐωχίαις ἐνασχολούμενοι διὰ τὴν βραχύτητα τῶν ἡμερῶν.

[30] p. 174.3 Wünsch: ὅθεν καὶ *βροῦμαν* αὐτὴν πατρίως ὠνόμασαν, οἱονεὶ βραχὺ ἦμαρ [the correct etymology]· *Βρουμάλια* δὲ οἱονεὶ χειμεριναὶ ἑορταί.

[31] p. 174.5 Wünsch: ἀργοῦντες οὖν τὸ τηνικάδε οἱ Ῥωμαῖοι μέχρι τῶν Αὐξιφωτίων ἐπὶ τῶν νυκτῶν χαιρετίζοντες ἐπευφήμουν ἀλλήλους, τῇ πατρίῳ φωνῇ λέγοντες 'βίβες ἄννους' οἷον 'ζῆθι εἰς χρόνους.'

He then returns to the three social groups, or rather the two that are inactive in winter, at least as to their proper activities: farmers and soldiers. There were some traditional activities for the farmers during this period: the herdsmen sacrificed animals, the agriculturists pigs to Kronos and Demeter, and the wine-growers billy-goats to Dionysos; the city-folk collected food stuff and made waterless cakes that they offered to the priest of the Mother.[32] This leads to the custom of the present day, with an important qualification:[33]

> This custom is still kept today, and in November and in December until the solstice they bring cakes to the priests; but to visit (a person of rank) by name at the Brumalia is more recent. But closer to the truth – and this is why the Church has banned them – they call them festivals of Kronos: they take place during the night because Kronos has been put into darkness when sent to Tartaros by Zeus, which allegorically means that the grain is distributed in the earth and does not remain visible anymore. This is closer to the truth, as I said, because their interest in the festival is to stroll around at night, so that the Brumalia truly are the festival of subterranean demons.

The cake offerings to the priests must be a popular custom of ordinary Christians in the cities who do not indulge in the Brumalia banquets of the ruling class, just as the farmers still slaughter pigs, although neither group sacrifices anymore to the pagan gods. In Lydus' reading, both customs are remnants of the pagan past, although harmless remnants; similarly, the cakes for the priests are an equivalent of the gifts to the pagan teachers that were mentioned by Tertullian. This conforms to Michael Maas' observation that "in book IV, Lydus limited himself almost exclusively to festivals from pagan Roman antiquity," not in order to defend paganism but to show how they were transformed "into a more acceptable ... practice."[34] The Brumalia, however (as Maas already saw), do not conform to this rule. Doubtless, to Lydus they are a transformation as well, this time from the pagan Saturnalia; it is the Brumalia with their banquets that were

---

[32] We have no other indication of such cakes for Magna Mater in Rome.
[33] p.174.19 Wünsch: φυλάττεται δὲ ἡ τοιαύτη συνήθεια ἔτι καὶ νῦν καὶ κατὰ τὸν Νοέμβριον καὶ Δεκέμβριον ἄχρι τῶν αὐξιφωτίων προσφέρουσιν αὐτὰ τοῖς ἱερεῦσιν. τὸ γὰρ κατ' ὄνομα χαιρετίζειν [χαιρετισμός is Polybius' term for the Roman custom of *salutatio*, 32.25.8] ἐν τοῖς Βρουμαλίοις νεώτερόν ἐστι· τὸ δὲ ἀληθέστερον, ἐξ οὗ καὶ ἡ ἐκκλησία ἀποτρέπεται αὐτά, Κρονίας ἑορτὰς αὐτὰς λέγουσιν. ἐν νυκτὶ δὲ γίνονται, ὅτι ἐν σκότει ἐστὶν ὁ Κρόνος ὡς ταρταρωθεὶς ὑπὸ τοῦ Διός, αἰνίττονται δὲ τὸν σῖτον ἀπὸ τοῦ ἐν τῇ γῇ σπαρῆναι καὶ τὸ λοιπὸν μὴ φαινομένου. τοῦτο δέ ἐστιν ἀληθέστερον ὡς εἴρηται, ὅτι νυκτιπόρος ἡ περὶ αὐτὰ σπουδή, ὥστε λοιπὸν κατὰ τὸ ἀληθὲς τῶν καταχθονίων δαιμόνων εἰσὶν ἑορταὶ τὰ Βρουμάλια.
[34] Maas (1992), 64.

celebrated at night, not the Saturnalia. But with the church authorities, Lydus understood this as highly problematical: the Saturnalia was the festival of the seed-god Kronos-Saturnus, whom Zeus imprisoned in Tartaros; therefore it is truly a "festival of an underground demon," no better than Satan and his demons. In this reading, Lydus' plural, καταχθόνιοι δαίμονες, is no more than a rhetorical amplification, adding Saturnus to all the other hellish demons into which Christianity has turned the pagan gods; or else he is quietly adding Demeter and Dionysos, the other recipients of sacrifices in his reconstruction of the winter rites of the pagan farmers. After all, both divinities have an association with the underworld, Demeter as the mother of Kore-Persephone, Dionysos as Persephone's son in the Orphic tradition.[35] From his antiquarian perspective, Lydus is also aware that the alphabetically organized visits are more recent: obviously, his research did not find this detail in the texts on the Saturnalia or other pagan winter customs that he consulted.

Incidentally, the custom of offering cakes during the Brumalia is attested in a poem by Christophoros of Mytilene "to his friend Nikephoros who had sent cakes at the time of the Brumalia." To judge from his preserved poems, the otherwise unknown Christophoros was a high official in Byzantium, active in the first half of the eleventh century.[36] The poem inscribes itself into the custom of Brumalia poems attested for several centuries, mostly at the Byzantine court, but also in sixth-century Egypt.[37] The poet teasingly corrects his friend:[38]

> Ἐκ ῥημάτων με δεξιοῦ, μὴ πεμμάτων·
> ἐμοὶ γὰρ ἡδὺ βρουμάλιον οἱ λόγοι,
> ὡς προσκυνητῇ καὶ λατρευτῇ τοῦ λόγου·
> τῶν δὲ σταλέντων πεμμάτων τίς μοι λόγος;

> Welcome me with words, not with cakes: to me, words are a sweet Brumalia present, since I adore and worship the Word; but what shall I say and care about the cakes you sent?

He plays with several meanings of λόγος, "word": the poetic word, the words one speaks about something, the Word that a Christian worships.[39] The text attests to the spread of the custom of giving cakes as a Brumalia

---

[35] The text thus should be added to the *testimonia* on the Orphic mythology of Dionysos.
[36] Kurtz (1903), iii–iv.   [37] Perpillou-Thomas (1993).
[38] Christophorus Mytilenaeus, *Poem* 115, Kurtz (1903) = De Groote (2012) (my translation).
[39] The singular βρουμάλιον can mean a single banquet, see Sophocles s.v. (add πρὸς τὴν βρουμάλιον τράπεζαν "to the Brumalia table i.e. banquet," Theodoros Daphnopates, *Epist.* 31 ed. Darrouzès and Westerink) or the presents given at the Brumalia.

present beyond the ritual act of thanking one's priests for their work, comparable to the Saturnalia presents for which Martial wrote the accompanying epigrams collected in his book 14, or the *strenae* given at New Year, attested in another poem of the same Christophoros.[40]

Lydus' account differs radically from the one given by Malalas. When Malalas focused almost exclusively on the potlatch aspects of the Brumalia with its enforced generosity, it was not because of his religious objections: the festival was instituted by Rhomos, the foundational predecessor of all Byzantine emperors, which legitimized and anchored it deeply in the Roman past. John Lydus, on the other hand, shared the Church's disapproval of the Brumalia. Thus, he identified the festival with the pagan Saturnalia, despite the different date of which he must have been well aware; this allowed him to connect the Brumalia with evil Kronos, the underground demon *par excellence*. "More truthfully," we deal with an old pagan festival that originated during the period of the year when the season imposed inactivity upon Roman society, and there existed other seasonal customs that derived from the same old period of inactivity – the slaughtering of the pigs, and bringing cakes to the priests.

At the same time, he connected it with a well-known social institution. The citizens are engaged in *salutationes* (χαιρετίζοντες), albeit at a somewhat unusual time: instead of early morning as in the standard *salutatio*, these inverted *salutationes* take place towards nighttime and are in reality banquets. As *salutationes* they are socially asymmetrical visits during which the powerful patrons received their dependents and clients; but unlike Malalas, John Lydus does not dwell on the social asymmetry. Instead, he dwells on the history: in earlier times guest and host greeted each other – reciprocally and symmetrically – with the formal wish for long life, *vives annos*. In more recent times, after the Brumalia have come into existence, these visits were also organized according to the alphabetical position of the name (κατ' ὄνομα χαιρετίζειν). Thus, Lydus' understanding of the Brumalia dinners as a specific expression of the traditional *salutatio* in a client system underlines that he, unlike Malalas, has no problem with the social aspect of the Brumalia but, like the orthodox church, takes offense at their "pagan" character, which comes from the fact that they are a transformation from the old Saturnalia.[41] Despite the different date – Brumalia from November 24 to December 17, Saturnalia from December 17 to 19 (in

---

[40] *Poem* 124, Kurtz (1903) = De Groote (2012), fragmentary.
[41] Kaldellis (2003) argues for (hidden) paganism of John Lydus; in this perspective, this passage would be tongue-in-cheek.

Republican times) or 21 (after Domitian) – they shared some common traits, especially the generous dinners offered by social superiors to their dependants, including the slaves, the giving of small gifts, and the calendar date in midwinter when all activities had ground to a halt.

From Bruma to Brumalia

It is now obvious that the Western Bruma festival, attested to in some detail by Tertullian, publicly still celebrated in Rome in the year 354, and somehow surviving even at the time of Charlemagne, has to be separated from the Eastern Brumalia.[42] The former was a one-day festival, celebrated on November 24 by the households with banquets, entertainments, and the exchange of small gifts; the latter was a prolonged festival and banqueting period that started on November 24 and lasted for as many days as there were letters in the Greek alphabet, that is twenty-four days until December 17.

Since the Western Bruma still retained its one day in 354, one has to assume that Constantine transferred the Bruma festival in its Roman shape to his new city, and that it was there that at some point it developed into the period of twenty-four festival days with their banquets. The most economic hypothesis is to assume that this happened in order to replace the Saturnalia and its divine recipient, the pagan demon Saturnus, with a less offensive celebration.[43] It need not have happened under pressure from the bishops – in fact, their ongoing objections (to which I will come back below) argue against such an assumption: the change must have been introduced by an emperor. An obvious date for it would be the time around Theodosius' repeated prohibition of pagan sacrifices in the 390s. Can this guess be substantiated?

The *Liber caerimoniarum* gives a short, but puzzling history of the festival. Telling us that the festival was abolished "in the reign of the tyrant Romanos" but reinstated by "the Christ-loving Konstantinos" – that is, abolished after Romanos Lekapenos' election as a co-emperor of Constantine VII in 921, and re-installed after Romanos and his sons fell from power in 945 – the author adds a severe criticism of the emperor Romanos:[44]

---

[42] Not all earlier authors have made this distinction, not even Wissowa (1912), 443 n. 1.
[43] See W. Pax, "Brumalia," *RAC* 2 (1954), 646–649.
[44] *Liber caerimoniarum* 2.16, p. 606 Reiske: ἰστέον, ὅτι ἡ τῶν βρουμαλίων αὕτη τάξις ἠλλοιώθη καὶ εἰς τὸ μηκέτι εἶναι παρήχθη ἐπὶ τῆς βασιλείας Ῥωμανοῦ δεσπότου. οὗτος γὰρ προσχήματι εὐλαβείας,

One has to understand that this arrangement of the Brumalia was changed and reduced to nothing under the despotic emperor Romanos. Under the pretext of solicitude, and deeming it not fitting for the Romans to celebrate the Brumalia according to the old customs of the Ausonians, he ordered it to stop. But he did not take seriously the former great and laudable emperors, not the great and laudable Constantine, nor Theodosius, nor Marcian, nor Leo Makelles,[45] nor Justinian, nor all the other Christ-loving emperors whom I would call demigods.

In this account, the Brumalia started well before Theodosius I, with none other than Constantine himself. We do not know on what evidence this is based or whether the claim is simply rhetorical, to bolster a polemical argument against the evil Romanos and to justify the restoration of the festival in the face of hostile bishops. Do we have other data that might be less biased?

As we saw, our main accounts of the festival are the ones in Malalas and in John Lydus. Both wrote in the time of Justinian, but this does not need to date the innovation this late, despite Lydus' information that "the greeting by name in the Brumalia is relatively new (νεώτερόν)": in the context of his discussion, this only means that it was added after the pagan phase of the festival.[46] Again, the time of Theodosius I offers itself as a possible *terminus post quem*. And there is at least evidence that the new festival pre-dates Justinian. We possess an anacreontic poem, written εἰς τὰ Βρουμάλια Κολλούθου τοῦ γραμματικοῦ, anonymous but attributed by a plurality of scholars to an evanescent Georgios Grammatikos.[47] If we do not know the author, we at least know the recipient: Kollouthos of Lycopolis lived under Anastasius (491–518), a century after Theodosius I; and the poem suggests that its author was a contemporary.[48] The title of the poem presupposes the alphabetic banquets, and its content confirms this. The unknown poet praises Kollouthos as "lord of the letters" because kappa precedes "the letter of the *logoi*" and thus "wakes up the dances of the Charites" (lines 15ff.), and the addressee suggests that the festival was

---

καὶ οὐχὶ δίκαιον εἶναι κατὰ τὰ παλαιὰ ἐθήματα Αὐσόνων Ῥωμαίοις βρουμαλίζειν νομίσας, ταῦτα σχολάζειν ἐκέλευσεν, οὐ κατὰ νοῦν λαβὼν τοὺς μεγάλους ἐκείνους καὶ ἀοιδίμους βασιλεῖς, οἷον· οὐ τὸν μέγαν ἐκεῖνον καὶ ἀοίδιμον Κωνσταντῖνον, οὐ Θεοδόσιον, οὐ Μαρκιανόν, οὐ Λέοντα τὸν Λεομακέλλην, οὐκ Ἰουστινιανόν, οὔτε τοὺς ἄλλους φιλοχρίστους, οὓς καὶ ἡμιθέους εἴποιμι ἄν. See Magdalino (1988), 115.

[45] Leo I Marcellus, nicknamed *Makelles* "the Butcher," ruled 457–474 and succeeded Marcian (ruled 450–457).

[46] p. 174.22 Wünsch: τὸ γὰρ κατ' ὄνομα χαιρετίζειν ἐν τοῖς Βρουμαλίοις νεώτερόν ἐστι.

[47] Georgios Grammaticus, *Poem 9*, in Ciccolella (2000), 252–263; on the author, 176–178; *anonymus* in Bergk, *Anthologia* 3.362.

[48] There is thus no need to assume that this Georgios was the much later Georgius Choeroboscus.

celebrated not only in Constantinople but in Egypt as well. This is confirmed from another and very different source, half a century later: the ledgers of Apion, a grandee with court ties at Oxyrhynchos, record, for Athyr 28 (= November 24) of the year 565, wine "at the happy Brumalia of our mighty Lord Apion."[49] Thus, wealthy Egyptians adopted the metropolitan custom of what Malalas described as an elite event, to offer a banquet according to the letter of one's name.

There is other evidence for the Brumalia outside of Constantinople; it is more ambiguous. Among the speeches of Choricius of Gaza, there is one held "for the Brumalia of Justinian": it was read when the emperor and the empress, Theodora, stayed in Gaza in November and December of 532.[50] But it is unclear whether the festival was regularly celebrated in Gaza or only during the imperial visit, to transfer momentarily what basically was a court festival to the host city. In his *Defense of the Mime*, Choricius describes the Brumalia ("the traditional festival" of the Romans, i.e. the Byzantines) as an imperial event during which mimes were enacted; this suggests a metropolitan festival only, and leaves Egypt as the only other place besides Constantinople where the festival was celebrated.[51] It is impossible to estimate how long it would take for such a custom to spread from the metropolis to Egypt, but a date at the time of Theodosius I is certainly not impossible.[52]

The Christian contestation

Lydus recorded the opposition of the Church: ἡ ἐκκλησία ἀποτρέπεται αὐτά, "the Church forbids it."[53] A century later, in 692, the Council in Trullo includes the Brumalia in its list of prohibited festivals: "The so-called Calends, and what are called Vota and Brumalia, and the festival which takes place on the first of March, we wish to be abolished from the life of the faithful."[54]

---

[49] *POxy.* XXVII 2480, line 37: ἐν τοῖς αἰσίοις Βρουαμλίοις τοῦ δεσπότου ἡμῶν τοῦ ὑπερφυεστάτου Ἀπίωνος. See Perpillou-Thomas (1993).

[50] Choricius, *Oratio* 13 ed. Foerster and Richtstein; see Litsas (1980), 231–234 and 310f.; (1982), 429–430.

[51] Choricius, *Or.* 32 (8).57, p. 357 Foerster and Richtscheid.

[52] *Ant. Pal.* 9.580, an anonymous and not easily datable poem on the month, makes the Brumalia banquets the characteristic event of November (8 δαῖτα φέρω χαρίεσσαν ἐς οὔνομα φωτὸς ἑκάστου). Line 5 makes August the month when the Nile is flooding: was it written in Egypt as well?

[53] *Mens.* 4.158 (p. 174.24 Wünsch).

[54] Trullo, canon 62: Τὰς οὕτω λεγομένας Καλάνδας καὶ τὰ λεγόμενα Βοτὰ καὶ τὰ καλούμενα Βρουμάλια καὶ τὴν ἐν τῇ πρώτῃ τοῦ Μαρτίου μηνὸς ἡμέραι ἐπιτελουμένην πανήγυριν καθάπαξ ἐκ τῆς τῶν πιστῶν πολιτείας περιαιρεθῆναι βουλόμεθα. – Text and translation after Nedungatt and

The Kalendae Ianuariae and *vota* were protected as an integral part of the legal calendar by Theodosius I, as we saw, and they retained this protection by their inclusion in the Codes of Theodosius II and Justinian – but this did not stop the ecclesiastical contestation in East and West which perhaps found most prominent expression in Augustine's Carthaginian sermon on January 1 of presumably the year 403. The festival (πανήγυρις) of March 1 continues the old Roman *Matronalia*: the festival was already attacked by Tertullian as one of the Roman customs continued by his Carthaginian Christians.[55] Christians must have been attracted both by its gift-giving – which gave harmless even if sometimes extravagant expression to a husband's gratitude or feeling of social obligation – and by its banquets, where the *matronae* dined with or served the slave women of the household.

The late antique history of the Matronalia is hazy. Among the manifold rituals of March 1, John Lydus mentions the sacrifice to Juno Lucina (whom he understands as the light-bringing moon, in an etymologically correct connection with *lux*, "light") and the *matronae* who were hosting the slaves (αἱ λεγόμεναι παρ'αὐτοῖς ματρῶναι ... τοὺς οἰκέτας εἰστίων); but he omits the festival name, nor does he suggest that the custom was still alive in his day.[56] If it survived in some form, the gift-giving and the banquets did so in a purely private setting, without any public manifestation: this explains their absence in Lydus or, for that matter, in the *Liber caerimoniarum*, but did not prevent the bishops from trying to repress it.[57] The same must have happened in the West: after Tertullian, no Christian author deals with the Matronalia anymore, with the exception, more than six centuries later, of Atto, between 914 and 961 bishop of Vercelli in Northwestern Italy (the Roman Vercellae where Marius routed the Cimbri and Teutones; today a sleepy provincial town between Turin and Milan). In a sermon on January 1 – in his time and world the *Octava Domini*, the eighth day after Christmas that recalled Christ's circumcision – Atto attacks some still surviving pagan customs of the Kalendae Ianuariae, but also those of the Kalendae Martiae: "In the same way, on the Kalends of March such people are accustomed to rave with many

---

Featherstone (1995), 142 who reprint the Greek text of 1962 by Périclès-Jean Joannou. There is also an English translation by Lames C. Skedros in Valantasis (2000), 299.

[55] On πανήγυρις "festival" see Lampe s.v. Tertullian, *De idololatria* 11.4.
[56] Lydus, *Mens.* 4.42. See also Macrob. *Sat.* 1.12.7 *servis cenas adponebant matronae, ut domini Saturnalibus* – not just to their slave girls, as among others Meslin (1970), 84 has it.
[57] See Sessa (2012) on the Roman bishops intervening in domestic matters.

deceits."[58] His verb, *debacchare*, points to somewhat euphoric rites, drinking and dancing. The details that Atto censures for the Kalendae Ianuariae do not correspond to the rather repetitive Christian contestation of the same festival in earlier authors: Atto, although a learned and well educated Christian, does not just reproduce earlier texts to signal to his congregation that he is paying attention to the purity of Christian practice as the Fathers of the Church had taught it, but engages with contemporary reality. Incidentally, the custom must have survived in the mountain towns to the north of Vercelli and the Po valley: some southern parts of the Swiss Grisons still celebrate Chalanda Marz, albeit transformed into an event for boys, who revel to the sound of large cowbells. If we assume that the bishops assembled in the Trullo were dealing with contemporary customs as well, we catch a glance of yet another "pagan survival" in Byzantine times that otherwise remains hidden, both before and after the council.

But the Trullo prohibition was much more general than this. In the long canon 62, the assembly prohibited also public dances of women, dances and initiations of men and women in the name of the pagan gods, cross-dressing, the wearing of "comic, satyric and tragic masks," the invocation of the "abominable Dionysos" at the wine-press, and ecstatic laughter when filling the wine casks – in short, a wide range of harmless private entertainments, not the least during the wine harvest. Kalendae, Vota, and Brumalia are part of these entertainments and were for centuries days of joyful relaxation both among pagans and Christians. More importantly, they were protected by imperial law from episcopal interference, if the emperor chose to do so. In his Novel 131, Justinian had accepted the parity of imperial law and ecclesiastical canons only as to the canons of the first four ecumenical councils; later canons needed explicit imperial approval to become law. The painstakingly precise definition that the Novel gives of these councils – "the one of Nicaea with three hundred and eighteen and the one of Constantinople with one hundred and fifty saintly fathers, the first council of Ephesos that condemned Nestorius, and the one in Chalcedon in which Eutychius was in the same way banned as was Nestorius" – looks as if it were designed to deter further discussions.[59]

---

[58] Atto Vercellianus, *Sermo iii in Octava Domini* (PL 134. 836A): *similiter etiam Kalendis Martiis hujusmodi homines multis solent debacchare praestigiis.*

[59] Justinian, *Novella* 131.1 *Sancimus igitur vicem legum obtinere sanctas ecclesiasticas regulas, quae a sanctis quattuor conciliis expositae sunt aut firmatae, hoc est in Nicaena trecentorum decem et octo et in Constantinopolitana sanctorum centum quinquaginta patrum et in Epheso Prima, in quo Nestorius est damnatus, et in Calcedone, in quo Eutychis cum Nestorio anathematizatus est. Praedictarum enim quattuor synodorum dogmata sicut sanctas scripturas accipimus et regulas sicut leges servamus.*

Later canons thus were at best advisory to the emperors; in a few cases, the bishops decided explicitly that a letter on a specific matter should be addressed to the rulers.[60] Sometimes, an emperor in search of allies might hope to gain ecclesiastical support by abolishing an offensive festival, as did Romanos with his short-lived suspension of the Brumalia. But overall, the Eastern bishops, it seems, were as humorless and severe in their understanding of Christian practice as their Western colleagues – and as inefficient at convincing all their colleagues, or moving imperial legislation their way.

The disappearance of the Brumalia

We do not know how long the Brumalia survived. They still existed at the court of Constantine Porphyrogennetos, as we saw. The *Klerologion* of Philotheos, written in 900 and added to the *Liber caerimoniarum*, lists the βρουμάλιον gifts handed out by the emperor Leo, his brother Alexander, and his wife Zoe on their respective days, twenty pounds, ten pounds, and eight pounds of gold, and has its own chapter "On the distributions of pious donations of the emperor at the Brumalia and the anniversaries of coronation and power."[61] The chapter on Constantine Porphyrogennetos in the collection called *Theophanes Continuatus*, the historians after Theophanes, describes Constantine's lavish *brumalion* banquet in great detail.[62] Theodoros Balsamon's commentary on canon 62 of the Trullo Council, on the other hand, differentiates between the Roman Kalendae where "the rustics" "up to the present day" were performing indecent rites, and the Vota and Brumalia that "were Hellenic [that is, pagan] festivals" celebrated in honor of Pan and Dionysos respectively.[63] If we take the change in tense seriously, the latter festivals had disappeared without a

---

[60] In 401, the African bishops assembled in Carthage decided on a petition to the emperor on, among other things, problems with pagan cult, Mansi 3.766 = Munier (1974), 196 can. 58 (African can. 51, Mansi 3.782) and 60.
[61] The single gifts: *Liber caerimoniarum* 2.52, p. 782 Reiske; the chapter: 2.53, p. 783ff. Reiske.
[62] *Theophanes Continuatus, Constantine* 15 p. 456 Bekker.
[63] Theodorus Balsamnon, *Commentary on Trullo*, PG 137. 728C εἴθισατο γοῦν παρὰ Ῥωμαίοις εἰς μνήμην τούτων πανηγυρίζειν καί τινα ἄσεμνα διαπράττεσθαι, ὅπερ μέχρι τοῦ νῦν παρά τινων ἀγροτῶν γίνεται κατὰ τὰς πρώτας ἡμέρας τοῦ Ἰανουαρίου μηνός, "the Romans had the custom to celebrate a festival in their honor and to perform some indecent things; this is done to the present day by some rustics during the first days of January" (Kalendae, Nonae, and Idus were Roman festivals in honor of three men with these names who saved the people from a famine). *Ibid.* 730A τὰ Βότα καὶ Βρουμάλια ἑορταί ἦσαν Ἑλληνικαί, ἡ μὲν τελουμένη χάριν τοῦ ψευδωνύμου θεοῦ Πανός ... ἡ δὲ χάριν τοῦ Διονύσου τοῦ σωτῆρος ὡς ἐκεῖνοι ἐβλασφήμουν "Vota and Brumalia were Hellenic festivals, the first celebrated because of Pan, falsely named a god ... the second because of Dionysos, the saviour as those blasphemous people said."

trace in the later twelfth century when Balsamon was writing, unlike the Kalendae that inspired celebrations in the countryside. The Brumalia most certainly had disappeared two centuries later when the monk Matthaios Blastares in the comment on canon 62 in his *Syntagma alphabeticon*, a handbook of canonical law, uses the past tense throughout: "They mention Kalendae and Vota and Brumalia and things like this, which the *Hellenes* used to perform as rituals. The Kalendae were celebrated on January 1."[64] In his interpretations of Vota and Brumalia as festivals of Pan and Dionysos, Blastares almost verbatim depends on Balsamon, but his use of tenses is more consistent: to him, all these festivals were a thing of the pagan past.

---

[64] Matthaios Blastares, *Collectio Alphabetica* E 3 (περὶ ἐθῶν ἑλληνικῶν): Καλάνδας γοῦν, καὶ Βοτὰ, καὶ Βρουμάλια, καὶ τοιαῦτα μέμνηται ἄττα, ἐν οἷς τελετὰς ἄγειν τοῖς Ἕλλησιν εἴθιστο. καὶ ἡ μὲν τῶν καλανδῶν ἑορτὴ, ἐτησίως ἐν τῇ α' τοῦ Ἰανουαρίου ἐτελεῖτο μηνός. Edition: M. Potles and G. A. Rhalles, Σύνταγμα τῶν θείων καὶ ἱερῶν κανόνων τῶν τε ἁγίων καὶ πανευφήμων ἀποστόλων, καὶ τῶν ἱερῶν οἰκουμενικῶν καὶ τοπικῶν συνόδων, καὶ τῶν κατὰ μέρος ἁγίων πατέρων (Athens: Αὐγή, 1859).

CHAPTER 8

Kalendae Ianuariae again, and again

The Kalendae Ianuariae, or in the Greek East often simply the Καλάνδαι, have come up rather frequently in the course of these chapters – as a Roman event rejected in the *Avodah Zarah*, as a festival that Theodosius in 389 made a legal holiday and by doing so legalized and legitimized for centuries to come; as a celebration attacked in forceful sermons by John Chrysostom, Augustine, and Asterius of Amaseia, partly at least in direct reaction to the imperial decision, and defended by Libanius, shortly before his death, in a rather nostalgic mood; as a festival that the bishops who assembled in East and West, most prominently 692 in the Trullo in Byzantium, banned as pagan but that still was celebrated by "rustics," as the bishops claimed; finally, as an entertainment on the streets of Rome that amused and scandalized Saint Boniface's recently converted Germans on pilgrimage to Rome so that pope Zachary again tried to ban it in the Council of Rome in 743 or 744. Although Michel Meslin's monograph is rather short on these later aspects of the Kalendae and concentrates on the West, their Byzantine history has recently been sketched by Anthony Kaldellis.[1] This short chapter intends to pull together some lose threads by describing how the Kalendae stood alongside the Brumalia, Vota, and Matronalia in Byzantium, and how it weathered the attacks of Christian bishops and, somewhat later, Muslim clerics.

Kalandai in twelfth-century Constantinople

We saw in Chapter 7 how the bishops in Trullo banned three named festivals, Καλάνδαι, Βοτά, and Βρουμάλια, and the unnamed "festival (πανήγυρις) performed on the first day of March," and how five centuries later Theodoros Balsamon mentioned the "first days of January" as the only event among the four that was still celebrated, albeit by "some rustics"

---
[1] Meslin (1970), 94–129; Kaldellis (2011).

only. His formulation hides the problem that, strictly speaking, the Vota of January 3 (or, as we shall see, maybe of January 2) were, in the fourth century, an integral part of the Kalendae Ianuariae whereas canon 62 treats them as two separate festivals; we shall have to come back to this. More importantly, Balsamon is fully aware that the Kalandai were Roman in origin, yet he turns all three festivals into Hellenic ones, and claims that at the Kalendae one worshipped the moon, at the Vota Pan the god of flocks, and at the Bruma Dionysos the god of wine. In a society in which the "Romans" were the Byzantines and the "Hellenes" the pagan ancestors, this distinction, surprising to us, makes much sense. Moreover, whereas to the bishops in Trullo "Hellenic" was simply "pagan," to a Byzantine of the twelfth century, "Hellenic" has acquired the double connotation of "pagan" and "Classical Greek," and the three festivals suddenly have become Greek festivals in honor of good Greek gods.[2]

There are a few other testimonies for the Kalandai in the later Byzantine world, all about contemporary with Balsamon. They prove that the beginning of January retained some ritual status among the inhabitants of Constantinople and beyond, and they contradict Balsamon's statement that it was only the rustics who celebrated during these days. In a poem on the months, Nikolaos Kallikles (*floruit* c.1130) described January as the month of the κάλανδα, as April is the month of Easter, and the festival is characterized by opulent drinking and eating – certainly not in the countryside, but among the urban intellectuals.[3] In a text that explains the term ἀγύρτης "begging priest," Ioannes Tzetzes (c.1110 – c.1180) compares the ancient begging priests with the contemporary begging monks (σιγνοφόροι) who at Christmas, the Kalandai, and Epiphany went from door to door, singing or reciting encomiastic prose and asking for a reward for their efforts, descendants of the begging children who annoyed Libanius and Asterios more than half a millennium before.[4] In a long and festive letter to his aristocratic friend Nikephoros Komnenos (died c.1173) – the more refined version, it seems, of the encomiastic prose of the begging monks – Eustathius archbishop of Thessalonica (c.1110–1198)

---

[2] Some contemporary scholars on Byzantium have followed this line of interpretation: see Trombley (1978) and Constantelos (1998), 163–171, an expanded version of his (1970) paper.
[3] Nikolaos Kallikles, *Poem* 37.61–66, in Sternbach (1903), 47. If he was the physician of Alexios I (Theophylaktos of Ohrid, *Letters* 531.1), who ruled from 1081–1118, he is a generation older than Balsamon.
[4] Ioannes Tzetzes, *Histories* 13.239–244 = Leone (1968), 523. They are *signiferi* presumably not because they carry flags (the military technical term is attested in Christian Latin, see Lampe s.v.) but because they carry sacred images, in a tradition of begging priests that goes back to the cult of the Great Mother. On the use of Latin in Byzantium, Kaldellis (2007), 69–70, with literature.

praises the Kalandai as a festival that all Byzantines (Ῥωμαῖοι) celebrate, and that they "count among the greatest of the days that lead to pleasure."[5] In his description of the festival, he refers back to "the impressive orator" (τὸν δεινὸν σοφιστὴν) Libanius and "the Syrophoenician Porphyry," and although the ritual details were different from those of his own time, they still shared the same atmosphere of friendship and togetherness.[6]

The concentration of the scant literary evidence in the twelfth century could lead to the suspicion that we are dealing with a custom revived by a few Hellenizing intellectuals who celebrated their nostalgic Hellenism.[7] But Balsamon's rustics, Eustathius' begging priests, and, to a lesser degree, the enthusiastic generalization of Callicles belie this suspicion. It looks as if people of all backgrounds still enjoyed banquets and generous giving at the Kalandai. Eustathius' reference to the pagan Libanius and to "the Syrophoenician Porphyry" simply serves to ennoble the customs that suspicious theologians rejected; it is the inversion of Balsamon's strategy of confining all this to rustics. It remains anybody's guess what the same theologians would have made of these references by the learned bishop to a pagan orator and a Neoplatonic philosopher whose books Theodosius had burned. The playful opening of the preceding letter to the same addressee and for the same festival implies that to celebrate the Kalandai might be controversial: "How long, mighty Komnenos" (writes the bishop) "will I draw such enemies upon me because of your Kalandai?" The enemies, it turns out, are the mice that invaded his house and among other damage ate the grapes destined for his friend as a Kalandai present; but the opening words gain additional wit if the celebration of the Kalandai roused other spirits as well.[8]

Vota and *ludi votivi*

When one goes back in time in order to fill the gap between the twelfth century and the time of Justinian, the main relevant text again is the *Liber caerimoniarum*. Surprisingly, the Kalandai do not appear among the imperial celebrations; obviously it was not a festival in which the emperor

---

[5] Τὰς νῦν καλάνδας πανηγυρίζουσι πάντες, οἷς τὰ Ῥωμαίων πρεσβεύεται, καὶ τῶν εἰς χαρμονὴν συντελουσῶν ἡμερῶν ταῖς μεγίσταις ἐγκρίνουσι: Eusthatios of Thessalonica, *Letter 7* in Kolovou (2006), 26–36, with a summary on 97*–101*; see also Tafel (1832), 314–317.
[6] line 172 Kolovou: συμμετέχειν ἔστι ἡμῖν ἀλλήλοις τῶν παρ᾽ ἑκάστοις καὶ κοινωνίαν φιλικὴν συνιστᾶν "We are allowed to share what belongs to an individual and to experience the community of friends."
[7] On the "Third Sophistic" under the Komnenoi see Kaldellis (2007), 225–316.
[8] Eustathios, *Letter 6*, in Kolovou (2006), 20–25 (summary, 94*–97*); see Tafel (1832), 311–313.

and his court were prominent. The *Klerologion* of Philotheos, added at the end of the *Liber*, suggests an explanation. During the twelve days between Christmas and Epiphany, the court offered a daily banquet to which the emperor invited a changing set of dignitaries, and sometimes the urban poor: the Kalandai or, for that matter, the fourth-century sequence of festival days between January 1 and January 5 was by now embedded in a much longer sequence of festivities; and sometimes one had to make choices. In accordance with the calendar of the Christian Church, the palace celebrated the entire Christmas Season, whose first day began on the evening of December 25, and did nothing to single out the Kalandai.

Or so it seems at first glance. One day, however, needs to be singled out. The eighth day, i.e. the day that began on the evening of January 1, is defined as the day when "the votive footrace is performed" (ἐκτελεῖται τὸ βοτὸν πεζοδρόμιον). The guests invited to the banquet are the private helpers of the emperor ("the leading members of the secret chamber", τοὺς προὔχοντας τῆς τάχεως τοῦ μυστικοῦ κουβουκλείου), and a large number of the poor. Both groups continue and transform the practice of the fourth-century households, to dine together with one's slaves and to invite the poor, and the "votive foot-race" recalls the foot race of the charioteers on the Lupercalia that I understand as an inversion of the usual chariot races; the same ritual inversion plays itself out on January 2. βοτόν, *votum* in the *Liber caerimoniarum*, a term whose reference baffled Reiske, must mean, as Albert Vogt saw, any *ludus votivus*, a public spectacle that resulted from a vow.[9] This explains why a βοτόν was not fixed in the calendar, could be either a chariot race or a foot race, and is once connected with the triumph.[10] This makes it likely that the *ludus votivus* of January 2 echoes the traditional *vota* of January 3, just placed a day earlier. If this is correct, this is the only trace left of the *vota* – and with it the entire complex of the Kalendae Ianuariae – after Trullo's canon 62 and the later commentators on this canon whose interest in their contemporary ritual practice is highly doubtful.

It is, however, plausible to assume that the public festivities on the streets that so incensed the bishops in Trullo were still going strong at the time of Constantine Porphyrogennetos and of Philotheos, since we

---

[9] Bafflement: Reiske, *Commentary* 327 (on his text p. 327.7): *Dies Votorum quam ob rem fuerit celebratus et quando, non liquet*. *Ludus votivus*: Vogt 2.2 (1940), 160.
[10] Not fixed in the calendar: *Liber caerimoniarum* 2.78 (69) (Vogt 2.129) uses "crosses made of flowers," thus cannot be a January event. Chariot race: *ibid*. 2.80 (71) (Vogt 2.158), an anecdote about a famous charioteer at a *votum*: ἱππικοῦ ἀγομένου, εἴτε καὶ βοτοῦ *ibid*. 2.20 (Reiske 612), as part of the triumph.

catch sight of them again in the twelfth century. This means that there is a split between what the people did on January 1 and what the court did. The court of the Christian emperor followed liturgical practice and celebrated the days between Christmas and Epiphany as a commemoration of Christ's life, the people followed a much older tradition and amused themselves on the Kalandai and the Vota. Incidentally, this can explain why canon 62 makes a distinction between the two festivals: in the spiritual trajectory from Christmas to Epiphany, January 1 and 3 – or perhaps already then January 2, the day when in the households masters and slaves shared meals and invited the poor – stood out, in an ecclesiastical perception, as days of unbridled sensuality that had its pagan roots. It is this pagan sensuality to which, as we saw, the Western bishops reacted with their three fasting days from January 1 to January 3, "which our ancestors instituted to stamp out the pagan habit," as the council of Tours self-consciously phrased it in 567, more than a century before Trullo.[11] The bishops assembled in Trullo shared that grim asceticism.

But there were other things that marked January 1 as a special day. For Ovid, it was the festive day when the new consuls entered office. By the fourth century, this political role was combined with the equally political *vota* to form the four or five festival days that Theodosius I made into a legal holiday. Although the consuls slowly lost real power and had become, as Justinian said about the consuls of his own time, an office that was "concerned solely with generous gift-giving" (*ad largitatem solam*), they still solemnly entered office on January 1.[12] Justinian made an effort to codify into a law the rules that governed their ceremonial appearances and the gifts (*sparsiones*) that they were allowed to scatter to the crowds on these occasions – not only, as he claims, to preserve an office that had existed for almost a millennium, but also to prevent an unhealthy competition between emperors and consuls that had led the emperor Marcian (ruled 450–457) to prohibit consular *sparsiones* altogether. Justinian found a diplomatic compromise. Unlike the emperors – or the aristocrats in Libanius' Antiocheia – the consuls were now only allowed to use silver coins, and not gold pieces; with this rule, Justinian renewed a ruling that was already given by Theodosius I (shrewd as ever) in 384 but had either never really caught on or was neglected later when not all emperors had

---

[11] Concilium Turonense, canon 18 = de Clerq (1963), 182; see also Isidore, *De ecclesiasticis officiis* 1.41 (*PL* 83.774D).
[12] See Sguaitamatti (2012), 137–157 on the festive inauguration of the new consul.

the political clout to enforce it over ambitious aristocrats.[13] Following Theodosius I, whose constitution on legal holidays had anchored the Kalendae in the public calendar of Rome and Constantinople, Justinian's law achieved the same by assigning the consuls a series of public appearances, from the solemn ingress on January 1 to the equally solemn withdrawal at the end of their tenure.

Already in Ovid's Rome the Kalendae were also the day of gift exchange; the same is true for Libanius' Antioch or Asterius' Amaseia. The line between gift and remuneration was and is always a problematic one, especially for public servants. Thus, in the later empire, January 1 was also the day when public servants received their salary, when the emperor rewarded advocates for their public service, and when doctors and craftsmen received a present which sometimes seems to have been mistaken by the giver for a salary, to the dismay of the recipient.[14]

Postscript from Muslim North Africa

Thus, although the details of the custom changed, the Kalendae Ianuariae remained a festive period where generosity and enjoyment played themselves out, and they must have remained so during most of the Byzantine epoch. They also entered the Muslim world, illustrating Fernand Braudel's insight that the Muslim Mediterranean "lived and breathed with the same rhythms" as the Christian.[15] A noteworthy passage in a treatise of an Arab doctor from Kairouan in Tunisia, written in the late tenth or early eleventh century, still deals with the presents given to doctors or teachers at certain festivals.[16] The French translation of the Arabic text reads: "De même, il est blamable d'accepter (des cadeaux) pour les fêtes des polythéistes, au nombre desquels sont Noël, Pâques et les Kalendes chez nous." Not unlike the Christian bishops, the author expands his argument to prohibit the adoption of all "polytheist" customs by pious Muslims, such as when children make "tabernacles" (whatever they are) at the Kalendae or the adults indulge in extraordinary meals at Christmas – customs and behaviors obviously current in Islamic North Africa. The editor of the text, Hady Roger Idris, argued that these customs were not survivals of local

---

[13] Justinian, *Novella* 105 (a. 536); he is very consciously promulgating this as a law, *in legis enim hoc ponimus schemate, ut transcendenti etiam poena quaedam inferatur competens*; the earlier law, *CTh* 15.9.1. On the public appearances of the consuls see Sguaitamatti (2012), 137–196.
[14] Public servants: *CJ* 12.19.14. Advocates: *CJ* 2.7.23 (under Anastasios, a. 506): *sollemni die festivitatis Kalendarum Ianuariarum.* Doctors and craftsmen: *Basilika* B XX.4.27 = D XIX.5.27.
[15] Braudel (1972), 450, cited in Broodbank (2013), 37.   [16] Idris (1954), 263–264.

pre-Islamic customs (be they Christian or pagan surviving in Christian times), but customs imported by Byzantine craftsmen and specialists who were attracted to Muslim Maroc: if this is correct, this is yet another piece of evidence that the Kalendae were fully integrated into the private festival calendars of the Byzantine world. The argument is, however, less cogent than Idris assumes: at least in the Maghreb, further West, the Ennaïr feast does not only preserve the Latin Ianuarius, but also continues customs such as eating sweet dates and adorning the house with greeneries – customs which seem to have been more at home in the Latin West than in the Greek East.[17]

---

[17] Doutté (1908), 544–551. Doutté's interpretative framework is much more indebted to Tylor and Frazer than to Émile Durkheim, whom, however, he dutifully cites in his first footnote. The dates already in Ovid, *Fasti* 1.185 (dates, figs, and honey); the greeneries are allegorized by John Chrysostom, *Hom. in Kalendas* 3.957 in Antioch, but also provoked the censure of Martin of Braga, *De correctione rusticorum* 16, in sixth-century Portugal, and their (late antique) prohibition was received into the canon law collection of Burchard of Worms in eleventh-century Germany, *Decretum* 10.15 (*PL* 140.835D): *non licet iniquas observationes agere Kalendarum . . . neque lauro, aut viriditate arborum cingere domos; omnis haec observatio paganorum est* ("it is not allowed to observe the unjust customs of the Kalendae . . . nor to adorn the houses with laurel and green tree branches: all this is a pagan custom").

CHAPTER 9

Christian liturgy and the imperial festival tradition

Introduction

A few years before the emperor Theodosius I spent a summer giving laws in the city of Rome, a religious lady from even further West, most likely Normandy, the lady Egeria, was making a pilgrimage to the holy places of the East. Entering the Holy Land from Egypt and the Sinai, she stayed at least three years in Jerusalem, from 381 to Easter 384, then moved on to Constantinople and home again. She wrote a report (*itinerarium*) of her experience to her sisters at home; chance has preserved a copy of it, albeit in a mutilated form that centers on the Sinai and Jerusalem.[1] As an appendix to the description of her time in Jerusalem, she gave a detailed description of the liturgy in the Holy City; despite a missing page at the beginning that truncates the section on the first celebration, Epiphany, this text remains the most important document on the fourth-century Christian liturgy, not only in Jerusalem, that we possess.[2]

The origins and the development of Christian liturgy are as intriguing for the historian of the religions of the Roman empire as they are little investigated except by members of the narrow circle of liturgy

---

[1] After the mutilated surviving manuscript had been found and published in 1884 in Arezzo, scholarship on her text – first philological and linguistic, more recently historical – has been growing steadily. The most recent critical editions are A. Franceschini and R. Weber, in: *Itineraria et alia Geographica* 1. Corpus Christianorum, series Latina 175 (Turnhout, 1965), 27–90 and Maraval (1982), 55–142 (with introduction, French translation, and notes), translation also in Maraval (2002b); an Italian edition and translation, Natalucci (1991); an annotated English translation, Wilkinson (1999). Her stay in Jerusalem, whose date was originally disputed, is now clearly dated, Wilkinson (1999), 169–171. Her origin is doubtless far in the West, presumably somewhere on the coast of the Atlantic Ocean; older suggestions such as Aquitania or Galicia have been rejected by Sirvan (1988a), who insisted on Gaul, and Clifford Weber (1989) has convincingly argued for the region of Mont St. Michel in Normandy; his paper came after the most influential scholars on early Western pilgrimage to Palestine, Wilkinson (1977; not even in the bibliography of the edition of 2002) and Maraval (1982) published their first studies and were not willing to change minds, and thus it is missing e.g. from the disappointing "Egeria Project," www.egeriaproject.net/.

[2] See Baldovin (1987), 55–64, Baldovin (1989), and Drijvers (2004), especially 65–96, 187–190.

specialists.[3] In 114 CE, when the younger Pliny in his famous report to Trajan tried to describe the rituals of the Bithynian Christians whom he was investigating, he did not come up with much: the Christians, he wrote, were accustomed to meet "on given days before dawn, to sing a hymn to Christ as their god, to give a mutual oath" of ethical behavior, and later in the day "to come together for a common meal, with varied food of an innocent character" (this last a reaction to rumors of child sacrifice).[4] Pliny had to rely on information from arrested Christians only: the rites were removed from public sight and knowledge and confined to private houses; private houses remained the places of Christian worship until the time of Constantine.[5] It was during the fourth century, when Christianity suddenly became public and Constantine and his successors sponsored major public cult buildings, that a public liturgy developed and inscribed Christian ritual not only into the interior spaces of the new Christian basilicae but also onto the public spaces of the cities.

Christian liturgy in Jerusalem

Palestine and especially Jerusalem, the place where Christ had lived and through his death and resurrection provided salvation to humanity, played a central role in this development.[6] Jerusalem Christians were aware of this already in the early third century. A century later Constantine reacted to it by reshaping the appearance of the city and its surroundings with three major buildings: the Birth Church in Bethlehem, the church on the Mount of Olives, and the basilica at Golgotha that Egeria calls either Martyrium or simply *ecclesia maior*, "Main Church," and that came to include not only the Holy Cross with its chapel but also the Calvary with its round church, the Anastasis.[7] This building program, doubtless helped and promoted by the bishop of Caesarea, Eusebius, emphasized the role of the Holy City

---

[3] Two monographs deserve to be singled out, Dix (1945) and Baldovin (1987); in many respects, Baldovin's is a sober historical reaction to Dix.
[4] Plin. *Ep.* 10.96.7 ... *soliti stato die ante lucem convenire, carmenque Christo quasi deo dicere secum invicem seque sacramento non in scelus aliquod obstringere, sed ne furta ne latrocinia ne adulteria committerent, ne fidem fallerent, ne depositum appellati abnegarent. quibus peractis morem sibi discedendi fuisse rursusque coeundi ad capiendum cibum, promiscuum tamen et innoxium.*
[5] Lact. *De mort. persec.* 12 mentions a clearly visible *ecclesia* or *fanum* in Nicomedia; it is unclear whether this is an anachronism or reflects the beginning of church-building in the East, but at any rate it was built in a densely built-up area of the city so that it could not be torched by the emperor.
[6] A short overview in Drijvers (2013).
[7] Overview in Baldovin (1987), 46–54. In what follows I will call it main church, the term cathedral being anachronistic for Egeria's time.

and its surroundings as the stage for the liturgical celebration of Christian belief: it was here that Christian leaders developed a stational liturgy, first and foremost presumably Cyril, the powerful and long-lived Jerusalem native who was bishop from about 351 to 389.[8]

Egeria's detailed descriptions more than the occasional allusions in Cyril's preserved writings show how, towards the end of the same century, the foremost sacred place of Christianity had developed a complex ritual calendar with liturgical forms that made ample use of the new buildings and of the sacred places inside and outside the city. Her report also attests to the interest she and her sisters in the Far West took in the forms of liturgy and in the many differences between what these Western Christians were used to and what the new and impressive forms were that the Jerusalem liturgy had developed from a basic Christian liturgical language and practice; she constantly compares her Jerusalem experience with that common liturgy that is *secundum consuetudinem, qua et ubique fit*, "according to custom as takes place everywhere."[9]

Scholars working on Christian liturgy agree that Christian liturgy in general and especially its rapid development in the fourth century has to be seen and understood in the common context of Mediterranean public religion: it resulted (to cite Gregory Dix's formulation) from "the blending of two things, of primitive Christian doctrine with the sort of expression the whole ancient world considered suitable for any public act."[10] The liturgical forms that church leaders in the fourth century developed were inscribed into a common background that rendered them understandable by a congregation most of whose members had been growing up with and were shaped by the experience of non-Christian festivals. Even when they had become Christians, many of them still participated in the traditional festivals of their own cities, such as the Brumalia or Kalendae, much to the chagrin of the bishops and Church fathers, from Tertullian to Augustine and beyond, as we saw, and as Faustus, the leading African Manichean, shrewdly and somewhat maliciously pointed out when he claimed that Christians were nothing but another pagan sect.[11] Even for Jerusalem, Cyril makes it clear that his Christians were living in a world also inhabited by

---

[8] See Drijvers (2004).
[9] Interest in liturgy: 24.1 (she tells them all this "knowing how much you like to know this," *sciens quia libenter haberetis haec cognoscere*); common Easter rites, 39.1; custom for Sunday rites, 25.1 and 2; differences are sometimes marked as such (e.g. 27.1: Lent lasts eight weeks unlike the forty days *apud nos*), but more commonly simply described. Western pilgrims had an interest in liturgy: Sivan (1988a), 69; on Egeria's community as not necessarily monastic, Sirvan (1988b).
[10] Dix (1945), 316; see Baldovin (1987), 102–103 and often.
[11] Faustus: Aug. *Contra Faustum* 20.4.

traditional pagans, whose rituals were a constant temptation and source of spiritual threats: in one of his catechetical lectures, he warns against participation in pagan sacrificial meals – "meat or bread, or other such things polluted by the invocation of the unclean spirits" – and in traditional pagan rituals, be it only to seek healing. Among the forbidden rites, he lists "prayer in idol temples; things done in honor of lifeless idols; the lighting of lamps, or burning of incense by fountains or rivers, as some persons cheated by dreams or by evil spirits do, thinking to find a cure even for their bodily ailments."[12]

The Jerusalem liturgy and ancient festivals

The overall characteristics of pagan festivals of the Imperial age – the characteristics that I developed in Chapter 1 for the Greek East and that informed the Roman festivals that I analyzed in the following chapters – thus must inform the Christian liturgy as well, not the least the new rites of Jerusalem.[13] In what follows I will concentrate on two salient traits: the lengthy celebration of certain festivals, and the important role of processions.

Festival periods

It has been often remarked how during Imperial times popular festivals became longer and longer, especially by the addition of circus races: the public happiness that the festival provided lasted longer and longer, to the detriment of the legal calendar, as we saw. The most obvious case is the Kalendae Ianuariae. From the one calendar day it grew into a celebration that lasted five days, first by the inclusion of the *vota* of January 3 and the elaboration of January 2 into a household festival, then by the addition of two days of circus games on January 4 and 5. But this is far from the only case, or the most extreme. The later calendars that we possess, the fragmentary Esquiline calendar from the late third century and the manuscript calendar of 354, demonstrate how this became a common practice in later

---

[12] Cyril, *Catechetical Lectures* 19 (= *Mystagogical Catechesis* 1), 7–8; see Drijvers (2013), 318 and the description of Jerusalem as a bustling city "full of all sorts of people" (*plena universi generis hominibus*) in Hieron. *Epist.* 58.4. On the authenticity of the *Mystagogical Catecheses* see Doval (2001), who defends their disputed authenticity.

[13] This is a very different argument from the one often made in the past that a specific pagan festival was replaced by a Christian one, such as the Lupercalia and *Purificatio Mariae*, or a festival of Sol and Christmas.

antiquity, and not just because several circus days were added to a city festival. The Hadrianic foundation of a *panegyris* in Oinoanda that lasted from Artemisios 1 to 23, the somewhat later transformation of the month Artemision in Ephesos into a month-long festival period dedicated to Artemis, or the extraordinary length of the Roman Capitolia at almost six weeks, attested at about the same time, show how already in the second century festivals went far beyond the three (or five) days of the Kalendae or any other celebration to whose main sacrificial day a few days with contests, games, and other spectacles were added. The fourth-century elaboration of the private one-day Bruma into the Brumalia with their sequence of twenty-four banquet days continued this into a time when the festival was shared by pagans and Christians.[14]

Thus, the lengthy Christian festivals in Jerusalem that Egeria described were far from unique even if one takes into account that they all were tied together by the thread of the salvation story that informed the sequence from Epiphany on January 6 to Pentecost Sunday in late Spring; Saints' days are conspicuously absent from her calendar and will appear only during the next half century, and the Encaeniae in mid-September are not connected with the salvation story. In this Christian calendar, only the celebrations of Presentation, Quadragesima, and Pentecost last one day. Epiphany and Encaeniae are part of an octave, eight days of which the main festival was held on the first day but whose following seven days contained specific ceremonies inside and outside of Jerusalem.

The celebrations that centered around Easter were considerably more intricate, and in a certain sense Quadragesima and Pentecost were specific festival days at the tail-end of a lengthy period that began with the Lent days. The fact that ordinary fasting was suspended between Easter and Pentecost provides a ritual expression to a sacred narrative that links Resurrection, Ascension, and Descent of the Holy Spirit; on the other hand, for a Christian inhabitant of Jerusalem, as for a practicing Christian today, there was enough daily life in between to count these three festivals as separate units, a daily life that was markedly different than the more narrow focus of the pilgrim who eagerly hastened from celebration to celebration and had no other purpose for her presence in the city.

Easter everywhere in the ancient world was preceded by a lengthy period of fasting; we do not know when this custom started, but it was part of the overall tendency to make fasting a distinctive trait of Christian festival

---

[14] Ephesos: *LSS* 101 = *I.Ephes.* 11; Oinoanda: Wörrle (1988), esp. 245–247; Capitolia: Fasti Ostienses, *I.Italiae* 13:1, 5 frg. xxvii (a. 146); Brumalia: above, Chapter 7.

culture. In Egeria's Jerusalem, the Lent period lasted eight weeks, more than the forty days Egeria and her sisters were used to in the West.[15] The reason was that the Western Lent was a solid period of fast days, whereas the Jerusalem Christians did not fast on Saturdays and Sundays: this left them forty-one days "that they call *heortae*," festivals, a local Greek term that neatly showcases the Christian intention of subverting the pagan festival tradition with its *euphrosynai*, banquets, and might well be Cyprian's invention, made in the same spirit that induced Augustine to insist on fasting during the Kalendae in Carthage.[16] The festival period proper began on the Saturday before Palm Sunday, Lazarus Day, which was celebrated outside the city at a shrine in Bethany where Mary, Lazarus' sister, had met Christ. This was the starting point of a series of extraordinary rituals, most of them celebrated in the double church space of the so-called Martyrium that combined Constantine's basilica at Golgotha with the adjacent Anastasis rotunda built over the rock of the Calvary; other rites took place outside the city and included the Mount of Olives and the spots of sacred commemoration that surrounded it. This intense ritual period led from Palm Sunday to Easter Sunday and into the following week, whose first Sunday marked its end.[17]

If we disregard the preceding Lent period, we can understand this as a complex sequence with at its centre the Holy Week from Palm Sunday to Easter Sunday, introduced by Lazarus Day outside the city and terminated by an octave a week after Easter Sunday. At the same time, the fifty days between Easter Sunday and Pentecost Sunday at least in Jerusalem were also regarded as a special period, insofar as the usual weekly fasting on Wednesdays and Fridays was suspended during their duration.[18] However, it contained two festival days only, both numbered: Quadragesima, the "Fortieth Day," a Thursday which in other places was understood as commemorating Christ's ascension (whereas in Jerusalem Ascension was part of Pentecost Sunday) and Pentecost itself, the "Fiftieth Day." The celebration of Quadragesima started on Wednesday night with a vigil in Bethlehem and continued in the morning with a service in Jerusalem; the Sunday of Pentecost was celebrated both as the Descent of the Holy Spirit and as Christ's Ascension – a very strenuous day marked by a number of rites in multiple locations.[19]

---

[15] Egeria 27.1. [16] *Quod hic appellant eortae, id est quadragesimas*: Egeria 27.1.
[17] On the sacred topography see Baldovin (1987), 46–53.
[18] *A pascha autem usque ad quinquagesima, id est pentecosten, hic penitus nemo ieiunat*: Egeria 41.
[19] *Quinquagesimarum autem die, id est dominica, qua die maximus labor est populo*: Egeria 43.1.

After this long and complex period, the rest of the liturgical year according to Egeria was almost empty, except for the Sunday services and the festival Encaeniae that commemorated not only the dedication of Constantine's Golgotha basilica and of the later adjacent Anastasis rotunda, but also the invention of the cross and Solomon's dedication of his temple, as Egeria explains (whose report breaks off during the description of the festival).[20] It again had an octave with celebrations in different places, and at least in mid-fifth century it was, like Easter, a day for Christian initiations.

Perhaps with the exception of the intricate Easter Period, the liturgical calendar of Egeria's Jerusalem must have felt familiar to any inhabitant of her world, pagan or Christian, with its lengthy festival periods; Easter was different only in degree. At the same time, one should not overlook that there were also some Jewish festivals of a comparable length that behaved in a way that was consistent with both Christian and pagan festivals, such as the seven (or nine) days of Sukkot and the eight days of Hannukah. And there might be more. The eight Encaeniae days took place in mid-September, at the time of a major Jewish holiday period, the equally joyful and splendid seven (or nine) days of Sukkot or "Feast of Tabernacles" that were celebrated in early autumn and started on the fifth day after another major Jewish Holiday, Yom Kippur; Egeria's reference to Solomon and his temple shows a vague awareness of such a Jewish background. Thus, it is conceivable that the one specific Jerusalem festival with its multiple references to events that commonly were only loosely datable (if at all) was consciously set into an important Jewish festival period, as Joshua Schwartz has suggested.[21] If so, it strikes one as no small irony – or an indication that the ways never really parted? – that the way Christian Jerusalem radically transformed Aelia Capitolina, turning Hadrian's minor garrison city into Christianity's most holy city by the construction of churches and by the invention of rituals that redefined public time and space, also brought back the resonances of Jerusalem's pre-Roman, Jewish past that Hadrian had hoped to obliterate.[22]

Processions

Whereas the new festival cycles redefined Jerusalem's sacred time both against pagan and Jewish traditions, the construction of churches and the

---

[20] Egeria 41.1; Sozomen. *Hist. eccl.* 2.26.   [21] Schwartz (1987).
[22] Irshai (2009) overlooks this in his post-colonial attempt to construe the Christian city as appropriating the Jewish past.

many processions to which Egeria testifies redefined public space. We saw in Chapter 1 how processions, πομπαί, were a vital part of ancient festival culture. The key role assigned to them in some of the novels shows their importance in the perception of the Imperial age: processions firmly belonged to festivals, and the more impressive they were, the better. This remained valid in the fourth century: on his way from Mt. Casius to Antioch, Julian imagined the splendor of the festival in Daphne that awaited him in terms of "a procession, like a man seeing visions in a dream, animals for sacrifice, libations, choruses in honor of the god, incense, and the ephebes there surrounding the shrine, their souls adorned with all holiness and themselves attired in white and splendid raiment"[23] – we know how deeply disappointed and frustrated the emperor would be when arriving in Antioch. The Christian perception fully agreed with the emperor's vision: πομπαί were a pagan thing, pagans or pseudo-Christians performed them publicly, and it was much worse when they were disguised by masks.[24] Through the baptismal renunciation "I renounce Satan and his works and processions and worship and his angels," πομπή/*pompa* was firmly associated with the *daimonia* of the pagans; and when Christ's grace expelled the demons, "the madness of oracles and prophecies ended, the annual processions and the blood stains in the hecatombs disappeared," according to a somewhat triumphalistic passage in the *Catechetical Oration* of Gregory of Nyssa.[25]

But this remained a matter of rhetoric, not of liturgical reality.[26] In the ritual tool-kit of the Jerusalem liturgy – as of any later stational liturgy – processions were very important, both inside and outside of a sanctuary. Already during the daily services in the liturgical center of Christian Jerusalem, there was a constant change of location between the main ritual spaces, the Martyrium basilica and the Anastasis rotunda;[27] the scholar of

---

[23] Julian, *Misopogon* 34, 361 D: ἀνέπλαττον παρ' ἐμαυτῷ πομπήν, ὥσπερ ὀνείρατα ὁρῶν, ἱερεῖα καὶ σπονδὰς καὶ χοροὺς τῷ θεῷ καὶ θυμιάματα καὶ τοὺς ἐφήβους ἐκεῖ περὶ τὸ τέμενος θεοπρεπέστατα μὲν τὰς ψυχὰς κατεσκευασμένους, λευκῇ δὲ ἐσθῆτι καὶ μεγαλοπρεπεῖ κεκοσμημένους. (Translation after W. C. Wright's Loeb edition.)
[24] A Christian topos, see e.g. *Martyrium Dasii* 3.2 and Kahlos (2005).
[25] Baptismal renunciation: *Constitutiones Apostolicae* 7.40.1: ἀποτάσσομαι τῷι Σατανᾶι καὶ τοῖς ἔργοις αὐτοῦ καὶ ταῖς πομπαῖς αὐτοῦ καὶ ταῖς λατρείαις αὐτοῦ καὶ τοῖς ἀγγέλοις αὐτοῦ. Greg. Nyss. *Or. Catechet.* 18 (*PG* 45.53D; p. 75 J. H. Shrawley [1903]): παύσασθαι μὲν τὰς τῶν χρηστηρίων καὶ μαντειῶν μανίας, ἀναιρεθῆναι δὲ τὰς ἐτησίους πομπὰς καὶ τὰ δι' αἱμάτων ἐν ταῖς ἑκατόμβαις μολύσματα.
[26] Justin, *Apologia* 1.13 defines Christian cult as διὰ λόγου πομπὰς καὶ ὕμνους πέμπειν, somewhat to the embarrassment of the commentator in *PG* 6.345B who understands πομπὰς not as processions (processions are pagan) but as rituals that are as impressive as the *spectacula gentium*.
[27] See Baldovin (1987), 58: "a great deal of movement inside the Golgotha complex" during ordinary service.

pagan cult is reminded of the sacrificial processions that took place both on the way to the shrine and inside the sanctuary space. During the Jerusalem festivals, there was even more processional movement in the Golgotha space, including the Cross and its chapel; and there were processional movements between this center and the outlying churches and sacred places, the Nativity church in Bethlehem, the Lazareum in Bethany, the church of Zion, and the church and the other holy places on the Mount of Olives.[28] In his fundamental analysis of the urban context of the ancient stational liturgies in Jerusalem, Rome, and Constantinople, John Baldovin has devoted a chapter to the importance of processions. He understood them as a natural consequence of the "out-door nature of Mediterranean culture" and inserted them into a wider religious perspective.[29] Although the reference to the "out-door nature" is somewhat too simplistic as an explanation, they point to the continuities between Christian and pre-Christian ritual, beyond all transformations; but more can be done. In what follows I will focus on the analysis of Egeria's description of two festivals, Palm Sunday and Pentecost.

Palm Sunday processions
The Palm Sunday cycle began on Saturday afternoon with a service in the church in Bethany that marked the spot where Mary, Lazarus' sister, met Christ. The bishop and the congregation then moved in a procession the half-mile to the Lazareum, Lazarus' grave site, for another service under open sky, the announcement of Easter and a reading from John 12 on Christ's awakening of Lazarus six days before Passover; Egeria explains the relevance of the Gospel reading for the festival.[30] From here, the participants returned individually and without forming a procession to the city and the Anastasis church for the Lamp-lighting ceremony (*lucernare*).

The following morning, a Sunday, began with the usual early morning service and the added announcement that daily during the Easter week they would meet at the ninth hour in the Martyrium church, and on this Sunday afternoon additionally at the seventh hour, on early afternoon, in the Eleona church on the Mount of Olives.[31] In this church, the bishop celebrated a service with hymns and readings "fit for the day." At the ninth hour, the congregation moved to the highest point, Imbomon, "from where the Lord ascended," for another open-air service that ended two

---

[28] Baldovin (1989), 100 underlines the high importance of mobility in the fourth- and fifth-century Jerusalem liturgy.
[29] Baldovin (1989), 234–238. [30] Egeria 29.5. [31] Egeria 31.1.

hours later, with a reading of the foundational Gospel text, John 12:12–13.[32] This immediately set a procession in motion, down from the Mount of Olives, with adults and children participating, the smallest ones carried by their parents, "all with branches, some of palm trees and some of olive trees."[33] They all together entered town through one of the Eastern gates in a slow procession and moved to Anastasis and from there to the Cross, where they prayed before being sent home.

In Gospel terms, this is a re-enactment of Christ's entry into Jerusalem from Bethany, with the bishop playing Christ, as Egeria insisted.[34] But the details of the rituals do not follow the sacred text that is regarded as their aetiology, so much so that at one point this distorts Egeria's memory of John's foundational words: unlike her paraphrase, the Gospel mentions neither children nor olive tree branches. Or rather, the ritual combines two Gospel stories, Christ's formal entry from Bethany after a dinner with the sisters of Lazarus that was told in John and alluded to in the Saturday ritual, and the final prayers in Gethsemane, at the foot of the Mount of Olives, that preceded his arrest.

To read the two days as two events in a public performance helps to understand the combination better. The rituals were two steps that led the Jerusalem Christians not only towards the Holy Week but announced the main festival to the entire city population, be they Christians or not. The Bethany liturgy appears to be tailored to Christian needs only, with its one-way procession from the Bethany church to Lazarus' grave, where Easter is announced to the participants, but without any formal, processional return to town; ritually, Bethany remains unconnected with Jerusalem. The Lazarus story introduces the key theological themes of Easter, the resurrection of the dead and Christ's divine powers that overcame death: both topics were again alluded to in the Sunday service on Imbomon, the highest point of the Mount of Olives from where Christ ascended to heaven. Otherwise, the Sunday ritual has a highly visible public face in its procession from the service under the open sky high up on Imbomon to the lamp-lighting in the main city church, in a centripetal

---

[32] "And on the next day, a great multitude that was come to the festival day, when they had heard that Jesus was coming to Jerusalem, took branches of palm trees and went forth to meet him and cried Hosanna." According to Egeria 31.2, "children" (*infantes*) with palm branches met Christ – against John but in accordance with the rite.

[33] Egeria 31.3 *quotquot sunt infantes in hisdem locis, usque etiam qui pedibus ambulare non possunt, quia teneri sunt, in collo illos parentes sui tenent, omnes ramos tenentes alii palmarum, alii oliuarum*: the syntax as well as her version of John 12:13 make the children carry branches.

[34] Egeria 31.3 *sic deducetur episcopus in eo typo, quo tunc Dominus deductus est*, "thus the bishop is escorted (from the Mount) in the form in which once Christ was escorted."

procession that leads from a starting point outside the city, in open nature, to its destination, the most holy document of Christ's passion, the Cross in the main city shrine where on Good Friday the most extraordinary ritual kissing of the Cross would take place.

In this structure, the Palm Sunday procession is akin to many processions in the ancient world that introduced major city festivals, such as the Panathenaia in Athens that led from outside the city gates to Athena's altar on the acropolis or, in a complex transformation, the Salutaris procession in Ephesos that ended in the theater, the public meeting place of the city.[35] And like these processions, it took over the city space and presented the celebrating group to the town – to itself, so to speak, in Athens or Ephesos, to itself and additionally a non-Christian city population in Jerusalem. It was performed by a large crowd of Christians who escorted (*deducunt*) the bishop into town, and Egeria is at pains to describe the large number of participants: not just the bishop, his clergy, and the monks and nuns, but *omnis populus* (31.1), *totus populus* (31.2) – adults and children, infants carried by their parents, *matronae* and *domini* (31.4), with branch-carrying children most memorably visible. We saw in Chapter 1 how important the renewal and invention of processions was to the revival of imperial festival culture: the Jerusalem Palm Sunday procession inscribes itself into the same typology and will have been immediately understood by participants and onlookers, Christians and non-Christians alike, unlike the more esoteric Saturday rite in Bethany. When talking about fifth- and sixth-century inscribed acclamations in Ephesos and Aphrodisias, Charlotte Roueché pointed out that they reflect a use of public space that is attested already by the Salutaris inscription and continues unbroken at least to the ceremonies described by Constantine Porphyrogennetos; the Jerusalem processions appear as just one link in a very long chain of continuity.[36]

Processions of Pentecost

In some respects, the rites of Pentecost – "the most strenuous day for the congregation"[37] – were an inversion of the Palm Sunday rites, but they also had a logic of their own. After a regular early Sunday morning service in the main church that had to end before the third hour and thus was somewhat shorter than usual, the congregation escorted the bishop to Zion, the spot

---

[35] On Athenian processions, Kavoulaki (1999); on Salutaris, above, Chapter 1; on the cross ritual, Egeria 37.1–3; see Drijvers (2013), 322.
[36] Roueché (1999), 163–164; see also Wickham (2005), 619 on "the Roman liking for expressing political affirmation through formal procession in wide streets."
[37] Egeria 43.1 *qua die maximus labor est populo*.

where the Holy Spirit descended and that in Egeria's time was marked by a new church. Zion was just outside the southern city wall and had its own gate, and the procession most likely moved from the main church along the main city street, the *cardo maximus* or Market Street that runs roughly from North to South, to exit the city space at the Zion Gate. A service with the appropriate reading from Acts 2:1–12 evoked the memory of the event. Then the congregation was sent home with the announcement to meet again at the sixth hour, immediately after lunch, at Inbomon on the Mount of Olives, the spot of Christ's ascension; they would go there individually, without any liturgical form.

At Inbomon, the bishop celebrated another service under open sky, with the appropriate reading of the ascension story. This lasted most of the afternoon; towards evening, bishop, clergy, and congregation descended the hill down to the Eleona church for a service that included the lighting of the lamps. After nightfall, the congregation slowly moved towards town, in a formal procession that escorted the bishop into the city; at the Eastern city gate burning church lamps were waiting to accompany the slow procession through the town into the main church for a nightly service. They entered through the main church gates from Market Street. After a nightly service, another procession led out of the city to Zion, where a final service took place before everybody went home, very late at night and again individually and informally.

On a theological level, the ritual experience moved the congregation from the morning ritual in which the descent of the Holy Spirit marked the last step of Christ's work on earth and the foundation of Christianity's apostolic expansion even to peoples of foreign tongues, to the afternoon, evening, and night rituals that commemorated Christ's ascension as the final shedding of his earthly nature; but it also brought back the memories of his Passion and again, late at night in Zion, of the descent of the Holy Spirit with its future promise. On a spatio-political level, and even more visibly than at Easter, the three processions took over the space of and around the city of Jerusalem. First came the centrifugal procession to Zion in the morning that was repeated late at night as the last stage of the long day, in both cases without a corresponding formal return into the city: this absence emphasized the expansive conquest of space outside of Jerusalem. In between these two processions, there was the centripetal long nocturnal procession from the Mount of Olives to the main church whose urban importance was emphasized by the church lights that awaited it at the city gate and thus had intruded from church space into city space, and by the entrance into the church through the main gates from the very heart of the city. The *deductio* of the bishop by his full congregation was made highly visible to all of Jerusalem, regardless of their religious adherence.

But this is not all there is: Christian ritual has also to be understood as a conscious and often provocative answer to pagan ritual traditions. The two later Pentecost processions took place at night and with artificial light – explicitly said so by Egeria for the procession from the Mount of Olives, assumed for the final procession out to Zion. Nocturnal processions were rare in the ancient world: I see them not just as an appropriation of urban space, but also of urban time, and as a Christian answer to the festive lighting of the city during prominent city festivals. At night, an ancient city ordinarily was dark, and its streets and squares were deserted; Christian poetry and ritual emphasized the uncanniness of night when the demons roamed, especially in the hymns that greeted the morning and ended the day.[38] But during the exceptional time of a festival, there was light, impressive and memorable. Libanius described the way Antioch was illuminated during the evening banquets and the ensuing reveling of the city festivals: "There are many lamps that fill the city with light, many revelers, the sounds of lutes and flutes, and songs through the streets . . .; and to drink oneself into drunkenness does not meet censure."[39] This was no exception in rich Antioch but the rule for all ancient cities, even if wealthy Antioch might have been somewhat more lavish. The orderliness and self-restraint of a Christian night procession thus appears as a conscious answer to the lack of discipline and restraint during pagan festivals (the bishops certainly were among those who censured drunkenness and worse), in the same way as the bishops understood fasting as an answer to exuberant pagan banqueting during city festivals and opposed Christian alms-giving to the distribution of *sportulae* during the Kalendae.

---

[38] See Prud. *Cathemerin.* 1 (*ad galli cantum*) and esp. 2 (*matutinus*) for the morning, 5 (*ad incensum lucernae*) and 6 (*ante somnum*) for the evening.

[39] Liban. *Progymn.* 12.29.10 ἔνθα δὴ πολλοὶ μὲν λαμπτῆρες ὡς ἐμπεπλῆσθαι φωτὸς τὸ ἄστυ, πολλοὶ δὲ κωμασταὶ καὶ αὐλῶν εἴδη καὶ συρίγγων <καὶ> ἐν στενωποῖς ᾠδαί . . . τότε καὶ εἰς μέθην πιεῖν οὐ πᾶν ὄνειδος.

PART III

Christianity and private ritual

Introduction

The final two chapters turn from collective festivals to the Christianization of individual religious action and experience exemplified in two specific institutions, incubation and magic rites. Incubation, the ritual of obtaining healing in a dream, is well established in healing sanctuaries of the Greek and Roman world, and its reappearance in Christian churches has been claimed as an obvious case of continuity, tolerated or encouraged by Christian authorities.[1] If this were correct, it would be an interesting contrast to the debate about the Roman (or, in the language of the Byzantine writers, Hellenic) festivals, and would add some background to that debate. Healing leads to magic and the complex ways emperors and bishops since Constantine dealt with it. Unlike incubation, but like festivals, it is an area where church and state were somewhat at odds and where the legal protection accorded to some "magic" rituals helped their survival against the objections of the church authorities. The Christianization of magic is thus an interesting parallel case to the continuity of festivals, where the two main contemporary sources of authority constructed religion in a contrasting way, and where many individuals preferred the freedom the state accorded to them over the constraints that the church imposed. Until recently, incubation and healing rites have not found much interest in scholarship on the ancient world for many decades now; magic, on the other hand, has been very present in contemporary research on ancient religions, yet there has been surprisingly little work done on the transition between the pagan and the Christian world.[2] In both cases, a new look at the evidence and the problems seems promising, well beyond the framework of this book.

---

[1] Most recently, and unhesitatingly, by Markschies (2007).
[2] I will give the relevant bibliography at the beginning of both chapters.

CHAPTER 10

Incubation in a Christian world

Introduction: a spa in the Holy Land

In the later part of the sixth century, about the year 570 CE, a group of pilgrims from Northern Italy, lead by one Antoninus of Piacenza, visited the Holy Land in a Grand Tour that brought them from Cyprus via Jerusalem and the Sinai to Mesopotamia. An otherwise unknown member of this group of Northern Italians left a lengthy report that is known as the *Itinerarium Placentinum,* "The Piacenza Itinerary," or *Itinerarium Placentini,* "The Itinerary of a Man from Piacenza."[3] It finds its place among several comparable reports from late antiquity and the early Middle Ages, all left by Western religious tourists.[4] This form of tourism had begun in the course of the fourth century, driven by the Western interest in the Holy Land and in the ascetic monks living in Egypt and Palestine. It helped that the famous Jerome and his wealthy lady friend Paula decided to live in Bethlehem and found their monasteries there. One of the earliest and, in modern scholarship, the most famous report has been vital to my Chapter 9 above, the *Peregrinatio Egeriae* written about a visit to the Sinai and the Holy Land in 381/384 and sent back to her co-religionists, *dominae sorores*. Thus from early on these travel texts must have had their readership in the Western monastic world. At about the time of Charlemagne, the Piacenza Itinerary created enough interest among the learned Benedictine monks of what was to become Switzerland that it was copied in St. Gall, and that a second contemporary copy was kept in the neighboring Reichenau library as a report about *loca sancta ultramarina*.[5]

---

[3] *Anonymus perperam Antoninus dictus Placentinus: Itinerarium*, in Geyer *et al.* (1965), 129–153, 157–174. Edition with Italian translation by Milani (1976); annotated French translation: Maraval (2002b), 203–235; annotated English translation for a wider readership: Wilkinson (2002), 129–151.
[4] The texts are edited in Geyer (1898) and Geyer *et al.* (1965); for Egeria see also Maraval (1982) and Natalucci (1991). A collection of annotated texts in English: Wilkinson (2002); a similar collection in French: Maraval (2002b); see also Maraval (1985) and the survey paper Maraval (2002a).
[5] See the description of the medieval manuscripts in Gildemeister (1889).

The anonymous author from Piacenza was not only interested in the usual Biblical monuments as were Egeria and other devoted Christians, but also in local customs and economies, and even in hot baths and thermal establishments – not unlike Michel de Montaigne, who, when traveling to Italy, was prone to make detours to check out all the spas in his way. The Piacenza pilgrim tells us how lepers were swimming in the Dead Sea to find purification or at least temporary relief, or how they were healed at the hot baths of Moses in Livias (Tell er-Ram), as were patients suffering from other ailments in the cold baths nearby, or he informs us about the healing baths of Siloa in Jerusalem.[6] In much more detail, however, he writes about the healing of lepers in the baths of Elija near Gadara (today Um Qaiss, East of the Jordan in Jordania):

> Three miles outside Gadara, there are hot springs that are called "Baths of Elija"; here the lepers are cleaned and entertained in the guest house at public expense. In the evening, they fill [or clean[7]] the baths. In front of the very exit of the water, there is a large tub; when it is filled, the doors are closed and the lepers are let in through the back with lamps and incense, and they sit the entire night in the tub. And when they fall asleep, the one that is to be healed has some dream vision (*visio*), and after he has narrated it, he will abstain from the bath for seven days, and after seven days, he is healed.[8]

Not all details of the report are clear; language and transmission create their problems, as does the confrontation with the archaeological record: the Roman thermal baths at Gadara are well excavated.[9] But this is irrelevant here, and it does not seriously infringe on the reliability of the report. The main point is that lepers are offered a special and segregated nighttime bath, performed with some ritual, incense burning, and the use of lamps. Through this, they all hope to be healed, or rather, as leprosy was understood as impurity, to be purified by divine grace. They do not expect treatment, they expect a sign that purification is on its way. But only a few find it. These chosen ones have a dream that they will tell the next morning (*recitarit*), presumably publicly rather than to a priest of whose existence we

---

[6] Dead Sea, 10.3; baths of Moses, 10.1f.; Siloa, 24.4.
[7] The older tradition has *mundantur*, the later *inundantur*; it is difficult to decide whether the later *recensio* misread or corrected the older tradition.
[8] 7.6–8 *In ista parte <Iordanis a> ciuitate ad milia tria sunt aquas calidas, quae appellantur Termas Heliae, ubi leprosi mundantur, qui e xenodochio habent de publicum delicias. hora uespertina inundantur termae. ante ipsum clibanum aquae est solius grandis, qui dum impletus fuerit, clauduntur omnia ostia, et per posticum mittuntur intus cum luminaria et incensum et sedent in illo solio tota nocte, et dum soporati fuerint, uidet ille, qui curandus est, aliquam uisionem, et dum eam recitarit, abstinentur ipsae termae septem diebus et intra septem dies mundatur.*
[9] See Belayche (2001).

do not hear; such a public announcement is common to pagans and Christians.[10] They then will segregate themselves by abstaining from bathing during the seven following nights, and on the eighth day they will be pure.

The reader of this report would not suspect that the pilgrims were in one of the most famous spas of the ancient world, "comparable only to Baiae in Italy," as Eunapius remarked when he told about Iamblichus' stay in this resort. For most of his teaching time, Iamblichus – who died in 327, ten years prior to Constantine – was living in Apameia in Northern Syria; the spa was thus in the neighborhood. To entertain his students, the philosopher provoked the apparition of Eros and Anteros, the tutelary gods of two of the several springs, Eros of a hot, Anteros of a cold one.[11] A century later, the empress Aelia Eudocia – the wife of Theodosius II, coming from a pagan Neoplatonic family in Athens and famous for her poetry – wrote a long ecphrastic poem about the place that she must have known well, as she lived in Jerusalem during her later years; it was found by the excavators a few years ago, inscribed on a large stone slab opposite the main entrance of the spa complex.[12] The poem evokes the splendor of the architecture, the sixteen pools or springs, each with its own name, and the crowd of marble statues that stood around them. None of these details is remarked upon by the Piacenza pilgrim, although he must have seen them as well; instead, he adds, local patriot that he is, that this was also the place where John of Piacenza, the husband of Saint Thekla, died. Which confirms that one sees only what one knows already.

Few scholars have noticed the Piacenza text. Nicole Belayche discussed it in her book on pagan cults in Palestine, where she regards the ritual as the survival of Graeco-Roman incubation in an unattested sanctuary of Asklepios: the temple, she thinks, must be hidden under a Christian church that still awaits excavation.[13] Belayche follows earlier scholars; only Pierre Maraval pointed out the obvious, that the Christian rite did

---

[10] On the public announcement of a healing dream see Tatian. *Adv. Graecos* 18; on the public recitation of a Christian healing miracle Aug. *De civ. D.* 22.8.22.
[11] Eunap. *VS* 5.2.2–7, p. 459.
[12] Published in *Israel Exploration Journal* 32 (1982), 77 no. 1; *Qadmoniot* 16 (1983) 28–36; *SEG* 32.1502; the excavators date it to about 455 CE. On Aelia Eudocia, wife of Theodosius II, as a learned poetess see Socrates, *Hist. eccl.* 7.21.8 (to celebrate Theodosius' victory over the Persians in 422, many praise texts were written): "The empress herself also composed a poem in heroic verse: for she had excellent literary taste; being the daughter of Leontius the Athenian sophist, she had been instructed in every kind of learning by her father. Atticus the bishop had baptized her a little while previous to her marriage with the emperor, and had then given her the Christian name of Eudocia, instead of her pagan one of Athenais."
[13] Belayche (2001), 268–273.

not take place in a sanctuary.[14] But things are not as simple as this, and Belayche's idea that this "originally" was a sanctuary of Asklepios, whose temple was covered by a sixth-century Byzantine church, is shaky at best. It is an argument based on nothing more than the fact that a Christian church was part of the late antique spa complex, and the probability that Christian churches continue pagan temples. No literary or epigraphical source attests any temple, of Asklepios or any other divinity; until the church is removed for further excavation, we do not know what is hiding under it.[15] The one detail that we can safely connect with earlier practices does not lead to pagan incubation, but to Jewish purification from leprosy. Already *Leviticus* 14 prescribes a period of seven days between the purification ritual and the moment when a leper is healed. On the seventh day, he shaves off "all his hair off his head and his beard and his eyebrows, even all his hair he shall shave off"; he washes all his clothes and his entire body, "and he shall be clean." On the eighth day, he sacrifices and is officially pronounced clean.[16] The same seven-day period was observed by Rabbinic Judaism; it must have still been alive at the time of the Piacenza pilgrim.

But there are other and perhaps more serious problems. Dream incubation is well attested in the ancient world since the Sumerians, but its status changed radically with Christianity.[17] Christian theologians early on had fundamental problems with dreaming. In a seminal paper, Jacques Le Goff had remarked on the odd character of dreaming in late antique and medieval Christianity; he called it "a society in which dreaming was impeded, which suffered from disorientation in the oniric realm," and more recent research has confirmed and refined his results.[18] Furthermore, there can be no simple continuation between a Graeco-Roman and a Christian incubation rite. We shall see how Theodosius' prohibition of pagan public cult put an end to all incubation rites, as it did to public sacrifice that was part of incubation rituals. Yet scholars insist on "the continuation, and even enthusiastic embracing, of incubation" in Christian late antique society.[19] It is far from clear in which respect this view is correct and how Christian, especially Byzantine, incubation related

---

[14] E.g. Wilkinson (2002), 133 n. 17; Talbot (2002); Maraval (2002b), 210 n. 2.
[15] The concept of a simple transition from a pagan to a Christian sanctuary has been questioned by archaeologists long ago: see the seminal papers by Frantz (1965) and Speiser (1976); more recently Foschia (2000), Pont (2004).
[16] Leviticus 14.8–9. I owe the reference to Michael Schwartz.
[17] On the Ancient Near East, see the rich monograph (with ample earlier bibliography) by Zgoll (2006); on incubation in general, a somewhat idiosyncratic approach in Patton (2004); more below.
[18] Le Goff (1988), the citation p. 211; Stroumsa (1999); Graf (2010).
[19] The citation is from the excellent introduction to Oberhelman (2008), 53.

to the previous Graeco-Roman ritual. I have to start with a short glance at the history of the scholarship.

Past scholarship

The term "Christian incubation" goes back to the slim but seminal doctoral dissertation of Ludwig Deubner, *De Incubatione Capita Quattuor*, defended and printed in 1900.[20] It almost immediately influenced an often-cited English book on the topic, Mary Hamilton's *Incubation, or The Cure of Disease in Pagan Temples and Christian Churches*, published in 1906 and at least partly stimulated by her interest in the psychology of dream healing. In her interest in the modern-day phenomenon, Hamilton goes well beyond Deubner, to whom she otherwise is heavily indebted, mostly without acknowledging it; it remained the task of Deubner's English wife to set the record straight.[21] Deubner collected an impressive amount of evidence from Latin Saints' Lives and from Byzantine sources on incubation healing and healers – the saints Cosmas and Damian, the most important incubation healers in the East, Saints Cyrus and John, and on Saint Thekla, Saint Michael, and a saint with the speaking name Therapon whose miracles he published in an appendix.

Deubner saw no reason not to understand Christian incubation as a simple continuation of the pagan ritual. Nobody had yet pointed out the peculiarity of Christian thought on dreaming; more importantly, Deubner wrote in the atmosphere of secularization and *Historismus* that characterized the study of ancient religions in the second half of the nineteenth century. Deubner was a student of Albrecht Dieterich in Giessen, to whom he dedicated his dissertation; Dieterich in turn was Hermann Usener's student and son-in-law, and he worked mainly on concepts of afterlife and apocalypticism that he analyzed in terms of pagan–Christian continuities. Deubner's position was shared by the leading scholars of his period, not the least the Bible scholars that we now loosely associate as the *Religionsgeschichtliche Schule* connected with the University of Göttingen;

---

[20] Deubner (1900).
[21] Hamilton (1906). The book received a glowing review by H. D. W. Rouse in *Classical Review* 21 (1907), 155. The reviewer did not notice the debts especially to Deubner's early Christian documentation, as "O. C. Deubner *née* Lindley" was quick to point out in the next issue of the journal, *ibid*. 220. Ottilie Caroline Lindley, daughter of Sir Walter Harlein Lindley, a hydraulic engineer and member of a family that pioneered water works in several European cities, married Ludwig Deubner in 1902; she died 1925. See *Neue Deutsche Biographie* 3 (1957), 621 (Deubner, Ludwig) and 14 (1986), 606–607 (Lindley, Sir William Harlein).

but it resonated also with the interests Usener already had in late antique Christianity and the Saints' Lives.[22]

Pagan incubation

Incubation, that is dreaming in a sanctuary sought intentionally for either information or healing, is an important part of ancient divination that in the course of the late sixth and fifth centuries BCE became specialized for ritual healing in the Graeco-Roman world, especially in the cult of Asklepios.[23] It is almost alone the private incubation rites of the Greek Magical Papyri, performed with the help of a miniaturized incubation shrine, that retain the primary oracular goal of incubation, to acquire superhuman knowledge through a dream.[24] Although primarily associated with the healer Asklepios, a son of the divinatory god Apollo, it was practiced also in the sanctuaries of other divinities and heroes, such as Sarapis in Alexandria, Isis on Delos and in Athens, or Amphiaraos in Oropos, almost exclusively again for healing purposes. It is a ritual complex on whose form in the shrines of Asklepios we are reasonably well informed, through a combination of literary texts from Aristophanes in late fifth century BCE Athens to Aristeides in second century CE Pergamon; inscriptions, most spectacularly the healing reports from several sanctuaries of Asklepios; and archaeological excavations.

As is typical for pagan Graeco-Roman religion, there is some variety among the local manifestations of ritual and cult; but overall, healing incubation is relatively uniform in its ritual structure and theological foundation. This might be due to its expansion from a few cult centers, mainly Epidauros and Kos; but even the cult of Amphiaraos in Oropos seems to have conformed to the same ritual pattern.[25] Thus, a summary can do better justice to the phenomenon than in most other cases of Greek religion. The summary does not take into account fictional narrations

---

[22] See Lüdemann (1996); Lüdemann and Schröder (1987); Colpe (1961). For Usener, most important in this context is his 1889 monograph (2nd edn. 1911; repr. 1969); see also his several editions of Saints' Lives: *Legenden der Pelagia* (Bonn: Georgi, 1879); *Cyrillus, Scythopolitanus: Vita S. Theodosii* (Bonn: Georgi, 1890); *Der heilige Theodosios: Schriften des Theodoros und Kyrillos* (Leipzig, 1890); *Acta SS. Anthusae, Athanasii Episcopi, Charisimi et Neopythi* (Brussels, 1893) = *Analecta Bollandiana* 12 (1893); *Acta martyris Anastasii Persae* (Bonn, 1894).
[23] The best detailed overview is Ehrenheim (2011), with the earlier bibliography.
[24] On these rites, see esp. Johnston (2008), 161–169. But there are vestiges of the divinatory function in an Epidaurian healing report, *SIG*³ 1169.19 no. xxiv = LiDonnici (1995), 102 B 4.
[25] Although Ehrenheim (2011) has shown that one should not underrate the diversity even among the incubation cults of Asklepios.

about people sleeping in temples where they experienced the dream apparition of a divinity, such as the pharaoh Sethos in Herodotus and his crisis dream in the temple of Hephaistos, or Bellerophon who was told by the seer Polyidos to sleep on Athena's altar, where in a dream the goddess gave him the bridle of Pegasos: these accounts typically do not concern healing, vary much more in their details, and are not necessarily anchored in ritual.[26]

In the typical incubation ritual, a human patient intentionally slept in the sanctuary of a healing divinity. In a dream, the sleeper met the divinity and received healing instructions or direct treatment and healing. The ritual thus enacted an individual encounter with the divinity that had one aim only, to heal a specific ailment; no expansion of human experience or knowledge was intended, unlike in theurgical or mystical rites. The ritual took place in the sanctuary, where a special space, the dormitory or incubation room (in Greek ἐγκοιμητήριον, "sleeping room," or ἄβατον "space that cannot be entered"), was set aside for the rite; the rooms were sometimes subdivided according to gender. One entered it in the evening after preparatory rites, and left it in the morning with other rites. Usually, a consultation with the priest, a dream interpreter, and sometimes a doctor followed; this consultation addressed questions of interpretation, the preparation of the prescribed medication, or other things that followed from the dream. The temple charged the patient a healing fee that in Pergamon was deposited in a cash box (*thesauros*) before one entered the incubation room.

The preparatory rituals varied somewhat from place to place, but the overall structure was the same. As always when entering Greek sacred space, basic purity was required, not the least to wash oneself after sexual activity and to wash and wait a few days after contact with birth or death. But this applied already to the general sacred space of the shrine, not the more specific space of the dormitory. On the day of incubation, one sacrificed an animal, a piglet or a sheep, on whose skin one sometimes slept. The animal sacrifice led to a common meal of the patients or their kin group. In the evening, before entering the dormitory, one prayed again and in Pergamon, where we have the most details, sacrificed cakes to a series of divinities, among them Themis (Divine Lawfulness) in order to dream a good dream (one recalls that dreams can be false), and Mnemosyne (Memory) in order to remember the dream, and one paid the fee. In the

---

[26] Sethos: Hdt. 2.141; Bellerophon: Pind. *Ol.* 13.63–82 (an aition for the cult of Athena Hippia in Corinth).

morning, one prayed and sacrificed again, and one consulted the priest. If healed, one often set up an inscription or a votive relief to commemorate publicly the helpful divine intervention – the epigraphical collections of healings, ἰάματα that are preserved from several sanctuaries claim to copy such votive inscriptions.[27]

Thus, Graeco-Roman incubation was well structured, both temporally and spatially. It took place in a space and a time of enhanced individual liminality that allowed the extraordinary experience of the healing dream and whose beginning and end was ritually and spatially marked. It also called for collaboration with the local priests for the sacrifices and prayers that were too complex for an unsupervised individual to perform, and again for the evaluation of the dream for which there often was a specialist available, the ὀνειροκρίτης or "dream interpreter." Some temple authority presumably must have helped also with the setting up of the votive gift, its iconography, and its wording. Incubation was usually undertaken on one's own initiative; we know very few cases where the god invited someone, in a dream or otherwise, to undertake incubation. This conforms to the general principle of Greek cult that participation was open to all members of a community as long as they fulfilled the purity requirements.

Dreaming among Christians

The dream was thus the key to incubation – and it was the dream with which Christianity began to have problems rather early on.[28] Greeks and Romans at all times were conscious and aware that dreams could be false. Homer expressed this in the famous image of the two gates through which dreams arrive on earth, a gate of ivory for the false dreams and a gate of horn for the true ones, and Agamemnon's dream in *Iliad* 2 shows a god-sent false dream and its consequences early in the poem.[29] Unlike some Ancient Near Eastern cultures, however, Greece did not have a ritual mechanism to test the veracity of a dream.[30] In incubation, we have to assume that the ritual precautions were thought to guarantee that all the dreams were true. It is consistent with general cultural assumptions among Greeks and Romans from the time of Homer onwards that some dreams at least were true divinatory messages, communicated by the divine to the

---

[27] For the Epidaurian *iamata*, the most extensive ones, see LiDonnici (1995); all the ancient texts in Girone (1998).
[28] Stroumsa (1999); Graf (2010).
[29] Gates of horn and ivory: Hom. *Od.* 19. 560–569; Agamemnon's dream: Hom. *Il.* 2.1–47.
[30] Zgoll (2006), 255–263 (especially in Mari).

human world, even if the gods could also send false dreams, and that one should not worry overmuch about those false dreams.

Inside this general cultural agreement, Christianity started to problematize dreams and dreaming, by inverting the relationship between true and false dreams: for Christians, true dreams were the exception. Of course, they existed: after all, both the Old and the New Testament knew of dreams in which God or his Angels intervened in the human world, and there was no good reason to reject these narrations. Like the pagans, Christianity had to make distinctions between true and false dreams, and to find criteria for these distinctions, and they came up with much fewer reliable dreams.

This process can be illustrated with two Western, Latin texts, the *Passio Perpetuae*, the prison diary of a young Christian woman in Carthage, written at the very beginning of the third century, and Tertullian's contemporary treatise *On the Soul*. In the *Passio Perpetuae*, dreams (*visiones*[31]) take the form of communications between the imprisoned young Christian mother Perpetua and God about the immediate future and about eschatology, a communication initiated by Perpetua, who knew that she was able, as she writes, to "chat with God" (*fabulari cum Deo*), and whom her fellow captives encouraged to do so because she had this extraordinary standing in God's eyes (*iam in magna dignatione es*). Not everybody can ask God for a true dream, it seems, but only those whom he favors. This continues Old Testament views and their reception in early Christian literature: Jacob or Daniel received true dreams from God as his elected, and Perpetua was another of God's elected.

In the literary form in which we have it, Perpetua's prison diary is not far in time, style, and implied theology from Tertullian, especially from Tertullian the Montanist with his acceptance of unmediated communication between individuals and God.[32] It is no surprise that his long chapters

---

[31] In the Latin terminology of Macrobius, *Somn.* 1.3.2, 9 *visio* is a dream that foretells the future in a clear and open way (1.3.9 *uisio est autem cum id quis uidet quod eodem modo quo apparuerat eueniet*, "It is a *visio* when someone sees something that will happen in the same way in which it was seen"); Perpetua's dreams do not conform to this but rather to Macrobius' *oraculum* (1.3.8 *cum in somnis parens uel alia sancta grauiuse persona seu sacerdos uel etiam deus aperte euenturum quid aut non euenturum, faciendum uitandumue denuntiat*, "when during sleep a parent or another revered and serious person or a priest or even a divinity tells clearly what will happen or not and what one should do or avoid") or *somnium* (1.3.10 *tegit figuris et uelat ambagibus non nisi interpretatione intellegendam significationem rei quae demonstratur*, "hides behind images and veils in ambiguities the meaning of the thing to which it points that can only be understood through interpretation"). But Macrobius' terminology is technical and formulaic, without necessarily corresponding to the non-technical usage of the terms in everyday language.
[32] Butler (2005). On Montanism, see Frend (1988); Hirschmann (2005).

on dreams in his treatise *De anima* (chapters 45–48) accept dreaming as legitimate communication between God and humans, as does Perpetua. But unlike Perpetua, Tertullian introduces an important note of caution and contradicts those pagan theoreticians – he mentions especially the Stoics – who put their faith in dream oracles and thought that "a most caring divinity had ... given dreams to a human institution, as the special comfort of a natural oracle." The Christian thinker had a serious problem with this: like all other oracular institutions, dream oracles were, in his own words, "a demonic institution, going back to those spirits who already then were dwelling in the very humans or who affected their memories with all their evilness" – spirits, that is, who manifested themselves in ecstatic prophecy such as that of the Sibyl or the Delphian Pythia, or in performance of the non-ecstatic professional soothsayers who relied on what they had learned; Tertullian follows the standard dichotomy between natural and artificial divination. In both cases, the demons "falsely claimed a divine nature, and ... they deceived through the benefits of medicine and of advice and foretelling, in order to do more damage by their very help: ... they divert humans from the search of the true divinity by suggesting a false one."[33] And given that demons are free agents who move around in the air without any restrictions and who certainly are not confined to the space of sanctuaries but can easily enter our bedrooms, he concludes that "most dreams are inspired by demons."[34] Only rare dreams come from God, who in this way fulfills his promised grace of prophecies. In this construction, there is no place for Christian incubation, nor is there a need; Tertullian does not even think of it. Neither is there a need for special incubation

---

[33] Tert. *De anima* 46.12: *Haec quantum ad fidem somniorum a nobis quoque consignandam et aliter interpretandam. nam de oraculis etiam ceteris, apud quae nemo dormitat, quid aliud pronuntiabimus quam daemonicam esse rationem eorum spirituum qui iam tunc in ipsis hominibus habitauerint uel memorias eorum affectauerint ad omnem malitiae suae scenam, in ista aeque specie diuinitatem mentientes eademque industria etiam per beneficia fallentes medicinarum et admonitionum, praenuntiationum, quo magis laedant iuuando, dum per ea quae iuuant ab inquisitione uerae diuinitatis abducunt ex insinuatione falsae?* "So much for the dreams to which credit has to be ascribed even by ourselves, although we must interpret them in another sense. As for all other oracles, at which no one ever dreams, what else must we declare concerning them, but that they are the diabolical contrivance of those spirits who even at that time dwelt in the persons themselves, or aimed at reviving the memory of them as the stage of their evil purposes, counterfeiting a divine power under their form, and, with equal persistence deceiving men by their very boons of remedies, warnings, and forecasts, to injure their victims the more they helped them; while the means whereby they rendered the help withdrew them from all search after the true God, by insinuating into their minds ideas of the false one?" (Translation after Peter Holmes, *The Ante-Nicene Fathers*.)

[34] *Ibid.* 47.12 (*a daemoniis plurimum incuti somnia*). This is why Zacharias, *Vita Severi* p. 17 can say that "notre philosophe imagina un oracle (ou plutôt il fut trompé par le démon figuré par Isis), d'après lequel la déesse lui promettait des enfants."

rooms: God shows his grace wherever he thinks fit to do so; Tertullian exempts no human space from divine or demonic presence. Perpetua, after all, was dreaming in prison, not in a sacred space, and she was an extraordinary human who possessed the necessary *dignatio*, grace.

Tertullian is not the first Christian author to connect dreaming with demons. Almost as soon as we see a Christian write about dreams, this devaluation and distrust of dreaming is obvious. Justin Martyr, who in the middle of the second century addressed an *Apologia* of Christianity to the emperor Antoninus Pius, warns the Christians that the demons "fight to make you slaves and servants; and sometimes through appearances in dreams, sometimes through acts of magic" they try to bring down weak Christians.[35] These demons were understood as the Fallen Angels who brought magic to humans but also, under the influence of Paul's identification of pagan gods and demons (δαιμόνια) in 1 Corinthians 10:20, as the pagan gods who manifest themselves in dreams.

Later Christian authors in East and West agreed. Despite Jerome's famous dream where God had him flogged for reading Cicero, dreams remained a problem for the church. Only Augustine moved from a position where he did not doubt that dreams were sent "by superior powers or demons," to an explication of ordinary dreams that did not rely on superhuman agency.[36] In the general opinion, dreams remained harmless only for the select few, mainly saints, bishops, and emperors, as Jacques Le Goff has pointed out.[37]

Several motives contributed to this distrust. The first is that dreams could be understood as unmediated communication with the superhuman world, as in Perpetua's case. The more the church installed its hierarchy and its control of teaching, the more it aimed to control such communication. The Montanists with their uncontrolled mediumship ended up as heretics.

---

[35] Justin. *Apologia* 1.14: Προλέγομεν γὰρ ὑμῖν φυλάξασθαι μὴ οἱ προδιαβεβλημένοι ὑφ' ἡμῶν δαίμονες ἐξαπατῶσιν ὑμᾶς καὶ ἀποτρέψωσιν ἀπὸ τοῦ ὅλως εὐτυχεῖν καὶ συνιέναι τὰ λεγόμενα· ἀγωνίζονται γὰρ ὑμᾶς ἔχειν δούλους καὶ ὑπηρέτας, καί ποτε μὲν δι' ὀνείρων ἐπιφανείας ποτὲ δ' αὖ διὰ μαγικῶν στροφῶν χειροῦνται πάντας τοὺς οὐκ ἔσθ' ὅπως ὑπὲρ τῆς αὑτῶν σωτηρίας ἀγωνιζομένους. "For we forewarn you to be on your guard, lest those demons whom we have been accusing should deceive you, and quite divert you from reading and understanding what we say. For they strive to hold you their slaves and servants; and sometimes by appearances in dreams, and sometimes by magical impositions, they subdue all who make no strong opposing effort for their own salvation." (Translation: Marcus Dods and George Reith, *The Ante-Nicene Fathers*.)

[36] Jerome, *Epist.* 22.30, with the insistence on their truthfulness, on which see Feichtinger (1997). Augustine: The earlier position in a letter to Nebridius from about 390 CE, *Epist.* 9; the later in a letter to Evodius, *Epist.* 159 (c.414/415 CE), where he also refers to book 12 of *De Genesi ad litteram*.

[37] Le Goff (1988), 220–223.

The second reason is that, as for example Tertullian had pointed out, dreams were part of the ancient divinatory system. Christian theology radically rejected divination, together with magic, as a private way of accessing the divine without the help of an ecclesiastical intermediary. Compared to the relative openness of Constantine, imperial legislation on divination and magic hardened during the fourth century, as did the position of the church. In Isidore of Seville, magic and divination, including dreams, were lumped together in one single chapter that would determine the medieval perception of these phenomena.[38] It was the institutional church that claimed a monopoly of foreknowledge, and the church was backed by the state. The emperors too had an urgent interest in monopolizing the knowledge of the future: in the past, this knowledge had been a dangerous weapon in the hand of potential usurpers.[39] For once, the reasons of state overlapped with the reasons of the church and its theologians.

There is an additional, powerful reason that transcends theology or politics. In its demonology, Christians problematized night as a dangerous time when demons were roaming freely, as for example Prudentius' collection of hymns sung during the day, the *Cathemerinon*, shows. The morning hymn *Ante galli cantum*, later a part of medieval liturgy, tells us that at sunrise "demons, roaming through the night, are frightened away by the crowing of the roosters."[40] Bishop's councils would prohibit *pervigiliae*, night rituals, even during Saints' festivals; the moralistic fervor that made Cicero prohibit female night rituals as a danger to matronal virtue easily blended with the belief that Satan was waiting out there in the night.[41] Dreams too are an affair of the night, as Prudentius tells us in his *Hymn Before Sleep*. Only the just dreamer will see God's truth, as did Perpetua; we lesser mortals better pray that we will

---

[38] This does not stop Isidore, *Etym.* 11.3.4 from accepting the divinatory value of portents, dreams, and oracles, since God sometimes wants to warn us: *Vult enim deus interdum ventura significare per aliqua nascentium noxia, sicut et per somnos et per oracula, qua praemoneat et significet quibusdam vel gentibus vel hominibus futuram cladem; quod plurimis etiam experimentis probatum est.* "God sometimes wants to point to the future through some damage to what is born as well as through dreams and oracles that warn groups or individuals of a future catastrophe; this is also proven by the experience of many people."

[39] Fögen (1997).

[40] Prud. *Cathem.* 1. 37 *Ferunt vagantes daemonas | laetos tenebris noctium, | gallo canente exterritos |* [40] *sparsim timere et cedere. || Invisa nam vicinitas | lucis, salutis, numinis | rupto tenebrarum situ |noctis fugat satellites.* "They say that roaming shadows, happy with the dark of night, are frightened by the crying cock and rush and flee everywhere; the hateful nearness of light, salvation, God breaks the dankness of night and drives away the followers of night."

[41] Autun, a. 561–605: de Clerq (1963), 265.7, 17; Cicero: *legg.* 2.21.11.

not dream at all, and perform the necessary ritual ablutions and signs of the cross to protect us against evil influences.[42]

Incubation among the Christians

Dreams, thus, are dangerous and might distract from true belief, not lead to it, because they might be sent by demons. It goes without saying that this influenced the Christian evaluation of incubation. Already a Greek contemporary of Justin Martyr, Tatian, made this clear when he explained that dream healing was just a trick by the demons to catch us unawares. The "so-called gods" first send us ailments, then appear in our dreams and make us publicly announce their dream appearance; then they heal us and disappear, leaving behind our admiration of their power.[43] In his denunciation of healing and oracular dreams as a trick by the demons to distract us from the search for God, Tertullian follows this explanatory paradigm; it would remain the basic Christian position on dream incubation for several centuries.

When Constantine took over the empire, in this as in other cases he showed restraint and toleration, with a few exceptions. One is the destruction of the cult place in Mamre and its replacement by a Christian basilica, another the destruction of the then famous incubation shrine of Asklepios in Aigai in Kilikia.[44] Eusebius, Constantine's biographer, claims that the emperor intervened in Aigai for religious reasons: "The demon worshipped in Kilikia, whom tens of thousands regarded with reverence as Savior and Healer and who sometimes appeared to those who passed the night in his temple ... was in reality a destroyer of souls who drew away deluded worshipers from the Savior to involve them

---

[42] Prud. *Cathem.* 6; see esp. vv. 73ff. *O quam profunda iustis | Arcana per soporem* |[75] *Aperit tuenda Christus! | Quam clara, quam tacenda!,* or vv. 113ff. *Tali sopore iustus | Mentem relaxat heros,* | [115] *Ut spiritu sagaci | Coelum peragret omne*; with the final wish 116ff. *Nos nil meremur horum, | Quos creber implet error. | Concreta quos malarum /*[120] *Vitiat cupido rerum. | Sat est quiete dulci | Fessum fovere corpus: | Sat, si nihil sinistrum | Vanae minentur umbrae.*

[43] Tatian. *Adv. Graecos* 18 οὕτω καὶ οἱ νομιζόμενοι θεοὶ τοῖς τινων ἐπιφοιτῶντες μέλεσιν, ἔπειτα δι' ὀνείρων τὴν εἰς αὐτοὺς πραγματευόμενοι δόξαν δημοσίαι τε τοὺς τοιούτους προϊέναι κελεύσαντες, πάντων ὁρώντων, ἐπειδὰν τῶν ἐγκοσμίων ἀπολαύσωσι ἀποπτόμενοι τῶν καμνόντων, ἣν ἐπραγματεύσαντο νόσον περιγράφοντες τοὺς ἀνθρώπους εἰς τὸ ἀρχαῖον ἀποκαθιστῶσιν. "Those who are thought to be gods, invading the bodies of certain persons, and producing a sense of their presence by dreams, command them to come forth into public and in the sight of all, when they have taken their fill of the things of this world, fly away from the sick and destroying the disease which they had produced restore men to their former state." (Translation after J. E. Ryland, *The Ante-Nicene Fathers*.)

[44] Mamre: Sozomen. *Hist.* 2.4.2–5; Aigai: Euseb. *V.Const.* 3.56.

in impious error."[45] But Constantine might have had another reason as well. He did not just destroy the shrine, he carried off the beautiful columns of the temple for his own building projects in Constantinople. It is possible that columns were more important than the cult; after all, incubation in Aigai seems to have continued until Julian's time, 361 CE, as did many other incubation cults.[46] Constantine's advisor Eusebius might have had an additional reason. The sanctuary at Aigai was not just, as Eusebius has it, "admired by the philosophers," it was also the place that had shaped young Apollonius of Tyana, whom Sossianus Hierocles, a high administrator under Diocletian, stylized as the pagan Christ; this had provoked Eusebius to a lengthy and somewhat violent refutation.[47]

Despite all this, dream healing is part of the story-telling of countless Christian saints' lives in East and West: saints and martyrs were the just ones to whom God granted dreams. More surprisingly, we have literary and archaeological records on ritual sleeping in churches, mostly near the grave of a saint: the saint in turn could procure true dreams for his worshipers. Scholars since Deubner called this Christian incubation. But the relationship between these Christian healing events and the Graeco-Roman incubation ritual needs more thought, both as to phenomenology and to chronology. Are the rituals close enough to vouchsafe the traditional assumption of continuity, and does chronology allow such an assumption?[48]

Archaeology: disputed cases

There is a curious time gap between the end of pagan incubation and the beginning of Christian stories about dream healing by Christian saints. During the fourth century, hostility was growing against pagan incubation sanctuaries, as against all oracular shrines. The imperial condemnation of divination that started in the middle of the century with a letter of Constans forbidding all divination and understanding divination as just another subcategory of sorcery must have addressed incubation as much as any other oracular method. On the other hand, dream healing begins to be

---

[45] Euseb. V. Const. 3.56.1 πολὺς ἦν ὁ τῶν δοκησισόφων περὶ τὸν Κιλίκων δαίμονα πλάνος, μυρίων ἐπτοημένων ἐπ' αὐτῷ ὡς ἂν ἐπὶ σωτῆρι καὶ ἰατρῷ, ποτὲ μὲν ἐπιφαινομένῳ τοῖς ἐγκαθεύδουσι... ψυχῶν δ' ἦν ὀλετὴρ ἄντικρυς οὗτος, τοῦ μὲν ἀληθοῦς ἀφέλκων σωτῆρος, ἐπὶ δὲ τὴν ἄθεον πλάνην κατασπῶν τοὺς πρὸς ἀπάτην εὐχερεῖς.
[46] On the later fate of the shrine see Cameron and Hall (1999), 303.
[47] See Eusebius, *Contra Hieroclem*; see the text with translation and notes by Christopher P. Jones (Loeb Classical Library, 2006).
[48] See Markschies (2007).

important in Christian story-telling – and, as far as we can see, in ritual practice – only in the fifth century, not long before Gregory of Tours and Isidore of Seville in the West formulated the first coherent Christian dream theories.[49] The Piacenza Pilgrim's report about Gadara, with its date around 570, belongs to this early phase. The same pilgrim tells us also that when in Jerusalem he fell seriously ill and was healed only when Saint Euphemia and his own local saint, Antony, appeared to him in his dream and healed him.[50] This is the personal experience of dream healing through the intercession of two saints, one of them the personal protector of the dreamer, not performed in a shrine or at a saint's grave but in the private space of a bedroom. It looks as if the hostility towards pagan incubation and the theological problems of dreams and dreaming delayed Christian saints from stepping into the gap left open by the demise of Asklepios or Isis.

There are only a few cases where we have enough data to see at least the outlines of a transition from pagan to Christian ritual practice. In three cases, scholars claim incubation healing on archaeological grounds; only in two cases, literary records confirm the presence of widespread and popular Christian incubation. This chapter deals with the cases that rest on archaeology alone.

Dor

In recent years, the excavator of a church at Dor (ancient Dora) south of Haifa made the claim that the Christian church succeeded a temple of Apollo with an incubation rite, and that incubation continued in the church. The church could have been built as early as the middle of the fourth century, according to a coin found under a wall foundation; extensive restorations took place after a fire in the middle of the fifth century.[51]

To date, it is impossible to check these claims; the details of the excavation are still unpublished. The published ground plan and the preliminary reports nevertheless allow a few observations and conclusions. The main conclusion is that the existence both of an Apollo temple and of incubation is conjectural at the very best. The church was built over a

---

[49] See Csepregi (2005); Talbot (2002).
[50] *Itinerarium* 46 *evidenter oculata fide vidi beatam Euphemiam per visionem et beatum Antonium quomodo venerunt et sanaverunt me*, "With the eye of my faith, I saw clearly in a dream Saint Ephemia and Saint Antony how they came and healed me."
[51] Dauphin (1986), (1997), (1999); Dauphin and Gibson (1993), 90–97. Markschies (2007), 180–182 follows Dauphin's assumptions.

pagan temple, with its adyton at the place of the later courtyard and its cistern. The attribution to Apollo seems to rest on two arguments alone: on the literary notice of an Apollo cult in Greek Dora, and on the idea that the cistern in the courtyard originally was a subterranean oracular grotto in the style of the grotto of Apollo's oracular shrine at Claros.[52] The subterranean construction of the Clarian temple is unique and cannot easily be exported to another place; as long as no archaeological data are published, the connection with Claros and thus with oracular Apollo remains a guess. Similarly, incubation in the church is not directly attested but rests on interpretation of the somewhat anomalous presence of five instead of three aisles of the basilica; this is read to mean that the traditional basilica was expanded on either side by a much wider "exterior aisle". The term "exterior aisle," however, hides some crucial facts: we deal with two additions to the church that run its entire length, including the sides of the courtyard; they were considerably wider than the side aisles of the basilica; and they comprised a series of rooms. These "exterior aisles" then might have functions that were not at all connected to the liturgical space of the basilica. The use of one of these aisles for incubation is rather unlikely, since Christian incubation took place in the church around a saint's monument. Until better archaeological data are available, it would thus be imprudent to assume church incubation in Dora, and even more so to think that a pagan incubation ritual was transformed into a Christian one.

Athens
The result is not dissimilar for the church that continued the Asklepieion in Athens.[53] Pagan cult in the Asklepios shrine on the south slope of the acropolis ended at some point before Marinus wrote his *Life of Proklos* not long after 485: when young Asklepiegeneia, "the wife of my contemporary Theagenes," was ill, Proklos prayed in the Asklepieion for her health, "since the city still was lucky to possess the undestroyed shrine of the savior."[54] This leaves it open whether the shrine was destroyed by a catastrophe or by Christian violence, and archaeology does not help. Not much later, a Christian church was built at the site, using the ancient walls

---

[52] Tac. *Ann.* 2.54.
[53] Gregory (1986), 237–241; Karivieri (1995); Markschies (2007), 178 ("das vielleicht beste archäologische Beispiel").
[54] Marinus, *Vita Procli* 29: καὶ γὰρ ηὐτύχει τούτου ἡ πόλις τότε καὶ εἶχεν ἔτι ἀπόρθητον τὸ τοῦ Σωτῆρος ἱερόν. Proklos lived from 412 to 485; Marinos must have written his life not much after his death.

as far as possible: the date oscillates between the late fifth century and some time after Justinian's closing of the Athenian schools in 529.[55] The late date has become improbable for several reasons, not the least because it contradicts what Marinus wrote: already in 485, the shrine did not function anymore. Arja Karivieri has made the appealing suggestion that the first Christian church in the monumental center of Athens was one in the so-called Library of Hadrian, built not long after Aelia Eudocia, the daughter of the pagan Athenian philosopher Leontios, converted and married the young Theodosius II on June 7, 421.[56] The church in the Asklepieion could have followed not much after 485, since the Christian builders made use of much of the earlier walls and the building materials. It is difficult to estimate how long the shrine remained an empty shell. Given the constraints of space on a terrace between the steep slope downwards and the even steeper cliffs towards the acropolis, the use of earlier walls seems reasonable, if not inevitable, and cannot be used to indicate a short time gap between destruction and reconstruction. Incubation is assumed because the small basilica had an additional fourth aisle that followed the outline of the former incubation stoa and incorporated the sacred spring; its interior wall consisted mostly of pillars or columns and communicated well with the basilica.[57] This, however, seems problematical: later Christian incubation churches had no incubation halls but used the interior space of the church, especially the space around a saint's grave, who healed through his dream apparitions. The inclusion of the sacred spring and its connection with the basilica could be read as providing ritual space for baptism at the spring, not for healing.

Santa Maria Antiqua, Rome

This does not mean that church incubation cannot be found solely with the help of archaeology, as the case of the Roman church of Santa Maria Antiqua shows. For its "Chapel of the Physicians," David Knipp has convincingly argued that from the seventh century onward, it was used as an incubation space in a church that mainly served the Byzantine community around the Palatine. Knipp's argument is based on the presence of frescoes that all depict healing saints and architectural details that are best explained by people sleeping on the chapel floor. But there is no

---

[55] Early date: Gregory (1986) and Karivieri (1995); late date: Frantz (1965), Aleshire (1989), 19–20.
[56] Karivieri (1995), 899–900.
[57] Gregory (1986), 238–239. Gregory's other argument for a Christian healing cult, a small inscription that mentions St. Andrews, a saint associated with healing (*Hesperia* 16, 1947, 29 no. XI), has been rejected by Karivieri (1995), 902, who suggests a dedication to Christ the Savior.

good reason to assume continuity of the rite. Earlier scholars argued that incubation in this church was transferred from an incubation rite either at the spring of Iuturna or in the temple of the Castores that both were nearby.[58] But incubation at one of these pagan shrines is a highly conjectural hypothesis, and chronology strongly argues against a transfer of the rite to St. Maria Antiqua. Before it was turned into a church, the building served administrative purposes, and the changes to the chapel that have been read as signs for incubation are not much later than the seventh century.[59]

Saints' lives, healing, and incubation stories

Saint Thekla

Matters get more complex as soon as we have more textual evidence, as in the case of the churches of St. Thekla in Seleukeia on the Kalykadnos (in Kilikia) and of Cyrus and John in Menouthis near Alexandria (today's Abukir). Seleukeia had an oracular cult of Apollo Sarpedonios, attested since Hellenistic times; the shrine was central to the city.[60] Zosimus preserves two hexametrical oracles that the god gave to the Romans and the Palmyraeans before Aurelian's attack on the troops of Zenobia in 272; he also informs us that the birds of the sanctuary helped against locusts.[61] The *Acts* and *Miracles* of Thekla, both written before 468, emphasize her hostility towards this sanctuary and its "varied deceit and false oracle" (ἀπάτη ποικίλη καὶ κίβδηλος χρησμολογία) whose owner could also be implored in case of an illness. This cry for help did not necessarily take the form of an incubation dream but could well have been a request for an oracle; the latter would be more consistent with the overall role of the god whom the *Acts of Thecla* call Apollo *Sarpedon*, whereas the *Miracles* call him Apollo *Sarpedonios*; the changing forms of the epithet suggests that the cult had stopped before the time of these two treatises.[62] Thekla, according to the *Acts*, intended to turn her own house into a healing center, ἰατρεῖον, for

---

[58] Deubner (1902) = (1982), 12–30, see also Deubner (1907), 56; accepted by Tea (1937); Osborne (1987), 207; see also Aronen (1989).

[59] Knipp (2002), 6f. on the hypothetical continuities.

[60] Proxeny decree to be set up in the sanctuary of Apollo (without an epiclesis); see Heberdey and Wilhelm (1896), 186 no. 108.

[61] The god is mentioned in Diod. 32.10.2f. (Phot. cod. 244, p. 377b Bekker) = Poseidonios frg. 85 Theiler (an ambivalent oracle to Alexander, fictitious?); Zosim. 1.57.2–4 (negative to the Palmyraeans).

[62] Originally ascribed to Basil of Seleukeia (*PG* 85, 477–617, after Pierre Pantin, Antwerp 1608), the *Acts* and the *Miracles* of Saint Thekla were "rendu à l'anonymat" by Dagron (1978) in the introduction to his excellent commented edition. See *Acts* 27 (τῷ δαίμονι τῷ Σαρπηδόνι with oracles); *Miracles* 2 (Sarpedonios, famous as a chresmodos and mantis), 11 (the nurse of a sick young man appeals in vain to Sarpedonios). The epiclesis is not attested epigraphically.

the entire region: this projects the fame of the shrine back to apostolic times.[63]

The *Miracles* show that the saint often appeared to sick people in a dream to provide healing. But she helped as often in other critical situations. During a war, she protected cities and individuals; when one traveled, she helped against robbers; after a theft she could like any oracle find the stolen object and denounce the thief.[64] The cases where a sick person is sleeping in the church are surprisingly rare. Of twelve helpful dreams, only two happen explicitly in the church; in a third, a patient is in the church, but it is too hot for sleeping. On the other hand, in five cases the dream explicitly or implicitly did not happen in the church.[65] The *Miracles* stress the helpful intervention of the saint, but make her help either through a dream or in any other way; they do not serve to legitimize dream incubation in Thekla's church. This must be the corollary of the fact that church incubation did not continue pagan divination or healing, even though Thekla's church seems to have been built at the very spot of Apollo's shrine.[66]

Saints Cyrus and John
The situation is different for the *Miracles* of Cyrus and John, the Hagioi Anargyroi, as narrated by Sophronius of Jerusalem in the years between 610 and 619, about 150 years after the two texts about Thekla.[67] Of the more than seventy miracle stories almost all are connected with incubation in the church of the two saints in Menouthis (modern Abuqir), about twelve miles east of Alexandria. In this respect, Sophronius' book feels like a Christian version of the pagan *iamata*, the healing miracles known through inscriptions from several sanctuaries of Asklepios, most famously from Epidauros. In Menouthis, the Christian cult was preceded by a famous healing cult of Isis and Sarapis with incubation; it is unclear how long the pagan sanctuary survived after the destruction of the Alexandrian Sarapeion in 392.[68] At some time around this date, patriarch Theophilos

---

[63] *Acts* 28: ὡς εἶναι πάνδημον ἰατρεῖον τὸν τόπον ... ἐπὶ θεραπείᾳ καὶ βοηθείᾳ τῶν συνεχόντων αὐτοὺς παθῶν καὶ ἀλγημάτων ἢ καὶ δαιμόνων.
[64] Theft: *Miracles* 21 and 22; protection in war: *Miracles* 5 and 6 (cities), 13, 16, and 27 (individuals); robbers: *Miracles* 28.
[65] In the church: *Miracles* 17 and 18b, cp. 19 (too hot for sleeping); clearly not in the church: *Miracles* 9a, 11, 12 (the narrator himself), 14, 18a.
[66] Basil, *Miracles* 1.
[67] For the text see *PG* 87:3, 3424B–3547D; translations with commentary, Fernández Marcos (1975) and Gascou (2006).
[68] On the date see Hahn (2006). The scenario presented in Athanassiadi (1993), 14f. ("Theophilus' monks overran the Canopus Serapeum, while they helped to convert the nearby temple of Isis into a church of the Evangelists") is somewhat implausible.

(ruled 384–412) built the church of the Holy Apostles in the vicinity of the Isis shrine in Menouthis, and in 417 his successor (and nephew) Cyril introduced into the same church the relics of Saints Cyrus and John, the "Healers Without Pay," in order to offer "a true healing place without commerce" instead of the dream orders given by Isis and Sarapis, "the Lady and the God."[69]

The polemical tone of Cyril could mean that the pagan shrine was not yet destroyed and covered under sand by the progression of the sea, as it certainly was when Paralios of Aphrodisias helped to expose the secret persistence of the Isis cult with its incubation in a private house of Menouthis in the 480s.[70] But even at this time, the cult had still its pagan officials and must have been protected by pagan intellectuals in Alexandria. When one opened the house, it was found that it contained a large number of pagan cult images; it must have served not only as a secret temple but also as a refuge for images from closed or destroyed temples.[71] Zacharias of Mytilene, who wrote an account of the affair in the 490s, is strangely impersonal when it comes to the agent of destruction of the shrine ("où quelqu'un a, accomplissant ainsi une bonne action, enfoui sous le sable le temple d'Isis"): he might well refer to natural or rather divine action, not to either of the great Alexandrian patriarchs. However that might be, pagan incubation survived even in a secret Iseion and was powerful enough to convince a noble citizen of Aphrodisias whose daughter was married to an Alexandrian living in Caria that the faraway goddess might heal the infertility of his daughter.[72]

---

[69] Cyril, *Oratiuncula* 3 (*PG* 77, 1105A): ἡκέτωσαν τοίνυν οἱ παλαὶ πλανώμενοι· ἐρχέσθωσαν εἰς ἀληθινὸν καὶ ἀκαπήλευτον ἰατρεῖον· οὐδεὶς γὰρ ἡμῖν ὀνείρατα πλάττεται· οὐδεὶς λέγει τοῖς ἐρχομένοις· "Εἴρηκεν ἡ Κυρά· Ποίησον τὸ καὶ τό· ὅλως Κυρὰ καὶ Θεὸς εἶναι δυνατός καὶ προσκυνεῖσθαι θέλει." ... πατήσαντες τοίνυν τὰ γραώδη μυθάρια καὶ τὰ πάλαι τῶν γοήτων ἐμπαίγματα, ἐρχέσθωσαν ἐπὶ τοὺς ἀληθινοὺς καὶ ἄνωθων ἰατρούς.

[70] Zacharias, *Vita Severi*, ed. Kugener (*PO* 2.1.6), p. 19: "Ménouthis, le village de la déesse, où quelqu'un a, accomplissant ainsi une bonne action, enfoui sous le sable le temple d'Isis, au point qu'on n'en voit même plus la trace." The Paralios affair is dated under the patriarch Petros Mongos who ruled from 482–490, *Vita Severi*, p. 30 Kugener; Watts (2005) dates the text to the 490s, as an originally independent account. On the underwater archaeology and its discovery of the Menouthis sanctuary, Goddio (2007).

[71] Cult officials: *Vita Severi*, p. 18 ("ceux qui interprétaient là-bas les songes et qui servaient le démon figuré par Isis"). Pagan intellectuals: *ibid*. p. 16 ("Horapollon, Héraïskos, Asklépiodotos, Ammonios, Isidore, et [les] autres philosophes qui étaient auprès d'eux"), cp. p. 22. Sacrifice to Isis: *ibid*. pp. 18 ("les sacrifices habituels"), 29 (when opening the secret room, they found "l'autel couvert de sang"). The many images: pp. 29–30 (a list; the damaged images are burnt, the others saved and inventoried), 33 (twenty camel-loads of images are brought to Alexandria).

[72] *Vita Severi*, pp. 16–18 Kugener.

This might well have happened at the very time when the Christian church attracted pilgrims from all over the East for its incubation healing at the grave of the two saints.[73] To Zacharias, Menouthis is only the village of Isis, despite its church, whose saints had been active healers for more than a half-century.

It is unclear whether already Cyril had introduced incubation healing, or whether he simply institutionalized the healing prayer at the grave of the two saints. The answer depends on how one understands his rejection of the dreams of Isis and Sarapis in his phrase οὐδεὶς γὰρ ἡμῖν ὀνείρατα πλάττεται, "nobody invents dreams for us": the most natural reading rejects all dreams, not just the invented dreams that come from the pagan demons.[74] Given the role of pagan incubation in the Paralios affair, one might also suspect that it had not yet started in the church of Menouthis at that time, but began as a reaction to the destruction of the secret sanctuary of Isis.

A third case might confirm these conclusions. The church of Saint Michael in Constantinople, according to Sozomenus founded by Constantine himself, was, in the words of the Church historian, a place "where one believes that the divine archangel Michael manifests himself (ἐπιφαίνεσθαι, with an already Hellenistic term for helpful divine manifestations)."[75] Among those whom Michael helped, Sozomenus explains, "there were some who were victims of bad luck or inescapable dangers, others of unknown diseases and ailments."[76] This might sound like an incubation church; but the historian offers only two detailed cases, and both contradict this assumption. The first story is that of Probianus, a semi-pagan court doctor, whom Michael tells in a dream in his home to find a remedy for his illness from a cross in his church – although it has some parallels in Sophronius' *Miracles*, this is a dream not intentionally sought, and not dreamt in a church. Its success hinges on the personal faith of the dreamer, this time the faith that Michael's relics have the power to heal.

The second case comes closer to what we understand as incubation, but still falls somewhat short of it. Aquilinus, a friend and colleague of the

---

[73] On Menouthis as a pilgrimage center see Montserrat (1998).
[74] Cyril, *Oratiuncula* 3 (*PG* 77.1105A). This is the understanding proposed by Montserrat (1998), 261–266 and followed by Knipp (2002), 1 and myself.
[75] Sozomen. *Hist. eccl.* 2.3. 9 πεπίστευται ἐνθάδε ἐπιφαίνεσθαι Μιχαὲλ τὸν θεῖον ἀρχάγγελον. On ἐπιφαίνεσθαι see *LSJ* s.v.
[76] *Ibid.* οἱ μὲν γὰρ περιπετείαις δειναῖς ἢ κινδύνοις ἀφύκτοις, οἱ δὲ νόσοις ἢ πάθεσιν ἀγνώστοις περιπεσόντες, εὐξάμενοι ἐνταῦθα τῷ θεῷ ἀπαλλαγὴν εὑρήκασιν τῶν συμφορῶν.

historian, fell ill with a heavy and incurable intestinal disease. When he felt that he was about to die, he told his servants to carry his bed into the church "where he either wanted to expire or to become healthy." During the night, "a divine power" (θεία δύναμις) appeared, revealed a prescription that Aquilinus' doctors first refused to implement because it radically contradicted their art – again as in Sophronius, where we noticed the opposition and rejection of professional medicine. The narrator leaves it open whether Aquilinus was seeking an incubation dream, expected another intervention by the saint, or simply wished to die in a sacred space. Sozomenus does not give us enough context to decide whether incubation dreams were customary in the church.

Thus here, as in Thekla's church in Seleukeia, dream incubation was the exception, not the rule. Again, chronology might be crucial: we are in the reign of Theodosius II, at best a few decades after Cyril's initiative in Menouthis, when the Christian church was still hesitant to accept incubation, unlike in later centuries.

Ritual differences

Whatever the origin of incubation in the church of Menouthis, its form was markedly different from what we know about the pagan rite. If we follow Sophronius as a guide, incubation was centered on the grave of the two saints; here as elsewhere, the remains of the holy man remained the center of power, and it was not uncommon that praying patients tried to touch the grave. The degree to which dreaming could take place elsewhere seems to have been changing from place to place, or from narrator to narrator, as we saw: in the case of Thekla's church in Seleukeia on Kalykadnos, whose miracles were narrated around 468, most dreaming happened elsewhere, whereas in Menouthis, narrated about 150 years later, dreaming in the sanctuary was the norm. The time in between must have seen the rise of pilgrimage to healing centers and thus the institutionalization of incubation, and Sophronius remains the best witness on the ritual realities.

Before incubation, one prayed and often shed tears. It is unclear whether there was also a more formal liturgy performed in the church. We hear of a procession with incense burners, but its relationship to incubation is never explained; it might be the regular church service that was unconnected with incubation.[77] This inverts the relationship between regular liturgy

[77] Sophronius, *Mir.* 31, col. 3520D.

and incubation in pagan sanctuaries, where most of the rites were centered around the incubation rite; in a Christian church, the mass liturgy remained the uncontested center. Special incubation halls are unknown; patients slept on the floor of the main church or in a side chapel dedicated to the healing saints, ordinarily on some bedding. If there were large numbers of visitors at big pilgrim centers such as Menouthis, the pilgrims were assigned their place by staff-members called πυλωροί, "gate-keepers."[78] One had to distinguish between a correct and a false dream (φαντασία), and it was extremely rare that already the first night provided a sleeper with a valid dream.[79] We are never told who made this distinction. Although ecclesiastics were living around the church, we never hear of priests or specialists interpreting the dreams; in one case at least, the decision was clearly the patient's own.[80] At least in Sophronius, the dream prescriptions were highly unusual in medical terms, and there was a marked tension between the healing saints and regular doctors who, as one case shows clearly, were not present nor even welcome in the sanctuary.[81] Furthermore, and in marked difference to pagan incubation, one very often needed several dreams in order to arrive at the final answer; Sophronius himself needed four different dreams during several nights in order to be fully healed from an eye disease.[82] Thus, prolonged stays in the sanctuary were the rule, not the exception. A prolonged stay in an Asklepieion – such as in the case of Aristeides in Pergamon or Apollonius of Tyana in Aigai – seems to be rare and has personal and not necessarily health-related reasons.

Narratives of dream healing

Besides dream incubation – pagan or Christian – there are narrations of dream healing: they form the bulk of Deubner's material on Christian incubation, but have to be kept strictly separate from incubation. Already Pierre Maraval's remark on the Gadara healings pointed in the direction of a clear terminological and factual distinction between incubation and dream healing. Incubation is a clearly defined ritual act of intentional sleeping in a sacred space in order to be healed by a superhuman healer in a dream; healing is obtained either by some medical intervention that happens during the dream, or by receiving a prescription for a medication

---

[78] *Mir.* 67, 3652D.　[79] *Mir.* 18. 3476B; *Mir.* 27, 3497B; *Mir.* 30, 3513C.　[80] *Mir.* 27, 3497B.
[81] Absence and rejection of regular doctors: *Mir.* 67, 3652D. See also the case of the learned doctor Gesios, *Mir.* 30, 3513C, who refused the irrational medicine of the saints and was punished.
[82] *Mir.* 70, 3662B.

to be used after waking up. This continues the two basic ways in which one obtained healing in the real world, roughly speaking through surgery or through pharmacology. This does not change much between the pagan *iamata* and Sophronius' report on healings in Menouthis. Dream healing, on the other side, is neither bound to a specific space nor to the intention of seeking a healing dream: it is the unsolicited manifestation of a benevolent saint that leads to healing that is not accompanied by any ritual. A few examples will be enough to show the difference – and make clear that although we have many instances of dream healing miracles, we possess only a narrowly circumscribed amount of Christian incubation. Following up on Le Goff's observation that bishops or comparable persons of proven faith were the most likely recipients of true dreams, I classify the stories into two groups, those that fit Le Goff's observation, and those that do not. For the first group, two stories should suffice.

Dream healing of bishops

In his *Dialogi*, Gregory the Great tells a story that is set shortly before the invasion of the Langobards in Lombardy in 568.[83] Redemptus, the bishop of Ferenti near Viterbo (whom we know from other sources; he died in about 586), when traveling on the regular visitation of his communities, one evening arrived at the church of Saint Euticius – in good Greek Eutychius – a local martyr. He put his bed up next to Euticius' grave, but could not fall asleep. During the night, the saint appeared in a *visio*, asked whether Redemptus was still awake (*Redempte, vigilas?*), which the bishop confirmed: *vigilo*. The saint reacted in a surprising way:

> He said: "The end of all flesh is near! The end of all flesh is near! The end of all flesh is near!" After this triple message, the apparition of the martyr that had appeared to the eyes of his mind, disappeared. The man of God got up and gave himself to mournful prayers.[84]

Although the bishop intentionally went to sleep near the tomb of the martyr (Gregory does not tell us why – maybe he simply wanted the closeness and protection of the saint), this is no incubation, because we do not deal with a dream, even if the Latin term *visio* can be used in

---

[83] Greg. *Dial.* 3.38; Deubner (1907), 57f.
[84] Greg. *Dial.* 3.38.2: *Qui ait: Finis venit universae carnis. Finis venit universae carnis. Finis venit universae carnis. post quam trinam vocem visio martyris, quae eius mentis oculis apparebat, evanuit. tunc vir Domini surrexit seque in orationis lamentum dedit.*

this sense, nor did Redemptus seek a vision, to be healed or to know the futures.[85] There is some emphasis on the fact that Redemptus could not sleep: "his mind was, as it happens sometimes, depressed by some weight, and stayed awake," says Gregory; the martyr and the bishop both insist on his being awake, *vigilans*. Thus, the apocalyptic prophecy – the simple sentence "The end of all flesh is near!", without any visual complement – is given as an oracular sentence with which the outside reality quickly corresponded: terrible signs appeared in the night sky. Shortly afterwards, but still in 568, the Langobards invaded the region and brought the usual barbarian destruction, "cities depopulated, castles uprooted, churches burnt down, monasteries destroyed."[86] Thus, the apparition of Saint Euticius was only the first sign in a chain of supernatural messages that led up to the apocalyptic invasion of yet another barbarian army. It was neither sought by the bishop nor dreamt in the church.

A second story, told by Bede in his *History of the English Church*, is similar. Under the second bishop of Canterbury, Laurence, the young local king who succeeded his baptized father remained pagan and even persecuted the Christians; in 614, the bishop decided to return to the safety of France. Wanting to spend his last night in Britain in the church of Peter and Paul that he himself had consecrated, the later Canterbury Cathedral, he had his bed put into the nave. In his sleep, Peter appeared to him, heavily censured him for leaving his flock, and flogged him. The next morning, Laurence went to the king, told his story and showed the king the vestiges of the apostolic flagellation on his body. Impressed, the king repented and converted.[87] Again, there is no intention to seek a dream, and although Laurence prayed before he fell asleep, praying is here not a formal ritual that would introduce an incubation rite, but the bishop's evening prayer. If anything, the story is modelled on Jerome's famous dream: in the same way Jerome repents and promises to become a better Christian, Laurence realizes his task as a bishop, and as a result the king is converted.[88] Thus, this is a double conversion miracle, triggered by the dream apparition of the apostle.

---

[85] The terminology is somewhat hazy. Macrob. *Somn.* 1.3.2 distinguishes *visio* (Greek ὄραμα) from other dreams and defines it as a straightforward divinatory dream; Isid. *Etym.* 7.35 distinguishes *visio* from *somnium*, the former being a vision during waking hours, the latter happening in sleep.
[86] Greg. *Dial.* 3.38.3 *depopulatae urbes, eversa castra, concrematae ecclesiae, destructa sunt monasteria*.
[87] Bede, *Historia ecclesiae Anglorum* 2.6. On the church and its consecration see *ibid.* 2.3.
[88] Jerome, *Epist.* 22.30.

Dream healing of commoners

Then there are the dreams in which a saint provides healing to a humble Christian. In some stories, dreaming is not associated with a church. The earliest instances are the two cases mentioned by the Piacenza Pilgrim: the institutionalized healing of lepers in Gadara and the occasional healing of the pilgrim himself, to whom his patron saint, Saint Anthony, and Saint Euphemia appeared in Jerusalem.

In a second subgroup are stories where dreaming takes place in a church or near a saint's grave. A first example is again associated with Canterbury Cathedral; it is very typical for at least the Latin sources. Augustine, who brought Christianity to Britain, had an immediate precursor in Lethardus (Saint-Léotard), bishop of Senlis and chaplain of the French queen Bertha, the wife of the Saxon king Ethelbert. (Lethardus' tomb was later transferred to Canterbury Cathedral.) A medieval collection of miracles of Lethardus, *præcursor et ianitor . . . Augustini*, tells how a lame man asked at his grave for help, and when he fell asleep, the saint appeared, asked him why he was disturbing his peace, and when being told the reason he first refused because he did not believe the man would change his bad ways, but finally healed one of his legs and promised that the other one would heal once he had become a good Christian.[89] This is one instance in a longer list of various miracles, and its main purpose is a lesson in religious ethics, that miraculous healing comes with a price tag attached: it is only granted when the dreamer promises moral improvement. To ask a saint for help at his grave has a long tradition that goes back at least to Saint Martin in Tours; some people fell asleep while waiting out the night, especially a lame man who must have been sitting or lying on the floor, many others did not. But the story does not introduce or legitimate healing incubations in Canterbury Cathedral: we have no testimony for such a ritual.

A second example obfuscates my categorization. In a story narrated by the sixth-century poet Venantius Fortunatus in a poem that lists the miracles of Saint Médard in Soissens that happened mostly at his grave, a man became ill and lost his sight, remained in bed for four months, and finally was admonished in a dream he dreamed in his bed that "he should quickly go to his church" (*tenderet ut velox ad tua templa gradum*).[90] But he goes rather slowly: first he plucks out his hair in order to create a tonsure ("without using scissors", the poet insists), then proceeds to the saint's

---

[89] *Acta Sanctorum* Febr., vol. 3 (Antwerp: Meursius, 1685), col. 470D = *Bibliotheca Hagiographica Latina antiquae et mediae aetatis*, no. 4893.
[90] Venant. Fortun. 2.16 (*MGH Scriptores: Auct. Ant.* 4.1), our story vv. 139–156.

grave, lies for two full days at the grave and in the end regains his sight; he does so not by a simple and invisible intercession of the saint, but because the blood that gushed from his self-made tonsure washed his eyes. Here, the dream admonishes the patient to go to church in order to find healing, but the healing itself is not performed in a dream but as the result of a somewhat idiosyncratic ritual that shows the Christian dedication of the man who was willing to exchange his hair for his sight, in an inversion of Leotard's doubts in the true Christianity of the lame man.

Thus, compared to the neatly structured, well institutionalized, and almost uniformly ritualized pagan incubation, the Christian cases are much more diverse, unstable, and somewhat chaotic. I read this as a consequence of the radically changed evaluation of dreaming. In the pagan dream world with the simple dichotomy between true and false dreams, the institution with its complex ritual apparatus guaranteed the true dream in the sanctuary. Patients rarely seem to have doubted that they would receive healing; and if they did, as in the one agnostic Epidaurian miracle story, the institution was at pains to reassure the doubters.[91] The Christian attitude to dreams could not allow an equally simple institutionalization, and it had to make sure that there were no demons involved; it thus destabilized institutionalization and introduced new ways of dealing with dreams. With the exception of dreamers of unquestionably high religious status (saints, bishops, kings – what one could call "professional believers"), a healing dream had to be legitimized. It was usually personal faith and dedication that did this (demons would not have answered to such intense faith), and it was often the saint who brought about the legitimization, by sending a patient to a church or even into contact with a relic. It is only slowly – and after the period I am interested in – that Christian churches institutionalized dream healing, as in the case of Cosmas and Damian: miracles resist institutionalization. The state did not intervene, because this was a pure matter of the church, and the church had no interest in preventing the miracles as soon as it was certain that they were genuine.

[91] No. IV in the numbering of Herzog (1931) and LiDonnici (1995).

CHAPTER 11

Magic in a Christian Empire

Augustine and magic

Augustine is not the most obvious place to look for magic in late antiquity – but he has more to say than one would expect, both on the theoretical and the practical aspects; and he is, here too, as we will see soon, quite opposed to the way the Late Roman State handled things.[1]

In a famous passage in Book 10 of the *City of God*, Augustine turns against the way *magia* was dichotomized into a harmless *theurgia* and an evil *goetia*. The passage is inserted into a discussion of true and false miracles; following a long-established tradition, the miracles performed by Pharaoh's magicians ("they did them through sorcery and magic spells to which the evil angels, that is the demons, are given") and those performed by Moses ("Moses outdid them easily and all the more powerfully because justly in the name of God, who created heaven and earth with the help of the angels") are emblematical for this dichotomy.[2] Augustine inserts Moses' Exodus miracles into a much longer list of miracles from the Old Testament. He sums them up in this way:[3]

> They all were done by simple faith and godly confidence, not by the incantations and charms composed under the influence of a criminal tampering with the unseen world, of an art which they call either magic (μαγίαν), or by the more abominable title sorcery (γοητίαν), or the more

---

[1] On Augustine and magic, see (among others) Dolbeau (2003) and Markus (1994); still worthwhile reading, Zellinger (1933).
[2] Aug. *De civ. D.* 10.8 *magi Pharaonis, hoc est regis Aegypti ... faciebant ueneficiis et incantationibus magicis, quibus sunt mali angeli, hoc est daemones, dediti; Moyses autem tanto potentius, quanto iustius, nomine Dei, qui fecit caelum et terram, seruientibus angelis eos facile superauit.*
[3] *Ibid.* 10.9 *Fiebant autem simplici fide atque fiducia pietatis, non incantationibus et carminibus nefariae curiositatis arte compositis, quam uel* magian *uel detestabiliore nomine* goetian *uel honorabiliore* theurgian *uocant, qui quasi conantur ista discernere et inlicitis artibus deditos alios damnabiles, quos et maleficos uulgus appellat (hos enim ad* goetian *pertinere dicunt), alios autem laudabiles uideri uolunt, quibus* theurgian *deputant; cum sint utrique ritibus fallacibus daemonum obstricti sub nominibus angelorum.*

honorable designation theurgy (θεουργίαν); for they wish to discriminate between those whom the people call sorcerers (*malefici*), who practise sorcery (γοητίαν), and are addicted to illicit arts and condemned, and those others who seem to them to be worthy of praise for their practice of theurgy, – the truth, however, being that both classes are the slaves of the deceitful rites of the demons whom they invoke under the names of angels.

Augustine, however, is not content with this simple identification of sorcery and theurgy. In two steps, he denounces theurgy as useless and dangerous, and he does so by citing extensively from Porphyry, as he claims from the treatise *De regressu animae* and from the famous *Letter to Anebo* that provoked Iamblichus to write his *On the Mysteries*. The nature of *De regressu* and its relationship to the *Letter* as well as to another famous work, *On Philosophy from the Oracles*, is heavily debated in contemporary scholarship but not very relevant for my purpose.[4]

First, and without referring to the famous *Letter*, he points out Porphyry's ambivalent attitude towards theurgy.[5] On the one hand, the philosopher had insisted that theurgy "makes the soul able to receive ghosts (*spiritus*) and angels (*angeli*) and to see the gods through some theurgic initiations that they call τελεταί." On the other hand, he concedes that the theurgic rites affect only the lower part of the soul that deals with the material world (*anima spiritalis*), not the intellectual part that is able to embrace the intelligible world, so that one would not need theurgy to purify the intellectual soul; and he refers to a "good Chaldaean," i.e. a theurgist, who complained that his purificatory rites did not succeed because he was defeated by another, envious, practitioner who was helped by more powerful beings who served his envy; from this Augustine concludes that theurgy is able to make use of beings that are subject to passions, that is demons.

---

[4] Augustine's indication of sources: *De civ. D.* 10.29.2 *in his ipsis libris, ex quibus multa posui, quos De regressu animae scripsit* (sc. Porphyrius); *De civ. D.* 10.32.1 *Porphyrius in primo iuxta finem De regressu animae libro; De civ. D.* 10.11.1 *Porphyrius, cum ad Anebontem scripsit Aegyptium*. O'Meara (1959) had argued for the identity of *On Philosophy* and *De regressu*; Beatrice (1989) accepted this and claimed that *On Philosophy* also contained the *Letter to Anebo* and was the only work of Porphyry Augustine knew. Edwards (2007) reports on the discussion, leans very much towards Beatrice and comes up with an intriguing compromise based on the Suda's entry. Smith (1993) keeps *De regressu* (319–350) and *De Philosophy* (351–407) apart, but does not include fragments from the *Letter*, for which he refers to Sodano (1958) (435).

[5] Aug. *De civ. D.* 10.9–10. It is unclear to me whether this already comes from the Letter or whether Augustine uses two different Porphyrian treatises; Andrew Smith ascribes the passage to *De regressu animae*.

He then presents a reading of the famous *Letter to Anebo*, which he uses to undercut any positive understanding of theurgy.[6] Although Porphyry, in Augustine's reading, is willing to grant that some demons are good-natured, overall they are treacherous and unreliable, and without a true knowledge of what is good. This radically devalues theurgy – and since theurgy not unlike sorcery (*goetia*) relies on these demons, there is no real difference between the two; this is highlighted by the fact that theurgists, like common diviners, use their encounter with divine knowledge to receive mundane information, "to find a run-away slave, to buy real estate, because of a wedding or a business venture, or similar things."[7] The real difference is between the miracles that are not concerned with the worship of God but still, being superhuman acts, are performed by superhuman beings, that is demons, and those that are concerned with true worship and are performed by the angels in the name of God.[8]

It makes sense that Augustine's discussion does not waste much time on goetic magic. As in the case of Pharaoh's *magi*, and as has been clear to Christians from early on, its miracles are the work of demons; goetic magic is easily and thoroughly rejected.[9] Theurgy is less easy to deal with: it has or claims to have no immediate practical aim (a claim Augustine contradicts) but intends to bring the practitioner close to the divine world; thus, it can be understood as a ritual way of mediation between humans and the divine. It also makes use not only of demons but also of what Porphyry called angels, superhuman beings that as beings of the aither are different from the demons that dwell in the air.

Given the binary oppositions that Augustine has been building up, a reader might even begin to wonder whether theurgy somehow could correspond to the good magic of Moses. This makes clear why Augustine selected Porphyry as his exponent of theurgy and not the founders of this art, the two Iuliani, or the Neoplatonist who answered the questions of Porphyry in the *Letter to Anebo*, Iamblichus.[10] He needed a prominent Neoplatonist whose doubts he could exploit for his own purpose of presenting magic as something that was indefensible and unacceptable. What Moses and Aaron had done at the court of the Pharaoh was radically

---

[6] For the Letter to Anebo and its reconstruction see Sodano (1958).
[7] Aug. *De civ. D.* 10.12 *ob inueniendum fugitiuum uel praedium comparandum, aut propter nuptias uel mercaturam uel quid huius modi.*
[8] *Ibid.* 10.12.
[9] See the rejection of magic and divination in the *Didache*, 2.2; 3.4; 5.1; Thee (1984), 319.
[10] It is irrelevant that he almost never cites Iamblichus, and does not prove that he did not read him, Edwards (2007), 116.

different from theurgy, since it served God's purpose; what might have attracted a religious thinker (and might have had some attraction even for Augustine), theurgy's offer of ritual means to help experience divine proximity and come into contact with divine wisdom, at a closer look proved to be dangerous, repulsive, and sometimes abused for very mundane purposes. It added additional weight that Porphyry was also a much reviled enemy of Christianity because of his anti-Christian writings. Not even such a pagan believed in theurgy without hesitations.[11]

Until two decades ago, these chapters in the tenth book of the *Civitas Dei* were the only place in which Augustine talked about theurgy, and they received relatively little attention. The reference to Porphyry, who had died half a century before Augustine was born, seemed somewhat scholarly and academic, even if theurgy was surviving among Neoplatonists as late as Proklos.[12] Here as elsewhere, the publication of sermon 26 Dolbeau on the Kalendae has changed our knowledge; given the importance of the text, a somewhat detailed discussion imposes itself.[13]

In the sermon, delivered on January 1 in Carthage presumably in the year 403, the introductory attack on the festivities of the Kalendae Ianuariae is only a minor topic; its main subject is the nature of the true mediator between humans and God, who is Christ. In a first step, Augustine rejects the religious role and importance of images and rituals. A Christian is prohibited to worship images or to use them as to mediate between God and man – again a not unexpected and traditional topic, since pagans are idolaters, and anti-pagan polemics are important in New Year sermons, with the pagan celebration being a noisy backdrop outside the church. Yet in the course of this argument, Augustine makes a distinction among the pagans he is talking about. Although all of mankind had turned away from God to the material world before Christ's advent, there were those who "turned their hearts upwards and sharpened them through study as much as possible in order to see something that their eyes could not see, transcending the earth they walked upon (an easy thing) and all that is on earth, transcending the sea and all that swims and crawls in it, transcending also the air and all birds . . . transcending the ethereal sky with all its lights"; at the end of their upward journey, they saw the immutable "Creator Spirit" (*creatorem spiritum*). But they were thrown back by the

---

[11] One still remembered Constantine's attempt to call the Arians *Porphyriani*; see Theodosius II in *CTh* 16.5.66.
[12] On Proklos and theurgy see Sheppard (1982); on the history of theurgy in later Neoplatonism, Tanaseanu-Döbler (2013).
[13] *Sermo* 198augm = 26 Dolbeau. See also above chapter 4, n. 44.

splendor of his wisdom and, once back "in the darkness of their flesh," they sought for a means to purify their souls from all carnal constrictions that impeded their intellect. They thought very highly of themselves, and this arrogance gave an opening to the devil, who suggested they purify themselves through the magical arts, *Chaldaica et magica sacra*.[14] Yet, as Augustine underlines somewhat later, not all pagans succumbed to the demons. Among those who were striving for contact with the divine were those philosophers who, although they did not know Christ, sought to contact the divine without any help of ritual means; these pagans earned Augustine's respect.[15]

This distinction corresponds to the dichotomy between the "pure" Platonists whom Augustine accepts, foremost Plato and Plotinus, and the theurgists, whom he rejects; Porphyry, whose name is not mentioned here, would sit uneasily between the two groups, even for Augustine. In the present sermon, Augustine deals only with the second group, with those who

> wanted to purify themselves with rituals, when they saw and believed that there was a god whom they could approach but did not trust their own strength. But full of vain curiosity and the teachings of demons, they thought they were better; and by this very arrogance they gave an entry to the devil and believed that they could purify themselves by the illusions and empty mysteries of the demons, that is the powers in the air ... Some of them extended themselves, traversed the entire creation and recognized the Creator above everything; but because they remained weak, they turned arrogant.[16]

Immediately before this, he had identified these rites as *Chaldaica et magica sacra*, that is as theurgic rituals.[17]

This is more than an academic disquisition, as Roberto Dodaro has pointed out.[18] The rituals were still being practiced, even after they were outlawed, as Augustine tells us: "In the same way that they had been private magical rites, they are still performed secretly, after their public performance has been prohibited."[19] Which must mean that they were not just performed anywhere, but where it mattered for the preaching bishop, in Carthage. There were theurgists – professionals and their clients – in the city who were performing these rites. They must have belonged to the

---

[14] *Sermo* 198augm = 26 Dolbeau, para. 27/28.   [15] See Solignac (1998).
[16] *Sermo* 198augm = 26 Dolbeau, para. 36.
[17] Ibid. *qui ... Chaldaicis et magicis sacris sese obstrinxerunt.*   [18] Dodaro (1998).
[19] *Sermo* 198augm = 26 Dolbeau, para. 28 *sicut antea magica privata, sic modo ista occulte fiunt, posteaquam prohibita sunt publice fieri.*

educated class, even the city elite: this is why the sermon singles them out and sets them off against the philosophers whom he respects, unlike the theurgists.[20]

Magic in imperial legislation

The basics

In his general rejection of magic, Augustine can rely on the emperors. "All this is already abolished in Christ's name by public laws and its performance has ended," he says in his Kalendae sermon with respect to the abolition of pagan rites under Theodosius II, and he includes the theurgic sacrifices in it.[21] Magic, however, had been affected by imperial legislation for much longer: its suppression – or, as Augustine might have felt, its partial suppression – went back to Constantine.

Unlike Christian theology that had always lumped magic and divination together, Constantine's legal decisions were much more differentiated and subtle. He made a clear difference between divination and magic. In divination, he only abolished private consultations but allowed public performance in the name of tradition: "We do not prohibit that the duties of a traditional activity are performed in open daylight."[22] In magic he made another distinction, between damaging and helpful rituals, as he instructed the Roman Praetorian Prefect on June 1, 321.[23] He prohibited magic that caused bodily harm or seduced innocent people, but allowed rituals that were used to heal and prevent ailments, or to protect the

---

[20] See Dodaro (1998), 378f.
[21] *Sermo* 198augm = 26 Dolbeau, para. 28 (*quae quidem omnia in nomine Christi iam sublata publicis legibus publice fieri destiterunt*).
[22] Divination: *CTh* 9.16.1 and 2, the citation from 9.16.2fin. *nec enim prohibemus praeteritae usurpationis officia libera luce tractari.*
[23] *CTh* 9.16.3: *Imp. Constantinus a. et c. ad Bassum pf. p. – Eorum est scientia punienda et severissimis merito legibus vindicanda, qui magicis accincti artibus aut contra hominum moliti salutem aut pudicos ad libidinem deflexisse animos detegentur. Nullis vero criminationibus implicanda sunt remedia humanis quaesita corporibus aut in agrestibus locis, ne maturis vindemiis metuerentur imbres aut ruentis grandinis lapidatione quaterentur, innocenter adhibita suffragia, quibus non cuiusque salus aut existimatio laederetur, sed quorum proficerent actus, ne divina munera et labores hominum sternerentur. – Dat. X. Kal. Iun. Aquileia, Crispo et Constantino caess. coss.*
"By the most severe laws one has to punish and deservedly to avenge the learning of those who, equipped with magic arts are found out to have worked against the safety of men or to have turned virtuous minds to lust. But no criminal accusations shall ensnare remedies sought for human bodies, nor in rural districts the harmless help that is employed in order that rains might not be feared for the ripe grape harvest nor that the harvests may be shattered by the prostrating stones of hail-storms, since by such devices no person's safety or reputation is injured, but these actions bring it about that divine gifts and the labors of men are not destroyed." Translation after Pharr (1952).

harvest, especially the vineyards, against rain and hailstorms. Yet in both cases, it was the intent and not the outcome that was relevant to the law, in accordance with the standard interpretation of the Lex Cornelia that formed the basis of legal proceedings against magic for most of the pre-Constantinian centuries.[24] This law had punished not only intentional death by armed hand and poison, but already the intention: the lex Cornelia punishes, as the Digest says, citing the law verbally, "who walks around with a weapon in order to kill or rob someone" and "who made, sold or possessed poison to kill someone."[25] As the jurist Paulus phrased it: "In the Lex Cornelia, evil intention is accepted as the crime."[26]

Constantine must have allowed protective rituals in the face of other, sterner interpretations that regarded them as sorcery no less than the forbidden rites. Such prohibitions must go back a long way to early Christianity, although only texts from the fourth century and later explicitly forbid amulets, that is protective charms. But the prohibition to become an "enchanter" (ἐπαοιδός) and "purifier" (περικθαίρων) that the early second-century *Didache* formulated in order to prevent pagan cult (εἰδωλολατρία) from encroaching must have included protective spells and rites.[27]

Constantine could make the distinction he made because he did not rely on demonology, unlike Christian theologians; it was the reference to demons that in the eyes of the theologians all types of magic shared which collapsed Constantine's two types of magic into the same idolatrous behavior. Constantine is as careful in his distinctions as were the jurists who were reflecting on the *Lex Cornelia de sicariis et veneficis* and who made not only a distinction between murder with a weapon and murder by *venenum*, "poison," but also between harmful and healing substances, and

---

[24] For the *lex Cornelia* see Bruns (1909), 92; Rotondi (1912), 357.
[25] *quive hominis occidendi furtive faciendi causa cum telo ambulaverit*, Marcian. *Inst.* 14 in *Digest*. 48.8.1; *qui venenum necandi hominis causa fecerit vel vendiderit vel habuerit*, Marcian. *Inst.* 14 in *Digest*. 48.8.3. (The jurist Aelianus Marcianus was mostly writing under Caracalla.)
[26] *In lege Cornelia dolus pro facto accipitur*. Paulus, in *Dig.* 48.8.7.
[27] *Didache* 3.4 τέκνον μου, μὴ γίνου οἰωνοσκόπος, ἐπειδὴ ὁδηγεῖ εἰς τὴν εἰδωλολατρίαν, μηδὲ ἐπαοιδὸς μηδὲ μαθηματικὸς μηδὲ περικαθαίρων, μηδὲ θέλε αὐτὰ βλέπειν [μηδὲ ἀκούειν], ἐκ γὰρ τούτων ἁπάντων εἰδωλολατρία γεννᾶται. "My child, do not become an augur, because this points the way to idolatry, nor a sorcerer, astrologer, or purification priest; nor seek to look into them, because all these arts create idolatry." Harmful magic, on the other hand, is forbidden in the list in 2.2 οὐ φονεύσεις, οὐ μοιχεύσεις, οὐ παιδοφθορήσεις, οὐ πορνεύσεις, οὐ κλέψεις, οὐ μαγεύσεις, οὐ φαρμακεύσεις, οὐ φονεύσεις, τέκνον ἐν φθορᾷ οὐδὲ γεννηθὲν ἀποκτενεῖς, "you will not kill, commit adultery or prostitution, you will not steal, use sorcery or poison, you will not kill a child in an abortion or when newborn." See *ibid.* 5.1. The date of the Didache is still somewhat disputed; I follow what I perceive to be the majority of scholars.

judged the healing substances not to be subsumed in this law.[28] Perhaps one can even hear a quiet polemic against such theological arguments in the fact that Constantine felt compelled to spell out his acceptance of protective spells, and that he explained this with a theological argument of his own: at least protective agrarian magic helped to preserve the gifts of god, *divina munera*. I imagine that Constantine's letter answered a question from his praetorian prefect, the chief law enforcement official, about how to deal with people accused by the clergy of being sorcerers.

This does not mean that the first Christian emperor took sorcery lightly, as two decisions on legal procedure show. In a letter that deals with the possibility of appeal, he denies appeal to those who were clearly convicted of or had confessed as "murderers, adulterers, sorcerers and poisoners, the most terrible crimes."[29] In another letter he admonishes the judges to remain calm and wait for a confession or a clear conviction before pronouncing a death sentence in the "accusations of adultery, murder or sorcery."[30] Consequently, when he granted a general amnesty in 322 to mark the birth of a son to his first-born Crispus and his wife Helena, he excluded adulterers, murderers, and *venefici* (i.e. poisoners and sorcerers).[31]

Four decades later, under the more volatile Constantius, the distinctions that were important to Constantine had disappeared. In a letter to the Roman people, read throughout the empire as a public proclamation, the emperor lumped divination and magic together and allowed no exceptions for any type of magic. The text is abrupt; its list of rejected professionals intends less to leave no loophole than to create the impression of a crowd of

---

[28] Marcianus, *Inst.* 14, in *Dig.* 48.8.3: 2. *adiectio autem ista 'veneni mali' ostendit esse quaedam et non mala venena. ergo nomen medium est et tam id, quod ad sanandum, quam id, quod ad occidendum paratum est, continet, sed et id quod amatorium appellatur: sed hoc solum notatur in ea lege, quod hominis necandi causa habet.* "The specification of 'an injurious substance' demonstrates that there are also substances that are not injurious. Thus the noun is neutral and means both what is able to heal and what is able to kill, and even what is called a love-potion; but this law is only concerned with what serves to kill a human being."

[29] *CTh* 11.36.1 (*homicidam vel adulterum vel maleficum vel veneficum, quae atrocissima crimina sunt*). On the use of *maleficium* and *maleficus* see below, n. 34.

[30] *CTh* 9.40.1 *in adulterii vel homicidii vel maleficii crimine.*

[31] *CTh* 9.38.1 *propter Crispi atque Helenae partum omnibus indulgemus praeter veneficos homicidas adulteros*. On the historical and genealogical problems see already Gothofredus 3.191–193, who could not accept an otherwise unattested third Helena, after Constantine's mother and daughter, as daughter-in-law, and an unnamed and otherwise unattested first grandson of the emperor, and proposed to change *partum* to *pactum* or *paratum*. Recent scholars were more willing to accept the text and its implications: see Pohlsander (1984), 83–85 with reference to an image of this Helena in Aachen (Diocesan Museum) first identified by Alföldi (1959/60), who adds a possible coin; B. Bleckmann, in *DNP* 3.233 ("eine nicht weiter bekannte Helena") thus is not correct, but still better than Guthrie (1966), 326: Crispus "married a woman whose name is not known."

evil professionals, and its vision of punishment is graphic. The text deserves to be read in its entirety:[32]

> Nemo haruspicem consulat aut mathematicum, nemo hariolum. augurum et vatum prava confessio conticescat. Chaldaei ac magi et ceteri, quos maleficos ob facinorum magnitudinem vulgus appellat, nec ad hanc partem aliquid moliantur. sileat omnibus perpetuo divinandi curiositas. etenim supplicium capitis feret gladio ultore prostratus, quicumque iussis obsequium denegaverit.

> Nobody shall consult a sooth-sayer or an astrologer, nobody a diviner. The wicked utterances of augurs and seers shall fall silent. The Chaldaeans and magicians and all the others whom the people call evildoers because of the magnitude of their crimes, shall not attempt anything of this sort. For all, the inquisitiveness of wanting to know the future shall be forever stifled. Whoever refuses to obey to these commands shall suffer execution, felled by the avenging sword.

This is the first imperial law that uses the popular term *maleficus*, "evildoer," to designate the sorcerer and distinguish him from what seems to be the more professional *Chaldaei et magi*.[33] This use is as old as Apuleius and might reflect spoken usage; in an earlier use that is as old as Plautus *maleficium* meant any evil deed, *maleficus* a person or act that caused harm.[34]

A similar emotionality is visible in another proclamation of Constantius, of which the Theodosian Code preserves only a short extract. In it, sorcerers are excluded from the community of humans – they are *naturae peregrini*, "alien to our nature" – and they are said to "disturb the elements, endanger the lives of innocent people, and promise to do away with anybody's personal adversaries by calling up the ghosts of the dead" – a description of binding spells that recall Plato's famous passage on the itinerant specialists and their claims.[35]

---

[32] *CTh* 9.16.4, dated January 25, 357. The translation again follows Pharr (1952), 237, but tries to better reproduce the rhetorical gestures of the text. The terms for the professionals are almost untranslatable, as is the speaking term *maleficus*.

[33] Clerc (1996) argues that *Chaldaei* in this letter designates the theurgists and confirms the statements by Aug. *De civ. D.* 10.16.2 and the story reported by Eunap. *VS* 6.10.7 that Sosipatra's son Julian refrained from using theurgical rites out of fear of the emperors (τὰς βασιλικὰς ὁρμὰς ὑφορώμενος). I agree with Clerc that *Chaldaei* could well mean "theurgist" (see Aug. *Serm.* 189augm/26 Dolbeau, para. 36), but I also think that Constantius' sweeping move remained somewhat isolated; theurgists could always be tried under the laws against sorcery and/or divination – see the definitions in *CTh* 9.38.6 (Gratian, a. 381).

[34] See *OLD* s.vv.

[35] *CTh* 9.16.5: *Idem* [i.e. Constantius a.] *ad populum. – Post alia: multi magicis artibus ausi elementa turbare vitas insontium labefactare non dubitant et manibus accitis audent ventilare, ut quisque suos conficiat malis artibus inimicos. Hos, quoniam naturae peregrini sunt, feralis pestis absumat. Dat. prid. Non. Decemb. Mediolano Constantio a. VIIII et Iuliano caes. II conss.* (357 dec. [?] 4). Compare Plato, *Rep.* 364BC.

Magic in a Christian Empire 277

There is a good reason for the emperor's emotionality, as we learn from Ammianus Marcellinus. Divinatory and magical rites could be wielded against the emperor as tools of usurpation; and Constantius was the target of such an usurpation by the short-lived pretender Magnentius, whom the armies of Gaul and then of the entire West elevated in 350 and whom Constantius deposed in 353.[36] Far from being confined to the lower classes, at this time sorcery and its twin sister, divination, had infected the court aristocracy. Another imperial letter, addressed again to the *Praefectus praetorio*, shows that the emperor is convinced of the presence of magicians and diviners in his entourage and that of his Caesar Julian. It threatens torture and execution despite the high rank of the criminal, "if some *magus* or a person adept at magical actions whom popular usage calls a sorcerer [*maleficus*], or haruspex, diviner, augur and also astrologer or someone who hides divination in telling dreams is apprehended in my entourage or that of the Caesar."[37]

After the interlude of Julian, sanity seemed to return. Not too long after Julian's death, the new emperor Valentinian addressed the problems of magic and of divination. In a letter sent in 371 to the Roman senate, and written by Valentinian (despite the signature by Valentinian, Valens, and Gratian), the emperor made a clear distinction between *haruspices* and *malefici*.[38] While rejecting the sorcerers, he was protecting traditional Roman *haruspicina* in the name of tradition, repeating his earlier, not preserved decision to grant liberty of worship: "Everybody is given the free possibility to worship whatever has touched his mind."[39] The senate will have appreciated it.

But it was also very clear that there were forms of divination or sorcery that could not be tolerated – in fact, most forms. Two letters, both written to the Praetorian Praefect, spell this out: astrology was a capital crime, as was "to perform at night-time unholy prayers, magical rituals, or impure sacrifices," *nocturnis temporibus aut nefarias preces aut magicos apparatus aut sacrificia funesta celebrare*.[40] While astrology could still be banned for reasons of imperial safety, the nocturnal rites had a wider but somewhat

---

[36] See Lizzi Testa (2004), 222–229 and (2009), 270.
[37] *CTh* 9.16.6: *si quis magus vel magicis contaminibus adsuetus, qui maleficus vulgi consuetudine nuncupatur, aut haruspex aut hariolus aut certe augur vel etiam mathematicus aut narrandis somniis occultans artem aliquam divinandi aut certe aliquid horum simile exercens in comitatu meo vel caesaris fuerit deprehensus.*
[38] *CTh* 9.16.9.
[39] *CTh* 9.16.9 *leges a me in exordio imperii mei datae quibus unicuique, quod animo inbibisset, colendi libera facultas tributa est.*
[40] Astrology: *CTh* 9.16.8; nocturnal rites: *CTh* 9.16.7.

fuzzy reach, from the perversion of traditional rituals to damage and death aimed at one's enemies.

Two other imperial letters, both addressed to the Urban Prefect, help us to understand the background. We deal with judicial procedures that were specific to the city of Rome, although their inclusion in the Theodosian and Justinian Codes suggests that they became models for other places as well. One letter, from 371, deals with the accusation of sorcery against members of the senate, born, as the letter states, from envy: if these cases were to run into problems at the urban prefecture, they should be handed over to the imperial *consistorium* for a final decision. One senses the emperor's confidence in his own abilities to move such accusations as far away as possible from the sphere of petty aristocratic envy where they originated.[41] There can be no doubt that accusations of sorcery were used as a political weapon among Rome's elite; the known cases reach from the accusations against Libo Drusus and Piso pater under Tiberius to those against Boethius under Theoderic.[42]

The abuse of accusations of magic is also behind Theodosius' law of August 16, 389 that reformed the trial of people accused of sorcery and that I discussed in the context of Theodosius' laws of that summer.[43] Theodosius recommended that a public trial had to follow immediately after an arrest under the accusation of sorcery, to prevent any unexplained death in custody that gave rise to the suspicion of a summary execution of the accused in order either to remove a personal enemy by a false accusation or to prevent a sorcerer from naming associates; the law mentioned explicitly the charioteers as instigators of such a murder.

Unlike the senate, which was a breeding ground of false accusations of magic, the circus and its chariot races were, in the late Roman Empire, the home of actual magic, well before Valentinian and long after his time, in the Eastern Empire no less than in the West; this explains why Theodosius' law was republished in Justinian's Code.[44] Shortly before Justinian's time, king Theoderic (or rather his chancellor Cassiodorus) was well aware of the problem created by the charioteers. In a letter, Theoderic wrote of a charioteer whom he admired, Thomas, that his stunning ability had brought him the – coveted, as Theoderic adds – reputation of someone who was heavily relying on magic: "One feels a need to refer to the

---

[41] *CTh* 9.16.10.
[42] Libo Drusus: Tac. *Ann.* 2.27. Piso pater: Tac. *Ann.* 3.13; Eck, Caballos, and Fernández (1996). Boethius: Rousseau (1979).
[43] *CTh* 9.16.11; for the background and a more detailed analysis see above, Chapter 3.
[44] *CJ* 9.18.9.

perversities of magic when one cannot attribute the victory to the abilities of the horses."[45] Thus, urban rumors as well as imperial law assumed that charioteers were among the prime users of magic against their rivals.

Christians did not always fully abstain from this practice. We possess a large number of binding spells against charioteers and their horses found in and around circus buildings all over the Roman world, from Rome and Carthage to Antioch and Alexandria; the largest number dates to the second and third century CE. They all attack a charioteer and the horses of another circus faction, often with long chains of names of demons, and almost equally long lists of horse names.[46] These spells survived into the Christian empire: Alexander Hollmann has published a text from sixth-century Antioch, found in the Princeton excavations of the local circus; it invokes thirty-nine demons and orders them to attack and slow down thirty-six horses of the blue faction.[47] As usual, the attacker does not identify himself; but we do not have a good reason not to assume him to be a Christian.[48]

Even pious Christians sometimes had to make compromises in this matter. In his *Life of Hilarion*, Jerome tells the story of how in Gaza during a main city festival (Jerome calls it Consualia, but this might be a learned interpretation since it concerned the local god Marnas) the two head officials, the *duumviri*, each had a team run against the other.[49] One year, one *duumvir* was pagan, the other Christian, and altogether typically the winning team was expected also to bring fame and victory to the winning cult, to Marnas or Christ. Rumors had it that the pagan contender intended to use magic to slow down his opponent, who, understandably worried, visited the local ascetic, Hilarion. The saint first did not want to intervene, but finally yielded and gave the *duumvir* a small flask with water from his personal water cup: he should sprinkle the horses and the stable with it. This worked, and Christ got his victory, with the Gazeans shouting acclamations to him. Jerome does not tell why it worked; but there is an obvious explanation: water that had been in contact with the body of the saint contained a special power and protected the Christian's team against the sorcery of his opponent. Whatever the mechanism, this is not very different from the way in which, according to Porphyry, one theurgist's

---

[45] Cassiodorus, *Variae* 3.51.2: *frequentia palmarum eum faciebat dici maleficum, inter quos magnum praeconium videtur esse ad talia crimina pervenire. necesse est enim ad perversitatem magicam referri, quando victoria equorum meritis non potest applicari.* See Lee-Stecum (2006), 226.
[46] Pavis d'Escurac (1987); Tremel (2004); Trzcionka (2007).　　[47] Hollmann (2003).
[48] See also, on an interesting case in fiction, Huttner (2012).
[49] Hieron. *V. Hilarionis* 11. On Consus: Belayche (2001), 253–255.

rites were outdone by another one's, or as Sosipatra, according to Eunapius, was protected against attacks of erotic magic by the more powerful rites of her protector Maximus.[50] If this is so, Jerome condones protective rituals against evil magic in the same way a Christian exorcist would have protected his clients from demonic attacks.

Theodosius' letter of August 389 to the city prefect is the last law against magic from both the Code of Theodosius and of Justinian; this latter Code contains several of the texts against magic and divination from its predecessor, sometimes with minor variations. In the section of the Theodosian Code on magic and divination, *De maleficis et mathematicis et ceteris similibus* (9.16), there is only one law that is later than 398. It was written in 409 in Ravenna by Honorius, with the very young Theodosius II added for form's sake, and it concerns not magic but astrology. It grants astrologers the chance of repentance, provided that they burned their books under the supervision of the local bishop, publicly profess their Catholic faith, and promise never to return to their error.[51]

Divinatory books, be they collections of unauthorized sayings or astrological treatises, are burnt by imperial law. On the other hand, the emperors never ordered the books of magic to be destroyed by fire, although in the late fourth century their possession could mean capital punishment.[52] Unlike astrology, which was always knowledge-based and therefore book-centered (a letter of Diocletian, preserved in Justinian's Code, makes a distinction between legal geometry and illegal astrology), for the law magic was based on ritual acts alone. Of course there were books of magic, and they were burned already in Paul's Ephesos, but that was a private decision, as *Acts* makes clear: "A good many of those who formerly practiced magic collected their books and burnt them publicly."[53] They might be included in the "books that provoke God's ire" and therefore have to be burnt, as Theodosius II and Valentinian write in the introduction to their decision to burn Porphyry's books; but no preserved law singles them out.[54] When contemporary scholars claim that Augustus burnt "two thousand magical scrolls," they confuse magic and divination: when entering office as Pontifex Maximus, Augustus collected and destroyed anonymous or otherwise "useless" divinatory books, to retain only the Sibylline Books.[55] This has nothing to do with magic, but

---

[50] Porphyry ap. Aug. *De civ. D.* 10.9.2, citing a Chaldaean; Eunap. *VS* 6.9.6.   [51] *CTh* 9.16.12.
[52] *CTh* 16.5.34, a. 398, under Arcadius and Honorius.   [53] *Acts* 19:19.
[54] *CJ* 1.1.3; see Speyer (1981), 34: "So sind natürlich auch die heidnischen Zauberbücher in den Augen Gottes ein Greuel."
[55] The mistaken information e.g. in Kieckhefer (1990), 20; I am unable to trace its source.

combines the cleaning up of the jungle of private divination that must have gone wild during the disturbances of the dying Republic with safeguarding the monopoly of the Sibyl, and with it that of the senate, on obtaining knowledge of the future.[56]

Only much later we hear of the burning of magical books in the presence of church and state; but again the initiative was private. When, in mid-fifth century Beirut, radical Christian students at the Beirut Law School found out about a fellow student, a young Christian from Egypt, who dabbled in magic to further a love affair, he himself burnt his books of magic – "some of them by Zoroaster the magos, some by Ostanes the sorcerer, some by Manetho" – in their presence and with tears of repentance.[57] When this led to other suspects and many more books, the students organized a public *autodafé*, with the permission of the bishop, who advised them to invite the city also to participate, in the form of Beirut's main law official (ἔκδικος) and members of the police (the δημόσιοι).[58] Although this act of book-burning went beyond what the imperial decrees provided for, the bishop wanted to make sure that at least on the local level church and state were perceived as collaborating powers in the eradication of sorcery.

These fifth-century events resonate with the collection of rules for the Egyptian clergy transmitted as the Canons of Athanasius that is contemporary with or older than the events in Beirut described by Zachariah.[59] Canon 71 deals with the sons of priests who use books of magic: young and educated Egyptian Christians, it seems, were somewhat prone to fall for this specific sin and bring punishment onto their fathers, as they did when they visited the theaters, another vice of the educated young (canon 75).[60] Canon 72 addresses the baptism of former sorcerers: they could only be baptized after sincere repentance, which began with burning their books and continued with three years of witnessed fasting and working with their hands: sorcerers are intellectuals, unused to the hard toil that helps focus one's mind.[61] These

---

[56] See e.g. MacMullen (1966), 128–130.
[57] Zachariah, *Vita Severi* (Syriac version) 15ff. (ed. Kugener, *Patrologia Orientalis* 2 p. 57ff.); the citation and burning, p. 62.
[58] *Ibid.* The public burning on p. 69, in Kugener's translation: "Nous nous occupâmes de brûler les livres de magie qui avaient été déjà saisis. C'est pourquoi, ayant pris avec nous, sous l'ordre de l'évêque, le défenseur (ἔκδικος) de la ville, les greffiers de l'état (δημόσιοι), et les membres de la clergé, nous allumâmes pour ces livres un feu devant l'église de la Sainte Vierge et Mère de Dieu, Marie."
[59] Riedel and Crum (1904). On date and authorship W. Riedel, in Riedel and Crum (1904), xiii–xvi (Athanasius; *c.*364 CE); René-Georges Coquin, "Canons of Pseudo-Athanasius," in *Copt. Enc.* 2.458 (unknown author, written before mid-fifth century).
[60] Riedel and Crum (1904), 48 (Arabic version), 135 (Coptic version, correcting a problematic translation of the Arabic version).
[61] Riedel and Crum (1904), 48 (Arabic), 135 (Coptic; lacunose).

canons fit the times even if they are not Athanasius'. During the magic trials under Valens, the last emperor to send Athanasius into exile, "in the Eastern provinces, entire libraries were burned by their owners out of fear" of trumped-up charges of sorcery, and the so-called "Anastasi cache" from Thebes in Upper Egypt demonstrates the interest such books must have roused among local intellectuals.[62] The multilingual library, bought and dispersed over several European collections after 1828 thanks to the entrepreneurship and connoisseurship of the Alexandrian merchant Giovanni Anastasi, contained both magical and alchemical papyri, written between the late third and earlier fourth century, manifest testimony to the interest of a learned and curious local collector.

The changes

Magic and divination

The examples just cited show how magic, *veneficium*, still existed in the Christian empire. The laws of Constantine, Constantius, and Valentinian also show a basic insecurity about whether divination was akin to magic, or different from it. Valentinian's attempt to correct Constantius' identification of the two was short-lived; in the following decades, the two were more and more often thrown together, and in the influential *Etymologies* of Isidore of Seville, in the early seventh century, sorcery had become just one subdivision of divination.[63] We also get at least a vague idea who the actors were: students who dabbled in magic out of curiosity, boredom, and a spirit of defiance of authorities; charioteers who made use of professionals; professionals who could even be members of the court, to believe Constantius or Ammianus; and some victims were sitting in high places and could be targeted by a binding spell or, worse, by the unfounded accusation of having used sorcery.

It needs to be underlined how strictly Constantine's responses were adhering to the way Roman laws had dealt with magic since time almost immemorial. Recognizing the intractable character of magic, the law never addressed it as such, but only its damaging impact on the rights and the integrity of a person. When, centuries earlier, the Twelve Tables forbade the use of spells to move harvests from one field to another (*incantare messis*), the law-giver did so because this infringed on the right of

---

[62] Fowden (1986), 168–171 (who also cites Ammian. 29.2.4).
[63] Already Thorndike (1915) pointed out the seminal role of Isidore, *Etym.* 8.9 (*De magis*), a passage widely received in medieval authors and council acts.

ownership. When Sulla brought in the *lex Cornelia de sicariis et veneficis*, he dealt with two closely related acts: to harm people with visible and invisible weapons (*tela* and *venenum*).[64] Originally, *venenum* was defined as something material that one could manufacture, sell, or possess;[65] later, the term acquired the double meaning Greek φάρμακον had in Plato, "poison" and "spell." The same reluctance to acknowledge magic as a crime in itself also meant that, even in Imperial times, an accusation of magic was always accessory to other accusations. Unlike other, more "mundane" accusations, it often did not make it into court, as famously happened in the case of Piso pater: Tacitus' account of the affair includes the instigation to sorcery, whereas the preserved minutes of the trial before the senate do not include it.[66]

This is different from the way Imperial law addressed divination as a crime, well before the Christian emperors. Diocletian, as we saw, prohibited astrology; more than a century earlier, in 199 CE, after Septimius Severus visited Egypt, his prefect of Egypt outlawed all temple oracles in the province.[67] Constantine suppressed only private divination, as we saw, presumably because he was concerned about its use as a secret tool for insurrection, but he followed tradition by protecting the public divinatory rites. In the case of magic, he was somewhat more innovative. Sorcerers "who are convicted of having moved against the health of people or of having deflected temperate minds towards lust" are severely punished, but the person who used spells and rites to protect health and harvests should remain unmolested: it was still the outcome that counted and not the intention.[68] Despite the fervor of Christian theologians, this remained the norm: Constantine's letter became part of the Code of Justinian. From there, it moved to later Byzantine codification, with some changes: still, it was the association with demons to do sorcery (γοητεία) that counted – that is, the aim was as punishable as the outcome.[69] Leo VI the Wise (reigned 886–912) changed this again and proposed to treat any sorcerer,

---

[64] See *Digest*. 48.8: the law speaks of *tela* and *venenum*, *Digest*. 48.8.
[65] Marcian. *Inst.* 14 in *Dig.* 48.8.3 echoes the text of the law: *qui venenum necandi hominis causa fecerit vel vendiderit vel habuerit*
[66] Tac. *Ann.* 3.13; the minutes: Eck, Caballos, and Fernández (1996).
[67] Diocletian: *CJ* 9.18.2 *ars autem mathematica damnabilis interdicta est*. Septimius Severus: P.Col. Youtie 130; see Parássoglou (1976); Rea (1977). Overall: Desanti (1990); Fögen (1997).
[68] *CTh* 9.16.3 = *CJ* 9.18.4.
[69] See the *Eklogai* published by Leo III the Isaurian in 726: Simon and Troianos (1977), 58–74, nos. 21 (οἱ γόητες οἱ ἐπὶ βλάβῃ ἀνθρώπων δαίμονας ἐπικαλούμενοι ἢ διὰ θυσιῶν μαντευόμενοι ξίφει τιμωρείσθωσαν) and 22 (οἱ φαρμάκοις τισὶ ἤγουν δηλητηρίοις ἀναιροῦντες ἑκουσίως ἀνθρώπους ξίφει τιμωρείσθωσαν); see also Zepos and Zepos (1931), 12–47, nos. 39 and 41.

regardless of his aim, in the same way the law treated an apostate: Leo saw sorcery, including weather charms and healing spells, as a relapse into paganism. We shall see that this joins the arguments of the theologians against amulets.[70]

After Constantine, things slowly changed. Terminology is a good indicator of such changes. Constantine's terminology was traditional and careful. In the amnesty proclamation of 322, he excluded *venefici* from amnesty, using the term proper to Roman law since Sulla's time. In the constitution that addressed magic properly but had nothing to do with poison (*CTh* 9.16.3), he circumscribed its practitioners as *magicis accinti artibus*, "armed with the science of magic"; *artes* points to the professionals of somewhat uncertain name – *venefici, magi, malefici* – but could also include the occasional non-professional. Constantius was more emotional and more explicit: twice in his constitutions against sorcery, he explained the term *maleficus* as a popular term, used for the sorcerer "because of the enormity of his crime" (*quos maleficos ob facinorum magnitudinem vulgus appellat*); Augustine later did the same.[71] The statement gains weight when one remembers that before the fourth century, *maleficium* was any "misdeed, crime," and *maleficus* an adjective for a person or an action that caused harm or was a crime, and that Apuleius was the first to attest its connection with sorcery;[72] in this general sense, *maleficus* is still used in an imperial letter by Constantine.[73] The wish to distinguish between *veneficium* and *maleficium*, "poisoning" and "sorcery," and the public fascination with the horrors of magic both contributed to the ascent of the term as an official legal term for the sorcerer and his art.

At the time of Valentinian I, the distinction became active also in the amnesty proclamations: twice, in 367 and in 368, the emperor referred to *malefici* or *maleficium* to exclude the sorcerers from his amnesty. In the earlier text, he simply used the double term *veneficus sive maleficus* that we met already earlier; in 368 he was carefully distinguishing the "crimes of the sorcerers" from the "secret attacks of the poisoners."[74] Fifteen years later,

---

[70] *Novella* 65; see Noailles and Dain (1944), 237f. See Troianos (1990), 50.
[71] *CTh* 9.16.4; see 9.16.6. Augustine: *De civ. D.* 10.9 *quos et maleficos uulgus appellat*.
[72] *Maleficium* "misdeed" and *maleficus* "wicked, nefarious" is as old as Plautus; *maleficium magicum* as the accusation: Apul. *Apol.* 1; *magus et maleficus homo ibid.* 51; see also Apul. *Met.* 3.16, 9.29.
[73] Constantine, a. 331: *CTh* 1.16.6 = *CJ* 1.40.3 on unjust and criminal (*iniusti et malefici*) judges; see also the letter by Hadrian used in *Dig.* 48.8.14, from Callistratus, *De cognitionibus* (under Caracalla) that states that *maleficium* is defined by intent, not outcome.
[74] *CTh* 9.38.3 *veneficus sive maleficus*; 9.38.4 *maleficiorum scelus, insidias venenorum* (in a longer list of the excluded crimes).

Gratian was even more explicit and verbosely precise.[75] He distinguished between "the person who has concocted poisons for mind and body with harmful herbs that he supplied, and terrible secrets that he murmured" on the one hand, and "the person who, learned in sacrilege, was imitating the sacred mouth and sought divine faces, giving shape to venerable forms." In plain words: on the one hand the emperor was concerned with the poisoner whose substances harm the body and the sorcerer whose spells harm the mind, on the other hand with the soothsayer who gave expression to a divine voice and the theurgist who strove to see the divinity face-to-face.[76]

From then on, these distinctions became current. In his amnesty proclamations, Gratian regularly excluded *venefici* and *malefici*, twice coupled with the counterfeiter of money, another figure who secretly and with bad intention perverted key values.[77] The same distinctions appeared with Theodosius I: unlike the transitional Constantine, who followed traditional Roman law, the later fourth century wanted to make a distinction between the poisoner, who used harmful substances but did not commit sacrilege, and the sorcerer, who relied on demons.[78]

A consequence of this transformation of magic is that the *Lex Cornelia* was no longer felt to be adequate to cover sorcery. Chapter 9.14 of the Theodosian Code, *Ad legem Corneliam de sicariis*, is concerned with two things only, infanticide and legitimate resistance against an attack by a robber or a burglar. In this changed world, magic has been removed into its own chapter, 9.16 *De maleficis et mathematicis et ceteris similibus*, where Constantine's echoes of the old Lex Cornelia sound almost out of place. It goes without saying that the Visigothic *breviarium* adopted this transformation.

Demonology and the law

At some point in the fourth or fifth century, there was another, even more momentous change: theology, or rather demonology, intruded into law.[79] None of the emperors of the fourth or fifth century ever referred to the

---

[75] *CTh* 9.38.6 *qui noxiis quaesita graminibus et diris inmurmurata secretis mentis et corporis venena composuit, aut qui sacri oris imitator et divinorum vultuum adpetitor venerabiles formas sacrilegio eruditus inpressit.*
[76] This is another overlooked attestation of theurgy in the late fourth century.
[77] *In lege Cornelia dolus* (i.e. evil intention) *pro facto accipitur*, Paulus in *Dig.* 48.8.7: the same, of course, is true for the counterfeiter.
[78] *CTh* 9.38.7 (a. 384: *homicidii veneficiique ac maleficiorum*), 9.38.8 (a. 385: *veneficus, maleficus adulteratorque monetae*); Theodosius I: *Const. Sirm.* 8 (*non aliquos in astra peccantes, non venenarios aut magos, non falsae monetae reos absolvendorum felicitati conectimus*).
[79] Rives (2003) sees this happening much earlier than I do.

supernatural agents of magic, unlike the bishops or, for that matter, the writers already before Apuleius or Jerome in his *Life of Hilarion*. The demons entered the venerable world of the Theodosian Code through the door of the *interpretationes*. Constantine's discerning law on sorcery received the interpretation that "sorcerers, singers of spells, those who send thunder-storms or who disturb human minds by invoking the demons, have to be punished very severely."[80] Thus, the interpretation not only did away with Constantine's distinctions, it turned the (permitted) ritual harvest protection into a (prohibited) magical causation of thunderstorms – which, incidentally, could still allow for amulets and spells to protect the fields. Similarly, Constantius' condemnation of sorcerers and diviners was understood, without much knowledge of traditional Roman divination, as "whoever out of curiosity for the future consults an invoker of demons, the seers that they call *harioli*, or a haruspex who collects birdsigns, shall suffer the death-sentence."[81] Valentinian I's condemnation of nocturnal rites means "whoever celebrates nocturnal sacrifices to demons or invokes in his spells the demons, suffers the death-sentence."[82] In short, where the imperial law-giver had avoided talking about supernatural agents, the later *interpretationes* bring them in, in order to underline the severity of the crime. The *interpretationes* are Western exegeses that the editors of the first Visigoth Code, the *Breviarium* of Alaric, added to the text which they took over from the Theodosian Code and which king Alaric published in 506, and that he elaborated "with the collaboration of priests and noblemen," as we already saw in the chapter about the calendar reform of Theodosius I (Chapter 3).[83] I suspect that it was especially the ecclesiastical commentators who had the interest in demonology; at any rate, it reflects practice and legal thought of a time and place that obviously was more attuned to accepting demonic intervention in human affairs than the imperial law-givers were.

Demonology explains magic in the East, as well as another distinction, the one between poisoning and sorcery, at least in the perception of

---

[80] *CTh* 9.16.3 (*Breviarium* 9.13.1) *Interpretatio. Malefici vel incantatores vel immissores tempestatum vel ii, qui per invocationem daemonum mentes hominum turbant, omni poenarum genere puniantur.*

[81] *CTh* 9.16.4 (*Breviarium* 9.13.2) *Interpretatio. Quicumque pro curiositate futurorum vel invocatorem daemonum vel divinos, quos hariolos appellant, vel haruspicem, qui auguria colligit, consuluerit, capite punietur.*

[82] *CTh* 9.16.7 (*Breviarium* 9.13.3) *Interpretatio: quicumque nocturna sacrificia daemonum celebraverit vel incantationibus daemones invocaverit, capite puniatur.*

[83] On the *interpretationes* see Gaudemet (1965), with earlier literature; the citation from Alaric's dedicatory letter, edited in Zeumer (1902), 465f., and in Mommsen's Prolegomena *to* CTh (Berlin: Weidmann, 1905), xxxiii.

Magic in a Christian Empire 287

educated persons, and thus perhaps also in the practice of the law. In his commentary on the hymns of Gregory of Nazianzus, Cosmas of Jerusalem (bishop of Maiuma after 743) makes the following distinction:[84]

> Magic (μαγεία) is different from sorcery (γοητεία): magic is the acclamation of beneficent demons to achieve some good thing, as the talismans of Apollonius of Tyana are serving a good purpose; sorcery is the invocation of maleficent demons for some bad purpose. These demons dwell around graves, and the term γοητεία is derived from dirges (ἀπὸ τῶν γόων) and laments around the graves. Poisoning is when it is given through the mouth as a love potion, in some deadly concoction.

The text replicates the legal distinction between benevolent and malevolent magical practices, both ascribed to the intervention of the demons whom we just saw intruding into legal texts in the West; good magic is exemplified by the talismanic statues of Apollonius of Tyana that were famous in the Byzantine world.[85] It also makes a clear distinction between sorcery and poisoning, in a move as old as Plato's distinction between the two actions inside his over-arching term φαρμακεία, the damage done to the body by a substance, and the damage done by μαγγανείαις ... καὶ ἐπῳδαῖς καὶ καταδέσεσι λεγομέναις, "sorcery, incantations, and so-called binding spells."[86]

The learned commentator is not alone with this distinction. The list of healing miracles at the incubation shrine of John and Cyrus in Menouthis near Alexandria, drawn up with often eloquent imagination by Sophronius of Jerusalem between 610 and 619, illustrates not only how pervasive the belief in sorcery as a source of incurable disease remained among the early Byzantines, it presents the same distinction. Among his seventy-odd cases of a disease that only the saints could cure, eight are cases of demonic possession without human agency.[87] Four are caused by a substance, δηλητήριον or φαρμακεία, administered by someone close to the victim – a rejected lover, greedy relatives, envious

---

[84] Cosmas, *Ad carmina S. Gregorii* 64 (*Patrologia Graeca* 36, 1024A): διαφέρει δὲ μαγεία γοητείας· ἡ μὲν μαγεία ἐπίκλησίς ἐστι δαιμόνων ἀγαθοποιῶν πρὸς ἀγαθοῦ τινος σύστασιν, ὥσπερ τὰ τοῦ Ἀπολλωνίου τοῦ Τυανέως θεσπίσματα δι᾽ ἀγαθῶν γεγόνασι· γοητεία δὲ ἐστιν ἐπίκλησις δαιμόνων κακοποιῶν περὶ τοὺς τάφους εἰλουμένων ἐπὶ κακοῦ τινος σύστασιν (γοητεία δὲ ἤκουσεν ἀπὸ τῶν γόων καὶ τῶν θρήνων τῶν περὶ τοὺς τάφους γινομένων)· φαρμακεία δὲ ὅταν διά τινος σκευασίας θανατοφόρου πρὸς φίλτρον δοθῆι τινι διὰ στόματος. The same definitions are varied in Georg. Monach. *Chron.* 1.74.10–20 de Boor = Suid. *s.v.* γοητεία (γ 365); the final definition of φαρμακεία is also in Georg. Monach. *Chron.* 1.74.18 de Boor = Suid. s.v. φαρμακεία (φ 100).
[85] On θέσπισμα "talisman" Sophocles. s.v., p. 581 (this passage); on the beliefs Dulière (1970).
[86] Plat. *Laws* 10.932E–933A.
[87] *Miracles* 14, 32, 40, 41, 54 (contracted in the bath: to add to the cases collected by Bonner [1932], 203–208), 56 (the demon had the shape of a rabbit that the victim was hunting), 57, 67.

sisters-in-law; in a fifth case the writer leaves it open whether the illness was caused by a substance or by demons.[88] Three other cases are unequivocally caused by demons sent by an enemy: in one of them with the help of a figurine; in another case the writer underlines that the patient was not "suffering sorcery through food or receiving deadly poison in a drink but hit hard by a demon," making clear that a noxious substance is what one might have expected.[89] Sophronius has a psychological explanation ready:

> If something hurtful has been done to us, or overpowered by brother-hating envy even when nothing has been done, we thrice unhappy people like to defend ourselves against fellow-humans not only with aggressive words, murderous tools and swords, but also take them down by sorcery (φαρμακεία), forgetting the natural love for our neighbor.[90]

Injustice, insult, or envy have been the forces behind magic for centuries. It is worthwhile to point out that in the reality of story-telling – and thus perhaps in the reality of suspicion behind an incurable illness – Sophronius felt in most cases able to make a distinction between the use of poison by relatives (φαρμακεία or δηλητήρια, in an age-old but still current term) and a demonic attack caused by someone unknown, even if he uses the term περιεργία for both, signaling how closely related the phenomena were, and how open the terminology remained.[91]

Amulets and the Christians

Constantine's toleration, which survived into the Code of Justinian and beyond, explains why so many Christian amulets and prayers to protect the harvest, especially the wine harvest, still survive.

---

[88] *Miracles* 12 (φαρμακεία), 27 (περιεργία, φάρμακον), 59 (φαρμακεία, δηλητήριον; proof is impossible), 68 (φάρμακον); the open case miracle, 21 (εἴτε οὖν δηλητηρίοις χρώμενοι εἴτε βλαπτικαῖς δαιμόνων ὁρμαῖς τε καὶ μάστιξιν).

[89] *Miracles* 35 περιεργία, γόητες σὺν μιαροῖς δαίμοσι; 55 ἀπὸ μαγείας; 63 οὐ μαγγανείαν ὑποστὰς διὰ βρώματος ἢ δηλητήριον λαβὼν διὰ πόσεως, ἀλλὰ πληγεὶς ἀφειδῶς διὰ δαίμονος.

[90] *Miracles* 27: φιλοῦμεν γὰρ οἱ τρισάθλιοι μὴ μόνον αἰκισμοῖς καὶ φονικοῖς ὀργάνοις καὶ ξίφεσι ἀμύνεσθαι τὸ ὁμόφυλον, εἴ τι τῶν λυπούντων εἰργάσατο, ἢ καὶ φθόνωι μισαδέλφωι κρατούμενοι καὶ εἰ μηδὲν εἰς ἡμᾶς ἐπλημμέλησεν, ἀλλὰ καὶ φαρμακείαις αὐτὸν κατεργάζεσθαι, τὴν πρὸς τὸν πέλας φυσικὸν στοργὴν ἀπολέσαντες.

[91] περιεργία with a substance: miracle 27; from demons: 35, 63; open miracle: 21. Unlike Cosmas, he uses μαγεία for bad magic, 55 (the only instance of the term, compared to the four instances of περιεργία and two of φαρμακεία, both times with a substance, as in Cosmas); once, he uses the rather obsolete (Platonic) μαγγανεία (63, with a substance). For δηλητήρια see the φάρμακα δηλητήρια in the so-called Dirae Teiorum, Meiggs and Lewis no. 30 a 1; for the Byzantine use, see Sophocles (1900), s.v.

Spells to protect the harvest come from all over the late Roman Empire, from Bithynia to Gaul.[92] A surprisingly large number has been found in late antique Sicily.[93] A typical example comes from Notion (Noto) in Sicily and is inscribed on the two sides of a limestone slab (fifth/sixth century).[94] One side has:

> + For the fruit-bearing of the places, and the vineyard.
> Angel of God Kramamila Phinael Louil Amegaoth Krephiel Phatoel Anemouel Moukathal Louechanda Eisdramal Meseel: we pray to you, Jesus Christ, give the harvest, the yield, to the vineyard of Kyriakos, son of Zosimos.
> Wherever this amulet is placed, Michael Gabriel Ouriel Rapahel and Muschouton, the powerful, give your benevolence to the harvest of grain, wine and oil of Kyriakos; of grain, wine and oil give plenty, Jesus Christ, yes, amen.+

It is a straightforward text that states its purpose, identifies the owner of the field, that is the beneficiary of divine intervention, and prays for a rich harvest to a long list of angels, some with easily recognizable names, others not, and to Christ. Thus, the fields are put under the protection of Christ and his angels; it remains open whether they are supposed to keep away damaging influence, or to actively influence the growth of grain, wine, and oil.

The other side of the same monument somewhat clarifies the issue, despite the gaps in the text. Again, it begins with a simple instruction before it enters the invocation:

> + Against hailstorms; place it in the three corners of the vineyard. Michael, Gabriel, Our(i)el, Raphel, Iaoa [sign of a sun or star] of God [—] the firmament of heaven [—] I lie. I implore the cloud-drivers in God's name: do not hit with hail the vineyard of Kyriakos, son of Zosimos, protect him day and night from the anger of the elements. + Christ overcomes; Christ, help the vineyard of Kyriakos.+

Whereas the somewhat vague concept of harvest growth can be seen as the result of divine benevolence and help, hailstorms can be constructed as a supernatural attack on human endeavors, here called the cloud-drivers, whoever they were. In the pagan world, there was a Zeus and an Apollo Chalazios and an Aither Alexichalazos who controlled these destructive

---

[92] Overview, with a collection of texts, Mastrocinque (2004).
[93] Manganaro Perrone (2007); Bevilacqua (1999). See also the prayer for the protection of vineyards and fields in Pradel (1907), 11, lines 15ff.
[94] See Bevilacqua and Giannobile (2000); Mastrocinque (2004), 815.

forces; already then, prayers tried to influence the powers that were imagined to be responsible for the destruction.[95] The same is true in the Christian world, where a prayer to Christ and the angels was supposed to help against similar powers.

As this text shows, the stone slabs bearing these inscribed prayers were placed along the border of the field; as long as the prayer remained there, it guaranteed protection. Other agricultural spells were written on lead tablets; we have to assume that they were buried or in some other way placed on the borders of the fields. Although they functioned in the same way as amulets worn against illness, the usual metals for amulet inscriptions, silver and gold, must have proved too much of a temptation to thieves, thus a less vulnerable support, a lead tablet or a stone slab, was thought preferable.

Amulets inscribed on thin gold and silver leaves and often carried in a container on one's body typically protected against ailments that were caused by demons and that resisted the art of the professional doctors.[96] Again, as with the binding spells on the race course, they did not end with Christianization; as in the protective harvest spells, a Christian origin is signaled by the sign of the cross or the invocation of Christ or the Virgin. A small gold lamella from Laodikeia (Latakia) in coastal Syria, dated to the fifth or sixth century, gives an interesting graphic expression to the function of providing health by inscribing the central text in a crudely drawn *tabula ansata* and framing it with two crosses and the invocation of the powerful names, partly as magical signs:

> + For health (?). (magic signs). Eloai, by the vigorous name, the crown of the Lord, give health.+ (Inserted: Give health and good favor).[97]

Eloia being Jewish as well, the crosses are the only unequivocal Christian sign.

Another text, perhaps from Tyre and with an uncertain date, starts its invocation against ophthalmia with a variation of the trinitarian formula that thus guarantees a Christian origin:

---

[95] Zeus Chalazios in a dedication from Kyzikos (first century BCE), *JHS* 24 (1904), 22, no. 4; Apollo Chalazios: Phot. s.v.; Aither Alexichalazios in a dedication from Roman Amaseia, *Studia Pontica* 3:1 (1910), 114a.
[96] Unlike with *defixiones*, we do not have a collection of the material, not even as old and thus incomplete as Audollent (1904). Kotansky (1994) marks an auspicious start but has not yet been continued, and there are amulets among the Coptic texts presented by Meyer and Smith (1994).
[97] *IGLSyr* 4 no. 1284; Kotansky (1994), 236 no. 45 (his translation).

In the name of God and Jesus Christ and the Holy Spirit, Raba Skanomena Loula Amrikto Rathên Athabatha Rourak, I pray to you, great name of Iaô, turn aside ophthalmia brought to me and do not let happen an onset of ophthalmia.[98]

Eye disease, together with head aches or tooth aches, is among the health problems against which doctors were almost helpless and which therefore called for ritual healing. In the Phrygian confessions stelai, eye disease is presented as being sent by a punishing deity, in the Epidaurian healing texts as something that only the god could heal.[99]

The short Christian text from Latakia used the Hebrew Eloia as the powerful name of God. Other amulet texts, some much longer and more complex, also use Jewish elements; not all are unequivocally Christian. This creates an interesting methodological quandary: how do we decide on the religious affiliation of the user of such texts? A look at three variations of an amuletic text will show the methodological problems.[100]

A fifth-century Oxyrrhynchos papyrus in Florence presents a long series of invocations in which one Paulus Iulianus asks for protection and power.[101] Thirteen invocations, all introduced by ἐπικαλοῦμαί σε, each address a power sitting over parts of the elements and the world and summarize these invocation with "I conjure you (ἐξορκίζω ὑμᾶς) in the name of the god of Abraham, Isaac and Jacob," followed by a list of what the praying person needs and summarized again by "I conjure you, Iaô Sabaôth, aô Sabaôth, ô Sabaôth, Sabaôth, abaôth, baôth, aôth, ôth, ô", with the decreasing formula depicting the slow achievement of the wish. Sabaôth and Iaô are names of the Jewish god, and a final group of formulas uses other Jewish elements. Prima facie, nothing forbids us to assume a Jewish origin and use of this amulet.

A second, longer version is found on a fifth-century gold leaf in a private collection in Bern (Switzerland) that still has traces of its use in an amulet capsule. It has the title "Seal of the Living God," then invokes (ὁρκίζω) "Sabaôth above the heavens, Edeôth above Echeiôth, Edeôth Chthodai" and commands him to protect Leontion "who wears this amulet from all demons, substances and binding spells, and all dangers and attacks of the opponent."[102] There follows a similar but longer invocation of the power over

---

[98] Kotansky (1994), 301 no. 53, late antiquity.
[99] Confession stelai: Petzl (1994), with an eye affliction mentioned in nos. 16, 45, 49, 50, 69, 85, 93, and eyes depicted on nos. 16, 50, 90. Epidaurian healing inscription: LiDonnici (1995).
[100] See Gelzer, Lurje, and Schäublin (1999).
[101] PGM 35, edited again by Gelzer, Lurja, and Schäublin (1999), 46–60.
[102] Gezler, Lurje, and Schäublin (1999), 3–13, 39–45: line 4 διαφύλαττε τὸ φοροῦντα τὸ φυλακτήριον τοῦτο Λεόντιον ἀπὸ πάντων δαιμονίων καὶ φαρμάκων καὶ καταδέσμων καὶ πάντων κινδύνων καὶ ἐπιβουλῶν τοῦ ἀντικειμένου.

the elements, again with the command to protect Leontion. The final section varies invocations, conjurations, and commands, insists again on protection against "*pharmaka*, spittle, binding spell, sorcery (γοητεία) or violence."[103] It ends with the prayer formula "for the eternity of all eternities, amen." This text does not mention the god of Abraham, Isaac, and Jacob, and its final formula is not uncommon in Christian texts.[104]

The third and longest variation is a fifth silver band from Beirut that is now in the Musée du Louvre.[105] It begins like the Bern text (but with minor textual variations) by invoking the Supreme God – "Thou, Sabaoth above Heaven, who went above Elaoth who is aboth Chthothai" – to protect "Alexandra whom Zoe has born, from every demon and every attack by demons and the powers of demons, from magical substances (φαρμακὰ μαγικά) and from binding spells (κατάδεσμοι)": we thus deal with an amulet providing general protection from demons, in a list that is somewhat different from the Bern list. After this, the text invokes a long list of twenty-three angels, again with vaguely Jewish names, from Marmarioth "who is sitting on the first sky" to Chara "sitting on the firmament"; like in the Oxyrrhynchos text the list ends with "God of Abraham, God of Isaac, God of Jacob." The text then addresses the very demon who could harm Alexandra "in the name of God living on Zaarabem … who is in Hebrew[106] Barbar Eipsathoathariath Phelpchaphion and whom all the evil things and all the binding spells fear." There follows a long list of everything that could harm Alexandra's virtue, from receiving a kiss to taking a bath. The text ends with what sounds like a Nestorian credo but feels somewhat tagged on: "One God and his Anointed, help Alexandra: Εἷς Θεὸς καὶ Χριστὲ αὐτοῦ, βόηθι Ἀλεξάνδραν."

Commentators all agree that the core of this text with its complex angelology and its resonances with the Hebrew Bible must be Jewish and perhaps go back to the famous Jewish exorcists mentioned already in *Acts* and, not much later, by the Elder Pliny.[107] But they also point out that the Bern and the Beirut text both end with a Christian formula that has been

---

[103] On this list see Gelzer, Lurje, and Schäublin (1999), 114–115.
[104] Gelzer, Lurje, and Schäublin (1999), 125, with reference *inter alia* to an amulet in Cologne, P. Colon. 8. 340, that cites John 1:1–11.
[105] Originally Héron de Villefosse (1911), republished by Jordan (1991), Kotansky (1994), 270 no. 52, with commentary 281–300, and Gelzer, Lurje, and Schäublin (1999), 14–22, 46–59.
[106] The text of the entire passage is corrupt. In 86 τὸν ΕΙΒΡΑΔΙΒΑΣ | βαρβλιοις Ειψαθω|αθαριαθ Φελχαφιαων, David Jordan (1991), 68 "guesses" "a phrase like Ἑβραϊστὶ Βαρβαρ κτλ."
[107] On Jewish exorcists of the Second Temple period see Bohak (2008), 88–114; on Jewish metal amulets of late antiquity (they did not yet exist in the Second Temple period), *ibid.* 149–153, 194–201.

tagged on, both from Christian liturgy. Although the rare use of Jesus' name in an Aramaic magic bowl shows that Jewish magical texts could use the power of Jesus' name, even for aggressive spells,[108] the appropriation of a liturgical formula – the end of a prayer or a variation of the creed – looks much more like an attempt to Christianize a powerful Jewish text and to legitimate its Christian use, in the same way as in the eye amulet from Tyre the trinitarian formula was used for the same purpose.[109] But as in the Graeco-Egyptian magical papyri, in this world of multicultural religious bricolage used to fight elementary fears and concerns certainty about religious affiliation of a text remains an illusion.

Not all amulets have to be inscribed on silver or gold. A bronze tablet from Xanthos in Lycia (fourth to sixth century) shows similar bricolage. The image of a fish alludes to its Christian affiliation, whereas the text is clearly Jewish:[110]

> God, help the wearer, Epiphanios whom Anastasia bore. I adjure you by Solomon, the great angel Michael, Gabriel, Uriel, Raphael; I adjure you by Abrasax. I adjure you in Hebrew Phthaobarao, in the name of Sabaoth, I Epiphanios. I adjure you by the great name of Abraham, Ado Adonai Ageleon Skiaraxou: deliver him who is living from the demon who has caught him.

The reference to the Hebrew name of God, this time without textual problems, replaces the pagan secret name in its "barbaric" form and grounds the text in the same Jewish background to which also Solomon, Abraham, and Adonai refer – it is left to the drawing of the fish to turn the text Christian. As to the reference to Abrasax, it should not surprise: the name is a common chronogram with the value of 365, the sum of days in the year, and thus guarantees permanence to the spell, beyond any fixed religious affiliation.[111]

The complex angelology and the reference to "Hebrew" names add an almost scholarly character to these amulets and harvest protection spells. The long and complex lists of demons in the so-called Sethian curse tablets evoke the skills of foreign specialists, and there can be no doubt that those

---

[108] Levene (1999); Shaked (1999) ("clearly borrowed from Christian usage"); see already Bonner (1943), 42, with reference to *Acts* 19:13–14.
[109] Christian appropriation in the case of the Beirut text: Kotansky (1994), 300; the Bern text, Gelzer, Lurje and Schäublin (1999), 128.
[110] Jordan and Kotansky (1996).
[111] Abrasax (or Abraxas, in a variation of the name that is uncommon in our texts but common in modern scholarship) is widespread in the magical papyri, but also in Basilidean gnosticism, Iren. *Adv. haer.* 1.24.7 (where the mss. have Abraxax, editors "correct" to Abraxas) and Hipp. *Ref.* 7.26.6 (Abrasax), both with a reference to the numeric value and its equivalence with the 365 days.

texts reflect the activity of itinerant Eastern practitioners with a knowledge of Jewish lore.[112] In a similar way, the complex Christian amulets and harvest spells presuppose a degree of Biblical and theological knowledge and expertise that one would expect of priests and monks rather than of lay Christians or pagans.

The prohibitions of the councils and synods confirm that priests freelancing as sorcerers or exorcists was a reality of the late antique Church. Already at the Council of Laodikeia in 364/365, the bishops forbade that "any priest or cleric ... acted as sorcerer or *magus* or fabricated amulets," and this prohibition was repeated over the centuries both in Eastern and in Western Christianity.[113] Thus, even in the Christian world professional magic both in its negative and its positive forms (which the church, unlike the state, did not separate and treat differently) remained the prerogative of the "professional of the sacred" as it had been already in Late Pharaonic Egypt, where the temple priests freelanced as sorcerers and healers.[114] Mediterranean constants die hard even when religious change is as momentous as in the Christianization of the ancient world.

Church and state

Amulets and paganism

This leads back to the different attitudes of church and state with regard to ritual healing and, to a lesser degree, harvest spells. One recalls that Augustine rejected both harmful sorcery (*goetia*) and harmless philosophical *theurgia* because they brought humans in contact with demons, whereas imperial legislation, as expressed in a rescript by Constantine, concerned itself only with preventing the damage done by sorcery to individuals and communities. Even if Augustine thought that the law also prohibited theurgy, as he claims in a somewhat allusive passage of the *City of God*, it is not clear on what he based this opinion – the only legal text he could have

---

[112] The name "Sethian" was given by the editor of the first comprehensive collection, Wünsch (1898); see now Gager (1992), 67 no. 13.

[113] Laodikeia, canon 36: Mansi 2.570. Agde, canon 78 (a. 506): *PL* 84.273A. *Collectio ii Decretorum Pontificum Romanorum collectioni I Dionysii Exigui addita*, canon 139, *PL* 67.168C. African synods: Munier (1974), 296 canon 110. See also Athanasius, *Syntagma ad monachos*, in Batiffol (1890), 122: γοητείας ἢ τὰ καλούμενα περίαπτά τε καὶ φυλακτήρια μήτε δρᾶν, μήτε ἑτέρων ποιεῖν βουλομένων εἰς αὐτὸν ἀνέχεσθαι "Not to perform acts of sorcery or the so-called attachments and amulets, nor to tolerate if someone else wants to do it for you."

[114] See Ritner (1993).

confidently relied upon was Constantius' very general prohibition of the *magi et Chaldaei*, where one could read *Chaldaei* as "theurgists."[115]

In the case of healing rituals, of which protective amulets were an integral part, there was an even greater distance between state and church. Constantine's protection of healing rites and harvest spells, accepted in both Codes, was far from being shared by the church fathers, who constantly and consistently opposed the use of amulets and healing spells. We are less well informed on the opposition to harvest incantations, not because they were less common but because, as a rural affair, they remained mostly outside the areas of concern for Christian teachers and theologians. Augustine shows once that he was aware of them, although in a somewhat oblique way. When, in interpreting a difficult verse of Psalm 70, he wanted to make a distinction between a bad profession and a bad professional, he introduced a farmer who was consulting a diviner to avert hailstorms and "God's tempests": this does not turn the farmer's profession into an ethical problem, Augustine explains, but only the single farmer, in the same way as the cheating merchant does not make the entire profession bad.[116] In Augustine's society, Christian farmers who employed ritual specialists to protect their harvests must have been about as common as cheating salesmen, but Augustine does not approve of either.

The disapproval of amulets and healing spells is much better attested, and not just in the fourth century with its outspoken fight against the survival of paganism. Already Clement of Alexandria rejected Christians "who trusted in sorcerers and accepted amulets and spells as helpful," instead of trusting in God's word alone.[117] The passage suggests how the association with sorcery (spells) could become harmful for amulets, even if this association was only regarded as a remnant from paganism; in later centuries, Christian thinkers almost automatically regarded amulets as part of sorcery.[118] In Christian thinking, heresy is not far away from sorcery: Epiphanius of Salamis lists among the books ascribed to the arch-heretic

---

[115] Clerc (1996) argues that *Chaldaei* here means theurgists; this might well be (see Aug. *Serm.* 189augm/26 Dolbeau, para. 36 and above n. 33), but Constantius' prohibition remained isolated and unnecessary: theurgists could always be tried under the laws against sorcery and/or divination; see the definitions in *CTh* 9.38.6 (Gratian, a. 381).

[116] Augustine, *In psalmum LXX enarratio (Sermo I)* 14.

[117] Clem. *Protr.* 11.115.2 (p. 81.14 Stählin): οἱ μὲν τοῖς γόησι πεπιστευκότες τὰ περίαπτα καὶ τὰς ἐποιδὰς ὡς σωτηρίους δῆθεν ἀποδέχονται. If he then talks about hanging the Gospel around one's neck, he either uses the verb metaphorically, or perhaps he thinks of tiny gospels used as amulets (see below).

[118] Most impressively Ephraem the Syrian, *Interrogationes et responsiones*, ed. Phrantzoles (1992), 89, among other execrations: Οὐαὶ τοῖς τὰ περίεργα ποιοῦσι, γοητείας καὶ μαντείας καὶ παιδοφθορίας καὶ περίαπτα, βάμματα καὶ πέταλα, ἅπερ ὀνομάζουσι φυλακτά, τῇ δὲ ἀληθείᾳ ὄντα φθορὰ καὶ

Mani a book about astrology, and adds: "They [*sc.* the Manichaeans] do not abstain from this unholy knowledge, rather their arrogance makes them interested in astrology and amulets (I mean those tied to one's body) and other forms of incantations and sorcery."[119] Philastrius, bishop of Brescia, who around 384 wrote a catalogue of heresies, condemned the use of incantations and amulets (*alligaturae et tutamina*) as remains of "pagan blindness," forbidden by God but still practiced by Jews.[120] Almost four centuries later, Boniface, the apostle of the Germans (died 754), complained about the same beliefs among his newly converted barbaric flock: they were relying on spells and oracles, believed in witches and werewolves, and were wearing amulets – all this was visibly idolatrous and Christianization had to eradicate it.[121] Yet Boniface spotted this not only among his Germans, but also in contemporary Rome: in a letter to pope Zachary that I discussed above, he complained that when his new Germanic Christians traveled to Rome, they would not only experience the ongoing carnival of the Kalendae Ianuariae but also see women who "in pagan fashion" were wearing amulets on their arms or legs; and amulets would even be for sale in the papal city – all this would quickly unravel his own missionary teaching.[122] The pope got the message and promised to Boniface to repress these customs – especially since they had been forbidden already by the fathers and more recently by his predecessor, Gregory III.[123]

Three centuries later, in the early eleventh century, Burchard, bishop of Worms 1000–1025, collected earlier canonical decisions in the twenty books of his influential *Decretum*; prohibitions of many rituals and

---

ἀπώλεια ψυχῆς καὶ σώματος ("Bad luck to those who practice the curious arts, sorcery, divination, child corruption, amulets, fringes and leaves that they call protection spells but that in reality destroy and ruin soul and body."). See also the *Ekloga*, the law collection that goes back to Leo III the Isaurian, where the condemnation of "those who make amulets with *charakteres*" immediately follows the condemnation of harmful magic.

[119] Epiphan. *Panarion* 2.66.13 (vol. 3 p. 35f. ed. Dummer, *CGS* 37): οὐ γὰρ ἀποδέουσι τῆς τοιαύτης περιεργίας· ἀλλὰ μᾶλλον αὐτοῖς ἐν προχείρωι καυχήματος κεῖται ἀστρονομία καὶ φυλακτήρια (φημὶ δὲ τὰ περίαπτα) καὶ ἄλλαι τινὲς ἐπωιδαὶ καὶ μαγγανεῖαι.

[120] *Liber de haeresibus* 21 (*PL* 12, 1132A). See also the *Liber de rectitudine catholicae conversationis* (*PL* 40.1169), ascribed in the Benedictine tradition to Augustine: *Ille itaque bonus christianus est, qui nulla phylacteria vel adinventiones diaboli credit, sed omnem suam spem in solo Christo ponit.* "This man is a good Christian who does not trust in any amulets or inventions of the devil but sets all his hope on Christ."

[121] Boniface, *Sermo* 6: *De capitalibus peccatis et praecipuis Dei praeceptis* (*PL* 89.855B).

[122] *Ep.* 49, to pope Zachary (a. 742; *PL* 89.747A = *MGH Epistulae: Epistolae Selectae* 1, no. 50, p. 301.8–27).

[123] Zacharias Papa, *Epistula* 2.6 (April 1, 734) (*PL* 89,921A), in *MGH Epistulae* among the letters of Boniface, *Epistolae Selectae* 1, no. 50, p. 304.32–305.7.

customs that his sources sometimes labelled as *ritus* or *consuetudo paganorum* run through his work, both the New Year rites and those of sorcery and divination.[124] The use of amulets is addressed in the final book, which Burchard called *Corrector vel Medicus* and where he decrees specific acts of penitence for misdeeds: the use of *phylacteria diabolica vel caracteres diabolicos* brings forty days of penitence with bread and water, that of *ligaturas et incantationes*, amulets and spells, penitence on all Christian holidays for two years.[125] All this material goes back to a sometimes long tradition. But Burchard claimed that the collection was destined "for the practical use of those who serve our Church," and modern scholars have accepted this claim as correct: there is thus not much doubt that these details not only reflect earlier rituals and customs, but also eminently those of his own time and place.[126] And when he (or his source) explains the eating of *idolothytum*, sacrificial meat with "offerings that happen in some places at graves, or at sources or trees or on crossroads," one senses in this explanatory note the intention to replace the anachronistic animal sacrifices in the Graeco-Roman world with more up-to-date Germanic rituals.[127]

Theology and amulets

But to describe the use of amulets as idolatrous and to associate it with sorcery, heresy, or Jewish rituals is to remain on the surface. Augustine offered a theologically more complex, although somewhat idiosyncratic analysis. He defined idolatry either as the worship of a part of the creation

---

[124] Both in the questions a bishop asks his congregation when opening a synod, *Decretum* 1.94 questions 42–44 (*PL* 140. 576AC) and in longer chapters in book 10 (*de incantatoribus et auguribus*) and 19 (*Corrector vel Medicus*). The Latin editio princeps of the *Decretum*, Cologne 1548, has been reprinted with supplements and an introduction by Fransen and Kölzer (1992); an independent Latin edition of the *Corrector* in Wasserschleben (1851), 624–982; English translation of the *Corrector* in McNeill and Gamer (1938) and Shinners (2007).

[125] *Ligaturas et incantationes PL* 140.961A = 644 no. 54 Wasserschleben (1851); *phylacteria diabolica vel caracteres diabolicos PL* 140.964B = 648 no. 80 Wasserschleben.

[126] *Ad necessarium Ecclesiae nostrae deservientium usum* ("for the practical use of those who serve our Church") in the overall introduction, PL 140.537A; the corrector *docet unumquemque sacerdotem, etiam simplicem, quomodo unicuique succurrere valeat* ("teaches all priests, even a simple one, how he could bring help to anybody"), PL 140.949A. Already Wasserschleben (1851), 90 claimed that the laws concerning superstition "aus dem Leben und der Praxis gegriffen zu sein scheinen, und ein charakteristisches Zeugnis der damaligen sittlichen und geistigen Kultur enthalten," taking the many traces of Germanic ritual terminology as a proof; for a much more thorough analysis with the same result see Austin (2009).

[127] *Corrector* (*Decretum* 19), PL 140 964C = 648 no. 82 Wasserschleben (1851): *Comedisti aliquid de idolothito, id est de oblationibus quae in quibusdam locis ad sepulcra mortuorum fiunt, vel ad fontes, aut ad arbores, aut ad lapides, aut ad bivia; idolothitum* is Jerome's Latinization of Paul's εἰδωλόθυτον, 1 Cor. 8:7, about the eating of which Paul was much more condoning than the later bishops.

instead of the creator, or to be in communication with demons. With this move, Augustine efficiently disqualified the entire complex of magic, divination, and amulets – "amulets that also the medical profession rejects," as he was quick to point out – without having to argue against each phenomenon separately.[128]

More often, Christian theologians argued somewhat differently. Typically, they said, people had recourse to amulets, incantations, and divination during a crisis in their lives, especially when they or members of their family fell ill.[129] Augustine pointed this out several times, as did others, and they insisted that a crisis was a test of faith, sent by God; to make use of forbidden practices instead of seeking his help in prayer was to turn away from him, to commit apostasy, the ultimate sin. "Believe me, brothers," thundered Ambrose in a sermon, "no-one is more guilty than the person who blasphemes and leaves God to worship idols; and no community can give up more than when it worships the demons and quits the Catholic church. Who despairs of God's mercy and does not believe in resurrection; who turns to augurs, lot-casters, soothsayers, seers and prophets, who trusts in amulets and magic signs (*charakteres*), in sneezing, bird-song, oracles and horoscopes or any other evil art: he will be damned."[130] In Alexandria, Athanasius made a similar argument: "If someone suffers from an incurable disease, he should pray: 'I say, Lord, have mercy upon me, heal my soul, because I sinned against you.' . . . Pray to the Lord, and he will heal you. Amulets and spells are useless remedies!" More importantly, they are not Christian: "For twenty obols or a quart of

---

[128] Main theoretical passage: *De doctrina Christiana* 2.20.30. On doctors and amulets, see the interesting passage in Alexander of Tralles where he yields to patients who cannot tolerate other methods of healing: Alexander of Tralles, lib. 12: *De podagra* (Puschmann vol. 2: 501–585): p. 579 ἐπειδή τινες οὔτε διαίτῃ προσκαρτερεῖν δυνάμενοι οὔτε φαρμακείαν ἀνέχεσθαι φυσικοῖς τε καὶ προσάπτοις ἀναγκάζουσι ἡμᾶς ἐπὶ ποδάγρας κεχρῆσθαι, ὥστε τὸν ἄριστον ἰατρὸν πανταχόθεν εὔπορον εἶναι καὶ πολυτρόπως βοηθεῖν τοῖς κάμνουσι, ἦλθον εἰς τοῦτο. πολλῶν δὲ ὄντων τούτων ἡμῖν δρᾶν πεφυκότων, τὰ πειραθέντα διὰ τῆς μακρᾶς πείρας γράφομεν. "Since some patients could not persist in a diet nor tolerate medication, they forced us to use spells and amulets against their gout in the feet; I went down this path because a very good doctor has to be on all accounts useful to his patients and help them in every way. And since there were many who made us do this, I write down what I have tried out in a risky attempt." Leg and feet ailments were among those sent by the gods as punishment and thus not curable by a doctor, according to the Phrygian Confession stelai: Petzl (1994), nos. 70, 89, 106.

[129] E.g. Augustine, *In psalmum L enarratio, sermo* i, 14 (*PL* 36. 887) or *Sermo* 286. 8.7 (*PL* 38.1300).

[130] Ambrose, *Sermo* 24.6 (*PL* 17.653B): *Firmiter mihi credite, fratres, quia nullus peiorem culpam habet, quam qui Deum blasphemans et derelinquens, idola colit: nec peior dissolutio esse potest in populo, quam quod daemonibus immoletur, et Ecclesiae catholicae derelinquantur: et qui de misericordia Domini desperat, et non credit in resurrectionem: et qui colunt augures, vel sortilegos, vel haruspices, divinos et praecantores, et qui confidunt in phylacteriis et characteribus, aut sternutationibus, avibus cantantibus, divinationibus, aut mathematicis, aut aliis quibuscumque malis artibus, damnabuntur.*

wine, the old woman will sing for you the spell of the snake – and you gape transfixed like a donkey, carrying on your neck the filth of animals, obliterating the seal of the Lord, the cross. This seal is feared not only by every illness, but also by the army of the demons: this is why a sorcerer remains unsealed."[131] Faith in the Lord and his cross should be enough; only sorcerers dedicate themselves to the demons, and they don't wear crucifixes.

In his teaching, John Chrysostom used similar arguments: "What would one say about those who use sorcery and amulets and tie bronze coins of Alexander the Great to their heads or feet? Tell me, is this what we hope after the cross and the death of our Lord, to pin our hopes for salvation on the image of a Greek king? ... And do you not only gain amulets for you but also spells, when you summon that drunken and crazy old woman into your house? Are you not ashamed of yourself?"[132] John continued his harangue with an important qualification: "When we censure these people and try to prohibit such things, they defend themselves by telling us that the woman who sings these spells is a good Christian and utters nothing else but the name of God."[133] Unlike Athanasius' old woman whose "spell of the snake" might have been a spell that was as traditionally Egyptian as some spells in the magical papyri, half a century later John's woman healer and her amuletic spells had turned entirely Christian and kept away from those pagan forms that made them an easy target of Christian accusations of idolatry. We saw in the case of the harvest spells how such a Christianization worked; the same is true for Christian amulets against illness, as many examples demonstrate. Here, too, one suspects that freelancing literary monks served as ritual experts.

---

[131] Athanasius, *Fragmenta* (PG 26, col. 1320): Ἐάν τις περιπέπτωκεν ἀνωμαλίᾳ δυσανιάτῳ, ψαλλέτω· "Ἐγὼ εἶπον, Κύριε, ἐλέησόν με, ἴασαι τὴν ψυχήν μου, ὅτι ἥμαρτόν σοι." ... εὔξαι Κυρίῳ, καὶ αὐτὸς ἰάσεταί σε. τὰ γὰρ περίαπτα καὶ αἱ γοητεῖαι μάταια βοηθήματα ὑπάρχουσιν. ... καταντλεῖ γάρ σοι γραῦς διὰ Κ ὀβολοὺς, ἢ τετάρτην οἴνου ἐπαοιδὴν τοῦ ὄφεως· καὶ σὺ ἕστηκας ὡς ὄνος χασμώμενος, φορῶν δὲ ἐπὶ τὸν αὐχένα τὴν ῥυπαρίαν τῶν τετραπόδων, παρακρουσάμενος τὴν σφραγῖδα τοῦ σωτηρίου σταυροῦ. ἣν σφραγῖδα οὐ μόνον νοσήματα δεδοίκασιν, ἀλλὰ καὶ πᾶν τὸ στῖφος τῶν δαιμόνων φοβεῖται καὶ τέθηπεν. ὅθεν καὶ πᾶς γόης ἀσφράγιστος ὑπάρχει.

[132] John Chrysostom, *Ad illuminandos catecheses* 1–2 (PG 49.240): Τί ἄν τις εἴποι περὶ τῶν ἐπῳδαῖς καὶ περιάπτοις κεχρημένων, καὶ νομίσματα χαλκᾶ Ἀλεξάνδρου τοῦ Μακεδόνος ταῖς κεφαλαῖς καὶ τοῖς ποσὶ περιδεσμούντων; αὗταί αἱ ἐλπίδες ἡμῶν, εἰπέ μοι, ἵνα μετὰ σταυρὸν καὶ θάνατον Δεσποτικὸν εἰς Ἕλληνος βασιλέως εἰκόνα τὰς ἐλπίδας τῆς σωτηρίας ἔχωμεν; ... οὐ περίαπτα δὲ μόνον, ἀλλὰ καὶ ἐπῳδὰς σαυτῷ περιάγεις, γραΐδια μεθύοντα καὶ παραπαίοντα εἰς τὴν οἰκίαν σου εἰσάγων· καὶ οὐκ αἰσχύνῃ οὐδὲ ἐρυθριᾷς;

[133] Ibid.: ὅταν γὰρ παραινῶμεν ταῦτα καὶ ἀπάγωμεν, δοκοῦντες ἀπολογεῖσθαί φασιν, ὅτι Χριστιανή ἐστιν ἡ γυνὴ ἡ ταῦτα ἐπᾴδουσα, καὶ οὐδὲν ἕτερον φθέγγεται, ἢ τὸ τοῦ Θεοῦ ὄνομα. See John Chrysostom, *In epistolam ad Collossenses homilia* (PG 62.357).

Compromises

In its opposition, the church fought an uphill battle. Since time immemorial, amulets were part of ancient medicine and remained so throughout and beyond antiquity. In a somewhat sarcastic list of medical procedures, Plato combines "technical" with "religious" medicine, drugs, burning, and cutting with spells and amulets: his wording suggests that spells and amulets belong to a different sphere than the rest; but they were all options that a sick person might have used.[134] This did not change through the centuries: when Libanius narrates the terrible accident that robbed his younger brother of his eyesight, he notes that the brother equally moved from "the hands of the doctors" through "medicines" to "amulets"; in the end, the patient rejected these techniques in favor of "altars, supplications, and the power of the gods."[135]

But not everybody approved of amulets and other irrational healing techniques, at least not among philosophers and doctors. If they allowed them, rationalists regarded them as means of last resort, not the least because they resisted explanation as much as other magical techniques.[136] With a sense of true piety that seems to be very close to the feelings of the Christian Fathers, Porphyry thought that holy people should not rely on them.[137] Although Augustine claimed that the teachings of the medical profession condemned all amulets and spells, the stance of doctors is more complex than this.[138] It does not come as a surprise that healers of the more irrational kind, such as Julius Africanus or an otherwise unknown Nepualios, recommended them, together with all other ritual techniques.[139] But even more serious doctors did not shy away from them. In

---

[134] Plato, *Rep.* 426AB: οὔτε φάρμακα οὔτε καύσεις οὔτε τομαὶ οὐδ' αὖ ἐπῳδαὶ αὐτὸν οὐδὲ περίαπτα οὐδὲ ἄλλο τῶν τοιούτων οὐδὲν ὀνήσει.

[135] Liban. *Or.* 1.201.

[136] Alexander of Aphrodisias, *De fato* 8, p. 174.20 (Bruns 1892, 164–212): ἄδηλα δὲ τὰ αἴτια ἀνθρωπίνῳ λογισμῷ ἐκείνων μᾶλλον ἃ κατά τινας ἀντιπαθείας γίνεσθαι πεπίστευται ἀγνοουμένης τῆς αἰτίας δι' ἣν γίνεται, ὁποῖα περίαπτά τέ τινα προσείληπται οὐδεμίαν εὔλογον καὶ πιθανὴν αἰτίαν τοῦ ταῦτα ποιεῖν ἔχοντα, ἔτι δὲ ἐπαοιδαὶ καί τινες τοιαῦται μαγγανεῖαι. "Obscure to human reasoning are rather the causes of those things which are believed to be in accordance with certain reactions, the cause through which they come to be being unknown, in the way that certain amulets are employed which have no reasonable and credible explanation for their acting in this way, also spells and certain trickeries of that sort." (Translation: R. W. Sharples, London: Duckworth, 1983.) The text is cited ap. Eusep. *Praep. Ev.* 6.9.24.

[137] Chaeremon, frg. 4 ap. Porph. *Abst.* 4.8, on Egyptian priests. For the opposite view see *Suid.* I 176, s.v. ἱερογραμματεῖς.

[138] Aug. *De Doctr. Christ.* 2.20.30.

[139] Recommendation: On Julius Africanus, see Thee (1984), 274–278; Nepualios: W. Gemoll, *Nepualii fragmentum* Περὶ τῶν κατὰ ἀντιπάθειαν καὶ συμπάθειαν *et Democriti* Περὶ συμπαθειῶν καὶ ἀντιπαθειῶν. Städtisches Realprogymnasium zu Striegau (1884), 1.

early Byzantine times, Alexander of Tralleis several times ended a list of cures with a reference to those amulets that in his experience were found to have some effect; in doing so, he relied on an illustrious predecessor, Archigenes – or rather, it seems, he followed in this the great Galen, who in turn had read Archigenes – "who is not just any doctor," as Galen wrote.[140] Even Galen, so much more rational than Alexander of Tralleis, did not entirely reject ritual healing. He was able to censure a predecessor, one Pamphilos, who wrote on plants and "used them for amulets and other hocus-pocus that is not just overwrought and outside the medical technique, but utterly wrong": for Galen, these are old wives' tales and Egyptian sorcery.[141] But at the same time, he read Archigenes' book on amulets against headaches and was willing to report from this book at least the things that made sense in medical terms, leaving aside only those items that "did not make medical sense to those who have tried them out."[142] When confronted with a famously difficult ailment such as headache, even scientific Greek doctors were willing to make a compromise, presumably because they understood the complex psychological problems to which chronic and incurable illnesses could lead.[143]

If even the science of doctors led them to make compromises with ailments they could neither understand nor cure, theological precision was even less capable of regulating the living tissue of human life. There remained gray areas between faith and the use of amulets and spells that even the bishops either quietly accepted or actively employed: the pressures

---

[140] Galen, *De compositione medicamentorum secundum locos* 2, vol. 12, p. 533 Kühn: ἐγένετο μὲν οὖν καὶ ὁ Ἀρχιγένης οὐ τῶν τυχόντων ἰατρῶν.

[141] Galen, *De simplicium medicamentorum temperamentis ac facultatibus* 6, vol. 11 p. 792 Kühn: ἐκεῖνος (Pamphilos) μὲν εἴς τε μύθους γραῶν τινας ἐξετράπετο καί τινας γοητείας Αἰγυπτίας ληρώδεις ἅμα τισὶν ἐπῳδαῖς, ἃς ἀναιρούμενοι τὰς βοτάνας ἐπιλέγουσι. καὶ δὴ κέχρηται πρὸς περίαπτα καὶ ἄλλας μαγγανείας οὐ περιέργους μόνον, οὐδ᾽ ἔξω τῆς ἰατρικῆς τέχνης, ἀλλὰ καὶ ψευδεῖς ἁπάσας: "This man turned to old wives' tales and frivolous Egyptian sorcery together with some spells used by those who extract plants. And it is used for amulets and other hocus-pocus that is not only futile and outside medical technique, but entirely false."

[142] Galen, *De compositione medicamentorum secundum locos* 2, vol. 12 p. 573 Kühn: Ἐπειδὴ δὲ καὶ περίαπτα τοῖς κεφαλαλγοῦσιν ἔγραψεν ὁ Ἀρχιγένης, ὅσα μὲν οὐδένα λόγον ἰατρικὸν ἔχει τοῖς πείρᾳ κεκρικόσι, ταῦτα παραλείπω κατά τινα θαυμαστὴν ἀντιπάθειαν ἄγνωστον ἀνθρώπῳ φάσκουσιν ἐνεργεῖν, ὅσα δὲ λόγον ἰατρικὸν ἔχει τῶν ὑπ᾽ Ἀρχιγένους γεγραμμένων ἐκλέξας ἐρῶ μόνα, κατὰ τὴν ἐκείνου λέξιν αὐτοῦ, καθάπερ ἄχρι δεῦρο περὶ τῶν φαρμάκων ἔπραξα: "Since Epigenes also wrote amulets for headaches that make no medical sense to those who have judged from practice, I leave them to those who claim that they have an effect according to some miraculous antipathy that is unknown to man, and having selected from among the writings of Archigenes the things that make medical sense, I will, following his own written word, talk only about what I did until now with drugs."

[143] Toothaches are another tricky problem, and here too Galen did not shy away from what we would call amulets: *De compositione medicamentorum secundum locos* 3, vol. 12 p. 874 Kühn.

of Christian life made them amenable to compromises. Augustine somewhat grudgingly accepted that some Christians pressed a gospel text against their heads to mitigate a headache instead of simply suffering and praying, and that some thought that this deserved praise when compared to the alternative, the use of an amulet; although he did not object to such a use of the sacred book, he read it as proof that many in his own society were still using amulets.[144] To make use of the sacred scripture to avert evil could make religious sense, and it narrowly avoided the accusation of idolatry even in Augustine's own definition: although the Bible as an object was part of the creation, yet it contained the very words of the creator, and the counter-spell was not the book, but the words contained in it. Augustine's Western contemporaries who suffered from headaches were not alone in this belief. John Chrysostom tells us that women and children in Antioch hung tiny copies of the gospel as protective amulets around their necks; he tolerated it as grudgingly as Augustine tolerated the use of the gospel against headaches.[145] Somewhat less hesitatingly, Isidore of Pelusium remarked on the same custom in Coptic Egypt: "magic" was less offensive in Egypt.[146]

But the search for healing did not stop with the use of the Bible, where one could argue that God's revealed word was much more powerful than any other utterance. Without flinching, Gregory the Great sent an amulet (*phylacta*) to the Langobardian king Aduolouvaldus; it consisted of a cross made from wood of the true cross and a gospel text "in a Persian box": this precious gift should flatter the powerful king.[147] Even if Gregory might have condescendingly assumed that such objects would delight barbarians only (but he never says so), he still was willing to go along with it. More importantly, here "amulet" comes close to "relic" – a piece of matter that had experienced closeness to God and that therefore could be exempted from the Augustinian prohibition on worshipping the creation. The other

---

[144] Aug. *In Ioanni evangelium tractatus* 7.12 (*PL* 35.1443).
[145] John Chrysostom, *Hom. de statuis* 19.4 (*PG* 49. 196).
[146] Isidore of Pelusium, *Letters* 2.150 (*PG* 78.604 C).
[147] Greg. *Ep.* 14.12 (PL 77. 1316A; *MGH Epistolae 2: Gregorii I papae registrum epistolarum. Libri VIII–XIV*, Berlin 1899): *excellentissimo autem filio nostro Adulouvaldo regi transmittere phylacta* [vl. *phylacteria*, given as text in *PL*, rejected in *MGH*] *curavimus, id est crucem cum ligno sanctae crucis Domini, et lectionem sancti Evangelii theca Persica inclusam.* "We arranged that a protective object [amulet] was sent to our most excellent son, king Adolouvaldus, a cross made from the wood of the Holy Cross and a reading from the Holy Gospel in a Persian box." The textual problem concerns only the question of whether the pope used a technical term with a long pre-Christian history, *phylacteria*/φυλακτήριον, or an otherwise unattested term with the same meaning ("protective object"); it does not change the fact that he sent the king a protective object and not just the word of God.

Gregory, the contemporary bishop of Tours, went one step further. A boy in Gregory's entourage fell ill, and without Gregory's knowledge, his people had summoned a diviner: "He murmurs spells, throws lots, hangs amulets around his neck" – he does everything that God and his bishops had prohibited. It should not surprise that the boy got much worse. When finally Gregory noticed all this, he was furious and ordered dust from Julian's grave to be brought to him: the boy drank it in water, and healing did not tarry.[148] This is only one small step beyond the horse-racing magic performed by Jerome's Hilarion of Gaza:[149] stories like these must be part of a discourse among the Fathers about the limits of healing rites.

A stipulation in the Byzantine *Eklogai*, the collection of laws organized by Zeno II the Isaurian, reveals another compromise. The section on sorcery that we already touched upon above contains a law on amulets or rather on the maker of amulets: it orders that any person "who makes amulets with *charakteres*," magical signs, should be flogged.[150] Agreeing with Ambrose's condemnation of amulets and *charakteres*,[151] but modifying the bishops' prohibition on ecclesiastics making amulets, the law punishes only the fabrication of those amulets that contain the strange signs that are known from the magical papyri but that survive well into the Middle Age and beyond. They still defy our understanding, although it is obvious that they somehow served to attract demons, as an alternative to the powerful name.[152]

A similar discourse is visible in another somewhat unexpected place. The so-called *Decretum Gelasianum de libris recipiendis et non recipiendis* is a document attributed to pope Gelasius I (492–496) or Hormisdas (514–520). It lists the books – biblical and otherwise – that the Church accepted or rejected as canonical. After the thorough and still valid study of Ernst von Dobschütz, the list is the work of private scholarship ("gelehrte Privatarbeit"), despite its high-sounding ascription to a pope; it was written in the sixth century but must contain material that went as far back as pope Gelasius.[153] The list of apocryphal books ends with magical and heretical

---

[148] Greg. Turon. *Libri miraculorum* 2.45 (PL 71.825C). [149] Hieron. *V. Hilarionis* 11.
[150] *Ecloga Aucta*: Simon and Troianos (1977), 58–74, no. 23: Οἱ τὰ περίαπτα ἔχοντα χαρακτῆρας ποιοῦντες τυπτέσθωσαν; the same as no. 40 in *Ecloga Aucta Privata*: Zepos and Zepos (1931), 12–47.
[151] Ambrosius, *Sermo* 24.6.
[152] An overview in Bohak (2008), 270–274; a beautiful example from late fifth- or early sixth-century Apameia in Syria in Gager (1992), 56 no. 6, another from the third century(?) in Istanbul in Jordan (1978). We urgently need a lexicon of these signs that appear in tablets of the Roman Age and survive until early modern Europe.
[153] Dobschütz (1912).

writings: an unknown treatise ascribed to Solomon,[154] *phylacteria*, and the writings of Simon Magus and other heretics (yet another indication of how closely late antique Christian thought associated heresy and magic). The passage on the phylacteries states:[155]

> Phylacteria omnia quae non angelorum, ut illi confingunt, sed daemonum magis nominibus conscripta sunt: apocrypha.
>
> Apocryphal: all phylacteries, if they are not written in the name of what they think to be the angels but of demons.

The document thus accepts all the amulets written in the name of angels, even if its author seems to realize the strangeness of some of the angels' names that are legitimized by the context of the better-known names, such as Gabriel or Uriel. By ascribing this text to one of the popes, the Catholic tradition was able to retain amulets like the ones we saw used for agrarian protection: in the long run, it was the pragmatism manifested in Constantine's magic law and not the rigidity of the church fathers that won the day.

---

[154] In the main recension *Scriptura quae appellatur Salomonis Interdictio*, in other traditions *Salomonis Contradictio*; neither title is otherwise attested, but either would make sense for a collection of exorcisms, building on the fame of Jewish exorcists. Dobschütz (1912), 316 is vague: "wohl der Titel eines Zauberbuches."

[155] Dobschütz (1912), 57f., l. 333–335.

EPILOGUE

The persistence of festivals and the end of sacrifices

The trajectory of this book has led us from the revival of festival traditions in the Greek cities in the first two centuries of the Imperial epoch to the celebration of Lupercalia and Kalendae in Byzantium under Justinian and later. What started as an inquiry into the festival culture of Greece and Asia Minor in the Imperial age and the reception of Roman city festivals in the cities of the Mediterranean East increasingly has become an investigation of some aspects of the religious transformation of the Eastern Mediterranean in the first five centuries CE, the ways in which this transformation was reflected in the urban festival culture and how this culture contributed to the change, and how the radical determination to change and innovate interacted with the need to follow or revive the traditions that determined identity; it also has become clear that the dichotomy of tradition versus innovation does not even roughly correspond to obvious dichotomies such as pagan versus Christian or emperors versus bishops. Almost inevitably, the focus of these studies was on the elites of cities and empire and their normative apex, the emperors and bishops of the later Roman Empire. Even when looking at two areas – dream healing and magic – where less exalted individuals, their actions, and their desires became more visible than in the realm of collective festivals, the reaction of the norm-giving elite, of imperial law-givers or censuring bishops, allowed us a glance into the world of the individual, and reflected this world in the various attempts at norm-giving, as in a multiplicity of mirrors, some clear, some opaque, and some distorting. It is time to pull in the loose threads and to weave the isolated strands of my narrative together. Two questions will serve as a coagulant for the many individual data and observations: Why did festivals survive, despite the onslaught of generations of bishops and their collective outcries? And how does this intersect with the problem made prominent in two independent investigations, namely the end of sacrifice, discussed in Guy Stroumsa's lectures at the Collège de France and in Maria-Zoe Petropolou's Oxford dissertation?[1]

The tenacity of festivals

The surprising resilience of festival traditions was visible from the start of this inquiry, in the way Epameinondas of Akraiphia renewed the local Ptoia, or how the Athenians in the Severan age regulated the procession during the Mysteria. Invented traditions and conscious innovations worked together to enhance the visual splendor of these rituals, in which the city presented itself to itself and to all the foreigners who cared to look and participate or who, like Vibius Salutaris in Ephesos, made their own contribution to the splendor. This revival of urban pride after the troubled period between the Mithridatic Wars and Nero's emancipation of all Greeks offered outstanding members of the civic elite large areas where they could contribute to their city's image and well-being, not the least by lavishly feeding citizens and foreign guests alike with the meat of the sacrifices and with whatever else took their fancy. The revival of the old splendor never was a simple restoration: even outside the field of consciously or unconsciously invented traditions, the city festivals helped to define the new world in which these independent Eastern cities operated and where Rome, its emperor, and its governor played a crucial role. Beyond the straightforward and well researched imperial cult, this new order expressed itself in more subtle ways, as demonstrated by the program of Salutaris' processions in Ephesos or the donation to celebrate a parallel series of Roman and local birthdays in Cretan Gortyn.

The city festivals of Rome that begin to become visible in the second century outside of Rome fit this pattern. The Kalendae and Saturnalia in Iudaea Palaestina or, attested not much later, in Tertullian's Carthage were first and foremost festivals celebrated by the Roman garrisons and the *municipia* implanted in conquered soil, to live and affirm their own Roman life regardless of their foreign surroundings.[2] Like the festivals celebrated in Rome itself, they were moments of lavish sacrifices and extravagant eating, drinking, and entertainment; exuberant merrymaking through the city streets was sometimes part of it.

---

[1] Stroumsa (2005); Petropoulou (2008); Heyman (2007) focuses on the opposition between emperor cult and cult of Christ and the martyrs. On the changes in time perception and organization see some of the sketches in Saggioro (2005), especially di Berardino (2005), 106–109 and Piccaluga (2005).

[2] See the overview of Ando (2003) and the reservations of Segenni (2007).

When a festival gave rise to a fair, such as the Saturnalia fair at Lykopolis/Beth Shean, it was attracting the people of the countryside and of neighboring cities, Romans, Greeks, and Jews alike. In most cases it remains unclear who took the initiative to start such a fair on the local level; but the Roman governor had to grant it to whoever had come up with the idea: thus local elites and Roman administrators had to work together.[3]

On these occasions, the borderlines between "idolatry" and permitted social interaction began to wear thin for Jews and Christians alike, unlike when people were "sitting down in temples" to dine on the slaughtered animals, with the altar still smoking nearby and the divine image looking out through the open temple doors. When groups of kin or neighbors were celebrating banquets and gift-exchange in the privacy of their houses, often temporarily obliterating the social hierarchies, as happened at the Kalendae or the Matronalia, the Christians in Carthage – or for that matter, I imagine, the Jews in Iudaea-Palaestina – were heavily tempted to join the celebration, to accept the invitation from pagan friends and neighbors, or, more exclusively if they felt more strongly about religious borderlines and idolatrous food, to come together for these festivals in a purely Christian or Jewish household and in their own way, without the pagan ritual paraphernalia. Already Paul in Corinth realized that at social gatherings and banquets diaspora Jews and Christians could not always reject an invitation from a friendly neighbor or non-Christian kinsman, and he provided his addressees with rules of behavior that, at least with regard to meat, amounted to a "don't ask don't tell" compromise. This allowed all possible forms of shared meals except the manifest "sitting down to a meal in a heathen temple" with which only Paul personally had no problems but that irked less self-assured Jews or Christians.[4] The members of the two guilds in Phrygian Hierapolis that in the early third century came together at Passover, Pentecost, and the Kalendae to crown the grave of a Jewish couple, on the other hand, would have known exactly what the diaspora Jew Paul was talking about. This turned into a problem in the heated atmosphere of the later fourth century with its increasing need to draw sharp boundaries, and an aggressively polemical observer such as the Manichean Faustus could easily turn participation against the mainstream Christians and their claims about themselves.

---

[3] On some of the conflicts in such a process see De Ligt (1993), 199–240.
[4] 1 *Cor.* 8–10. See Marshal (1987), 290–291.

Reasons for survival

Several factors helped this double transfer and adaptation, from the *urbs* to the *polis* and from the "idolaters" to the "just," be they Jewish or Christian.

Encounters and identity

One was the inherent nature of festivals as spaces of enjoyment and social encounter. In their eagerness to draw sharp boundaries, rabbis and bishops continuously underrated this basic human need – most famously perhaps Augustine and his fellow bishops who tried to impose a period of fasting during the Kalendae. They could have learned from the more thoughtful Origen, had they been open to a more nuanced approach. Kelsos had suggested that Christians should feel no hesitation to participate in public festivals since they shared with pagans the basic understanding of divinity – that "god is the god of all alike; he is good, he stands in need of nothing, and he is without jealousy."[5] Origen responds to this tricky invitation by pointing out the duality of human nature: the human body is in need of the pleasures and relaxation that the festivals provide, whereas the human soul, if purified, is permanently with god, celebrates permanently, and thus would not need a special festival day.[6] But the pure are a minority; the rest, ordinary humans, are in the quandary that they need festivals although they should not need them. This explains why the ascetic solution proposed by John Chrysostom or Augustine never was as realistic and as lasting as Origen's compromise, Christian festivals for the less pure souls ("Sundays, Paraskevi, Easter, Pentecost"), has become the reality of Christian life.

Not all new festivals were radically new; some successfully replaced problematical older festivals, in the same way as relics or the use of gospel texts replaced rejected amulets. The Brumalia combined with the Twelve Days of Christmas efficiently eclipsed the Saturnalia, but, interestingly enough, did not remove the Kalendae and Vota, not even in Byzantium, where the Court celebrated the Twelve Days with daily dinner invitations while the city people danced on the streets at the Kalendae and Vota. Nor did the placement of the Jerusalem Encaeniae in the period between Rosh Hashana and Sokkut have a lasting impact on the Jewish festivals, except perhaps for converted Jews. But the replacement strategy was used less often than modern scholars have imagined, despite the idea of Augustine to turn pagan festivals into saints' days.[7] The Lupercalia was never replaced by

---

[5] Kelsos ap. Origen, *Contra Celsum* 8.21; see Dihle (1992), 328–329.
[6] Origen, *Contra Celsum* 8.22–23. [7] Aug. *Ep.* 29.9.

the Christian *Purificatio Mariae*, nor did Christmas replace an imaginary festival of Sol; Easter and Pentecost found their dates independently from the pagan festival calendar.[8]

A second factor was the ability of festivals to express and create local or translocal identities, and the human need for such identities. The wish to belong to Carthage and to celebrate the common Matronalia in the same way as all the neighbors did could be stronger than the wish to stand out as a Christian, and not all Christians were willing to pay for their religious choice with the loss of local identity, or were able to cling to their new, Christian identity alone. And once everybody was Christian, it did not matter anyway, and one could just go on with celebrating what one had celebrated all the time, to the revulsion of some more radical bishops.[9]

Festival names
A third factor was the fact that some festival names lent themselves better to this sort of globalization than others. Most often, a Greek or Roman festival name contained the name of a divinity – Artemisia and Panathenaia, Cerialia or Neptunalia. A few names, such as Kalendae (Ianuariae) or Matronalia, were neutrally descriptive names: they concern the beginning of January or the honors of the *matronae*. In his poem "On the Festivals of Rome," *De feriis Romanis*, Ausonius, the Christian aristocrat from Bordeaux, is aware of both of these possibilities: in his somewhat nostalgic and antiquarian verses, he easily juxtaposed *Vulcani dies* and "the rites the *matronae* perform to praise their husbands," the festivals of Mercurius and Diana, and the one that recalled the expulsion of the tyrants.[10] Emperors or their advisors understood the political possibilities of these descriptive names. In a very conscious decision, Hadrian changed the name Parilia to *Natalis Urbis* and made the festival accessible to an empire outside of but dependent on the *urbs*: out in the empire, at best a few learned men had ever heard of the Italian goddess Pales, but it could seem a good thing to celebrate the birthday of the Ruling City. But this was an exceptional decision that had to do with a politically important cult that served to ritually express the unity of the empire, as did Kalendae and Vota; and it is no coincidence that the initiative was that of the most Hellenizing emperor with a clear imperial outlook.

---

[8] On Christmas and the cult of Sol see Förster (2007).
[9] In the Latin West, Burchard of Worms (early eleventh century) still instructed the bishops to ask what festivals were celebrated, *Corrector* 94 interrogatio 72 (PL 140.578C).
[10] Ausonius, *Eclogae* (14) 16 Hall.

A parallel case demonstrates how well such functional names could survive because of their openness to interpretation: it concerns a festival known only from the Latin West, the "Day of Torches," *dies lampadarum* (or *lampadis*), celebrated on June 24, that does not appear before the mid-fourth century. In the calendar of 354, a torch is depicted among the symbols of June, and the epigram that explains the image describes the torch as a sign for the mature sheaves of Ceres' wheat (*lampas maturas Cereris designat aristas*). Stern connected the torch with the *dies lampadarum*, attested in several late sources for June 24, whereas the codex calendar on this day only notes the solstice.[11] The festival is attested by Fulgentius, who connects it with the torches that Ceres used to search for her daughter, with her joy of finding her, and with the torch as a symbol of the Summer solstice.[12] Christians connected it with John the Baptist, whom they celebrated on June 24 by lighting torches and celebrating the day with singing, dancing, and feasting, according to a newly found anonymous Latin sermon from fifth- or sixth-century Africa.[13] The anonymous preacher has no problems with this (and unwittingly proves the point of the Manichaean Faustus that there was no real difference between mainstream Christians and pagans) – unlike Augustine, who rejects the celebration as a relic of paganism and stresses in his detailed description not the joy and light but the dark smoke of the torches.[14] It is obvious from the other Christian testimonies that Augustine's severe radicalism did not stop the festival (although he had the law on his side, at least after 407), and its name with its polysemic symbol let it easily be adapted by Christians on all levels of meaning, agricultural, astronomical, and theological.[15]

Another strategy for neutralizing the festival names must have been inspired by the success of the Kalendae: some festival names simply expressed calendrical or seasonal time. The *dies lampadarum*, as we just saw, had a seasonal and calendrical aspect, combining two emotionally charged moments, the Summer Solstice and the beginning of the annual grain harvest. The substitution of the Saturnalia by the Brumalia – a rearrangement of the festival calendar, not just a change of name – was such a move as well. It must have happened after the founding of the New Rome in 330 CE and involved a double change of tradition – to expand the

---

[11] Stern (1953), 252–258; Salzman (1991), 91–92.   [12] Fulgentius, *Mitologiae* 1.10–11.
[13] Published by Dolbeau and Étaix (2003), with an introduction that presents the evidence for the *dies lampadarum* that goes well beyond Stern (1953).
[14] Aug. Serm. 293B 5.
[15] On another case, where Augustine refers to *recentissimae leges* (Aug. *Ep.* 91.8), see di Berardino (2005), 98–99; the law in question is Honorius' rescript of Nov. 15 (25), 407, *CTh* 16.10.19.

one-day household festival of the Bruma into a series of twenty-three public festival days, outdoing the lengthy Saturnalia, and to change the unusual name Bruma, acceptable in an informal festival of the local households, into the more typical festival name Brumalia. Date and agents of these changes are unknown. One can imagine that the foundation of Constantinople brought with it a rethinking of the festival calendar: in this new situation, the calendar had on the one hand to guarantee and express the traditional Roman identity of the new city, on the other hand to demonstrate the presence of the Christian faith in its ideological fabric as well. We do not know whether this was a one-time decision or a long-drawn-out process. The rejection of Saturnus by the church was still a living memory for John Lydus under Justinian: this might exclude a mid-fourth century date for the change and argue for a long-drawn-out process.

The flip side of this strategy is that in the Christian empire, the bishops were at pains to detect even in the most neutral festival names a trace of idolatry by exploiting the regular connection between a festival and a pagan divinity. Pope Gelasius found the shadowy god Februus (or an invented Februarius) in the Lupercalia, in a construction that was as unjustified as it was artificial. In the same way, the Byzantine theologians in Trullo and after connected the Vota with the Arcadian Pan and the Brumalia with ecstatic Dionysos; the pagans now were the Ἕλληνες, so the gods had to be those they knew from reading their Greek classics. To assign a festival to a specific divinity is a mental habit deeply familiar to scholars and hard to eradicate, even after the realization of how questionable it is. Books on Greek festivals, such as Deubner's *Attische Feste* or Graf's *Nordionische Kulte*, in a handy classification still arrange the festivals according to the divinities, and some modern Byzantine scholars have followed their theological ancestors in their attribution of the Vota and Brumalia to Dionysos and Pan.

Christian festival names, by the way, could be similarly non-committal. Easter, Pascha, the oldest festival, adopted the Jewish name attested in the Gospels: but this remains the exception. Epiphany, the name for the Eastern nativity festival, was semantically charged during centuries of Greek vocabulary: since Hellenistic times, the ἐπιφάνεια of the θεὸς ἐπιφανής, the "manifestation" of the "helping divinity," is constitutive of gods and godlike kings – this background resonates with Christians as well, although the reinterpretation of the festival after the dating of the nativity on December 25 attenuated this meaning. The names of two other major festivals were simply numerals: *tesserakoste* (*quadragesimae post Pascha* in Egeria) for the fortieth day after Easter, in the West the celebration of

Christ's ascension, in Jerusalem a festival day of somewhat vaguer contours; and *pentekoste* (*quinquagesimae*), the fiftieth day after Easter, for the descent of the Holy Spirit and in Jerusalem the ascension. In a pluralistic religious environment, on the marketplace of religions that existed for most of the fourth century, these vaguely defined names must have been more attractive than well-defined "brand-names."

It is less easy to assess how much the imperial protection of Kalendae and Vota helped their survival; an alternative view would be to suspect that Theodosius and his successors backed festivals that had such deep popular support that they would have survived against whatever opposition. In a way, the same question can be asked with regard to the imperial protection of agrarian magic that survived into Christian times: did they survive because of this protection, or did the emperor react to a deeply ingrained urge to rely on such protective rites that assured their survival? The survival of amulets to protect one's person might help to formulate an answer. These rituals were in a legal limbo: the prohibition of magic did not concern them, nor did the guarantee of agrarian protective rituals help them, or only very indirectly. The church rejected them unanimously, and not just after Constantine. But they survived into the Middle Ages, protected again by the same over-arching need for superhuman protection when scientific medicine gave out that also helped the resurgence of incubation; this ritual too had not been touched by imperial legislation. Thus, at least with private rituals, imperial protection did not really matter for their survival – but if a ritual was performed under the umbrella of an institution, as was the case for the Kalendae, this certainly helped.

The spread of neutral festival names is far from innocent, however. As Mona Ozouf has shown in her classical work on the festivals of the French Revolution, the revolutionaries radically rethought the function of festivals, abolished the traditional Christian festivals and created new ones in order to give expression to the new society that was being invented.[16] These festivals all had descriptive names, such as "Fête de la Jeunesse," or "Fête des Époux," or "Agriculture." At the same time, they were all consciously anchored in the seasonal structure of the year: the Festival of Youth was celebrated in early Spring, on Germinal 10 (i.e. March 29 or 30); the Festival of Married Couples a month later during the flower season, on Floréal 10; Agriculture at the start of the harvest season, Messidor 10 (i.e. June 28 or 29). Season and society became metaphors of each other. Imperial Rome and Byzantium did not go as far as this, but the function

---

[16] Ozouf (1976).

of festivals as expressions of the season was well known. This helps to understand the career of Bruma and Brumalia as a seasonally anchored festival with a descriptive name: there must have been a similar will to "secularize," or rather to make the festival palatable in a Christian state; "secularization," in this context, is a somewhat misleading term because it implies a conscious opposition and even rejection of religion, which certainly was not what motivated whoever introduced the Brumalia to Byzantium. A comparable strategy was at work in the Byzantine transformation of the Lupercalia ritual: we saw that it was reinterpreted as a Spring festival, with the young man whom I understand as a transformation of the Luperci expressing the youthful vigor of the season, in a metaphor that comes very close to the French Revolution's move.

This should remind us that the conscious tying of a festival to the season is far from being a feature of the archaic religion of primeval farmers, whatever James G. Frazer imprinted onto the newly urbanized Western consciousness. It is mostly a recent and secondary intellectual move in order to free the festivals from their religious ballast and to make them acceptable in a new religious framework, not a survival of early agricultural societies. The classification of festivals as spring festival and autumn festival in the Hittite cult inventories could follow another but equally modern logic: they might well describe the local festivals that the king had to attend from the perspective of the classifying palace scribes.[17]

Festivals and gods

There is another insight to gain – or rather a confirmation of what we should have known anyway. Gods can disappear from festivals but the festivals themselves remain or undergo minor changes. If push comes to shove, the gods reveal themselves as less well anchored in the collective hearts and minds than ritual group experience. What counts to the celebrating people is the celebration as such, the ritual acts, not the divine recipient – despite the fact that many festival names derive from the name of a god, and that the intellectual reflection centers on the gods, as Ovid's *Fasti* show even to a superficial reader.[18] This is different from what we saw happen in incubation. There, the ritual acts themselves disappeared, with only the core belief surviving, that dreams can be a window to a

---

[17] Hazenbos (2003); a summary in Hazenbos (2004).
[18] This reacts to statements such as that of Fraschetti (2005), 124: "I *ludi* e i *dies festi* a Roma e nel mondo romano non sono semplici festività, ma si intendevano supratutto come celebrazioni in onore degli dei."

superhuman, helpful world. Unlike the collective festivals, pagan individual incubation was so closely tied to an institution that the disappearance of the institution made the ritual disappear, only to be recreated in a different form by the underlying driving constant.

In a related move, pagan ritual language and its innovations and developments in later antiquity lent themselves to the inventors of a Christian urban liturgy in fourth-century Jerusalem that became the model for Rome and Constantinople. Processions, present in urban ritual since the Bronze Age cultures of the Near East, became a major tool to express Christian theological and political messages in the recently Christianized space of Jerusalem;[19] the growing length of festivals during the Imperial age accommodated equally long Christian festivals, some of which added an octave, an entire special week, to their main day. In this way even the Easter period that lasted (not counting the Lent period) from Palm Sunday to the Sunday after Easter or even, as the counting of days suggests, until the fiftieth day, Pentecost, follows models that were present in the religious culture of the late Imperial age. The custom of modern European Protestants of adding Boxing Day or the Monday of Easter and Pentecost to the festival period appears just as an extreme attenuation of this tradition.

Bottom up and top down

We noticed that there is a good reason to assume that Kalendae and Saturnalia of the first and second centuries spread from garrisons and *coloniae* outwards, without any intervention from the emperors or the provincial governors, whereas at least the name change from Parilia to Natalis Urbis made me assume a central decision; but the adoption of this festival in an individual city again remained the decision of the city, not the result of pressure from the center. On the other hand, the introduction of the Brumalia in Constantinople and the reinterpretation of the Lupercalia in Byzantine court ceremonial could only be a central decision, as was Theodosius' decision to declare Kalendae, Vota, and Natalis Urbis as days without legal business; the changes that affected the Lupercalia in Rome before Gelasius' time, however, could again only be caused by local forces and actors, presumably approved or even instigated by the Roman senate, but without any imperial intervention.

---

[19] See for the Near East Pongratz-Leisten (1994); on the *longue durée* in the Roman world, Wickham (2005), 619.

There is thus not one bottom-up or top-down movement, but individual developments according to place and time that defy a unifying description. There remains the question of what prompted emperors to intervene as innovators or protectors of such festivals, both in the pre-Christian centuries and even more so after Constantine, against continuing resistance and objection by powerful individual preachers such as John Chrysostom or Augustine, and by the many local councils in East and West that often seem to repeat a predecessor's canons, and what made their interventions successful or not.

The question is easier to answer for the second and third centuries than for Christian late antiquity. The emperors between Nerva and Caracalla – and, in a somewhat idiosyncratic way, already Nero – were concerned with the unity of the empire and realized the potential of festivals to create such an imperial ideology.[20] Besides the festivals of the imperial cult – accession days, anniversaries of emperors, members of the imperial family, and of signal events – other festivals could fulfill a similar purpose, such as Vota, Kalendae, or Natalis Urbis. Some of the emperors might have also been acutely aware that this mission was better accomplished if it provided the citizens with entertainment and relaxation: this must be the deeper reason why Hadrian founded so many contests all over Greece and helped the Guild of Itinerant Stage Artists of Dionysos against local moves to abolish games and contests to save money.[21]

In this respect, my analysis corrects Jörg Rüpke's claim that "religious practices did not create the empire."[22] Agreed, the festivals did not create the empire; but they helped to hold it together by suggesting a unity well beyond the administrative structures that always could be debated, changed, or rejected. With the exception of the moralists – who might well have a political agenda as well, as the Palestinian rabbis did – nobody argued about festivals.

For Christian late antiquity, Nicole Belayche tried to sketch a tentative answer to the same question.[23] Starting from two pre-Constantinian acclamations from Cyprus, one to Constantius Chlorus, the other to Maximianus, that praise them as "origin of public joy and all ceremonies" (*laetitiae publicae caerimoniarumque omnium auctori*), she generalized this role of the emperors for the fourth and fifth centuries.[24] She

---

[20] See e.g. Ando (2007).   [21] Petzl and Schwertheim (2006).
[22] Rüpke (2011), 243: "Nicht die religiösen Praktiken schufen das Reich, sondern das Reich schuf die 'Religion'."
[23] Belayche (2007); see also Dihle (1992).
[24] Pouilloux, Roesch, and Marcillet-Jaubert (1987), nos. 130 and 131; Belayche (2007), 44.

finds confirmation in a rescript of Constantius to the prefect of Rome, written in 342:[25]

> Although all superstition has to be totally eradicated, we nevertheless want the temples that are outside the city walls to remain intact and undamaged. Since some of them were the origin of circus games and athletic contests, one should not destroy what offers to the Roman people the celebration of traditional pleasure.

The circumstances under which this decree was issued confirm Belayche's insight and demonstrate the tensions to which all the emperors saw themselves being subjected, well beyond the fourth century. The decree reacts to the much more radical decree of 341 with which Constantius harshly and in surprisingly emotional language ordered the acting Pretorian Prefect to terminate all sacrifices, and with them the traditional festivals: *cesset superstitio, sacrificiorum aboleatur insania*.[26] One senses popular protests in Rome against the attempts of the imperial authorities to take away all the entertainment in the name of Christianity. The Urban Prefect asked the emperor for help, and Constantius (or his advisers) reacted with the insight that he had gone too far: the Roman people – both, narrowly, the people of Rome and, more generally, the subjects of the emperor – needed the pleasures of the traditional festivals, and they expected the emperor to guarantee it. Constantius retracted in a way that saved his face: the law of 342 on the surface dealt not with spectacles and games but with sanctuaries; the *solemnitas voluptatum* entered only in a somewhat circuitous way. But still, the emperor recognized the need of his people for joyful moments and guaranteed them.

Although Theodosius' decision to free the Kalendae and Votae from legal business – a decision made in the city of Rome forty-five years after Constantius' self-correction – sets itself into a different tradition, the tradition of the good emperor who cares for the smooth function of the law courts, Theodosius might well have been aware of this other tradition and could even have profited from Constantius' experience. And even if this was not Theodosius' intention in August 389, the outcome of his legislation was that it protected the Kalendae and Vota against the episcopal attempts to do away with them and with the widespread *prisca voluptas*

---

[25] *CTh* 16.10.3 *Quamquam omnis superstitio penitus eruenda sit, tamen volumus, ut aedes templorum, quae extra muros sunt positae, intactae incorruptaeque consistant. Nam cum ex nonnullis vel ludorum vel circensium vel agonum origo fuerit exorta, non convenit ea convelli, ex quibus populo Romano praebeatur priscarum sollemnitas voluptatum.*

[26] *CTh* 16.10.2, to the acting Praetorian Prefect. On these two decrees see Gaudemet, Siniscalco, and Falchi (2000), 29–30.

the people of the empire gained from them, as John Chrysostom, Augustine, and other irascibly ascetic bishops were quick to realize. Ten years after the Rome edict – well after his repeated prohibition of animal sacrifice, but more aware of the consequences than Constantius had been – Honorius explicitly protected public festivals, be they pagan or Christian, because they brought *communis laetitia*, "good cheer to all." Shortly before this, Augustine had succeeded in abolishing the *laetitia*, the public banquet, for Saint Leontius in Hippo as being a pagan remnant.[27] For his line of argument, revelry – be it as Christian as it might be – was no more than disguised paganism.

That is: imperial involvement was a constant in the entertainment culture, well beyond Hadrian's direct intervention, and it had sound political reasons that in the Christian empire sometimes antagonized the bishops. New contests were founded all over the Eastern provinces, very often the prestigious panhellenic *agones hieroi kai stephanitai*; their foundation was only possible with permission of the emperor, and they provided not only happiness but also economic stimuli.[28] Mostly, these new contests were connected with the imperial cult, or then existing festivals were expanded with an imperial element; this too could not be done without imperial permission. All this is a phenomenon of a very *longue durée*. The association of festivals with joy and relaxation was a constant in Greek and Roman culture, expressed already by Plato and Democritus and repeated by many later authors, and has its parallels already in the urban cultures of the Ancient Near East.[29] Honorary decrees over and over praised a member of the urban elite or the imperial administration for the pleasure of festivals they provided: the inscriptions reach from the lavish honors bestowed on the Hellenistic *stephanophoroi* of Priene via the praise for an Epameinondas of Akraiphia in the time of Claudius and Nero for, among many other things, his lavish festivities to a late fourth- or early fifth-century imperial official, Alexandros from Aphrodisias, whom the Phrygians praised both for his justice and the "good cheer," εὐφροσύνη (the equivalent of Latin *laetitia*), that he had provided to them during his administration; the same word might have been used to designate the festival ("Happiness Day") that one Aurelius Marcus founded in 263 in

---

[27] *CTh* 16.1017; Augustine, *Ep.* 29; for the affair see Lancel (1999), 227–229.
[28] An overview in Klose (2004).
[29] For Greece see the texts in Dihle (1992), 323–326; Burkert (2012). For the Ancient Near East, see e.g. the complaint of the Babylonian king Kadašman-Enlil to Amenophis III in Moran (1992), 7 no. EA 3.13–33: "When you celebrated a great festival, you did not send a messenger to me saying: 'Come to eat and drink'."

the small Phrygian mountain town Orkistos.³⁰ To the contemporaries of Theodosius I, good government – local rule in this case – still manifested itself both in justice and the creation of festive happiness. In fifth-century Trier, heavily damaged by repeated barbarian incursions, the city aristocrats still asked the emperor for circus games, *circenses*, to the utter (and, not surprisingly, vociferous) dismay of Salvian of Marseilles, who castigated this clinging to *voluptas*.³¹ But the Bishops and moralists were fighting a lost cause.

The way magic developed is illustrative of the forces at work, and their respective success. Here too, both bishops and emperors intervened, and again the bishops were more radical than most emperors, with the exception once again of Constantius. But in the long run it was again the need of the people that dominated. Binding spells almost disappeared from the realities of the Christian world, although they survived in narrative fiction. Ritual protection of body and fields, however, survived much more tenaciously, to the extent that the ritual benediction of cattle and fields at some point was quietly taken over by the Catholic Church, to survive in some parts, such as rural Bavaria or Switzerland, well into the modern world. And Christian theologians themselves could be shockingly ambivalent, condemning traditional amulets as pagan but easily accepting their Christian equivalents, be it Ambrose praising his brother for the use of eucharistic bread wrapped in a prayer text and hung around his neck to save himself from a shipwreck or Gregory of Nyssa talking about Macrina's use of the "phylactery of the cross."³²

The end of sacrifice, and the continuity of festivals

We saw how urban benefactors in the early empire were praised for their lavish festivals, from whose sacrifices entire cities could be fed; this

---

[30] Priene: most impressive, *I.Priene* 113 and 114 (Aulos Aimilios Zosimos), after 84 BCE. Epameinondas: above Chapter 1. Alexandros of Aphrodisias: Roueché (1989), no. 32, with an ample commentary: εἰκόνα λαϊνέην μὲν Ἀλεξάνδροιο δικαίου ἡ Φρυγίης μήτηρ μητέρι τῆι Καρίης τῆς ζαθέης ἀρχῆς τέκμαρ ἄμβροτον ἐνθάδ᾽ ἔπεμψεν· πᾶς δὲ λόγος μείων ἀνδρὸς εὐφροσύνης. "The metropolis of Phrygia has sent a stone statue of the just Alexander to the metropolis of Caria here, as an immortal witness of his sacred rule. No word is large enough for the good cheer of this man." Orkistos: Buckler (1937). εὐφροσύνη for "banquet" is older: already the Kyrbantes Euphronisioi in fourth-century BCE Erythrai must have presided over banquets with ample drinking; see *IErythrai* 201 a 62; Graf (1985), 325–328.

[31] Salvian, *De gubernatione Dei* 6.85; see Van Dam (2007), 69f. and, for the context, Brown (2012), 433–453.

[32] Ambros. *De excessu fratris* 1.43; Greg. Nyss. *Vita Macrinae* 20, 990CD; more in Bradshaw (2002), 221.

The persistence of festivals 319

continued strong Hellenistic traditions of *euergesia* as a way of elite self-representation and legitimization through social work. The praise of urban benefaction continued through the centuries, and lavish festivals still played their role, although in the praise of local benefactors over time their building activities became more important. The Christianized elite of the empire, including many bishops, seamlessly continued this tradition. Several inscriptions from fifth-century Aphrodisias praise local grandees who restored many public buildings, mostly, it seems, with their own money and not with public funding.[33] In a sign of the times, an epigram on the base of the marble statue of governor Dulcitius claims that the dedicator would not have hesitated to dedicate a golden image, "if it had been allowed," εἰ θέμις ἦν: but in this time and age, gold images were only allowed for emperors: the prohibition is used as a neat springboard for praise.[34] At about the same time, the *comes* Diogenes son of Archelaos recorded in Megara that he had contributed to the restoration of the city walls, "caring for the cities of Greece as if it were his own house ... and deeming nothing more honorable than to be a benefactor to the Greeks and to renew their cities."[35]

A praise poem from Hierapolis (Pammukkale) in Phrygia, inscribed around 355 CE, presents an interesting transitional case. The poem praises one Flavius Magnus, most likely the vicarius Asianae between 353 and 358 and a well known imperial aristocrat and administrator, for his restoration of the local theater.[36] This thus places Magnus among the building benefactors of the area. One couplet, however, seems ambivalent:

[καὶ] νυ[μ]φῶ[ν τέ]μενος ῥέξεν [πόλι]ν ἀγλαομήτης |
καὶ θαλίαις ἐραταῖς θῆκεν ἀγαλλομένην.

A man of rare wisdom, he made the city a shrine of the nymphs and made it blooming with lovely revelries.

θαλία is the usual term for a banquet, but this meaning is too narrow here.[37] The preceding line expresses the new-found beauty of the city – a

---

[33] See Roueché (1989), nos. 38, 42–44 (Ampelius); cp. 39–41 (governor Dulcitius); 53–54 (Asklepiodotes); 56, 58 (Pytheas).
[34] *StEGO* 02/09/10; the relevant law *CJ* 1.24.1 (a. 398) permits only marble, bronze, and silver images for officials (*iudices*), and even those only with imperial permission. More in the commentary of Merkelbach and Stauber.
[35] *IG* vii 26. On the *comes* Diogenes see *PLRE* 2.360 s.v. Diogenes 5.
[36] *StEGO* 02/12/06; see Jones (1997); Ritti (1986). For Magnus see *PLRE* 1.535, Magnus 9 and Jones (1997), 211–212.
[37] Belayche (2007), 44 translates "[Magnus] a fait qu'elle [i.e. la cité] se réjouisse par des fêtes aimables": this might be too narrow; I follow the translation of Jones (1997), 204.

spa city, after all, thanks to the hot springs of what is nowadays the tourist attraction Pammukkale – with an image that exploits the association of the nymphs with any *locus amoenus*. The pentameter, as usual, gives a variation of the same thought: Magnus turned the city into a place that "blooms with lovely revelries." The poet might still feel that Magnus' munificence resonates with the lush banquets of earlier benefactors, but these new banquets have become more enticing for the eyes than for the stomach.

This late antique transition from banquets to buildings recalls the problems P. Vedius Antoninus incurred with his building program in Ephesos, and the backing he received from an emperor, Antoninus Pius, who encouraged the local rich to invest in building projects. But the emperor did not oppose banquets, he did not even mention them, he opposed "shows, distributions, and the spectacles of games": we can read from this that already in the later second century Eastern city elites had begun to replace the traditional city-wide banquets with Roman forms of keeping the urban masses. City-wide banquets were the result of lavish animal sacrifices: it is no coincidence that at about the same time, we begin to sense an opposition to them. As we saw above, it is not only intellectuals that articulate it, people such as Porphyry, the Lucian of *On Sacrifices*, or Apollonius of Tyana in Philostratus' account that might go back to a second-century local writer, Maximus of Aigai. Inscriptions begin to express similar reservations – an oracle of Ammon in Cyzicus of about 130 CE, the Didymaean oracle that recommends hymns instead of sacrifices and is vaguely dated to the later second or third century, a contemporary epigram from Hadrianoi in Mysai that prefers incense burning to meat, or a grave epigram that praises a local aristocrat for having enjoyed himself as prytanis among his fellow citizens with libations, ἐν σπουδαῖσι.[38] Thus, for reasons that need more research but that are much more complex than any monocausal theory could explain, ancient cultures moved away from large sacrifices as a way in which urban elites demonstrated their status and earned the mostly justified gratitude of their fellow citizens.

Large banquets, however, did not fully disappear even with the abolition of sacrifices, as we just saw. Local authorities were reading the prohibition of sacrifices in this way; but they were wrong. In a letter that Honorius addressed to the proconsul of Africa in 399, the emperor insisted that the

---

[38] Ammon oracle from Kyzikos: *StEGO* 08/01/0; oracle from Didyma: *I.Didyma* 217; epigram from Hadrianoi: *StEGO* 08/08/03; grave epigram fom Kyzikos: *StEGO* 08/01/53.

prohibition of sacrifices did not mean the suppression of common festivals and their joyful atmosphere; he obviously was asked what the abolition of sacrifices meant for the performance of large public festivals. He made clear that he saw no connection between the two facts: "We decree that, according to ancient custom, entertainment shall be given to the people, although without sacrifices and damnable superstitions, and they shall be allowed to attend festive banquets whenever public desire so demands."[39] The emperor thus attests to the intention not to utterly disrupt city traditions despite the prohibition of sacrifices. Nor did this prohibition mean the wholesale destruction of public temples, as the same emperor made clear in the same year.[40] It looks as if over-eager provincial authorities were drawing hasty conclusions from Theodosius' prohibition of sacrifices that his successor corrected in the name of tradition.

Still, public banquets thus were no more a given, but could take place "whenever public desire so demands"; local elites thus looked for alternative outlets of their munificence. Building programs were one possibility, and as we saw, it was taken up. But it rarely created the immediate pleasure that splendid banquets had offered, perhaps with the exception of fountain houses and baths; the restoration of theaters and city walls needed the pressure of destruction and damage to become really satisfactory. This is why games, spectacles, and distributions offered such an allure, to the chagrin of Antoninus Pius. Games, spectacles, and *sparsiones*, however, were a mainly Roman thing; they needed vehicles to arrive in the East. Gladiatorial games arrived early and found enthusiastic crowds; but they did not stay. It was the horse races and the *sparsiones* that made the largest impact, and they came with Roman festivals, not the least with the Kalendae – we saw how in Libanius' Antioch the horse-racing aristocrats threw gold coins to the crowds on their way to and from the temple, and how the final three days after the Vota were defined by the horse races. Banquets were still there as well, but they were kept to the houses, the great and the smaller ones; only distributions and races were really public. I am inclined to understand already the money distributed to the local guilds by a Jewish couple in early third-century Hierapolis as a local form of distribution – it was far from the liberal throwing of coins to the circus crowds, and it implied that the recipients would celebrate the grave crowning instead; but it still is distribution of coins to groups, and

---

[39] *CTh* 16.10.17 *Unde absque ullo sacrificio atque ulla superstitione damnabili exhiberi populo voluptates secundum veterem consuetudinem, iniri etiam festa convivia, si quando exigunt publica vota, decernimus.* (Translation after Pharr 1952.)
[40] *CTh* 16.10.15.

is a form of munificence and of redistribution of wealth. We still have a long way to go to the times when the emperors had to prohibit the distribution of gold coins by consuls and other members of the urban elite; but the foundation of the second Rome with its Roman festivals, the Kalendae, Vota, Brumalia and Lupercalia, marked a major step in that direction.

References

Editions of inscriptions and papyri are cited in full when they appear, except those contained in the major corpora, for which see the list of abbreviations. Articles in *DNP* are not listed.

d'Agostino, Fred (2001) "Rituals of impartiality," *Social Theory and Practice* 27.1, 65–81
Agusta-Boularot, Sandrine, Joëlle Beaucamp, Anne-Marie Bernardi, and Emmanuèle Caire, eds. (2006) *Recherches sur la Chronique de Jean Malalas* (Paris: Association des Amis du Centre d'Histoire et Civilisation de Byzance)
Ahlbäck, Tore, ed. (1993) *The Problem of Ritual: Based on Papers Read at the Symposium on Religious Rites Held at Åbo, Finland on the 13–16 August 1991* (Åbo and Stockholm: Donner Institute and Almqvist & Wiksell)
Aleshire, Sarah B. (1989) *The Athenian Asklepieion: The People, their Dedications, the Inventories* (Amsterdam: Gieben)
Alföldi, Andreas (1937) *A Festival of Isis in Rome under the Christian Emperors of the IVth Century*. Dissertationes Pannonicae ser. 2 fasc. 7 (Budapest: Institute of Numismatics and Archaeology of the Pázmany-University)
Alföldi, Andreas (1974) *Die Struktur des voretruskischen Römerstaates* (Heidelberg: Winter)
Alföldi, Maria R. (1959/60) "*Helena nobilissima femina*. Zur Deutung der Trierer Deckengemälde," *Jahrbuch für Numismatik* 10, 79–90
Alföldy, Géza (1989) "Die Krise des Imperium Romanum und die Religion Roms," in: Werner Eck, ed., *Religion und Gesellschaft in der römischen Kaiserzeit: Kolloqium zu Ehren von Friedrich Vittinghoff* (Cologne: Böhlau), 53–102
Ameling, Walter, ed. (2004) *Inscriptiones Judaicae Orientis*, vol. 2: *Kleinasien* (Tübingen: Mohr Siebeck)
Anderson, Galusha, and Edgar Johnson Goodspeed, eds. (1904) *Ancient Sermons for Modern Times, by Asterius, Bishop of Amasia circa 375–405, A.D.* (New York, Boston, Chicago: The Pilgrim Press)
Ando, Clifford (2003) "A religion for the empire," in: A. J. Boyle and W. J. Dominik, eds., *Flavian Rome: Culture, Image, Text* (Leiden: Brill), 323–344
Ando, Clifford (2007) "Exporting Roman religion," in: Jörg Rüpke, ed., *A Companion to Roman Religion* (Malden, Mass.: Blackwell), 429–445

Applebaum, S. (1978) "The Roman Theatre of Scythopolis", *Scripta Classica Israelica* 4, 77–105
Arbesmann, Rudolph (1979) "The *cervuli* and *anniculae* in Caesarius of Arles", *Traditio* 35, 89–119
Arena, Patrizia (2009) "The *pompa circensis* and the *domus Augusta* (1st–2nd c. A.D.)," in: Olivier Hekster, Sebastian Schmidt-Hofner, and Christian Witschel, eds., *Ritual Dynamics and Religious Change in the Roman Empire: Proceedings of the Eighth Workshop of the International Network 'Impact of Empire', Heidelberg, July 5–7, 2007* (Leiden: Brill), 77–93
Arena, Patrizia (2010) *Feste e Rituali a Roma: Il Principe Incontra il Popolo nel Circo Massimo* (Bari: Edipuglia)
Aronen, Jaako (1989) "La sopravvivenza dei culti pagani e la topografia cristiana dell'area di Giuturna e delle sue adiacenze," in Eva Margareta Steinby, ed., *Lacus Iuturnae*, vol. 1 (Rome: De Luca), 148–174
Athanassiadi, Polymnia (1993) "Persecution and response in late paganism. The evidence of Damascius," *Journal of Hellenic Studies* 113, 1–29
Audollent, Auguste (1904) *Defixionum Tabellae Quotquot Innotuerunt* (Paris: Fontemoing) (repr. Frankfurt: Minerva, 1967)
Auffarth, Christoph, ed. (2009) *Religion auf dem Lande: Entstehung und Veränderung von Sakrallandschaft unter römischer Herrschaft* (Stuttgart: Steiner)
Austin, Greta (2009) *Shaping Church Law Around the Year 1000: The Decretum of Burchard of Worms* (Farnham: Ashgate)
Bacher, Wilhelm (1909) "Der Jahrmarkt an der Terebinthe bei Hebron," *Zeitschrift für die alttestamentliche Wissenschaft* 29, 148–152
Baldovin, John Francis (1987) *The Urban Character of Christian Worship*. Orientalia Christiana Analecta 228 (Rome: Pontificium Institutum Studiorum Orientalium)
Baldovin, John Francis (1989) *Liturgy in Ancient Jerusalem*. Alcuin/GROW Liturgical Studies 9 (Nottingham: Grove Books)
Bandy, Anastasius C. (2013) *Ioannes Lydus: On the Months (De mensibus). The Three Works of Ioannes Lydus*, vol. 1 (Lewiston, Queenston, and Lampeter: Edwin Mellen Press)
Barceló, Pedro (2003) "Beobachtungen zur Verehrung des christlichen Kaisers in der Spätantike," in: Cancik and Hitzl, 313–339
Barlow, Claude W. ed. (1950) *Martini Episcopi Bracarensis Opera Omnia*. Papers and Monographs of the American Academy in Rome 12 (New Haven: Yale University Press)
Baronius, Caesar [Cesare Baronio] (1864–1884) *Annales ecclesiastici: Denuo excussi et ad nostra usque tempora perducti*, ed. Augustin Theiner (Barri-Ducis: Louis Guerrin) (last edition published by the author [*editio postrema ab ipsomet aucta et recognita*], Mainz: Lippius et Albinus, 1601–1608, 12 parts in 6 vols.)
Barton, Carlin A. (1989) "The scandal of the arena," *Representations* 27, 1–36
Batiffol, Pierre (1890) *Studia patristica: Études d'ancienne littérature chrétienne*, fasc. 2 (Paris: Leroux)

Beard, Mary (1987) "A complex of times. No more sheep on Romulus' birthday," *Proceedings of the Cambridge Philological Society* 33.213, 1–15
Beard, Mary, John North, and Simon Price (1998) *Religions of Rome*, 2 vols. (Cambridge: Cambridge University Press)
Beatrice, Pier Franco (1989) "*'Quosdam libros Platonicos'*. The Platonic Reading of Augustine in Milan," *Vigiliae Christianae* 43, 248–281
Beaujeu, Jean (1955) *La religion romaine à l'apogée de l'Empire*, vol. 1 (Paris: Les Belles Letters)
Belayche, Nicole (2001) *Iudaea-Palaestina: The Pagan Cults in Roman Palestine (Second to Fourth Century)* (Tübingen: Mohr Siebeck)
Belayche, Nicole (2004) "Une panégyrie antéochienne: Les Maïouma," *Topoi Orient-Occident. Supplement* 5, 401–415
Belayche, Nicole (2007) "Des lieux pour le 'profane' dans l'antiquité tardo-antique? Les fêtes entre *koinônia* sociale et espaces de rivalités religieuses," *Antiquité Tardive* 15, 35–46
Belayche, Nicole (2011) "Entre deux éclats de rire. Sacrifice et représentation du divin dans le traité 'Sur les sacrifices' de Lucien," in: Vincianne Pirenne Delforge and Francesca Prescendi, eds., *Nourrir les dieux? Sacrifice et représentation du divin*. Kernos Supplément 21 (Liège: Centre International d'Étude de la Religion Grecque Antique), 321–334
Bell, Sinclair and Glenys Davies, eds. (2004) *Games and Festivals in Classical Antiquity: Proceedings of the conference held in Edinburgh 10–12 July 2000* (Oxford: Archaeopress)
Berardino, Angelo di (2005) "Tempo sociale pagano e cristiano nel IV secolo," in: Saggioro, 95–121
Bernardi, Anne-Marie (2006) "Regards croisée sur les origines de Rome. La fête des Brumalia chez Jean Malalas et Jean Lydos," in: Sandrine Agusta-Boulardot, Joëlle Beaucamp, Anne-Marie Bernardi, and Emmanuèle Caire, eds., *Recherches sur la Chronique de Jean Malalas*, vol. 2 (Paris: Association des Amis du Centre d'Histoire et Civilisation de Byzance), 53–66
Berner, Ulrich (1979) "Der Begriff 'Synkretismus': Ein Instrument historischer Erkenntnis?," *Saeculum* 30, 68–85
Bernstein, Frank (1997) "Verständnis- und Entwicklungsstufen der archaischen Consualia. Römisches Substrat und griechische Überlagerung," *Hermes* 125, 411–446
Bevilacqua, Gabriella (1999) "Le epigrafi magiche," in: Maria Ida Gulletta, ed., *Sicilia Epigrafica: Atti del convegno internazionale, Erice, 15–18 ottobre 1998*. Annali della Scuola Normale Superiore di Pisa. Quaderni 1 (Pisa: Classe di Lettere e Filosofia), 65–88
Bevilacqua, Gabriella, and Sergio Giannobile (2000) "'Magia' rurale siciliano. Iscrizioni di Noto e Modica," *Zeitschrift für Papyrologie und Epigraphik* 133, 135–146
Bianchi, Lorenzo (1914) *Der Kalender des sogenannten Clodius Tuscus*. Sitzungsberichte der Heidelberger Akademie der Wissenschaften 1914:3 (Heidelberg: Winter)

Bickerman, Elias (1933) *Chronologie* (Leipzig: Teubner)
Binder, Stéphanie E. (2012) *Tertullian, On Idolatry and Mishnah 'Avodah Zarah: Questioning the Parting of the Ways between Christians and Jews in Late Antiquity*. Jewish and Christian Perspectives 22 (Leiden and Boston: Brill)
Blaufuss, Hans (1909) *Römische Feste und Feiertage nach den Traktaten über fremden Dienst (Aboda zara) in Mischna, Tosefta, Jerusalemer und babylonischem Talmud*. Beilage zum Jahresbericht des Königlichen Neuen Gymnasiums in Nürnberg für das Schuljahr 1908/09 (Nuremberg: Stich)
Bloi, Lukas de, Peter Funke, and Johannes Hahn, eds. (2006) *The Impact of Imperial Rome on Religions, Ritual, and Religious Life in the Roman Empire: Proceedings of the Fifth Workshop of the International Network Impact of Empire (Roman Empire, 200 B.C. – A. D. 476), Münster, June 30 – July 4, 2004* (Leiden: Brill)
Blömer, Michael, Margherita Facella, and Engelbert Winter, eds. (2009) *Lokale Identitäten im Römischen Nahen Osten* (Stuttgart: Steiner)
Blümel, Wolfgang (1997) "Ein weiteres Fragment des Kultgesetzes aus Bargylia," *Epigraphica Anatolica* 28, 153–156
Blümel, Wolfgang (2000) "Ein dritter Teil des Kultgesetzes aus Bargylia," *Epigraphica Anatolica* 32, 89–93
Boatwright, Mary Taliaferro (2000) *Hadrian and the Cities of the Roman Empire* (Princeton: Princeton University Press)
Bohak, Gideon (2008) *Ancient Jewish Magic: A History* (Cambridge: Cambridge University Press)
Boin, Douglas R. (2010) "A hall for Hercules at Ostia and a farewell to the Late Antique 'Pagan Revival'," *American Journal of Archaeology* 114, 253–266
Bonner, Campbell (1932) "Demons of the bath," in: *Studies Presented to F. L. Griffiths* (London: Egypt Exploration Society), 203–208
Bonner, Campbell (1943) "The technique of exorcism," *Harvard Theological Review* 36, 39–49
Botte, Bernard (1932) *Les origines de la Noël et de l'Épiphanie: Étude historique*. Textes et Études Liturgiques 1 (Louvain: Abbaye du Mont César) (repr. 1970)
Bowersock, Glen W. (1978) *Julian the Apostate* (London: Duckworth)
Bradshaw, Paul F. (2002) *The Search for the Origins of Christian Worship: Sources and Methods for the Study of Early Liturgy* (Oxford and New York: Oxford University Press)
Bradshaw, Paul F., and Maxwell E. Johnson (2011) *The Origins of Feasts, Fasts, and Seasons in Early Christianity* (London: SPCK, and Collegeville, Minn.: Liturgical Press)
Brandt, J. Rasmus, and Jon W. Iddeng, eds. (2012) *Greek and Roman Festivals: Content, Meaning, and Practice* (Oxford: Oxford University Press)
Braudel, Fernand (1972) "Personal testimony," *Journal of Modern History* 44, 448–467
Bremmer, Jan N. (1987) "Romulus, Remus and the foundation of Rome," in: Jan N. Bremmer and Nicholas M. Horsfall, *Roman Myth and Mythography* (London: Institute for Classical Studies), 25–48

Bremmer, Jan N. (1993) "Three Roman aetiological myths," in: Fritz Graf, ed., *Mythos in mythenloser Gesellschaft: Das Paradigma Roms*. Colloquia Raurica 3 (Stuttgart and Leipzig: Teubner), 158–175

Bremmer, Jan N. (2002) "How old is the ideal of holiness (of mind) in the Epidaurian temple inscription and the Hippocratic oath?", *Zeitschrift für Papyrologie und Epigraphik* 141, 106–108

Briggs, Charles (1996) "The politics of discursive authority in research on the invention of tradition," *Cultural Anthropology* 11, 435–469

Briquel, Dominique (1997) *Chrétiens et haruspices* (Paris: Presses de l'École Normale Supérieure)

Broodbank, Cyprian (2013) *The Making of the Middle Sea: A History of the Mediterranean from the Beginning to the Emergence of the Classical World* (Oxford: Oxford University Press)

Brown, Peter (1967) *Augustine of Hippo: A Biography* (London: Faber and Faber)

Brown, Peter (1988) *The Body and Society: Men, Women and Sexual Renunciation in Early Christianity* (New York: Columbia University Press)

Brown, Peter (1996) *The Rise of Western Christendom: Triumph and Diversity, AD 200–1000* (Oxford: Blackwell)

Brown, Peter (1998) "Augustine and a Practice of the Imperiti. Qui adorant columnas in ecclesia (S. Dolbeau 26.10.232/Mayence 62)," in: Madec, 367–375

Brown, Peter (2012) *Through the Eye of a Needle: Wealth, the Fall of Rome, and the Making of Christianity in the West, 350–550 AD* (Princeton: Princeton University Press)

Bruggisser, Philippe (1987) *Romulus Servianus: La légende de Romulus dans les "Commentaires à Virgile" de Servius. Mythographie et idéologie à l'époque de la dynastie théodosienne* (Bonn: Habelt)

Bruns, Carl Georg (1909) *Fontes iuris Romani antiqui, post curas Theodori Mommseni editionibus quintae et sextae adhibitas septimum edidit Otto Gradenwitz* (Tübingen: Mohr)

Bruns, Ivo (1892) *Alexandri Aphrodisiensis praeter commentaria scripta minora*. Commentaria in Aristotelem Graeca suppl. 2.2 (Berlin: Reimer)

Buckler, William H. (1937) "A charitable foundation of 237 A.D.," *Journal of Hellenic Studies* 57, 1–10

Buraselis, Kostas (2008) "Priesthoods for sale. Comments on ideological and financial aspects of the sale of priesthoods in the Greek cities of the Hellenistic and Roman periods," in: Anders-Holm Rasmussen and Susanne Williams Rasmussen, eds., *Religion and Society: Rituals, Resources and Identity in the Ancient Graeco-Roman World. The Bomos-Conferences 2002–2005* (Rome: Quasar), 125–132

Burkert, Walter (1992) "Athenian cults and festivals," in: *The Cambridge Ancient History* (2nd edn) (Cambridge: Cambridge University Press), 5: 245–267. Reprinted in: *Kleine Schriften*, vol. 6, ed. Eveline Krummen (Göttingen: Vandenhoeck & Ruprecht, 2011), 208–230

Burkert, Walter (1994) *'Vergeltung' zwischen Ethologie und Ethik* (Munich: Siemens Stiftung)

Burkert, Walter (2011) *Kleine Schriften* IV, ed. Fritz Graf (Göttingen: Vandenhoeck & Rupprecht)
Burkert, Walter (2012) "Ancient views on festivals. A case of Near Eastern Mediterranean koine," in: J. Rasmus Brandt and Jon W. Iddeng, eds., *Greek and Roman Festivals: Content, Meaning, and Practice* (Oxford: Oxford University Press), 39–51
Butler, Rex (2005) *The New Prophecy and New Visions: Evidence of Montanism in the Passion of Perpetua and Felicitas*. Patristic Monograph Series 18 (Washington, D.C.: Catholic University of America Press)
Caldelli, Maria Letizia (1993) *L'Agon Capitolinus: Storia e protagonisti dall'istituzione domizianea al IV° secolo* (Rome: Istituto Italiano per la Storia Antica)
Cameron, Alan (2011) *The Last Pagans of Rome* (Oxford: Oxford University Press)
Cameron, Averil and Stuart G. Hall (1999) *Eusebius: Life of Constantine* (Oxford: Clarendon Press)
Cancik, Hubert and Jörg Rüpke, eds. (1997) *Römische Reichsreligion und Provinzialreligion* (Tübingen: Mohr Siebeck)
Cancik, Hubert, and Conrad Hitzl, eds. (2003) *Die Praxis der Herrscherverehrung in Rom und seinen Provinzen* (Tübingen: Mohr Siebeck)
Caner, Daniel F. (2013) "Alms, Blessings, Offerings: The Repertoire of Christian Gifts in Early Byzantium", in: Michael L. Satlow, ed.: *The Gift in Antiquity* (Malden, Mass. and Oxford: Wiley-Blackwell), 25–44
Carafa, Paolo (2006) "I Lupercali", in: Andrea Carandini, ed., *La leggenda di Roma*, vol. 1: *Dalla Nascita dei Gemelli alla Fondazione della Città* (Milan: Fondazione Lorenzo Valla/Mondadori), 477–493
Carandini, Andrea (2008) (with Daniela Bruno) *La Casa di Augusto, dai "Lupercalia" al Natale* (Rome and Bari: Laterza)
Castello, C. (1991) "Cenni sulla repressione del reato di magia dagli inizi del principato fino a Costanzo II," in: G. Crifò and S. Giglio, eds., *VIII° Convegno Internazionale dell'Accademia Romanistica Constantiniana* (Naples: Edizioni Scientifiche Internazionali), 665–692
Cerfaux, Lucien, and Jules Tondriau (1957) *Un concurrent du Christianisme: Le culte des souverains dans la civilisation gréco-romaine*. Bibliothèque de Théologie 3 (Paris: Desclée)
Chadwick, Henry (1981) *Boethius: The Consolation of Music, Logic, Theology and Philosophy* (Oxford: Clarendon Press)
Chaniotis, Angelos (1991) "Gedenktage der Griechen. Ihre Bedeutung für das Geschichtsbewusstsein griechischer Poleis," in: Jan Assmann and Theo Sundermeier, eds., *Das Fest und das Heilige*. Studien zum Verstehen fremder Religionen 1 (Gütersloh: Bertelsmann), 123–145
Chaniotis, Angelos (1995) "Sich selbst feiern? Städtische Feste des Hellenismus im Spannungsfeld von Religion und Politik," in: Michael Wörrle and Paul Zanker, eds., *Stadtbild und Bürgerbild im Hellenismus*. Vestigia. Beiträge zur Alten Geschichte 47 (Munich: Beck), 147–172

Chaniotis, Angelos (2003) "Negotiating religion in the cities of the Eastern Roman Empire," *Kernos* 16, 177–190
Chaniotis, Angelos (2004) "Das Bankett des Damas und der Hymnos des Sosandros. Öffentlicher Diskurs über Rituale in den griechischen Städten der Kaiserzeit," in: Dieter Harth and Gerrit Jasper Schenk, eds., *Ritualdynamik: Kulturübergreifende Studien zur Theorie und Geschichte rituellen Handelns* (Heidelberg: Synchron), 291–304
Chaniotis, Angelos (2013) "Processions in Hellenistic cities. Contemporary discourses and ritual dynamics," in: Richard Alston, Onno M. van Nijf, and Christina G. Williamson, eds., *Cults, Creeds and Identities in the Greek City After the Classical Age* (Leuven: Peeters), 21–47
Chastagnol, André (1960) *La préfecture urbaine à Rome sous le Bas-Empire* (Paris: Presses Universitaires de France)
Chastagnol, André (1962) *Les fastes de la Préfecture de Rome au Bas-Empire* (Paris: Nouvelles Éditions Latines)
Ciccolella, Francesca (2000) *Cinque Poeti Bizantini: Anacreontee dal Barberiniano Greco 310* (Alessandria: Edizioni dell'Orso)
Clavel Levêque, Monique (1984) *L'empire en jeu* (Paris: Éditions du CNRS)
Clerc, Benoît (1996) "Theurgica legibus prohibita. A propos de l'interdiction de la théurgie," *Revues des Études Augustiniennes* 42, 57–64
Clercq, Charles de, ed. (1963) *Concilia Galliae a. 511–695*. Corpus Christianorum Series Latina 148A (Turnhout: Brepols)
Clifford, James (2004) "Looking several ways. Anthropology and native heritage in Alaska," *Current Anthropology* 45:1, 5–30. Reprinted in: *Returns: Becoming Indigenous in the Twenty First Century* (Harvard University Press, 2013), 213–259
Clinton, Kevin (1974) *The Sacred Officials of the Eleusinian Mysteries*. Proceedings of the American Philosophical Society 64:3 (Philadelphia: American Philosophical Society)
Clinton, Kevin (1992) *Myth and Cult: The Iconography of the Eleusinian Mysteries*. Nilsson Lectures 1 (Stockholm: Aström)
Cloud, J. D. (1979) "Numa's calendar in Livy and Plutarch," *Liverpool Classical Monthly* 4:4, 65–71
Cohen, A. (1988) *Hebrew–English Edition of the Babylonian Talmud: Abodah Zarah* (London: Soncino Press)
Collins, John J. (2003) "The zeal of Phinehas. The Bible and the legitimation of violence," *Journal of Biblical Literature* 122, 3–21
Colpe, Carsten (1961) *Die religionsgeschichtliche Schule: Darstellung und Kritik ihres Bildes vom gnostizistischen Erlösermythos* (Göttingen: Vandenhoeck & Ruprecht)
Conrat, Max (1903) *Breviarium Alaricianum: Römisches Recht im fränkischen Reich* (Leipzig: Hinrichs)
Constantelos, Demetrios J. (1970) "Canon 62 of the Synod in Trullo and the Slavic problem," *Byzantina* 2, 23–35. Reprinted as "Church Canons and cultural realities. Canon sixty-two of the Synod in Trullo. A case study," in Constantelos (1998), 163–171

Constantelos, Demetrios J. (1998) *Christian Hellenism: Essays and Studies in Continuity and Change* (New Rochelle, N.Y. and Athens: Caratzas)

Cotton, Hannah (1999) "Some aspects of the Roman administration of Judaea/Syria-Palaestina", in: Werner Eck, ed., *Lokale Autonomie und römische Ordnungsmacht in den kaiserzeitlichen Provinzen vom 1. bis 3. Jahrhundert*. Schriften des Historischen Kollegs Kolloquium 3 (Munich: Beck), 75–81

Crawford, John R. (1914–1919) "De Bruma et Brumalibus festis," *Byzantinische Zeitschrift* 22, 365–396

Cribiore, Raffaella (2013) *Libanius the Sophist: Rhetoric, Reality and Religion in the Fourth Century* (Ithaca, N.Y.: Cornell University Press)

Croke, Brian (1990) "Malalas, the man and his work," in: Jeffreys (1990a), 1–25

Csepregi, Ildikó (2005) "Mysteries for the uninitiated. The role and symbolism of the Eucharist in Miraculous Dream Healing," in: István Perczel, *The Eucharist in Theology and Philosophy* (Leuven: Leuven University Press), 97–130

Dagron, Gilbert (1974) *Naissance d'une capitale. Constantinople et ses institutions de 330 à 451* (Paris: Presses Universitaires de France)

Dagron, Gilbert, ed. (1978) *Vie et miracles de sainte Thècle: Texte grec, traduction et commentaire*. Subsidia Hagiographica 62 (Brussels: Société des bollandistes)

Dagron, Gilbert (1984) *Constantinople imaginaire: Études sur le recueil des "Patria"* (Paris: Presses Universitaires de France)

Datema, Cornelis (1970) *Asterius of Amasea: Homilies I–XIV* (Leiden: Brill)

Dauphin, Claudine (1986) "Temple grec, église byzantine et cimetière musulman: la basilique de Dor en Israël," *Proche-Orient Chrétien* 36 14–22

Dauphin, Claudine (1997) "On the Pilgrim's Way to the Holy City of Jerusalem: The Basilica of Dor in Israel," in: J. R. Barlett, ed., *Archaeology and Biblical Interpretation* (London: Routledge), 145–166

Dauphin, Claudine (1999) "From Apollo and Asclepius to Christ: Pilgrimage and healing at the temple and episcopal basilica of Dor," *Liber Annuus* 49, 397–429

Dauphin, Claudine, and S. Gibson (1993) "Dor-Dora: A station for pilgrims in the Byzantine period on their way to Jerusalem," in: Y. Tsafir, ed., *Ancient Churches Revealed* (Jerusalem: Israel Exploration Society), 90–97

De Groote, Marc, ed. (2012) *Christophori Mitylenaii versuum variorum collectio Cryptensis*. Corpus Christianorum, series Graeca 74 (Turnhout: Brepols)

Degrassi, Attilio, ed. (1963) *Fasti Anni Numani et Iuliani, accedunt ferialia, menologia rustica, parapegmata*. Inscriptiones Italiae 13: Fasti et elogia, fasc. 2 (Rome: Libreria dello Stato)

Demougin, Ségolène, Hubert Devijver, and Marie-Thérèse Raepsaet-Charlier, eds. (1999) *L'ordre équestre: Histoire d'une aristocratie* (Rome: École Française de Rome)

Desanti, Luigi (1990) *Sileat Omnibus Perpetuo Divinandi Curiositas: Indovini e sanzioni nel diritto Romano*. Università di Ferrara. Pubblicazioni della Facoltà Giuridica, Ser. 2:26 (Ferrara: Università)

Deshours, Nadine (2006) *Les mystères d'Andania: Étude d'épigraphie et d'histoire religieuse* (Pessac: Ausonius)

References

Deubner, Ludwig (1900) *De Incubatione Capita Quattuor. Accedit Laudatio in Miracula Sancti Hieromartyris Therapontis e Codice Messanensi Denuo Edita* (Leipzig: Teubner)
Deubner, Ludwig (1902) "Juturna und die Ausgrabungen auf dem römischen Forum," *Neue Jahrbücher* 9, 370–388
Deubner, Ludwig (1907) *Kosmas und Damian* (Berlin: Teubner)
Deubner, Ludwig (1932) *Attische Feste* (Berlin: Teubner)
Deubner, Ludwig (1982) *Kleine Schriften zur klassischen Altertumskunde*, ed. Otfried Deubner (Königstein: Hain)
Dignas, Beate, and Kai Trampedach, eds. (2008) *Practitioners of the Sacred: Greek Priests and Religious Officials from Homer to Heliodorus* (Washington, D.C.: Center for Hellenic Studies)
Dijkstra, Jitse, Justin Kroesen, and Yme Kuiper, eds. (2010) *Myths, Martyrs, and Modernity: Studies in the History of Religions in Honor of Jan N. Bremmer* (Leiden: Brill)
Dihle, Albrecht (1992) "La fête chrétienne," *Revue des Études Augustiniennes* 38, 323–335
Dindorf, Ludwig, ed. (1831) *Ioannis Malalae Chronographia*. Corpus Scriptorum Historiae Byzantinae (Bonn: Weber)
Dix, Gregory (1945) *The Shape of the Liturgy* (London: Dacre)
Dobschütz, Ernst von (1912) *Das Decretum Gelasianum de libris recipiendis et non recipiendis*. Texte und Untersuchungen zur Geschichte der altchristlichen Literatur 38 (Leipzig: Hinrich)
Dodaro, Roberto (1998) "Christus Sacerdos. Augustine's Preaching Against Pagan Priests in the Light of S. Dolbeau 26 and 23," *Augustin Prédicateur: Actes du colloque de Chantilly (5–7 Septembre 1996)* (Paris: Institut d'Études Augustiniennes), 377–393
Dolbeau, François (1990) "Sermons inédits de S. Augustin dans un manuscript de Mayence (*Stadtbibliothek*, I 9)," *Revue d'Études Augustinennes* 36, 355–359
Dolbeau, François (1992) "Sermons inédits de Saint Augustin prêchés en 397 (2ème série)," *Revue Bénédictine* 102, 33–74
Dolbeau, François, ed. (1996) *Augustin d'Hippone: Vingt-six sermons au peuple d'Afrique* (Paris: Institut d'Études Augustiniennes)
Dolbeau, François (2003) "Le combat pastoral d'Augustin contre les astrologues, les devins et les guérisseurs," in: Pierre-Yves Fux, Jean-Michel Roessli, and Otto Wermelinger, eds., *Augustinus Afer: Saint Augustin; africanité et universalité* (Fribourg: Universitätsverlag), 167–82
Dolbeau, François, and Raymond Étaix (2003) "Le 'jour des torches' (24 juin), d'après un sermon inédit d'origine africaine," *Archiv für Religionsgeschichte* 5, 243–359
Domenici, Ilaria, ed. (2007) *Giovanni Lido, Sui segni celesti* (Milan: Medusa)
Doutté, Edmond (1908) *Magie et religion dans l'Afrique du Nord* (Alger: Jourdain) (repr. Paris: Geuthner, 1985)

Doval, Alexis James (2001) *Cyril of Jerusalem, Mystagogue: The Authorship of the Mystagogic Catecheses* (Washington, D.C.: The Catholic University of America Press)
Drijvers, Jan Willem (2004) *Cyril of Jerusalem: Bishop and City* (Leiden: Brill)
Drijvers, Jan Willem (2013) "Transformation of a city. The Christianization of Jerusalem in the fourth century,"in: Richard Alston, Onno M. van Nijf, and Christina G. Williamson, eds., *Cults, Creeds and Identities in the Greek City After the Classical Age* (Leuven: Peeters), 309–329
Drobner, Hubertus R., ed. (2010) *Augustinus von Hippo: Predigten zu Neujahr und Epiphanie (Sermones 196/A–204/A)*. Patrologia 22 (Frankfurt am Main: Peter Lang)
Dulière, Walter Louis (1970) "Protection permanente contre des animaux nuisibles assurée par Apollonius de Tyana dans Byzance et Antioche. Evolution de son mythe," *Byzantinische Zeitschrift* 63, 247–277
Dunand, Françoise, ed. (1981) *La fête, pratique et discours: D'Alexandrie hellénistique à la mission de Besançon*. Annales littéraires de l'Université de Besançon (Paris: Belles Lettres)
Duval, Yves Marie (1976) "Les Lupercales, Junon et le printemps," *Annales de la Bretagne et des Pays de l'Ouest* 83, 253–272
Duval, Yves Marie (1977) "Des Lupercales de Constantinople aux Lupercales de Rome," *Revue des Études Latines* 55, 222–227
Eck, Werner, Antonio Caballos, and Fernando Fernández (1996) *Das Senatus Consultum de Cn. Pisone Patre*. Vestigia 48 (Munich: Beck)
Edelmann, Babett (2008) "Pompa und Bild im Kaiserkult des römischen Ostens," in: Jörg Rüpke, ed., *Festrituale in der römischen Kaiserzeit* (Tübingen: Mohr Siebeck), 153–167
Edwards, Mark (2007) "Porphyry and the Christians," in: George Karamanolis and Anne Sheppard, eds., *Studies on Porphyry* (London: Institute of Classical Studies), 112–116
Ehrenberg, Victor, and A. H. M. Jones, eds. (1955) *Documents Illustrating the Reigns of Augustus and Tiberius* (Oxford: Clarendon Press)
Ehrenheim, Hedvig von (2011) *Greek Incubation Rituals in Classical and Hellenistic Times* (Stockholm: Stockholm University, Department of Archaeology and Classical Studies)
Errington, R. Malcolm (1997) "Church and state in the first years of Theodosius I," *Historia* 27, 21–72
Feeney, Denis (2007) *Caesar's Calendar: Ancient Time and the Beginning of History*. Sather Lectures 65 (Berkeley, Los Angeles, London: University of California Press)
Feichtinger, Barbara (1997) "'Nec vero sopor ille fuerat aut vana somnia...' (Hier., ep. 22, 30, 6). Überlegungen zum geträumten Selbst des Hieronymus," *Revue des Études Augustiniennes* 43, 41–61
Fernández Marcos, Natalio, ed. (1975) *Los Thaumata de Sofronio: Contribución al estudio de la incubatio cristiana* (Madrid: Instituto Antonio de Nebrija)
Ferriès, Marie-Claire (2009) "Luperci et Lupercalia de César à Auguste," *Latomus* 68, 373–392

Fink, Robert O., A. S. Hoey, and W. F. Snyder, eds. (1940) *The Feriale Duranum*. Yale Classical Studies 7 (New Haven: Yale University Press)
Finn, Richard D. (2006) *Almsgiving in the Later Roman Empire: Christian Promotion and Practice (313–450)* (Oxford and New York: Oxford University Press)
Fishwick, Duncan (1987–2005) *The Imperial Cult in the Latin West*, 3 vols. (Leiden: Brill)
Fishwick, Duncan (1988) "Dated inscriptions and the Feriale Duranum," *Syria* 65, 349–361
Fleischer, Robert (1973) *Artemis von Ephesos und verwandte Kultstatuen aus Anatolien und Syrien*. EPRO 35 (Leiden: Brill)
Fögen, Marie Theres (1997) *Die Enteignung der Wahrsager: Studien zum kaiserlichen Wissensmonopol in der Spätantike* (Frankfurt: Suhrkamp) (orig. 1993)
Fontenrose, Joseph (1978) *The Delphic Oracle: Its Responses and Operations* (Berkeley: University of California Press)
Förster, Hans (2007) *Die Anfänge von Weihnachten und Epiphanias: Eine Anfrage an die Entstehungshypothesen*. Studien und Texte zu Antike und Christentum 46 (Tübingen: Mohr Siebeck)
Foschia, Laurence (2000) "La réutilisation des sanctuaires païens par les chrétiens en Grèce continentale (IVè–VIIè s.)," *Revue des Études Grecques* 113, 413–434
Fowden, Garth (1986) *The Egyptian Hermes: A Historical Approach to the Late Pagan Mind* (Princeton: Princeton University Press)
Fowler, William Warde (1899) *The Roman Festivals* (London: MacMillan)
Frankfurter, David (2005) "Beyond magic and superstition," in: Virginia Burrus, ed., *Late Ancient Christianity* (Minneapolis: Fortress), 255–284, 309–312
Franse, Gérard, and Theo Kölzer, eds. (1992) *Burchardi Wormatiensis Ecclesiae Episcopi Decretorum Libri Viginti: Ergänzter Neudruck der Editio Princeps Köln 1548* (Aalen: Scientia)
Frantz, Allison (1965) "From paganism to Christianity in the temples of Athens," *Dumbarton Oaks Papers* 19, 187–205
Fraschetti, Augusto (1999) *La Conversione: Da Roma Pagana a Roma Cristiana* (Rome and Bari: Laterza)
Fraschetti, Augusto (2005) "Principi cristiani, templi e sacrifici nel Codice Teodosiano e in altre testimonianze parallele," in Saggioro, 123–140
Frend, W. H. C. (1988) "Montanism. A movement of prophecy and regional identity in the early Church," *Bulletin of the John Rylands Library* 70, 25–34
Friedheim, Emmanuel (2006) *Rabbinisme et paganisme en Palestine romaine: Étude historique des realia talmudiques (Ier–IVème siècles)*. Religions in the Graeco-Roman World 157 (Leiden and Boston: Brill)
Friedländer, Ludwig (1921) *Darstellungen aus der Sittengeschichte Roms*, vol. 4, 9th/10th edn. (Leipzig: Hirzel)
Friesen, Steven J. (2001) *Imperial Cults and the Apocalypse of John: Reading Revelation in the Ruins* (Oxford and New York: Oxford University Press)
Fuks, Gideon (1982) "The Jews of Hellenistic and Roman Scythopolis," *Journal of Jewish Studies* 33, 407–416

Funari, Rodolfo, ed. (2011) *Titus Livius. Corpus dei Papiri Storici Greci e Latini*, B:1:1 (Pisa and Rome: Fabrizio Serra editore)

Furley, William D., and Jan Maarten Bremer, eds. (2001) *Greek Hymns: Selected Cult Songs From the Archaic to the Hellenistic Period*. Studien und Texte zu Antike und Christentum 9 and 10 (Tübingen: Mohr Siebeck)

Gager, John G. (1992) *Curse Tablets and Binding Spells from the Ancient World* (Oxford: Oxford University Press)

Gascou, Jean, ed.(2006) *Sophrone de Jérusalem: Miracles des saints Cyr et Jean (BHGI 477–479)* (Paris: De Boccard)

Gaudemet, Jean (1965) *Le Bréviaire d'Alaric et les Epitomes*. Ius Romanum Medii Aevi (Milan: Giuffrè)

Gaudemet, Jean, Paolo Siniscalco, and Gian Luigi Falchi (2000) *Legislazione imperiale e religione nel IV secolo*. Sussidi Patristici 11 (Rome: Istituto Patristico "Augustinianum")

Gauthier, Philippe (1985) *Les cités grecques et leur bienfaiteurs (IVe–Ier siècle avant J.-C.)*. Bulletin de Correspondance Hellénique, supplément 12 (Athens: École Française)

Gauthier, Philippe and Miltiades B. Hatzopoulos (1993) *La loi gymnasiarchique de Béroia*. Μελετήματα 16 (Athens: National Hellenic Research Foundation)

Gawlinski, Laura (2011) *The Sacred Law of Andania: A New Text with Commentary* (Berlin and New York: De Gruyter)

Gelzer, Thomas (1992) "Die Alte Komödie in Athen und die Basler Fasnacht," in: Fritz Graf, ed., *Klassische Antike und neue Wege der Kulturwissenschaften: Symposium Karl Meuli* (Basel: Verlag der Schweizerischen Gesellschaft für Volkskunde), 29–61

Gelzer, Thomas, Michael Lurje, and Christoph Schäublin (1999) *Lamella Bernensis: Ein spätantikes Goldamulett mit christlichem Exorzismus und verwandte Texte*. Beiträge zur Altertumskunde 124 (Stuttgart and Leipzig: Teubner)

Geominy, W. (1989) "Eleusinische Priester," in: *Festschrift für Nikolaus Himmelmann* (Mainz: Zabern), 253–264

Georgidou, Stella (1990) *Des chevaux et des boeufs dans le monde grec* (Paris and Athens: Daedalus)

Geyer, Paul, ed. (1898) *Itinera hierosolymitana saeculi IIII–VIII*. Corpus Scriptorum Ecclesiasticorum Latinorum 39 (Vienna: Tempsky)

Geyer, Paul, Otto Cuntz, Ezio Franceschini, Robert Weber, Ludwig Bieler, Jean Fraipont, and François Glorie, eds. (1965) *Itineraria et alia geographica*. Corpus Christianorum Series Latina 175 (Turnhout: Brepols)

Gildemeister, Johann, ed. (1889) *Antonini Placentini Itinerarium im unentstellten Text* (Berlin: Reuther)

Ginzburg, Carlo (1991) "Représentation. Le mot, l'idée, la chose," *Annales Économies, Sociétés, Civilizations* 16, 1219–1234

Girone, Maria (1998) *Iamata: Guarigioni miracolose di Asclepio in testi epigrafici*. Pinakes 3 (Bari: Levante)

Gleason, Maud W. (1986) "Festive Satire. Julian's Mysopogon and the New Year at Antioch," *Journal of Roman Studies* 76, 106–119

Goddio, Franck (2007) *The Topography and Excavation of Heracleion-Thonis and East Canopus* (1996–2006). Underwater Archaeology in the Canopic Region in Egypt. OCMA Monograph 1 (Oxford: Oxford Centre for Maritime Archaeology)

Godefroy, Jacques (1736–1745) *Codex Theodosianus cum perpetuis commentariis Jacobi Gothofredi*, ed. Johann Daniel Ritter (Leipzig: Weidmann)

Goodman, Martin (1983) *State and Society in Roman Galilee, A. D. 132–212* (Totowa, N.J.: Rowman and Allanheld)

Gouw, Patrick (2008) "Hadrian and the Calendar of Greek Agonistic Festivals. A New Proposal for the Third Year of the Olympic Cycle," *Zeitschrift für Papyrologie und Epigraphik* 165, 96–104

Graf, Fritz (1985) *Nordionische Kulte: Religionsgeschichtliche und epigraphische Untersuchungen zu den Kulten von Chios, Erythrai, Klazomenai und Phokaia*. Bibliotheca Helvetica Romana 21 (Rome: Institut Suisse de Rome)

Graf, Fritz (1984–1985) "Maximos von Aigai. Ein Beitrag zur Überlieferung über Apollonios von Tyana," *Jahrbuch für Antike und Christentum* 27/28, 65–73

Graf, Fritz (1996) "Pompai in Greece. Some considerations about space and ritual in the Greek Polis," in: Robin Hägg, ed., *The Role of Religion in the Early Greek Polis*. Acta Instituti Atheniensis Regni Sueciae, Series in 8°, Vol. 14 (Stockholm: Aström), 55–65

Graf, Fritz (2001) "Pedestals of the Gods," *Zeitschrift für Papyrologie und Epigraphik* 141, 137–138

Graf, Fritz (2002) "Roman Festivals in Syria Palaestina," in: Peter Schäfer, ed., *The Talmud Yerushalmi and Graeco-Roman Culture*, vol. 3 (Tübingen: Mohr Siebeck), 435–451

Graf, Fritz (2010) "Dreams, visions and revelations: Dreams in the thought of the Latin Fathers," in: Christina Walde and Emma Scioli, eds., *Sub Imagine Somni: Nighttime Phenomena in Greco-Roman Culture* (Pisa: ETS), 211–231

Graf, Fritz (2011a) "Ritual restoration and innovation in the Greek cities of the Roman Imperium," in: Angelos Chaniotis, ed., *Ritual Dynamics in the Ancient Mediterranean: Agency, Emotion, Gender, Representation* (Stuttgart: Steiner), 105–117

Graf, Fritz (2011b) "A Satirist's sacrifices. Lucian's *On Sacrifices* and the contestation of religious traditions," in: Jenny Knust and Zsuzsana Varhélyi, eds., *Sacrifice in the Ancient Mediterranean: Images, Acts, Meanings* (New York and Oxford: Oxford University Press), 203–213

Graf, Fritz (2014) "Laying down the law in *Ferragosto*. The Roman visit of Theodosius in summer 389," *Journal of Early Christian Studies* 22, 219–242

Greatrex, Geoffrey and John W. Watt (1999) "One, two or three feasts? The Brytae, the Maiuma and the May Festival at Edessa," *Oriens Christianus* 83, 1–21

Green, M. (1931) "The Lupercalia in the fifth century," *Classical Philology* 26, 60–69

Gregory, Timothy E. (1986) "The survival of paganism in Christian Greece: A critical essay," *American Journal of Philology* 107, 229–242

Grumel, Venance (1936) "Le commencement et la fin de l'année des jeux à l'Hippodrome de Constantinople," *Echos d'Orient* 35, 428–435

Guggenheimer, Heinrich W., ed. (2011) *The Jerusalem Talmud. Fourth Order: Neziqin. Tractates Ševi'it and Avodah Zarah* (Berlin and New York: De Gruyter)
Günther, Otto, ed. (1895) *Epistolae imperatorum pontificum aliorum inde ab a. CCCLXVII usque DLIII datae Avellana quae dicitur Collectio.* Corpus Scriptorum Ecclesiasticorum Latinorum 35:1 (Prague and Vienna: Tempsky; Leipzig: Freytag)
Guthrie, Patrick (1966) "The execution of Crispus," *Phoenix* 20, 325–331
Hadas-Lebel, Mireille (1979) "Le paganisme à travers les sources rabbiniques des IIe et IIIe siècles. Contribution à l'étude du syncrétisme religieux," in: *Aufstieg und Niedergang der Römischen Welt* 2.19.2 (Berlin and New York: De Gruyter), 397–485
Hadas-Lebel, Mireille (1990) *Jérusalem contre Rome* (Paris: Cerf)
Hahn, Johannes (2006) "'Vetustus error extinctus est': Wann wurde das Sarapeion von Alexandria zerstört?," *Historia* 55, 368–383
Hamilton, Mary (1906) *Incubation, or The Cure of Disease in Pagan Temples and Christian Churches* (London: Simpkin, Marshall and Co.)
Hanson, John Arthur (1959) *Greek Theatre Temples* (Princeton: Princeton University Press)
Harder, Richard (1956) "Inschriften von Didyma no. 217 Vers 4," in: *Navicula Chiloniensis: Studia philologa Felici Jacoby professori Chiloniensi emerito octogenario oblata* (Leiden: Brill), 88–97
Hardie, Philip (1998) "A reading of Heliodorus 3.4.1–5.2," in: Richard L. Hunter, ed., *Studies in Heliodorus* (Cambridge: Cambridge University Press), 19–39
Harl, Monique (1981) "La dénonciation des festivités profanes dans le discours épiscopal et monastique en Orient chrétien à la fin du IVe siècle," in: Dunand, 123–147
Harland, Philip A. (2006) "Acculturation and identity in the diaspora: A Jewish family and 'pagan' guilds at Hierapolis," *Journal of Jewish Studies* 57, 222–244
Hartung, I. A. (1836) *Die Religion der Römer, nach den Quellen dargestellt* (Erlangen: Palm & Enke)
Hawkins, Tom (2011) "Jester for a day, master for a year. Julian's Misopogon and the Kalends of 363 CE," *Archiv für Religionsgeschichte* 13, 161–173
Hazenbos, Joost J. M. (2003) *The Organization of the Anatolian Local Cults During the 13th Century: An Appraisal of the Hittite Cult Inventories.* Cuneiform Monographs 21 (Leiden: Brill)
Hazenbos, Joost J. M. (2004) "Die lokalen Herbst- und Frühlingsfeste in der späten hethitischen Grossreichszeit," in: Manfred Hutter and Sylvia Hutter-Braunsar, eds., *Offizielle Religion, lokale Kulte und individuelle Religiosität: Akten des religionsgeschichtlichen Symposiums "Kleinasien und angrenzende Gebiete vom Beginn des 2. bis zur Mitte des 1. Jahrtausends v.Chr." (Bonn, 20.–22. Februar 2003)* (Münster: Ugarit-Verlag), 241–248
Heberdey, Rudolf, and Adolf Wilhelm (1896) *Reisen in Kilikien*. Denkschriften der Akademie Wien 44:6
Hénaff, Marcel (2013) "Ceremonial gift-giving. The lessons of anthropology from Mauss and beyond," in: Michael L. Satlow, ed., *The Gift in Antiquity* (Malden, Mass. and Oxford: Wiley-Blackwell), 12–24

Heller, Anna and Anne-Valérie Pont, eds. (2012) *Patrie d'origine et patries électives: Les citoyennetés multiples dans le monde grec d'époque romaine*. Actes du colloque international de Tours, 6–7 novembre 2009 (Pessac: Ausonius)

Hennecke, Edgar (1965) *New Testament Apocrypha*, vol. 2 (London: Lutterworth) (Orig. pub. as *Neutestamentliche Apokryphen in deutscher Übersetzung*, ed. Wilhelm Schneemelcher, Tübingen: Mohr, 1964)

Héron de Villefosse, Antoine (1911) "Tablette magique de Beyrouth, conservée au musée du Louvre," in: *Florilegium ou, Recueil de travaux d'érudition dédiés à Monsieur le marquis Melchior de Vogüé à l'occasion du quatre-vingtième anniversaire de sa naissance, 18 octobre 1909* (Paris: Imprimerie Nationale), 287–295

Herz, Peter (2003) "Neue Forschungen zum Festkalender der römischen Kaiserzeit," in: Cancik and Hitzl, 47–67

Herzog, Rudolf (1931) *Die Wunderheilungen von Epidauros*. Philologus, Supplement 22:3 (Leipzig: Teubner)

Hevelone-Harper, Jennifer L. (2005) *Disciples of the Desert: Monks, Laity, and Spiritual Authority in Sixth-Century Gaza* (Baltimore and London: Johns Hopkins University Press)

Heyman, George (2007) *The Power of Sacrifice: Roman and Christian Discourse in Conflict* (Washington, D.C.: Catholic University of America)

Hill, Edmond, ed. (1997) *Saint Augustine, The Works: A Translation for the 21st Century. Part 3: Homilies.* 11: *Sermons Various (Newly Discovered)* (Hyde Park, N.Y.: New City Press)

Hirschmann, Vera-Elisabeth (2005) *Horrenda Secta: Untersuchungen zum frühchristlichen Montanismus und seinen Verbindungen zur paganen Religion Phrygiens*. Historia Einzelschriften 179 (Stuttgart: Steiner)

Hobsbawm, Eric and Terence Ranger, eds. (1983) *The Invention of Tradition* (Cambridge: Cambridge University Press)

Hoey, Allan S. (1937) "Rosaliae Signorum," *Harvard Theological Review* 30, 15–35

Holleman, Aloysius W. J. (1974) *Pope Gelasius I and the Lupercalia* (Amsterdam: Hakkert)

Hollmann, Alexander (2003) "A curse tablet from the circus at Antioch," *Zeitschrift für Papyrologie und Epigraphik* 145, 67–82

Hörling, Elsa (1980) *Mythos und Pistis: Zur Deutung heidnischer Mythen in der christlichen Weltchronik des Johannes Malalas* (Lund: [s.n.])

Hotz, Stephan (2005) "Bigger, better, more. Die Kleinstadt Bargylia im Bann eines Festes," in: Claus Ambos, Stephan Hotz, Gerald Schwedler, and Stefan Weinfurter, eds., *Die Welt der Rituale: Von der Antike bis heute* (Darmstadt: Wissenschaftliche Buchgesellschaft), 59–65

Hunt, D. W. S. (1947) "Feudal Survivals in Ionia," *JHS* 67, 68–76

Huttner, Ulrich (2012) "Der Fluch des Apostels. Magie in den Philippusakten," in: Lutz Popko, Nadine Quenouille, and Michaela Rücker, eds., *Von Sklaven, Pächtern und Politikern: Beiträge zum Alltag in Ägypten, Griechenland und Rom*. Archiv für Papyrusforschung und verwandte Gebiete. Beiheft 33 (Berlin and New York: DeGruyter), 18–32

Idris, Hady R. (1954) "Fêtes chrétiennes en Ifriqiya à l'époque zîrîde," *Revue africaine* 98, 261–276
Irshai, Oded (2009) "The Christian appropriation of Jerusalem in the fourth century: The case of the Bordeaux Pilgrim," *Jewish Quarterly Review* 99, 465–498
Jacobs, Martin (1998) "Theatres and performances as reflected in the Talmud Yerushalmi," in: Schäfer, 327–347
Jeffreys, Elizabeth (1979) "The attitudes of Byzantine chroniclers towards ancient history," *Byzantion* 49, 199–238
Jeffreys, Elizabeth, ed. (1990a) *Studies in John Malalas*. Byzantina Australiensia 6 (Sydney: Australian Association for Byzantine Studies)
Jeffreys, Elizabeth (1990b) "Malalas' world view," in Jeffreys (1990a), 55–66
Jeffreys, Elizabeth, Michael Jeffreys, Roger Scott et al. (1986) *John Malalas: The Chronicle* (Melbourne: Australian Association for Byzantine Studies)
Johnston, David (1989) "Justinian's *Digest*: The interpretation of interpolation," *Oxford Journal of Legal Studies* 9, 149–166
Johnston, Sarah Iles (2008) *Ancient Greek Divination* (Oxford: Blackwell)
Jones, Christopher E. (1997) "Epigrams from Hierapolis and Aphrodisias," *Hermes* 125, 203–214
Jones, Christopher E. (1999) "A decree from Thyatira in Lydia," *Chiron* 29, 1–28
Jones, Christopher E. (2012) "The fuzziness of 'paganism'," *Common Knowledge* 18, 249–254
Jordan, David R. (1978) "A silver phylactery at Istanbul," *Zeitschrift für Papyrologie und Epigraphik* 28, 84–86
Jordan, David R. (1991) "A new reading of a phylactery from Beirut," *Zeitschrift für Papyrologie und Epigraphik* 88, 61–69
Jordan, David R., and Roy Kotansky (1996) "Two phylacteries from Xanthos," *Révue Archéologique*, 161–174
Jules-Rosette, Bennetta (1994) "Decentering ethnography: Victor Turner's vision of anthropology," *Journal of Religion in Africa* 24, 160–81
Jüthner, Julius (1902) "Die Augusteia in Olbasa," *Wiener Studien* 24, 285–291
Kahlos, Maijastina (2005) "Pompa diaboli. The grey area of urban festivals in the fourth and fifth centuries," in: Charles Deroux, ed., *Studies in Latin Literature and Roman History* 12 (Brussels: Latomus), 467–483
Kaldellis, Anthony (2003) "The religion of Ioannes Lydos," *Phoenix* 57, 300–316
Kaldellis, Anthony (2007) *Hellenism in Byzantium: The Transformations of Greek Identity and the Reception of the Classical Tradition* (Cambridge: Cambridge University Press)
Kaldellis, Anthony (2011) "The Kalends in Byzantium, 400–1200 AD: A new interpretation," *Archiv für Religionsgeschichte* 13, 187–203
Kalinowski, Angela (2002) "The Vedii Antonini. Aspects of patronage and benefaction in second-century Ephesos," *Phoenix* 56, 108–149
Kantiréa, Maria (2007) *Les dieux et les dieux Augustes: Le culte impérial en Grèce sous les Julio-claudiens et les Flaviens* (Athens: Center for Greek and Roman Antiquity)

Karivieri, Arja (1995) "The Christianization of an ancient pilgrimage site. A case study of the Athenian Asklepieion," in: *Akten des* XII. *Internationalen Kongresses für christliche Archäologie.* Jahrbuch für Antike und Christentum, Ergänzungsband 20:2 (Münster: Aschendorff), 898–905

Kavoulaki, Athena (1999) "Processional performances and the democratic polis," in: Simon Goldhill and Robin Osborne, eds., *Performance Culture and Athenian Democracy* (Cambridge: Cambridge University Press), 293–320

Kehati, Pinhas (1987) "Avodah Zarah," in: *Avodah Zarah, Avot, Horayot: The Mishnah, Seder Nezsikin*, vol. 4 (Jerusalem: Eliner Library)

Kieckhefer, Richard (1990) *Magic in the Middle Ages* (Cambridge: Cambridge University Press)

Klose, Dietrich A. (2004) "Festivals and games in the East during the Roman Empire," in: Christopher Howgego, Volker Heuchert, and Andrew Burnett, eds., *Coinage and Identity in the Roman Provinces* (Oxford: Oxford University Press), 125–142

Knipp, David (2002) "The Chapel of Physicians at Santa Maria Antiqua," *Dumbarton Oaks Papers* 56, 1–23

Knoepfler, Denis (2004) "Les Rômaia de Thèbes: un nouveau concours musical (et athlétique ?) en Béotie," *Comptes Rendus de l'Académie des Inscriptions et Belles-Lettres*, 1241–79

Kofsky, Aryeh (1998) "Mamre: A case of a regional cult?" in: Aryeh Kofsky and Guy G. Stroumsa, eds., *Sharing the Sacred: Religious Contacts and Conflicts in the Holy Land. First–Fifth Centuries* CE (Jerusalem: Yad Izhak Ben-Zvi Publications), 19–30

Kokkinia, Christina (1999) "Rosen für die Toten im griechischen Raum und eine neue ῥοδισμός-Inschrift aus Bithynien," *Museum Helveticum* 56, 204–221

Kokkinia, Christina (2003) "Letters of Roman authorities on local dignitaries. The case of Vedius Antoninus," *Zeitschrift für Papyrologie und Epigraphik* 142, 197–213

Kolovou, Foteini, ed. (2006) *Die Briefe des Eustathios von Thessalonike* (Munich: Saur)

Kotansky, Roy (1994) *Greek Magical Amulets: The Inscribed Gold, Silver, Copper and Bronze Lamellae*, Part 1: *Published Texts of Known Provenance.* Papyrologica Colonensia 22/1 (Opladen: Westdeutscher Verlag)

Krauss, Samuel (1899) *Griechische und lateinische Lehnwörter in Talmud, Midrasch und Targum*, vol. 2 (Berlin: Calvary)

Kurtz, Eduard, ed. (1903) *Die Gedichte des Christophoros Mitylenaios* (Leipzig: Neumann)

Lambot, Cyril (1950) *Sermones selecti duodeviginti* (Utrecht: Spectrum)

Lana, Italo (1951) "I ludi Capitolini di Domiziano," *Rivista di Filologia ed Istruzione Classica* 79, 145–160

Lancel, Serge (1999) *Saint Augustin* (Paris: Fayard) (English trans.: 2002)

Landes, Christian, and Jean-Michel Carrié, eds. (2007) "Jeux et spectacles dans l'Antiquité tardive," *Antiquité Tardive* 15, 9–219

Lane Fox, Robin (1987) *Pagans and Christians* (New York: Harper Collins)

Le Goff, Jacques (1988) "Christianity and dreams (second to seventh century)," in: *The Medieval Imagination* (Chicago: University of Chicago Press), 193–231, 271–277 (orig. "Le christianisme et les rêves (IIe–VIIe siècles)," in: Tullio Gregory, ed., *I sogni nel Medioevo: Seminario Internazionale, Roma, 2–4 Ottobre 1983*, Rome: Istituto per il Lessico Intellettuale Europeo, 1985)

Lee-Stecum, Parshia (2006) "Dangerous reputations. Charioteers and magic in fourth-century Rome," *Greece & Rome* 53, 224–234

Leone, Petrus A., ed. (1968) *Ioannis Tzetzae Historiae* (Naples: Libreria Scientifica Editrice)

Lepelley, Jacques (1999) "Du triomphe à la disparition. Le destin de l'ordre équestre de Dioclétien à Théodose," in: Demougin, Devijver, and Raepsaet-Charlier, 629–646

Levene, Dan (1999) "«... and by the name of Jesus ...». An unpublished magic bowl in Jewish Aramaic," *Jewish Studies Quarterly* 6, 283–308

Levine, Lee I., ed. (1992) *The Galilee in Late Antiquity* (New York: Jewish Theological Seminary of America)

LiDonnici, Lynn R. (1995) *The Epidaurian Miracle Inscriptions: Text, Translation and Commentary*. Texts and Translations 36: Graeco-Roman Series 11 (Atlanta, Ga.: Scholars Press)

Liebermann, Saul (1964) *Midrash Debarim Rabbah* (Jerusalem: Wahrmann)

Liebs, Detlef (1997) "Strafprozesse wegen Zauberei. Magie und politisches Kalkül in der römischen Geschichte," in: Ulrich Manthe and Jürgen von Ungern-Sternberg, eds., *Grosse Prozesse der römischen Antike*, (Munich: Beck), 146–158

Liénart, Edmond (1934) "Un courtisan de Théodose," *Revue Belge de Philologie et d'Histoire* 13, 57–82

Lifshitz, Baruch (1977) "Scythopolis. L'histoire, les institutions et les cultes de la ville à l'époque hellenistique et imperiale", in: *Aufstieg und Niedergang der Römischen Welt* 2.8 (Berlin and New York: De Gruyter), 262–94

Ligt, Luuk de (1993) *Fairs and Markets in the Roman Empire: Economic and Social Aspects of Periodic Trade in a Pre-industrial Society* (Amsterdam: Gieben)

Litsas, Fotios K. (1980) *Choricius of Gaza: An Approach to his Work. Introduction, Translation, Commentary*. Dissertation, University of Chicago

Litsas, Fotios K. (1982) "Choricius of Gaza and his description of festivals at Gaza," *Jahrbuch der Österreichischen Byzantinistik* 32, 427–436

Lizzi Testa, Rita (2004) *Senatori, popolo, papi: Il governo di Roma al tempo dei Valentiniani* (Bari: Laterza)

Lizzi Testa, Rita (2009) "*Augures et pontifices*. Public sacred law in late antique Rome," in: Andrew Cain and Noel Lenski, eds., *The Power of Religion in Late Antiquity* (Farnham: Ashgate)

Lüdemann, Gerd, ed. (1996) *Die "Religionsgeschichtliche Schule": Facetten eines theologischen Umbruchs* (Frankfurt am Main: Peter Lang)

Lüdemann, Gerd, and Martin Schröder (1987) *Die religionsgeschichtliche Schule in Göttingen: Eine Dokumentation* (Göttingen: Vandenhoeck & Ruprecht)

Maas, Michael (1992) *John Lydus and the Roman Past: Antiquarianism and Politics in the Age of Justinian* (London and New York: Routledge)

Maas, Paul (1933) "Epidaurische Hymnen," *Schriften der Königsberger Gelehrten Gesellschaft* 9, *Geisteswissenschaftliche Klasse* 3, 127–161

MacMullen, Ramsay (1966) *Enemies of the Roman Order: Treason, Unrest, and Alienation in the Empire* (London: Routledge)

Madec, Goulven, ed. (1998) *Augustin Prédicateur (395–411)* (Paris: Institut des Études Augustiniennes)

Magdalino, Paul (1988) "The Bath of Leo the Wise and the 'Macedonian Renaissance' revisited: Topography, iconography, ceremonial, ideology," *Dumbarton Oaks Papers* 42, 97–118

Magi, Filippo (1972) *Il calendario dipinto sotto Santa Maria Maggiore.* Atti delle Pontificia Accademia Romana di Archeologia, serie 3. Memorie 11:1 (Rome: Tipografia Poliglotta Vaticana)

Malay, Hasan (1994) *Greek and Latin Inscriptions in the Manisa Museum* (Vienna: Verlag der Österreichischen Akademie der Wissenschaften)

Malay, Hasan (1999) *Researches in Lydia, Mysia and Aiolis.* Tituli Asiae Minoris, Ergänzungsband 23 (Denkschriften der Akademie Wien 279) (Vienna: Verlag der Österreichischen Akademie der Wissenschaften)

Manganaro Perrone, Giacomo (2007) "Magia 'benefica' nella Sicilia Tardoantica," *Epigraphica* 69, 263–285

Maraval, Pierre, ed. (1982) *Égérie: Journal de voyage (Itinéraire).* Sources Chrétiennes 296 (Paris: Cerf)

Maraval, Pierre (1985) *Lieux saints et pèlerinages d'Orient: Histoire et géographie des origines à la conquête arabe* (Paris: Cerf)

Maraval, Pierre (2002a) "The earliest phase of Christian pilgrimage in the Near East (before the 7th century)," *Dumbarton Oaks Papers* 56, 63–74

Maraval, Pierre, ed. (2002b) *Récits des premiers pèlerins chrétiens au Proche-Orient (IVe–VIIe siècle)* (Paris: Cerf)

Mărghitan, Liviu, and Constantin C. Petolescu (1976) "*Vota Pro Salute Imperatoris* in an inscription at Ulpia Traiana Sarmizegetusa," *Journal of Roman Studies* 66, 84–86

Markschies, Christoph (2007) "Gesund werden im Schlaf – Einige Rezepte aus der Antike," in: Hugo Brandenburg, Stefan Heid, and Christoph Markschies, eds.: *Salute e Guarigione nella Tarda Antichità: Atti della Giornata Tematica dei Seminari di Archeologia Cristiana (Roma – 20 maggio 2004)* (Vatican City: Pontificio Istituto di Archeologia Cristiana), 165–198

Markus, Robert A. (1990) *The End of Ancient Christianity* (Cambridge: Cambridge University Press)

Markus, Robert A. (1994) "Augustine on magic: A neglected semiotic theory," *Revue des Études Augustiniennes* 40, 375–388 Reprinted in: *Signs and Meanings: World and Text in Ancient Christianity* (Liverpool: Liverpool University Press, 1996), 125–146

Marshall, Peter (1987) *Enmity in Corinth: Social Conventions in Paul's Relations with the Corinthians.* Wissenschaftliche Untersuchungen zum Neuen Testament 2: 23 (Tübingen: Mohr Siebeck)

Martin, René (1972) "Apulée dans les *Géoponiques*," *Revue de Philologie* 98, 246–255

Mass, Michael (1992) *John Lydus and the Roman Past* (London: Routledge)
Massen, Friedrich, ed. (1893) *Concilia Aevi Merivingici*. MGH Leges: Concilia I (Hannover: Hahn)
Mastandrea, Paolo (1979) *Un neoplatonico Latino: Cornelio Labeone* (Leiden: Brill)
Mastrocinque, Attilio (2004) "Magia agraria nell'Impero Cristiano," *Mediterraneo Antico* 7, 795–836
Matthews, John F. (2000) *Laying Down the Law: A Study of the Theodosian Code* (New Haven: Yale University Press)
Maxwell, Jaclyn L. (2006) *Christianization and Communication in Late Antiquity: John Chrysostom and his Congregation in Antioch* (Cambridge: Cambridge University Press)
Mazza, Roberta (2005) "Dalla Bruma ai Brumalia. Modelli di cristianizzazione tra Roma e Constantinopoli," in: Saggioro, 161–178
McClymond, Kathryn (2008) *Beyond Sacred Violence: A Comparative Study of Sacrifice* (Baltimore: Johns Hopkins University Press)
McCormick, Michael (1986) *Eternal Victory: Triumphal Rulership in Late Antiquity, Byzantium and the Early Medieval West* (Cambridge: Cambridge University Press)
McGinn, Thomas A. J. (1998) *Prostitution, Sexuality, and Law in Ancient Rome* (New York and Oxford: Oxford University Press)
McLynn, Neil (2008) "Crying wolf: The pope and the Lupercalia," *Journal of Roman Studies* 98, 161–175
McNeill, John T., and Helena M. Gamer (1938) *Medieval Handbooks of Penance: A Translation of the Principal Libri Poenitentiales and Selections from Related Documents* (New York: Columbia University Press)
Mellor, Ronald (1975) *ΘΕΑ ΡΩΜΗ: The Worship of the Goddess Roma in the Greek World* (Göttingen: Vandenhoeck & Ruprecht)
Meslin, Michel (1970) *La fête des calendes de janvier sous l'Empire romain*. Collection Latomus 115 (Brussels: Latomus)
Meyer, Marvin, and Richard Smith, eds. (1994) *Ancient Christian Magic: Coptic Texts of Ritual Power* (San Francisco: Harper)
Michels, Agnes Kirsopp (1953) "The topography and interpretation of the Lupercalia," *Transactions of the American Philological Association* 84, 35–59
Michels, Agnes Kirsopp (1967) *The Calendar of the Roman Republic* (Princeton: Princeton University Press)
Milani, Celestina (1976) *Itinerarium Antonini Piacentini: Un viaggio in Terra Santa nel 560–570 d.C.* (Milan: Vita e Pensiero)
Millar, Fergus (1993) *The Roman Near East 31 B.C. – A.D. 337* (Cambridge, Mass.: Harvard University Press)
Millar, Fergus (2006) *A Greek Roman Empire: Power and Belief Under Theodosius II (408–450)*. Sather Classical Lectures 46 (Berkeley: University of California Press)
Miranda, Elena (1999) "La comunità giudaica di Hierapolis di Frigia," *Epigraphica Anatolica* 31, 109–155
Mitchell, Stephen (1990) "Festivals, games, and civic life in Roman Asia Minor," *Journal of Roman Studies* 80, 183–193

Moffatt, Ann, and Maxeme Tall, eds. (2012) *Constantine Porphyrogennetos: The Book Of Ceremonies.* Byzantina Australiensia 18 (Canberra: Australian Association for Byzantine Studies)

Montserrat, Dominique (1998) "Pilgrimage to the Shrine of SS Cyrus and John at Menouthis in Late Antiquity," in: David Frankfurter, ed., *Pilgrimage and Holy Space in Late Antique Egypt* (Leiden: Brill), 257–279

Moran, William L. (1992) *The Amarna Letters* (Baltimore: Johns Hopkins University Press) (French original: Paris, Cerf, 1987)

Moretti, Luigi, ed. (1953) *Iscrizioni Agonistiche Greche* (Rome: Signorelli)

Motte, André and Charles-Marie Ternes, eds. (2003) *Dieux, fêtes, sacré dans la Grèce et la Rome antiques.* Actes du Colloque tenu à Luxembourg du 24 au 26 octobre 1999 (Turnhout: Brepols)

Munier, Charles, ed. (1963) *Concilia Galliae a. 314–506.* Corpus Christianorum Series Latina 148 (Turnhout: Brepols)

Munier, Charles, ed. (1974) *Concilia Africae a. 345–525.* Corpus Christianorum Series Latina 149 (Turnhout: Brepols)

Munzi, Massimiliano (1994) "Sulla topografia dei Lupercalia. Il contributo di Constantinopoli," *Studi Classici e Orientali* 44, 347–364

Murgia, Charles E. (2003) "The dating of Servius revisited," *Classical Philology* 98, 45–69

Natalucci, Nicoletta, ed. (1991) *Pellerinaggio in Terra Santa: Itinerarium Egeriae* (Florence: Nardini)

Nedungatt, George, and Michael Featherstone (1995) *The Council in Trullo Revisited.* Kanonika 6 (Rome: Pontificio Instituto Orientale)

Nervegna, Sebastiana (2007) "Staging scenes or plays? Theatrical revivals of old Greek drama in antiquity," *Zeitschrift für Papyrologie und Epigraphik* 162, 14–42

Nielsen, Inge (2002) *Cultic Theatres and Ritual Drama: A Study in Regional Development and Religious Interchange Between East and West in Antiquity* (Aarhus: Aarhus University Press)

Nigdelis, P. M. and G. A. Souris (2005) Ανθύπατος λέγει: Ενα διάταγμα των αυτοκρατορικών χρώνων γιά τό γυμνάσιο της Βεροίας (Thessalonica: [s.n.])

Nijf, Onno van (2001) "Local heroes. Athletics, festivals and elite self-fashioning in the Roman East," in: Simon Goldhill, ed., *Being Greek Under Rome: Cultural Identity, the Second Sophistic and the Development of Empire* (Cambridge: Cambridge University Press)

Nilsson, Martin P. (1906) *Griechische Feste* (Berlin and Leipzig: Teubner)

Nilsson, Martin P. (1951) *Geschichte der griechischen Religion*, vol. 2 (2nd edn.). Handbuch der Altertumswissenschaft (Munich: Beck)

Nisbet, R. G. (1918) "The *festuca* and the *alapa* of manumission," *Journal of Roman Studies* 8, 1–14

Nixon, C. E. V. (1987) *Pacatus: Panegyric to the Emperor Theodosius* (Liverpool: Liverpool University Press)

Noailles, Pierre, and Alphonse Dain, eds. (1944) *Les Novelles de Léon VI le Sage* (Paris: Belles Lettres)

Nock, Arthur Darby (1972) *Essays on Religion and the Ancient World*, ed. Zeph Stewart (Oxford: Clarendon Press)
North, John A. (2008) "Caesar at the Lupercalia," *Journal of Roman Studies* 98, 144–160
North, John A., and Neil McLynn (2008) "Postscript to the Lupercalia. From Caesar to Andromachus," *Journal of Roman Studies* 98, 176–181
O'Meara, John J. (1959) *Porphyry's Philosophy from Oracles in Augustine* (Paris: Institut Augustinienne)
Oberhelman, Steven M. (2008) *Dreambooks in Byzantium: Six Oneirocritica in Translation* (Aldershot: Ashgate)
Opelt, Ilona (1970) "Die Volcanalia in der Spätantike," *Vigiliae Christianae* 24, 59–65
Oppenheimer, Aharon (1992) "Roman rule and the cities of the Galilee in Talmudic literature," in: Levine, 21–125
Ors, Alvaro d' (1986) *La ley Flavia Municipal* (Rome: Pontificia Universitas Lateranensis)
Osborne, John (1987) "The atrium of S. Maria Antiqua, Rome: A history in art," *Papers of the British School in Rome* 55, 186–223
Ozouf, Mona (1976) *La fête révolutionnaire: 1789–1799* (Paris: Gallimard) (English trans.: *Festivals and the French Revolution*, Cambridge, Mass.: Harvard University Press, 1988)
Parássoglou, Georg M. (1976) "Circular from a prefect. 'Sileat omnibus perpetuo divinandi curiositas'," in: Ann Ellis Hanson, ed., *Collectanea Papyrologica: Texts Published in Honor of H. C. Youtie* (Bonn: Habelt), 261–274
Parker, Robert (2011) "The Thessalian Olympia," *Zeitschrift für Papyrologie und Epigraphik* 177, 111–118
Paschoud, François (1971) "Zosime 2, 29 et la version païenne de la conversion de Constantin," *Historia* 20, 334–353
Patton, Kimberley C. (2004) "'A great and strange correction': Intentionality, locality, and epiphany in the category of dream incubation," *History of Religions* 43, 194–223
Pavis d'Escurac, Henriette (1987) "Magie et cirque dans la Rome antique," *Byzantinische Forschungen* 12 (= Mélanges F. Thiriet), 449–467
Peek, Werner (1971) "Milesische Versinschriften, Nr. 4," *Zeitschrift für Papyrologie und Epigraphik* 7, 196–200
Pellizani, Andrea (2003) *Servio: Storia, Cultura e Istituzioni nell'Opera di un Grammatico Tardodantico* (Florence: Olschki)
Perlman, Paula J. (2000)*City and Sanctuary in Ancient Greece: The theorodokia in the Peloponnese* (Göttingen: Vandenhoeck & Ruprecht)
Perpillou-Thomas, Françoise (1993) "Les Brumalia d'Apion II," *Tyche* 8, 107–109
Petit, Paul (1951) "Sur la date du *Pro Templis* de Libanius," *Byzantion* 21, 285–309
Petit, Paul (1956) "Recherches sur la publication et la diffusion des discours de Libanius," *Historia* 5, 479–509
Petrakos, Vasileios B. (1997) *Epigraphes tou Oropou* (Athens: Archaiologike Hetairia)

Petropoulou, Maria-Zoe (2008) *Animal Sacrifice in Ancient Greek Religion, Judaism, and Christianity, 100 BC – AD 200* (Oxford: Oxford University Press)
Petzl, Georg, ed. (1982) *Die Inschriften von Smyrna, Teil 1*. Inschriften griechischer Städte aus Kleinasien 23 (Bonn: Habelt)
Petzl, Georg, ed. (1994) "Die Beichtinschriften Westkleinasiens," *Epigraphica Anatolica* 22, 1–174
Petzl, Georg and Elmar Schwertheim (2006) *Hadrian und die dionysischen Künstler: Drei in Alexandreia Troas neugefundene Briefe des Kaisers an die Künstler-Vereinigung*. Asia Minor Studien 58 (Bonn: Habelt)
Pharr, Clyde (1952) *The Theodosian Code and Novels and the Sirmondian Constitutions: A Translation with Commentary, Glossary and Bibliography* (Princeton: Princeton University Press)
Phillips, C. Robert III (2007) "Approaching Roman religion. The case for *Wissenschaftsgeschichte*," in: Jörg Rüpke, ed., *A Companion to Roman Religion* (Malden, Mass.: Blackwell), 10–28
Phrantzoles, Konstantinos G., ed. (1992) Ὁσίου Ἐφραίμ τοῦ Σύρου ἔργα (Thessalonica: To Perivoli tis Panagias)
Piccaluga, Giulia (1981) "L'olocausto di Patrai," in: Olivier Reverdin and Bernard Grange, eds., *Le sacrifice dans l'antiquité*. Entretiens sur l'antiquité classique (Vandoeuvres and Geneva: Fondation Hardt), 243–277
Piccaluga, Giulia (2005) "La gestione sacrale della realtà," in: Saggioro, 193–200
Pirenne-Delforge, Vinciane (2006) "Ritual dynamics in Pausanias. The Laphria," in: Eftychia Stavrianopoulou, ed., *Ritual and Communication in the Graeco-Roman World*. Kernos Supplément 16 (Liège: Centre International d'Étude de la Religion Grecque Antique), 111–129
Pirenne-Delforge, Vinciane (2008) *Retour à la source: Pausanias et la religion grecque*. Kernos Supplément 16 (Liège: Centre International d'Étude de la Religion Grecque Antique)
Pirenne-Delforge, Vinciane (2010) "Mnasistratos, the 'hierophant' in Andania (IG 5.1.1390 and Syll.^{3} 735)," in: Dijkstra, Kroesen, and Kuiper, 219–35
Pleket, Harry W. (1970) "Nine Greek Inscriptions from the Cayster-Valley in Lydia: a republication," *Talanta* 2, 55–88
Pohlsander, Hans A. (1984) "Crispus: Brilliant career and tragic end," *Historia* 33, 79–106
Pomarès, Gilbert, ed. (1959) *Gélase Ier: Letter contre les Lupercales et dix-huit messes du sacramentaire Léonien*. Sources Chrétiennes 65 (Paris: Cerf)
Pongratz-Leisten, Beate (1994) *Ina šulmi īrub: Die kulttopographische und ideologische Programmatik der akītu-Prozession in Babylonien und Assyrien im 1. Jahrtausend v. Chr.* (Mainz: Von Zabern)
Pont, Anne-Valérie (2004) "Le paysage religieux grec traditionel dans les cités de l'Asie Mineure occidentale, au IVe et au début du Ve siècle," *Revue des Études Grecques* 117, 546–577
Pont, Anne-Valérie (2010) *Orner la cité: Enjeux culturels et politiques du paysage urbain dans l'Asie gréco-romaine*. Scripta Antiqua 24 (Pessac: Ausonius)

Portefaix, Lilian (1993) "Ancient Ephesus. Processions as media of religious and secular propaganda," in: Ahlbäck, 195–210

Pouilloux, Jean, Paul Roesch, and Jean Marcillet-Jaubert, eds. (1987) *Testimonia Salaminia*, vol. 2: *Corpus épigraphique*. Salamine de Chypre 13 (Paris: Boccard)

Pradel, Fritz (1907) *Griechische und süditalienische Gebete, Beschwörungen und Rezepte des Mittelalters*. Religionsgeschichtliche Versuche und Vorarbeiten 3:3 (Giessen: Alfred Töpelmann)

Price, Simon R. F. (1984) *Rituals and Power: The Roman Imperial Cult in Asia Minor* (Cambridge: Cambridge University Press)

Prickett, Stephen (2009) *Modernity and the Reinvention of Tradition: Backing into the Future* (Cambridge: Cambridge University Press)

Quet, Marie-Henriette (1981) "Remarques sur la place de la fête dans le discours des moralistes grecs et dans l'éloge des cités et des évergètes aux premiers siècles de l'Empire," in: Dunand, 39–84

Rea, John (1977) "A new version of P.Yale Inv. 299," *Zeitschrift für Papyrologie und Epigraphik* 27, 151–160

Reiske, Johann Jacob (1829–1830) *Constantini Porphyrogeniti imperatoris de cerimoniis aulae Byzantinae libri duo*, 2 vols. Corpus Scriptorum Historiae Byzantinae (Bonn: Weber)

Reynolds, Joyce M. (1962) "Vota pro salute imperatoris," *Papers of the British School at Rome* 30, 33–36

Reynolds, Joyce M. (1965) "Notes on Cyrenaican inscriptions," *Papers of the British School at Athens* 33, 52–55

Reynolds, Joyce (1982) *Aphrodisias and Rome: Documents from the Excavation of the Theatre at Aphrodisias Conducted by Professor Kenan T. Erim, Together with Some Related Texts* (London: Society for the Promotion of Roman Studies)

Riedel, Wilhelm, and W. E. Crum, eds. (1904) *The Canons of Athanasius of Alexandria: The Arabic and Coptic Versions* (Oxford: Williams & Norgate)

Ritner, Robert Kriech (1993) *The Mechanics of Ancient Egyptian Magical Practice* (Chicago: Chicago University Press)

Ritti, Tullia (1986) "Un epigramma del tardo impero da Hierapolis," *Annali della Scuola Normale Superiore di Pisa* 16, 691–716

Ritti, Tullia (1992–93) "Nuovi dati su una nota epigrafe sepolcrale con stefanotico da Hierapolis di Frigia," *Scienze dell'Antichità Storia Archeologia Antropologia* 6–7, 41–68

Rives, James B. (1999) "The decree of Decius and the religion of Empire," *Journal of Roman Studies* 89, 135–154

Rives, James B. (2003) "Magic in Roman law. The reconstruction of a crime," *Classical Antiquity* 22, 312–339

Rizakis, Athanassios (2008) "Langue et culture, ou les ambiguïtés identitaires des notables des cités grecques sous l'empire de Rome," in: Frédérique Biville, Jean-Claude Decourt, and Georges Rougement, eds., *Bilinguisme Gréco-Latin et épigraphie* (Lyon: Maison de l'Orient et de la Méditerranée), 17–34

Robert, Louis (1933) "Sur des inscriptions de Chios," *Bulletin de Correspondance Hellénique* 57, 505–543 (= *OMS* 1.473–529)

Robert, Louis (1935) "Études sur les inscriptions et la topographie de la Grèce Centrale. VI. Décrets d'Akraiphia," *Bulletin de Correspondance Hellénique* 59, 438–542 (= *OMS* 1.279–293)
Robert, Louis (1940) *Les gladiateurs dans l'Orient grec* (Paris: Champion)
Robert, Louis (1960a) *Hellenica: Recueil d'épigraphie de numismatique et d'antiquités grecques*, vol. 11–12 (Limoges: Bontemps) (repr. Paris: Maisonneuve, 1961)
Robert, Louis (1960b) "Études épigraphiques," *Revue des Études Anciennes* 62, 276–361 (= *OMS* 2.792–877)
Robert, Louis (1966) "Sur un decret d'Ilion et sur un papyrus concernant les cultes royaux," in: A. E. Samuel, ed., *Essays in Honour of Bradford Welles*. American Studies in Papyrology 1 (New Haven: American Society of Papyrologists), 175–211 (= *OMS* 7.599–635)
Robert, Louis (1970) "Deux concours grecs à Rome," *Comptes rendus de l'Académie des Inscriptions et Belles-Lettres*, 6–27. Reprinted in: Denis Rousset, ed., *Louis Robert: Choix d'écrits* (Paris: Belles Lettres, 2007), 247–266
Rogers, Guy M. (1991) *The Sacred Identity of Ephesos: Foundation Myths of a Roman City* (London and New York: Routledge)
Rotondi, Giovanni (1912) *Leges Publicae Populi Romani* (Milano: SEL) (repr. Hildesheim: Olms, 1962)
Roueché, Charlotte (1989) *Aphrodisias in Late Antiquity* (London: Society for the Promotion of Roman Studies) (The second edition of 2004 is electronic only: http://insaph.kcl.ac.uk/ala2004/inscription/index.html)
Roueché, Charlotte (1999) "Looking for late antique ceremonial: Ephesos and Aphrodisias," in: Herwig Friesinger and Fritz Krinzinger, eds., *100 Jahre Österreichische Forschungen in Ephesos: Akten des Symposions Wien 1995* (Vienna: Verlag der Österreichischen Akademie der Wissenschaften), 161–168
Rousseau, Philip (1979) "The death of Boethius. The charge of maleficium," *Studi Medievali* 20, 871–889
Roussel, Pierre (1931) "Le miracle de Zeus Panamaros," *Bulletin de Correspondance Héllenique* 55, 70–116
Ruiz-Montero, Consuelo (1999) Review of James N. O'Sullivan, "Xenophon of Ephesus. His Compositional Technique and the Birth of the Novel," *Gnomon* 71, 303–306
Rüpke, Jörg (1995) *Kalender und Öffentlichkeit: Die Geschichte der Repräsentation und religiösen Qualifikation von Zeit in Rom*. Religionsgeschichtliche Versuche und Vorarbeiten 40 (Berlin and New York: De Gruyter)
Rüpke, Jörg (2001) *Die Religion der Römer: Eine Einführung* (Munich: Beck) (Engl. trans.: *Religion of the Romans*, Cambridge: Polity Press, 2007)
Rüpke, Jörg (2005) *Fasti Sacerdotum: Die Mitglieder der Priesterschaften und das sakrale Funktionspersonal römischer, griechischer, orientalischer und jüdisch-christlicher Kulte in der Stadt Rom von 300 v. Chr. bis 499 n. Chr.* (Stuttgart: Steiner)
Rüpke, Jörg (2008a) *Fasti Sacerdotum: A Prosopography of Pagan, Jewish, and Christian Religious Officials in the City of Rome, 300 BC to AD 499* (Oxford: Oxford University Press)

Rüpke, Jörg, ed. (2008b) *Festrituale in der römischen Kaiserzeit* (Tübingen: Mohr Siebeck)
Rüpke, Jörg (2011) *Von Jupiter zu Christus: Religionsgeschichte in römischer Zeit* (Darmstadt: Wissenschaftliche Buchgesellschaft)
Russell, David A., ed. (1992) *Dio Chrysostom: Orations VII, XII and XXXVI* (Cambridge: Cambridge University Press)
Rutherford, Ian (2013) *State Pilgrims and Sacred Observers in Ancient Greece: A Study of Theōriā and Theōroi* (Cambridge: Cambridge University Press)
Sabbatucci, Dario (1988) *La religione di Roma Antica: dal calendario festivo all'ordine cosmico* (Milan: Mondadori)
Sacco, Giulia (1984) *Iscrizioni Greche d'Italia: Porto* (Rome: Edizioni di storia e letteratura)
Safrai, Zeva (1992) "The Roman army in the Galilee," in: Levine, 103–114
Saggioro, Alessandro, ed. (2005) *Diritto Romano e Identità Cristiana: Definizioni Storico-religiose e Confronti Interdisciplinari* (Rome: Carocci)
Salzman, Michele R. (1991) *On Roman Time: The Codex-Calendar of 354 and the Rhythms of Urban Life in Late Antiquity* (Berkeley, Los Angeles, and Oxford: University of California Press)
Samuel, Alan E. (1972) *Greek and Roman Chronology: Calendars and Years in Classical Antiquity* (Munich: Beck)
Sandwell, Isabella (2005) "Outlawing 'magic' or outlawing 'religion'? Libanius and the Theodosian Code as evidence for legislation against 'pagan' practices," in: William Harris, ed., *Understanding the Spread of Christianity in the First Four Centuries: Essays in Explanation* (Leiden: Brill), 87–124
Sandwell, Isabella (2007) *Religious Identity in Late Antiquity: Greeks, Jews and Christians in Antioch* (Cambridge: Cambridge University Press)
Sartre, Maurice (1995) *L'Asie Mineure et l'Anatolie d'Alexandre à Dioclétien* (Paris: Colin)
Sartre, Maurice (2001) *D'Alexandre à Zénobie* (Paris: Fayard)
Sartre, Maurice (2005) *The Middle East Under Rome*. English abridged edition of Sartre (2001). (Cambridge, Mass.: Harvard University Press)
Schachter, Albert (1981) *The Cults of Boiotia*, vol. 1: *Acheloos to Hera* (London: Institute for Classical Studies)
Schäfer, Peter (1979) "Die Flucht Johanan b. Zakais aus Jerusalem und die Gründung des 'Lehrhauses' in Jabne," in: *Aufstieg und Niedergang der römischen Welt 2.19.2* (Berlin and New York: De Gruyter), 43–101
Schäfer, Peter, ed. (1998) *The Talmud Yerushalmi and Graeco-Roman Culture* (Tübingen: Mohr Siebeck)
Schäfer, Peter (2002) "Jews and Gentiles in Yerushalmi Avodah Zarah," in: Peter Schäfer, ed., *The Talmud Yerushalmi and Graeco-Roman Culture*, vol. 3 (Tübingen: Mohr Siebeck), 335–352
Schäfer, Peter and Catherine Hezser, eds. (2000) *The Talmud Yerushalmi and Graeco-Roman Culture*, vol. 2 (Tübingen: Mohr Siebeck)
Schäublin, Christoph (1995) "Lupercalien und Lichtmess," *Hermes* 123, 117–125

Scheid, John (1975) *Les frères Arvales: Recrutement et origine sociale sous les empereurs julio-claudiens*. Bibliothèque de l'École des Hautes Études. Sciences religieuses (Paris: Presses Universitaires de France)

Scheid, John, ed. (1998) *Commentarii Fratrum Arvalium qui supersunt: Les copies épigraphiques des protocoles annuels de la Confrérie Arvale (21 av.–304 ap. J.C.)* (Rome: École Française de Rome)

Scheid, John, and Maria Grazia Granino Cecere (1999) "Les sacerdoces publiques équestres," in Demougin, Devijver, and Raepsaet-Charlier, 79–189

Scheltema, Jan Herman and Nicolaas van der Wal, eds. (1955) *Basilicorum libri LX. Series A, volumen 1: Textus librorum I–VIII* (Groningen and s'Gravenhage: J. B. Wolters and Martinus Nijhoff)

Schiller, Isabella, Dorothea Weber and Clemens Weidmann (2009) "Sechs neue Augustinuspredigten. Teil 2 mit Edition dreier Sermones zum Thema Almosen," *Wiener Studien* 122, 171–213

Schmid, Max (1911) *Beiträge zur Lebensgeschichte des Asterios von Amasea und zur philologischen Würdigung seiner Schriften* (Borna-Leipzig: Noske)

Schmidlin, Bruno, and Alfred Dufour, eds. (1991) *Jacques Godefroy (1587–1652) et l'humanisme juridique à Genève* (Basel: Helbing et Lichtenhahn)

Schmidt, Wilhelm (1908) *Geburtstag im Altertum*. Religionsgeschichtliche Versuche und Vorarbeiten 7.1 (Giessen: Töpelmann)

Scholz, Udo W. (1981) "Zur Erforschung der römischen Opfer (Beispiel: die Lupercalia)," in: Jean Rudhart and Olivier Reverdin, eds., *Le sacrifice dans l'antiquité*. Entretiens sur l'antiquité classique 27 (Vandoeuvres-Genève: Fondation Hardt), 289–328

Scholz, Udo W. (1993) "Consus und Consualia," in: Joachim Dalfen, Gerhard Petersmann, and Franz Ferdinand Schwarz, eds., *Religio Graeco-Romana: Festschrift für Walter Pötscher* (Horn: Berger), 195–213

Schürer, Emil (1973–1979) *The History of the Jewish People in the Age of Jesus Christ*, ed. Géza Vermès and Fergus Millar, 3 vols. (Edinburgh: Clark) (orig. German, *Geschichte des jüdischen Volkes im Zeitalter Jesu Christi*, 3 vols., Leipzig: Hinrichs, 1886–1911)

Schwartz, Joshua (1987) "The Encaenia of the Church of the Holy Sepulchre, the Temple of Solomon and the Jews," *Theologische Zeitschrift* 43, 265–281

Scott, Roger (1981) "The classical tradition in Byzantine historiography," in: Margaret Mullett and Roger Scott, eds., *Byzantium and the Classical Tradition* (Birmingham: Centre for Byzantine Studies, University of Birmingham), 61–74

Scott, Roger (1990a) "Malalas and his contemporaries," in: Jeffreys (1990a), 67–86

Scott, Roger (1990b) "Malalas' view of the classical past," in: Graeme Clark, ed., *Reading the Past in Late Antiquity* (Canberra: Australian National University Press), 147–164

Scullard, Howard H. (1981) *Festivals and Ceremonies of the Roman Republic* (London: Thames and Hudson)

Segal, Alan (1995) *Theatres in Roman Palestine and the Provincia Arabia* (Leiden: Brill), 56–61

Segenni, Simonetta (2007) "Calendari e vita municipale (Riflessioni su CIL, XI 1420–1421)," *Epigraphica* 69, 99–115

Sessa, Kristina (2012) *The Formation of Papal Authority in Late Antique Italy* (Cambridge: Cambridge University Press)

Selinger, Reinhard (2004 [2002]) *The Mid-third Century Persecutions of Decius and Valerian* (Frankfurt am Main: Peter Lang)

Sguaitamatti, Lorenzo (2012) *Der spätantike Konsulat*. Paradosis 53 (Fribourg: Presses Universitaires)

Shaked, Saul (1999) "Jesus in the magic bowls. Apropos Dan Levene's «... and by the name of Jesus ...»," *Jewish Quarterly Review* 6, 309–319

Sheppard, Anne (1982) "Proclus' attitude to theurgy," *Classical Quarterly* 32, 212–224

Shinners, John (2007) *Medieval Popular Religion, 1000–1500: A Reader*, 2nd edn. (Peterborough, Ontario: Broadview) (1st edn. 1997)

Simon, Dieter, and Spyros Troianos, eds. (1977) *Eklogadion und Ecloga privata aucta*. Forschungen zur Byzantinischen Rechtsgeschichte 3, Fontes Minores 2 (Frankfurt am Main: Vittorio Klostermann)

Sivan, Hagith (1988a) "Who was Egeria? Piety and pilgrimage in the age of Gratian," *Harvard Theological Review* 81, 59–72

Sivan, Hagith (1988b) "Holy Land pilgrimage and Western audiences: Some reflections on Egeria and her circle," *Classical Quarterly* 38, 528–53

Slater, William (2007) "Deconstructing festivals," in: Peter Wilson, ed., *The Greek Theatre and Festivals: Documentary Studies* (Oxford: Oxford University Press), 21–47

Smith, Andrew, ed. (1993) *Porphyrii Philosophi fragmenta* (Stuttgart and Leipzig: Teubner)

Smith, Jonathan Z. (1987) "The domestication of sacrifice," in Robert G. Hamerton-Kelly, ed., *Violent Origins: Walter Burkert, René Girard and Jonathan Z. Smith on Ritual Killing and Cultural Formation* (Stanford: Stanford University Press), 191–205

Snyder, Walter F. (1940) "Public anniversaries in the Roman Empire," *Yale Classical Studies* 7, 225–317

Sodano, Angelo Raffaele (1958) *Porfirio: Lettera Ad Anebo* (Naples: L'Arte Tipografica)

Sogno, Cristiana (2006) *Q. Aurelius Symmachus: A Political Biography* (Ann Arbor: University of Michigan Press)

Soler, Emmanuel (2006) *Le sacré et le salut à Antioche au IVe siècle apr. J.-C.: Pratiques festives et comportements religieux dans le processus de christianisation de la cité*. Institut Français du Prochain Orient, Bibliothèque Archéologique et Historique 176 (Beirut: Institut Français du Prochain Orient)

Solignac, Aimé (1998) "Le salut des païens d'après la prédication d'Augustin," in: Madec, 419–428

Sophocles, E. A. (1900) *Greek Lexicon of the Roman and Byzantine Periods (from B.C. 146 to A.D. 1100)* (New York: Scribners)

Speiser, Jean-Marie (1976) "La christianisation des sanctuaires païens en Grèce," in: Ulf Jantzen, ed., *Neue Forschungen in griechischen Heiligtümern* (Tübingen: Wasmuth), 309–320

Speyer, Wolfgang (1981) *Büchervernichtung und Zensur des Geistes bei Heiden, Juden und Christen* (Stuttgart: Hiersemann)
Steinby, Eva Margareta, ed. (1993–2000) *Lexicon topographicum urbis Romae* (Rome: Edizioni Quasar)
Stern, Henri (1953) *Le calendrier de 354: Étude sur son texte et ses illustrations*. Institut Français de Beyrouth. Bibliothèque archéologique et historique 55 (Paris: Geuthner)
Sternbach, Leon, ed. (1903) *Nicolai Calliclis carmina* (Cracow: Cracoviae Academiae Litterarum)
Strack, Paul L. (1933) *Untersuchungen zur römischen Reichsprägung des zweiten Jahrhunderts*, vol. 2: *Die Reichsprägung zur Zeit des Hadrian* (Stuttgart: Kohlhammer)
Stroumsa, Guy G. (1999) "Dreams and visions in Early Christian discourse," in: David Shulman and Guy G. Stroumsa, eds., *Dream Cultures: Explorations in the Comparative History of Dreaming* (New York; Oxford: Oxford University Press), 189–212. Reprinted in: *Barbarian Philosophy: The Religious Revolution of Early Christianity* (Tübingen: Mohr Siebeck, 1999), 204–237
Stroumsa, Guy G. (2005) *La fin du sacrifice: Les mutations religieuses de l'Antiquité tardive* (Paris: Jacob) (English trans.: *The End of Sacrifice*, Chicago: University of Chicago Press, 2009)
Syme, Roland (1961) "Who was Vedius Pollio?", *Journal of Roman Studies* 51, 23–30. Reprinted in: *Roman Papers*, vol. 2 (Oxford: Oxford University Press, 1979), 518–529
Taeger, Fritz (1960) *Charisma: Studien zur Geschichte des antiken Herrscherkults*, 2 vols. (Stuttgart: Kohlhammer)
Tafel, Gottlieb (Theophilus) Lucas Friedrich, ed. (1832) *Eustathii metropolitae Thessalonicensis opuscula* (Frankfurt: Schmerber) (repr. Amsterdam: A. M. Hakkert, 1964)
Talbot, Alice-Mary (2002) "Pilgrimage to healing shrines: The evidence of miracle accounts," *Dumbarton Oaks Papers* 56, 153–173
Tanaseanu-Döbler, Ilinca (2013) *Theurgy in Late Antiquity: The Invention of a Ritual Tradition* (Göttingen: Vandenhoeck & Ruprecht)
Tea, Eva (1937) *La Basilica di Santa Maria Antiqua* (Milan: Vita e Pensiero), 48–54
Thee, Francis C. R. (1984) *Julius Africanus and the Early Christian View of Magic*. Hermeneutische Untersuchungen zur Theologie 19 (Tübingen: Mohr)
Thiel, Andreas, ed. (1868) *Epistolae Romanorum pontificum genuinae*, vol. 1 (Braunsberg: Peter)
Thorndike, Lynn (1915) "Some medieval conceptions of magic," *The Monist* 25, 107–135
Thurn, Ioannes, ed. (2000) *Ioannis Malalae Chronographia*. Corpus Fontium Historiae Byzantinae (Berlin and New York: De Gruyter)
Torrelli, Mario (1992) *Typology and Structure of Roman Historical Reliefs* (Ann Arbor: University of Michigan Press)

Tortorella, Stefano (2000) "Luperci e Lupercalia. La documentazione iconografica," in: Andrea Carandini and Renata Capella, eds., *Roma: Romolo, Remo e la Fondazione della Città*. Catalogo della mostra (Milan: Electa), 244–255

Tremel, Jan (2004) *Magica Agonistica: Fluchtafeln im antiken Sport*. Nikephoros. Beiheft 10 (Hildesheim: Olms Weidmann)

Troianos, Spyros N. (1990) "Zauberei und Giftmischerei in mittelbyzantinischer Zeit," in: Günter Prinzing and Dieter Simon, eds., *Fest und Alltag in Byzanz* (Munich: Beck), 37–51, 184–188

Trombley, Frank R. (1978) "The council in Trullo (691–692). A study of the canons relating to paganism, heresy, and the invasions," *Comitatus* 9, 1–18

Trzcionka, Silke (2007) *Magic and the Supernatural in Fourth-Century Syria* (London: Routledge)

Turcan-Verkerk, Anne-Marie (2003) *Un poète latin chrétien redécouvert: Latinius Pacatus Drepanius, panégyriste de Théodose*. Collection Latomus 276 (Brussels: Latomus)

Turner, Victor (1969) *The Ritual Process: Structure and Anti-Structure* (Ithaca, N.Y.: Cornell University Press)

Ulf, Christoph (1982) *Das römische Luperkalienfest* (Darmstadt: Wissenschaftliche Buchgesellschaft)

Ullmann, Walter (1962) *The Growth of Papal Government in the Middle Ages: A Study in the Ideological Relation of Clerical to Lay Power* (London: Methuen)

Usener, Hermann (1911) *Das Weihnachtsfest*. Religionsgeschichtliche Untersuchungen 1 (2nd edn.) (Bonn: Friedrich Cohen) (orig. 1889; repr. 1969)

Valantasis, Richard, ed. (2000) *Religions of Late Antiquity in Practice* (Princeton: Princeton University Press)

Valli, Barbara (2007) "*Lupercis nudis lustratur antiquum oppidum Palatinum*: Alcune reflessioni sui Lupercalia," *Florentia* 2, 101–154

Van Andringa, William (2003) "Cités et communautés d'expatriés dans l'empire romain: le cas des *cives Romani consistentes*," in: Nicole Belayche and Simon C. Mimouni, eds., *Les communautés religieuses dans le monde gréco-romain: Essais de définition* (Louvain: Peeters), 49–60

Van Dam, Raymond (2007) *The Roman Revolution of Constantine* (Cambridge: Cambridge University Press)

Van Ess, Josef (2014) *Im Halbschatten: Der Orientalist Hellmut Ritter (1892–1971)* (Wiesbaden: Harrassowitz)

Van Straten, Folkert T. (1995) *Hiera Kala: Images of Animal Sacrifice in Archaic and Classical Greece*. Religions in the Graeco-Roman World 127 (Leiden: Brill)

Veltri, Giuseppe (2000) "Römische Religion an der Peripherie des Reiches. Ein Kapitel rabbinischer Rhetorik," in: Schäfer and Hezser, 81–138

Verbraken, P.-P. (1974) "Les fragments conservés des sermons perdus de saint Augustin," *Revue Bénédictine* 84, 245–270

Versnel, Hendrik S. (1993) *Inconsistencies in Greek and Roman Religion*, vol. 2: *Transition and Reversal in Myth and Ritual* (Leiden: Brill)

Veyne, Paul (1960) "Iconographie de la 'transvectio equitum' et des Lupercales," *Revue des Études Anciennes* 62, 100–112

Veyne, Paul (1976) *Le pain et le cirque: Sociologie historique d'un pluralisme politique* (Paris: Seuil)
Vogt, Albert, ed. (1935–1940) *Constantin VII Porphyrogénète: Le livre des cérémonies*. 2 vols. (Paris: Belles Lettres)
Wachsmuth, Curt (1897) *Iohannis Laurentii Lydi liber de ostentis et calendaria graeca omnia* (Leipzig: Teubner)
Walt, Siri (1997) *Der Historiker C. Licinius Macer: Einleitung, Fragmente, Kommentar*. Beiträge zur Altertumskunde 103 (Stuttgart: Teubner)
Wasserschleben, Friedrich Wilhelm H., ed. (1851) *Die Bußordnungen der abendländischen Kirche* (Halle: Graeger) (repr. Graz: Styria, 1958)
Waszink, J. H., and J. C. M. van Weiden, eds. (1987) *Tertullianus: De Idololatria*. Supplements to Vigiliae Christianae 1 (Leiden: Brill)
Watson, Alan, ed. (1998) *The Digest of Justinian: Translation* (Baltimore: Johns Hopkins University Press)
Watts, Edward (2005) "Winning the intracommunal dialogues: Zacharias Scholasticus' Life of Severus," *Journal of Early Christian Studies* 13, 437–464
Weber, Clifford (1989) "Egeria's Norman Homeland," *Harvard Studies in Classical Philology* 92, 437–456
Weber, Ronald J. (1989) "Albinus. The living memory of a fifth-century personality," *Historia* 38, 472–497
Wehrli, Fritz (1964) *Hauptrichtungen des griechischen Denkens* (Zurich: Artemis)
Weinstock, Stefan (1948) "A new Greek calendar and festivals of the Sun," *Journal of Roman Studies* 38, 37–42
Weinstock, Stefan (1964) "Saturnalien und Neujahrsfest in den Märtyrerakten," in: A. Stuiber and A. Hermann, eds., *Mullus: Festschrift für Theodor Klauser*. Jahrbuch für Antike und Christentum, Ergänzungsband 1 (Münster: Aschendorff), 391–400
Weir, Robert G. A. (2004) *Roman Delphi and its Pythian Games* (Oxford: Archaeopress)
Weiss, Peter (1991) "Auxe Perge. Beobachtungen zu einem bemerkenswerten städtischen Dokument," *Chiron* 21, 353–392
Wermighoff, Albert, ed. (1906/1908) *Concilia Aevi Karolini (742–842)*. MGH Leges: Concilia 2.1–2 (Hannover: Hahn)
Whitmarsh, Tim (2013) *Beyond the Second Sophistic: Adventures in Greek Postclassicism* (Berkeley and Los Angeles: University of California Press)
Wickham, Chris (2005) *Framing the Early Middle Ages: Europe and the Mediterranean 400–800* (Oxford: Oxford University Press)
Wilkinson, John (1999) *Egeria's Travels*, 3rd edn. (Warminster: Aris & Phillips) (first publ. 1971)
Wilkinson, John (2002) *Jerusalem Pilgrims Before the Crusades*, 2nd edn. (Warminster: Aris & Phillips) (first edn. 1977)
Wilson, Peter, ed. (2007) *The Greek Theatre and Festivals: Documentary Studies* (Oxford: Oxford University Press)
Wiseman, Peter (1995) *Remus: A Roman Myth* (Cambridge: Cambridge University Press)

Wissowa, Georg (1912) *Religion und Kultus der Römer* (2nd edn.). Handbuch der Altertumswissenschaft 5:4 (Munich: C.H.Beck) (First edn. 1892)

Wittenburg, Andreas (1990) *Il testamento di Epikteta* (Trieste: Giulip Bernardi)

Wörrle, Michael (1988) *Stadt und Fest im kaiserzeitlichen Kleinasien: Studien zu einer agonistischen Stiftung aus Oinoanda*. Vestigia. Beiträge zur Alten Geschichte 39 (Munich: Beck)

Wünsch, Richard (1898) *Sethianische Verfluchungstafeln aus Rom* (Leipzig: Teubner)

Yavetz, Zvi (1969) *Plebs and Princeps* (London: Oxford University Press) (repr. New Brunswick: Transaction Books, 1988; orig. Hebrew *Hamon U-Manhigim Be-Romi*, Tel Aviv: Devir, 1966)

York, Michael (1986) *The Roman Festival Calendar of Numa Pompilius*. American University Studies. Classical Languages and Literature 17:2 (New York, Bern, and Frankfurt: Peter Lang)

Zellinger, Joseph (1933) *Augustin und die Volksfrömmigkeit: Blicke in den frühchristlichen Alltag* (Munich: Max Hueber)

Zepos, Ioannes, and Panayotis Zepos, eds. (1931) *Jus Graecoromanum*, vol. 6: *Ecloga Privata Aucta* (Athens: Fexis)

Zeumer, Karl, ed. (1902) *Leges Visigothorum*. MGH Leges: Leges nationum Germanicarum 1 (Hannover and Lepizig: Hahn)

Zgoll, Annette (2006) *Traum und Welterleben im antiken Mesopotamien: Traumtheorie und Traumpraxis im 3.–1. Jahrtausend v. Chr. als Horizont einer Kulturgeschichte des Träumens*. Alter Orient und Altes Testament 333 (Münster: Ugarit-Verlag)

Ziegler, Ruprecht (1985) *Städtisches Prestige und kaiserliche Politik: Studien zum Festwesen in Ostkilikien im 2. und 3. Jahrhundert n. Chr.* (Düsseldorf: Schwann)

Index

Acca Larentia, 191
acclamations, 178, 236, 315
Adam, 69
Aelia Eudocia, 243, 257
Aelius Tubero, frg. 3, 165
Aigai, Asklepieion, 52, 253, 263, 320
Akraiphia, 22
Akraiphia, Ptoia, 18–20
alapa and manumission, 196
Alaric, *Breviarium*, 123
Albinus. *See* Caeionius Rufius A.
Alexander of Tralleis, on amulets, 301
Alföldy, Géza, 15
Almoura (Lydia), 26
Ambarvalia, 46
Ambrose, on amulets, 298
Amphiaraos, 246
amulet, 274, 288–294, 312
    Church opposition, 295–303
    from Beirut, 292
    from Laodikeia, 290
    from Oxyrrhynchos, 291
    from Tyre (?), 290
    from Xanthos, 293
    in Bern, 291
    in Byzantine law, 303
Anastasi, Giovanni, 282
Andania, mysteries, 26–27
Andromachus, 168
angels, 268, 269, 270, 289, 292, 293
Antioch, 103
    Kalendae, 128–138
    Olympic games, 50, 56
Antoninus Pius, 39, 251, 320
Anysius, 170, 183
Aphrodisias, 97, 317, 319
    imperial letters, 40
Apion of Oxyrhynchos, 214
Apollo Chalazios, 289
Apollo Sarpedonios, oracle in Seleukeia, 258
Apollonius of Tyana, 52, 254, 263, 287, 320

Apuleius, 192, 203, 276, 284
Arcadius, 122
Ares, festival of, 64 n. 13
Aristophanes, 33, 36
army
    festivals, 64, 71, 76, 100
    and Parilia, 83
    and Saturnalia, 87
    and Vota, 74, 87
Artemis Orthia, altar of, Sparta, 35
Ascension (festival), 125, 231
Asklepios, 29, 37, 244, 246, 256, 259
    in Aigai, 253
Asterius of Amaseia, 74
    on festivals, 138
    Hom. 4, On the Kalendae, 138–140
    on Kalendae, 75
    and Libanius, 139
astrology, 277, 280
Athanasius
    on amulets, 298
    Canons, 121, 281
Athena Pammousos, 43
Athenaios of Naukratis, *Deipn.* 8.63, 93
Athens, Asklepieion, 256
Atto of Vercelli, *Sermo III in festo Octavae Domini*, 215
Augustine, 113, 144, 159, 161, 169, 294, 317
    amulets, 297
    Christmas and Epiphany, 121
    De civ. Dei 1.8, 268
    Kalendae, 75, 140–144
    magic, 268–273
    ritual harvest protection, 295
    ritual healing, 302
    sermo 26 Dolbeau, 140–144, 268–273; date, 140 n. 44
    sermon Erfurt 4, 162
Augustus, 42, 74, 115, 280
    and Lupercalia, 163
    reform of legal calendar, 120

Index

Aurelius, bishop of Carthage, 152, 158
Autun, synod, 147
Avodah Zarah
  1:1, 83
  1:3, 62, 66–72
  1:4, 81
  1:7, 82

Baldovin, John, 234
banquets, 157, 202, 320
  replaced by other rites, 58
Baronius, Caesar, 167
Bede, *Historia ecclesiae Anglorum* 2.6, 265
Beirut Law School, and magic, 281
Belayche, Nicole, 243, 315
Beroia phallos procession, 23, 28
bilingualism, 47 n. 126
bishops
  destruction of images and temples, 156
  and emperors on festivals, 162; games, 94
  limits of power, 162
  opposed by local officials, 157
  pagan festivals, 65, 75, 147–162
  ritual healing, 302; radicalization, 152
  succeed wealthy sponsors, 161
  against Theodosius' calendar reform, 128
  Visigoth, on Kalendae, 150
Boniface
  amulets, 296
  Kalendae, 206, 219
book-burning, 280–281
Braudel, Fernand, 224
Bremmer, Jan, 53
Brown, Peter, 7, 161
Bruggisser, Philippe, 186
bruma (day), 204
  and Bruma (festival), 205
  and Brumalia, 204, 208
Bruma (festival), 77, 192, 201–207, 220
  date, 203
  gift-giving, 201
  in eighth-cent. Rome, 206
  under Charlemagne, 206
Brumae (festival), 202
Brumalia, 62, 76, 185, 192, 207–214, 230
  cake offerings, 209, 210
  in Egypt, 214
  etymology in John Malalas, 190, 191
  gift-giving, 211; John Malalas, 189–192
  opposed by the Church, 211, 214–217
  salutationes, 211
  Saturnalia, 211, 212
  survival in Byzantium, 217
Brutus, in John Malalas, 192–199
Burchard of Worms, 158 n. 108, 225, 296

cacologia, 169
Caecina Paetus, 38
Caeionius Rufius Albinus, 108
calendar
  Clodius the Etruscan, 204
  cod. Baroccianus 131, 207
  Feriale Duranum, 63, 74
  Hermes Trismegistos, 204
  Menologia Rustica, 91
  of 354 (Philocalus), 63, 65, 73, 76, 116, 119
  Polemius Silvius, 65, 76, 95, 116, 120, 165, 189
  Santa Maria Maggiore, 65
candles, 89, 135, 206
Canterbury, 265, 266
Capitolia (games), 95–98
  length of, 230
Cara Cognatio, 201
Carandini, Andrea, 180
Carthage, 140–144
Carthage, council of (401), 153–154
  against idolatry, 154
  pagan festivals, 153
Cassianus Bassus, 203
Cassiodorus, *Variae* 3.51.2, 112, 278
Chalanda Marz, 1, 216
charakteres, 298, 303
charioteers
  foot race, 179, 180, 222
  and sorcery, 112, 278, 282
Choricius of Gaza, 131
  Or. 13, 214
Christianization, 5, 120, 162, 166, 206, 239, 296
Christmas, 120, 125, 126
Christophoros of Mytilene
  Poem 124 Kurtz, 210
chrysophoroi, 43, 44
church
  and emperors (church and state), 114, 144–146, 157, 162, 216, 239
  and Theodosius' legal calendar, 150
Cicero, 12
circumcision, Christ's, 125, 148, 215
circus
  games, festival of Mars, 189
  games, *Parilia*, 93
  Lupercalia in Byzantium, 177
  sorcery, 112, 278
Claudius, 115
Clement of Alexandria, on amulets, 295
Clodius Tuscus, 204
coins, distribution of
  in Oinoanda, 58
  in Syros, 58
  See also sparsiones
Columella, 204

Commodus, 90
Consilia, 185
  etymology, 198
  festival, 192–199
  meaning, 193
  meaning in Malalas, 198
Constantine
  building program in Jerusalem, 227
  on divination, 283
  on imperial cult, 114
  on magic, 273–275, 283
  sacrifice to Jupiter, 152
Constantine Porphyrogennetos, 236
  Liber caerimoniarum: on Kalendae and Vota, 221–222; on the Lupercalia, 175–181; 1.82 Vogt, 175–181; 2.16 p. 606 Reiske, 212
Constantinople
  foundation day, 61, 114, 117, 120
  Hippodrome, 180
  lupercal, 181
  Saint Michael as healer, 261
Constantius, 316
  and magic, 275
  on sorcery, 284
Consualia, 194, 279
consuls, 131, 139, 223
contests, 38, 70, 78
  athletic, at the Ptoia, 19
  in Syria-Palaestina, 78–79
  musical: Eretria, 36; Oinoanda, 30, 51; Ptoia, 19
  Pan-Lycian, in Oinoanda, 58
  sacred, in Ephesos, 31, 43
continuity
  Eleusis, 24–25
  Hellenistic festivals, 35–36
  incubation, 255–262
  Kalendae, 207
  processions, 234–236
  Ptoia, 18–20
Cornelius Labeo, 172
Cosmas of Jerusalem, *Ad carm. S. Greg.* 64, 287
councils
  Braga, 147
  Carthage, 153
  Eliberi, 152
  Laodikeia, 152, 294
  Rome, 206, 219
  Toledo, 149, 150
  Tours, 147, 148, 152, 223
  Trullo, 74, 136, 147, 148, 214, 216
Crawford, John R., 5, 62
Crepereius Rogatus, Lucius, 164
Cyril of Alexandria, 260
  Oratiuncula 3, 261
Cyril of Jerusalem, on liturgy, 227–229

Dagron, Gilbert, 186, 188, 258 n. 62
Daphne near Antioch, 133, 233
Decius, emperor, 15
Decretum Gelasianum, on amulets, 303
Democritus, 204
demonology and laws on magic, 286
demons, 34, 134, 135, 159, 209, 233, 250, 251, 269
Deubner, Ludwig, 245
Didyma oracle, 56, 320
dies lampadarum, 310
Dieterich, Albrecht, 245
Dio Chrysostom
  benefactor of Prusa, 39
  on festival spending, 55
  Or. 12.85, 11
Dionysiac artists, 40, 97, 315
Dionysos, 79, 217, 220
distributions, 161. *See also sparsiones*
divination, 254, 273
Dix, Gregory, 228
doctors and amulets, 298 n. 128, 300
Domitian, 96
Dor (Dora) incubation shrine, 255
dream healing Christian, 255
  Christian narrations, 263–267
  and incubation, 263
  rejected, 253
  ritual, Christian, 262–263
  Thekla, 259
dreams
  in Augustine, 251
  in Christian theology, 244, 249–253
  and demons, 251, 253
  and divination, 252; in *Passio Perpetuae,* 249
  terminology, 249 n. 31
  in Tertullian, 249–251
  veracity, 248
Drepanius Pacatus, 107

Easter, 114, 117, 118, 230, 231
Edessa, 155
Egeria, 118, 121, 226, 241
  in Jerusalem, 117
  Itinerary, 227–229
Eleusis, mysteries, 24
Eliberi, council, 152
Elpinike Regilla, 24
emperors
  and bishops on festivals, 156, 162
  city autonomy, 40–41
  public entertainment, 94, 174, 315–318
Encaeniae, 230, 308
  and Sukkot, 232
Ennaïr (festival in the Maghreb), 225
Epameinondas of Akraiphia, 18–20

ephebes, 17, 19, 24–25, 28, 34, 35 n. 87, 44, 233
Ephesos, 39
　Artemision, 42, 45; cult reform, 28–29
　imperial letters, 40
　Rome, 43
　sacred month, 33, 230
　Salutaris procession, 31–32, 41–46, 236
Epidauros, 246
　purity inscription, 52
　See also incubation, *iamata*
Epiphany (festival), 120, 126, 230, 311
Eretria, Artemisia in, 36
euergetism, 37–40
　banquets vs. construction, 57, 320
　building program, 39, 319
　Christian, 319
Eunapius, *VS* 5.2.2–7, 243
Eusebius of Caesarea, 227, 253
Eustathius of Thessalonica, *Epist.* 7, 220
Euticius, Saint, 264–265
exorcists, 292, 294

fairs, 78, 81
fasting, 161, 223, 230, 231, 238
　Christian festivals, 230
　Kalendae, 142, 143, 148, 152, 308
　See also heortae
Faustulus, 189, 190
Februarius, alleged Roman god, 169–170
Februus, alleged Roman god, 169
Feriae, legal, summer and
　　harvest, 114, 115
Feriale Duranum, 63, 64, 74
festival names, 309, 310
　abstract nouns, 33, 68, 86, 159
　Christian, 311
　Parilia, 95
　politics, 312
　εὐφροσύνη, 33
　Ἡλιοδυσία, 207
　Καλάνδαι, 67, 132
festivals
　agency of distribution, 314–318
　and daily life, 59–60; economic impact, 160
　　(*see also* fairs)
　and enjoyment, 308
　foundation, agency, 99–101
　and gods, 313
　Hellenistic, 35
　joyful occasion, 32
　length, 33, 229
　and seasons, 313
　See individual festival names
festivals, Christian
　and Theodosius' reform, 120–122

length, 230
replacing non-Christian festivals, 308
See also individual festival names
festivals, Jewish
　and Christian festivals, 232, 311
　definitory, 67
　duration, 232
　See also individual festival names
Fraschetti, Augusto, 107
Frazer, Sir James G., 313

Gadara, hot springs, 241–245
Galen, on amulets, 301
games, 40, 321
　Capitolia in Rome, 96
　gladiatorial, 55, 82, 321
　Olympic, 50
　Olympic, in Antioch, 51, 56
　See also contests
Gauthier, Philippe, 37
Gaza
　Brumalia, 214
　Consualia, 279
　festival of Marnas, 80, 194
Gelasius (pope)
　Decretum Gelasianum, 303
　letter on Lupercalia, 168–175; pub. by
　　Baronius, 167; title, 168
　Lupercalia in Constantinople, 175
Gelzer, Thomas, 173
Geoponica
　1.1.9, 203
　1.5.3–4, 203
Georgios Grammatikos, *Poem* 9 Ciccolella, 213
Georgios Kedrenos, on Brumalia, 205
gift-giving, 77, 132, 201, 202
　cakes, 209
　candles, 89
　criticism, 138, 142, 143, 161
　Kronia, 88
　βρουμάλιον, 217
Godefroy, Jacques, 106, 106 n. 5, 114,
　　122, 129
Gortyn, 89
gospel book, as amulet, 302
Gothofredus. *See* Godefroy, Jacques
Greek, used in official documents, 47
Greek words
　βρουμάλιον, 192, 210 n. 39
　γοητεία, 287
　δαίμων, 133
　ἐπιφανέστατος (of the emperor), 41
　ἐπιφανής, 311
　εὐταξία, 35
　εὐφροσύνη, 33, 318 n. 30

Καλάνδαι, 132
κράτησις, 68, 86
φάρμακον, 283
Greekness, 51
Gregory the Great
 and amulets, 302
 Dial. 3.38, 264–265

Hadrian, 40, 93
 Dionysiac artists, 40
 Zeus Panhellenios, 41
Hamilton, Mary, 245
Hannukah, 232
harvest protection spell, 274, 286, 288, 289–290, 295
healing, 56, 111, 183, 187, 229, 241–245. *See also* *iamata*, incubation
healing miracle, doubts, 267
Hebrew
 Greek words in, 68, 69, 70
 names in invocations, 291, 292, 293
Heliodorus, 16
Hellenic, meanings, 220
heortae, fast-days in Jerusalem, 231
Hermes Trismegistos, 204
Herodes Atticus, 24, 25, 33
Herodian, 15
Hierapolis (Pammukkale), 84–85, 307, 319
Hobsbawm, Eric, 25
Holleman, A. W. J., 5
Hollmann, Alexander, 279
Holy Week, 118
Honorius, 154, 156
Horace, *Epode* 16, 187
hymns, 28, 29, 30, 56, 178

iamata, 248, 259, 264
Iamblichus, 243, 270
idolothytum, 297
Idris, Hady Roger, 224
Ildephonsus of Toledo, 167 n. 23
images
 allegorical, 47
 See also under procession
imperial cult, 22, 30, 41, 317
 Accession Day, 69, 90, 114
 birthdays, 70–71, 90, 99, 114
 commemoration of death, 72
incense, 58, 80, 155, 229, 233, 242, 320
incubation
 Christian, 241–245, 262–263
 continuity, 255–258
 pre-Christian, 246–248
 ritual structure, 247

incubation church, continuity, 258–262
inscriptions
 bilingual, 48–49
 luperci, 164–165
 protecting harvest, 289–290
inscriptions (individual)
 Ameling (2004), 414 no. 196 (Hierapolis/ Pammukkale), 84–85
 CIL 6.2160, 164
 CIL 6 31413, 31414, 36969, 36960 (Rome), 108, 109
 I.Cret. 4.300 (Gortyn), 89
 I.Didyma 217, 29, 56, 320
 I.Ephes. 27, 41–46
 I.Ephes. 29, 48–49
 I.Ephes. 3801, 70
 I.Stratonikeia 1101, 29
 IG ii² 1078, 24–25
 IG v 1.1390 (Andania), 26–27
 IvP 2.347, 99
 StEGO 02/09/10, 319
 StEGO 02/12/06 (Hierapolis), 319
 StEGO 08/01/01, 320
 StEGO 08/01/53, 320
Ioannes Tzetzes, *Histories* 13.239–244, 220
Isidore of Seville, on the Kalendae, 149
Isis, 5, 246, 261
 Menouthis, 260
 Ostia, 159
Isis and Sarapis, healing, 259
Itinerarium Placentinum
 46, 255, 266
 7.6–8, 241–245, 266
 manuscripts, 241

Jerome, *Vita Hilarionis* 11, 279
Jewish elements in spells, 291–293
John Chrysostom, 144
 on amulets, 299
 date, 134
 Hom. in Kalendas, 134–138
 Libanius, 134, 137–138
John Lydus
 De mensibus 4.158, 208
 De mensibus 4.25, 172
 De ostentis 69, 204
John Malalas, 184–200
 Chron. 7.2., 185–189
 Chron. 7.3, 188
 Chron. 7.7, 189–192
 Chron. 7.9, 192–199
 Livy, 193
 narrative traditions, 189, 199
Julian
 in Antioch, 133

Julian (cont.)
    Misopogon 34, 233
Julius Africanus, 300
Jupiter Optimus Maximus, New Year's
    sacrifice, 152
Justin Martyr
    Apologia 1.13, 233 n. 26
    Apologia 1.14, 251
Justinian Code, interpolation, 127

Kairouan, 224
Kaldellis, Anthony, 219
Kalendae Ianuariae, 77, 98, 114, 115,
    197, 202
    African bishops, 162
    alms-giving, 143
    army, 139
    Asterius of Amaseia, 138–140
    Augustine, 140–144
    banquets, 130, 144
    begging, 139
    carnival, 133, 134, 215
    contested, 146–151
    date, in the Greek East, 86
    duration, 73
    Eastern bishops on, 147
    fasting, 142, 148, 152, 308
    generosity, 131, 142
    gift-giving, 161
    horse races, 132
    in Africa, 86
    in Byzantium, 126, 217, 219–221
    in Carthage, 140–144
    in eighth-cent. Rome, 206
    in Hierapolis, 84–85
    in medieval Tunisia, 224–225
    in Pergamon, 100
    in the Talmud, 67, 69
    John Chrysostom, 134–138
    Libanius, 128–132
    masks, 133, 135, 147, 149
    minor Latin sermons, 144
    Western bishops on, 147
Kalendae Martiae, 215. *See also* Matronalia
Karavieri, Arja, 257
Knipp, David, 257
Kollouthos of Lycopolis, 213
Kos, 246
Kronia. *See* Saturnalia

laetitia, 94, 160
Laetitia (festival in Hippo), 159, 317
lampoons
    against pope Symmachus, 174
    at Kalendae, 133, 139
    at Lupercalia, 173
lamps, 229, 237, 238, 242
Laodikeia, council, 152, 294
Laphria, in Patrai, 34
Latte, Kurt, 63
law
    amulets, 303
    closing temples, 129, 155, 157
    collapse of legal tradition, 151
    divination, 283
    festivals, 105–106, 125–127, 131, 150, 151, 155,
        216, 223
    magic, 111–112, 273–288
Le Goff, Jacques, 244, 264
legal texts
    Basilika, 115, 124, 127
    Breviarium of Alaric, 123
    CJ 3.12.6, 105–106, 124 n. 79, 126
    CJ 9.18.9, 112
    CTh 2.8.19, 105–106
    CTh 2.8.22, 122
    CTh 9.16.11, 111
    CTh 9.16.3, 273, 283
    CTh 9.16.4, 276
    CTh 9.16.5, 276 n. 35
    CTh 16.10.16, 156, 160
    CTh 16.10.17, 155, 320
    CTh 16.10.18, 154, 155
    CTh 16.10.19, 156
    CTh 16.10.2, 316
    CTh 16.10.3, 316; *interpretatio* on *CTh*
        2.8.18, 125
    Justinian, Novella 131, 216
    laws of the Burgundian kings, 150
    laws of the Visigoth kings, 150
    Liber iudiciorum, 124, 125
Leontius, Saint, 159, 317
leprosy, 242, 244
Lethardus, Saint, 266
Lex Cornelia de sicariis et veneficis, 274, 285
Libanius, 57, 144, 221, 238
    Asterius of Amaseia, 139
    John Chrysostom, 134, 137–138
    local Olympics, 51
    Or. 30, *On the Temples*, 129, 145, 155
    Or. 9, *On the Kalendae*, 128–132, 133; date, 129
    panegyric on Julian, 133
    Progymn. 12.5, 129
libation, 24, 32, 38, 58, 233, 320
Licinius Macer, 191
Lindley, Ottilie Caroline, 245 n. 21
liturgy
    Christian: origins, 226; pagan parallels,
        229–232, 234–238
    Jerusalem, 227–229

Livy, 171
  and John Malalas, 193
Lucian
  On sacrifices, 52
  on the Kronia, 89
ludus votivus, 222
lupercal in Constantinople, 181
Lupercalia, 62
  after Constantine, 165
  before Constantine, 163–168
  Byzantium, 163–183
  fifth-cent. Rome, 168–175
  good harvests, 171
  horse race, 177–179
  Purificatio Mariae, 166
luperci
  actors, 173
  Circus Maximus, 180
  iconography, 164
  inscriptions, 164–165
  nudi, 164
  race, 164, 180
  statues of, 163
  transformed in Byzantium, 179–181
Lykaina, 189, 190
Lyttos, 70

Maas, Michael, 209
Macrobius, *Saturnalia*, 76, 108, 169
magic, magician, 294
  Augustine, 268–273
  Beirut law school, 281
  Christian, 279
  Constantine, 111, 273–275, 283
  Constantius, 276, 284
  imperial legislation, 273–288
  Isidore of Sevil, 252
  Justinian's Code, 280
  Roman law, 111–112
  Theodosius I, 278
  Valentinian I, 277
Magnentius, 277
Maiouma, 5
maleficus, 276, 284, 285
Mamre, 79, 253
  fair, 81
Manichaeans, 112
  and sorcery, 296
Mansi, Gian Domenico, 146
manumission, 195–198
  manumissio apud consilium, 195
  manumissio vindicta, 195
Maraval, Pierre, 243, 263
Marc Anthony, as *lupercus*, 172
Marcus Aurelius, speech to the senate, 116

Marnas, 80, 194, 279
Martin of Braga, 147, 148, 158, 225
Martin, René, 203
masks, 59, 136, 147, 233
  at the Kalendae, 135, 147
Matronalia, 77, 202
  John Lydus, *De mensibus*, 215
  opposed by the Church, 215
Matthews, John, 6, 123
Maximus of Aigai, 320
McLynn, Neil, 168
Menander Rhetor, 13, 14
Menardus, Hugo, 167
Menologia Rustica, 91
Menouthis, 259–261
Meslin, Michel, 5, 63, 219
Miletos, Kabeiroi, 38
Millar, Fergus, 6, 107
Mnasistratos of Andania, 26
Moses, 268
  baths of, 242
Munzi, Massimiliano, 181
myth in Byzantium, 184–200

Natalis Urbis, 89–95, 98, 99, 116
Nepualios, 300
Nero Zeus Eleutherios, 23
night, 238, 252
Nikolaos Kallikles, *Poem* 37.61–66, 220
Nilsson, Martin P., 13
Notion, 289

Oinoanda, 58
  Demostheneia, 30, 51, 230
  Euaresteia, 24
Olbasa and Capitolia, 97
oracle
  Ammon, on sacrifice, 320
  Didyma, 56, 320
  Mnasistratos of Andania, 27
  Ptoion, 19, 20, 22
  Sarpedon, 258 n. 62
  Trophonios, 21
Origen
  Contra Celsum 8.22–23, 308
  on Christian holidays, 120
  on festivals, 308
Orkistos, 33, 318
Ostia, temple of Isis, 159
Ovid
  Fasti 1.63–88, 73
  luperci, 164
Oxyrrhynchos, Capitolia, 97
Ozouf, Mona, 4, 312

paean, 24, 29, 56
Pan, 217, 220
Panathenaia, procession, 236
panegyric, 99, 107, 133, 134
Parilia, 83, 89–95, 127
  foundation of Rome, 91
  renamed Natalis Urbis, 93; reason, 95
  shepherds' festival, 91
  urban ritual, 92
  See also Natalis Urbis
Passover, 85, 311
Paul, 45, 54, 134, 142, 143, 152, 251, 307. *See also* Peter and Paul
Paulus, jurist, 195, 274
Pausanias, 12
Pentecost, 85, 119 n. 62, 120, 121, 125, 230
Pergamon, 99
Pesah, 67, 311
Peter and Paul (festival), 119, 121
Petropolou, Maria-Zoe, 306
Philastrius of Brescia, on amulets, 296
Philocalus. *See under* calendar
Philostratus, *Apollonius of Tyana*, 52
Philotheos, *Klerologion*, 217, 222
Phinehas, 136
Plato on healing methods, 300
Pliny the Elder, 204, 292
Pliny the Younger, 13, 15
  and benefactions, 39
  Ep. 10.96, 227
Plutarch, 12, 24, 166
  on festival spending, 55–56
Polemius Silvius. *See under* calendar
pompa and the Devil, 233
Pompeius Trogus on Pan Lupercus, 165
Porphyry, 221, 280
  amulets, 300
  De regressu animae, 269, 269 n. 4
  Letter to Anebo, 270
  On abstinence, 52
Price, Simon, 41, 72
priests, 299
  amulets, 294
  as sorcerers and exorcists, 294
procession, 17, 24, 26, 233
  centrifugal, 44
  Christian liturgy, 232–234
  circular, 46
  Eleusinian Mysteries, 24
  Ephesos, Salutaris, 31–32, 41–46, 236
  Golgatha liturgy, 234
  nighttime, 238
  Palm Sunday in Jerusalem, 234–236
  Pentecost in Jerusalem, 236–238
  pompa circensis, 47

pompa funebris, 47
  with images, 34, 36, 41–46
  with masks, 34
  πομπή, meaning, 17 n. 21
Proculus, *praef. urbi* of Constantinople, 108
Prudentius, *C. Symmachum* 816, 165
Ptoion
  festival Ptoia, 19
  history, 20–22
  Ptoia Kaisareia, 24
  Πτοῖα καὶ Καισηρεῖα, 19
Purim, 159
purity, 51–53, 136, 242, 247

Quadragesima, 230

Ranger, Terence, 25
religion and business
  in Imperial times, 53
Remus, murder and placation, 185–189
Rhodiapolis Asklepieia, 37
Rhomos. *See* Romulus
Ritter, Hellmut, 20 n. 32
Robert, Louis, and euergetism, 37
Rogers, Guy M., 46
Rome, council of (743/744)
  canon 9, 206
Romulus
  and the emperor, 187
  in John Malalas, 184–192
  and *pluralis maiestatis*, 187
Rosalia, 5
Roueché, Charlotte, 236
Rüpke, Jörg, 315

Sabbath, 123
sacrifice, 24, 32, 38, 129, 131, 154, 186, 233, 320
sale of priesthoods, prohibition of, 53
Salutaris, C. Vibius, 41–46
Salvian of Marseilles, 318
Santa Maria Antiqua church, Rome, 257
Sarapis, 246, 261
Saturnalia, 77, 98, 202, 209
  Avodah Zarah, 67
  fair at Beth Shean, 76
  feriae servorum, 76; Lucian, 89
  Syria-Palaestina, 76–77
  Vindolanda letters, 87
Schäublin, Christoph, 167
Schwartz, Joshua, 232
Scythopolis, festival of Dionysos, 79
Sechseläuten, 1, 25
senators
  accused of sorcery, 278
  and Lupercalia, 173

Index

Septimius Severus, 283
  and Capitolia, 97
Servius on Romulus and Remus, 185
Sidonius Apollinaris, *Carmen* 2.544–548, 196
Siricius (pope), 113
Soler, Emmanuel, 103
Solomon, 232
Sophronius
  Miracles of the Hagioi Anargyroi, 259–261
  sorcery and healing, 288
sorcery
  charioteers, 112, 278, 282
  disease, 287
  distinct from magic, 269, 287
  γοητεία, 269
Sozomenus, *Hist. eccl.* 2.3. 9, 261
sparsiones, 161, 223, 321
spectacles, 321
  church services, 154
  prohibited, 126, 176
  Sundays, 176
Syria-Palaestina, 82
statue, 31, 42, 47, 59, 89, 108, 153, 156, 163, 165, 188
Stratonikeia, 29
strenae, 132, 142, 144, 147
Suetonius, *Domit.*4.4, on Capitolia, 96
Sukkot, 67, 232, 308
  and Encaeniae in Jerusalem, 232
Sunday
  as legal holiday, 118
  spectacles, 176
Symmachus, Q. Aurelius (orator), 107, 113, 165
Symmachus (pope), 174
Syros, 70
  Vota, 57
syrtoi dancers, 19, 20

Tatian, *Adv. Graecos* 18, 253
temples and Christians, 13, 153, 154, 156, 159, 229, 321
Tertullian, 86, 152, 192, 212
  De anima 45–48, 249–251
  De idol. 10.3, 201
  De idol. 11.4, 215
  De idol. 14.4–6, 77
  De idol. 14.6, 202
  on the Vota, 74
Thekla
  incubation church in Seleukeia on the Kalykadnos, 258–259
  Miracles, 258–259

Theoderic, 278
Theodoros Balsamon, 219
  Commentary on Trullo, canon 62, 217
Theodosius I, 107–113, 278
  Church reaction to his legal calendar, 145
  in Rome, 107–108
  festivals, 61, 105–106
  laws promulgated in Rome, 109
  reform of legal calendar, 119–123
Theodosius II on Purim, 159
Theophanes of Mytilene, 23 n. 43
Thermantia, mother of Theodosius I, 109
Thespiai, Mouseia, 51
theurgy, 145, 269, 272, 273, 294
  practiced in Carthage, 272
Tiberius, 41
Toledo, council, 149, 150
Tours, council, 147, 148, 152, 223
tradition, invented, 20, 25
Trier, 99, 318
Trullo, council, 74, 136, 147, 148, 214, 216

Valentinian I, 277
  on sorcery, 284
Valerius Maximus on Lupercalia, 164
Vedii Antonini, family in Ephesos, 54
Vedius Antoninus, P., 39, 50, 320
Venantius Fortunatus, *Carmen* 2.6, 266
veneficus, 284, 285
venenum, 283
Venus and Roma, temple of, 94
Veyne, Paul, 37, 164
Vindolanda, Saturnalia, 87
Visigoths, 127, 150
  and Roman law, 124 n. 80
visuality, 34, 59
Volcanalia, 5, 62, 148
Vota, 57, 74, 100, 132, 133, 147, 160, 220, 222
  army, 74, 87
  Syria-Palestine, 74–75
  Talmud, 75

Whirling Dervishes, 20, 20 n. 32
Wilson, Peter, 3
Wörrle, Michael, 3

Xenophon of Ephesos, 16

Zacharias of Mytilene, 260
Zeus Chalazios, 289
Zeus Driktes, 41
Ziegler, Ruprecht, 97